PRINCIPLES OF
MICRO
ECONOMICS

2024 Release

ROBERT H. FRANK

Cornell University

BEN S. BERNANKE

Brookings Institution [affiliated]
Former Chair, Board of Governors of the Federal Reserve System

KATE ANTONOVICS

University of California, San Diego

ORI HEFFETZ

Cornell University and the Hebrew University of Jerusalem

PRINCIPLES OF MICROECONOMICS, 2024 RELEASE

1 2 3 4 5 6 7 8 9 LKV 29 28 27 26 25 24

ISBN 978-1-265-39967-2 (bound)
MHID 1-265-39967-0 (bound)
ISBN 978-1-265-41812-0 (loose-leaf)
MHID 1-265-41812-8 (loose-leaf)

Portfolio Director: *Anke Weekes*
Associate Portfolio Manager: *Jonathan Hsu*
Senior Product Developer: *Christina Kouvelis*
Senior Marketing Manager: *Carla Villani*
Lead Assessment Content Project Manager: *Bruce Gin*
Lead Core Content Project Manager: *Susan Trentacosti*
Manufacturing Senior Project Manager: *Laura Fuller*
Manager, Content Licensing: *Brianna Kirschbaum*
Cover Image: *Shutterstock/photoff*
Compositor: *Aptara®, Inc.*

Library of Congress Cataloging-in-Publication Data

Names: Frank, Robert H., author. | Bernanke, Ben, author. | Antonovics, Kate L., author. | Heffetz, Ori, 1973- author.
Title: Principles of microeconomics / Robert H. Frank, Cornell University, Ben S. Bernanke, Brookings Institution [affiliated], Former Chair, Board of Governors of the Federal Reserve System, Kate L. Antonovics, University of California, San Diego, Ori Heffetz, Cornell University and the Hebrew University of Jerusalem.
Description: 2024 Release | New York, NY : McGraw Hill Education, [2024] | Series: Principles of macroeconomics | 2024 Release | Audience: Ages 18+ | Audience: Grades 10-12
Identifiers: LCCN 2024000956 (print) | LCCN 2024000957 (ebook) | ISBN 9781265399672 (hardcover) | ISBN 9781265418120 (spiral bound) | ISBN 9781265425760 (ebook)
Subjects: LCSH: Economics.
Classification: LCC HB171.5 .F734 2024b (print) | LCC HB171.5 (ebook) | DDC 338.5—dc23/eng/20240131
LC record available at https://lccn.loc.gov/2024000956
LC ebook record available at https://lccn.loc.gov/2024000957

mheducation.com/highered

DEDICATION

For Ellen
R. H. F.

For Anna
B. S. B.

For Fiona and Henry
K. A.

For Katrina, Eleanor, Daniel, and Amalia
O. H.

ROBERT H. FRANK

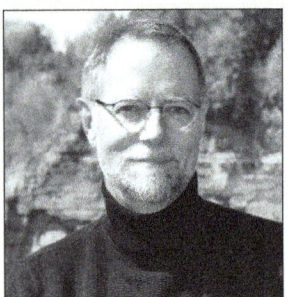

Courtesy of Robert H. Frank

Robert H. Frank is the H. J. Louis Professor of Management and Professor of Economics, emeritus, at Cornell's Johnson School of Management, where he taught from 1972 to 2020. After receiving his B.S. from Georgia Tech in 1966, he taught math and science for two years as a Peace Corps Volunteer in rural Nepal. He received his M.A. in statistics in 1971 and his Ph.D. in economics in 1972 from The University of California at Berkeley. He also holds honorary doctorate degrees from the University of St. Gallen and Dalhousie University. During leaves of absence from Cornell, he has served as chief economist for the Civil Aeronautics Board (1978–1980), a Fellow at the Center for Advanced Study in the Behavioral Sciences (1992–1993), Professor of American Civilization at l'Ecole des Hautes Etudes en Sciences Sociales in Paris (2000–2001), and the Peter and Charlotte Schoenfeld Visiting Faculty Fellow at the NYU Stern School of Business in 2008–2009. His papers have appeared in the *American Economic Review, Econometrica,* the *Journal of Political Economy,* and other leading professional journals, and for more than two decades, his economics columns appeared regularly in *The New York Times.*

Professor Frank is the author of a best-selling intermediate economics textbook—*Microeconomics and Behavior* (McGraw Hill, 2024). His research has focused on rivalry and cooperation in economic and social behavior. His books on these themes include *Choosing the Right Pond* (Oxford, 1985), *Passions Within Reason* (W. W. Norton, 1988), *What Price the Moral High Ground?* (Princeton, 2004), *Falling Behind* (University of California Press, 2007), *The Economic Naturalist* (Basic Books, 2007), *The Economic Naturalist's Field Guide* (Basic Books, 2009), *The Darwin Economy* (Princeton, 2011), *Success and Luck* (Princeton, 2016), and *Under the Influence* (Princeton, 2020), which have been translated into 24 languages. *The Winner-Take-All Society* (The Free Press, 1995), co-authored with Philip Cook, received a Critic's Choice Award, was named a Notable Book of the Year by *The New York Times,* and was included in *BusinessWeek*'s list of the 10 best books of 1995. *Luxury Fever* (The Free Press, 1999) was named to the *Knight-Ridder* Best Books list for 1999.

Professor Frank is a co-recipient of the 2004 Leontief Prize for Advancing the Frontiers of Economic Thought. He was awarded the Johnson School's Stephen Russell Distinguished Teaching Award in 2004, 2010, 2012, and 2018, and the School's Apple Distinguished Teaching Award in 2005. His introductory microeconomics course has graduated more than 7,000 enthusiastic economic naturalists over the years.

BEN S. BERNANKE

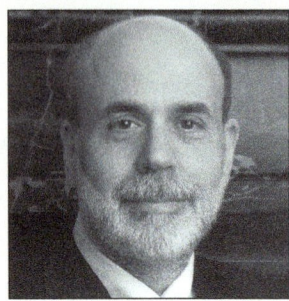

Ben S. Bernanke

Professor Bernanke received his B.A. in economics from Harvard University in 1975 and his Ph.D. in economics from MIT in 1979. He taught at the Stanford Graduate School of Business from 1979 to 1985 and moved to Princeton University in 1985, where he was named the Howard Harrison and Gabrielle Snyder Beck Professor of Economics and Public Affairs and where he served as chair of the Economics Department. Professor Bernanke is currently a Distinguished Fellow in Residence with the Economic Studies Program at the Brookings Institution.

Professor Bernanke was sworn in on February 1, 2006, as chair and a member of the Board of Governors of the Federal Reserve System; his second term expired January 31, 2014. Professor Bernanke also served as chair of the Federal Open Market Committee, the Fed's principal monetary policymaking body. Professor Bernanke was also chair of the President's Council of Economic Advisers from June 2005 to January 2006.

Professor Bernanke's intermediate textbook, with Andrew Abel and Dean Croushore, *Macroeconomics,* Tenth Edition (Pearson, 2021), is a best seller in its field. He has authored numerous scholarly publications in macroeconomics, macroeconomic history, and finance. He has done significant research on the causes of the Great Depression, the role of financial markets and institutions in the business cycle, and measurement of the effects of monetary policy on the economy.

Professor Bernanke has held a Guggenheim Fellowship and a Sloan Fellowship, and he is a Fellow of the Econometric Society and of the American Academy of Arts and Sciences. He served as the director of the Monetary Economics Program of the National Bureau of Economic Research (NBER) and as a member of the NBER's Business Cycle Dating Committee. From 2001 to 2004 he served as editor of the *American Economic Review,* and as president of the American Economic Association in 2019. Professor Bernanke's work with civic and professional groups includes having served two terms as a member of the Montgomery Township (New Jersey) Board of Education. In 2022 Professor Bernanke was awarded the Nobel Prize in Economics for his research on the Great Depression, which suggested that among the contributing factors were credit market stress and a failing gold standard.

KATE ANTONOVICS

Kate Antonovics

Professor Antonovics received her B.A. from Brown University in 1993 and her Ph.D. in economics from the University of Wisconsin in 2000. Shortly thereafter, she joined the faculty in the Economics Department at the University of California,

San Diego. Professor Antonovics is also currently serving as the Provost of UC San Diego's Seventh College.

Professor Antonovics is known for her excellence in teaching and her innovative use of technology in the classroom. Her popular introductory-level microeconomics courses have regularly enrolled over 900 students each fall. She also teaches labor economics at both the undergraduate and graduate level. She has received numerous teaching awards, including the UCSD Department of Economics award for Best Undergraduate Teaching, the UCSD Academic Senate Distinguished Teaching Award, and the UCSD Chancellor's Associates Faculty Excellence Award in Undergraduate Teaching.

Professor Antonovics's research has focused on racial discrimination, gender discrimination, affirmative action, intergenerational income mobility, learning, and wage dynamics. Her papers have appeared in the *American Economic Review,* the *Review of Economics and Statistics,* the *Journal of Labor Economics,* and the *Journal of Human Resources.* She is a member of both the American Economic Association and the Society of Labor Economists.

ORI HEFFETZ

Ori Heffetz

Professor Heffetz received his B.A. in physics and philosophy from Tel Aviv University in 1999 and his Ph.D. in economics from Princeton University in 2005. He is an Associate Professor of Economics at the Samuel Curtis Johnson Graduate School of Management at Cornell University, and at the Economics Department at the Hebrew University of Jerusalem.

Bringing the real world into the classroom, Professor Heffetz has created a unique macroeconomics course that introduces basic concepts and tools from economic theory and applies them to current news and global events. His popular classes are taken by hundreds of students every year on Cornell's Ithaca and New York City campuses and via live videoconferencing in dozens of cities across the United States, Canada, and Latin America.

Professor Heffetz's research studies the social and cultural aspects of economic behavior, focusing on the mechanisms that drive consumers' choices and on the links between economic choices, individual well-being, and policymaking. He has published scholarly work on household consumption patterns, individual economic decision making, and survey methodology and measurement. He was a visiting researcher at the Bank of Israel during 2011, is currently a Research Associate at the National Bureau of Economic Research (NBER), and serves on the editorial board of *Social Choice and Welfare.*

FOCUSED ON SEVEN CORE PRINCIPLES TO PRODUCE ECONOMIC NATURALISTS THROUGH ACTIVE LEARNING

Our 2024 release arrives in the midst of some of the most dramatic upheavals ever witnessed, both in the economy generally and in higher education in particular. The COVID-19 pandemic produced levels of unemployment not seen since the Great Depression and created dramatic changes in the ways we teach across educational institutions at every level.

These developments have reinforced our confidence in the instructional philosophy that motivated us to produce our first edition—the need to strip away clutter and focus more intensively on central concepts. This approach, we believe, is especially well-suited for the new environment.

In earlier editions, we noted that although many millions of dollars are spent each year on introductory economics instruction in American colleges and universities, the return on this investment has been disturbingly low. Studies have shown, for example, that several months after having taken a principles of economics course, former students are no better able to answer simple economics questions than others who never even took the course. Most students, it seems, leave our introductory courses without having learned even the most important basic economic principles. Such dismal performance, never defensible, has become even more difficult to justify in the face of looming resource shortages in higher education.

The problem, in our view, has almost always been that courses try to teach students far too much. In the process, really important ideas get little more coverage than minor ones, and everything ends up going by in a blur. The human brain tends to ignore new information unless it comes up repeatedly. That's hardly surprising, since only a tiny fraction of the terabytes of information that bombard us each day is likely to be relevant for anything we care about. Only when something comes up a third or fourth time does the brain start laying down new circuits for dealing with it. Yet when planning their lectures, many instructors ask themselves, "How much can I cover today?" And because modern electronic media enable them to click through upward of 100 PowerPoint slides in an hour, they feel they better serve their students when they put more information before them. But that's not the way learning works. Professors should instead be asking, "How much can my students absorb?"

Our approach to this text was inspired by our conviction that students will learn far more if we attempt to cover much less. Our basic premise is that a small number of basic principles do most of the heavy lifting in economics, and that if we focus narrowly and repeatedly on those principles, students can actually master them in just a single semester. The enthusiastic reactions of users of previous editions of our textbook affirm the validity of this premise. Avoiding excessive reliance on formal mathematical derivations, we present concepts intuitively through examples drawn from familiar contexts. We rely throughout on a well-articulated list of seven Core Principles, which we reinforce repeatedly by illustrating and applying each principle in numerous contexts. We ask students periodically to apply these principles themselves to answer related questions, exercises, and problems.

Another distinguishing feature of this text is its explicit recognition of the pedagogical challenge posed by the broad variance in students' quantitative backgrounds and in instructor preferences about the optimal level of mathematical detail for the course. We confront this challenge by relegating more detailed mathematical treatment of selected topics to chapter appendices. For example, Chapter 5, *Demand,* emphasizes the key intuition that underpins utility maximization, and relegates the formal presentation of indifference curves and budget constraints to the appendix, allowing instructors the freedom to choose the approach that best suits their needs. Similarly, Chapter 25, *Spending and Output in the Short Run,* uses diagrams and numerical examples to convey the main ideas behind the basic Keynesian model (the "Keynesian cross"), saving a more general algebraic analysis to Appendix A and a derivation of the multiplier formula to Appendix B—again providing flexibility to instructors. Many adopters have cited this additional flexibility as a reason for having chosen our book.

Throughout the body of the text, however, our principal focus is not on quantitative detail but rather on students to become "economic naturalists," people who employ basic economic principles to understand and explain what they observe in the world around them. An economic naturalist understands, for example, that infant safety seats are required in cars but not in airplanes because the marginal cost of space to accommodate these seats is typically zero in cars but often hundreds of dollars in airplanes. Scores of such examples are sprinkled throughout

the book. Each one, we believe, poses a question that should make any curious person eager to learn the answer. These examples stimulate interest while teaching students to see each feature of their economic landscape as the reflection of one or more of the Core Principles. Students talk about these examples with their friends and families. Learning economics is like learning a language. In each case, there is no substitution for actually speaking. By inducing students to speak economics, The Economic Naturalist examples serve this purpose.

For those who would like to learn more about the role of examples in learning economics, Bob Frank's lecture on this topic is posted on YouTube's "Authors@Google" series (www.youtube.com/watch?v=QalNVxeIKEE), or search "Authors@Google Robert Frank."

KEY THEMES AND FEATURES

Emphasis on Seven Core Principles

Because a few Core Principles do most of the work in economics, focusing almost exclusively on these principles ensures that students leave the course with a deep mastery of them. In contrast, traditional encyclopedic texts so overwhelm students with detail that they often leave the course with little useful working knowledge at all.

1. **The Scarcity Principle:** Although we have boundless needs and wants, the resources available to us are limited. So having more of one good thing usually means having less of another.

2. **The Cost-Benefit Principle:** An individual (or a firm or a society) should take an action if, and only if, the extra benefits from taking the action are at least as great as the extra costs.

3. **The Incentive Principle:** A person (or a firm or a society) is more likely to take an action if its benefit rises, and less likely to take it if its cost rises. In short, incentives matter.

4. **The Principle of Comparative Advantage:** Everyone does best when each concentrates on the activity for which his or her opportunity cost is lowest.

5. **The Principle of Increasing Opportunity Cost:** In expanding the production of any good, first employ those resources with the lowest opportunity cost, and only afterward turn to resources with higher opportunity costs.

6. **The Efficiency Principle:** Efficiency is an important social goal because when the economic pie grows larger, everyone can have a larger slice.

7. **The Equilibrium Principle:** A market in equilibrium leaves no unexploited opportunities for individuals but may not exploit all gains achievable through collective action.

Economic Naturalism

Our ultimate goal is to produce economic naturalists—people who see each human action as the result of an implicit or explicit cost-benefit calculation. The economic naturalist sees mundane details of ordinary existence in a new light and becomes actively engaged in the attempt to understand them. Some representative examples:

- Why do movie theaters offer discount tickets to students?

- Why do we often see convenience stores located on adjacent street corners?

- Why do supermarket checkout lines all tend to be roughly the same length?

Economic Naturalist Video Series: We are very excited to offer a video series based on The Economic Naturalist examples. A series of videos covering some of our favorite micro- and macro-focused examples can be used as part of classroom presentations or assigned for homework along with accompanying questions within McGraw Hill Connect®. These fascinating, fun, and thought-provoking applications of economics in everyday life encourage students to think like an economist. Refer to the distinguishing features pages of the preface for additional information. You can view one of these dynamic videos here: http://econeveryday.com/why-do-cooked-rotisserie-chickens-cost-less-than-fresh-uncooked-chickens.

Active Learning Stressed

The only way to learn to hit an overhead smash in tennis is through repeated practice. The same is true for learning economics. Accordingly, we consistently introduce new ideas in the context of simple examples and then follow them with applications showing how they work in familiar settings. At frequent intervals, we pose self-tests that both test and reinforce the understanding of these ideas. The end-of-chapter questions and problems are carefully crafted to help students internalize and extend basic concepts and are available within Connect as assignable content so that instructors can require students to engage with this material. Experience with earlier editions confirms that this approach

really does prepare students to apply basic economic principles to solve economic puzzles drawn from the real world.

Learning Glass Lecture Videos: A collection of brief instructional videos featuring the authors Kate Antonovics and Ori Heffetz utilize learning glass technology to provide students with an overview of important economic concepts. Perfect for an introduction to basic concepts before coming to class, or as a quick review, these videos, with accompanying questions, can be assigned within Connect or used as part of classroom discussion.

Both The Economic Naturalist and Learning Glass videos and accompanying multiple-choice questions that test students' understanding of the principles illustrated in the videos have become valued tools for instructors who incorporate elements of the flipped-classroom approach in their teaching, or those who are relying more heavily on other forms of remote learning.

Modern Microeconomics

Economic surplus is more fully developed here than in any other text. This concept underlies the argument for economic efficiency as an important social goal. Rather than speak of trade-offs between efficiency and other goals, we stress that maximizing economic surplus facilitates the achievement of *all* goals.

One of the biggest hurdles to the fruitful application of cost-benefit thinking is to recognize and measure the relevant costs and benefits. Common decision pitfalls identified by 2002 Nobel laureate Daniel Kahneman and others—such as the tendency to ignore implicit costs, the tendency not to ignore sunk costs, and the tendency to confuse average and marginal costs and benefits—are introduced in Chapter 1, *Thinking Like an Economist,* and discussed repeatedly in subsequent chapters.

There is perhaps no more exciting toolkit for the economic naturalist than a few principles of elementary game theory. In Chapter 9, *Games and Strategic Behavior,* we show how these principles enable students to answer a variety of strategic questions that arise in the marketplace and everyday life. In new Chapter 10, *An Introduction to Behavioral Economics,* we survey many of the most exciting developments in what has become the economics profession's most vibrant new field. We believe that the insights of Nobel laureate Ronald Coase are indispensable for understanding a host of familiar laws, customs, and social norms. In Chapter 11, *Externalities, Property Rights, and the Environment,* we show how such devices function to minimize misallocations that result from externalities.

CHANGES IN THE 2024 RELEASE

Changes Common to All Chapters

In all chapters, the narrative has been tightened. Many of the examples have been updated, with a focus on student-centered examples that connect to current topics such as the COVID-19 pandemic and bank failures. Data have been updated throughout.

Chapter-by-Chapter Changes

Chapter 1

- Updated the list of important pitfalls that occur when applying the Cost-Benefit Principle inconsistently from three to four pitfalls.

- Added a new section and new learning objective introducing invisible hand theory.

- Replaced Economic Naturalist 1.2 with an updated example on check-splitting moved to this chapter from Chapter 14.

- New and updated end-of-chapter problems that reinforce the chapter's learning objectives, including the new learning objective added to reflect invisible hand theory.

Chapter 2

- New Economic Naturalist 2.3 "How will climate change affect wine-industry specialization?"

- Economic Naturalist 2.3 and 2.4 renumbered to Economic Naturalist 2.4 and 2.5, respectively.

Chapter 3

- Economic Naturalist 3.4 moved earlier in the chapter and now appears as The Economic Naturalist 3.3. The subsequent Economic Naturalist example renumbered accordingly.

- Rewording of some examples related to climate change and vaccines in the narrative for clarity and currency.

- New Economic Naturalist 3.5 "Why do physicians tend to overprescribe antibiotics?" added at the end of the chapter.

Chapter 4

- Added a new learning objective "Show how values of long-run price elasticities of demand influence the design of the economic policy." All subsequent learning objectives renumbered accordingly in the chapter narrative and among the end-of-chapter questions.

- "Using Price Elasticity of Demand" was promoted to a first-level head and two entirely new subsections, "Social Contagion and the Long-Run Price Elasticity of Demand" and "The Long-Run Response to a Carbon Tax" were added.

- Reversed the order of Economic Naturalist 4.1 and 4.2.

- New end-of-chapter problem added to reflect the new learning objective.

Chapter 5

- Updated Economic Naturalist 5.4 and gasoline examples with updated data in the chapter narrative.

Chapter 6

- No substantive changes.

Chapter 7

- "Smart for One, Dumb for All" subsection rewritten to draw in invisible hand theory and market failure.

Chapter 8

- Minor updates to a few end-of-chapter problems.

- No substantive changes.

Chapter 9

- New Example 9.4 "Will firms voluntarily incur costs to adopt cleaner production methods?" further illustrates why the prisoner's dilemma is a powerful metaphor for describing why markets don't always deliver the best outcomes possible.

- Subsequent examples renumbered accordingly.

- Minor updates to a few end-of-chapter problems.

Chapter 10

- Economic Naturalist 10.5 moved to Chapter 14.

- Adjustments made to end-of-chapter problem 7.

Chapter 11

- Subsection "Controlling Multinational Environmental Pollution" changed to "Controlling Emissions of Greenhouse Gases."

- Updated climate change section.

- Updated end-of-chapter problem 7.

Chapter 12

- No substantive changes.

Chapter 13

- Updated student-centered examples, such as Serena Williams and Taylor Swift.

- Updated discussion of recent trends in inequality.

Chapter 14

- Added discussion describing the case for Pigouvian taxes as source of revenue for public goods.

- Added material here from Chapter 10 related to cognitive illusions and added a related learning objective.

- New subsection on how government policy matters and how data on the determinants of human flourishing inform the debate on how extensive the government's role should be. A new associated learning objective added to reflect this new material as well.

Chapter 15

- Updated Economic Naturalist 15.2 to highlight the imposition of tariffs on imports from China.

- Replaced Economic Naturalist 15.3 with a new example that answers the question "Why did the U.S. impose restrictions on exports to China?"

A NOTE ON THE WRITING OF THIS EDITION

Ben Bernanke was sworn in on February 1, 2006, as chair and a member of the Board of Governors of the Federal Reserve System, a position to which he was reappointed in January 2010. From June 2005 until January 2006, he served as chair of the President's Council of Economic Advisers. These positions have allowed him to play an active role in making U.S. economic policy, but the rules of government service have restricted his ability to participate in the preparation of previous editions. Since his second term as chair of the Federal Reserve has completed, we are happy that Ben is actively involved in the revision of the macro portion of this edition.

EVERGREEN

Content and technology are ever-changing, and it is important that you can keep your course up to date with the latest information and assessments. That's why we want to deliver the most current and relevant content for your course, hassle-free.

Frank, Bernanke, Antonovics, and Heffetz *Principles of Economics* is moving to an Evergreen delivery model, which means it has content, tools, and technology that are updated and relevant, with updates delivered directly to your existing McGraw Hill Connect® course. Engage students and freshen up assignments with up-to-date coverage of select topics and assessments, all without having to switch editions or build a new course.

Reflecting the Diverse World around Us

McGraw Hill believes in unlocking the potential of every learner at every stage of life. To accomplish that, we are dedicated to creating products that reflect, and are accessible to, all the diverse, global customers we serve. Within McGraw Hill, we foster a culture of belonging, and we work with partners who share our commitment to equity, inclusion, and diversity in all forms. In McGraw Hill Higher Education, this includes, but is not limited to, the following:

- Refreshing and implementing inclusive content guidelines around topics including generalizations and stereotypes, gender, abilities/disabilities, race/ethnicity, sexual orientation, diversity of names, and age.

- Enhancing best practices in assessment creation to eliminate cultural, cognitive, and affective bias.

- Maintaining and continually updating a robust photo library of diverse images that reflect our student populations.

- Including more diverse voices in the development and review of our content.

- Strengthening art guidelines to improve accessibility by ensuring meaningful text and images are distinguishable and perceivable by users with limited color vision and moderately low vision.

ACKNOWLEDGMENTS

Our thanks first and foremost go to our portfolio manager, Jonathan Hsu and our product developer, Christina Kouvelis. Jonathan encouraged us to think deeply about how to improve the book and helped us transform our ideas into concrete changes. Christina shepherded us through the revision process with intelligence, sound advice, and good humor. We are grateful as well to the production team, whose professionalism (and patience) was outstanding: Susan Trentacosti, content project manager; Bruce Gin, assessment project manager; Matt Diamond, lead designer; and all of those who worked on the production team to turn our manuscript into the text you see now. Finally, we also thank Carla Villani, marketing manager, for getting our message into the wider world.

Special thanks to Paul Fisher, Henry Ford College, and Per Norander, University of North Carolina at Charlotte, for their energy, creativity, and help in refining the assessment material in Connect; Sukanya Kemp, University of Akron, for her detailed accuracy check of the learning glass and economic naturalist videos; Alvin Angeles and team at the University of California, San Diego, for their efforts in the production and editing of the learning glass videos; and Kevin Bertotti and the team at ITVK for their creativity in transforming The Economic Naturalist examples into dynamic and engaging video vignettes.

Finally, our sincere thanks to the following teachers and colleagues, whose thorough reviews and thoughtful suggestions led to innumerable substantive improvements to *Principles of Economics*.

Mark Abajian, *San Diego Mesa College*

Richard Agesa, *Marshall University*

Seemi Ahmad, *Dutchess Community College*

Donald L. Alexander, *Western Michigan University*

Jason Aimone, *Baylor University*

Chris Azevedo, *University of Central Missouri*

Narine Badasyan, *Murray State University*

Sigridur Benediktsdottir, *Yale University*

Robert Blewett, *St. Lawrence University*

Brian C. Brush, *Marquette University*

Christopher Burkart, *University of West Florida*

Colleen Callahan, *American University*

Giuliana Campanelli Andreopoulos, *William Paterson University*

J. Lon Carlson, *Illinois State University*

David Chaplin, *Northwest Nazarene University*

Monica Cherry, *Saint John Fisher College*

Joni Charles, *Texas State University*

Anoshua Chaudhuri, *San Francisco State University*

Xudon Chen, *Baldwin Wallace University*

Nan-Ting Chou, *University of Louisville*

Maria Luisa Corton, *University of South Florida-St. Petersburg*

Manabendra Dasgupta, *University of Alabama at Birmingham*

Craig Dawkins, *Rose State College*

Craig Dorsey, *College of DuPage*

Dennis Edwards, *Coastal Carolina University*

Tracie Edwards, *University of Missouri-St. Louis*

Roger Frantz, *San Diego State University*

Mark Frascatore, *Clarkson University*

Amanda Freeman, *Kansas State University*

Greg George, *Macon State College*

Seth Gershenson, *Michigan State University*

Amy D. Gibson, *Christopher Newport University*

Rajeev Goel, *Illinois State University*

Reginald Gray, *Dallas College Mountain View*

Mehdi Haririan, *Bloomsburg University of Pennsylvania*

Susan He, *Washington State University*

John Hejkal, *University of Iowa*

Kuang-Chung Hsu, *Kishwaukee College*

Greg Hunter, *California State University-Pomona*

Nick Huntington-Klein, *California State University-Fullerton*

Andres Jauregui, *Columbus State University*

David W. Johnson, *University of Wisconsin-Madison*

Derek Johnson, *University of Connecticut*

Sukanya Kemp, *University of Akron*

Brian Kench, *University of Tampa*

Fredric R. Kolb, *University of Wisconsin-Eau Claire*

Daniel D. Kuester, *Kansas State University*

Nakul Kumar, *Northern Virginia Community College*

Sunita Kumari, *St. Petersburg College*

Valerie Lacarte, *American University*

Donald J. Liu, *University of Minnesota-Twin Cities*

Brian Lynch, *Lake Land College*

Christine Malakar, *Lorain Community College*

Ida Mirzaie, *The Ohio State University*

Steven Nafziger, *Williams College*

THE ECONOMIC NATURALIST EXAMPLES

Each Economic Naturalist example starts with a question to spark curiosity and interest in learning an answer. These examples fuel interest while teaching students to see economics in the world around them.

Videos of select Economic Naturalist examples are denoted in the margin of the material to which they pertain and they are housed within Connect as assignable content with accompanying questions. A full list of Economic Naturalist examples and videos can be found in the following pages.

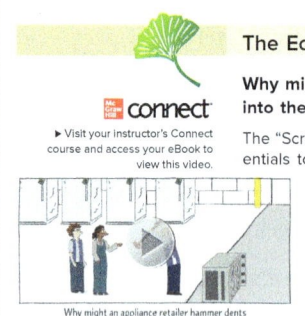

The Economic Naturalist 8.3

▶ Visit your instructor's Connect course and access your eBook to view this video.

Why might an appliance retailer instruct its clerks to hammer dents into the sides of its stoves and refrigerators?

The "Scratch 'n' Dent Sale" is another example of how retailers use quality differentials to segregate buyers according to their reservation prices. Many stores hold an annual sale in which they display appliances with minor scratches and blemishes in the parking lot at deep discounts. People who don't care much about price are unlikely to turn out for these events, but those with very low reservation prices often get up early to be first in line. Indeed, these sales have proven so popular that it might even be in a retailer's interest to put dents in some of its sale items deliberately.

Why might an appliance retailer hammer dents into the sides of its stoves and refrigerators?

ECONOMIC NATURALISM

With the rudiments of the cost-benefit framework under your belt, you are now in a position to become an "economic naturalist," someone who uses insights from economics to help make sense of observations from everyday life. People who have studied biology are able to observe and marvel at many details of nature that would otherwise have escaped their notice. For example, on a walk in the woods in early April, the novice may see only trees. In contrast, the biology student notices many different species of trees and understands why some are already in leaf while others still lie dormant. Likewise, the novice may notice that in some animal species males are much larger than females, but the biology student knows that pattern occurs only in species in which males take several mates. Natural selection favors larger males in those species because their greater size helps them prevail in the often bloody contests among males for access to females. In contrast, males tend to be roughly the same size as females in monogamous species, in which there is much less fighting for mates.

▶ Visit your instructor's Connect course and access your eBook to view this video.

Why does the light come on when you open the refrigerator door but not when you open the freezer?

NUMBERED EXAMPLES

Throughout the text, numbered and titled examples are referenced and called out to further illustrate concepts. Our engaging questions and examples from everyday life highlight how each human action is the result of an implicit or explicit cost-benefit calculation.

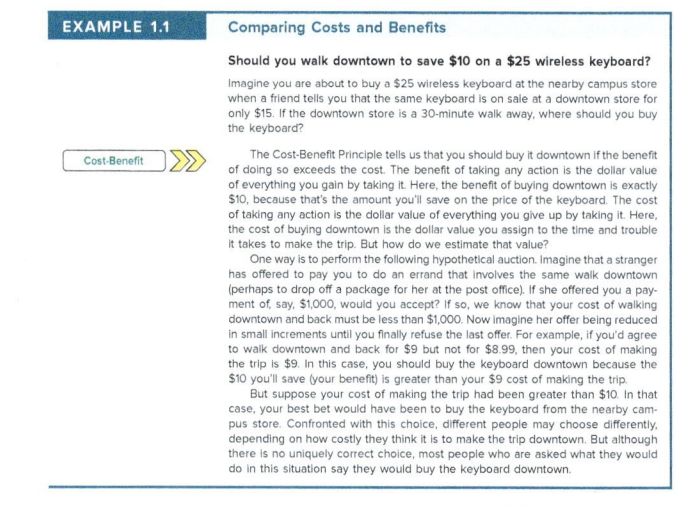

EXAMPLE 1.1   **Comparing Costs and Benefits**

Should you walk downtown to save $10 on a $25 wireless keyboard?

Imagine you are about to buy a $25 wireless keyboard at the nearby campus store when a friend tells you that the same keyboard is on sale at a downtown store for only $15. If the downtown store is a 30-minute walk away, where should you buy the keyboard?

Cost-Benefit ≫

The Cost-Benefit Principle tells us that you should buy it downtown if the benefit of doing so exceeds the cost. The benefit of taking any action is the dollar value of everything you gain by taking it. Here, the benefit of buying downtown is exactly $10, because that's the amount you'll save on the price of the keyboard. The cost of taking any action is the dollar value of everything you give up by taking it. Here, the cost of buying downtown is the dollar value you assign to the time and trouble it takes to make the trip. But how do we estimate that value?

One way is to perform the following hypothetical auction. Imagine that a stranger has offered to pay you to do an errand that involves the same walk downtown (perhaps to drop off a package for her at the post office). If she offered you a payment of, say, $1,000, would you accept? If so, we know that your cost of walking downtown and back must be less than $1,000. Now imagine her offer being reduced in small increments until you finally refuse the last offer. For example, if you'd agree to walk downtown and back for $9 but not for $8.99, then your cost of making the trip is $9. In this case, you should buy the keyboard downtown because the $10 you'll save (your benefit) is greater than your $9 cost of making the trip.

But suppose your cost of making the trip had been greater than $10. In that case, your best bet would have been to buy the keyboard from the nearby campus store. Confronted with this choice, different people may choose differently, depending on how costly they think it is to make the trip downtown. But although there is no uniquely correct choice, most people who are asked what they would do in this situation say they would buy the keyboard downtown.

EXCHANGE AND OPPORTUNITY COST

Scarcity ≫

The Scarcity Principle (see Chapter 1, *Thinking Like an Economist*) reminds us that the opportunity cost of spending more time on any one activity is having less time available to spend on others. As the following example makes clear, this principle helps explain why everyone can do better by concentrating on those activities at which they perform best relative to others.

CORE PRINCIPLES

There are seven Core Principles that we focus on to ensure student mastery. Throughout the text, these principles are called out and are denoted by an icon in the margin. Again, the seven Core Principles are: scarcity, cost-benefit, incentive, comparative advantage, increasing opportunity cost, efficiency, and equilibrium.

SELF-TESTS

These self-test questions in the body of the chapter enable students to determine whether the preceding material has been understood and reinforce understanding before reading further. Detailed answers to the self-test questions are found at the end of each chapter.

 SELF-TEST 3.1

In Figure 3.1, what is the marginal buyer's reservation price when the quantity of pizza sold is 10,000 slices per day? For the same demand curve, what will be the quantity of pizza demanded at a price of $2.50 per slice?

RECAP

RECAP↑

MARKET EQUILIBRIUM

Market equilibrium, the situation in which all buyers and sellers are satisfied with their respective quantities at the market price, occurs at the intersection of the supply and demand curves. The corresponding price and quantity are called the *equilibrium price* and the *equilibrium quantity*.

Unless prevented by regulation, prices and quantities are driven toward their equilibrium values by the actions of buyers and sellers. If the price is initially too high, so that there is excess supply, frustrated sellers will cut their price in order to sell more. If the price is initially too low, so that there is excess demand, competition among buyers drives the price upward. This process continues until equilibrium is reached.

Sprinkled throughout each chapter are Recap boxes that underscore and summarize the importance of the preceding material and key concept takeaways.

WORKED PROBLEM VIDEOS

Brief videos work through end-of-chapter problems to aid in student understanding of core economic concepts and offer assistance with more challenging material. The videos are available as hints within Connect.

To earn extra money in the summer, you grow tomatoes and sell them at a local farmers' market for 30 cents per pound. By adding compost to your garden, you can increase your yield as shown in the table below. If compost costs 50 cents per pound and your goal is to make as much profit as possible, how many pounds of compost should you add?

Additional cost (or marginal cost)

Pounds of compost	Pounds of tomatoes	Additional pounds of tomatoes	Additional revenue (or marginal benefit)	
	100			
1	120	20	$6.00	✓
2	125	5	$1.50	✓
3	128			
4	130			
5	131			
6	131.5			

LEARNING GLASS VIDEOS

Dozens of lecture videos featuring authors Kate Antonovics and Ori Heffetz utilize learning glass technology to provide you with an overview of important concepts. These videos can be accessed as resources within SmartBook® or as assignable content with accompanying questions via Connect.

Asymmetric Information: Why do "almost new" used cars sell for so much less than brand new ones?

Behavioral Economics: Why do real estate agents often show clients two nearly identical houses, even though one is both cheaper and in better condition than the other?

Comparative Advantage: iPhones: Designed in California, but assembled in China

Cost Benefit 1: Why does the light come on when you open the refrigerator door but not when you open the freezer?

Cost Benefit 2: Why are child safety seats required in automobiles but not in airplanes?

Discount Pricing: Why might an appliance retailer hammer dents into the sides of its stoves and refrigerators?

Elasticity: Why do people buy the same amount of salt as before even when the price of salt doubles?

Incentive Problems and Inefficiency: Why does the practice of check splitting cause people to spend more at restaurants?

Monopolistic Competition: Why do we often see convenience stores located on adjacent street corners?

Prisoner's Dilemma: Why do people shout at parties?

Production Costs: Why are brown eggs more expensive than white ones?

Supply and Demand: Why are rotisserie chickens less expensive than fresh chickens?

Tariffs: Why do consumers in the United States often pay more than double the world price for sugar?

The Invisible Hand: Why do supermarket checkout lines all tend to be roughly the same length?

The Law of Demand: Why are smaller automobile engines more common in Europe than in the United States?

The Optimal Amount of Information: Why might a patient be more likely to receive an expensive magnetic resonance imaging (MRI) exam for a sore knee if covered under a conventional health insurance rather than a health maintenance organization (HMO) plan?

The Tragedy of the Commons and Property Rights: Why do blackberries in public parks get picked before they're completely ripe?

THE ECONOMIC NATURALIST EXAMPLES

SUPPLEMENTS

The following ancillaries are available for quick download and convenient access via the Instructor Resource material available through McGraw Hill Connect®.

Solutions Manual

Prepared by the authors, this manual provides detailed answers to the end-of-chapter review questions and problems.

Test Bank

The test bank has been carefully revised and reviewed for accuracy. Thousands of questions have been categorized by chapter learning objectives, AACSB learning categories, Bloom's Taxonomy objectives, and level of difficulty.

Test Builder in Connect

Available within Connect, Test Builder is a cloud-based tool that enables instructors to format tests that can be printed or administered within an LMS. Test Builder offers a modern, streamlined interface for easy content configuration that matches course needs, without requiring a download.

Test Builder allows you to:

- access all test bank content from a particular title.

- easily pinpoint the most relevant content through robust filtering options.

- manipulate the order of questions or scramble questions and/or answers.

- pin questions to a specific location within a test.

- determine your preferred treatment of algorithmic questions.

- choose the layout and spacing.

- add instructions and configure default settings.

Test Builder provides a secure interface for better protection of content and allows for just-in-time updates to flow directly into assessments.

PowerPoints

Presentation slides contain a detailed, chapter-by-chapter review of the important ideas presented in the textbook, accompanied by animated graphs and slide notes. You can edit, print, or rearrange the slides to fit the needs of your course.

Customizable Micro Lecture Notes

One of the biggest hurdles to an instructor considering changing textbooks is the prospect of having to prepare new lecture notes and slides. For the microeconomics chapters, this hurdle no longer exists. A full set of lecture notes for *Principles of Microeconomics*, prepared by Bob Frank for his award-winning introductory microeconomics course at Cornell University, is available as Microsoft Word files that instructors are welcome to customize as they see fit. The challenge for any instructor is to reinforce the lessons of the text in lectures without generating student unrest by merely repeating what's in the book. These lecture notes address that challenge by constructing examples that run parallel to those presented in the book, yet are different from them in interesting contextual ways.

ReadAnywhere®

Read or study when it's convenient for you with McGraw Hill's free ReadAnywhere® app. Available for iOS or Android smartphones or tablets, ReadAnywhere gives users access to McGraw Hill tools including the eBook and SmartBook® 2.0 or Adaptive Learning Assignments in Connect. Take notes, highlight, and complete assignments offline—all of your work will sync when you open the app with Wi-Fi access. Log in with your McGraw Hill Connect username and password to start learning—anytime, anywhere!

Remote Proctoring & Browser-Locking Capabilities

New remote proctoring and browser-locking capabilities, hosted by Proctorio within Connect, provide control of the assessment environment by enabling security options and verifying the identity of the student.

Seamlessly integrated within Connect, these services allow instructors to control students' assessment experience by restricting browser activity, recording students' activity, and verifying students are doing their own work.

Instant and detailed reporting gives instructors an at-a-glance view of potential academic integrity concerns, thereby avoiding personal bias and supporting evidence-based claims.

FOR MORE INFORMATION ABOUT CONNECT AND ITS AVAILABLE RESOURCES, REFER TO THE PAGES THAT FOLLOW.

Course Challenges

Connect Solutions

Student Preparedness

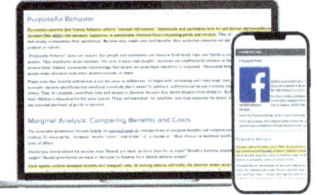

Adaptive Econ Prep: Math & Graphing is designed for students to gain knowledge and build understanding of the basic math and graphing content they need to be successful in any principles course. The result? Modules provide students with a refresher of prerequisite content in an adaptive environment, personalizing the learning experience, leading to a greater level of preparedness.

SmartBook® 2.0 personalizes learning to individual student needs, continually adapting to pinpoint knowledge gaps and focus learning on concepts requiring additional study. For instructors, SmartBook tracks student progress and provides insights that guide teaching strategies and advanced instruction, for a more dynamic class experience. The result? An adaptive reading experience that has been made more personal, accessible, productive, and mobile that improves comprehension and builds student confidence.

The ReadAnywhere® App is a free, downloadable app that allows your students to read their eBook anytime, anywhere or complete their SmartBook 2.0 assignments. Any notes or highlights they make in the eBook will sync across platforms. The result? Students are much more likely to have read the materials, completed their assignments, and be more prepared for class.

Personalized & Conceptualized Feedback

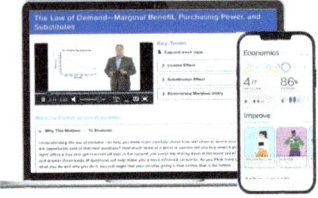

Adaptive Learning Assignment provides each student a personalized path to learning concepts instructors assign in their course. The assignments continually adapt to the individual, identify knowledge gaps, and focus on areas where remediation is needed. All adaptive content—including questions and integrated concept resources—is specifically targeted and directly aligned with individual learning objectives. The result? Students gain targeted learning to help with their specific areas of need.

Sharpen is a study app that highlights and emphasizes the key learning objectives most frequently assigned by faculty and most frequently missed by learners. The result? Sharpen provides students with vetted and credible supplemental resources that complement McGraw Hill Principles of Economics titles.

Math & Graphing Skills

Graphing Homework Exercises go beyond the basics to apply and practice what students now know by demonstrating understanding through translating data and plotting points, shifting curves, calculating values, and identifying areas within graphs. The result? Learning is reinforced by applying knowledge to translating data and answering questions.

Interactive Graphs help students visualize and interpret economic concepts, graphs, and real data. All graphs are accompanied by assignable assessment questions and feedback to guide students through the experience of learning to read and interpret graphs and data. The result? Interactive graphs provide a much easier way to teach complex topics in a visual way.

Perceived Course Relevance

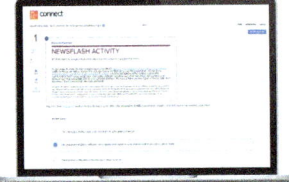

New in Economics!* Newsflash Activities assignable within Connect, students interact with relevant news articles and are graded on their ability to connect the content to key economics topics. The result? Students deepen their understanding of difficult concepts using content that is relevant to their everyday lives.

Application-Based Activities (ABA) prepare students for the real-world through highly interactive, assignable exercises that boost engagement while providing immersive way to apply concepts learned to Economics-specific activities. The result? Students benefit from the application of multiple concepts, providing the ability to synthesize information and use critical-thinking skills to solve realistic scenarios.

Course Challenges

Connect Solutions

Student Engagement

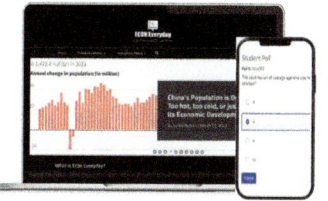

Videos from engaging explanations that help students grasp challenging concepts, to videos that bring economics to life with relevant real-world examples or an experienced instructor walking students through a step-by-step end-of-chapter problem; there are thousands of short, succinct videos to help bridge the gaps in students' understanding across our portfolio. The result? This dynamic media offers extra support and another avenue to help aid in understanding.

Polling within Connect allows you to discover where your students are in real time. Engage students and help them create connections with your course content while gaining valuable insight during your lecture. The result? Leveraging polling data helps deliver personalized instruction when and where it is needed most. All at no additional cost.

EconEveryday Blog saves faculty time by bringing relevant, engaging, student-centered content into Principles-level courses all semester long. Short articles are written for Principles students and tagged by topic for easy search. Discussion questions are provided to help drive the conversation forward. **Visit www.econeveryday.com** to explore and subscribe for updates. The result? Blog content provides extra support, engagement, and current events for you and your students.

Asset Alignment with Bloom's Taxonomy Economics

	SmartBook® 2.0	Adaptive Learning Assignment	Adaptive Econ Prep	Videos	Exercises	Interactive Graphs	Application-Based Activities	Newsflash Activities & Econ Everyday Blog	Writing Assignments
Create									✓
Evaluate							✓	✓	✓
Analyze					✓	✓	✓	✓	✓
Apply		✓	✓	✓	✓	✓	✓	✓
Understand	✓	✓	✓	✓	✓	✓	✓	✓	✓
Remember	✓	✓	✓	✓	✓	✓	✓	✓	✓

What Instructors Are Saying...

"Students report that they like the Application-Based Activities assignments because they are practical and give them a chance to put their knowledge into practice."

Dr. Michelle Hampton, Cuyahoga Community College

A complete course platform

Connect enables you to build deeper connections with your students through cohesive digital content and tools, creating engaging learning experiences. We are committed to providing you with the right resources and tools to support all your students along their personal learning journeys.

65%
Less Time Grading

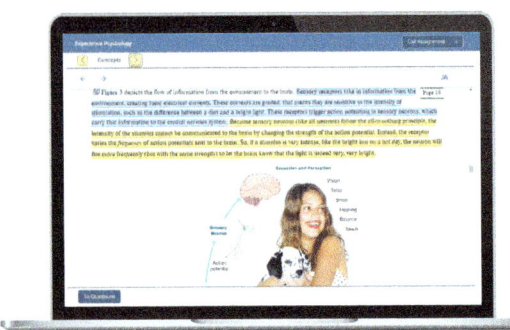

Laptop: Getty Images; Woman/dog: George Doyle/Getty Images

Every learner is unique

In Connect, instructors can assign an adaptive reading experience with SmartBook® 2.0. Rooted in advanced learning science principles, SmartBook 2.0 delivers each student a personalized experience, focusing students on their learning gaps, ensuring that the time they spend studying is time well spent. **mheducation.com/highered/connect/smartbook**

Study anytime, anywhere

Encourage your students to download the free ReadAnywhere® app so they can access their online eBook, SmartBook® 2.0, or Adaptive Learning Assignments when it's convenient, even when they're offline. And since the app automatically syncs with their Connect account, all of their work is available every time they open it. Find out more at **mheducation.com/readanywhere**

"I really liked this app— it made it easy to study when you don't have your textbook in front of you."

Jordan Cunningham, a student at *Eastern Washington University*

Effective tools for efficient studying

Connect is designed to help students be more productive with simple, flexible, intuitive tools that maximize study time and meet students' individual learning needs. Get learning that works for everyone with Connect.

Education for all

McGraw Hill works directly with Accessibility Services departments and faculty to meet the learning needs of all students. Please contact your Accessibility Services Office, and ask them to email accessibility@mheducation.com, or visit mheducation.com/about/accessibility for more information.

Affordable solutions, added value

Make technology work for you with LMS integration for single sign-on access, mobile access to the digital textbook, and reports to quickly show you how each of your students is doing. And with our Inclusive Access program, you can provide all these tools at the lowest available market price to your students. Ask your McGraw Hill representative for more information.

Solutions for your challenges

A product isn't a solution. Real solutions are affordable, reliable, and come with training and ongoing support when you need it and how you want it. Visit supportateverystep.com for videos and resources both you and your students can use throughout the term.

Updated and relevant content

Our new Evergreen delivery model provides the most current and relevant content for your course, hassle-free. Content, tools, and technology updates are delivered directly to your existing McGraw Hill Connect® course. Engage students and freshen up assignments with up-to-date coverage of select topics and assessments, all without having to switch editions or build a new course.

Principles of Economics provides enhanced coverage, offers more topics, and more mathematical rigor. *Principles of Economics: A Streamlined Approach* is a stripped down version of the big book featuring core content with a less is more approach. See which product is right for you!

Comparison Guide

Principles of Economics, 2024 Release				Principles of Economics: A Streamlined Approach, 4th edition			
Chapter Title	Econ	Micro	Macro	Chapter Title	Streamlined 4e Econ	Streamlined 4e Micro	Streamlined 4e Macro
Thinking Like an Economist	1	1	1	Thinking Like An Economist	1	1	1
Comparative Advantage	2	2	2				
Supply and Demand	3	3	3	Supply and Demand	2	2	2
Elasticity	4	4		Demand and Elasticity	3	3	
Demand	5	5					
Perfectly Competitive Supply	6	6		Perfectly Competitive Supply	4	4	
Efficiency, Exchange, and the Invisible Hand in Action	7	7		Efficiency, Exchange, and the Invisible Hand in Action	5	5	
Monopoly, Oligopoly, and Monopolistic Competition	8	8		Monopoly, Oligopoly, and Monopolistic Competition	6	6	
Games and Strategic Behavior	9	9		Games and Strategic Behavior	7	7	
An Introduction to Behavioral Economics	10	10		An Introduction to Behavioral Economics (NEW)	8	8	
Externalities, Property Rights, and the Environment	11	11		Externalities and Property Rights	9	9	
The Economics of Information	12	12		Using Economics to Make Better Policy Decisions	10	10	
Labor Markets, Poverty, and Income Distribution	13	13					
Public Goods and Tax Policy	14	14					
International Trade and Trade Policy	15	15	16	International Trade and Trade Policy	11	11	12
Macroeconomics: The Bird's-Eye View of the Economy	16		4	Macroeconomics: The Bird's Eye View of the Economy	12		3
Measuring Economic Activity: GDP and Unemployment	17		5	Measuring Economic Activity: GDP, Unemployment, and Inflation	13		4
Measuring the Price Level and Inflation	18		6				
Economic Growth, Productivity, and Living Standards	19		7	Economic Growth, Productivity, and Living Standards	14		5
The Labor Market: Workers, Wages, and Unemployment	20		8	The Labor Market: Workers, Wages, and Unemployment	15		6
Saving and Capital Formation	21		9	Saving and Capital Formation	16		7
Money, Prices, and the Federal Reserve	22		10	Money, The Federal Reserve, and Global Financial Markets	17		8
Financial Markets and International Capital Flows	23		11				
Short-Term Economic Fluctuations: An Introduction	24		12	Short-Term Economic Fluctuations and Fiscal Policy	18		9
Spending and Output in the Short Run	25		13				
Stabilizing the Economy: The Role of the Fed	26		14	Stabilizing the Economy: The Role of the Fed	19		10
Aggregate Demand, Aggregate Supply, and Inflation	27		15	Aggregate Demand, Aggregate Supply, and Inflation	20		11
Exchange Rates and the Open Economy	28		17	Exchange Rates and the Open Economy	21		13

BRIEF CONTENTS

CONTENTS

Thinking Like an Economist

People often make bad decisions because they fail to compare the relevant costs and benefits.

Nick Dolding/Cultura/Corbis

How many students are in your introductory economics class? Some classes have just 20 or so. Others average 35, 100, or 200 students. At some schools, introductory economics classes may have as many as 2,000 students. What size is best?

If cost were no object, the best size might be a single student. Think about it: the whole course, all term long, with just you and your professor! Everything could be custom-tailored to your own background and ability. You could cover the material at just the right pace. The tutorial format also would promote close communication and personal trust between you and your professor. And your grade would depend more heavily on what you actually learned than on your luck when taking multiple-choice exams. Let's suppose, for the sake of discussion, that students have been shown to learn best in the tutorial format.

Why, then, do so many introductory classes still have hundreds of students? The simple reason is that costs *do* matter. They matter not just to the university administrators who must build classrooms and pay faculty salaries, but also to *you*. The direct cost of providing you with your own personal introductory economics course might easily top $50,000. *Someone* has to pay these costs. In private universities, a large share of the cost would be recovered directly from higher tuition payments. In state universities, the burden

Are small classes "better" than large ones?

economics the study of how people make choices under conditions of scarcity and of the results of those choices for society

  Scarcity

 Cost-Benefit

would be split between higher tuition payments and higher tax payments. But, in either case, the course would be unaffordable for most students.

With larger classes, of course, the cost per student goes down. For example, an introductory economics course with 300 students might cost as little as $200 per student. But a class that large could easily compromise the quality of the learning environment. Compared to the custom tutorial format, however, it would be dramatically more affordable.

In choosing what size introductory economics course to offer, then, university administrators confront a classic economic trade-off. In making the class larger, they risk lowering the quality of instruction—a bad thing. At the same time, they reduce costs and hence the tuition students must pay—a good thing.

In this chapter, we'll introduce three simple principles that will help you understand and explain patterns of behavior you observe in the world around you. These principles also will help you avoid four pitfalls that plague decision makers in everyday life.

ECONOMICS: STUDYING CHOICE IN A WORLD OF SCARCITY

Even in rich societies like the United States, *scarcity* is a fundamental fact of life. There is never enough time, money, or energy to do everything we want to do or have everything we'd like to have. **Economics** is the study of how people make choices under conditions of scarcity and of the results of those choices for society.

In the class-size example just discussed, a motivated economics student might definitely prefer to be in a class of 20 rather than a class of 100, everything else being equal. But other things, of course, are not equal. Students can enjoy the benefits of having smaller classes, but only at the price of having less money for other activities. The student's choice inevitably will come down to the relative importance of competing activities.

That such trade-offs are widespread and important is one of the core principles of economics. We call it the *Scarcity Principle* because the simple fact of scarcity makes trade-offs necessary. Another name for the scarcity principle is the *No-Free-Lunch Principle* (which comes from the observation that even lunches that are given to you are never really free—somebody, somehow, always has to pay for them).

The Scarcity Principle (also called the No-Free-Lunch Principle): Although we have boundless needs and wants, the resources available to us are limited. So having more of one good thing usually means having less of another.

Inherent in the idea of a trade-off is the fact that choice involves compromise between competing interests. Economists resolve such trade-offs by using cost-benefit analysis, which is based on the disarmingly simple principle that an action should be taken if, and only if, its benefits exceed its costs. We call this statement the *Cost-Benefit Principle,* and it, too, is one of the core principles of economics:

The Cost-Benefit Principle: An individual (or a firm or a society) should take an action if, and only if, the extra benefits from taking the action are at least as great as the extra costs.

With the Cost-Benefit Principle in mind, let's think about our class-size question again. Imagine that classrooms come in only two sizes—100-seat lecture halls and 20-seat classrooms—and that your university currently offers introductory economics courses to classes of 100 students. Question: Should administrators reduce the class size to 20 students? Answer: Reduce if, and only if, the value of the improvement in instruction outweighs its additional cost.

This rule sounds simple. But to apply it we need some way to measure the relevant costs and benefits, a task that's often difficult in practice. If we make a few simplifying assumptions, however, we can see how the analysis might work. On the cost side, the primary expense of reducing class size from 100 to 20 is that we'll now need five professors instead of just one. We'll also need five smaller classrooms rather than a single big one, and this too may add slightly to the expense of the move. Let's suppose that classes with 20 cost $1,000 per student more than those with 100. Should administrators switch to the smaller class size? If they apply the Cost-Benefit Principle, they will realize that *doing so makes sense only if the value of attending the smaller class is at least $1,000 per student greater than the value of attending the larger class.*

Would you (or your family) be willing to pay an extra $1,000 for a smaller class? If not, and if other students feel the same way, then sticking with the larger class size makes sense. But if you and others would be willing to pay the extra tuition, then reducing the class size makes good economic sense.

Notice that the "best" class size, from an economic point of view, will generally not be the same as the "best" size from the point of view of an educational psychologist. That's because the economic definition of "best" takes into account both the benefits *and* the costs of different class sizes. The psychologist ignores costs and looks only at the learning benefits of different class sizes.

In practice, of course, different people feel differently about the value of smaller classes. People with high incomes, for example, tend to be willing to pay more for the advantage. That helps explain why average class size is smaller, and tuition higher, at private schools whose students come predominantly from high-income families.

The cost-benefit framework for thinking about the class-size problem also suggests a possible reason for the gradual increase in average class size that has been taking place in American colleges and universities. During the last 30 years, professors' salaries have risen sharply, making smaller classes more costly. During the same period, median family income—and hence the willingness to pay for smaller classes—has remained roughly constant. When the cost of offering smaller classes goes up but willingness to pay for smaller classes does not, universities shift to larger class sizes.

Scarcity and the resulting trade-offs also apply to resources other than money. Jeff Bezos is one of the richest people on Earth. His wealth is estimated at more than $116 billion. That's more than the combined wealth of the poorest 54 percent of Americans. Bezos could buy more houses, cars, vacations, and other consumer goods than he could possibly use. Yet he, like the rest of us, has only 24 hours each day and a limited amount of energy. So even he confronts trade-offs. Any activity he pursues—whether it be building his business empire or redecorating his mansion—uses up time and energy that he could otherwise spend on other things. Indeed, someone once calculated that the value of Bezos's time is so great that pausing to pick up a $100 bill from the sidewalk simply wouldn't be worth his while.

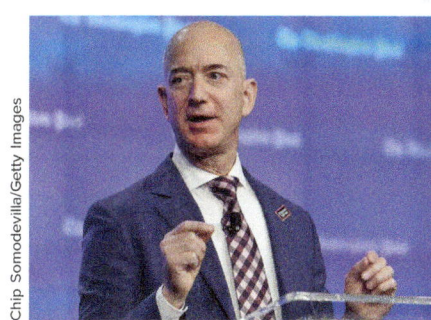

If Jeff Bezos saw a $100 bill lying on the sidewalk, would it be worth his time to pick it up?

APPLYING THE COST-BENEFIT PRINCIPLE ⟶

In studying choice under scarcity, we'll usually begin with the premise that people are **rational**, which means they have well-defined goals and try to fulfill them as best they can. The Cost-Benefit Principle is a fundamental tool for the study of how rational people make choices.

rational person someone with well-defined goals who tries to fulfill those goals as best he or she can

As in the class-size example, often the only real difficulty in applying the cost-benefit rule is to come up with reasonable measures of the relevant benefits and costs. Only in rare instances will exact dollar measures be conveniently available. But the cost-benefit framework can lend structure to your thinking even when no relevant market data are available.

To illustrate how we proceed in such cases, the following example asks you to decide whether to perform an action whose cost is described only in vague, qualitative terms.

EXAMPLE 1.1   **Comparing Costs and Benefits**

Should you walk downtown to save $10 on a $25 wireless keyboard?

Imagine you are about to buy a $25 wireless keyboard at the nearby campus store when a friend tells you that the same keyboard is on sale at a downtown store for only $15. If the downtown store is a 30-minute walk away, where should you buy the keyboard?

The Cost-Benefit Principle tells us that you should buy it downtown if the benefit of doing so exceeds the cost. The benefit of taking any action is the dollar value of everything you gain by taking it. Here, the benefit of buying downtown is exactly $10, because that's the amount you'll save on the price of the keyboard. The cost of taking any action is the dollar value of everything you give up by taking it. Here, the cost of buying downtown is the dollar value you assign to the time and trouble it takes to make the trip. But how do we estimate that value?

One way is to perform the following hypothetical auction. Imagine that a stranger has offered to pay you to do an errand that involves the same walk downtown (perhaps to drop off a package for her at the post office). If she offered you a payment of, say, $1,000, would you accept? If so, we know that your cost of walking downtown and back must be less than $1,000. Now imagine her offer being reduced in small increments until you finally refuse the last offer. For example, if you'd agree to walk downtown and back for $9 but not for $8.99, then your cost of making the trip is $9. In this case, you should buy the keyboard downtown because the $10 you'll save (your benefit) is greater than your $9 cost of making the trip.

But suppose your cost of making the trip had been greater than $10. In that case, your best bet would have been to buy the keyboard from the nearby campus store. Confronted with this choice, different people may choose differently, depending on how costly they think it is to make the trip downtown. But although there is no uniquely correct choice, most people who are asked what they would do in this situation say they would buy the keyboard downtown.

ECONOMIC SURPLUS

economic surplus the benefit of taking an action minus its cost

Suppose that in Example 1.1 your "cost" of making the trip downtown was $9. Compared to the alternative of buying the keyboard at the campus store, buying it downtown resulted in an **economic surplus** of $1, the difference between the benefit of making the trip and its cost. In general, your goal as an economic decision maker is to choose those actions that generate the largest possible economic surplus. This means taking all actions that yield a positive total economic surplus, which is just another way of restating the Cost-Benefit Principle.

Note that the fact that your best choice was to buy the keyboard downtown doesn't imply that you *enjoy* making the trip, any more than choosing a large class means that you prefer large classes to small ones. It simply means that the trip is less unpleasant than the prospect of paying $10 extra for the keyboard. Once again, you've faced a trade-off. In this case, the choice was between a cheaper keyboard and the free time gained by avoiding the trip.

OPPORTUNITY COST

opportunity cost the value of what must be forgone to undertake an activity

Of course, your mental auction could have produced a different outcome. Suppose, for example, that the time required for the trip is the only time you have left to study for a difficult test the next day. Or suppose you are watching one of your favorite shows on Netflix, or that you are tired and would love a short nap. In such cases, we say that the **opportunity cost** of making the trip—that is, the value of what you must sacrifice to walk downtown and back—is high and you are more likely to decide against making the trip.

Strictly speaking, your opportunity cost of engaging in an activity is the value of everything you must sacrifice to engage in it. For instance, if seeing a movie requires not only that you buy a $10 ticket, but also that you give up a $20 dogwalking job that you would have been willing to do for free, then the opportunity cost of seeing the film is $30.

Under this definition, *all* costs—both implicit and explicit—are opportunity costs. Unless otherwise stated, we will adhere to this strict definition.

We must warn you, however, that some economists use the term *opportunity cost* to refer only to the implicit value of opportunities forgone. Thus, in the example just discussed, these economists wouldn't include the $10 ticket price when calculating the opportunity cost of seeing the film. But virtually all economists would agree that your opportunity cost of not doing the dogwalking job is $20.

In the previous example, if watching another hour of your favorite show on Netflix is the most valuable opportunity that conflicts with the trip downtown, the opportunity cost of making the trip is the dollar value you place on pursuing that opportunity. It is the largest amount you'd be willing to pay to avoid watching your show at another time. Note that the opportunity cost of making the trip is not the combined value of *all* possible activities you could have pursued, but only the value of your *best* alternative—the one you would have chosen had you not made the trip.

Throughout the text we'll pose self-tests like the one that follows. You'll find that pausing to answer them will help you master key concepts in economics. Because doing these self-tests isn't very costly (indeed, many students report that they're actually fun), the Cost-Benefit Principle indicates that it's well worth your while to do them.

 SELF-TEST 1.1

You would again save $10 by buying the wireless keyboard downtown rather than at the campus store, but your cost of making the trip is now $12, not $9. By how much would your economic surplus be smaller if you bought the keyboard downtown rather than at the campus store?

THE ROLE OF ECONOMIC MODELS

Economists use the Cost-Benefit Principle as an abstract model of how an idealized rational individual would choose among competing alternatives. (By "abstract model" we mean a simplified description that captures the essential elements of a situation and allows us to analyze them in a logical way.) A computer model of a complex phenomenon like climate change, which must ignore many details and includes only the major forces at work, is an example of an abstract model.

Noneconomists are sometimes harshly critical of the economist's cost-benefit model on the grounds that people in the real world never conduct hypothetical mental auctions before deciding whether to make trips downtown. But this criticism betrays a fundamental misunderstanding of how abstract models can help explain and predict human behavior. Economists know perfectly well that people don't conduct hypothetical mental auctions when they make simple decisions. All the Cost-Benefit Principle really says is that a rational decision is one that is explicitly or implicitly based on a weighing of costs and benefits.

Most of us make sensible decisions most of the time, without being consciously aware that we are weighing costs and benefits, just as most people ride a bike without being consciously aware of what keeps them from falling. Through trial and error, we gradually learn what kinds of choices tend to work best in different contexts, just as bicycle riders internalize the relevant laws of physics, usually without being conscious of them.

Even so, learning the explicit principles of cost-benefit analysis can help us make better decisions, just as knowing about physics can help in learning to ride a bicycle. For instance, when a young economist was teaching his oldest son to ride a bike, he followed the time-honored tradition of running alongside the bike and holding onto his son, then giving him a push and hoping for the best. After several hours and painfully skinned elbows and knees, his son finally got it. A year later, someone pointed out that the trick to riding a bike is to turn slightly in whichever direction the bike is leaning. Of course! The economist passed this information along to his second son, who learned to ride almost instantly. Just as knowing a little physics can help you learn to ride a bike, knowing a little economics can help you make better decisions.

RECAP

COST-BENEFIT ANALYSIS

Scarcity is a basic fact of economic life. Because of it, having more of one good thing almost always means having less of another (the *Scarcity Principle*). The *Cost-Benefit Principle* holds that an individual (or a firm or a society) should take an action if, and only if, the extra benefit from taking the action is at least as great as the extra cost. The benefit of taking any action minus the cost of taking the action is called the *economic surplus* from that action. Hence, the Cost-Benefit Principle suggests that we take only those actions that create additional economic surplus.

FOUR IMPORTANT DECISION PITFALLS[1]

Rational people will apply the Cost-Benefit Principle most of the time, although probably in an intuitive and approximate way, rather than through explicit and precise calculation. Knowing that rational people tend to compare costs and benefits enables economists to predict their likely behavior. As noted earlier, for example, we can predict that students from wealthy families are more likely than others to attend colleges that offer small classes. (Again, while the cost of small classes is the same for all families, their benefit, as measured by what people are willing to pay for them, tends to be higher for wealthier families.)

Yet researchers have identified situations in which people tend to apply the Cost-Benefit Principle inconsistently. In these situations, the Cost-Benefit Principle may not predict behavior accurately. But it proves helpful in another way, by identifying specific strategies for avoiding bad decisions.

PITFALL 1: MEASURING COSTS AND BENEFITS AS PROPORTIONS RATHER THAN ABSOLUTE DOLLAR AMOUNTS

As the next example makes clear, even people who seem to know they should weigh the pros and cons of the actions they are contemplating sometimes don't have a clear sense of how to measure the relevant costs and benefits.

EXAMPLE 1.2 | **Comparing Costs and Benefits**

Should you walk downtown to save $10 on a $2,020 laptop computer?

You are about to buy a $2,020 laptop computer at the nearby campus store when a friend tells you that the same computer is on sale at a downtown store for only $2,010. If the downtown store is half an hour's walk away, where should you buy the computer?

---

[1]The examples in this section are inspired by the pioneering research of Daniel Kahneman and the late Amos Tversky. Kahneman was awarded the 2002 Nobel Prize in Economics for his efforts to integrate insights from psychology into economics. You can read more about this work in Kahneman's brilliant 2011 book, *Thinking Fast and Slow* (New York: Macmillan).

Assuming that the laptop is light enough to carry without effort, the structure of this example is exactly the same as that of Example 1.1. The only difference is that the price of the laptop is dramatically higher than the price of the wireless keyboard. As before, the benefit of buying downtown is the dollar amount you'll save, namely, $10. And because it's exactly the same trip, its cost also must be the same as before. So if you are perfectly rational, you should make the same decision in both cases. Yet when people are asked what they would do in these situations, the overwhelming majority say they'd walk downtown to buy the keyboard but would buy the laptop at the campus store. When asked to explain, most of them say something like, "The trip was worth it for the keyboard because you save 40 percent, but not worth it for the laptop because you save only $10 out of $2,020."

This is faulty reasoning. The benefit of the trip downtown is not the *proportion* you save on the original price. Rather, it is the *absolute dollar amount* you save. The benefit of walking downtown to buy the laptop is $10, exactly the same as for the wireless keyboard. And because the cost of the trip must also be the same in both cases, the economic surplus from making both trips must be exactly the same. That means that a rational decision maker would make the same decision in both cases. Yet, as noted, most people choose differently.

The pattern of faulty reasoning in the decision just discussed is one of several decision pitfalls to which people are often prone. In the discussion that follows, we will identify two additional decision pitfalls. In some cases, people ignore costs or benefits that they ought to take into account. On other occasions they are influenced by costs or benefits that are irrelevant.

 SELF-TEST 1.2

Which is more valuable: saving $100 on a $2,000 plane ticket to Tokyo or saving $90 on a $200 plane ticket to Chicago?

PITFALL 2: IGNORING IMPLICIT COSTS

Sherlock Holmes, Arthur Conan Doyle's legendary detective, was successful because he saw details that most others overlooked. In *Silver Blaze*, Holmes is called on to investigate the theft of an expensive racehorse from its stable. A Scotland Yard inspector assigned to the case asks Holmes whether some particular aspect of the crime requires further study. "Yes," Holmes replies, and describes "the curious incident of the dog in the nighttime." "The dog did nothing in the nighttime,"[2] responds the puzzled inspector. But, as Holmes realized, that was precisely the problem! The watchdog's failure to bark when Silver Blaze was stolen meant that the watchdog knew the thief. This clue ultimately proved the key to unraveling the mystery.

Just as we often don't notice when a dog fails to bark, many of us tend to overlook the implicit value of activities that fail to happen. As discussed earlier, however, intelligent decisions require taking the value of forgone opportunities properly into account.

The opportunity cost of an activity, once again, is the value of all that must be forgone in order to engage in that activity. If buying a wireless keyboard downtown means not watching another hour of your favorite show on Netflix, then the value to you of watching the show is an implicit cost of the trip. Many people make bad decisions because they tend to ignore the value of such forgone opportunities. To avoid overlooking implicit costs, economists often translate questions like "Should I walk downtown?" into ones like "Should I walk downtown or watch another hour of my favorite show?"

Implicit costs are like dogs that fail to bark in the night. Many of us tend to overlook activities that fail to happen.

[2]Arthur Conan Doyle, "The Adventure of Silver Blaze," *The Memoirs of Sherlock Holmes* (London: George Newnes Ltd., 1893).

| EXAMPLE 1.3 | **Implicit Cost** |

Should you use your frequent-flyer coupon to fly to Cancun for spring break?

With spring break only a week away, you are still undecided about whether to go to Cancun with a group of classmates at the University of Iowa. The round-trip airfare from Cedar Rapids is $500, but you have a frequent-flyer coupon you could use for the trip. All other relevant costs for the vacation week at the beach total exactly $1,000. The most you would be willing to pay for the Cancun vacation is $1,350. That amount is your benefit of taking the vacation. Your only alternative use for your frequent-flyer coupon is for a trip to Boston the weekend after spring break to attend your brother's wedding. (Your coupon expires shortly thereafter.) If the Cedar Rapids–Boston round-trip airfare is $400, should you use your frequent-flyer coupon to fly to Cancun for spring break?

The Cost-Benefit Principle tells us that you should go to Cancun if the benefits of the trip exceed its costs. If not for the complication of the frequent-flyer coupon, solving this problem would be a straightforward matter of comparing your benefit from the week at the beach to the sum of all relevant costs. And because your airfare and other costs would add up to $1,500, or $150 more than your benefit from the trip, you would not go to Cancun.

But what about the possibility of using your frequent-flyer coupon to make the trip? Using it for that purpose might make the flight to Cancun seem free, suggesting you'd reap an economic surplus of $350 by making the trip. But doing so also would mean you'd have to fork over $400 for your airfare to Boston. So the implicit cost of using your coupon to go to Cancun is really $400. If you use it for that purpose, the trip still ends up being a loser because the cost of the vacation, $1,400, exceeds the benefit by $50. In cases like these, you're much more likely to decide sensibly if you ask yourself, "Should I use my frequent-flyer coupon for this trip or save it for an upcoming trip?"

Is your flight to Cancun "free" if you travel on a frequent-flyer coupon?

We cannot emphasize strongly enough that the key to using the Cost-Benefit Principle correctly lies in recognizing precisely what taking a given action prevents us from doing. Self-Test 1.3 illustrates this point by modifying the details of Example 1.3 slightly.

 SELF-TEST 1.3

Refer to given information in Example 1.3, but this time your frequent-flyer coupon expires in a week, so your only chance to use it will be for the Cancun trip. Should you use your coupon?

PITFALL 3: TAKING SUNK COSTS INTO ACCOUNT

When deciding whether to take an action, the only relevant costs and benefits are those that would occur as a result of taking the action. Sometimes people are influenced by costs they ought to ignore. Other times they compare the wrong costs and benefits. *The only costs that should influence a decision about whether to take an action are those we can avoid by not taking the action. Similarly, the only benefits we should consider are those that would not occur unless the action were taken.* As a practical matter, however, many decision makers appear to be influenced by costs or benefits that would have occurred no matter what. Thus, people are often influenced by **sunk costs**—costs that are beyond recovery at the moment a decision is made. For example, money spent on a nontransferable, nonrefundable airline ticket is a sunk cost.

sunk cost a cost that is beyond recovery at the moment a decision must be made

As the following example illustrates, sunk costs must be borne *whether or not an action is taken,* so they are irrelevant to the decision of whether to take the action.

EXAMPLE 1.4   Sunk Cost

How much should you eat at an all-you-can-eat restaurant?

Sangam, an Indian restaurant in Philadelphia, offers an all-you-can-eat lunch buffet for $10. Customers pay $10 at the door, and no matter how many times they refill their plates, there is no additional charge. One day, as a goodwill gesture, the owner of the restaurant tells 20 randomly selected guests that they can eat at the all-you-can-eat buffet for free. The remaining guests pay the usual price. If all diners are rational, will those who are able to eat at the buffet for free consume a different amount of food, on average, than those who have to pay $10 for the buffet?

Having eaten their first helping, diners in each group confront the following question: "Should I go back for another helping?" For rational diners, if the benefit of doing so exceeds the cost, the answer is yes; otherwise it is no. Note that at the moment of decision, the $10 charge for the lunch is a sunk cost. Those who paid it have no way to recover it. Thus, for both groups, the (extra) cost of another helping is exactly zero. And because the people who received the free lunch were chosen at random, there's no reason their appetites or incomes should be any different from those of other diners. The benefit of another helping thus should be the same, on average, for people in both groups. And because their respective costs and benefits are the same, the two groups should eat the same number of helpings, on average.

Psychologists and economists have experimental evidence, however, that people in such groups do *not* eat similar amounts.[3] In particular, those who have to pay for the all-you-can-eat buffet tend to eat substantially more than those for whom the buffet is free. People in the former group somehow seem determined to "get their money's worth." Their implicit goal is apparently to minimize the average cost per bite of the food they eat. Yet minimizing average cost is not a particularly sensible objective. The irony is that diners who are determined to get their money's worth usually end up eating too much.

The fact that the cost-benefit criterion failed the test of prediction in Example 1.4 does nothing to invalidate its advice about what people *should* do. If you are letting sunk costs influence your decisions, you can do better by changing your behavior.

PITFALL 4: FAILURE TO APPRECIATE THE DISTINCTION BETWEEN MARGINAL AND AVERAGE COSTS AND BENEFITS

In addition to paying attention to costs and benefits that should be ignored, people often use incorrect measures of the relevant costs and benefits. This error often occurs when we must choose the *extent* to which an activity should be pursued (as opposed to choosing whether to pursue it at all). We can apply the Cost-Benefit Principle in such situations by repeatedly asking the question, "Should I increase the level at which I am currently pursuing the activity?"

In attempting to answer this question, the focus should always be on the benefit and cost of an *additional* unit of activity. To emphasize this focus, economists refer to the cost of an additional unit of activity as its **marginal cost**. Similarly, the benefit of an additional unit of the activity is its **marginal benefit**.

marginal cost the increase in total cost that results from carrying out one additional unit of an activity

marginal benefit the increase in total benefit that results from carrying out one additional unit of an activity

[3]See, for example, Richard Thaler, "Toward a Positive Theory of Consumer Choice," *Journal of Economic Behavior and Organization* 1, no. 1 (1980).

When the problem is to discover the proper level for an activity, the cost-benefit rule is to keep increasing the level as long as the marginal benefit of the activity exceeds its marginal cost. As the following example illustrates, however, people often fail to apply this rule correctly.

| EXAMPLE 1.5 | **Focusing on Marginal Costs and Benefits** |

Should SpaceX expand its launch program from four launches per year to five?

SpaceX accountants have estimated that the gains from the company's jumbo rocket launch program are currently $24 billion a year (an average of $6 billion per launch) and that its costs are currently $20 billion a year (an average $5 billion per launch). On the basis of these estimates, they have recommended that the company increase its number of launches. Should SpaceX CEO Elon Musk follow their advice?

To discover whether the advice makes economic sense, we must compare the marginal cost of a launch to its marginal benefit. The accountants' estimates, however, tell us only the **average cost** and **average benefit** of the program. These are, respectively, the total cost of the program divided by the number of launches and the total benefit divided by the number of launches.

average cost the total cost of undertaking n units of an activity divided by n

average benefit the total benefit of undertaking n units of an activity divided by n

Knowing the average benefit and average cost per launch for all rockets launched thus far is simply not useful for deciding whether to expand the program. Of course, the average cost of the launches undertaken so far *might* be the same as the cost of adding another launch. But it also might be either higher or lower than the marginal cost of a launch. The same holds true regarding average and marginal benefits.

Suppose, for the sake of discussion, that the benefit of an additional launch is in fact the same as the average benefit per launch thus far, $6 billion. Should SpaceX add another launch? Not if the cost of adding the fifth launch would be more than $6 billion. And the fact that the average cost per launch is only $5 billion simply does not tell us anything about the marginal cost of the fifth launch.

Suppose, for example, that the relationship between the number of rockets launched and the total cost of the program is as described in Table 1.1. The average cost per launch (third column) when there are four launches would then be $20 billion/4 = $5 billion per launch, just as the accountants reported. But note in the second column of the table that adding a fifth launch would raise costs from $20 billion to $32 billion, making the marginal cost of the fifth launch $12 billion. So if the benefit of an additional launch is $6 billion, increasing the number of launches from four to five would make absolutely no economic sense.

TABLE 1.1
How Total Cost Varies with the Number of Launches

Number of launches	Total cost ($ billions)	Average cost ($ billion/launch)
0	0	0
1	3	3
2	7	3.5
3	12	4
4	20	5
5	32	6.4

The following example illustrates how to apply the *Cost-Benefit Principle* correctly in this case.

| EXAMPLE 1.6 | Focusing on Marginal Costs and Benefits |

How many rockets should SpaceX launch?

SpaceX must decide how many rockets to launch. The benefit of each launch is estimated to be $6 billion, and the total cost of the program again depends on the number of launches as shown in Table 1.1. How many rockets should SpaceX launch?

SpaceX should continue to launch its jumbo rockets as long as the marginal benefit of the program exceeds its marginal cost. In this example, the marginal benefit is constant at $6 billion per launch, regardless of the number of rockets launched. SpaceX should thus keep launching rockets as long as the marginal cost per launch is less than or equal to $6 billion.

Applying the definition of marginal cost to the total cost entries in the second column of Table 1.1 yields the marginal cost values in the third column of Table 1.2. (Because marginal cost is the change in total cost that results when we change the number of launches by one, we place each marginal cost entry midway between the rows showing the corresponding total cost entries.) Thus, for example, the marginal cost of increasing the number of launches from one to two is $4 billion, the difference between the $7 billion total cost of two launches and the $3 billion total cost of one launch.

TABLE 1.2
How Marginal Cost Varies with the Number of Launches

Number of launches	Total cost ($ billions)	Marginal cost ($ billion/launch)
0	0	
		3
1	3	
		4
2	7	
		5
3	12	
		8
4	20	
		12
5	32	

As we see from a comparison of the $6 billion marginal benefit per launch with the marginal cost entries in the third column of Table 1.2, the first three launches satisfy the cost-benefit test, but the fourth and fifth launches do not. SpaceX should thus launch three rockets.

 SELF-TEST 1.4

If the marginal benefit of each launch had been not $6 billion but $9 billion, how many rockets should SpaceX have launched?

The cost-benefit framework emphasizes that the only relevant costs and benefits in deciding whether to pursue an activity further are *marginal* costs and benefits—measures that correspond to the *increment* of activity under consideration. In many contexts, however, people seem more inclined to compare the *average* cost and benefit of the activity. As Example 1.5 made clear, increasing the level of an activity may not be justified, even though its average benefit at the current level is significantly greater than its average cost.

 SELF-TEST 1.5

Should a basketball team's best player take all the team's shots?

A professional basketball team has a new assistant coach. The assistant notices that one player scores on a higher percentage of her shots than other players. Based on this information, the assistant suggests to the head coach that the star player take *all* the shots. That way, the assistant reasons, the team will score more points and win more games.

On hearing this suggestion, the head coach fires her assistant for incompetence. What was wrong with the assistant's idea?

RECAP ↑

FOUR IMPORTANT DECISION PITFALLS

1. **The pitfall of measuring costs or benefits proportionally.** Many decision makers treat a change in cost or benefit as insignificant if it constitutes only a small proportion of the original amount. Absolute dollar amounts, not proportions, should be employed to measure costs and benefits.
2. **The pitfall of ignoring implicit costs.** When performing a cost-benefit analysis of an action, it is important to account for all relevant costs, including the implicit value of alternatives that must be forgone in order to carry out the action. A resource (such as a frequent-flyer coupon) may have a high implicit cost, even if you originally got it "for free," if its best alternative use has high value. The identical resource may have a low implicit cost, however, if it has no good alternative uses.
3. **The pitfall of taking sunk costs into account.** When deciding whether to perform an action, the only costs and benefits that are relevant are those that would result from taking the action. It is important to ignore sunk costs—those costs that cannot be avoided even if the action isn't taken. Even though a ticket to a concert may have cost you $100, if you've already bought it and cannot sell it to anyone else, the $100 is a sunk cost and shouldn't influence your decision about whether to go to the concert.
4. **The pitfall of failure to think at the margin.** It's also important not to confuse average costs and benefits with marginal costs and benefits. Decision makers often have ready information about the total cost and benefit of an activity, and from these it's simple to compute the activity's average cost and benefit. A common mistake is to conclude that an activity should be increased if its average benefit exceeds its average cost. The Cost-Benefit Principle tells us that the level of an activity should be increased if, and only if, its *marginal* benefit exceeds its *marginal* cost.

Some costs and benefits, especially marginal costs and benefits and implicit costs, are important for decision making, while others, like sunk costs and average costs and benefits, are essentially irrelevant. This conclusion is implicit in our original statement of the Cost-Benefit Principle (an action should be taken if, and only if, the extra benefits of taking it exceed the extra costs). When we encounter additional examples of decision pitfalls, we will flag them by inserting the icon for the Cost-Benefit Principle as shown here.

NORMATIVE ECONOMICS VERSUS POSITIVE ECONOMICS

The examples discussed in the preceding section make the point that people *sometimes* choose irrationally. We must stress that our purpose in discussing these examples was not to suggest that people *generally* make irrational choices. On the contrary, most people appear to choose sensibly most of the time, especially when their decisions are important or familiar ones. The economist's focus on rational choice thus offers not only useful advice about making better decisions, but also a basis for predicting and explaining human behavior. We used the cost-benefit approach in this way when discussing how rising faculty salaries have led to larger class sizes. And as we will see, similar reasoning helps explain human behavior in virtually every other domain.

The Cost-Benefit Principle is an example of a **normative economic principle**, one that provides guidance about how we *should* behave. For example, according to the Cost-Benefit Principle, we should ignore sunk costs when making decisions about the future. As our discussion of the various decision pitfalls makes clear, however, the Cost-Benefit Principle is not always a **positive**, or **descriptive**, **economic principle**, one that describes how we actually *will* behave. As we saw, the Cost-Benefit Principle can be tricky to implement, and people sometimes fail to heed its prescriptions.

That said, we stress that knowing the relevant costs and benefits surely does enable us to predict how people will behave much of the time. If the benefit of an action goes up, it is generally reasonable to predict that people will be more likely to take that action. And conversely, if the cost of an action goes up, the safest prediction will be that people will be less likely to take that action. This point is so important that we designate it as the *Incentive Principle*.

normative economic principle one that says how people should behave

positive (or **descriptive**) **economic principle** one that predicts how people will behave

The Incentive Principle: A person (or a firm or a society) is more likely to take an action if its benefit rises, and less likely to take it if its cost rises. In short, incentives matter.

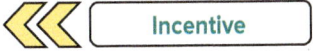 Incentive

The Incentive Principle is a positive economic principle. It stresses that the relevant costs and benefits usually help us predict behavior, but at the same time does not insist that people behave rationally in each instance. For example, if the price of heating oil were to rise sharply, we would invoke the Cost-Benefit Principle to say that people *should* turn down their thermostats, and invoke the Incentive Principle to predict that average thermostat settings *will* in fact go down.

THE INVISIBLE HAND

Adam Smith, an eighteenth-century Scottish moral philosopher, is widely regarded as the father of economics. To him we owe what is perhaps our discipline's most celebrated idea, the Invisible Hand Theory, developed in his landmark 1776 treatise, *The Wealth of Nations*. Smith began with the observation that self-interested business owners introduce product design improvements and cost-saving innovations not for the benefit of society but to lure customers away from rival firms. Smith was not the first to characterize the motives of business owners in this way. His real contribution was to describe the dynamic that unfolds in response to an innovation's appearance. The self-interested owners of rival firms are quick to copy the innovation in hope of recapturing lost sales, Smith argued. And when the competitive churning settles, consumers are the ultimate beneficiaries: They enjoy cheaper, better products, while firms earn no more than necessary to cover their new lower costs of production.

It's an elegant narrative, but Smith was more circumspect about the consequences of self-serving behavior than many modern accounts suggest. In his description of the business owner, for example, he wrote,

> . . . he intends only his own gain; and he is in this, as in many other cases, led by an invisible hand to promote an end which was no part of his intention.

Adam Smith: 1723–1790. Smith's modern disciples often oversimplify his message.

Nor is it always the worse for the society that it was no part of it. By pursuing his own interest, he *frequently* promotes that of the society more effectually than when he really intends to promote it.[4] [Emphasis added]

Contrast Smith's cautious language in this passage with that many of his modern disciples, who denounce any attempt to regulate private markets as a grave threat to human welfare. As the conservative Nobel economist Milton Friedman is said to have once remarked, "If you put the federal government in charge of the Sahara Desert, in five years there'd be a shortage of sand."

Although Smith emphasized that the pursuit of private gain often benefits society, he also understood that markets often fail when exchange is accompanied by side effects, which economists now call *externalities*. Externalities can be either positive, as when the planting of apple trees boosts honey production in nearby apiaries, or negative, as when factory smokestacks emit greenhouse gases. The question of how externalities affect resource allocation will be a recurrent theme in future chapters.

But if it is a mistake to assume that markets always deliver the best possible outcomes, it is also an error to fail to appreciate their extraordinary power. For all but a tiny slice of human history, most people performed most of life's daily tasks for themselves. In Chapter 2, we'll discuss why existence on those terms was, in the words of the seventeenth-century philosopher Thomas Hobbes, "solitary, poor, nasty, brutish, and short."[5]

As shown in Figure 1.1, income per capita hovered close to Hobbesian subsistence levels before Smith's birth in 1723. Since his death in 1790, it has grown at rates our ancestors never could have imagined. The modern marketplace, which began to spread in earnest only during Smith's lifetime, has changed living conditions dramatically, and the invisible-hand narrative explains much of that change.

The income gains made possible by markets have eliminated an enormous amount of human suffering. In Smith's Scotland, a family with three children could expect to see one of them die before reaching the age of 15; today, the likelihood that all three would survive into adulthood is more than 99 percent.

Of course, recent income gains have also been accompanied by significant new challenges. Had it not been for the fossil-fuel driven industrial age of the last two centuries, for example, we would not be facing a serious climate crisis today. But Smith's economic insights also inform the design of policies that can help defuse that crisis. To be sure, many of the measures we'll need to adopt will be extremely costly. But as we'll see going

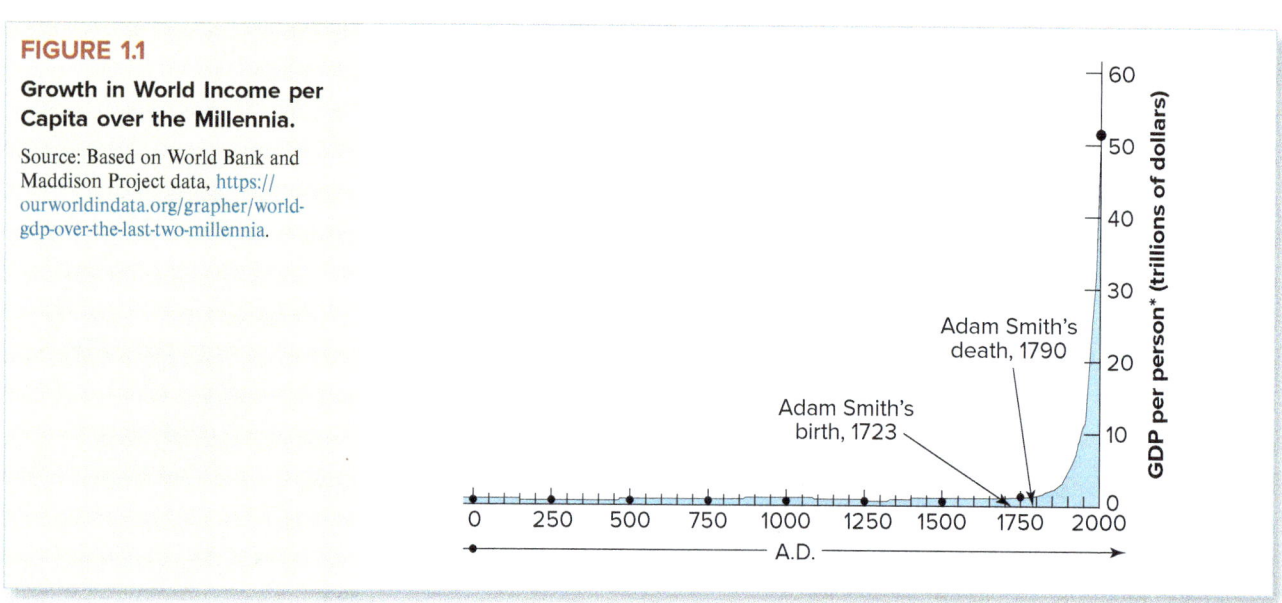

FIGURE 1.1

Growth in World Income per Capita over the Millennia.

Source: Based on World Bank and Maddison Project data, https:// ourworldindata.org/grapher/world-gdp-over-the-last-two-millennia.

[4]Adam Smith, *The Wealth of Nations*, Chapter 2, www.onlineliterature.com/view/php/wealth_nations /24?term=invisible%hand.
[5]Thomas Hobbes, *Leviathan*, 1651, Chapter 12.

forward, their costs turn out to be little more than a rounding error in comparison with the income gains that markets have made possible.

WHEN INDIVIDUAL AND COLLECTIVE INTERESTS ARE IN CONFLICT

Because of externalities, choices that look best to us individually often look much less attractive to the larger groups to which we belong. In the familiar stadium metaphor, for example, all stand to get a better view, yet no one sees any better than if all had remained comfortably seated. As the following example suggests, vehicle purchase decisions often entail a similar conflict between individual and collective interests.

EXAMPLE 1.7   **Individual and Collective Interests in Conflict**

How Big a Car Should I Buy?

You and other motorists in your community currently drive compact cars weighing 2,000 pounds. Your own car has begun to break down frequently and you're shopping for a replacement. The auto dealer who sells your favorite brand urges you to consider the company's new 7,000-pound SUV, citing evidence that people who drive it are rarely injured seriously in collisions with 2,000-pound compacts. You also care about air quality and fuel economy, but because safety is your highest concern, you decide to buy the SUV.

Regarding the decision of how big a car to buy, individual and collective interests often conflict sharply.

A side effect of your decision is to put others in your community at greater risk. Let's assume, plausibly, that because safety is also their main concern, they too switch to SUVs when replacement time comes. The result is that every driver will then be at greater risk of injury and death than if everyone had stuck with their 2,000-pound compacts. And since SUVs emit approximately 14 percent more CO_2 per mile than small cars, a second negative externality is an increase in greenhouse gas emissions.[6]

As even the most ardent market enthusiasts acknowledge, externalities can cause problems like the ones illustrated in this example. Their concern, however, is that government attempts to intervene in the marketplace can also cause problems. It's a concern worth taking seriously.

A government prohibition on the sale of vehicles weighing more than 2,000 pounds, for example, would take little account of tradespeople and others whose needs can be met only by larger vehicles. But less intrusive interventions are also possible, ones that preserve far greater freedom of individual action. If the problem is that heavier vehicles are misleadingly attractive to individuals, a simple solution would be to tax vehicles by weight. Those who feel they have pressing needs for larger vehicles could then pay the additional tax, which would enable those who continue driving smaller vehicles to be taxed less heavily.

That people generally dislike taxes would not argue against this policy. A country without taxes could field no army and would soon be taken over by another country that had one, and its citizens would then be taxed by the conquering country. Since we must tax something, why not tax activities that cause harm to others? As we'll see in Chapter 11, taxes on activities that generate negative externalities can increase total economic surplus substantially.

ECONOMICS: MICRO AND MACRO

By convention, we use the term **microeconomics** to describe the study of individual choices and of group behavior in individual markets. **Macroeconomics**, by contrast, is the study of the performance of national economies and of the policies that governments use to try to improve that performance. Macroeconomics tries to understand the determinants of such things as the national unemployment rate, the overall price level, and the total value of national output.

microeconomics the study of individual choice under scarcity and its implications for the behavior of prices and quantities in individual markets

macroeconomics the study of the performance of national economies and the policies that governments use to try to improve that performance

---

[6]Oliver Milman, "How SUVs Conquered the World—At the Expense of Its Climate," *The Guardian*, September 1, 2020.

Our focus in this chapter is on issues that confront the individual decision maker, whether that individual confronts a personal decision, a family decision, a business decision, a government policy decision, or indeed any other type of decision. Further on, we'll consider economic models of groups of individuals such as all buyers or all sellers in a specific market. Later still we'll turn to broader economic issues and measures.

No matter which of these levels is our focus, however, our thinking will be shaped by the fact that, although economic needs and wants are effectively unlimited, the material and human resources that can be used to satisfy them are finite. Clear thinking about economic problems must therefore always take into account the idea of trade-offs—the idea that having more of one good thing usually means having less of another. Our economy and our society are shaped to a substantial degree by the choices people have made when faced with trade-offs.

THE APPROACH OF THIS TEXT

Choosing the number of students to register in each class is just one of many important decisions in planning an introductory economics course. Another, to which the Scarcity Principle applies just as strongly, concerns which topics to include on the course syllabus. There's a virtually inexhaustible set of issues that might be covered in an introductory course, but only limited time in which to cover them. There's no free lunch. Covering some inevitably means omitting others.

All textbook authors are forced to pick and choose. A textbook that covered *all* the issues would take up more than a whole floor of your campus library. It is our firm view that most introductory textbooks try to cover far too much. One reason that each of us was drawn to the study of economics is that a relatively short list of the discipline's core ideas can explain a great deal of the behavior and events we see in the world around us. So rather than cover a large number of ideas at a superficial level, our strategy is to focus on this short list of core ideas, returning to each entry again and again, in many different contexts. This strategy will enable you to internalize these ideas remarkably well in the brief span of a single course. And the benefit of learning a small number of important ideas well will far outweigh the cost of having to ignore a host of other, less important ones.

So far, we've already encountered three core ideas: the Scarcity Principle, the Cost-Benefit Principle, and the Incentive Principle. As these core ideas reemerge in the course of our discussions, we'll call your attention to them. And shortly after a *new* core idea appears, we'll highlight it by formally restating it.

A second important element in our philosophy is a belief in the importance of active learning. In the same way that you can learn Spanish only by speaking and writing it, or tennis only by playing the game, you can learn economics only by *doing* economics. And because we want you to learn how to do economics, rather than just to read or listen passively as the authors or your instructor does economics, we'll make every effort to encourage you to stay actively involved.

For example, instead of just telling you about an idea, we'll usually first motivate the idea by showing you how it works in the context of a specific example. Often, these examples will be followed by self-tests for you to try, as well as applications that show the relevance of the idea to real life. Try working the self-tests *before* looking up the answers (which are at the end of each chapter).

Think critically about the applications: Do you see how they illustrate the point being made? Do they give you new insight into the issue? Work the problems at the end of the chapters and take extra care with those relating to points that you don't fully understand. Apply economic principles to the world around you. (We'll say more about this in the following discussion of economic naturalism.) Finally, when you come across an idea or example that you find interesting, tell a friend about it. You'll be surprised to discover how much the mere act of explaining it helps you understand and remember the underlying principle. The more actively you can become engaged in the learning process, the more effective your learning will be.

ECONOMIC NATURALISM

With the rudiments of the cost-benefit framework under your belt, you are now in a position to become an "economic naturalist," someone who uses insights from economics to help make sense of observations from everyday life. People who have studied biology are able to observe and marvel at many details of nature that would otherwise have escaped their notice. For example, on a walk in the woods in early April, the novice may see only trees. In contrast, the biology student notices many different species of trees and understands why some are already in leaf while others still lie dormant. Likewise, the novice may notice that in some animal species males are much larger than females, but the biology student knows that pattern occurs only in species in which males take several mates. Natural selection favors larger males in those species because their greater size helps them prevail in the often bloody contests among males for access to females. In contrast, males tend to be roughly the same size as females in monogamous species, in which there is much less fighting for mates.

Learning a few simple economic principles broadens our vision in a similar way. It enables us to see the mundane details of ordinary human existence in a new light. Whereas the uninitiated often fail even to notice these details, the economic naturalist not only sees them, but also becomes actively engaged in the attempt to understand them. We'll now consider a few examples of questions economic naturalists might pose for themselves, the first of which provides another illustration of how individuals and collective interests can diverge.

▶ Visit your instructor's Connect course and access your eBook to view this video.

Why does the light come on when you open the refrigerator door but not when you open the freezer?

The Economic Naturalist 1.1

Why does an accident in the northbound lanes of a divided highway cause a traffic jam in the southbound lanes?

When an accident occurs in the northbound lanes of an expressway, it's easy to see why traffic gets backed up in those lanes. The damaged cars, ambulances, and police cars often make the northbound lanes impassable for hours. But why should the accident cause traffic to back up—often for miles—in the southbound lanes?

As they approach the scene of the accident, southbound drivers make a simple cost-benefit calculation. The cost of slowing down to take a closer look at the accident scene is that they will be delayed by several seconds. The benefit is that by so doing, they will satisfy their curiosity. To judge from their behavior, the benefit seems to exceed the cost for most motorists. What most motorists do not consider, of course, is that one's decision to slow down for several seconds also creates several seconds of delay for each of the hundreds or thousands of motorists behind them. The cost of getting a better look at the accident might thus be a delay of more than an hour per motorist.

It seems unlikely that many motorists would be willing to endure an hour's delay to get a better look at an accident scene. If drivers could take a binding vote on the matter, they would almost surely elect not to slow down. But they make their decisions on this issue one by one when they reach the spot of the accident. At that point, having already paid the cost of others' curiosity, most motorists—even those in a hurry—choose to slow down.

The rubber-necker's curiosity: Is the delay worth it?

▶ Visit your instructor's Connect course and access your eBook to view this video.

Why are child safety seats required in automobiles but not in airplanes?

The Economic Naturalists 1.2 and 1.3 suggest plausible answers to the following strange questions.

The Economic Naturalist 1.2

Why does check-splitting make the total restaurant bill higher?

▶ Visit your instructor's Connect course and access your eBook to view this video.

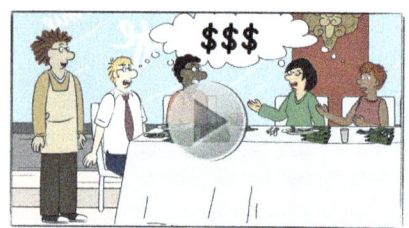

Why does the practice of check splitting cause people to spend more at restaurants?

Sven Torvaldsen and nine friends are having dinner at La Maison de La Casa House, a four-star restaurant in Minneapolis. To simplify the task of paying for their meal, they have agreed in advance to split the cost of their meal equally, with each paying one-tenth of the total check. Having cleared the entree dishes, the server arrives with the dessert menu, on which Sven's two favorite items are pumpkin bread pudding ($10) and chocolate mousse ($6). Sven's reservation prices for these items are $4 and $3, respectively. Will he order dessert, and, if so, which one? Would he order dessert if he were dining by himself?

When Sven and his friends split the total check equally, Sven's payment goes up by one-tenth of the menu price of any dessert he orders. Thus, the prices—to him—of the bread pudding and chocolate mousse are $1 and 60 cents, respectively. Because he gets $4 − $1 = $3 of consumer surplus from the bread pudding and only $3 − $0.60 = $2.40 from the chocolate mousse, he will order the bread pudding. If Sven were dining alone, however, his bill would increase dollar for dollar with the menu price of any dessert he ordered. And since the menu prices exceed his corresponding reservation prices, he would not order dessert at all.

The irony, of course, is that if Sven's nine friends have the same preferences regarding dessert, each will order bread pudding and each person's share of the total bill will rise not by $1 but by the full $10. Compared to the alternative of no one having dessert, each diner suffers a $6 loss in consumer surplus. Still, it made sense for each to order bread pudding since failure to do so would have reduced each diner's bill by only $1.

✅ **SELF-TEST 1.6**

In The Economic Naturalist 1.2 example, would Sven have ordered dessert if there had been only 5 people splitting the check instead of 10?

The Economic Naturalist 1.3

Why do the keypad buttons on drive-up automated teller machines have Braille dots?

Braille dots on elevator buttons and on the keypads of walk-up automated teller machines enable blind people to participate more fully in the normal flow of daily activity. But even though blind people can do many remarkable things, they cannot drive automobiles on public roads. Why, then, do the manufacturers of automated teller machines install Braille dots on the machines at drive-up locations?

Why do the keypad buttons on drive-up automated teller machines have Braille dots?

The answer to this riddle is that once the keypad molds have been manufactured, the cost of producing buttons with Braille dots is no higher than the cost of producing smooth buttons. Making both would require separate sets of molds and two different types of inventory. If the patrons of drive-up machines found buttons with Braille dots harder to use, there might be a reason to incur these extra costs. But since the dots pose no difficulty for sighted users, the best and cheapest solution is to produce only keypads with dots.

The preceding example was suggested by Cornell student Bill Tjoa, in response to the following assignment:

 SELF-TEST 1.7

In 500 words or less, use cost-benefit analysis to explain some pattern of events or behavior you have observed in your own environment.

There is probably no more useful step you can take in your study of economics than to perform several versions of the assignment in Self-Test 1.7. Students who do so almost invariably become lifelong economic naturalists. Their mastery of economic concepts not only does not decay with the passage of time, but it actually grows stronger. We urge you, in the strongest possible terms, to make this investment!

SUMMARY

• Economics is the study of how people make choices under conditions of scarcity and of the results of those choices for society. Economic analysis of human behavior begins with the assumption that people are rational—that they have well-defined goals and try to achieve them as best they can. In trying to achieve their goals, people normally face trade-offs: Because material and human resources are limited, having more of one good thing means making do with less of some other good thing. *(LO1)*

• Our focus in this chapter has been on how rational people make choices among alternative courses of action. Our basic tool for analyzing these decisions is cost-benefit analysis. The Cost-Benefit Principle says that a person should take an action if, and only if, the benefit of that action is at least as great as its cost. The benefit of an action is defined as the largest dollar amount the person would be willing to pay in order to take the action. The cost of an action is defined as the dollar value of everything the person must give up in order to take the action. *(LO2)*

• In using the cost-benefit framework, we need not presume that people choose rationally all the time. Indeed, we

identified four common pitfalls that plague decision makers in all walks of life: a tendency to treat small proportional changes as insignificant, a tendency to ignore implicit costs, failing to ignore sunk costs, or by failing to compare marginal costs and benefits. *(LO3)*

• Often the question is not whether to pursue an activity but rather how many units of it to pursue. In these cases, the rational person pursues additional units as long as the marginal benefit of the activity (the benefit from pursuing an additional unit of it) exceeds its marginal cost (the cost of pursuing an additional unit of it). *(LO4)*

• Adam Smith's Invisible Hand Theory describes how the self-seeking actions of individual business owners often lead to beneficial results for society. But markets often produce less attractive results when transactions are accompanied by side effects or externalities. *(LO5)*

• Microeconomics is the study of individual choices and of group behavior in individual markets, while macroeconomics is the study of the performance of national economics and of the policies that governments use to try to improve economic performance.

CORE PRINCIPLES

 The Scarcity Principle (also called the No-Free-Lunch Principle)
Although we have boundless needs and wants, the resources available to us are limited. So having more of one good thing usually means having less of another.

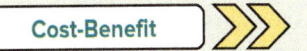 **The Cost-Benefit Principle**
An individual (or a firm or a society) should take an action if, and only if, the extra benefits from taking the action are at least as great as the extra costs.

 The Incentive Principle
A person (or a firm or a society) is more likely to take an action if its benefit rises, and less likely to take it if its cost rises. In short, incentives matter.

KEY TERMS

average benefit

average cost

economic surplus

economics

macroeconomics

marginal benefit

marginal cost

microeconomics

normative economic principle

opportunity cost

positive (or descriptive) economic
 principle

rational person

sunk cost

REVIEW QUESTIONS

1. A friend of yours on the tennis team says, "Private tennis lessons are definitely better than group lessons." Explain what you think they mean by this statement. Then use the Cost-Benefit Principle to explain why private lessons are not necessarily the best choice for everyone. *(LO2)*

2. True or false: Your willingness to drive downtown to save $30 on a new appliance should depend on what fraction of the total selling price $30 is. Explain. *(LO3)*

3. Why might someone who is trying to decide whether to see a movie be more likely to focus on the $10 ticket price than on the $20 one would fail to earn by not dogwalking? *(LO3)*

4. Many people think of their air travel as being free when they use frequent-flyer coupons. Explain why these people are likely to make wasteful travel decisions. *(LO3)*

5. Is the nonrefundable tuition payment you made to your university this semester a sunk cost? How would your answer differ if your university were to offer a full tuition refund to any student who dropped out of school during the first two months of the semester? *(LO3)*

PROBLEMS

1. Suppose your school is considering whether to spend $20 million building a new state-of-the-art recreation facility. All of the students agree that the existing facility is in disrepair and that a new facility would be much nicer. Despite this, however, when students are asked to vote on whether they would like the school to build the new recreation facility, over 78 percent vote no. Why might such a large fraction of students vote no even though they all agree that a new recreation facility would be much nicer than the existing one? *(LO1)*

2. Suppose the most you would be willing to pay to have a freshly washed car before going out on a date is $6. The smallest amount for which you would be willing to wash someone else's car is $3.50. You are going out this evening and your car is dirty. How much economic surplus would you receive from washing it? *(LO2)*

3. To earn extra money in the summer, you grow tomatoes and sell them at a local farmers' market for 30 cents per pound. By adding compost to your garden, you can increase your yield as shown in the accompanying table. If compost costs 50 cents per pound and your goal is to make as much profit as possible, how many pounds of compost should you add? *(LO2)*

Pounds of compost	Pounds of tomatoes
	100
1	120
2	125
3	128
4	130
5	131
6	131.5

4.* You and your friend Jamal have identical tastes. At 2 p.m., you go to the local Ticketmaster outlet and buy a nonrefundable $50 ticket to a basketball game to be played that night in Syracuse, 50 miles north of your home in Ithaca. Jamal plans to attend the same game, but because he cannot get to the Ticketmaster outlet, he plans to buy his ticket at the game. Tickets sold at the game cost only $40 because they carry no Ticketmaster surcharge. (Many people nonetheless pay the higher price at Ticketmaster, to be sure of getting good seats.) At 4 p.m., an unexpected snowstorm begins, making the prospect of the drive to Syracuse much less attractive than before (but ensuring the availability of good seats). If both you and Jamal are rational, is one of you more likely to attend the game than the other? *(LO2)*

*Denotes more difficult problem.

5. Kenya is a mushroom farmer. She invests all her spare cash in additional mushrooms, which grow on otherwise useless land behind her barn. The mushrooms double in weight during their first year, after which time they are harvested and sold at a constant price per pound. Kenya's friend Fatima asks Kenya for a loan of $200, which she promises to repay after one year. How much interest will Fatima have to pay Kenya in order for Kenya to recover her opportunity cost of making the loan? Explain briefly. *(LO3)*

6. Suppose that in the last few seconds you devoted to question 1 on your physics exam you earned 4 extra points, while in the last few seconds you devoted to question 2 you earned 10 extra points. You earned a total of 48 and 12 points, respectively, on the two questions, and the total time you spent on each was the same. If you could take the exam again, how—if at all—should you reallocate your time between these questions? *(LO3)*

7. Monica and Rachel have the same preferences and incomes. Just as Monica arrived at the theater to see a play, she discovered that she had lost the $10 ticket she had purchased earlier. Rachel also just arrived at the theater planning to buy a ticket to see the same play when she discovered that she had lost a $10 bill from her wallet. If both Monica and Rachel are rational and both still have enough money to pay for a ticket, is one of them more likely than the other to go ahead and see the play anyway? *(LO3)*

8. Residents of your city are charged a fixed weekly fee of $6 for garbage collection. They are allowed to put out as many cans as they wish. The average household disposes of three cans of garbage per week under this plan. Now suppose that your city changes to a "tag" system. Each can of garbage to be collected must have a tag affixed to it. The tags cost $2 each and are not reusable. What effect do you think the introduction of the tag system will have on the total quantity of garbage collected in your city? Explain briefly. *(LO4)*

9. Once a week, Hector purchases a six-pack of cola and puts it in his refrigerator for his two children. He invariably discovers that all six cans are gone on the first day. Jin also purchases a six-pack of cola once a week for his two children, but unlike Hector, he tells them that each

may drink no more than three cans per week. If the children use cost-benefit analysis each time they decide whether to drink a can of cola, explain why the cola lasts much longer at Jin's house than at Hector's. *(LO4)*

10.* Suppose there is only one electric scooter company in Adriana's hometown. Currently, the company charges 20 cents per minute, and there is no fee to unlock a scooter. The scooter company is considering changing its pricing plan so that it would charge $1 to unlock a scooter and 10 cents per minute. If Adriana never takes a ride that lasts less than 10 minutes, then what will happen to the average length of her rides if the scooter company switches to the new pricing plan? Explain. *(LO4)*

11.* The meal plan at University A lets students eat as much as they like for a fixed fee of $500 per semester. The average student there eats 250 pounds of food per semester. University B charges $500 for a book of meal tickets that entitles the student to eat 250 pounds of food per semester. If the student eats more than 250 pounds, they pay $2 for each additional pound; if the student eats less, they get a $2 per pound refund. If students are rational, at which university will average food consumption be higher? Explain briefly. *(LO4)*

12. Discuss how one individual's decision to smoke cigarettes could harm other consumers. When someone makes a decision about whether to smoke, are they likely to account fully for any costs that smoking imposes on others? Why or why not? *(LO5)*

13. Suppose Ms. Green's home currently uses electricity produced from a coal-fired power plant. To save money, she is considering installing rooftop solar panels. She estimates that over the lifetime of the panels, their cost would be $150 per month and they would reduce her monthly electric bill by $125. The panels would also reduce damage from sulfur dioxide and carbon dioxide emissions from the coal plant by $35 per month. If Ms. Green bases her decision on only her private costs and benefits (that is, if she ignores how others will benefit from pollution reduction), will she install solar panels? From society's perspective, would their installation be justified? *(LO5)*

ANSWERS TO SELF-TESTS

1.1 The benefit of buying the wireless keyboard downtown is again $10 but the cost is now $12, so your economic surplus would be $2 smaller than if you'd bought it at the campus store. *(LO2)*

1.2 Saving $100 is $10 more valuable than saving $90, even though the percentage saved is much greater in the case of the Chicago ticket. *(LO3)*

1.3 Since you now have no alternative use for your coupon, the opportunity cost of using it to pay for the Cancun trip is zero. That means your economic surplus from the trip will be $1,350 − $1,000 = $350 > 0, so you should use your coupon and go to Cancun. *(LO3)*

1.4 The marginal benefit of the fourth launch is $9 billion, which exceeds its marginal cost of $8 billion, so the

*Denotes more difficult problem.

fourth launch should be added. But the fifth launch should not, because its marginal cost ($12 billion) exceeds its marginal benefit ($9 billion). *(LO3)*

1.5 If the star player takes one more shot, some other player must take one less. The fact that the star player's *average* success rate is higher than the other players' does not mean that the probability of making her *next* shot (the marginal benefit of having her shoot once more) is higher than the probability of another player making her next shot. Indeed, if the best player took all her team's shots, the other team would focus its defensive effort entirely on her, in which case letting others shoot would definitely pay. *(LO3)*

1.6 If Sven orders bread pudding, his share of the bill would now go up by $2 instead of $1. If he orders chocolate mousse, his share of the bill would go up by $1.20 instead of $0.60. So he would still order the bread pudding (surplus = $4 − $2 = $2) rather than the chocolate mousse (surplus = $3 − $1.20 − $1.80). *(LO3)*

1.7 Answers will vary.

Working with Equations, Graphs, and Tables

lthough many of the examples and most of the end-of-chapter problems in this book are quantitative, none requires mathematical skills beyond rudimentary high school algebra and geometry. In this brief appendix, we review some of the skills you'll need for dealing with these examples and problems.

One important skill is to be able to read simple verbal descriptions and translate the information they provide into the relevant equations or graphs. You'll also need to be able to translate information given in tabular form into an equation or graph, and sometimes you'll need to translate graphical information into a table or equation. Finally, you'll need to be able to solve simple systems with two equations and two unknowns. The following examples illustrate all the tools you'll need.

USING A VERBAL DESCRIPTION TO CONSTRUCT AN EQUATION

We begin with an example that shows how to construct a billing equation for a ride on an electric scooter from a verbal description of the billing plan.

EXAMPLE 1A.1 — A Verbal Description

An electric scooter company charges $1 to unlock a scooter plus 20 cents per minute. Write an equation that describes your bill for riding this scooter.

An **equation** is a simple mathematical expression that describes the relationship between two or more **variables**, or quantities, that are free to assume different values in some range. The most common type of equation we'll work with contains two types of variables: **dependent variables** and **independent variables**. In this example, the dependent variable is the dollar amount of your scooter bill and the independent variable is the variable on which your bill depends, namely, the number of minutes you ride the scooter. Your bill also depends on the $1 fee to unlock the scooter and the 20 cents per minute charge. But, in this example, those amounts are **constants**, not variables. A constant, also called a **parameter**, is a quantity in an equation that is fixed in value, not free to vary. As the terms suggest, the dependent variable describes an outcome that depends on the value taken by the independent variable.

Once you've identified the dependent variable and the independent variable, choose simple symbols to represent them. In algebra courses, X is typically used to represent the independent variable and Y the dependent variable. Many people find it easier to remember what the variables stand for, however, if they choose symbols that are linked in some straightforward way to the quantities

equation a mathematical expression that describes the relationship between two or more variables

variable a quantity that is free to take a range of different values

dependent variable a variable in an equation whose value is determined by the value taken by another variable in the equation

independent variable a variable in an equation whose value determines the value taken by another variable in the equation

constant (or **parameter**) a quantity that is fixed in value

23

that the variables represent. Thus, in this example, we might use B to represent your scooter *bill* in dollars and T to represent the total *time* in minutes of your ride.

Having identified the relevant variables and chosen symbols to represent them, you are now in a position to write the equation that links them

$$B = 1 + 0.20T, \tag{1A.1}$$

where B is your scooter bill in dollars and T is the number of minutes you spend riding the scooter. The fee to unlock the scooter (1) and the charge per minute (0.20) are parameters in this equation. Note the importance of being clear about the units of measure. Because B represents the scooter bill in dollars, we must also express the fee to unlock the scooter and the per-minute charge in dollars, which is why the latter number appears in Equation 1A.1 as 0.20 rather than 20. Equation 1A.1 follows the normal convention in which the dependent variable appears by itself on the left-hand side while the independent variable or variables and constants appear on the right-hand side.

Once we have the equation for the scooter bill, we can use it to calculate how much you'll owe as a function of the number of minutes you spend riding. For example, if you ride the scooter for 16 minutes, you can calculate your scooter bill by simply substituting 16 minutes for T in Equation 1A.1

$$B = 1 + 0.20(16) = 4.20. \tag{1A.2}$$

Your scooter bill when you ride for 16 minutes is thus equal to $4.20.

 SELF-TEST 1A.1

Under the scooter billing plan described in Example 1A.1, how much would you owe for a 22-minute ride?

GRAPHING THE EQUATION OF A STRAIGHT LINE

The next example shows how to portray the billing plan described in Example 1A.1 as a graph.

EXAMPLE 1A.2	Graphing an Equation

Construct a graph that portrays the scooter billing plan described in Example 1A.1, putting your total bill, in dollars, on the vertical axis and the length of your ride, in minutes, on the horizontal axis.

The first step in responding to this instruction is the one we just took, namely, to translate the verbal description of the billing plan into an equation. When graphing an equation, the normal convention is to use the vertical axis to represent the dependent variable and the horizontal axis to represent the independent variable. In Figure 1A.1, we therefore put B on the vertical axis and T on the horizontal axis. One way to construct the graph shown in the figure is to begin by plotting the bill values that correspond to several different ride lengths. For example, someone who rides for 10 minutes would have a bill of $B = 1 + 0.20(10) = \$3$. Thus, in Figure 1A.1 the value of 10 minutes on the horizontal axis corresponds to a bill of $3 on the vertical axis (point A). Someone who rides for 15 minutes

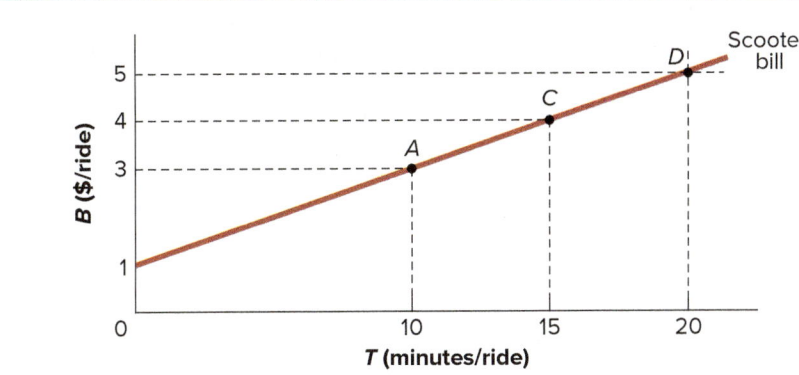

FIGURE 1A.1

The Scooter Billing Plan in Example 1A.1.

The graph of the equation $B = 1 + 0.20T$ is the straight line shown. Its vertical intercept is 1 and its slope is 0.20.

would have a bill of $B = 1 + 0.20(15) = \$4$, so the value of 15 minutes on the horizontal axis corresponds to \$4 on the vertical axis (point C). Similarly, someone who rides for 20 minutes would have a bill of $B = 1 + 0.20(20) = \$5$, so the value of 20 minutes on the horizontal axis corresponds to \$5 on the vertical axis (point D). The line joining these points is the graph of the billing Equation 1A.1.

As shown in Figure 1A.1, the graph of the equation $B = 1 + 0.20T$ is a straight line. The parameter 1 is the **vertical intercept** of the line—the value of B when $T = 0$, or the point at which the line intersects the vertical axis. The parameter 0.20 is the **slope** of the line, which is the ratio of the **rise** of the line to the corresponding **run**. The ratio rise/run is simply the vertical distance between any two points on the line divided by the horizontal distance between those points. For example, if we choose points A and C in Figure 1A.1, the rise is $4 - 3 = 1$ and the corresponding run is $15 - 10 = 5$, so rise/run $= 1/5 = 0.20$. More generally, for the graph of any equation $Y = a + bX$, the parameter a is the vertical intercept and the parameter b is the slope.

vertical intercept in a straight line, the value taken by the dependent variable when the independent variable equals zero

slope in a straight line, the ratio of the vertical distance the straight line travels between any two points *(rise)* to the corresponding horizontal distance *(run)*

DERIVING THE EQUATION OF A STRAIGHT LINE FROM ITS GRAPH

The next example shows how to derive the equation for a straight line from a graph of the line.

EXAMPLE 1A.3   Deriving an Equation from a Graph

Figure 1A.2 shows the graph of the billing plan for an electric scooter company. What is the equation for this graph? How much is the fee to unlock a scooter under this plan? How much is the charge per minute?

The slope of the line shown is the rise between any two points divided by the corresponding run. For points A and C, rise $= 3.50 - 3 = 0.50$ and run $= 15 - 10 = 5$, so the slope equals rise/run $= 0.50/5 = 0.10$. And since the horizontal intercept of the line is 2, its equation must be given by

$$B = 2 + 0.10T. \tag{1A.3}$$

Under this plan, the fee to unlock a scooter is the value of the bill when $T = 0$, which is \$2. The charge per minute is the slope of the billing line, 0.10, or 10 cents per minute.

FIGURE 1A.2

Another Scooter Billing Plan.
The vertical distance between points A and C is $3.50 - 3 = 0.50$ units, and the horizontal distance between points A and C is $15 - 10 = 5$, so the slope of the line is $0.50/5 = 0.10$. The vertical intercept (the value of B when $T = 0$) is 2. So the equation for the billing plan shown is $B = 2 + 0.10T$.

SELF-TEST 1A.2

Write the equation for the billing plan shown in the accompanying graph. How much does it cost to unlock a scooter? What is the charge per minute?

CHANGES IN THE VERTICAL INTERCEPT AND SLOPE

The next two examples and self-tests provide practice in seeing how a line shifts with a change in its vertical intercept or slope.

EXAMPLE 1A.4   **Change in Vertical Intercept**

Show how the billing plan whose graph is in Figure 1A.2 would change if the fee to unlock a scooter were increased from $2 to $3.

An increase in the fee to unlock a scooter from $2 to $3 would increase the vertical intercept of the billing plan by $1 but would leave its slope unchanged. An increase in the fee to unlock a scooter thus leads to a parallel upward shift in the billing plan by $1, as shown in Figure 1A.3. For any given number of minutes the new bill will be $1 higher than the old bill. Thus, a 10-minute ride cost $3 under the original plan (point A) but $4 under the new plan (point A'). A 15-minute

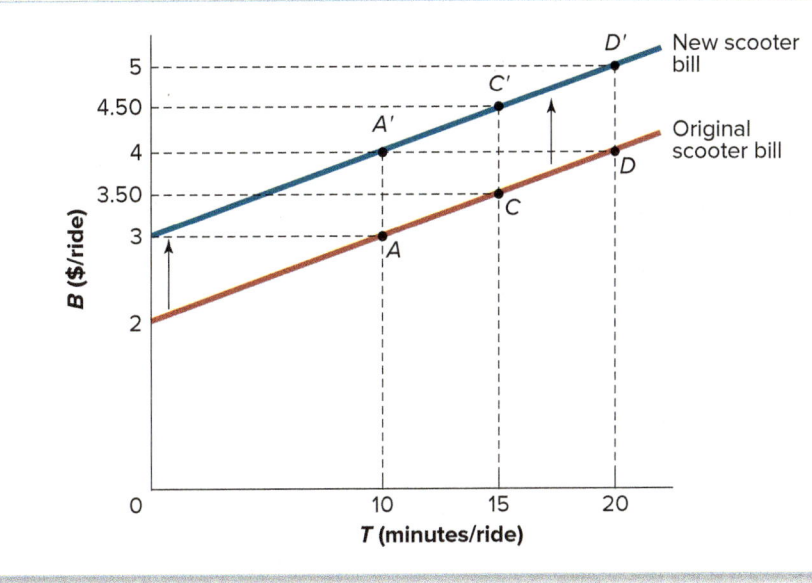

FIGURE 1A.3

The Effect of an Increase in the Vertical Intercept.

An increase in the vertical intercept of a straight line produces an upward parallel shift in the line.

ride cost $3.50 under the original plan (point *C*), but $4.50 under the new plan (point *C'*). And a 20-minute ride cost $4 under the original plan (point *D*), but $5 under the new plan (point *D'*).

 SELF-TEST 1A.3

Show how the billing plan whose graph is in Figure 1A.2 would change if the fee to unlock a scooter were reduced from $2 to $1.

EXAMPLE 1A.5   Change in Slope

Show how the billing plan whose graph is in Figure 1A.2 would change if the charge per minute were increased from 10 cents to 20 cents.

Because the fee to unlock a scooter is unchanged, the vertical intercept of the new billing plan continues to be 2. But the slope of the new plan, shown in Figure 1A.4,

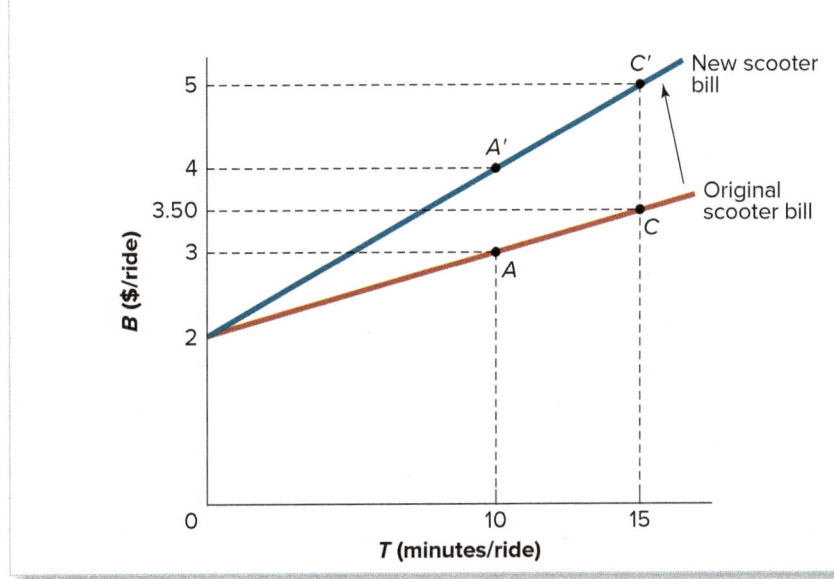

FIGURE 1A.4

The Effect of an Increase in the Charge per Minute.

Because the fixed monthly fee continues to be $2, the vertical intercept of the new plan is the same as that of the original plan. With the new charge per minute of 20 cents, the slope of the billing plan rises from 0.10 to 0.20.

is 0.20, or twice the slope of the original plan. More generally, in the equation $Y = a + bX$, an increase in b makes the slope of the graph of the equation steeper.

 SELF-TEST 1A.4

Show how the billing plan whose graph is in Figure 1A.2 would change if the charge per minute were reduced from 10 cents to 5 cents.

Self-Test 1A.4 illustrates the general rule that in an equation $Y = a + bX$, a reduction in b makes the slope of the graph of the equation less steep.

CONSTRUCTING EQUATIONS AND GRAPHS FROM TABLES

The next example and self-test show how to transform tabular information into an equation or graph.

EXAMPLE 1A.6   **Transforming a Table to a Graph**

Table 1A.1 shows four points from a scooter billing equation. If all points on this billing equation lie on a straight line, find the vertical intercept of the equation and graph it. What is the fee to unlock a scooter? What is the charge per minute? Calculate the total bill for a 30-minute ride.

TABLE 1A.1
Points on a Scooter Billing Plan

Total bill ($/ride)	Length of ride (minutes/ride)
2.50	5
3.75	10
5.00	15
6.25	20

One approach to this problem is simply to plot any two points from the table on a graph. Because we are told that the billing equation is a straight line, that line must be the one that passes through any two of its points. Thus, in Figure 1A.5 we use A to denote the point from Table 1A.1 for which a bill of $3.75 corresponds to a 10-minute ride (second row) and C to denote the point for which a bill of $6.25 corresponds to a 20-minute ride (fourth row). The straight line passing through these points is the graph of the billing equation.

Unless you have a steady hand, however, or use extremely large graph paper, the method of extending a line between two points on the billing plan is unlikely to be very accurate. An alternative approach is to calculate the equation for the billing plan directly. Because the equation is a straight line, we know that it takes

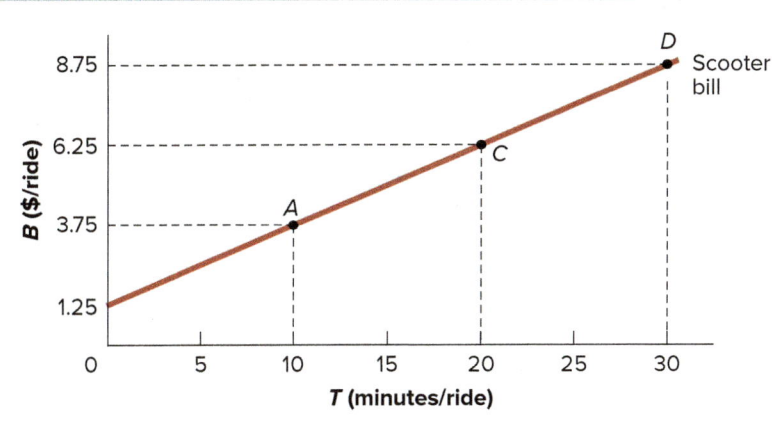

FIGURE 1A.5

Plotting the Scooter Billing Plan from a Sample of Points.

Point A is taken from row 2, Table 1A.1, and point C from row 4. The billing plan is the straight line that passes through these points.

the general form $B = f + sT$, where f is the fixed monthly fee and s is the slope. Our goal is to calculate the vertical intercept f and the slope s. From the same two points we plotted earlier, A and C, we can calculate the slope of the billing plan as $s = $ rise/run $= 2.50/10 = 0.25$.

So all that remains is to calculate f, the fee to unlock a scooter. At point C on the billing plan, the total bill is \$6.25 for 20 minutes, so we can substitute $B = 6.25$, $s = 0.25$, and $T = 20$ into the general equation $B = f + sT$ to obtain

$$6.25 = f + 0.25(20), \tag{1A.4}$$

or

$$6.25 = f + 5, \tag{1A.5}$$

which solves for $f = 1.25$. So the billing equation must be

$$B = 1.25 + 0.25T. \tag{1A.6}$$

For this billing equation, the fee to unlock a scooter is \$1.25, the charge per minute is 25 cents (\$0.25/minute), and the total bill for a 30-minute ride is $B = 1.25 + 0.25(30) = \$8.75$, just as shown in Figure 1A.5.

 SELF-TEST 1A.5

The following table shows four points from a scooter billing plan.

Total bill ($/ride)	Length of ride (minutes/ride)
2.50	5
4.25	10
6.00	15
7.75	20

If all points on this billing plan lie on a straight line, find the vertical intercept of the corresponding equation without graphing it. What is the fee to unlock a scooter? What is the charge per minute? How much would the charges be for a 30-minute ride?

SOLVING SIMULTANEOUS EQUATIONS

The next example and self-test demonstrate how to proceed when you need to solve two equations with two unknowns.

EXAMPLE 1A.7

Solving Simultaneous Equations

Suppose you are trying to choose between two electric scooter companies, each with a different pricing plan. If you choose Company 1, your charges will be computed according to the equation

$$B = 0.50 + 0.30T, \tag{1A.7}$$

where B is again your bill in dollars and T is the length of your ride in minutes. If you choose Company 2, your bill will be computed according to the equation

$$B = 2 + 0.15T. \tag{1A.8}$$

How many minutes long would your ride have to be to make Company 2 cheaper?

Company 1 has the attractive feature of a relatively low fee to unlock a scooter, but also the unattractive feature of a relatively high rate per minute. In contrast, Company 2 has a relatively high fee to unlock a scooter but a relatively low rate per minute. Someone who wanted to make a short ride (for example, 4 minutes) would do better under Company 1 (bill = $1.70) than under Company 2 (bill = $2.60) because the low fee to unlock a scooter for Company 1 would more than compensate for its higher rate per minute. Conversely, someone who wanted to make a long ride (say, 15 minutes) would do better under Company 2 (bill = $4.25) than under Company 1 (bill = $5.00) because Company 2's lower rate per minute would more than compensate for its higher fee to unlock a scooter.

Our task here is to find the break-even ride length, which is the ride length for which the bill is the same under the two plans. One way to answer this question is to graph the two billing plans and see where they cross. At that crossing point, the two equations are satisfied simultaneously, which means that the length of the rides will be the same, as will the bills.

In Figure 1A.6, we see that the graphs of the two plans cross at A, where both yield a bill of $3.50 for a 10-minute ride. The break-even ride length for these two

---

FIGURE 1A.6

The Break-Even Volume of Ride Length.

For 10-minute rides, your bill will be the same under both plans. For longer rides, Company 2 is cheaper; Company 1 is cheaper for shorter rides.

companies is thus 10 minutes. If the length of your ride is longer than that, you will save money by choosing Company 2. For example, if you take a 20-minute ride, your bill under Company 2 ($5) will be $1.50 cheaper than under Company 1 ($6.50). Conversely, if you ride for less than 10 minutes, you will do better under Company 1. For example, if you take a 5-minute ride, your bill under Company 1 ($2) will be 75 cents cheaper than under Company 2 ($2.75). For 10-minute rides, the two companies cost exactly the same ($3.50).

The question posed here also may be answered algebraically. As in the graphical approach just discussed, our goal is to find the point (T, B) that satisfies both billing equations simultaneously. As a first step, we rewrite the two billing equations, one on top of the other, as

$$B = 0.50 + 0.30T \qquad \text{(Company 1)}.$$
$$B = 2 + 0.15T \qquad \text{(Company 2)}.$$

As you'll recall from high school algebra, if we subtract the terms from each side of one equation from the corresponding terms of the other equation, the resulting differences must be equal. So if we subtract the terms on each side of the Company 2 equation from the corresponding terms in the Company 1 equation, we get

$$B = 0.50 + 0.30T \qquad \text{(Company 1)}.$$
$$-B = -2 - 0.15T \qquad \text{(−Company 2)}.$$
$$\overline{}$$
$$0 = -1.5 + 0.15T \qquad \text{(Company 1 − Company 2)}.$$

Finally, we solve the last equation (Company 1 − Company 2) to get $T = 10$.

Plugging $T = 10$ into either plan's equation, we then find $B = 3.50$. For example, Company 1's equation yields $0.5 + 0.30(10) = 3.50$, as does Company 2's $2 + 0.15(10) = 3.50$.

Because the point $(T, B) = (10, 3.50)$ lies on the equations for both plans simultaneously, the algebraic approach just described is often called the *method of simultaneous equations*.

 SELF-TEST 1A.6

Suppose you are trying to choose between two electric scooter companies. If you choose Company 1, your bill will be computed according to the equation

$$B = 0.20 + 0.40T \qquad \text{(Company 1)},$$

where B is again your bill in dollars and T is the length of your ride in minutes. If you choose Company 2, your bill will be computed according to the equation

$$B = 5 + 0.10T \qquad \text{(Company 2)}.$$

Use the algebraic approach described in the preceding example to find the break-even ride length for these plans.

KEY TERMS

constant (or parameter)	independent variable	slope
dependent variable	rise	variable
equation	run	vertical intercept

ANSWERS TO APPENDIX SELF-TESTS

1A.1 To calculate your bill for a 22-minute ride, substitute 22 minutes for T in Equation 1A.1 to get $B = 1 + 0.20(22) = \$5.40$.

1A.2 Calculating the slope using points A and C, we have rise $= 4.50 - 3 = 1.50$ and run $= 20 - 10 = 10$, so rise/run $= 1.5/10 = 0.15$. And since the horizontal intercept of the line is 1.5, its equation is $B = 1.5 + 0.15T$. Under this plan, the fee to unlock a scooter is $1.50 and the charge per minute is the slope of the billing line, 0.15, or 15 cents per minute.

1A.3 A $1 reduction in the fee to unlock a scooter would produce a downward parallel shift in the billing plan by $1.

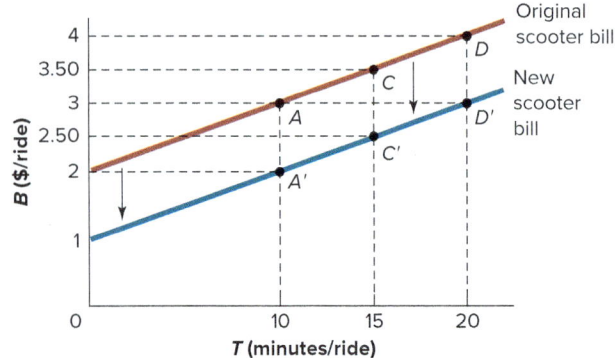

1A.4 With the fee to unlock a scooter unchanged, the vertical intercept of the new billing plan continues to be 2. The slope of the new plan is 0.05, half the slope of the original plan.

1A.5 Let the billing equation be $B = f + sT$, where f is the fee to unlock a scooter and s is the slope. From the first two points in the table, calculate the slope $s =$ rise/run $= 1.75/5 = 0.35$. To calculate f, we can use the information in the first row of the table to write the billing equation as $2.50 = f + 0.35(5)$ and solve for $f = 0.75$. So the billing equation must be $B = 0.75 + 0.35T$. For this billing equation, the fee to unlock a scooter is 75 cents, the charge per minute is 35 cents, and the total bill for a 30-minute ride is $B = 0.75 + 0.35(30) = \$11.25$.

1A.6 Subtracting the Company 2 equation from the Company 1 equation yields the equation

$$0 = -4.8 + 0.30T \qquad \text{(Company 1} - \text{Company 2),}$$

which solves for $T = 16$. So if you ride for more than 16 minutes, you'll do better with Company 2.

CHAPTER 2

Comparative Advantage

Always pick the low-hanging fruit first.

LEARNING OBJECTIVES

After reading this chapter, you should be able to:

LO1 Explain and apply the *Principle of Comparative Advantage* and explain how it differs from absolute advantage.

LO2 Explain and apply the *Principle of Increasing Opportunity Cost* (also called the *Low-Hanging-Fruit Principle*). Use a production possibilities curve to illustrate opportunity cost and comparative advantage.

LO3 Identify factors that shift the menu of production possibilities.

LO4 Explain the role of comparative advantage in international trade and describe why some jobs are more vulnerable to outsourcing than others.

During a stint as a Peace Corps volunteer in rural Nepal, a young economic naturalist employed a cook named Birkhaman, who came from a remote Himalayan village in neighboring Bhutan. Although Birkhaman had virtually no formal education, he was spectacularly resourceful. His primary duties, to prepare food and maintain the kitchen, he performed extremely well. But he also had other skills. He could thatch a roof, butcher a goat, and repair shoes. An able tinsmith and a good carpenter, he could sew and fix a broken alarm clock, as well as plaster walls. And he was a local authority on home remedies.

Birkhaman's range of skills was broad even in Nepal, where the least-skilled villager could perform a wide range of services that most Americans hire others to perform. Why this difference in skills and employment?

One might be tempted to answer that the Nepalese are simply too poor to hire others to perform these services. Nepal is indeed a poor country, whose income per person is less than one-sixtieth that of the United States. Few Nepalese have spare cash to spend on outside services. But as reasonable as this poverty explanation may seem, the reverse is actually the case. The Nepalese do not perform their own services because they are poor; rather, they are poor largely *because* they perform their own services.

The alternative to a system in which everyone is a jack-of-all-trades is one in which people *specialize* in particular goods and services and then satisfy their needs by trading among themselves. Economic systems based on specialization and the exchange of goods and services are generally far more productive than those with little specialization. Our task in this chapter is to investigate why this is so.

As this chapter will show, the reason that specialization is so productive is *comparative advantage*. Roughly, a person has a comparative advantage at producing a particular good or service (say, haircuts) if that person is *relatively* more efficient at producing haircuts than at producing other goods or services. We will see that we can all have more of *every* good and service if each of us specializes in the activities at which we have a comparative advantage.

Did this man perform most of his own services because he was poor, or was he poor because he performed most of his own services?

This chapter also will introduce the *production possibilities curve*, which is a graphical method of describing the combinations of goods and services that an economy can produce. This tool will allow us to see more clearly how specialization enhances the productive capacity of even the simplest economy.

EXCHANGE AND OPPORTUNITY COST

Scarcity

The Scarcity Principle (see Chapter 1, *Thinking Like an Economist*) reminds us that the opportunity cost of spending more time on any one activity is having less time available to spend on others. As the following example makes clear, this principle helps explain why everyone can do better by concentrating on those activities at which they perform best relative to others.

EXAMPLE 2.1	Scarcity Principle

Should Kelly Wearstler design her own web page?

Kelly Wearstler is among the most famous and influential interior designers in the United States today. She has received numerous accolades for her commercial and residential design work, has completed projects for top celebrities such as Cameron Diaz, Gwen Stefani, and Ben Stiller, and boasts more than 2 million followers on Instagram.

Although Kelly devotes most of her time and talent to interior design, she is well equipped to do a broad range of other design work. Suppose Kelly could design her own web page in 300 hours, half the time it would take any other web designer. Does that mean that Kelly should design her own web page?

Suppose that on the strength of her talents as an interior designer, Kelly earns more than $1 million a year, implying that the opportunity cost of any time she spent designing her web page would be over $500 per hour. Kelly would have little difficulty engaging a highly qualified web designer whose hourly wage is considerably less than $500 per hour. So even though Kelly's substantial skills might enable her to design her web page more quickly than most web designers, it would not be in her interest to do so.

Should Kelly Wearstler design her own web page?

In Example 2.1, economists would say that Wearstler has an **absolute advantage** at designing her web page but a **comparative advantage** at interior design. She has an absolute advantage at designing her web page because she can perform that task in less time than a web designer could. Even so, the web designer has a comparative advantage at designing web pages because his or her opportunity cost of performing that task is lower than Wearstler's.

Example 2.1 makes the implicit assumption that Wearstler would be equally happy to spend an hour designing her web page or working on an interior design project. But suppose she is tired of interior design work and feels it might be enjoyable to try her hand at web design. Designing her own web page might then make perfect sense! But unless she expects to gain extra satisfaction from performing that task, she almost certainly will do better to hire a web designer. The web designer will also benefit, or else the designer wouldn't have offered to design web pages for the stated price.

absolute advantage one person has an absolute advantage over another if one takes fewer hours to perform a task than the other person

comparative advantage one person has a comparative advantage over another if his or her opportunity cost of performing a task is lower than the other person's opportunity cost

THE PRINCIPLE OF COMPARATIVE ADVANTAGE

One of the most important insights of modern economics is that when two people (or two nations) have different opportunity costs of performing various tasks, they can always increase the total value of available goods and services by trading with one another. The following example captures the logic behind this insight.

EXAMPLE 2.2	Comparative Advantage

Should Ana update her own web page?

Consider a small community in which Ana is the only professional bicycle mechanic and Xin is the only professional web designer. If the amount of time for each of them to update a web page and repair a bicycle is as shown in Table 2.1, and if each regards the two tasks as equally pleasant (or unpleasant), does the fact that Ana can update a web page faster than Xin imply that Ana should update her own web page?

TABLE 2.1
Productivity Information for Ana and Xin

	Time to update a web page	Time to complete a bicycle repair
Ana	20 minutes	10 minutes
Xin	30 minutes	30 minutes

The entries in the table show that Ana has an absolute advantage over Xin in both activities. While Ana, the mechanic, needs only 20 minutes to update a web page, Xin, the web designer, needs 30 minutes. Ana's advantage over Xin is even greater when the task is fixing bikes: She can complete a repair in only 10 minutes, compared to Xin's 30 minutes.

But the fact that Ana is a better web designer than Xin does *not* imply that Ana should update her own web page. Xin has a comparative advantage over Ana at web design: She is *relatively* more productive at updating a web page than Ana. Similarly, Ana has a comparative advantage in bicycle repair. (Remember that a person has a comparative advantage at a given task if their opportunity cost of performing that task is lower than another person's.)

What is Xin's opportunity cost of updating a web page? Because she takes 30 minutes to update each page—the same amount of time she takes to fix a bicycle—her opportunity cost of updating a web page is one bicycle repair. In other words, by taking the time to update a web page, Xin is effectively giving up the opportunity to do one bicycle repair. Ana, in contrast, can complete two bicycle repairs in the time she takes to update a single web page. For her, the opportunity cost of updating a web page is two bicycle repairs. Ana's opportunity cost to update a web page, measured in terms of bicycle repairs forgone, is twice as high as Xin's. Thus, Xin has a comparative advantage at web design.

The interesting and important implication of the opportunity cost comparison summarized in Table 2.2 is that the total number of bicycle repairs and web updates accomplished if Xin and Ana both spend part of their time at each activity will always be smaller than the number accomplished if each specializes in the activity in which she has a comparative advantage. Suppose, for example, that people in their community demand a total of 16 web page updates per day. If Ana spent half her time updating web pages and the other half repairing bicycles, an 8-hour workday would yield 12 web page updates and 24 bicycle repairs. To complete the remaining 4 updates, Xin would have to spend 2 hours web designing, which would leave her 6 hours to repair bicycles. And because she takes 30 minutes to do each repair, she would have time to complete 12 of them. So when the two women try to be jacks-of-all-trades, they end up completing a total of 16 web page updates and 36 bicycle repairs.

TABLE 2.2
Opportunity Costs for Ana and Xin

	Opportunity cost of updating a web page	Opportunity cost of a bicycle repair
Ana	2 bicycle repairs	0.5 web page update
Xin	1 bicycle repair	1 web page update

Consider what would have happened had each woman specialized in her activity of comparative advantage. Xin could have updated 16 web pages on her own and Ana could have performed 48 bicycle repairs. Specialization would have created an additional 12 bicycle repairs out of thin air.

When computing the opportunity cost of one good in terms of another, we must pay close attention to the form in which the productivity information is presented. In Example 2.2, we were told how many minutes each person needed to perform each task. Alternatively, we might be told how many units of each task each person can perform in an hour. Work through the following self-test to see how to proceed when information is presented in this alternative format.

 SELF-TEST 2.1

Should Miguel update his own web page?

Consider a small community in which Miguel is the only professional bicycle mechanic and Monique is the only professional web designer. If their productivity rates at the two tasks are as shown in the table, and if each regards the two tasks as equally pleasant (or unpleasant), does the fact that Miguel can update a web page faster than Monique imply that Miguel should update his own web page?

	Productivity in web design	Productivity in bicycle repair
Monique	2 web page updates per hour	1 repair per hour
Miguel	3 web page updates per hour	3 repairs per hour

The principle illustrated by the preceding examples is so important that we state it formally as one of the core principles of the course:

The Principle of Comparative Advantage: Everyone does best when each person (or each country) concentrates on the activities for which their opportunity cost is lowest.

Comparative Advantage

Indeed, the gains made possible from specialization based on comparative advantage constitute the rationale for market exchange. They explain why each person does not devote 10 percent of his or her time to producing cars, 5 percent to growing food, 25 percent to building housing, 0.0001 percent to performing brain surgery, and so on. By concentrating on those tasks at which we are relatively most productive, together we can produce vastly more than if we all tried to be self-sufficient.

This insight brings us back to Birkhaman the cook. Though Birkhaman's versatility was marvelous, he was neither as good a doctor as someone who has been trained in medical school, nor as good a repair person as someone who spends each day fixing things. If a number of people with Birkhaman's native talents had joined together, each of them specializing in one or two tasks, together they would have enjoyed more and better goods and services than each could possibly have produced independently. Although there is much to admire in the resourcefulness of people who have learned through necessity to rely on their own skills, that path is no route to economic prosperity.

Specialization and its effects provide ample grist for the economic naturalist. Here's an example from the world of sports.

The Economic Naturalist 2.1

Where have all the .400 hitters gone?

In baseball, a .400 hitter is a player who averages at least four hits every 10 times he comes to bat. Though never common in professional baseball, .400 hitters used to appear relatively frequently. Early in the twentieth century, for example, a player known as Wee Willie Keeler batted .432, meaning that he got a hit in over 43 percent of his times at bat. But since Ted Williams of the Boston Red Sox batted .406 in 1941, there hasn't been a single .400 hitter in the major leagues. Why not?

Why has no major league baseball player batted .400 since Ted Williams did it more than half a century ago?

Some baseball buffs argue that the disappearance of the .400 hitter means today's baseball players are not as good as yesterday's. But that claim does not withstand close examination. For example, today's players are bigger, stronger, and faster than those of Willie Keeler's day. (Wee Willie himself was just a little over 5 feet 4 inches and weighed only 140 pounds.)

Bill James, a leading analyst of baseball history, argues that the .400 hitter has disappeared because the quality of play in the major leagues has *improved*, not declined. In particular, pitching and fielding standards are higher, which makes batting .400 more difficult.

Why has the quality of play in baseball improved? Although there are many reasons, including better nutrition, training, and equipment, specialization also has played an important role.[1] At one time, pitchers were expected to pitch for the entire game. Now pitching staffs include pitchers who specialize in starting the game ("starters"), others who specialize in pitching two or three innings in the middle of the game ("middle relievers"), and still others who specialize in pitching only the last inning ("closers"). Each of these roles requires different skills and tactics. Pitchers also may specialize in facing left-handed or right-handed batters, in striking batters out, or in getting

---

[1]For an interesting discussion of specialization and the decline of the .400 hitter from the perspective of an evolutionary biologist, see Stephen Jay Gould, *Full House* (New York: Three Rivers Press, 1996), part 3.

batters to hit balls on the ground. Similarly, few fielders today play multiple defensive positions; most specialize in only one. Some players specialize in defense (to the detriment of their hitting skills); these "defensive specialists" can be brought in late in the game to protect a lead. Even in managing and coaching, specialization has increased markedly. Relief pitchers now have their own coaches, and statistical specialists use computers to discover the weaknesses of opposing hitters. The net result of these increases in specialization is that even the weakest of today's teams play highly competent defensive baseball. With no "weaklings" to pick on, hitting .400 over an entire season has become a near-impossible task.

SOURCES OF COMPARATIVE ADVANTAGE

At the individual level, comparative advantage often appears to be the result of inborn talent. For instance, some people seem to be naturally gifted at programming computers while others seem to have a special knack for fixing bikes. But comparative advantage is more often the result of education, training, or experience. Thus, we usually leave the design of kitchens to people with architectural training, the drafting of contracts to people who have studied law, and the teaching of physics to people with advanced degrees in that field.

At the national level, comparative advantage may derive from differences in natural resources or from differences in society or culture. The United States, which has a disproportionate share of the world's leading research universities, has a comparative advantage in the design of electronic computing hardware and software. Canada, which has one of the world's highest per-capita endowments of farm and forest land, has a comparative advantage in the production of agricultural products. Topography and climate explain why Colorado specializes in the skiing industry while Hawaii specializes as an ocean resort.

Seemingly noneconomic factors also can give rise to comparative advantage. For instance, the emergence of English as the de facto world language gives English-speaking countries a comparative advantage over non-English-speaking nations in the production of books, movies, and popular music. Even a country's institutions may affect the likelihood that it will achieve comparative advantage in a particular pursuit. For example, cultures that encourage entrepreneurship will tend to have a comparative advantage in the introduction of new products, whereas those that promote high standards of care and craftsmanship will tend to have a comparative advantage in the production of high-quality variants of established products.

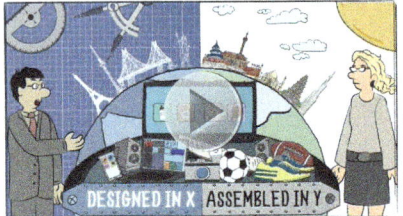

▶ Visit your instructor's Connect course and access your eBook to view this video.

Why are many products designed in one place yet assembled in another?

The Economic Naturalist 2.2

What happened to the U.S. lead in the television market?

Televisions were developed and first produced in the United States, but today this country accounts for only a minuscule share of the total world production of TVs. The early lead is explained in part by this country's comparative advantage in technological research, which in turn was supported by the country's outstanding system of higher education. Other contributing factors were high expenditures on the development of electronic components for the military and a culture that actively encourages entrepreneurship. As for the production of these products, the United States enjoyed an early advantage partly because the product designs were themselves evolving rapidly at first, which favored production facilities located in close proximity to the product designers. Early production techniques also relied intensively on skilled labor, which is abundant in the United States. In time, however, product designs stabilized and many of the more complex manufacturing operations were automated. Both of these changes gradually led to greater reliance on relatively less-skilled production workers. And at that point, factories located in high-wage countries like the United States could no longer compete with those located in low-wage areas overseas.

Why was the United States unable to remain competitive as a manufacturer of televisions and other electronic equipment?

RECAP ↑

EXCHANGE AND OPPORTUNITY COST

Gains from exchange are possible if trading partners have comparative advantages in producing different goods and services. You have a comparative advantage in producing, say, web pages if your opportunity cost of producing a web page—measured in terms of other production opportunities forgone—is smaller than the corresponding opportunity costs of your trading partners. Maximum production is achieved if each person specializes in producing the good or service in which he or she has the lowest opportunity cost (the *Principle of Comparative Advantage*). Comparative advantage makes specialization worthwhile even if one trading partner is more productive than others, in absolute terms, in every activity.

COMPARATIVE ADVANTAGE AND PRODUCTION POSSIBILITIES

Comparative advantage and specialization allow an economy to produce more than if each person tries to produce a little of everything. In this section, we gain further insight into the advantages of specialization by introducing a graph that can be used to describe the various combinations of goods and services that an economy can produce.

THE PRODUCTION POSSIBILITIES CURVE

We begin with a hypothetical economy in which only two goods are produced: coffee and pine nuts. It's a small island economy and "production" consists either of picking coffee beans that grow on small bushes on the island's central valley floor or of gathering pine nuts that fall from trees on the steep hillsides overlooking the valley. The more time workers spend picking coffee beans, the less time they have available for gathering nuts. So if people want to drink more coffee, they must make do with a smaller amount of nuts.

If we know how productive workers are at each activity, we can summarize the various combinations of coffee beans and nuts they can produce each day. This menu of possibilities is known as the **production possibilities curve (PPC)**.

To keep matters simple, we begin with an example in which the economy has only a single worker, who can divide her time between the two activities.

production possibilities curve (PPC) a graph that describes the maximum amount of one good that can be produced for every possible level of production of the other good

| EXAMPLE 2.3 | Production Possibilities Curve |

What is the production possibilities curve for an economy in which Krisha is the only worker?

Consider a society consisting only of Krisha, who allocates her production time between coffee beans and nuts. She has nimble fingers, a quality that makes her more productive at picking coffee beans than at gathering nuts. She can gather 2 pounds of nuts or pick 4 pounds of coffee beans in an hour. If she works a total of 6 hours per day, describe her production possibilities curve—the graph that displays, for each level of nut production, the maximum amount of coffee beans that she can pick.

The vertical axis in Figure 2.1 shows Krisha's daily production of coffee beans and the horizontal axis shows her daily production of nuts. Let's begin by looking at two extreme allocations of her time. First, suppose she employs her entire workday (6 hours) picking coffee beans. In that case, since she can pick 4 pounds of coffee beans per hour, she would pick 24 pounds per day of coffee beans and gather zero pounds of nuts. That combination of coffee beans and nut production is represented by point *A* in Figure 2.1. It is the vertical intercept of Krisha's production possibilities curve.

FIGURE 2.1

Krisha's Production Possibilities.

For the production relationships given, the production possibilities curve is a straight line.

Krisha's PPC: All combinations of coffee beans and nuts that can be produced with Krisha's labor

Now suppose, instead, that Krisha devotes all her time to gathering nuts. Since she can gather 2 pounds of nuts per hour, her total daily production would be 12 pounds of nuts. That combination is represented by point D in Figure 2.1, the horizontal intercept of Krisha's PPC. Because Krisha's production of each good is exactly proportional to the amount of time she devotes to that good, the remaining points along her PPC will lie on the straight line that joins A and D.

For example, suppose that Krisha devotes 4 hours each day to picking coffee beans and 2 hours to gathering nuts. She will then end up with (4 hours/day) × (4 pounds/hour) = 16 pounds of coffee beans per day and (2 hours/day) × (2 pounds/hour) = 4 pounds of nuts. This is the point labeled B in Figure 2.1. Alternatively, if she devotes 2 hours to coffee beans and 4 hours to nuts, she will get (2 hours/day) × (4 pounds/hour) = 8 pounds of coffee beans per day and (4 hours/day) × (2 pounds/hour) = 8 pounds of nuts. This alternative combination is represented by point C in Figure 2.1.

Because Krisha's PPC is a straight line, its slope is constant. The absolute value of the slope of Krisha's PPC is the ratio of its vertical intercept to its horizontal intercept: (24 pounds of coffee beans/day)/(12 pounds of nuts/day) = (2 pounds of coffee beans)/(1 pound of nuts). (Be sure to keep track of the units of measure on each axis when computing this ratio.) *This ratio means that Krisha's opportunity cost of an additional pound of nuts is 2 pounds of coffee beans.*

Note that Krisha's opportunity cost (*OC*) of nuts can also be expressed as the following simple formula:

$$OC_{nuts} = \frac{\text{loss in coffee beans}}{\text{gain in nuts}}, \tag{2.1}$$

where "loss in coffee beans" means the amount of coffee beans given up and "gain in nuts" means the corresponding increase in nuts. Likewise, Krisha's opportunity cost of coffee is expressed by this formula:

$$OC_{coffee} = \frac{\text{loss in nuts}}{\text{gain in coffee beans}}. \tag{2.2}$$

To say that Krisha's opportunity cost of an additional pound of nuts is 2 pounds of coffee beans is thus equivalent to saying that her opportunity cost of a pound of coffee beans is ½ pound of nuts.

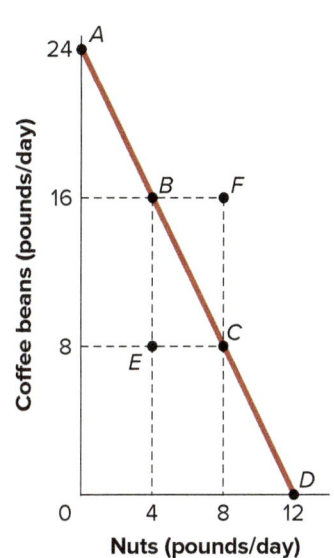

FIGURE 2.2

Attainable and Efficient Points on Krisha's Production Possibilities Curve.

Points that lie either along the production possibilities curve (for example, *A, B, C,* and *D*) or within it (for example, *E*) are said to be attainable. Points that lie outside the production possibilities curve (for example, *F*) are unattainable. Points that lie along the curve are said to be efficient, while those that lie within the curve are said to be inefficient.

The downward slope of the production possibilities curve shown in Figure 2.1 illustrates the Scarcity Principle—the idea that because our resources are limited, having more of one good thing generally means having to settle for less of another (see Chapter 1, *Thinking Like an Economist*). Krisha can have an additional pound of coffee beans if she wishes, but only if she is willing to give up half a pound of nuts. If Krisha is the only person in the economy, her opportunity cost of producing a good becomes, in effect, its price. Thus, the price she has to pay for an additional pound of coffee beans is half a pound of nuts, or the price she has to pay for an additional pound of nuts is 2 pounds of coffee beans.

 Scarcity

Any point that lies either along the production possibilities curve or within it is said to be an **attainable point**, meaning that it can be produced with currently available resources. In Figure 2.2, for example, points *A, B, C, D,* and *E* are attainable points. Points that lie outside the production possibilities curve are said to be **unattainable**, meaning that they cannot be produced using currently available resources. In Figure 2.2, *F* is an unattainable point because Krisha cannot pick 16 pounds of coffee beans per day *and* gather 8 pounds of nuts. Points that lie within the curve are said to be **inefficient**, in the sense that existing resources would allow for production of more of at least one good without sacrificing the production of any other good. At *E,* for example, Krisha is picking only 8 pounds of coffee beans per day and gathering 4 pounds of nuts. This means that she could increase her coffee beans harvest by 8 pounds per day without giving up any nuts (by moving from *E* to *B*). Alternatively, Krisha could gather as many as 4 additional pounds of nuts each day without giving up any coffee beans (by moving from *E* to *C*). An **efficient point** is one that lies along the production possibilities curve. At any such point, more of one good can be produced only by producing less of the other.

attainable point any combination of goods that can be produced using currently available resources

unattainable point any combination of goods that cannot be produced using currently available resources

inefficient point any combination of goods for which currently available resources enable an increase in the production of one good without a reduction in the production of the other

efficient point any combination of goods for which currently available resources do not allow an increase in the production of one good without a reduction in the production of the other

 SELF-TEST 2.2

For the PPC shown in Figure 2.2, state whether the following points are attainable and/or efficient:

a. 20 pounds per day of coffee beans, 4 pounds per day of nuts.

b. 12 pounds per day of coffee beans, 6 pounds per day of nuts.

c. 4 pounds per day of coffee beans, 8 pounds per day of nuts.

HOW INDIVIDUAL PRODUCTIVITY AFFECTS THE SLOPE AND POSITION OF THE PPC

To see how the slope and position of the production possibilities curve depend on an individual's productivity, let's compare Krisha's PPC to that of Tom's, who is less productive at picking coffee beans but more productive at gathering nuts.

| EXAMPLE 2.4 | Productivity Changes |

How do changes in productivity affect the opportunity cost of nuts?

Tom is short and has keen eyesight, qualities that make him especially well suited for gathering nuts that fall beneath trees on the hillsides. He can gather 4 pounds of nuts or pick 2 pounds of coffee beans per hour. If Tom were the only person in the economy, describe the economy's production possibilities curve.

We can construct Tom's PPC the same way we did Krisha's. Note first that if Tom devotes an entire workday (6 hours) to coffee bean picking, he ends up with (6 hours/day) × (2 pounds/hour) = 12 pounds of coffee beans per day and zero pounds of nuts. So the vertical intercept of Tom's PPC is A in Figure 2.3. If instead he devotes all his time to gathering nuts, he gets (6 hours/day) × (4 pounds/hour) = 24 pounds of nuts per day and no coffee beans. That means the horizontal intercept of his PPC is D in Figure 2.3. Because Tom's production of each good is proportional to the amount of time he devotes to it, the remaining points on his PPC will lie along the straight line that joins these two extreme points.

For example, if he devotes 4 hours each day to picking coffee beans and 2 hours to gathering nuts, he'll end up with (4 hours/day) × (2 pounds/hour) = 8 pounds of coffee beans per day and (2 hours/day) × (4 pounds/hour) = 8 pounds of nuts per day. This is the point labeled B in Figure 2.3. Alternatively, if he devotes 2 hours to coffee beans and 4 hours to nuts, he'll get (2 hours/day) × (2 pounds/hour) = 4 pounds of coffee beans per day and (4 hours/day) × (4 pounds/hour) = 16 pounds of nuts. This alternative combination is represented by point C in Figure 2.3.

How does Tom's PPC compare with Krisha's? Note in Figure 2.4 that because Tom is absolutely less productive than Krisha at picking coffee beans, the vertical intercept of his PPC lies closer to the origin than Krisha's. By the same token, because Krisha is absolutely less productive than Tom at gathering nuts, the horizontal intercept of her PPC lies closer to the origin than Tom's. For Tom, the opportunity cost of an additional pound of nuts is ½ pound of coffee beans, which

FIGURE 2.3

Tom's Production Possibilities Curve.

Tom's opportunity cost of producing 1 pound of nuts is only ½ pound of coffee beans.

Tom's PPC: All combinations of coffee beans and nuts that can be produced with Tom's labor

Coffee beans (pounds/day)

Nuts (pounds/day)

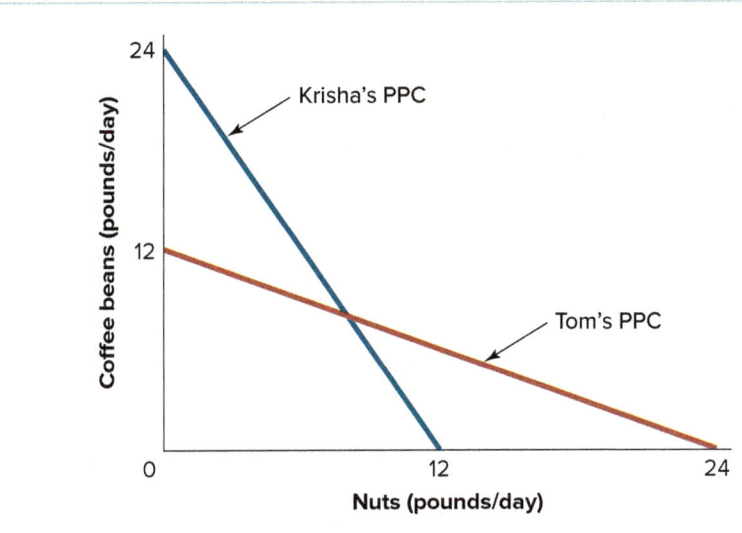

FIGURE 2.4

Individual Production Possibilities Curves Compared.

Tom is less productive in coffee beans than Krisha, but more productive in nuts.

is one-fourth Krisha's opportunity cost of nuts. This difference in opportunity costs shows up as a difference in the slopes of their PPCs: The absolute value of the slope of Tom's PPC is ½, whereas Krisha's is 2.

In this example, Tom has both an absolute advantage and a comparative advantage over Krisha in gathering nuts. Krisha, for her part, has both an absolute advantage and a comparative advantage over Tom in picking coffee beans.

We cannot emphasize strongly enough that the principle of comparative advantage is a relative concept—one that makes sense only when the productivities of two or more people (or countries) are being compared.

 SELF-TEST 2.3

Suppose Krisha can pick 2 pounds of coffee beans per hour or gather 4 pounds of nuts per hour; Tom can pick 1 pound of coffee beans per hour or gather 1 pound of nuts per hour. What is Krisha's opportunity cost of gathering a pound of nuts? What is Tom's opportunity cost of gathering a pound of nuts? Where does Krisha's comparative advantage now lie?

THE GAINS FROM SPECIALIZATION AND EXCHANGE

Earlier we saw that a comparative advantage arising from disparities in individual opportunity costs creates gains for everyone (see Examples 2.1 and 2.2). The following example shows how the same point can be illustrated using production possibility curves.

EXAMPLE 2.5 Specialization

How costly is failure to specialize?

Suppose that in Example 2.4 Krisha and Tom had divided their time so that each person's output consisted of half nuts and half coffee beans. How much of each good would Tom and Krisha have been able to consume? How much could they have consumed if each had specialized in the activity for which he or she enjoyed a comparative advantage?

FIGURE 2.5

Production without Specialization.

When Tom and Krisha divide their time so that each produces the same number of pounds of coffee beans and nuts, they can consume a total of 16 pounds of coffee beans and 16 pounds of nuts each day.

Because Tom can produce twice as many pounds of nuts in an hour as pounds of coffee beans, to produce equal quantities of each, he must spend 2 hours picking coffee beans for every hour he devotes to gathering nuts. And since he works a 6-hour day, that means spending 2 hours gathering nuts and 4 hours picking coffee beans. Dividing his time in this way, he'll end up with 8 pounds of coffee beans per day and 8 pounds of nuts. Similarly, since Krisha can produce twice as many pounds of coffee beans in an hour as pounds of nuts, to pick equal quantities of each, she must spend 2 hours gathering nuts for every hour she devotes to picking coffee beans. And because she too works a 6-hour day, that means spending 2 hours picking coffee beans and 4 hours gathering nuts. So, like Tom, she'll end up with 8 pounds of coffee beans per day and 8 pounds of nuts. (See Figure 2.5.) Their combined daily production will thus be 16 pounds of each good. By contrast, had they each specialized in their respective activities of comparative advantage, their combined daily production would have been 24 pounds of each good.

If they exchange coffee beans and nuts with one another, each can consume a combination of the two goods that would have been unattainable if exchange had not been possible. For example, Krisha can give Tom 12 pounds of coffee beans in exchange for 12 pounds of nuts, enabling each to consume 4 pounds per day more of each good than when each produced and consumed alone. Note that point *E* in Figure 2.5, which has 12 pounds per day of each good, lies beyond each person's PPC, yet is easily attainable with specialization and exchange.

As the following self-test illustrates, the gains from specialization grow larger as the difference in opportunity costs increases.

 SELF-TEST 2.4

How do differences in opportunity cost affect the gains from specialization?

Krisha can pick 5 pounds of coffee beans or gather 1 pound of nuts in an hour. Tom can pick 1 pound of coffee beans or gather 5 pounds of nuts in an hour. Assuming they again work 6-hour days and want to consume coffee and nuts in equal quantities, by how much will specialization increase their consumption compared to the alternative in which each produced only for his or her own consumption?

Although the gains from specialization and exchange grow with increases in the differences in opportunity costs among trading partners, these differences alone still seem insufficient to account for the enormous differences in living standards between rich and poor countries. Average income in the 20 richest countries in the year 2019, for example, was over $60,000 per person, compared to roughly $600 per person in the 20 poorest countries.[2] Although we will say more later about specialization's role in explaining these differences, we first discuss how to construct the PPC for an entire economy and examine how factors other than specialization might cause it to shift outward over time.

As the following Economic Naturalist notes, geographical specialization patterns in wine production have been significantly altered by changing weather.

The Economic Naturalist 2.3

How will climate change affect wine-industry specialization?

As a possibly apocryphal story has it, when the eminent British economist John Maynard Keynes was asked on his deathbed whether he had any regrets, he responded, "I wish I'd drunk more champagne." What's not in doubt, however, is that not a single ounce of whatever champagne Mr. Keynes did drink was produced in his native England. It was imported from producers in a small region in the northeast of France, an area whose cool climate was perfectly suited for growing pinot noir and chardonnay, the two grape varieties used most extensively in champagne production. Because of its colder temperatures, no viticulturist would have recommended planting those varieties in England.

But warming temperatures have called traditional agricultural specialties into question. In recent years, vintners have been busily buying up acreage along England's southern coast, where champagne-style wine production is forecast to exceed even that of France if warming trends continue.

A PRODUCTION POSSIBILITIES CURVE FOR A MANY-PERSON ECONOMY

Although most actual economies consist of millions of workers, the process of constructing a production possibilities curve for an economy of that size is really no different from the process for a one-person economy. Consider again an economy in which the only two goods are coffee beans and nuts, with coffee beans again on the vertical axis and nuts on the horizontal axis. The vertical intercept of the economy's PPC is the total amount of coffee beans that could be picked if all available workers worked full time picking coffee beans. Thus, the maximum attainable amount of coffee bean production is shown for the hypothetical economy in Figure 2.6 as 100,000 pounds per day (an amount chosen arbitrarily, for illustrative purposes). The horizontal intercept of the PPC is the amount of nuts that could be gathered if all available workers worked full time gathering nuts, shown for this same economy as 80,000 pounds per day (also an amount chosen arbitrarily). But note that the PPC shown in the diagram is not a straight line—as in the earlier examples involving only a single worker—but rather a curve that is bowed out from the origin.

We'll say more in a moment about the reasons for this shape. But first note that a bow-shaped PPC means that the opportunity cost of producing nuts increases as the economy produces more of them. Notice, for example, that when the economy moves from *A,* where it is producing only coffee beans, to *B,* it gets 20,000 pounds of nuts per day by giving up only

[2]The 20 richest countries tracked by the International Monetary Fund: Australia, Austria, Belgium, Canada, Denmark, Finland, France, Germany, Iceland, Ireland, Luxembourg, Netherlands, Norway, Qatar, San Marino, Singapore, Sweden, Switzerland, United Kingdom, and United States. The 20 poorest countries tracked by the International Monetary Fund: Afghanistan, Burkina Faso, Burundi, Central African Republic, Comoros, Democratic Republic of the Congo, Haiti, Liberia, Madagascar, Malawi, Mozambique, Niger, Rwanda, Sierra Leone, South Sudan, Sudan, Tajikistan, The Gambia, Togo, and Uganda. (Source: IMF World Economic Outlook Database, April 2019, www.imf.org/external/pubs/ft/weo/2019/01/weodata/download.aspx.)

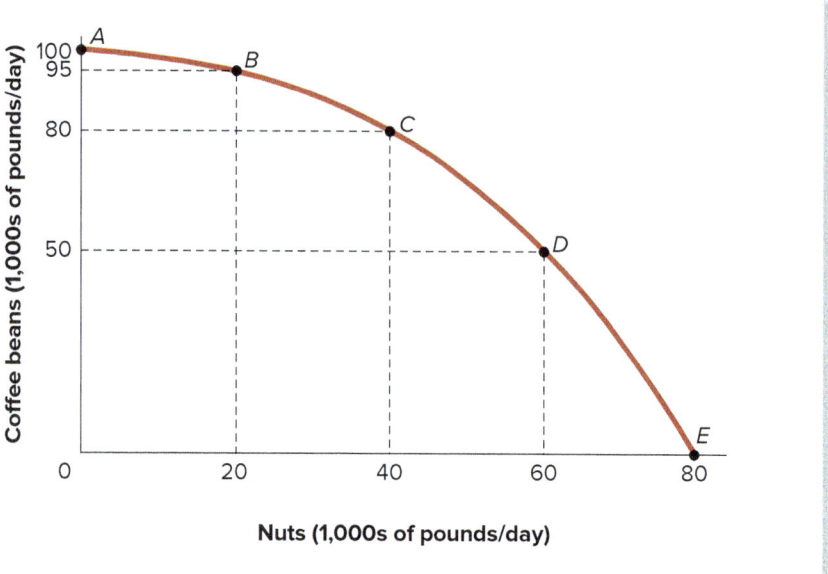

FIGURE 2.6

Production Possibilities Curve for a Large Economy.

For an economy with millions of workers, the PPC typically has a gentle outward bow shape.

5,000 pounds per day of coffee beans. When nut production is increased still further, however—for example, by moving from *B* to *C*—the economy again gains 20,000 pounds of nuts each day, but this time gives up 15,000 pounds of coffee beans. This pattern of increasing opportunity cost persists over the entire length of the PPC. For example, note that in moving from *D* to *E,* the economy again gains 20,000 pounds of nuts per day, but now gives up 50,000 pounds of coffee beans. Note, finally, that the same pattern of increasing opportunity cost applies to coffee beans. Thus, as more coffee beans are produced, the opportunity cost of producing additional coffee beans—as measured by the amount of nuts that must be sacrificed—also rises.

Why is the PPC for the multiperson economy bow-shaped? The answer lies in the fact that some resources are relatively well suited for gathering nuts while others are relatively well suited for picking coffee beans. If the economy is initially producing only coffee beans and wants to begin producing some nuts, which workers will it reassign? Recall Krisha and Tom, the two workers discussed in the preceding example, in which Tom's comparative advantage was gathering nuts and Krisha's comparative advantage was picking coffee beans. If both workers were currently picking coffee beans and you wanted to reassign one of them to gather nuts instead, whom would you send? Tom would be the clear choice because his departure would cost the economy only half as much coffee beans as Krisha's and would augment nut production by twice as much.

The principle is the same in any large multiperson economy, except that the range of opportunity cost differences across workers is even greater than in the earlier two-worker example. As we keep reassigning workers from coffee bean production to nut production, sooner or later we must withdraw even coffee bean specialists like Krisha from coffee production. Indeed, we must eventually reassign others whose opportunity cost of producing nuts is far higher than hers.

The shape of the production possibilities curve shown in Figure 2.6 illustrates the general principle that when resources have different opportunity costs, we should always exploit the resource with the lowest opportunity cost first. We call this the *Low-Hanging-Fruit Principle,* in honor of the fruit picker's rule of picking the most accessible fruit first:

The Principle of Increasing Opportunity Cost (also called the "Low-Hanging-Fruit Principle"): In expanding the production of any good, first employ those resources with the lowest opportunity cost, and only afterward turn to resources with higher opportunity costs.

A Note on the Logic of the Fruit Picker's Rule

Why should a fruit picker harvest the low-hanging fruit first? This rule makes sense for several reasons. For one, the low-hanging fruit is easier (and hence cheaper) to pick, and if he planned on picking only a limited amount of fruit to begin with, he would clearly come out ahead by avoiding the less-accessible fruit on the higher branches. But even if he planned on picking all the fruit on the tree, he would do better to start with the lower branches first because this would enable him to enjoy the revenue from the sale of the fruit sooner.

The fruit picker's job can be likened to the task confronting a new CEO who has been hired to reform an inefficient, ailing company. The CEO has limited time and attention, so it makes sense to focus first on problems that are relatively easy to correct and whose elimination will provide the biggest improvements in performance—the low-hanging fruit. Later on, the CEO can worry about the many smaller improvements needed to raise the company from very good to excellent.

Again, the important message of the Low-Hanging-Fruit Principle is to be sure to take advantage of your most favorable opportunities first.

> *RECAP*↑
>
> ### COMPARATIVE ADVANTAGE AND PRODUCTION POSSIBILITIES
>
> For an economy that produces two goods, the production possibilities curve describes the maximum amount of one good that can be produced for every possible level of production of the other good. Attainable points are those that lie on or within the curve and efficient points are those that lie along the curve. The slope of the production possibilities curve tells us the opportunity cost of producing an additional unit of the good measured along the horizontal axis. The *Principle of Increasing Opportunity Cost*, or the *Low-Hanging-Fruit Principle*, tells us that the slope of the production possibilities curve becomes steeper as we move downward to the right. The greater the differences among individual opportunity costs, the more bow-shaped the production possibilities curve will be; and the more bow-shaped the production possibilities curve, the greater the potential gains from specialization will be.

FACTORS THAT SHIFT THE ECONOMY'S PRODUCTION POSSIBILITIES CURVE

As its name implies, the production possibilities curve provides a summary of the production options open to any society. At any given moment, the PPC confronts society with a trade-off. The only way people can produce and consume more nuts is to produce and consume less coffee. In the long run, however, it is often possible to increase production of all goods. This is what is meant when people speak of economic growth. As shown in Figure 2.7, economic growth is an outward shift in the economy's production possibilities curve. It can result from increases in the amount of productive resources available or from improvements in knowledge or technology that render existing resources more productive.

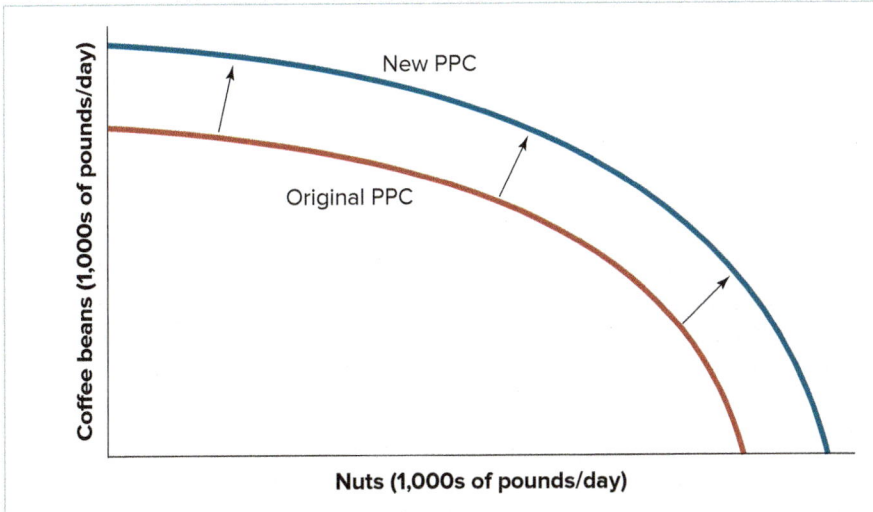

FIGURE 2.7

Economic Growth: An Outward Shift in the Economy's PPC.

Increases in productive resources (such as labor and capital equipment) or improvements in knowledge and technology cause the PPC to shift outward. They are the main factors that drive economic growth.

What causes the quantity of productive resources to grow in an economy? One factor is investment in new factories and equipment. When workers have more and better equipment to work with, their productivity increases, often dramatically. This is surely an important factor behind the differences in living standards between rich and poor countries. According to one study, for example, the value of capital investment per worker in the United States is about 30 times as great as in Nepal.[3]

Such large differences in capital per worker don't occur all at once. They are a consequence of decades, even centuries, of differences in rates of savings and investment. Over time, even small differences in rates of investment can translate into extremely large differences in the amount of capital equipment available to each worker. Differences of this sort are often self-reinforcing: Not only do higher rates of saving and investment cause incomes to grow, but the resulting higher income levels also make it easier to devote additional resources to savings and investment. Over time, then, even small initial productivity advantages from specialization can translate into very large income gaps.

Population growth also causes an economy's PPC curve to shift outward and thus is often listed as one of the sources of economic growth. But because population growth also generates more mouths to feed, it cannot by itself raise a country's standard of living. Indeed it may even cause a decline in the standard of living if existing population densities have already begun to put pressure on available land, water, and other resources.

Perhaps the most important sources of economic growth are improvements in knowledge and technology. As economists have long recognized, such improvements often lead to higher output through increased specialization. Improvements in technology often occur spontaneously. More frequently they are directly or indirectly the result of increases in education.

Earlier we discussed a two-person example in which individual differences in opportunity cost led to a tripling of output from specialization (Self-Test 2.4). Real-world gains from specialization often are far more spectacular than those in the example. One reason is that specialization not only capitalizes on preexisting differences in individual skills but also deepens those skills through practice and experience. Moreover, it eliminates many of the switching and start-up costs people incur when they move back and forth among numerous tasks. These gains apply not only to people but also to the tools and equipment they use. Breaking down a task into simple steps, each of which can be performed by a different machine, greatly multiplies the productivity of individual workers.

Even in simple settings, these factors can combine to increase productivity hundreds- or even thousands-fold. Adam Smith, the Scottish philosopher who is remembered today as the founder of modern economics, was the first to recognize the enormity of the gains made possible by the division and specialization of labor. Consider, for instance, his description of work in an eighteenth-century Scottish pin factory:

> One man draws out the wire, another straightens it, a third cuts it, a fourth points it, a fifth grinds it at the top for receiving the head; to make the head requires two or three distinct operations . . . I have seen a small manufactory of this kind where only ten men were employed . . . [who] could, when they exerted themselves, make among them about twelve pounds of pins in a day. There are in a pound upwards of four thousand pins of middling size. Those ten persons, therefore, could make among them upwards of forty-eight thousand pins in a day. Each person, therefore, making a tenth part of forty-eight thousand pins, might be considered as making four thousand eight hundred pins in a day. But if they had all wrought separately and independently, and without any of them having been educated to this peculiar business, they certainly could not each of them have made twenty, perhaps not one pin in a day.[4]

[3]Alan Heston and Robert Summers, "The Penn World Table (Mark 5): An Expanded Set of International Comparisons, 1950-1988," *Quarterly Journal of Economics,* May 1991, pp. 327-368.
[4]Adam Smith, *The Wealth of Nations* (New York: Everyman's Library, Book 1, 1910).

The gains in productivity that result from specialization are indeed often prodigious. They constitute the single most important explanation for why societies that don't rely heavily on specialization and exchange have failed to keep pace.

WHY HAVE SOME COUNTRIES BEEN SLOW TO SPECIALIZE?

You may be asking yourself, "If specialization is such a great thing, why don't people in poor countries like Nepal just specialize?" If so, you're in good company. Adam Smith spent many years attempting to answer precisely the same question. In the end, his explanation was that population density is an important precondition for specialization. Smith, ever the economic naturalist, observed that work tended to be far more specialized in the large cities of England in the eighteenth century than in the rural Highlands of Scotland:

> In the lone houses and very small villages which are scattered about in so
> desert a country as the Highlands of Scotland, every farmer must be butcher,
> baker, and brewer for his own family. . . . A country carpenter . . . is not
> only a carpenter, but a joiner, a cabinet maker, and even a carver in wood,
> as well as a wheelwright, a ploughwright, a cart and waggon maker.[5]

In contrast, each of these same tasks was performed by a different specialist in the large English and Scottish cities of Smith's day. Scottish Highlanders also would have specialized had they been able to, but the markets in which they participated were simply too small and fragmented. Of course, high population density by itself provides no guarantee that specialization will result in rapid economic growth. But especially before the arrival of modern shipping and electronic communications technology, low population density was a definite obstacle to gains from specialization.

Nepal remains one of the most remote and isolated countries on the planet. As recently as the mid-1960s, its average population density was less than 30 people per square mile (as compared, for example, to more than 1,200 people per square mile in New Jersey). Specialization was further limited by Nepal's rugged terrain. Exchanging goods and services with residents of other villages was difficult, because the nearest village in most cases could be reached only after trekking several hours, or even days, over treacherous Himalayan trails. More than any other factor, this extreme isolation accounts for Nepal's long-standing failure to benefit from widespread specialization.

Population density is by no means the only important factor that influences the degree of specialization. Specialization may be severely impeded, for example, by laws and customs that limit people's freedom to transact freely with one another. The communist governments of North Korea and the former East Germany restricted exchange severely, which helps explain why those countries achieved far less specialization than South Korea and the former West Germany, whose governments were far more supportive of exchange.

CAN WE HAVE TOO MUCH SPECIALIZATION?

Of course, the mere fact that specialization boosts productivity does not mean that more specialization is always better than less, for specialization also entails costs. For example, most people appear to enjoy variety in the work they do, yet variety tends to be one of the first casualties as workplace tasks become ever more narrowly specialized.

Indeed, one of Karl Marx's central themes was that the fragmentation of workplace tasks often exacts a heavy psychological toll on workers. Thus, he wrote,

> All means for the development of production . . . mutilate the laborer into
> a fragment of a man, degrade him to the level of an appendage of a machine,
> destroy every remnant of charm in his work and turn it into hated toil.[6]

Charlie Chaplin's 1936 film *Modern Times* paints a vivid portrait of the psychological costs of repetitive factory work. As an assembly worker, Chaplin's only task, all day every day, is to tighten the nuts on two bolts as they pass before him on the assembly line. Finally, he snaps and staggers from the factory, wrenches in hand, tightening every nutlike protuberance he encounters.

[5]Adam Smith, *The Wealth of Nations* (New York: Everyman's Library, Book I, 1910).
[6]Karl Marx, *Das Kapital* (New York: Modern Library, 1906), pp. 708, 709.

Do the extra goods made possible by specialization simply come at too high a price? We must certainly acknowledge at least the *potential* for specialization to proceed too far. Yet specialization need not entail rigidly segmented, mind-numbingly repetitive work. And it is important to recognize that *failure* to specialize entails costs as well. Those who don't specialize must accept low wages or work extremely long hours.

When all is said and done, we can expect to meet life's financial obligations in the shortest time—thereby freeing up more time to do whatever else we wish—if we concentrate at least a significant proportion of our efforts on those tasks for which we have a comparative advantage.

COMPARATIVE ADVANTAGE AND OUTSOURCING

The same logic that leads the individuals in an economy to specialize and exchange goods with one another also leads nations to specialize and trade among themselves. As with individuals, each nation can benefit from exchange, even though one may be generally more productive than the other in absolute terms.

The Economic Naturalist 2.4

If trade among nations is so beneficial, why are free-trade agreements so controversial?

One of the most heated issues in the 1996 presidential campaign was President Clinton's support for the North American Free Trade Agreement (NAFTA), a treaty to sharply reduce trade barriers between the United States and its immediate neighbors north and south. The treaty attracted fierce opposition from third-party candidate Ross Perot, who insisted that it would mean unemployment for millions of American workers. If exchange is so beneficial, why does anyone oppose it?

If free trade is so great, why do so many people oppose it?

The answer is that, while reducing barriers to international trade increases the total value of all goods and services produced in each nation, it does not guarantee that each individual citizen will do better. One specific concern regarding NAFTA was that it would help Mexico exploit a comparative advantage in the production of goods made by unskilled labor. Although U.S. consumers would benefit from reduced prices for such goods, many Americans feared that unskilled workers in the United States would lose their jobs to workers in Mexico.

In the end, NAFTA was enacted over the vociferous opposition of American labor unions. So far, however, studies have failed to detect significant overall job losses among unskilled workers in the United States, although there have been some losses in specific industries. Nonetheless, opposition to NAFTA has remained fervent, and when U.S. president Donald Trump took office, he pledged to renegotiate NAFTA. The resulting new agreement, the United States–Mexico–Canada Agreement (or USMCA, for short), which has a wide range of new provisions, went into effect on July 1, 2020.

OUTSOURCING

outsourcing a term increasingly used to connote having services performed by low-wage workers overseas

An issue very much in the news in recent years has been the **outsourcing** of U.S. service jobs. Although the term once primarily meant having services performed by subcontractors anywhere outside the confines of the firm, increasingly it connotes the act of replacing relatively expensive American service workers with much cheaper service workers in overseas locations.

A case in point is the transcription of medical records. In an effort to maintain accurate records, many physicians dictate their case notes for later transcription after examining their patients. In the past, transcription was often performed by the physician's secretary in spare moments. But secretaries also must attend to a variety of other tasks that disrupt concentration. They must answer phones, serve as receptionists, prepare correspondence, and so on. As insurance disputes and malpractice litigation became more frequent during the 1980s and 1990s, errors in medical records became much more costly to physicians. In response, many turned to independent companies that offered transcription services by full-time, dedicated specialists.

These companies typically served physicians whose practices were located in the same community. But while many of the companies that manage transcription services are still located in the United States, an increasing fraction of the actual work itself is now performed outside the United States. For example, Eight Crossings, a company headquartered in northern California, enables physicians to upload voice dictation files securely to the Internet, whereupon they are transmitted to transcribers who perform the work in India. The finished documents are then transmitted back, in electronic form, to physicians, who may edit and even sign them online. The advantage for physicians, of course, is that the fee for this service is much lower than for the same service performed domestically because wage rates in India are much lower than in the United States.

In China, Korea, Indonesia, India, and elsewhere, even highly skilled professionals still earn just a small fraction of what their counterparts in the United States are paid. Accordingly, companies face powerful competitive pressure to import not just low-cost goods from overseas suppliers, but also a growing array of professional services.

As Microsoft chair Bill Gates put it in a 1999 interview,

> As a business manager, you need to take a hard look at your core competencies. Revisit the areas of your company that aren't directly involved in those competencies, and consider whether Web technologies can enable you to spin off those tasks. Let another company take over the management responsibilities for that work, and use modern communication technology to work closely with the people—now partners instead of employees are doing the work. In the Web work style, employees can push the freedom the Web provides to its limits.[7]

In economic terms, the outsourcing of services to low-wage foreign workers is exactly analogous to the importation of goods manufactured by low-wage foreign workers. In both cases, the resulting cost savings benefit consumers in the United States. And in both cases, jobs in the United States may be put in jeopardy, at least temporarily. An American manufacturing worker's job is at risk if it is possible to import the good he produces from another country at lower cost. By the same token, an American service worker's job is at risk if a lower-paid worker can perform that same service somewhere else.

The Economic Naturalist 2.5

Is PBS economics reporter Paul Solman's job a likely candidate for outsourcing?

Paul Solman produces video segments that provide in-depth analysis of current economic issues for the PBS evening news program *PBS NewsHour*. Is it likely that his job will someday be outsourced to a low-wage reporter from Hyderabad, India?

In the book *The New Division of Labor*, economists Frank Levy and Richard Murnane attempt to identify the characteristics of a job that make it a likely candidate for outsourcing.[8] In their view, any job that is amenable to computerization is also vulnerable to outsourcing. To computerize a task means to break it down into units that can be managed with simple rules. ATMs, for example, were able to replace many of the tasks that bank tellers once performed because it was straightforward to reduce these tasks to a simple series of questions that a

[7]Bill Gates, *Business @ The Speed of Thought: Using a Digital Nervous System* (New York: Warner Books, March 1999).
[8]Frank Levy and Richard Murnane, *The New Division of Labor: How Computers Are Creating the Next Job Market* (Princeton, NJ: Princeton University Press, 2004).

machine could answer. By the same token, the workers in offshore call centers who increasingly book our airline and hotel reservations are basically following simple scripts much like computer programs.

So the less rules-based a job is, the less vulnerable to outsourcing it is. Safest of all are those that Levy and Murnane describe as "face-to-face" jobs. Unlike most rules-based jobs, these jobs tend to involve complex face-to-face communication with other people, precisely the kind of communication that dominates Solman's economics reporting.

In an interview for PBS *NewsHour*, Solman asked Levy what he meant, exactly, by "complex communication":

> "Suppose I say the word *bill*," Levy responded, "and you hear that. And the question is what does that mean? . . . Am I talking about a piece of currency? Am I talking about a piece of legislation, the front end of a duck? The only way you're going to answer that is to think about the whole context of the conversation. But that's very complicated work to break down into some kind of software."[9]

Levy and Murnane describe a second category of tasks that are less vulnerable to outsourcing—namely, those that for one reason or another require the worker to be physically present. For example, it is difficult to see how someone in China or India could build an addition to someone's house in a Chicago suburb or repair a blown head gasket on someone's Chevrolet Corvette in Atlanta or fill a cavity in someone's tooth in Los Angeles.

So on both counts, Paul Solman's job appears safe for the time being. Because it involves face-to-face, complex communication, and because many of his interviews can be conducted only in the United States, it is difficult to see how a reporter from Hyderabad could displace him.

Of course, the fact that a job is relatively safe does not mean that it is completely sheltered. For example, although most dentists continue to think themselves immune from outsourcing, it is now possible for someone requiring extensive dental work to have the work done in New Delhi and still save enough to cover his airfare and a two-week vacation in India.

There are more than 160 million Americans in the labor force. Each month almost 4 percent of workers leave their jobs and a roughly equal number find new ones.[10] At various points in your life, you are likely to be among this group in transition. In the long run, the greatest security available to you or any other worker is the ability to adapt quickly to new circumstances. Having a good education provides no guarantee against losing your job, but it should enable you to develop a comparative advantage at the kinds of tasks that require more than just executing a simple set of rules.

RECAP ↑

COMPARATIVE ADVANTAGE AND OUTSOURCING

Nations, like individuals, can benefit from exchange, even though one trading partner may be more productive than the other in absolute terms. But expansions of exchange do not guarantee that each individual citizen will be better off. For example, unskilled workers in high-wage countries may be hurt in the short run by the reduction of barriers to trade with low-wage nations.

---

[9]www.pbs.org/newshour/bb/business-july-dec04-jobs_8-16.
[10]www.bls.gov/jlt/#data.

SUMMARY

- One person has an *absolute* advantage over another in the production of a good if she can produce more of that good than the other person. One person has a *comparative* advantage over another in the production of a good if she is relatively more efficient than the other person at producing that good, meaning that her opportunity cost of producing it is lower than her counterpart's. Specialization based on comparative advantage is the basis for economic exchange. When each person specializes in the task at which he or she is relatively most efficient, the economic pie is maximized, making possible the largest slice for everyone. *(LO1)*

- At the individual level, comparative advantage may spring from differences in talent or ability or from differences in education, training, and experience. At the national level, sources of comparative advantage include those innate and learned differences, as well as differences in language, culture, institutions, climate, natural resources, and a host of other factors. *(LO1)*

- The production possibilities curve is a simple device for summarizing the possible combinations of output that a society can produce if it employs its resources efficiently. In a simple economy that produces only coffee beans and nuts, the PPC shows the maximum quantity of coffee bean production (vertical axis) possible at each level of nut production (horizontal axis). The slope of the PPC at any point represents the opportunity cost of nuts at that point, expressed in pounds of coffee beans. *(LO2)*

- The gains from specialization and exchange tend to be larger the larger the differences are between trading partners' opportunity costs. *(LO2)*

- All production possibilities curves slope downward because of the *Scarcity Principle*, which states that the only way a consumer can get more of one good is to settle for less of another. In economies whose workers have different opportunity costs of producing each good, the slope of the PPC becomes steeper as consumers move downward along the curve. This change in slope illustrates the *Principle of Increasing Opportunity Cost (or the Low-Hanging-Fruit Principle)*, which states that in expanding the production of any good, a society should first employ those resources that are relatively efficient at producing that good, only afterward turning to those that are less efficient. *(LO2)*

- Factors that cause a country's PPC to shift outward over time include investment in new factories and equipment, population growth, and improvements in knowledge and technology. *(LO3)*

- The same logic that prompts individuals to specialize in their production and exchange goods with one another also leads nations to specialize and trade with one another. Just because a country as a whole benefits from trade, however, does not mean that each individual citizen will be better off. For example, trade between nations may lead some workers to lose their jobs due to outsourcing. *(LO4)*

CORE PRINCIPLES

The Principle of Comparative Advantage
Everyone does best when each person (or each country) concentrates on the activities for which his or her opportunity cost is lowest.

The Principle of Increasing Opportunity Cost (also called the "Low-Hanging-Fruit Principle")
In expanding the production of any good, first employ those resources with the lowest opportunity cost, and only afterward turn to resources with higher opportunity costs.

KEY TERMS

absolute advantage
attainable point
comparative advantage

efficient point
inefficient point
outsourcing

production possibilities curve (PPC)
unattainable point

REVIEW QUESTIONS

1. Explain what "having a comparative advantage" at producing a particular good or service means. What does "having an absolute advantage" at producing a good or service mean? *(LO1)*

2. What factors have helped the United States to become the world's leading exporter of movies, books, and popular music? *(LO1)*

3. Why does saying that people are poor because they do not specialize make more sense than saying that people perform their own services because they are poor? *(LO2, LO3)*

4. How will a reduction in the number of hours worked each day affect an economy's production possibilities curve? *(LO3)*

5. How will technological innovations that boost labor productivity affect an economy's production possibilities curve? *(LO3)*

PROBLEMS

1. Ted can wax a car in 20 minutes or wash a car in 60 minutes. Ishana can wax a car in 15 minutes or wash a car in 30 minutes. What is each person's opportunity cost of washing a car? Who has a comparative advantage in washing cars? *(LO1)*

2. Ted can wax 4 cars per day or wash 12 cars. Ishana can wax 3 cars per day or wash 6 cars. What is each person's opportunity cost of washing a car? Who has a comparative advantage in washing cars? *(LO1)*

3. Isabella and Antonio are auto mechanics. Isabella takes 4 hours to replace a clutch and 2 hours to replace a set of brakes. Antonio takes 6 hours to replace a clutch and 2 hours to replace a set of brakes. State whether anyone has an absolute advantage at either task and, for each task, identify who has a comparative advantage. *(LO1)*

4. Consider a society consisting only of Helen, who allocates her time between sewing dresses and baking bread. Each hour she devotes to sewing dresses yields 4 dresses and each hour she devotes to baking bread yields 8 loaves of bread. *(LO2)*
   a. If Helen works a total of 8 hours per day, graph her production possibilities curve.
   b. Using your graph, which of the points listed below are attainable and/or efficient?
      28 dresses per day, 16 loaves per day.
      16 dresses per day, 32 loaves per day.
      18 dresses per day, 24 loaves per day.

5. Suppose that in Problem 4 a new sewing machine is introduced that enables Helen to sew 8 dresses per hour rather than only 4. *(LO3)*
   a. Show how this development shifts her production possibilities curve.
   b. Indicate if the following points are attainable and/or efficient before and after the introduction of the sewing machine.
      16 dresses per day, 48 loaves per day.
      24 dresses per day, 16 loaves per day.

c. Explain what is meant by the following statement: "An increase in productivity with respect to any one good increases our options for producing and consuming all other goods."

6. Krisha can pick 4 pounds of coffee beans in an hour or gather 2 pounds of nuts. Tom can pick 2 pounds of coffee beans in an hour or gather 4 pounds of nuts. Each works 6 hours per day. *(LO2)*
   a. Together, what is the maximum number of pounds of coffee beans the two can pick in a day? What is the maximum number of pounds of nuts the two can gather in a day?
   b. Now suppose Krisha and Tom were gathering the maximum number of pounds of nuts when they decided that they would like to begin picking 8 pounds of coffee beans per day. Who would pick the coffee beans, and how many pounds of nuts would they still be able to gather?
   c. Would it be possible for Krisha and Tom in total to gather 26 pounds of nuts and pick 20 pounds of coffee beans each day? If so, how much of each good should each person pick?
   d. Is the point at 30 pounds of coffee beans per day, 12 pounds of nuts per day an attainable point? Is it an efficient point?
   e. On a graph with pounds of coffee beans per day on the vertical axis and pounds of nuts per day on the horizontal axis, show all the points you identified in parts a–d.

7.* Refer to the two-person economy described in Problem 6. *(LO2)*
   a. Suppose that Krisha and Tom could buy or sell coffee beans and nuts in the world market at a price of $2 per pound for coffee beans and $2 per pound for nuts. If each person specialized completely in the good for which he or she had a comparative advantage, how much could they earn by selling all they produce?
   b. At the prices just described, what is the maximum amount of coffee beans Krisha and Tom could buy

*Denotes more difficult problem.

in the world market with the income they earned? What is the maximum amount of nuts? Would it be possible for them to consume 40 pounds of nuts and 8 pounds of coffee beans each day?

c. In light of their ability to buy and sell in world markets at the stated prices, show on the same graph all combinations of the two goods it would be possible for them to consume.

8. Which of the following U.S. jobs is likely to be the most vulnerable to outsourcing: an in-home health care provider, a hairstylist, or a computer programmer? Explain. *(LO4)*

ANSWERS TO SELF-TESTS

2.1

	Productivity in web design	Productivity in bicycle repair
Monique	2 web page updates per hour	1 repair per hour
Miguel	3 web page updates per hour	3 repairs per hour

The entries in the table tell us that Miguel has an absolute advantage over Monique in both activities. While Miguel, the mechanic, can update 3 web pages per hour, Monique, the web designer, can update only 2. Miguel's absolute advantage over Monique is even greater in the task of fixing bikes—3 repairs per hour versus Monique's 1.

But as in the second example in this chapter, the fact that Miguel is a better web designer than Monique does not imply that Miguel should update his own web page. Miguel's opportunity cost of updating a web page is 1 bicycle repair, whereas Monique must give up only half a repair to update a web page. Monique has a comparative advantage over Miguel at web design and Miguel has a comparative advantage over Monique at bicycle repair. *(LO1)*

2.2 In the accompanying graph, *A* (20 pounds per day of coffee beans, 4 pounds per day of nuts) is unattainable; *B* (12 pounds per day of coffee beans, 6 pounds per day of nuts) is both attainable and efficient; and *C* (4 pounds per day of coffee beans, 8 pounds per day of nuts) is attainable and inefficient. *(LO2)*

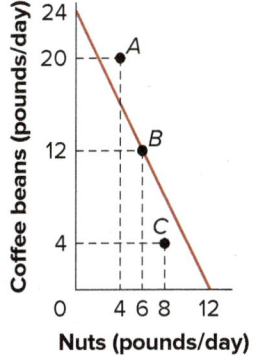

2.3 Krisha's opportunity cost of gathering a pound of nuts is now ½ pound of coffee beans and Tom's opportunity cost of gathering a pound of nuts is now only 1 pound of coffee beans. So Tom has a comparative advantage at picking coffee beans and Krisha has a comparative advantage at gathering nuts. *(LO2)*

2.4 Because Tom can produce five times as many pounds of nuts in an hour as pounds of coffee beans, to produce equal quantities of each, he must spend 5 hours picking coffee for every hour he devotes to gathering nuts. And because he works a 6-hour day, that means spending 5 hours picking coffee beans and 1 hour gathering nuts. Dividing his time in this way, he will end up with 5 pounds of each good. Similarly, if she is to produce equal quantities of each good, Krisha must spend 5 hours gathering nuts and 1 hour picking coffee beans. So she, too, produces 5 pounds of each good if she divides her 6-hour day in this way. Their combined daily production will thus be 10 pounds of each good. By working together and specializing, however, they can produce and consume a total of 30 pounds per day of each good. *(LO2)*

CHAPTER 3

Supply and Demand

When there's excess demand for a product, its price tends to rise.

Johnny Michael/Shutterstock

The stock of foodstuffs on hand at any moment in New York City's grocery stores, restaurants, and private kitchens is sufficient to feed the area's 10 million residents for at most a week or so. Since most of these residents have nutritionally adequate and highly varied diets, and since almost no food is produced within the city proper, provisioning New York requires that millions of pounds of food and drink be delivered to locations throughout the city each day.

No doubt many New Yorkers, buying groceries at their favorite local markets or eating at their favorite Italian restaurants, give little or no thought to the nearly miraculous coordination of people and resources required to feed city residents on a daily basis. But near-miraculous it is, nevertheless. Even if the supplying of New York City consisted only of transporting a fixed collection of foods to a given list of destinations each day, it would be quite an impressive operation, requiring at least a small (and well-managed) army to carry out.

Yet the entire process is astonishingly more complex than that. For example, the system must somehow ensure that not only *enough* food is delivered to satisfy New Yorkers' discriminating palates, but also the *right kinds* of food. There can't be too much pheasant and not enough smoked eel, or too much bacon and not enough eggs, or too much caviar and not enough canned tuna, and so on. Similar judgments must be made *within* each category of food and drink: there must be the right amount of Swiss cheese and the right amounts of provolone, gorgonzola, and feta.

But even this doesn't begin to describe the complexity of the decisions and actions required to provide our nation's largest city with its daily bread. Someone has to decide where each particular type of food gets produced, and how, and by whom. Someone must decide how much of each type of food gets delivered to *each* of the tens of thousands of restaurants and grocery stores in the city. Someone must determine whether the deliveries should be made in big trucks or small ones, arrange that the trucks be in the right place at the right time, and ensure that gasoline and qualified drivers be available.

Thousands of individuals must decide what role, if any, they will play in this collective effort. Some people—just the right number—must choose to drive food delivery trucks rather than trucks that deliver lumber. Others—again, just the right number—must become the mechanics who fix these trucks rather than carpenters who build houses. Others must become farmers rather than architects or bricklayers. Still others must become chefs in upscale restaurants, or flip burgers at McDonald's, instead of becoming plumbers or electricians.

Yet despite the almost incomprehensible number and complexity of the tasks involved, somehow the supplying of New York City manages to get done remarkably smoothly. Oh, a grocery store will occasionally run out of flank steak or a diner will sometimes be told that someone else has just ordered the last serving of roast duck. But if episodes like these stick in memory, it is only because they are rare. For the most part, New York's food delivery system—like that of every other city in the country—functions so seamlessly that it attracts virtually no notice.

The situation is strikingly different in New York City's rental housing market. According to one estimate, growth in the city's population has long outstripped growth in the

city's supply of housing units (with the exception of a recent surge in construction of ultra-luxury condominiums).[1] As a result, America's most densely populated city has been experiencing a protracted housing shortage. Yet, paradoxically, in the midst of this shortage, apartment houses are being demolished; and in the vacant lots left behind, people from the neighborhoods are planting flower gardens!

New York City is experiencing not only a growing shortage of rental housing, but also chronically strained relations between landlords and tenants. In one all-too-typical case, for example, a photographer living in a loft on the Lower East Side waged an eight-year court battle with his landlord that generated literally thousands of pages of legal documents. "Once we put up a doorbell for ourselves," the photographer recalled, "and [the landlord] pulled it out, so we pulled out the wires to his doorbell."[2] The landlord, for his part, accused the photographer of obstructing his efforts to renovate the apartment. According to the landlord, the tenant preferred for the apartment to remain in substandard condition since that gave him an excuse to withhold rent payments.

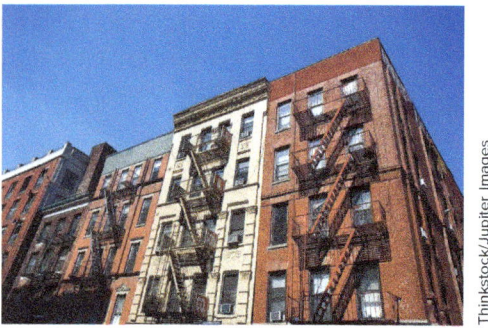

Same city, two strikingly different patterns: In the food industry, goods and services are available in wide variety and people (at least those with adequate income) are generally satisfied with what they receive and the choices available to them. In contrast, in the rental housing industry, chronic shortages and chronic dissatisfaction are rife among both buyers and sellers. Why this difference?

The brief answer is that New York City relies on a complex system of administrative rent regulations to allocate housing units but leaves the

Melissamn/Shutterstock

Thinkstock/Jupiter Images

Why does New York City's food distribution system work so much better than its housing market?

[1]For additional information see www.citylab.com/equity/2017/05/is-housing-catching-up/528246.
[2]John Tierney, "The Rentocracy: At the Intersection of Supply and Demand," *New York Times Magazine,* May 4, 1997, p. 39.

allocation of food essentially in the hands of market forces—the forces of supply and demand. Although intuition might suggest otherwise, both theory and experience suggest that the seemingly chaotic and unplanned outcomes of market forces, in most cases, can do a better job of allocating economic resources than can (for example) a government agency, even if the agency has the best of intentions.

In this chapter we'll explore how markets allocate food, housing, and other goods and services, usually with remarkable efficiency despite the complexity of the tasks. To be sure, markets are by no means perfect, and our stress on their virtues is to some extent an attempt to counteract what most economists view as an underappreciation by the general public of their remarkable strengths. But, in the course of our discussion, we'll see why markets function so smoothly most of the time and why bureaucratic rules and regulations rarely work as well in solving complex economic problems.

To convey an understanding of how markets work is a major goal of this course, and in this chapter we provide only a brief introduction and overview. As the course proceeds, we'll discuss the economic role of markets in considerably more detail, paying attention to some of the problems of markets as well as their strengths.

WHAT, HOW, AND FOR WHOM? CENTRAL PLANNING VERSUS THE MARKET

No city, state, or society—regardless of how it is organized—can escape the need to answer certain basic economic questions. For example, how much of our limited time and other resources should we devote to building housing, how much to the production of food, and how much to providing other goods and services? What techniques should we use to produce each good? Who should be assigned to each specific task? And how should the resulting goods and services be distributed among people?

In the thousands of different societies for which records are available, issues like these have been decided in essentially one of two ways. One approach is for all economic decisions to be made centrally, by an individual or small number of individuals on behalf of a larger group. For example, in many agrarian societies throughout history, families or other small groups consumed only those goods and services that they produced for themselves, and a single clan or family leader made most important production and distribution decisions. On an immensely larger scale, the economic organization of the former Soviet Union (and other communist countries) was also largely centralized. In so-called centrally planned communist nations, a central bureaucratic committee established production targets for the country's farms and factories, developed a master plan for how to achieve the targets (including detailed instructions concerning who was to produce what), and set up guidelines for the distribution and use of the goods and services produced.

Neither form of centralized economic organization is much in evidence today. When implemented on a small scale, as in a self-sufficient family enterprise, centralized decision making is certainly feasible. For the reasons discussed in the preceding chapter, however, the jack-of-all-trades approach was doomed once it became clear how dramatically people could improve their living standards by specialization—that is, by having each individual focus his or her efforts on a relatively narrow range of tasks. And with the fall of the Soviet Union and its satellite nations in the late 1980s, there are now only three communist economies left in the world: Cuba, North Korea, and China. The first two of these appear to be on their last legs, economically speaking, and China has largely abandoned any attempt to control production and distribution decisions from the center. The major remaining examples of centralized allocation and control now reside in the bureaucratic agencies that administer programs like New York City's rent controls—programs that are themselves becoming increasingly rare.

At the beginning of the twenty-first century, we are therefore left, for the most part, with the second major form of economic system, one in which production and distribution decisions are left to individuals interacting in private markets. In the so-called capitalist, or free-market, economies, people decide for themselves which careers to pursue and which products to produce or buy. In fact, there are no *pure* free-market economies today. Modern industrial countries are more properly described as "mixed economies." Their goods and services are allocated by a combination of free markets, regulation, and other forms of collective control. Still, it makes sense to refer to such systems as free-market economies because people are for the most part free to start businesses, shut them down, or sell them. And within broad limits, the distribution of goods and services is determined by individual preferences backed by individual purchasing power, which in most cases comes from the income people earn in the labor market.

In country after country, markets have replaced centralized control for the simple reason that they tend to assign production tasks and consumption benefits much more effectively. The popular press and conventional wisdom often assert that economists disagree about important issues. (As someone once quipped, "If you lay all the economists in the world end to end, they still wouldn't reach a conclusion.") The fact is, however, that there is overwhelming agreement among economists about a broad range of issues. A substantial majority believes that markets are the most effective means for allocating society's scarce resources. For example, a recent survey found that more than 90 percent of American professional economists believe that rent regulations like the ones implemented by New York City do more harm than good. That the stated aim of these regulations—to make rental housing more affordable for middle- and low-income families—is clearly benign was not enough to prevent them from wreaking havoc on New York City's housing market. To see why, we must explore how goods and services are allocated in private markets and why nonmarket means of allocating goods and services often do not produce the expected results.

BUYERS AND SELLERS IN MARKETS

market the market for any good consists of all buyers or sellers of that good

Beginning with some simple concepts and definitions, we will explore how the interactions among buyers and sellers in markets determine the prices and quantities of the various goods and services traded. We begin by defining a market: the **market** for any good consists of all the buyers and sellers of that good. So, for example, the market for pizza on a given day in a given place is just the set of people (or other economic actors such as firms) potentially able to buy or sell pizza at that time and location.

In the market for pizza, sellers comprise the individuals and companies that either do sell—or might, under the right circumstances, sell—pizza. Similarly, buyers in this market include all individuals who buy—or might buy—pizza.

In most parts of the country, a decent pizza can still be had for less than $10. Where does the market price of pizza come from? Looking beyond pizza to the vast array of other goods that are bought and sold every day, we may ask, "Why are some goods cheap and others expensive?" Aristotle had no idea. Nor did Plato, or Copernicus, or Newton. On reflection, it is astonishing that, for almost the entire span of human history, not even the most intelligent and creative minds on Earth had any real inkling of how to answer that seemingly simple question. Even Adam Smith, the Scottish moral philosopher whose *Wealth of Nations* launched the discipline of economics in 1776, suffered confusion on this issue.

Smith and other early economists (including Karl Marx) thought that the market price of a good was determined by its cost of production. But although costs surely do affect prices, they cannot explain why one of Claude Monet's paintings sells for so much more than one of Pierre-Auguste Renoir's.

Why do Claude Monet's paintings sell for so much more than Pierre-Auguste Renoir's?

Metropolitan Museum of Art

Stanley Jevons and other nineteenth-century economists tried to explain price by focusing on the value people derived from consuming different goods and services. It certainly seems plausible that people will pay a lot for a good they value highly. Yet willingness to pay cannot be the whole story, either. Deprive a person in the desert of water, for example, and he will be dead in a matter of days, and yet water sells for less than a penny a gallon. By contrast, human beings can get along perfectly well without gold, and yet gold sells for more than $1,800 an ounce.

Cost of production? Value to the user? Which is it? The answer, which seems obvious to today's economists, is that both matter. Writing in the late nineteenth century, the British economist Alfred Marshall was among the first to show clearly how costs and value interact to determine both the prevailing market price for a good and the amount of it that is bought and sold. Our task in the pages ahead will be to explore Marshall's insights and gain some practice in applying them. As a first step, we introduce the two main components of Marshall's pathbreaking analysis: the demand curve and the supply curve.

A Pierre-Auguste Renoir painting.

THE DEMAND CURVE

In the market for pizza, the **demand curve** for pizza is a simple schedule or graph that tells us how many slices people would be willing to buy at different prices. By convention, economists usually put price on the vertical axis of the demand curve and quantity on the horizontal axis.

A fundamental property of the demand curve is that it is downward-sloping with respect to price. For example, the demand curve for pizza tells us that as the price of pizza falls, buyers will buy more slices. Thus, the daily demand curve for pizza in Chicago on a given day might look like the curve seen in Figure 3.1. (Although economists usually refer to demand and supply "curves," we often draw them as straight lines in examples.)

The demand curve in Figure 3.1 tells us that when the price of pizza is low—say, $2 per slice—buyers will want to buy 16,000 slices per day, whereas they will want to buy only 12,000 slices at a price of $3 and only 8,000 at a price of $4. The demand curve for pizza—as for any other good—slopes downward for multiple reasons. Some have to do with the individual consumer's reactions to price changes. Thus, as pizza becomes more expensive, a consumer may switch to chicken sandwiches, hamburgers, or other foods that substitute for pizza. This is called the **substitution effect** of a price change. In addition, a price increase reduces the quantity demanded because it reduces purchasing power: a consumer simply can't afford to buy as many slices of pizza at higher prices as at lower prices. This is called the **income effect** of a price change.

demand curve a schedule or graph showing the quantity of a good that buyers wish to buy at each price

substitution effect the change in the quantity demanded of a good that results because buyers switch to or from substitutes when the price of the good changes

income effect the change in the quantity demanded of a good that results because a change in the price of a good changes the buyer's purchasing power

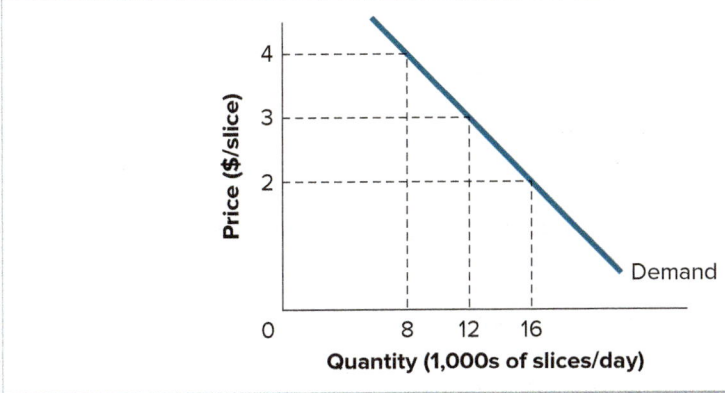

FIGURE 3.1

The Daily Demand Curve for Pizza in Chicago.

The demand curve for any good is a downward-sloping function of its price.

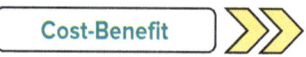

buyer's reservation price
the largest dollar amount the buyer would be willing to pay for a good

Another reason the demand curve slopes downward is that consumers differ in terms of how much they're willing to pay for the good. The Cost-Benefit Principle tells us that a given person will buy the good if the benefit she expects to receive from it exceeds its cost. The benefit is the **buyer's reservation price**, the highest dollar amount she'd be willing to pay for the good. The cost of the good is the actual amount that the buyer actually must pay for it, which is the market price of the good. In most markets, different buyers have different reservation prices. So, when the good sells for a high price, it will satisfy the cost-benefit test for fewer buyers than when it sells for a lower price.

To put this same point another way, the fact that the demand curve for a good is downward-sloping reflects the fact that the reservation price of the marginal buyer declines as the quantity of the good bought increases. Here the marginal buyer is the person who purchases the last unit of the good sold. If buyers are currently purchasing 12,000 slices of pizza a day in Figure 3.1, for example, the reservation price for the buyer of the 12,000th slice must be $3. (If someone had been willing to pay more than that, the quantity demanded at a price of $3 would have been more than 12,000 to begin with.) By similar reasoning, when the quantity sold is 16,000 slices per day, the marginal buyer's reservation price must be only $2.

We defined the demand curve for any good as a schedule telling how much of it consumers wish to purchase at various prices. This is called the *horizontal interpretation* of the demand curve. Using the horizontal interpretation, we start with price on the vertical axis and read the corresponding quantity demanded on the horizontal axis. Thus, at a price of $4 per slice, the demand curve in Figure 3.1 tells us that the quantity of pizza demanded will be 8,000 slices per day.

The demand curve also can be interpreted in a second way, which is to start with quantity on the horizontal axis and then read the marginal buyer's reservation price on the vertical axis. Thus, when the quantity of pizza sold is 8,000 slices per day, the demand curve in Figure 3.1 tells us that the marginal buyer's reservation price is $4 per slice. This second way of reading the demand curve is called the *vertical interpretation*.

 SELF-TEST 3.1

In Figure 3.1, what is the marginal buyer's reservation price when the quantity of pizza sold is 10,000 slices per day? For the same demand curve, what will be the quantity of pizza demanded at a price of $2.50 per slice?

THE SUPPLY CURVE

supply curve a graph or schedule showing the quantity of a good that sellers wish to sell at each price

In the market for pizza, the **supply curve** is a simple schedule or graph that tells us, for each possible price, the total number of slices that all pizza vendors would be willing to sell at that price. What does the supply curve of pizza look like? The answer to this question is based on the logical assumption that suppliers should be willing to sell additional slices as long as the price they receive is sufficient to cover their opportunity cost of supplying them. Thus, if what someone could earn by selling a slice of pizza is insufficient to compensate her for what she could have earned if she had spent her time and invested her money in some other way, she will not sell that slice. Otherwise, she will.

Just as buyers differ with respect to the amounts they are willing to pay for pizza, sellers also differ with respect to their opportunity cost of supplying pizza. For those with limited education and work experience, the opportunity cost of selling pizza is relatively low (because such individuals typically do not have a lot of high-paying alternatives). For others, the opportunity cost of selling pizza is of moderate value, and for still others—like rock stars and professional athletes—it is prohibitively high. In part because of these differences in opportunity cost among people, the daily supply curve of pizza will be *upward-sloping* with respect to price. As an illustration, see Figure 3.2, which shows a hypothetical supply curve for pizza in the Chicago market on a given day.

FIGURE 3.2

The Daily Supply Curve of Pizza in Chicago.
At higher prices, sellers generally offer more units for sale.

The fact that the supply curve slopes upward may be seen as a consequence of the Low-Hanging-Fruit Principle, discussed in Chapter 2, *Comparative Advantage.* This principle tells us that as we expand the production of pizza, we turn first to those whose opportunity cost of producing pizza is lowest, and only then to others with a higher opportunity cost.

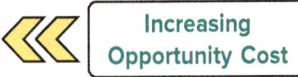

Increasing Opportunity Cost

Like the demand curve, the supply curve can be interpreted either horizontally or vertically. Under the horizontal interpretation, we begin with a price and then go over to the supply curve to read the quantity that sellers wish to sell at that price on the horizontal axis. For instance, at a price of $2 per slice, sellers in Figure 3.2 wish to sell 8,000 slices per day.

Under the vertical interpretation, we begin with a quantity and then go up to the supply curve to read the corresponding marginal cost on the vertical axis. Thus, if sellers in Figure 3.2 are currently supplying 12,000 slices per day, the opportunity cost of the marginal seller is $3 per slice. In other words, the supply curve tells us that the marginal cost of producing the 12,000th slice of pizza is $3. (If someone could produce a 12,001st slice for less than $3, she would have an incentive to supply it, so the quantity of pizza supplied at $3 per slice would not have been 12,000 slices per day to begin with.) By similar reasoning, when the quantity of pizza supplied is 16,000 slices per day, the marginal cost of producing another slice must be $4. The **seller's reservation price** for selling an additional unit of a good is her marginal cost of producing that good. It is the smallest dollar amount for which she would not be worse off if she sold an additional unit.

seller's reservation price the smallest dollar amount for which a seller would be willing to sell an additional unit, generally equal to marginal cost

 SELF-TEST 3.2

In Figure 3.2, what is the marginal cost of a slice of pizza when the quantity of pizza sold is 10,000 slices per day? For the same supply curve, what will be the quantity of pizza supplied at a price of $3.50 per slice?

RECAP↑

DEMAND AND SUPPLY CURVES

The *market* for a good consists of the actual and potential buyers and sellers of that good. For any given price, the *demand curve* shows the quantity that demanders would be willing to buy and the *supply curve* shows the quantity that suppliers of the good would be willing to sell. Suppliers are willing to sell more at higher prices (supply curves slope upward) and demanders are willing to buy less at higher prices (demand curves slope downward).

MARKET EQUILIBRIUM

equilibrium a balanced or unchanging situation in which all forces at work within a system are canceled by others

The concept of **equilibrium** is employed in both the physical and social sciences, and it is of central importance in economic analysis. In general, a system is in equilibrium when all forces at work within the system are canceled by others, resulting in a balanced or unchanging situation. In physics, for example, a ball hanging from a spring is said to be in equilibrium when the spring has stretched sufficiently that the upward force it exerts on the ball is exactly counterbalanced by the downward force of gravity. In economics, a market is said to be in equilibrium when no participant in the market has any reason to alter his or her behavior, so that there is no tendency for production or prices in that market to change.

equilibrium price and equilibrium quantity the price and quantity at the intersection of the supply and demand curves for the good

If we want to determine the final position of a ball hanging from a spring, we need to find the point at which the forces of gravity and spring tension are balanced and the system is in equilibrium. Similarly, if we want to find the price at which a good will sell (which we will call the **equilibrium price**) and the quantity of it that will be sold (the **equilibrium quantity**), we need to find the equilibrium in the market for that good. The basic tools for finding the equilibrium in a market for a good are the supply and demand curves for that good. For reasons we will explain, the equilibrium price and equilibrium quantity of a good are the price and quantity at which the supply and demand curves for the good intersect. For the hypothetical supply and demand curves shown earlier for the pizza market in Chicago, the equilibrium price will therefore be $3 per slice, and the equilibrium quantity of pizza sold will be 12,000 slices per day, as shown in Figure 3.3.

Note that at the equilibrium price of $3 per slice, both sellers and buyers are "satisfied" in the following sense: buyers are buying exactly the quantity of pizza they wish to buy at that price (12,000 slices per day) and sellers are selling exactly the quantity of pizza they wish to sell (also 12,000 slices per day). And since they are satisfied in this sense, neither buyers nor sellers face any incentives to change their behavior.

market equilibrium occurs in a market when all buyers and sellers are satisfied with their respective quantities at the market price

Note the limited sense of the term *satisfied* in the definition of **market equilibrium**. It doesn't mean that sellers would be displeased to receive a price higher than the equilibrium price. Rather, it means only that they're able to sell all they wish to sell at that price. Similarly, to say that buyers are satisfied at the equilibrium price doesn't mean that they wouldn't be happy to pay less than that price. Rather, it means only that they're able to buy exactly as many units of the good as they wish to at the equilibrium price.

Note also that if the price of pizza in our Chicago market were anything other than $3 per slice, either buyers or sellers would be frustrated. Suppose, for example, that the price of pizza were $4 per slice, as shown in Figure 3.4. At that price, buyers wish to buy only 8,000 slices per day, but sellers wish to sell 16,000. And since no one can force someone to buy a slice of pizza against her wishes, this means that buyers will buy only the 8,000 slices they wish to buy. So when price exceeds the equilibrium price, it is sellers

FIGURE 3.3

The Equilibrium Price and Quantity of Pizza in Chicago.

The equilibrium price and quantity of a product are the values that correspond to the intersection of the supply and demand curves for that product.

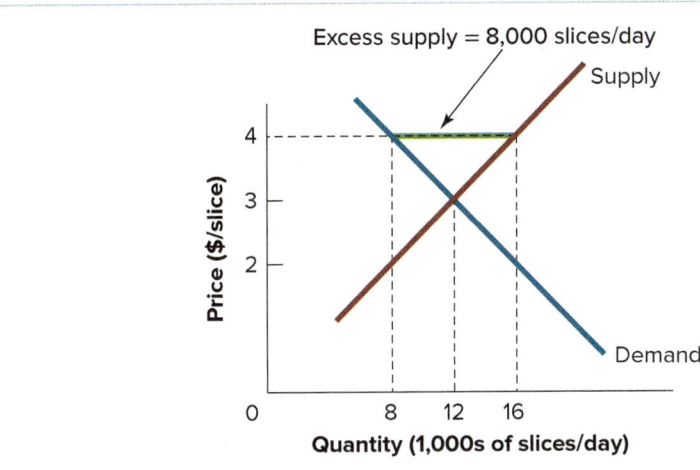

FIGURE 3.4

Excess Supply.

When price exceeds equilibrium price, there is excess supply, or surplus, the difference between quantity supplied and quantity demanded.

who end up being frustrated. At a price of $4 in this example, they are left with an **excess supply**, or **surplus**, of 8,000 slices per day.

Conversely, suppose that the price of pizza in our Chicago market were less than the equilibrium price—say, $2 per slice. As shown in Figure 3.5, buyers want to buy 16,000 slices per day at that price, whereas sellers want to sell only 8,000. And since sellers cannot be forced to sell pizza against their wishes, this time it is the buyers who end up being frustrated. At a price of $2 per slice in this example, they experience an **excess demand**, or **shortage**, of 8,000 slices per day.

An extraordinary feature of private markets for goods and services is their automatic tendency to gravitate toward their respective equilibrium prices and quantities. This tendency is a simple consequence of the Incentive Principle. The mechanisms by which the adjustment happens are implicit in our definitions of excess supply and excess demand. Suppose, for example, that the price of pizza in our hypothetical market was $4 per slice, leading to excess supply as shown in Figure 3.4. Because sellers are frustrated in the sense of wanting to sell more pizza than buyers wish to buy, sellers have an incentive to take whatever steps they can to increase their sales. The simplest strategy available to them is to cut their price slightly. Thus, if one seller reduced her price from $4 to, say, $3.95 per slice, she would attract many of the buyers who had been paying $4 per slice for pizza supplied by other sellers. Those sellers, in order to recover their lost business, would then have an incentive to match the price cut. But notice that if all sellers lowered their prices to $3.95 per slice, there would still be considerable excess supply. So sellers would face continuing incentives to cut their prices. This pressure to cut prices won't go away until prices fall all the way to $3 per slice.

excess supply (or **surplus**) the amount by which quantity supplied exceeds quantity demanded when the price of the good exceeds the equilibrium price

excess demand (or **shortage**) the amount by which quantity demanded exceeds quantity supplied when the price of a good lies below the equilibrium price

Incentive

FIGURE 3.5

Excess Demand.

When price lies below equilibrium price, there is excess demand, the difference between quantity demanded and quantity supplied.

Conversely, suppose that price starts out less than the equilibrium price–say, $2 per slice. This time it is buyers who are frustrated. A person who can't get all the pizza she wants at a price of $2 per slice has an incentive to offer a higher price, hoping to obtain pizza that would otherwise have been sold to other buyers. And sellers, for their part, will be only too happy to post higher prices as long as queues of frustrated buyers remain.

The upshot is that price has a tendency to gravitate to its equilibrium level under conditions of either excess supply or excess demand. And when price reaches its equilibrium level, both buyers and sellers are satisfied in the technical sense of being able to buy or sell precisely the amounts of their choosing.

EXAMPLE 3.1   Market Equilibrium

Samples of points on the demand and supply curves of a pizza market are provided in Table 3.1. Graph the demand and supply curves for this market and find its equilibrium price and quantity.

TABLE 3.1
Points along the Demand and Supply Curves of a Pizza Market

Demand for Pizza		Supply of Pizza	
Price ($/slice)	Quantity demanded (1,000s of slices/day)	Price ($/slice)	Quantity supplied (1,000s of slices/day)
1	8	1	2
2	6	2	4
3	4	3	6
4	2	4	8

The points in the table are plotted in Figure 3.6 and then joined to indicate the supply and demand curves for this market. These curves intersect to yield an equilibrium price of $2.50 per slice and an equilibrium quantity of 5,000 slices per day.

FIGURE 3.6

Graphing Supply and Demand and Finding Equilibrium Price and Quantity.

To graph the demand and supply curves, plot the relevant points given in the table and then join them with a line. Equilibrium price and quantity occur at the intersection of these curves.

We emphasize that market equilibrium doesn't necessarily produce an ideal outcome for all market participants. Thus, in Example 3.1, market participants are satisfied with the amount of pizza they buy and sell at a price of $2.50 per slice, but for a poor buyer this may signify little more than that he *can't* buy additional pizza without sacrificing other more highly valued purchases.

Indeed, buyers with extremely low incomes often have difficulty purchasing even basic goods and services, which has prompted governments in almost every society to attempt to ease the burdens of the poor. Yet the laws of supply and demand cannot simply be repealed by an act of the legislature. In the next section, we'll see that when legislators attempt to prevent markets from reaching their equilibrium prices and quantities, they often do more harm than good. Fortunately, there are other, more effective, ways of providing assistance to families in need.

RENT CONTROLS RECONSIDERED

Consider again the market for rental housing units in New York City and suppose that the demand and supply curves for one-bedroom apartments are as shown in Figure 3.7. This market, left alone, would reach an equilibrium monthly rent of $1,600, at which 2 million one-bedroom apartments would be rented. Both landlords and tenants would be satisfied, in the sense that they would not wish to rent either more or fewer units at that price.

This wouldn't necessarily mean, of course, that all is well and good. Many potential tenants, for example, might simply be unable to afford a rent of $1,600 per month and thus be forced to remain homeless (or to move out of the city to a cheaper location). Suppose that, acting purely out of benign motives, legislators made it unlawful for landlords to charge more than $800 per month for one-bedroom apartments. Their stated aim in enacting this law was that no person should have to remain homeless because decent housing was unaffordable.

But note in Figure 3.8 that when rents for one-bedroom apartments are prevented from rising above $800 per month, landlords are willing to supply only 1 million apartments per month, 1 million fewer than at the equilibrium monthly rent of $1,600. Note also that at the controlled rent of $800 per month, tenants want to rent 3 million one-bedroom apartments per month. (For example, many people who would have decided to live in New Jersey rather than pay $1,600 a month in New York will now choose to live in the city.) So when rents are prevented from rising above $800 per month, we see an excess demand for one-bedroom apartments of 2 million units each month. Put another way, the rent controls result in a housing shortage of 2 million units each month. What is more, the number of apartments actually available *declines* by 1 million units per month.

If the housing market were completely unregulated, the immediate response to such a high level of excess demand would be for rents to rise sharply. But here the law prevents them from rising above $800. Many other ways exist, however, in which market participants

Quantity (millions of apartments/month)

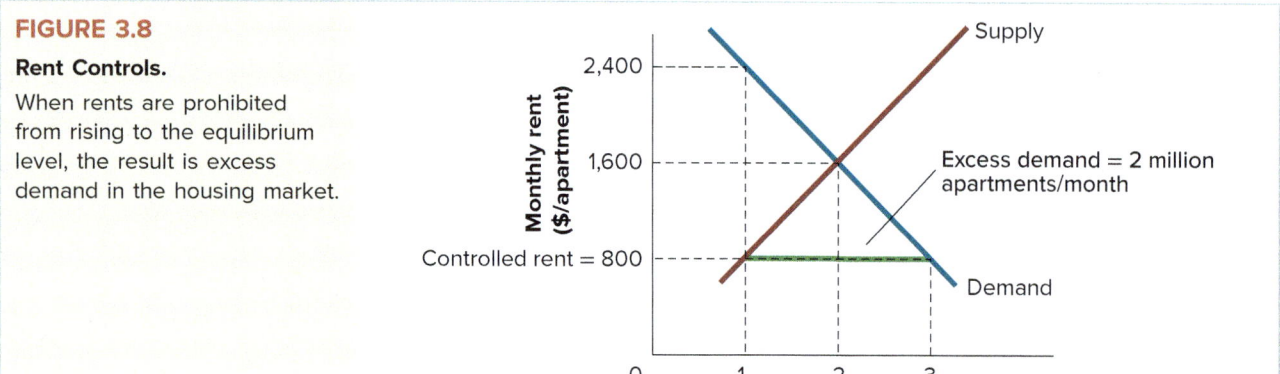

FIGURE 3.8

Rent Controls.

When rents are prohibited from rising to the equilibrium level, the result is excess demand in the housing market.

can respond to the pressures of excess demand. For instance, owners will quickly learn that they are free to spend less on maintaining their rental units. After all, if there are scores of renters knocking at the door of each vacant apartment, a landlord has considerable room to maneuver. Leaking pipes, peeling paint, broken furnaces, and other problems are less likely to receive prompt attention—or, indeed, any attention at all—when rents are set well below market-clearing levels.

Nor are reduced availability of apartments and poorer maintenance of existing apartments the only difficulties. With an offering of only 1 million apartments per month, we see in Figure 3.8 that there are renters who'd be willing to pay as much as $2,400 per month for an apartment. As the Incentive Principle suggests, this pressure will almost always find ways, legal or illegal, of expressing itself. In New York City, for example, it is not uncommon to see "finder's fees" or "key deposits" as high as several thousand dollars. Owners who cannot charge a market-clearing rent for their apartments also have the option of converting them to condominiums or co-ops, which enables them to sell their assets for prices much closer to their true economic value.

Even when rent-controlled apartment owners don't hike their prices in these various ways, serious misallocations result. For instance, ill-suited roommates often remain together despite their constant bickering because each is reluctant to reenter the housing market. Or a widow might steadfastly remain in her seven-room apartment even after her children have left home because it is much cheaper than alternative dwellings not covered by rent control. It would be much better for all concerned if she relinquished that space to a larger family that valued it more highly. But under rent controls, she has no economic incentive to do so.

There's also another more insidious cost of rent controls. In markets without rent controls, landlords cannot discriminate against potential tenants on the basis of race, religion, sexual orientation, physical disability, or national origin without suffering an economic penalty. Refusal to rent to members of specific groups would reduce the demand for their apartments, which would mean having to accept lower rents. When rents are artificially pegged below their equilibrium level, however, the resulting excess demand for apartments enables landlords to engage in discrimination with no further economic penalty.

Rent controls are not the only instance in which governments have attempted to repeal the law of supply and demand in the interest of helping the poor. During the late 1970s, for example, the federal government tried to hold the price of gasoline below its equilibrium level out of concern that high gasoline prices imposed unacceptable hardships on low-income drivers. As with controls in the rental housing market, unintended consequences of price controls in the gasoline market made the policy an extremely costly way of trying to aid the poor. For example, gasoline shortages resulted in long lines at the pumps, a waste not only of valuable time, but also of gasoline as cars sat idling for extended periods.

In their opposition to rent controls and similar measures, are economists revealing a total lack of concern for the poor? Although this claim is sometimes made by those who don't understand the issues, or who stand to benefit in some way from government regulations, there is little justification for it. *Economists simply realize that there are much more effective ways to help poor people than to try to give them apartments and other goods at artificially low prices.*

One straightforward approach would be to give the poor additional income and let them decide for themselves how to spend it. True, there are also practical difficulties involved in transferring additional purchasing power into the hands of the poor—most importantly, the difficulty of targeting cash to the genuinely needy without weakening others' incentives to fend for themselves. But there are practical ways to overcome this difficulty. For example, for far less than the waste caused by price controls, the government could afford generous subsidies to the wages of the working poor and could sponsor public-service employment for those who are unable to find jobs in the private sector.

Regulations that peg prices below equilibrium levels have far-reaching effects on market outcomes. The following self-test asks you to consider what happens when a price control is established at a level above the equilibrium price.

✅ SELF-TEST 3.3

In the rental housing market whose demand and supply curves are shown below, what will be the effect of a law that prevents rents from rising above $1,200 per month?

PIZZA PRICE CONTROLS?

The sources of the contrast between the rent-controlled housing market and the largely unregulated food markets in New York City can be seen more vividly by trying to imagine what would happen if concern for the poor led the city's leaders to implement price controls on pizza. Suppose, for example, that the supply and demand curves for pizza are as shown in Figure 3.9 and that the city imposes a **price ceiling** of $2 per slice, making it unlawful to charge more than that amount. At $2 per slice, buyers want to buy 16,000 slices per day, but sellers want to sell only 8,000.

price ceiling a maximum allowable price, specified by law

At a price of $2 per slice, every pizza restaurant in the city will have long queues of buyers trying unsuccessfully to purchase pizza. Frustrated buyers will behave rudely to clerks, who will respond in kind. Friends of restaurant managers will begin to get preferential treatment. Devious pricing strategies will begin to emerge (such as the $2 slice of pizza sold in combination with a $5 cup of Coke). Pizza will be made from poorer-quality ingredients. Rumors will begin to circulate about sources of black-market pizza. And so on.

FIGURE 3.9

Price Controls in the Pizza Market.

A price ceiling below the equilibrium price of pizza would result in excess demand for pizza.

The very idea of not being able to buy a pizza seems absurd, yet precisely such things happen routinely in markets in which prices are held below the equilibrium levels. For example, prior to the collapse of communist governments, it was considered normal in those countries for people to stand in line for hours to buy bread and other basic goods, while the politically connected had first choice of those goods that were available.

> **RECAP** ↑
>
> **MARKET EQUILIBRIUM**
>
> *Market equilibrium*, the situation in which all buyers and sellers are satisfied with their respective quantities at the market price, occurs at the intersection of the supply and demand curves. The corresponding price and quantity are called the *equilibrium price* and the *equilibrium quantity*.
>
> Unless prevented by regulation, prices and quantities are driven toward their equilibrium values by the actions of buyers and sellers. If the price is initially too high, so that there is excess supply, frustrated sellers will cut their price in order to sell more. If the price is initially too low, so that there is excess demand, competition among buyers drives the price upward. This process continues until equilibrium is reached.

PREDICTING AND EXPLAINING CHANGES IN PRICES AND QUANTITIES

If we know how the factors that govern supply and demand curves are changing, we can make informed predictions about how prices and the corresponding quantities will change. But when describing changing circumstances in the marketplace, we must take care to recognize some important terminological distinctions. For example, we must distinguish between the meanings of the seemingly similar expressions **change in the quantity demanded** and **change in demand**. When we speak of a "change in the quantity demanded," this means the change in the quantity that people wish to buy that occurs in response to a change in price. For instance, Figure 3.10(a) depicts an increase in the quantity demanded that occurs in response to a reduction in the price of tuna. When the price falls from $2 to $1 per can, the quantity demanded rises from 8,000 to 10,000 cans per day. By contrast, when we speak of a "change in demand," this means a *shift in the entire demand curve*. For example, Figure 3.10(b) depicts an increase in demand, meaning that at every price the quantity demanded is higher than before. In summary, a "change in the quantity demanded" refers to a movement *along* the demand curve and a "change in demand" means a *shift* of the entire curve.

change in the quantity demanded a movement along the demand curve that occurs in response to a change in price

change in demand a shift of the entire demand curve

FIGURE 3.10

An Increase in the Quantity Demanded versus an Increase in Demand.

(a) An increase in quantity demanded describes a downward movement along the demand curve as price falls.
(b) An increase in demand describes an outward shift of the demand curve.

A similar terminological distinction applies on the supply side of the market. A **change in supply** means a shift in the entire supply curve, whereas a **change in the quantity supplied** refers to a movement along the supply curve.

Alfred Marshall's supply and demand model is one of the most useful tools of the economic naturalist. Once we understand the forces that govern the placements of supply and demand curves, we're suddenly in a position to make sense of a host of interesting observations in the world around us.

change in supply a shift of the entire supply curve

change in the quantity supplied a movement along the supply curve that occurs in response to a change in price

SHIFTS IN DEMAND

To get a better feel for how the supply and demand model enables us to predict and explain price and quantity movements, it's helpful to begin with a few simple examples. The first one illustrates a shift in demand that results from events outside the particular market itself.

EXAMPLE 3.2 | **Complements**

What will happen to the equilibrium price and quantity of tennis balls if court-rental fees decline?

Let the initial supply and demand curves for tennis balls be as shown by the curves *S* and *D* in Figure 3.11, where the resulting equilibrium price and quantity are $1 per ball and 40 million balls per month, respectively. Tennis courts and tennis balls are what economists call **complements**, goods that are more valuable when used in combination than when used alone. Tennis balls, for example, would be of little value if there were no tennis courts on which to play. (Tennis balls would still have *some* value even without courts—for example, to the parents who pitch them to their children for batting practice.) As tennis courts become cheaper to use, people will respond by playing more tennis, and this will increase their demand for tennis balls. A decline in court-rental fees will thus shift the demand curve for tennis balls rightward to *D'*. (A "rightward shift" of a demand curve also can be described as an "upward shift." These distinctions correspond, respectively, to the horizontal and vertical interpretations of the demand curve.)

Note in Figure 3.11 that, for the illustrative demand shift shown, the new equilibrium price of tennis balls, $1.40, is higher than the original price and the new equilibrium quantity, 58 million balls per month, is higher than the original quantity.

complements two goods are complements in consumption if an increase in the price of one causes a leftward shift in the demand curve for the other (or if a decrease causes a rightward shift)

FIGURE 3.11

The Effect on the Market for Tennis Balls of a Decline in Court-Rental Fees.

When the price of a complement falls, demand shifts right, causing equilibrium price and quantity to rise.

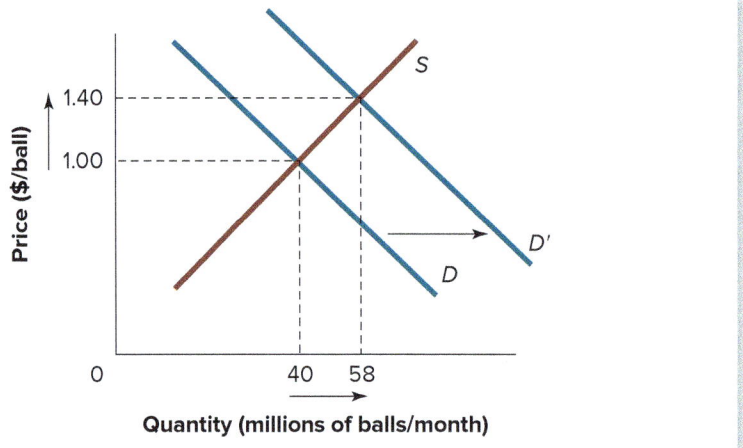

EXAMPLE 3.3   Substitutes

What will happen to the equilibrium price and quantity of print ads as the price of digital ads falls?

Most businesses purchase a mix of digital and print ads to promote their products. Suppose the initial supply and demand curves for print ads are as shown by the curves *S* and *D* in Figure 3.12, and the resulting equilibrium price and quantity are denoted *P* and *Q*. Print ads and digital ads are examples of what economists call **substitutes**, meaning that, in many applications at least, the two serve similar functions. (Many noneconomists would call them substitutes, too. Economists don't *always* choose obscure terms for important concepts!) When two goods or services are substitutes, a decrease in the price of one will cause a leftward shift in the demand curve for the other. (A "leftward shift" in a demand curve can also be described as a "downward shift.") Diagrammatically, the demand curve for print ads shifts from *D* to *D'* in Figure 3.12.

substitutes two goods are substitutes in consumption if an increase in the price of one causes a rightward shift in the demand curve for the other (or if a decrease causes a leftward shift)

FIGURE 3.12

The Effect on the Market for Print Ads of a Decline in the Price of Digital Ads.

When the price of a substitute falls, demand shifts left, causing equilibrium price and quantity to fall.

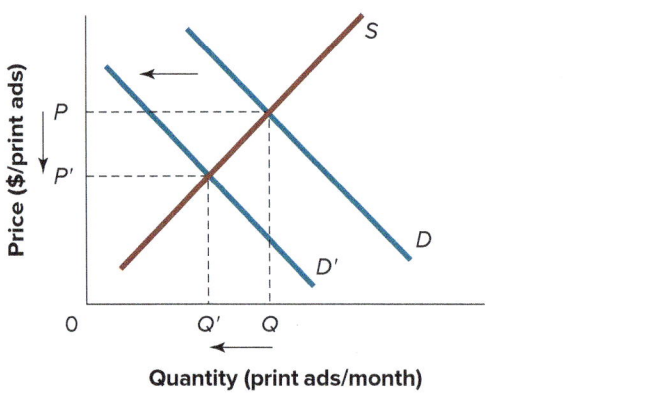

As the figure shows, both the new equilibrium price, *P'*, and the new equilibrium quantity, *Q'*, are lower than the initial values, *P* and *Q*. Cheaper digital ads probably won't put print advertising companies out of business, but it will definitely lead to a drop in sales.

To summarize, economists define goods as substitutes if an increase in the price of one causes a rightward shift in the demand curve for the other. By contrast, goods are complements if an increase in the price of one causes a leftward shift in the demand curve for the other.

The concepts of substitutes and complements enable you to answer questions like the one posed in Self-Test 3.4.

▶ Visit your instructor's Connect course and access your eBook to view this video.

 SELF-TEST 3.4

How will a decline in airfares affect intercity bus fares and the price of hotel rooms in resort communities?

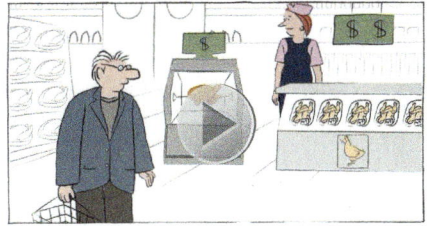

Why are rotisserie chickens less expensive than fresh chickens?

Demand curves are shifted not just by changes in the prices of substitutes and complements but also by other factors that change the amounts people are willing to pay for a given good or service. One of the most important such factors is income.

The Economic Naturalist 3.1

When the federal government implements a large pay increase for its employees, why do rents for apartments located near Washington Metro stations go up relative to rents for apartments located far away from Metro stations?

For the citizens of Washington, D.C., a substantial proportion of whom are government employees, it's more convenient to live in an apartment located 1 block from the nearest subway station than to live in one that is 20 blocks away. Conveniently located apartments thus command relatively high rents. Suppose the initial demand and supply curves for such apartments are as shown in Figure 3.13. Following a federal pay raise, some government employees who live in less convenient apartments will be willing and able to use part of their extra income to bid for more conveniently located apartments, and those who already live in such apartments will be willing and able to pay more to keep them. The effect of the pay raise is thus to shift the demand curve for conveniently located apartments to the right, as indicated by the demand curve labeled D'. As a result, both the equilibrium price and quantity of such apartments, P' and Q', will be higher than before.

Who gets to live in the most conveniently located apartments?

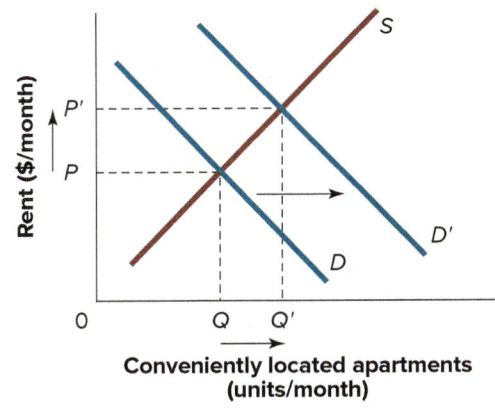

FIGURE 3.13

The Effect of a Federal Pay Raise on the Rent for Conveniently Located Apartments in Washington, D.C.

An increase in income shifts demand for a normal good to the right, causing equilibrium price and quantity to rise.

It might seem natural to ask how there could be an increase in the number of conveniently located apartments, which might appear to be fixed by the constraints of geography. But the Incentive Principle reminds us never to underestimate the ingenuity of sellers when they confront an opportunity to make money by supplying more of something that people want. For example, if rents rose sufficiently, some landlords might respond by converting warehouse space to residential use. Or perhaps people with cars who do not place high value on living near a subway station might sell their co-op apartments to landlords, thereby freeing them for people eager to rent them. (Note that these responses constitute movements along the supply curve of conveniently located apartments, as opposed to shifts in that supply curve.)

When incomes increase, the demand curves for most goods will behave like the demand curve for conveniently located apartments, and in recognition of that fact, economists have chosen to call such goods **normal goods**.

normal good a good whose demand curve shifts rightward when the incomes of buyers increase and leftward when the incomes of buyers decrease

Not all goods are normal goods, however. In fact, the demand curves for some goods actually shift leftward when income goes up. Such goods are called **inferior goods**.

inferior good a good whose demand curve shifts leftward when the incomes of buyers increase and rightward when the incomes of buyers decrease

When would having more money tend to make you want to buy less of something? In general, this happens with goods for which there exist attractive substitutes that sell for only slightly higher prices. Apartments in unsafe, inconveniently located neighborhoods are an example. Most residents would choose to move out of such neighborhoods as soon as they could afford to, which means that an increase in income would cause the demand for such apartments to shift leftward.

 SELF-TEST 3.5

How will a large pay increase for federal employees affect the rents for apartments located far away from Washington Metro stations?

Ground beef with high fat content is another example of an inferior good. For health reasons, most people prefer grades of meat with low fat content, and when they do buy high-fat meats it's usually a sign of budgetary pressure. When people in this situation receive higher incomes, they usually switch quickly to leaner grades of meat.

Preferences, or tastes, are another important factor that determines whether the purchase of a given good will satisfy the Cost-Benefit Principle. The release of each Marvel Studio film appears to kindle a powerful preference among children for Marvel action figures. When these films are released, the demand for Marvel action figures shifts sharply to the right. And the same children who can't get enough Marvel action figures suddenly lose interest in their other toys, whose respective demand curves shift to the left.

Expectations about the future are another factor that may cause demand curves to shift. If Apple users hear a credible rumor, for example, that a cheaper or significantly upgraded model will be introduced next month, the demand curve for the current model is likely to shift leftward.

SHIFTS IN THE SUPPLY CURVE

The preceding examples involved changes that gave rise to shifts in demand curves. Next, we'll look at what happens when supply curves shift. Because the supply curve is based on costs of production, anything that changes production costs will shift the supply curve, resulting in a new equilibrium quantity and price.

EXAMPLE 3.4   Increasing Opportunity Cost

What will happen to the equilibrium price and quantity of skateboards if the price of fiberglass, a substance used for making skateboards, rises?

Suppose the initial supply and demand curves for skateboards are as shown by the curves S and D in Figure 3.14, resulting in an equilibrium price and quantity

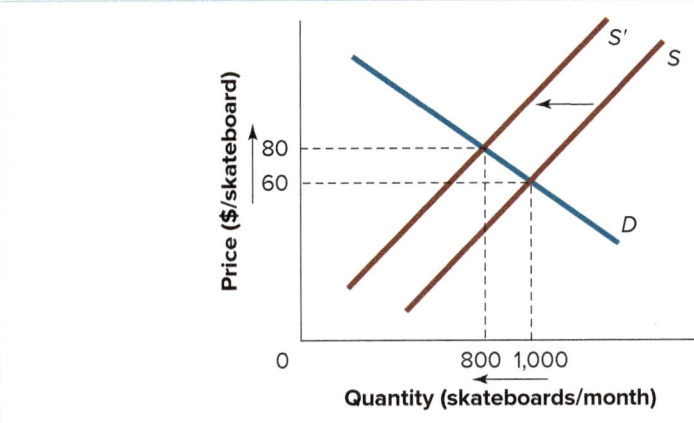

FIGURE 3.14

The Effect on the Skateboard Market of an Increase in the Price of Fiberglass.

When input prices rise, supply shifts left, causing equilibrium price to rise and equilibrium quantity to fall.

of $60 per skateboard and 1,000 skateboards per month, respectively. Since fiberglass is one of the materials used to produce skateboards, the effect of an increase in its price is to raise the marginal cost of producing skateboards. How will this affect the supply curve of skateboards?

Recall that the supply curve is upward-sloping because when the price of skateboards is low, only those potential sellers whose marginal cost of making skateboards is low can sell boards profitably, whereas at higher prices, those with higher marginal costs also can enter the market profitably (again, the Low-Hanging-Fruit Principle). So if the cost of one of the materials used to produce skateboards rises, the number of potential sellers who can profitably sell skateboards at any given price will fall. And this, in turn, implies a leftward shift in the supply curve for skateboards. Note that a "leftward shift" in a supply curve also can be viewed as an "upward shift" in the same curve. The first corresponds to the horizontal interpretation of the supply curve, while the second corresponds to the vertical interpretation. We will use these expressions to mean exactly the same thing. The new supply curve (after the price of fiberglass rises) is the curve labeled S' in Figure 3.14.

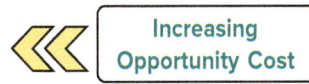

Increasing Opportunity Cost

Does an increase in the cost of fiberglass have any effect on the demand curve for skateboards? The demand curve tells us how many skateboards buyers wish to purchase at each price. Any given buyer is willing to purchase a skateboard if her reservation price for it exceeds its market price. And since each buyer's reservation price, which is based on the benefits of owning a skateboard, does not depend on the price of fiberglass, there should be no shift in the demand curve for skateboards.

In Figure 3.14, we can now see what happens when the supply curve shifts leftward and the demand curve remains unchanged. For the illustrative supply curve shown, the new equilibrium price of skateboards, $80, is higher than the original price, and the new equilibrium quantity, 800 per month, is lower than the original quantity. (These new equilibrium values are merely illustrative. There is insufficient information provided in the example to determine their exact values.) People who don't place a value of at least $80 on owning a skateboard will choose to spend their money on something else.

The effects on equilibrium price and quantity run in the opposite direction whenever marginal costs of production decline, as illustrated in the next example.

EXAMPLE 3.5 | Reduction of Marginal Cost

What will happen to the equilibrium price and quantity of new houses if the wage rate of carpenters falls?

Suppose the initial supply and demand curves for new houses are as shown by the curves S and D in Figure 3.15, resulting in an equilibrium price of $120,000

FIGURE 3.15

The Effect on the Market for New Houses of a Decline in Carpenters' Wage Rates.

When input prices fall, supply shifts right, causing equilibrium price to fall and equilibrium quantity to rise.

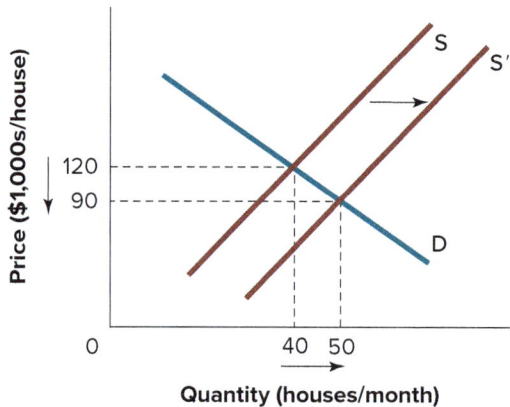

per house and an equilibrium quantity of 40 houses per month, respectively. A decline in the wage rate of carpenters reduces the marginal cost of making new houses, and this means that, for any given price of houses, more builders can profitably serve the market than before. Diagrammatically, this means a rightward shift in the supply curve of houses, from S to S'. (A "rightward shift" in the supply curve also can be described as a "downward shift.")

Does a decrease in the wage rate of carpenters have any effect on the demand curve for houses? The demand curve tells us how many houses buyers wish to purchase at each price. Because carpenters are now earning less than before, the maximum amount that they are willing to pay for houses may fall, which would imply a leftward shift in the demand curve for houses. But because carpenters make up only a tiny fraction of all potential home buyers, we may assume that this shift is negligible. Thus, a reduction in carpenters' wages produces a significant rightward shift in the supply curve of houses, but no appreciable shift in the demand curve.

We see from Figure 3.15 that the new equilibrium price, $90,000 per house, is lower than the original price and the new equilibrium quantity, 50 houses per month, is higher than the original quantity.

Examples 3.4 and 3.5 involved changes in the cost of a material, or input, in the production of the good in question—fiberglass in the production of skateboards and carpenters' labor in the production of houses. As the following example illustrates, supply curves also shift when technology changes.

The Economic Naturalist 3.2

Why do major term papers go through so many more revisions today than in the 1970s?

Students in the dark days before word processors were in widespread use could not make even minor revisions in their term papers without having to retype their entire manuscript from scratch. The availability of word-processing technology has, of course, radically changed the picture. Instead of having to retype the entire draft, now only the changes need be entered.

In Figure 3.16, the curves labeled *S* and *D* depict the supply and demand curves for revisions in the days before word processing, and the curve *S′* depicts the supply curve for revisions today. As the diagram shows, the result is not only a sharp decline in the price per revision, but also a corresponding increase in the equilibrium number of revisions.

Why does written work go through so many more revisions now than in the 1970s?

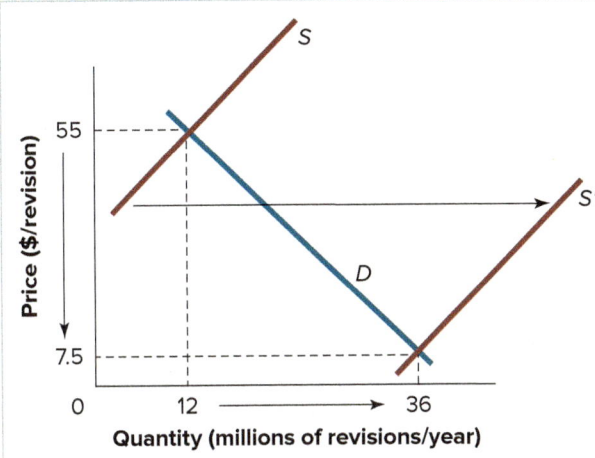

FIGURE 3.16

The Effect of Technical Change on the Market for Term-Paper Revisions.

When a new technology reduces the cost of production, supply shifts right, causing equilibrium price to fall and equilibrium quantity to rise.

Note that in The Economic Naturalist 3.2 we implicitly assumed that students purchased typing services in a market. In fact, however, many students type their own term papers. Does that make a difference? Even if no money actually changes hands, students pay a price when they revise their term papers—namely, the opportunity cost of the time it takes to perform that task. Because technology has radically reduced that cost, we would expect to see a large increase in the number of term-paper revisions even if most students type their own work.

Changes in input prices and technology are two of the most important factors that give rise to shifts in supply curves. In the case of agricultural commodities, weather may be another important factor, with favorable conditions shifting the supply curves of such products to the right and unfavorable conditions shifting them to the left. (Weather also may affect the supply curves of nonagricultural products through its effects on the national transportation system.) Expectations of future price changes also may shift current supply curves, as when the expectation of poor crops from a current drought causes suppliers to withhold supplies from existing stocks in the hope of selling at higher prices in the future. Changes in the number of sellers in the market also can cause supply curves to shift.

FOUR SIMPLE RULES

For supply and demand curves that have the conventional slopes (upward-sloping for supply curves, downward-sloping for demand curves), the preceding examples illustrate the four basic rules that govern how shifts in supply and demand affect equilibrium prices and quantities. These rules are summarized in Figure 3.17.

FIGURE 3.17

Four Rules Governing the Effects of Supply and Demand Shifts.

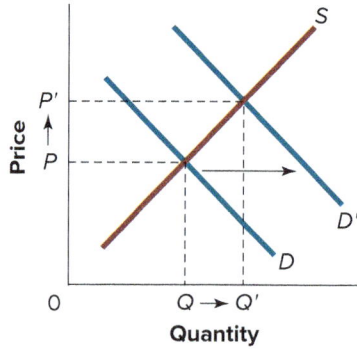

An increase in demand will lead to an increase in both the equilibrium price and quantity.

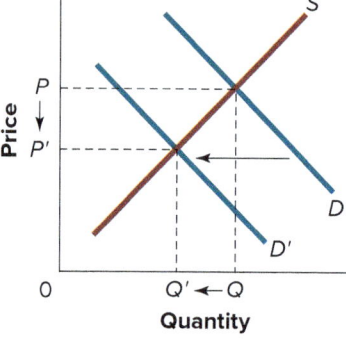

A decrease in demand will lead to a decrease in both the equilibrium price and quantity.

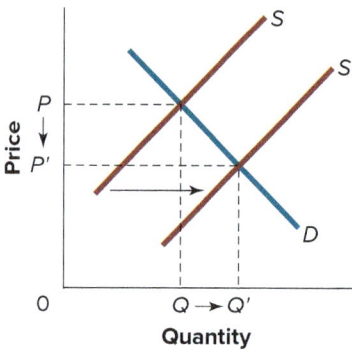

An increase in supply will lead to a decrease in the equilibrium price and an increase in the equilibrium quantity.

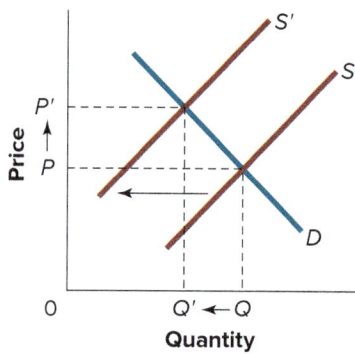

A decrease in supply will lead to an increase in the equilibrium price and a decrease in the equilibrium quantity.

RECAP

FACTORS THAT SHIFT SUPPLY AND DEMAND

Factors that cause an increase (rightward or upward shift) in demand:

1. A decrease in the price of complements to the good or service.
2. An increase in the price of substitutes for the good or service.
3. An increase in income (for a normal good).
4. An increased preference by demanders for the good or service.
5. An increase in the population of potential buyers.
6. An expectation of higher prices in the future.

When these factors move in the opposite direction, demand will shift left.

Factors that cause an increase (rightward or downward shift) in supply:

1. A decrease in the cost of materials, labor, or other inputs used in the production of the good or service.
2. An improvement in technology that reduces the cost of producing the good or service.
3. An improvement in the weather (especially for agricultural products).
4. An increase in the number of suppliers.
5. An expectation of lower prices in the future.

When these factors move in the opposite direction, supply will shift left.

The qualitative rules summarized in Figure 3.17 hold for supply or demand shifts of any magnitude, provided the curves have their conventional slopes. But as the next example demonstrates, when both supply and demand curves shift at the same time, the direction in which equilibrium price or quantity changes will depend on the relative magnitudes of the shifts.

EXAMPLE 3.6   Shifts in Supply and Demand

How do shifts in *both* demand and supply affect equilibrium quantities and prices?

What will happen to the equilibrium price and quantity in the corn tortilla chip market if both of the following events occur: (1) researchers prove that the oils in which tortilla chips are fried are harmful to human health and (2) the price of corn harvesting equipment falls?

The conclusion regarding the health effects of the oils will shift the demand for tortilla chips to the left because many people who once bought chips in the belief that they were healthful will now switch to other foods. The decline in the price of harvesting equipment will shift the supply of chips to the right because additional farmers will now find it profitable to enter the corn market. In Figure 3.18(a) and 3.18(b), the original supply and demand curves are denoted by S and D, while the new curves are denoted by S' and D'. Note that in both panels the shifts lead to a decline in the equilibrium price of chips.

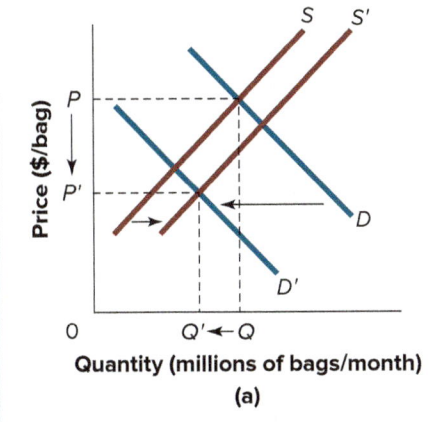

Quantity (millions of bags/month)

(a)

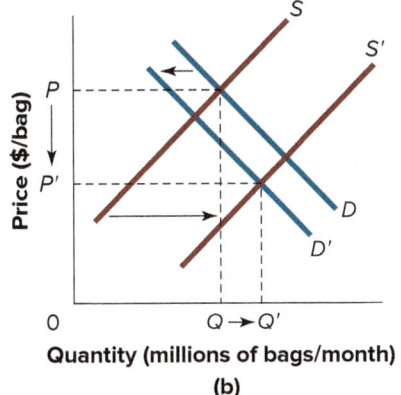

Quantity (millions of bags/month)

(b)

FIGURE 3.18

The Effects of Simultaneous Shifts in Supply and Demand.

When demand shifts left and supply shifts right, equilibrium price falls, but equilibrium quantity may either rise (b) or fall (a).

But note also that the effect of the shifts on equilibrium quantity cannot be determined without knowing their relative magnitudes. Taken separately, the demand shift causes a decline in equilibrium quantity, whereas the supply shift causes an increase in equilibrium quantity. The net effect of the two shifts thus depends on which of the individual effects is larger. In Figure 3.18(a), the demand shift dominates, so equilibrium quantity declines. In Figure 3.18(b), the supply shift dominates, so equilibrium quantity goes up.

The following Self-Test 3.6 asks you to consider a simple variation on the problem posed in the previous example.

SELF-TEST 3.6

What will happen to the equilibrium price and quantity in the corn tortilla chip market if both of the following events occur: (1) researchers discover that a vitamin found in corn helps protect against cancer and heart disease and (2) a swarm of locusts destroys part of the corn crop?

The Economic Naturalist 3.3

Why was there a shortage of toilet paper during the COVID-19 pandemic?

During the COVID-19 pandemic, many consumers in search of toilet paper arrived at their local grocery stores only to be faced with empty shelves. If prices are supposed to adjust to equate the quantity supplied and the quantity demanded, then why was there a shortage of toilet paper during the COVID-19 pandemic?

Faced with the public health crisis brought about by COVID-19, many, if not most, consumers in the United States stocked up on essential items such as toilet paper. Indeed, some consumers purchased excessive quantities of these items, and this type of hoarding behavior received much of the blame for the shortage of toilet paper during the pandemic.

But there is another important factor as well. The toilet paper market in the United States is divided into two distinct segments. There is a market for the lower-quality commercial-grade toilet paper, typically used in restaurants, schools, workplaces, and other public venues, and a separate market for the higher-quality consumer-grade toilet paper, generally used in people's homes. Even though the overall use of toilet paper did not substantially change during the pandemic, there was a large shift away from commercial-grade toilet paper toward consumer-grade toilet paper. That is, the widespread stay-at-home orders led to a sharp decrease in the demand for commercial-grade toilet paper, and an equally abrupt increase in the demand for consumer-grade toilet paper, and toilet paper producers, who are accustomed to relatively stable demand, had difficulty adjusting to this rapid change.

Of course, in normal times, an increase in demand would not lead to a shortage. Instead we would expect prices to rise. During times of emergency, however, both social norms and price gouging laws limit retailers' ability to raise prices. Thus while the demand for consumer-grade toilet paper surged during the pandemic (both because of hoarding and the shift away from commercial-grade toilet paper), prices did not adjust, leading to empty shelves and anxious consumers.

The Economic Naturalist 3.4

Why do the prices of some goods, like airline tickets to Europe, go up during the months of heaviest consumption, while others, like sweet corn, go down?

Seasonal price movements for airline tickets are primarily the result of seasonal variations in demand. Thus, ticket prices to Europe are highest during the summer months because the demand for tickets is highest during those months, as shown in Figure 3.19(a), where the w and s subscripts denote winter and summer values, respectively.

FIGURE 3.19

Seasonal Variation in the Air Travel and Corn Markets.

(a) Prices are highest during the period of heaviest consumption when heavy consumption is the result of high demand. (b) Prices are lowest during the period of heaviest consumption when heavy consumption is the result of high supply.

Why are some goods cheapest during the months of heaviest consumption, while others are most expensive during those months?

By contrast, seasonal price movements for sweet corn are primarily the result of seasonal variations in supply. The price of sweet corn is lowest in the summer months because its supply is highest during those months, as seen in Figure 3.19(b).

EFFICIENCY AND EQUILIBRIUM

Markets represent a highly effective system of allocating resources. When a market for a good is in equilibrium, the equilibrium price conveys important information to potential suppliers about the value that potential demanders place on that good. At the same time, the equilibrium price informs potential demanders about the opportunity cost of supplying the good. This rapid, two-way transmission of information is the reason that markets can coordinate an activity as complex as supplying New York City with food and drink, even though no one person or organization oversees the process.

But are the prices and quantities determined in market equilibrium socially optimal, in the sense of maximizing total economic surplus? That is, does equilibrium in unregulated markets always maximize the difference between the total benefits and total costs experienced by market participants? As we'll see, the answer is "it depends": a market that is out of equilibrium, such as the rent-controlled New York housing market, always creates opportunities for individuals to arrange transactions that will increase their individual economic surplus. As we'll also see, however, a market for a good that is in equilibrium makes the largest possible contribution to total economic surplus only when its supply and demand curves fully reflect all costs and benefits associated with the production and consumption of that good.

CASH ON THE TABLE

In economics we assume that all exchange is purely voluntary. This means that a transaction cannot take place unless the buyer's reservation price for the good exceeds the seller's reservation price. When that condition is met and a transaction takes place, both parties receive an economic surplus. The **buyer's surplus** from the transaction is the difference between his or her reservation price and the price he or she actually pays. The **seller's surplus** is the difference between the price he or she receives and his or her reservation price. The **total surplus** from the transaction is the sum of the buyer's surplus and the seller's surplus. It is also equal to the difference between the buyer's reservation price and the seller's reservation price.

buyer's surplus the difference between the buyer's reservation price and the price he or she actually pays

seller's surplus the difference between the price received by the seller and his or her reservation price

total surplus the difference between the buyer's reservation price and the seller's reservation price

FIGURE 3.20

Price Controls in the Pizza Market.

A price ceiling below the equilibrium price of pizza would result in excess demand for pizza.

Suppose there is a potential buyer whose reservation price for an additional slice of pizza is $4 and a potential seller whose reservation price is only $2. If this buyer purchases a slice of pizza from this seller for $3, the total surplus generated by this exchange is $4 − $2 = $2, of which $4 − $3 = $1 is the buyer's surplus and $3 − $2 = $1 is the seller's surplus.

A regulation that prevents the price of a good from reaching its equilibrium level unnecessarily prevents exchanges of this sort from taking place, and in the process reduces total economic surplus. Consider again the effect of price controls imposed in the market for pizza. The demand curve in Figure 3.20 tells us that if a price ceiling of $2 per slice were imposed, only 8,000 slices of pizza per day would be sold. At that quantity, the vertical interpretations of the supply and demand curves tell us that a buyer would be willing to pay as much as $4 for an additional slice and that a seller would be willing to sell one for as little as $2. The difference–$2 per slice–is the additional economic surplus that would result if an additional slice were produced and sold. As noted earlier, an extra slice sold at a price of $3 would result in an additional $1 of economic surplus for both buyer and seller.

cash on the table an economic metaphor for unexploited gains from exchange

When a market is out of equilibrium, it's always possible to identify mutually beneficial exchanges of this sort. When people have failed to take advantage of all mutually beneficial exchanges, we often say that there's "**cash on the table**"–the economist's metaphor for unexploited opportunities. When the price in a market is below the equilibrium price, there's cash on the table because the reservation price of sellers (marginal cost) will always be lower than the reservation price of buyers. In the absence of a law preventing buyers from paying more than $2 per slice, restaurant owners would quickly raise their prices and expand their production until the equilibrium price of $3 per slice were reached. At that price, buyers would be able to get precisely the 12,000 slices of pizza they want to buy each day. All mutually beneficial opportunities for exchange would have been exploited, leaving no more cash on the table.

With the Incentive Principle in mind, it should be no surprise that buyers and sellers in the marketplace have an uncanny ability to detect the presence of cash on the table. It is almost as if unexploited opportunities give off some exotic scent triggering neurochemical explosions in the olfactory centers of their brains. The desire to scrape cash off the table and into their pockets is what drives sellers in each of New York City's thousands of individual food markets to work diligently to meet their customers' demands. That they succeed to a far higher degree than participants in the city's rent-controlled housing market is plainly evident. Whatever flaws it might have, the market system moves with considerably greater speed and agility than any centralized allocation mechanisms yet devised. But as discussed in Chapter 1, markets often fail to deliver the greatest good for the greatest number when transactions entail side effects, or externalities. The following section provides additional examples.

SMART FOR ONE, DUMB FOR ALL

The **socially optimal quantity** of any good is the quantity that maximizes the total economic surplus that results from producing and consuming the good. From the Cost-Benefit Principle, we know that we should keep expanding production of the good as long as its marginal benefit is at least as great as its marginal cost. This means that the socially optimal quantity is that level for which the marginal cost and marginal benefit of the good are the same.

When the quantity of a good is less than the socially optimal quantity, boosting its production will increase total economic surplus. By the same token, when the quantity of a good exceeds the socially optimal quantity, reducing its production will increase total economic surplus. **Efficiency**, or **economic efficiency**, occurs when all goods and services in the economy are produced and consumed at their respective socially optimal levels.

Efficiency is an important social goal. Failure to achieve efficiency means that total economic surplus is smaller than it could have been. Movements toward efficiency make the total economic pie larger, making it possible for everyone to have a larger slice. The importance of efficiency will be a recurring theme as we move forward, and we state it here as one of the core principles:

The Efficiency Principle: Efficiency is an important social goal because when the economic pie grows larger, everyone can have a larger slice.

Is the market equilibrium quantity of a good efficient? That is, does it maximize the total economic surplus received by participants in the market for that good? When the private market for a given good is in equilibrium, we can say that the cost *to the seller* of producing an additional unit of the good is the same as the benefit *to the buyer* of having an additional unit. If all costs of producing the good are borne directly by sellers, and if all benefits from the good accrue directly to buyers, it follows that the market equilibrium quantity of the good will equate the marginal cost and marginal benefit of the good. And this means that the equilibrium quantity also maximizes total economic surplus.

But sometimes the production of a good entails costs that fall on people other than those who sell the good. This will be true, for instance, for goods whose production emits significant levels of greenhouse gases. As extra units of these goods are produced, the emissions contribute to climate change, which damages not only buyers and sellers of these goods, but also all other current and future inhabitants of our planet. In the market equilibrium for such goods, the *private* benefit *to buyers* of the last good produced is, as in other markets, equal to the private cost incurred by sellers to produce that good.

But since producing that good also imposes pollution costs on others, we know that the *full* marginal cost of the last unit produced—the seller's private marginal cost plus the marginal pollution cost borne by others—must be higher than the benefit of the last unit produced. So, in this case, the market equilibrium quantity of the good will be larger than the socially optimal quantity. Total economic surplus would be higher if output of the good were lower. Yet neither sellers nor buyers have any incentive to alter their behavior.

Another source of market failure is that people other than those who buy a good may receive significant benefits from it. For instance, when someone receives a COVID-19 vaccine, she not only protects herself against serious illness and death, but also makes it less likely that others will catch the disease. The marginal benefit of getting vaccinated or of wearing a mask in indoor settings is not only the value of the protection these steps provide to the person taking them, but also the protection they provide for others. Many people, however, tend to ignore effects on others when deciding what to do. In such cases, the market equilibrium quantities of vaccines taken and masks worn will be smaller than the quantities that maximize total economic surplus. Adam Smith's invisible hand again breaks down: Purely self-interested individuals would have no incentive to alter their behavior.

socially optimal quantity the quantity of a good that results in the maximum possible economic surplus from producing and consuming the good

Cost-Benefit

efficiency (or **economic efficiency**) a condition that occurs when all goods and services are produced and consumed at their respective socially optimal levels

Efficiency

Producers and consumers often give too little weight to externalities that accompany their transactions.

Situations like the ones just discussed provide examples of behaviors that we may call "smart for one but dumb for all." In each case, the individual actors are behaving rationally. They are pursuing their goals as best they can, and yet there remain unexploited opportunities for gain from the point of view of the whole society. The difficulty is that these opportunities cannot be exploited by individuals acting alone. In subsequent chapters, we will see how people can often organize collectively to exploit such opportunities. For now, we simply summarize this discussion in the form of the following core principle:

The Equilibrium Principle (also called the No-Cash-on-the-Table Principle): A market in equilibrium leaves no unexploited opportunities for individuals but may not exploit all gains achievable through collective action.

The Economic Naturalist 3.5

Why do physicians tend to overprescribe antibiotics?

When patients complain of minor ear and respiratory infections, many doctors prescribe antibiotics. If the infection was caused by bacteria (as opposed to viruses), antibiotic treatment is likely to speed recovery. But each time a patient takes antibiotics, there is a small risk that a drug-resistant strain of bacteria will emerge. Public health officials therefore urge physicians to prescribe antibiotics only in response to serious infections. Why, then, do so many physicians continue to prescribe them for minor ones?

Overprescription of antibiotics is much like the overharvesting of fish in the oceans, another instance in which the invisible hand tends to break down. Just as the amount of fish caught by an individual fisherman cannot by itself cause a fish population to crash, no single prescription of antibiotics can produce lethal drug-resistant bacteria. Yet the side-effects of individual prescriptions cumulate over time. Each time an antibiotic is prescribed, at least some of the bacteria that caused the patient's infection tend to survive. Individual bacterial cells in the colony are all different, and the ones most likely to survive a course of antibiotic treatment are those least vulnerable to the drug. These survivors may still be susceptible to higher doses, but as additional mutations accumulate over time, drug resistance in the surviving bacteria becomes more powerful.

The dilemma confronting doctors is that patients demand antibiotics in the belief that taking them will hasten their recovery. Some physicians refuse to treat minor infections in this way but others give in, knowing that their patients may seek other doctors if they do not. The Centers for Disease Control estimates that roughly one-third of the 150 million antibiotic prescriptions written each year are unnecessary.

RECAP

EFFICIENCY AND EQUILIBRIUM

When the supply and demand curves for a good reflect all significant costs and benefits associated with the production and consumption of that good, the market equilibrium will result in the largest possible economic surplus. But if people other than buyers benefit from the good, or if people other than sellers bear costs because of it, market equilibrium need not result in the largest possible economic surplus.

SUMMARY

- The demand curve is a downward-sloping line that tells what quantity buyers will demand at any given price. The supply curve is an upward-sloping line that tells what quantity sellers will offer at any given price. *(LO1)*

- Alfred Marshall's model of supply and demand explains why neither cost of production nor value to the purchaser (as measured by willingness to pay) is, by itself, sufficient to explain why some goods are cheap and others are expensive. To explain variations in price, we must examine the interaction of cost and willingness to pay. As we've seen in this chapter, goods differ in price because of differences in their respective supply and demand curves. *(LO2)*

- Market equilibrium occurs when the quantity buyers demand at the market price is exactly the same as the quantity that sellers offer. The equilibrium price–quantity pair is the one at which the demand and supply curves intersect. In equilibrium, market price measures both the value of the last unit sold to buyers and the cost of the resources required to produce it. *(LO2)*

- When the price of a good lies above its equilibrium value, there is an excess supply of that good. Excess supply motivates sellers to cut their prices and price continues to fall until equilibrium price is reached. When price lies below its equilibrium value, there is excess demand. With excess demand, frustrated buyers are motivated to offer higher prices and the upward pressure on prices persists until equilibrium is reached. A remarkable feature of the market system is that, relying only on the tendency of people to respond in self-interested ways to market price signals, it somehow manages to coordinate the actions of literally billions of buyers and sellers worldwide. When excess demand or excess supply occurs, it tends to be small and brief, except in markets where regulations prevent full adjustment of prices. *(LO2)*

- The basic supply and demand model is a primary tool of the economic naturalist. Changes in the equilibrium price of a good, and in the amount of it traded in the marketplace, can be predicted on the basis of shifts in its supply or demand curves. The following four rules hold for any good with a downward-sloping demand curve and an upward-sloping supply curve:
  1. An increase in demand will lead to an increase in equilibrium price and quantity.
  2. A reduction in demand will lead to a reduction in equilibrium price and quantity.

  3. An increase in supply will lead to a reduction in equilibrium price and an increase in equilibrium quantity.
  4. A decrease in supply will lead to an increase in equilibrium price and a reduction in equilibrium quantity. *(LO3)*

- Incomes, tastes, population, expectations, and the prices of substitutes and complements are among the factors that shift demand schedules. Supply schedules, in turn, are primarily governed by such factors as technology, input prices, expectations, the number of sellers, and, especially for agricultural products, the weather. *(LO3)*

- The efficiency of markets in allocating resources does not eliminate social concerns about how goods and services are distributed among different people. For example, we often lament the fact many buyers enter the market with too little income to buy even the most basic goods and services. Concern for the well-being of the poor has motivated many governments to intervene in a variety of ways to alter the outcomes of market forces. Sometimes these interventions take the form of laws that peg prices below their equilibrium levels. Such laws almost invariably generate harmful, if unintended, consequences. Programs like rent-control laws, for example, lead to severe housing shortages, black marketeering, and a rapid deterioration of the relationship between landlords and tenants. *(LO4)*

- If the difficulty is that the poor have too little money, the best solution is to discover ways of boosting their incomes directly. The law of supply and demand cannot be repealed by the legislature. But legislatures do have the capacity to alter the underlying forces that govern the shape and position of supply and demand schedules. *(LO4)*

- When the supply and demand curves for a good reflect all significant costs and benefits associated with the production and consumption of that good, the market equilibrium price will guide people to produce and consume the quantity of the good that results in the largest possible economic surplus. This conclusion, however, does not apply if others, besides buyers, benefit from the good (as when someone benefits from his neighbor's purchase of a vaccination against measles) or if others besides sellers bear costs because of the good (as when its production generates pollution). In such cases, market equilibrium does not result in the greatest gain for all. *(LO4)*

CORE PRINCIPLES

The Efficiency Principle

Efficiency is an important social goal because when the economic pie grows larger, everyone can have a larger slice.

The Equilibrium Principle (also called the No-Cash-on-the-Table Principle)

A market in equilibrium leaves no unexploited opportunities for individuals but may not exploit all gains achievable through collective action.

KEY TERMS

buyer's reservation price
buyer's surplus
cash on the table
change in demand
change in supply
change in the quantity
  demanded
change in the quantity
  supplied
complements

demand curve
efficiency (or economic efficiency)
equilibrium
equilibrium price and equilibrium
  quantity
excess demand (or shortage)
excess supply (or surplus)
income effect
inferior good
market

market equilibrium
normal good
price ceiling
seller's reservation price
seller's surplus
socially optimal quantity
substitutes
substitution effect
supply curve
total surplus

REVIEW QUESTIONS

1. Explain the distinction between the horizontal and vertical interpretations of the demand curve. *(LO1)*

2. Why isn't knowing the cost of producing a good sufficient to predict its market price? *(LO2)*

3. In recent years, a government official proposed that gasoline price controls be imposed to protect the poor from rising gasoline prices. What evidence could you consult to discover whether this proposal was enacted? *(LO2)*

4. Distinguish between the meaning of the expressions "change in demand" and "change in the quantity demanded." *(LO3)*

5. Give an example of behavior you have observed that could be described as "smart for one but dumb for all." *(LO4)*

PROBLEMS

1. How would each of the following affect the U.S. market supply curve for corn? *(LO1)*
   a. A new and improved crop rotation technique is discovered.
   b. The price of fertilizer falls.
   c. The government offers new tax breaks to farmers.
   d. A tornado sweeps through Iowa.

2. Indicate how you think each of the following would shift demand in the indicated market. *(LO1)*
   a. The incomes of buyers in the market for Adirondack vacations increase.

   b. Buyers in the market for pizza read a study linking pepperoni consumption to heart disease.
   c. Buyers in the market for gas-powered cars learn of an increase in the price of electric cars (a substitute for gas-powered cars).
   d. Buyers in the market for electric cars learn of an increase in the price of electric cars.

3. An Arizona student claims to have spotted a UFO over the desert outside of Tucson. How will this claim affect the *supply* (not the quantity supplied) of binoculars in Tucson stores? *(LO1)*

4. Suppose that when milk sells for $4.50 per gallon, the quantity of milk demanded is 3,250 gallons per day and

the quantity of milk supplied is 3,860 gallons per day. Will the equilibrium price of milk be greater than, less than, or equal to $4.50 per gallon? Explain. *(LO2)*

5. State whether the following pairs of goods are complements, substitutes, or both. *(LO3)*
   a. Washing machines and dryers.
   b. Tennis rackets and tennis balls.
   c. Birthday cake and birthday candles.
   d. Cloth diapers and disposable diapers.

6. How will an increase in the birth rate affect the equilibrium price of land? *(LO3)*

7. What will happen to the equilibrium price and quantity of beef if the price of chickenfeed increases (assume that chicken and beef are substitutes)? *(LO3)*

8. How will a new law mandating an increase in required levels of automobile insurance affect the equilibrium price and quantity in the market for new automobiles? *(LO3)*

9. Predict what will happen to the equilibrium price and quantity of oranges if the following events take place. *(LO3)*
   a. A study finds that a daily glass of orange juice reduces the risk of heart disease.
   b. The price of grapefruit falls drastically.
   c. The wage paid to orange pickers rises.
   d. Exceptionally good weather provides a much greater than expected harvest.

10. Suppose the current issue of *The New York Times* reports an outbreak of mad cow disease in Nebraska, as well as the discovery of a new breed of chicken that gains more weight than existing breeds that consume the same amount of food. How will these developments affect the equilibrium price and quantity of chickens sold in the United States? *(LO3)*

11. Twenty-five years ago, tofu was available only from small businesses operating in predominantly Asian sections of large cities. Today tofu has become popular as a high-protein health food and is widely available in supermarkets throughout the United States. At the same time, tofu production has evolved to become factory-based using modern food-processing technologies. Draw a diagram with demand and supply curves depicting the market for tofu 25 years ago and the market for tofu today. Given the information above, what does the demand–supply model predict about changes in the volume of tofu sold in the United States between then and now? What does it predict about changes in the price of tofu? *(LO3)*

12. For each of the following statements about a market equilibrium, identify whether the statement is always true, never true, or sometimes true. *(LO4)*
   a. A market equilibrium maximizes total economic surplus.
   b. A market equilibrium exploits all gains achievable through collective action.
   c. A market equilibrium leaves no unexploited opportunities for individuals.

13. In March 2020, global crude oil prices tumbled from over $50 a barrel to below $23 per barrel, bringing prices to their lowest level in nearly two decades. This precipitous drop in crude oil prices was fueled by two major shocks to the oil market. First, the COVID-19 pandemic led to a massive reduction in all forms of travel as large numbers of people around the world were advised to shelter in place. Second, Russia, Saudi Arabia, and a number of other major oil-producing nations typically reach collective agreements to limit the world supply of oil in order to keep prices high, but these negotiations broke down in March 2020, prompting a sharp increase in oil production. Using a supply and demand graph, show how each of these factors affected the market price and quantity of crude oil. *(LO3)*

ANSWERS TO SELF-TESTS

3.1 At a quantity of 10,000 slices per day, the marginal buyer's reservation price is $3.50 per slice. At a price of $2.50 per slice, the quantity demanded will be 14,000 slices per day. *(LO1)*

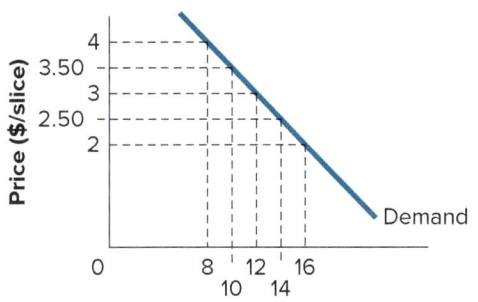

Quantity (1,000s of slices/day)

3.2 At a quantity of 10,000 slices per day, the marginal cost of pizza is $2.50 per slice. At a price of $3.50 per slice, the quantity supplied will be 14,000 slices per day. *(LO1)*

Quantity (1,000s of slices/day)

3.3 Because landlords are permitted to charge less than the maximum rent established by rent-control laws, a law that sets the maximum rent at $1,200 will have no effect on the rents actually charged in this market, which will settle at the equilibrium value of $800 per month. *(LO2)*

3.4 Travel by air and travel by intercity bus are substitutes, so a decline in airfares will shift the demand for bus travel to the left, resulting in lower bus fares and fewer bus trips taken. Travel by air and the use of resort hotels are complements, so a decline in airfares will shift the demand for resort hotel rooms to the right, resulting in higher hotel rates and an increase in the number of rooms rented. *(LO3)*

3.5 Apartments located far from Washington Metro stations are an inferior good. A pay increase for federal workers will thus shift the demand curve for such apartments downward, which will lead to a reduction in their equilibrium rent. *(LO3)*

3.6 The vitamin discovery shifts the demand for tortilla chips to the right and the crop losses shift the supply of tortilla chips to the left. Both shifts result in an increase in the equilibrium price of tortilla chips. But depending on the relative magnitude of the shifts, the equilibrium quantity of tortilla chips may either rise (top panel) or fall (bottom panel). *(LO3)*

**Quantity
(millions of bags/month)**

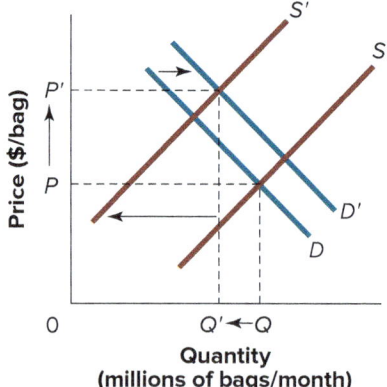

**Quantity
(millions of bags/month)**

The Algebra of Supply and Demand

n the text of this chapter, we developed supply and demand analysis in a geometric framework. The advantage of this framework is that many find it an easier one within which to visualize how shifts in either curve affect equilibrium price and quantity.

It is a straightforward extension to translate supply and demand analysis into algebraic terms. In this brief appendix, we show how this is done. The advantage of the algebraic framework is that it greatly simplifies computing the numerical values of equilibrium prices and quantities.

Consider, for example, the supply and demand curves in Figure 3A.1, where P denotes the price of the good and Q denotes its quantity. What are the equations of these curves?

The equation of a straight-line demand curve must take the general form $P = a + bQ^d$, where P is the price of the product (as measured on the vertical axis), Q^d is the quantity demanded at that price (as measured on the horizontal axis), a is the vertical intercept of the demand curve, and b is its slope. For the demand curve shown in Figure 3A.1, the vertical intercept is 16 and the slope is -2. So the equation for this demand curve is

$$P = 16 - 2Q^d. \tag{3A.1}$$

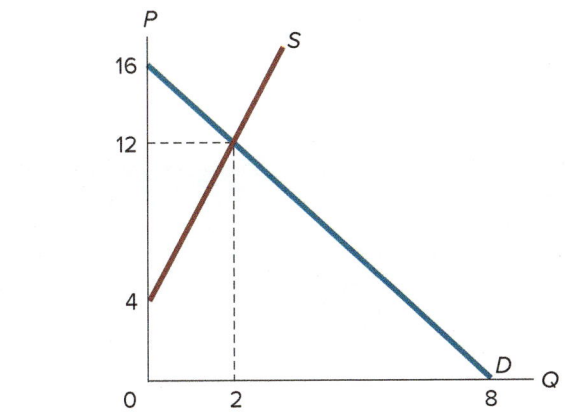

FIGURE 3A.1

Supply and Demand Curves.

Similarly, the equation of a straight-line supply curve must take the general form $P = c + dQ^s$, where P is again the price of the product, Q^s is the quantity supplied at that price, c is the vertical intercept of the supply curve, and d is its slope. For the supply curve shown in Figure 3A.1, the vertical intercept is 4 and the slope is also 4. So the equation for this supply curve is

$$P = 4 + 4Q^s. \tag{3A.2}$$

If we know the equations for the supply and demand curves in any market, it is a simple matter to solve them for the equilibrium price and quantity using the method of simultaneous equations. The following example illustrates how to apply this method.

EXAMPLE 3A.1   **Simultaneous Equations**

If the supply and demand curves for a market are given by $P = 4 + 4Q^s$ and $P = 16 - 2Q^d$, respectively, find the equilibrium price and quantity for this market.

In equilibrium, we know that $Q^s = Q^d$. Denoting this common value as Q^*, we may then equate the right-hand sides of Equations 3A.1 and 3A.2 and solve

$$4 + 4Q^* = 16 - 2Q^*, \tag{3A.3}$$

which yields $Q^* = 2$. Substituting $Q^* = 2$ back into either the supply or demand equation gives the equilibrium price $P^* = 12$.

Of course, having already begun with the graphs of Equations 3A.1 and 3A.2 in hand, we could have identified the equilibrium price and quantity by a simple glance at Figure 3A.1. (That is why it seems natural to say that the graphical approach helps us visualize the equilibrium outcome.) As the following Self-Test 3A.1 illustrates, the advantage of the algebraic approach to finding the equilibrium price and quantity is that it is much less painstaking than having to produce accurate drawings of the supply and demand schedules.

 SELF-TEST 3A.1

Find the equilibrium price and quantity in a market whose supply and demand curves are given by $P = 2Q^s$ and $P = 8 - 2Q^d$, respectively.

ANSWER TO APPENDIX SELF-TEST

3A.1 Let Q^* denote the equilibrium quantity. Since the equilibrium price and quantity lie on both the supply and demand curves, we equate the right-hand sides of the supply and demand equations to obtain

$$2Q^* = 8 - 2Q^*,$$

which solves for $Q^* = 2$. Substituting $Q^* = 2$ back into either the supply or demand equation gives the equilibrium price $P^* = 4$.

CHAPTER 4

Elasticity

If the demand for illegal drugs is inelastic, increased arrests of illegal-drug sellers will increase total expenditures on illegal drugs.

Bikeriderlondon/Shutterstock

Many illicit-drug users commit crimes to finance their addiction. The connection between drugs and crime has led to calls for more vigorous efforts to stop the smuggling of illicit drugs. But can such efforts reduce the likelihood that your iPhone or laptop computer will be stolen? If attempts to reduce the supply of illicit drugs are successful, our basic supply and demand analysis tells us that the supply curve for drugs will shift to the left and the market price of drugs will increase. Given that demand curves are downward-sloping, drug users will respond by consuming a smaller quantity of drugs. But the amount of crime drug users commit depends not on the *quantity* of drugs they consume, but rather on their *total expenditure* on drugs. Depending on the specific characteristics of the demand curve for illicit drugs, a price increase might reduce total expenditure on drugs, but it also could raise total expenditure.

Suppose, for example, that extra border patrols shift the supply curve in the market for illicit drugs to the left, as shown in Figure 4.1. As a result, the equilibrium quantity of drugs would fall from 50,000 to 40,000 ounces per day and the price of drugs would rise from $50 to $80 per ounce. The total amount spent on drugs, which was $2,500,000 per day (50,000 ounces/day × $50/ounce), would rise to $3,200,000

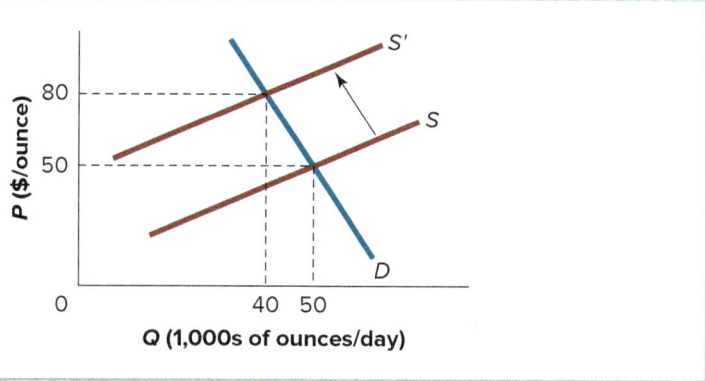

FIGURE 4.1

The Effect of Extra Border Patrols on the Market for Illicit Drugs.

Extra patrols shift supply leftward and reduce the quantity demanded, but they may actually increase the total amount spent on drugs.

Could reducing the supply of illegal drugs cause an increase in drug-related burglaries?

per day (40,000 ounces/day × $80/ounce). In this case, then, efforts to stem the supply of drugs would actually increase the likelihood of your laptop being stolen.

Other benefits from stemming the flow of illicit drugs might still outweigh the resulting increase in crime. But knowing that the policy might increase drug-related crime would clearly be useful to law-enforcement authorities.

Our task in this chapter will be to introduce the concept of elasticity, a measure of the extent to which quantity demanded and quantity supplied respond to variations in price, income, and other factors. In Chapter 3, *Supply and Demand,* we saw how shifts in supply and demand curves enabled us to predict the direction of change in the equilibrium values of price and quantity. An understanding of price elasticity will enable us to make even more precise statements about the effects of such changes. In the illicit-drug example just considered, the decrease in supply led to an increase in total spending. In many other cases, a decrease in supply will lead to a reduction in total spending. Why this difference? The underlying phenomenon that explains this pattern, as we'll see, is price elasticity of demand. We'll explore why some goods have higher price elasticity of demand than others and the implications of that fact for how total spending responds to changes in prices. We'll also discuss price elasticity of supply and examine the factors that explain why it takes different values for different goods.

PRICE ELASTICITY OF DEMAND

When the price of a good or service rises, the quantity demanded falls. But to predict the effect of the price increase on total expenditure, we also must know by how much quantity falls. The quantity demanded of some goods such as salt is not very sensitive to changes in price. Indeed, even if the price of salt were to double, or to fall by half, most people would hardly alter their consumption of it. For other goods, however, the quantity demanded is extremely responsive to changes in price. For example, when a luxury tax was imposed on yachts in the early 1990s, purchases of yachts plummeted sharply. (Refer to The Economic Naturalist 4.2 example presented later in this chapter.)

PRICE ELASTICITY DEFINED

price elasticity of demand the percentage change in the quantity demanded of a good or service that results from a 1 percent change in its price

The **price elasticity of demand** for a good is a measure of the responsiveness of the quantity demanded of that good to changes in its price. Formally, the price elasticity of demand for a good is defined as the percentage change in the quantity demanded that results from a 1 percent change in its price. For example, if the price of beef falls by 1 percent and the quantity demanded rises by 2 percent, then the price elasticity of demand for beef has a value of −2.

Although the definition just given refers to the response of quantity demanded to a 1 percent change in price, it also can be adapted to other variations in price, provided they're relatively small. In such cases, we calculate the price elasticity of demand as the percentage change in quantity demanded divided by the corresponding percentage change in price. Thus, if a 2 percent reduction in the price of pork led to a 6 percent increase in the quantity of pork demanded, the price elasticity of demand for pork would be

$$\frac{\text{Percentage change in quantity demanded}}{\text{Percentage change in price}} = \frac{6 \text{ percent}}{-2 \text{ percent}} = -3. \qquad (4.1)$$

Strictly speaking, the price elasticity of demand will always be negative (or zero) because price changes are always in the opposite direction from changes in quantity demanded. So for convenience, we drop the negative sign and speak of price elasticities in terms of absolute value. The demand for a good is said to be **elastic** with respect to price if the absolute value of its price elasticity is greater than 1. It is said to be **inelastic** if the absolute value of its price elasticity is less than 1. Finally, demand is said to be **unit elastic** if the absolute value of its price elasticity is equal to 1. (See Figure 4.2.)

elastic the demand for a good is elastic with respect to price if its price elasticity of demand is greater than 1

inelastic the demand for a good is inelastic with respect to price if its price elasticity of demand is less than 1

unit elastic the demand for a good is unit elastic with respect to price if its price elasticity of demand equals 1

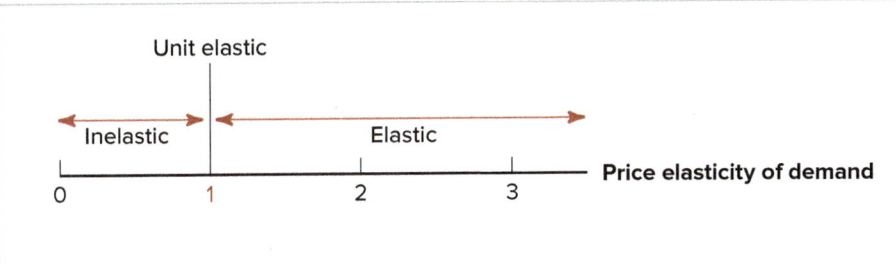

FIGURE 4.2
Elastic and Inelastic Demand.
Demand for a good is called elastic, unit elastic, or inelastic with respect to price if the price elasticity is greater than 1, equal to 1, or less than 1, respectively.

EXAMPLE 4.1   Elasticity of Demand

What is the elasticity of demand for pizza?

When the price of pizza is $1 per slice, buyers wish to purchase 400 slices per day, but when price falls to $0.97 per slice, the quantity demanded rises to 404 slices per day. At the original price, what is the price elasticity of demand for pizza? Is the demand for pizza elastic with respect to price?

The fall in price from $1 to $0.97 is a decrease of 3 percent. The rise in quantity demanded from 400 slices to 404 slices is an increase of 1 percent. The price elasticity of demand for pizza is thus (1 percent)/(3 percent) = 1/3. So when the initial price of pizza is $1, the demand for pizza is not elastic with respect to price; it is inelastic.

 SELF-TEST 4.1

What is the elasticity of demand for season ski passes?
When the price of a season ski pass is $400, buyers, whose demand curve for passes is linear, wish to purchase 10,000 passes per year, but when price falls to $380, the quantity demanded rises to 12,000 passes per year. At the original price, what is the price elasticity of demand for ski passes? Is the demand for ski passes elastic with respect to price?

DETERMINANTS OF PRICE ELASTICITY OF DEMAND

What factors determine the price elasticity of demand for a good or service? To answer this question, recall that before a rational consumer buys any product, the purchase decision must first satisfy the Cost-Benefit Principle. For instance, consider a good (such as a dorm refrigerator) that you buy only one unit of (if you buy it at all). Suppose that, at the current price, you have decided to buy it. Now imagine that the price goes up by 10 percent. Will a price increase of this magnitude be likely to make you change your mind? The answer will depend on factors like the following.

Substitution Possibilities

When the price of a product you want to buy goes up significantly, you're likely to ask yourself, "Is there some other good that can do roughly the same job, but for less money?" If the answer is yes, then you can escape the effect of the price increase by simply switching to the substitute product. But if the answer is no, you are more likely to stick with your current purchase.

These observations suggest that demand will tend to be more elastic with respect to price for products for which close substitutes are readily available. Salt, for example, has no close substitutes, which is one reason that the demand for it is highly inelastic. Note, however, that while the quantity of salt people demand is highly insensitive to price, the same cannot be said of the demand for any *specific brand* of salt. After all, despite what salt manufacturers say about the special advantages of their own labels, consumers tend to regard one brand of salt as a virtually perfect substitute for another. Thus, if Morton were to raise the price of its salt significantly, many people would simply switch to some other brand.

The vaccine against rabies is another product for which there are essentially no attractive substitutes. A person who is bitten by a rabid animal and does not take the vaccine faces a certain and painful death. Most people in that position would pay any price they could afford rather than do without the vaccine.

If the price of salt were to double, would you use less of it?

▶ Visit your instructor's Connect course and access your eBook to view this video.

Why do people buy the same amount of (table) salt—even when the price rises substantially?

Budget Share

Suppose the price of key rings suddenly were to double. How would that affect the number of key rings you buy? If you're like most people, it would have no effect at all. Think about it—a doubling of the price of a $1 item that you buy only every few years is simply nothing to worry about. By contrast, if the price of the new car you were about to buy suddenly doubled, you would definitely want to check out possible substitutes such as a used car or a smaller new model. You also might consider holding on to your current car a little longer. The larger the share of your budget an item accounts for, the greater is your incentive to look for substitutes when the price of the item rises. Big-ticket items, therefore, tend to have higher price elasticities of demand.

Time

Home appliances come in a variety of models, some more energy-efficient than others. As a general rule, the more efficient an appliance is, the higher its price. Suppose that you were about to buy a new air conditioner and electric rates suddenly rose sharply. It would probably be in your interest to buy a more efficient machine than you'd originally planned. However, what if you'd already bought a new air conditioner before you learned of the rate increase? You wouldn't think it worthwhile to discard the machine right away and replace it with a more efficient model. Rather, you'd wait until the machine wore out, or until you moved, before making the switch.

As this example illustrates, substitution of one product or service for another takes time. Some substitutions occur in the immediate aftermath of a price increase, but many others take place years or even decades later. For this reason, the price elasticity of demand for any good or service will be higher in the long run than in the short run.

RECAP ↑

FACTORS THAT INFLUENCE PRICE ELASTICITY

The price elasticity of demand for a good or service tends to be larger when substitutes for the good are more readily available, when the good's share in the consumer's budget is larger, and when consumers have more time to adjust to a change in price.

SOME REPRESENTATIVE ELASTICITY ESTIMATES

The entries in Table 4.1 show that the price elasticities of demand for different products often differ substantially—in this sample, ranging from a high of 3.5 for public transportation to a low of 0.1 for food. This variability is explained in part by the determinants of elasticity just discussed. Note, for example, that the price elasticity of demand for green peas is more than nine times that for coffee, reflecting the fact that there are many more close substitutes for green peas than for coffee.

TABLE 4.1

Historical Price Elasticity of Demand Estimates for Selected Products

Product or service	Estimated price elasticity
Food	0.1
Coffee	0.3
Magazines and newspapers	0.3
Housing	0.6
Tobacco	0.6
Clothing	0.6
Medical care	0.8
Oil	0.9
Motor vehicles	1.1
Beer	1.2
Furniture	1.3
Restaurant meals	1.6
Household electricity	1.9
Boats, pleasure aircraft	2.4
Green peas	2.8
Public transportation	3.5

Sources: K. Elzinga, "The Beer Industry," *The Structure of American Industry*, ed. Walter Adams (New York: Macmillan, 1977); R. Fisher, *State and Local Public Finance* (Chicago, IL: Irwin, 1996); H. S. Houthakker and L. Taylor, *Consumer Demand in the United States: Analyses and Projections*, 2nd ed. (Cambridge, MA: Harvard University Press, 1970); A. Mansur and J. Whalley, "Numerical Specification of Applied General Equilibrium Models: Estimation, Calibration, and Data," *Applied General Equilibrium Analysis*, ed. Herbert Scarf and John Shoven (New York: Cambridge University Press, 1984); J. Möller, "Income and Price Elasticities in Different Sectors of the Economy—An Analysis of Structural Change for Germany, the U.K., and the U.S.A.," in T. Ten Raa and R. Schettkat (eds.), *The Growth of Service Industries: The Paradox of Exploding Costs and Persistent Demand* (Cheltenham, UK: Edward Elgar Publishing, 2001), pp. 167–208; L. Taylor, "The Demand for Electricity: A Survey," *Bell Journal of Economics*, Spring 1975; H. Theil, C. Chung, and J. Seale, "Advances in Econometrics," Supplement I, *International Evidence on Consumption Patterns* (Greenwich, CT: JAI Press, 1989).

Note also the contrast between the low price elasticity of demand for food and the high price elasticity of demand for green peas. Unlike green peas, food occupies a substantial share of most family budgets and there are few substitutes for broad spending categories like food.

USING PRICE ELASTICITY OF DEMAND

An understanding of the factors that govern price elasticity of demand is necessary not only to make sense of consumer behavior, but also to design effective public policy. Consider, for example, the debate about luxury taxes.

The Economic Naturalist 4.1

Why was the luxury tax on yachts such a disaster?

In 1990, Congress imposed a luxury tax on yachts costing more than $100,000, along with similar taxes on a handful of other luxury goods. Before these taxes were imposed, the Joint Committee on Taxation estimated that they would yield more than $31 million in revenue in 1991. However, the tax actually generated only a bit more than half that amount, $16.6 million.[1] Several years later, the Joint Economic Committee estimated that the tax on yachts had led to a loss of 7,600 jobs in the U.S. boating industry. Taking account of lost income taxes and increased unemployment benefits, the U.S. government actually came out $7.6 million behind in fiscal 1991 as a result of its luxury taxes—almost $39 million worse than the initial projection. What went wrong?

Why did the luxury tax on yachts backfire?

The 1990 law imposed no luxury taxes on yachts built and purchased outside the United States. What Congress failed to consider was that foreign-built yachts are almost perfect substitutes for yachts built and purchased in the United States. And, no surprise, when prices on domestic yachts went up because of the tax, yacht buyers switched in droves to foreign models. A tax imposed on a good with a high price elasticity of demand stimulates large rearrangements of consumption but yields little revenue. Had Congress done the economic analysis properly, it would have predicted that this particular tax would be a big loser. Facing angry protests from unemployed New England shipbuilders, Congress repealed the luxury tax on yachts in 1993.

SOCIAL CONTAGION AND THE LONG-RUN PRICE ELASTICITY OF DEMAND

As discussed earlier, the price elasticity of demand is higher in the long run than in the short run, in part because responses to price changes take time to implement. Short-run responses can also be muted by uncertainty over whether price changes are permanent.

[1]For an alternative view, see Dennis Zimmerman, "The Effect of the Luxury Excise Tax on the Sale of Luxury Boats," Congressional Research Service, February 10, 1992.

For example, each of the large increases in gasoline prices that happened in the wake of oil supply interruptions during the 1970s and at the time of the Russian invasion of Ukraine in 2022 was followed just months later by an equally sharp price decline. For a price change to alter people's choices significantly, it must be durable.

The long-run responses to durable price changes are shaped not only by individuals acting in isolation, but also by broader social and cultural forces. **Social contagion** is the term used by behavioral scientists to describe how behaviors often spread from person to person in ways that resemble the spread of memes on social media. As Economic Naturalist 4.2 suggests, models of behavior that incorporate social contagion support substantially larger long-run price elasticity estimates than those implied by models that fail to account for it.

social contagion a term used by behavioral scientists to describe how behaviors often spread from person to person in ways that resemble the spread of memes on social media

The Economic Naturalist 4.2

Will a higher tax on cigarettes curb teenage smoking?

Consultants hired by the tobacco industry have testified in Congress against higher cigarette taxes aimed at curbing teenage smoking. The main reason teenagers smoke is that their friends smoke, these consultants testified, and they concluded that higher taxes would have little effect. Does the consultants' testimony make economic sense?

The consultants were right that peer influence is the most important determinant of teen smoking. Thus, according to one study, if the proportion of smokers among an adolescent's close friends rose by 10 percentage points, her probability of smoking would rise by 5 percentage points.[2]

Although consultants were correct to assert that the initial impact of cigarette taxes on teenage smoking decisions would be small, it was not zero. Because most teenagers have little money to spend at their own discretion, cigarette purchases constitute a significant share of their budgets. For at least some teenagers, a higher tax would make smoking unaffordable. And even among those who could afford the higher prices, at least some others would choose to spend their money on other things.

Given that the tax would affect at least *some* teenage smokers, the consultants' argument begins to unravel. In addition to its direct effect on the price of cigarettes, the tax also deters others indirectly, by reducing the number of peers who smoke. Those who refrain because of these indirect effects no longer influence others to smoke, and so on. So even if the direct effect of higher cigarette taxes on teen smoking was small in the short run, the cumulative indirect effect of the resulting social contagion was far larger. The mere fact that peer pressure may be the primary determinant of teen smoking therefore simply does not imply that higher cigarette taxes would have no significant impact on the number of teens who smoke. On the contrary, social contagion's effect was in fact to amplify the direct effect of price increases alone.

Do high cigarette prices discourage teen smoking?

The U.S. Surgeon General's Report on Smoking and Tobacco Use, published in 1964, put Americans on notice that smoking posed significant risks to health and longevity. For almost the next two decades, however, the government remained reluctant to regulate

[2]Mir M. Ali and Debra S. Dwyer, "Estimating Peer Effects in Adolescent Smoking Behavior: A Longitudinal Analysis," *Journal of Adolescent Health,* 45, no. 4 (October 2009), pp. 402–408.

smoking. That attitude changed after the appearance of studies showing that exposure to second-hand smoke contributed to serious health problems in nonsmokers. This evidence made officials more receptive to antismoking measures, and the early 1980s saw the adoption of heavy cigarette taxes and bans on smoking in various public spaces. Individuals have a right to harm themselves, proponents of these measures argued, but not a right to harm innocent bystanders.

Citing evidence that nicotine is highly addictive, critics claimed that although cigarette taxation might discourage some from taking up the habit, it would have virtually no impact on smokers themselves. Even more so than in the case of teen smoking just discussed, that claim proved correct in the short run: Most adult smokers simply paid the taxes and stuck with their habit. But here, too, the long-run response was a different matter. The new taxes initially led at least a few people to quit smoking or refrain from starting, which meant that each adult peer group had a lower proportion of smokers than before, which in turn produced cascades like the ones seen for teenagers. Without reference to social contagion, it's difficult to explain how adult smoking rates fell from 33 percent in 1980 to less than 13 percent today. The social environment often changes slowly, but its influence on long-run demand elasticities is profound.

THE LONG-RUN RESPONSE TO A CARBON TAX

Social contagion also promises to boost the long-run response to a carbon tax, one of the most important policy tools with which governments around the world have been attempting to mitigate climate change. Under a carbon tax, the price of each good or service is boosted by a tax levied in proportion to the carbon emissions associated with its production and use. The traditional economic argument is that by making goods with heavy carbon footprints more expensive, this tax would encourage people to switch to less polluting alternatives. In response, many climate pessimists complain that because price elasticities of demand for energy-intensive activities are typically small, the response to a carbon tax would be too little too late. But because many of the behaviors that have contributed to the climate crisis are as socially contagious as smoking, the long-run response to a carbon tax would be larger than many of these pessimists expect.

People live in big houses, drive big cars, stage destination weddings, and engage in a host of other energy-intensive behaviors less because those activities are priced incorrectly than because that's what peers do.[3] The implication is that, as in the case of cigarette taxation, behavioral models that incorporate social contagion predict substantially larger responses to carbon taxation than predicted by traditional models.

The adoption of rooftop photovoltaic solar panels is an instructive case in point. Early adoptions were encouraged by government subsidies, which were equivalent to a price reduction. That these adoptions were contagious can be seen by entering an address into Google's Project Sunroof website, which will then display aerial photos of the surrounding neighborhood in which houses with solar panels are identified by red dots on their roofs. Those with red dots are almost invariably adjacent to other houses that also have them, while those without dots are similarly clustered. That pattern is a signature feature of contagion.

Further support for the contagiousness of solar panel adoption comes from a careful statistical analysis of early adoption patterns. Controlling for all factors known to influence adoption decisions, the researchers found that each new installation stimulated a copycat installation (one that would not have occurred otherwise) in the same ZIP code within four months' time, on average.[4] A new installation on January 1 of a given year would thus spawn a copycat by May 1, and these two would spawn two more by September 1, and so on. There would thus be 8 new installations by the end of the first year and 64 by the end of year 2.

Since these are just the new installations that occur in the same ZIP code, total contagion must be appreciably larger, because most people have closer ties to friends and relatives in distant locations than to fellow ZIP code residents. Like the adoptions

[3]For a survey of evidence in support of this claim, see R. H. Frank, *Under the Influence: Putting Peer Pressure to Work* (Princeton: Princeton University Press 2020).
[4]Bryan Bollinger and Kenneth Gillingham, "Peer Effects in the Diffusion of Photovoltaic Solar Panels," *Marketing Science*, 31, August 15, 2012, pp. 900–912.

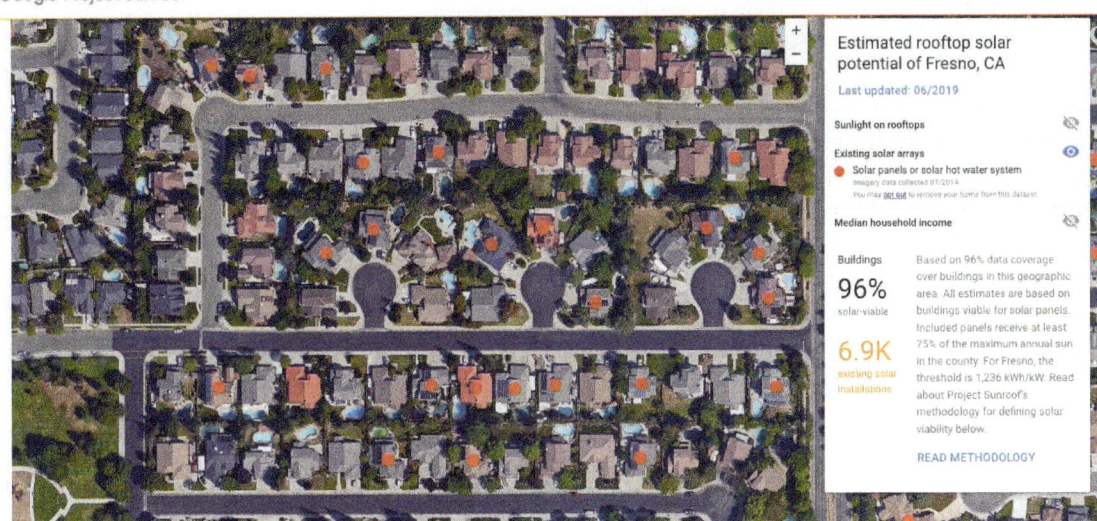

Social Contagion in Rooftop Solar Panel Adoption
Most houses with solar panels (those with red dots) are adjacent to others that also have them.

stimulated by the initial subsidies, those stimulated by a carbon tax that makes fossil-fuel energy more expensive would launch a similar contagion process.

Carbon taxation would have analogous effects in other domains of energy use. When some buy electric vehicles because a carbon tax makes gasoline more expensive, friends and neighbors become more likely to consider them.[5] And when some eat less beef after a carbon tax makes its heavy carbon footprint more costly, peers tend to rethink their own diets.[6] One reason for cautious optimism, then, is that because social contagion is so powerful, any policy that alters individual energy usage directly will also generate ripple effects that exceed the direct effects, often by substantial multiples.

A GRAPHICAL INTERPRETATION OF PRICE ELASTICITY

For small changes in price, price elasticity of demand is the proportion by which quantity demanded changes divided by the corresponding proportion by which price changes. This formulation enables us to construct a simple expression for the price elasticity of demand for a good using only minimal information about its demand curve.

Look at Figure 4.3. P represents the current price of a good and Q the quantity demanded at that price. ΔP represents a small change in the current price, and the resulting change in quantity demanded is given by ΔQ. The expression $\Delta P/P$ will then stand for the proportion by which price changes and $\Delta Q/Q$ will stand for the corresponding proportion by which quantity changes. These two expressions, along with our definition of the price elasticity of demand (Equation 4.1), give us the formula for price elasticity

$$\text{Price elasticity} = \in = \frac{\Delta Q/Q}{\Delta P/P}. \qquad (4.2)$$

Suppose, for example, that 20 units were sold at the original price of 100 and that when price rose to 105, quantity demanded fell to 15 units. Neglecting the negative sign of the quantity change, we would then have $\Delta Q/Q = 5/20$ and $\Delta P/P = 5/100$ which yields $\in = (5/20)/(5/100) = 5$.

[5]Jesper Berggreen, "Almost One-Third of All New Car Sales in Norway in 2018 Were for Pure Electric Vehicles," *CleanTechnica.com*, January 3, 2019.
[6]Nicholas A. Christakis and James H. Fowler, "The Spread of Obesity in a Large Social Network over 32 Years," *New England Journal of Medicine*, July 26, 2007, pp. 370–379.

FIGURE 4.3

A Graphical Interpretation of Price Elasticity of Demand.

Price elasticity of demand at any point along a straight-line demand curve is the ratio of price to quantity at that point times the reciprocal of the slope of the demand curve.

One attractive feature of this formula is that it has a straightforward graphical interpretation. Thus, if we want to calculate the price elasticity of demand at point A on the demand curve shown in Figure 4.3, we can begin by rewriting the right-hand side of Equation 4.2 as $(P/Q) \times (\Delta Q/\Delta P)$. And since the slope of the demand curve is equal to $\Delta P/\Delta Q$, $\Delta Q/\Delta P$ is the reciprocal of that slope: $\Delta Q/\Delta P = 1/\text{slope}$. The price elasticity of demand at point A, denoted $\in_A$, therefore has the following simple formula

$$\in_A = \frac{P}{Q} \times \frac{1}{\text{slope}}. \tag{4.3}$$

To demonstrate how convenient this graphical interpretation of elasticity can be, suppose we want to find the price elasticity of demand at point A on the demand curve in Figure 4.4. The slope of this demand curve is the ratio of its vertical intercept to its horizontal intercept: $20/5 = 4$. So $1/\text{slope} = 1/4$. (Actually, the slope is -4, but we again ignore the minus sign for convenience since price elasticity of demand always has the same sign.) The ratio P/Q at point A is 8/3, so the price elasticity at point A is equal to $(P/Q) \times (1/\text{slope}) = (8/3) \times (1/4) = 2/3$. This means that when the price of the good is 8, a 3 percent reduction in price will lead to a 2 percent increase in quantity demanded.

FIGURE 4.4

Calculating Price Elasticity of Demand.

The price elasticity of demand at A is given by $(P/Q) \times (1/\text{slope}) = (8/3) \times (1/4) = 2/3$.

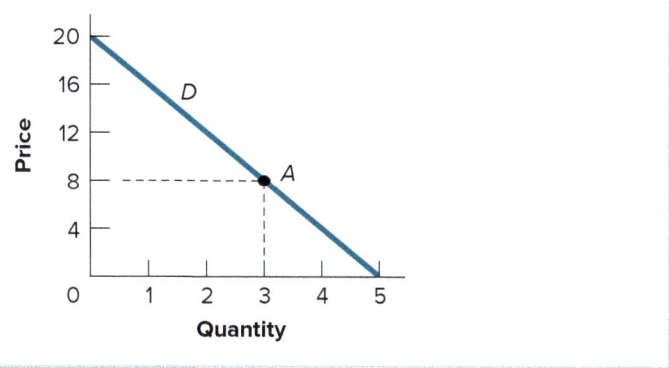

✅ SELF-TEST 4.2

What is the price elasticity of demand when $P = 4$ on the demand curve in Figure 4.4?

EXAMPLE 4.2   The Relationship between Elasticity and Slope

For the demand curves D_1 and D_2 shown in Figure 4.5, calculate the price elasticity of demand when $P = 4$. What is the price elasticity of demand on D_2 when $P = 1$?

These elasticities can be calculated easily using the formula $\in = (P/Q) \times (1/\text{slope})$. The slope of D_1 is the ratio of its vertical intercept to its horizontal intercept: 12/6 = 2. So (1/slope) is 1/2 for D_1. Similarly, the slope of D_2 is the ratio of its vertical intercept to its horizontal intercept: 6/12 = 1/2. So the reciprocal of the slope of D_2 is 2. For both demand curves, $Q = 4$ when $P = 4$, so $(P/Q) = 4/4 = 1$ for each. Thus the price elasticity of demand when $P = 4$ is $(1) \times (1/2) = 1/2$ for D_1 and $(1) \times (2) = 2$ for D_2. When $P = 1$, $Q = 10$ on D_2, so $(P/Q) = 1/10$. Thus price elasticity of demand $= (1/10) \times (2) = 1/5$ when $P = 1$ on D_2.

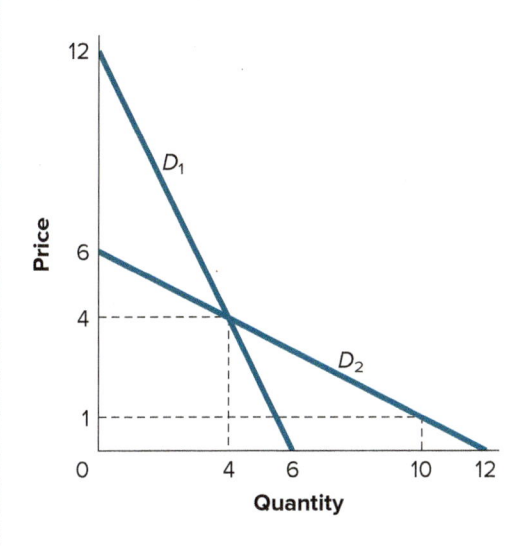

FIGURE 4.5

Price Elasticity and the Steepness of the Demand Curve.

When price and quantity are the same, price elasticity of demand is always greater for the less steep of two demand curves.

This example illustrates a general rule: If two demand curves have a point in common, the steeper curve must be the less price-elastic of the two with respect to price at that point. However, this does not mean that the steeper curve is less elastic at *every* point. Thus, we saw that at $P = 1$, price elasticity of demand on D_2 was only 1/5, or less than half the corresponding elasticity on the steeper D_1 at $P = 4$.

PRICE ELASTICITY CHANGES ALONG A STRAIGHT-LINE DEMAND CURVE

As a glance at our elasticity formula makes clear, price elasticity has a different value at every point along a straight-line demand curve. The slope of a straight-line demand curve is constant, which means that 1/slope is also constant. But the price–quantity ratio P/Q declines as we move down the demand curve. The elasticity of demand thus declines steadily as we move downward along a straight-line demand curve.

Since price elasticity is the percentage change in quantity demanded divided by the corresponding percentage change in price, this pattern makes sense. After all, a price movement of a given absolute size is small in percentage terms when it occurs near the top of the demand curve, where price is high, but large in percentage terms when it occurs near the bottom of the demand curve, where price is low. Likewise, a quantity movement of a given absolute value is large in percentage terms when it occurs near the top of the demand curve, where quantity is low, and small in percentage terms when it occurs near the bottom of the curve, where quantity is high.

The graphical interpretation of elasticity also makes it easy to see why the price elasticity of demand at the midpoint of any straight-line demand curve must always be 1. Consider, for example, the price elasticity of demand at point A on the demand curve D shown in Figure 4.6. At that point, the ratio P/Q is equal to 6/3 = 2. The slope of this

FIGURE 4.6

Elasticity at the Midpoint of a Straight-Line Demand Curve.

The price elasticity of demand at the midpoint of any straight-line demand curve always takes the value 1.

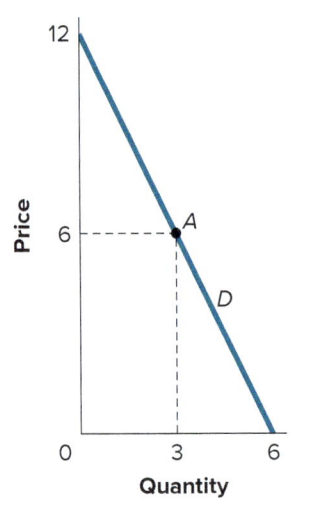

demand curve is the ratio of its vertical intercept to its horizontal intercept, $12/6 = 2$. So $(1/\text{slope}) = 1/2$ (again, we neglect the negative sign for simplicity). Inserting these values into the graphical elasticity formula yields $\in_A = (P/Q) \times (1/\text{slope}) = (2) \times (1/2) = 1$.

This result holds not just for Figure 4.6, but also for any other straight-line demand curve.[7] A glance at the formula also tells us that since P/Q declines as we move downward along a straight-line demand curve, price elasticity of demand must be less than 1 at any point below the midpoint. By the same token, price elasticity must be greater than 1 for any point above the midpoint. Figure 4.7 summarizes these findings by denoting the elastic, inelastic, and unit elastic portions of any straight-line demand curve.

TWO SPECIAL CASES

FIGURE 4.7

Price Elasticity Regions along a Straight-Line Demand Curve.

Demand is elastic on the top half, unit elastic at the midpoint, and inelastic on the bottom half of a straight-line demand curve.

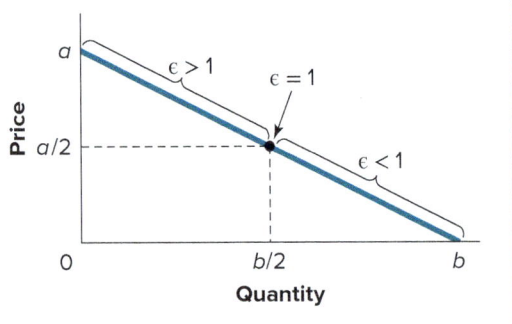

There are two important exceptions to the general rule that elasticity declines along straight-line demand curves. First, the horizontal demand curve in Figure 4.8(a) has a slope of zero, which means that the reciprocal of its slope is infinite. Price elasticity of demand is thus infinite at every point along a horizontal demand curve. Such demand curves are said to be **perfectly elastic**.

Second, the demand curve in Figure 4.8(b) is vertical, which means that its slope is infinite. The reciprocal of its slope is thus equal to zero. Price elasticity of demand is thus exactly zero at every point along the curve. For this reason, vertical demand curves are said to be **perfectly inelastic**.

perfectly elastic demand
demand is perfectly elastic with respect to price if price elasticity of demand is infinite

perfectly inelastic demand
demand is perfectly inelastic with respect to price if price elasticity of demand is zero

---

RECAP

CALCULATING PRICE ELASTICITY OF DEMAND

The price elasticity of demand for a good is the percentage change in the quantity demanded that results from a 1 percent change in its price. Mathematically, the elasticity of demand at a point along a demand curve is equal to $(P/Q) \times (1/\text{slope})$, where P and Q represent price and quantity and $(1/\text{slope})$ is the reciprocal of the slope of the demand curve at that point. Demand is elastic with respect to price if the absolute value of its price elasticity exceeds 1; inelastic if price elasticity is less than 1; and unit elastic if price elasticity is equal to 1.

---

[7]To see why, note that at the midpoint of any such curve, P is exactly half the vertical intercept of the demand curve and Q is exactly half the horizontal intercept. Since the ratio of the vertical intercept to the horizontal intercept is the slope of the demand curve, the ratio (P/Q) must also be equal to the slope of the demand curve. And this means that $(1/\text{slope})$ will always be equal to (Q/P). Thus, the product $(P/Q) \times (1/\text{slope}) = (P/Q) \times (Q/P)$ will always be exactly 1 at the midpoint of any straight-line demand curve.

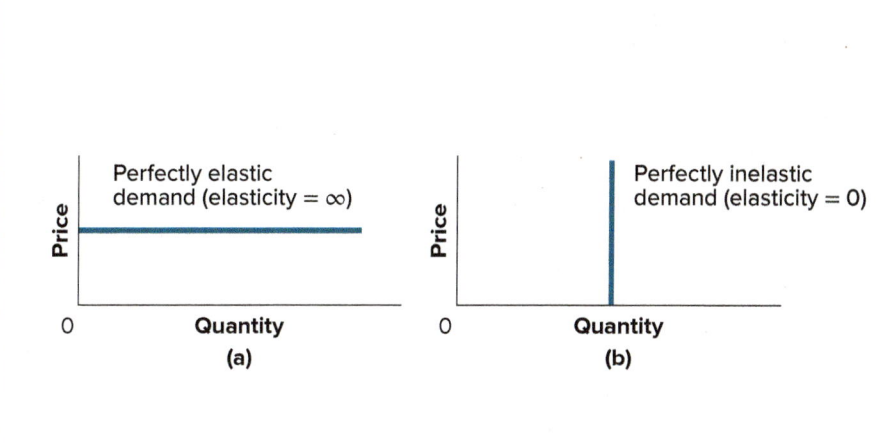

FIGURE 4.8
Perfectly Elastic and Perfectly Inelastic Demand Curves.

The horizontal demand curve (a) is perfectly elastic, or infinitely elastic, at every point. Even the slightest increase in price leads consumers to desert the product in favor of substitutes. The vertical demand curve (b) is perfectly inelastic at every point. Consumers do not, or cannot, switch to substitutes even in the face of large increases in price.

ELASTICITY AND TOTAL EXPENDITURE

Sellers of goods and services have a strong interest in being able to answer questions like "Will consumers spend more on my product if I sell more units at a lower price or fewer units at a higher price?" As it turns out, the answer to this question depends critically on the price elasticity of demand. To see why, let's first examine how the total amount spent on a good varies with the price of the good.

The total daily expenditure on a good is simply the daily number of units bought times the price for which it sells. The market demand curve for a good tells us the quantity that will be sold at each price. We can thus use the information on the demand curve to show how the total amount spent on a good will vary with its price.

To illustrate, let's calculate how much moviegoers will spend on tickets each day if the demand curve is as shown in Figure 4.9 and the price is $2 per ticket (a). The demand curve tells us that at a price of $2 per ticket, 500 tickets per day will be sold, so total expenditure at that price will be $1,000 per day. If tickets sell not for $2 but for $4 apiece, 400 tickets will be sold each day (b), so total expenditure at the higher price will be $1,600 per day.

(a)

(b)

FIGURE 4.9
The Demand Curve for Movie Tickets.

An increase in price from $2 to $4 per ticket increases total expenditure on tickets.

total expenditure (or **total revenue**) the dollar amount that consumers spend on a product ($P \times Q$) is equal to the dollar amount that sellers receive

Note that the total amount consumers spend on a product each day must equal the total amount sellers of the product receive. That is, the terms **total expenditure** and **total revenue** are simply two sides of the same coin:

> **Total expenditure = Total revenue:** The dollar amount that consumers spend on a product ($P \times Q$) is equal to the dollar amount that sellers receive.

It might seem that an increase in the market price of a product should always result in an increase in the total revenue received by sellers. Although that happened in the case we just saw, it needn't always be so. The law of demand tells us that when the price of a good rises, people will buy less of it. The two factors that govern total revenue—price and quantity—will thus always move in opposite directions as we move along a demand curve. When price goes up and quantity goes down, the product of the two may go either up or down.

Note, for example, that for the demand curve shown in Figure 4.10 (which is the same as the one in Figure 4.9), a rise in price from $8 per ticket (a) to $10 per ticket (b) will cause total expenditure on tickets to go down. Thus people will spend $1,600 per day on tickets at a price of $8, but only $1,000 per day at a price of $10.

FIGURE 4.10

The Demand Curve for Movie Tickets.

An increase in price from $8 to $10 per ticket results in a fall in total expenditure on tickets.

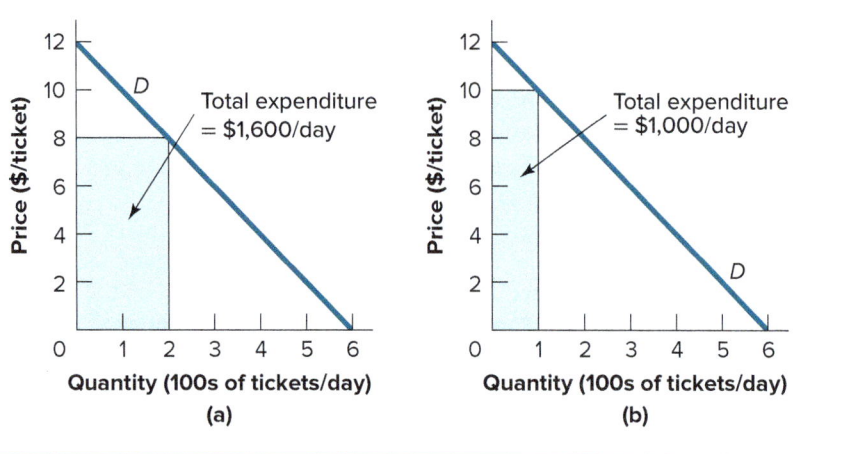

The general rule illustrated by Figures 4.9 and 4.10 is that a price increase will produce an increase in total revenue whenever it is greater, in percentage terms, than the corresponding percentage reduction in quantity demanded. Although the two price increases (from $2 to $4 and from $8 to $10) were of the same absolute value—$2 in each case—they are much different when expressed as a percentage of the original price. An increase from $2 to $4 represents a 100 percent increase in price, whereas an increase from $8 to $10 represents only a 25 percent increase in price. And although the quantity reductions caused by the two price increases were also equal in absolute terms, they too are very different when expressed as percentages of the quantities originally sold. Thus, although the decline in quantity demanded was 100 tickets per day in each case, it was just a 20 percent reduction in the first case (from 500 units to 400 in Figure 4.9) but a 50 percent reduction in the second (from 200 units to 100 in Figure 4.10). In the second case, the negative effect on total expenditure of the 50 percent quantity reduction outweighed the positive effect of the 25 percent price increase. The reverse happened in the first case: The 100 percent increase in price (from $2 to $4) outweighed the 20 percent reduction in quantity (from 500 units to 400 units).

The following example provides further insight into the relationship between total revenue and price.

EXAMPLE 4.3	**Elasticity and Total Expenditure**

For the demand curve shown in Figure 4.11, draw a separate graph showing how total expenditure varies with the price of movie tickets.

The first step in constructing this graph is to calculate total expenditure for each price shown in the graph and record the results, as in Table 4.2. The next step is to plot total expenditure at each of the price points on a graph, as in Figure 4.12. Finally, sketch the curve by joining these points. (If greater accuracy is required, you can use a larger sample of points than the one shown in Table 4.2.)

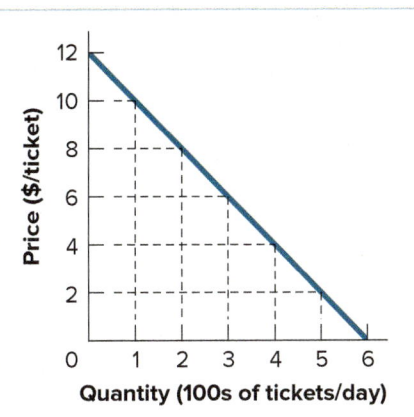

FIGURE 4.11

The Demand Curve for Movie Tickets.

TABLE 4.2
Total Expenditure as a Function of Price

Price ($/ticket)	Total expenditure ($/day)
12	0
10	1,000
8	1,600
6	1,800
4	1,600
2	1,000
0	0

FIGURE 4.12
Total Expenditure as a Function of Price.

For a good whose demand curve is a straight line, total expenditure reaches a maximum at the price corresponding to the midpoint of the demand curve.

   Note in Figure 4.12 that as the price per ticket increases from $0 to $6, total expenditure increases. But as the price rises from $6 to $12, total expenditure decreases. Total expenditure reaches a maximum of $1,800 per day at a price of $6.

The pattern observed in the preceding example holds true in general. For a straight-line demand curve, total expenditure is highest at the price that lies on the midpoint of the demand curve.

Bearing in mind these observations about how expenditure varies with price, let's return to the question of how the effect of a price change on total expenditure depends on the price elasticity of demand. Suppose, for example, that the business manager of a rock band knows she can sell 5,000 tickets to the band's weekly summer concerts if she sets the price at $20 per ticket. If the elasticity of demand for tickets is equal to 3, will total ticket revenue go up or down in response to a 10 percent increase in the price of tickets?

Total revenue from tickets sold is currently ($20/ticket) × (5,000 tickets/week) = $100,000 per week. The fact that the price elasticity of demand for tickets is 3 implies that a 10 percent increase in price will produce a 30 percent reduction in the number of tickets sold, which means that quantity will fall to 3,500 tickets per week. Total expenditure on tickets will therefore fall to (3,500 tickets/week) × ($22/ticket) = $77,000 per week, which is significantly less than the current spending total.

What would have happened to total expenditure if the band manager had *reduced* ticket prices by 10 percent, from $20 to $18? Again assuming a price elasticity of 3, the result would have been a 30 percent increase in tickets sold—from 5,000 per week to 6,500 per week. The resulting total expenditure would have been ($18/ticket) × (6,500 tickets/week) = $117,000 per week, significantly more than the current total.

These examples illustrate the following important rule about how price changes affect total expenditure for an elastically demanded good:

Rule 1: When price elasticity of demand is greater than 1, changes in price and changes in total expenditure always move in opposite directions.

Let's look at the intuition behind this rule. Total expenditure is the product of price and quantity. For an elastically demanded product, the percentage change in quantity will be larger than the corresponding percentage change in price. Thus the change in quantity will more than offset the change in revenue per unit sold.

Now let's see how total spending responds to a price increase when demand is *inelastic* with respect to price. Consider a case like the one just considered except that the elasticity of demand for tickets is not 3 but 0.5. How will total expenditure respond to a 10 percent increase in ticket prices? This time the number of tickets sold will fall by only 5 percent to 4,750 tickets per week, which means that total expenditure on tickets will rise to (4,750 tickets/week) × ($22/ticket) = $104,500 per week, or $4,500 per week more than the current expenditure level.

In contrast, a 10 percent price reduction (from $20 to $18 per ticket) when price elasticity is 0.5 would cause the number of tickets sold to grow by only 5 percent, from 5,000 per week to 5,250 per week, resulting in total expenditure of ($18/ticket) × (5,250 tickets/week) = $94,500 per week, significantly less than the current total.

As these examples illustrate, the effect of price changes on total expenditure when demand is inelastic is precisely the opposite of what it was when demand was elastic:

Rule 2: When price elasticity of demand is less than 1, changes in price and changes in total expenditure always move in the same direction.

Again, the intuition behind this rule is straightforward. For a product whose demand is inelastic with respect to price, the percentage change in quantity demanded will be smaller than the corresponding percentage change in price. The change in revenue per unit sold (price) will thus more than offset the change in the number of units sold.

The relationship between elasticity and the effect of a price change on total revenue is summarized in Figure 4.13, where the symbol $\in$ is used to denote elasticity.

Recall that in the example with which we began this chapter, an increase in the price of drugs led to an increase in the total amount spent on drugs. That will happen whenever

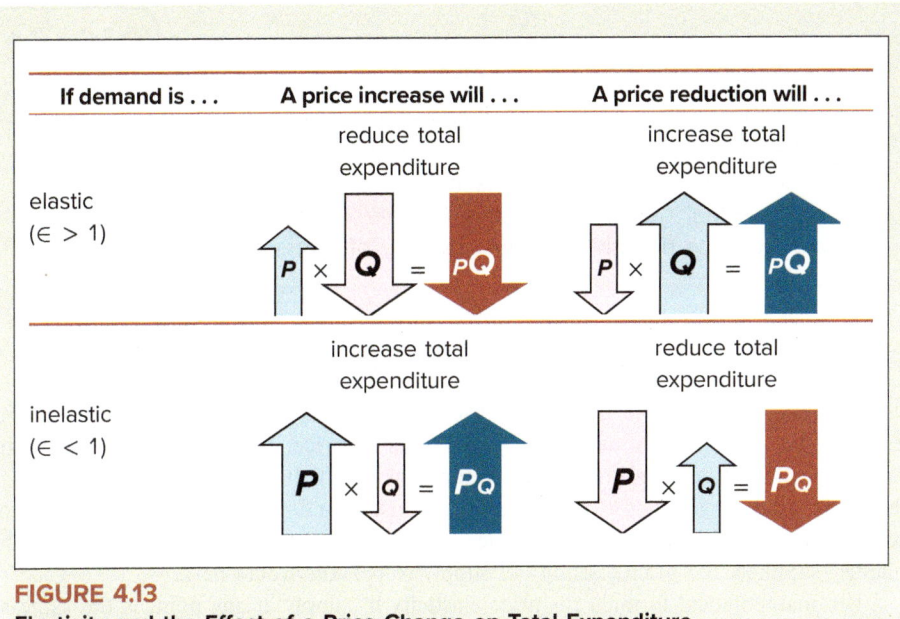

FIGURE 4.13
Elasticity and the Effect of a Price Change on Total Expenditure.

the demand for drugs is inelastic with respect to price, as it was in that example. Had the demand for drugs instead been elastic with respect to price, the drug supply interruption would have led to a reduction in total expenditure on drugs.

INCOME ELASTICITY AND CROSS-PRICE ELASTICITY OF DEMAND

The elasticity of demand for a good can be defined not only with respect to its own price but also with respect to the prices of substitutes or complements, or even to income. For example, the elasticity of demand for peanuts with respect to the price of cashews—also known as the **cross-price elasticity of demand** for peanuts with respect to cashew prices—is the percentage by which the quantity of peanuts demanded changes in response to a 1 percent change in the price of cashews. The **income elasticity of demand** for peanuts is the percentage by which the quantity demanded of peanuts changes in response to a 1 percent change in income.

Unlike the elasticity of demand for a good with respect to its own price, these other elasticities may be either positive or negative, so it is important to note their algebraic signs carefully. The income elasticity of demand for inferior goods, for example, is negative, whereas the income elasticity of demand for normal goods is positive. When the cross-price elasticity of demand for two goods is positive—as in the peanuts–cashews example—the two goods are substitutes. When it is negative, the two goods are complements. The elasticity of demand for tennis racquets with respect to court rental fees, for example, is less than zero.

cross-price elasticity of demand the percentage by which the quantity demanded of the first good changes in response to a 1 percent change in the price of the second

income elasticity of demand the percentage by which a good's quantity demanded changes in response to a 1 percent change in income

> ✅ **SELF-TEST 4.3**
>
> If a 10 percent increase in income causes the number of students who choose to attend private universities to go up by 5 percent, what is the income elasticity of demand for private universities?

RECAP↑

CROSS-PRICE AND INCOME ELASTICITIES

When the cross-price elasticity of demand for one good with respect to the price of another good is positive, the two goods are substitutes; when the cross-price elasticity of demand is negative, the two goods are complements. A normal good has positive income elasticity of demand and an inferior good has negative income elasticity of demand.

THE PRICE ELASTICITY OF SUPPLY

price elasticity of supply
the percentage change in quantity supplied that occurs in response to a 1 percent change in price

On the buyer's side of the market, we use price elasticity of demand to measure the responsiveness of quantity demanded to changes in price. On the seller's side of the market, the analogous measure is **price elasticity of supply**. It is defined as the percentage change in quantity supplied that occurs in response to a 1 percent change in price. For example, if a 1 percent increase in the price of peanuts leads to a 2 percent increase in the quantity supplied, the price elasticity of supply of peanuts would be 2.

The mathematical formula for price elasticity of supply at any point is the same as the corresponding expression for price elasticity of demand

$$\text{Price elasticity of supply} = \frac{\Delta Q/Q}{\Delta P/P}, \tag{4.4}$$

where P and Q are the price and quantity at that point, ΔP is a small change in the initial price, and ΔQ the resulting change in quantity.

As with the corresponding expression for price elasticity of demand, Equation 4.4 can be rewritten as $(P/Q) \times (\Delta Q/\Delta P)$. And since $(\Delta Q/\Delta P)$ is the reciprocal of the slope of the supply curve, the right-hand side of Equation 4.4 is equal to $(P/Q) \times (1/\text{slope})$–the same expression we saw in Equation 4.3 for price elasticity of demand. Price and quantity are always positive, as is the slope of the typical supply curve, so price elasticity of supply will be a positive number at every point.

Consider the supply curve shown in Figure 4.14. The slope of this supply curve is 2, so the reciprocal of this slope is 1/2. Using the formula, this means that the price elasticity of supply at A is $(8/2) \times (1/2) = 2$. The corresponding expression at B is $(10/3) \times (1/2) = 5/3$, a slightly smaller value.

 SELF-TEST 4.4

For the supply curve shown in Figure 4.14, calculate the elasticity of supply when $P = 6$.

FIGURE 4.14

A Supply Curve for Which Price Elasticity Declines as Quantity Rises.

For the supply curve shown, (1/slope) is the same at every point, but the ratio P/Q declines as Q increases. So elasticity = $(P/Q) \times (1/\text{slope})$ declines as quantity increases.

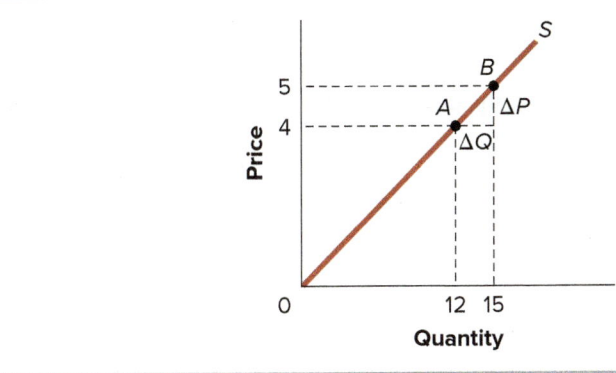

FIGURE 4.15

Calculating the Price Elasticity of Supply Graphically.

Price elasticity of supply is $(P/Q) \times (1/\text{slope})$, which at A is $(4/12) \times (12/4) = 1$, exactly the same as at B. The price elasticity of supply is equal to 1 at any point along a straight-line supply curve that passes through the origin.

Not all supply curves, however, have the property that price elasticity declines as quantity rises. Consider, for example, the supply curve shown in Figure 4.15. Because the ratio P/Q is the same at every point along this supply curve, and because the slope of the supply curve is also constant, price elasticity of supply will take exactly the same value at every point along this curve. At A, for example, price elasticity of supply = $(P/Q) \times (1/\text{slope}) = (4/12) \times (12/4) = 1$. Similarly, at B price elasticity of supply = $(5/15) \times (12/4) = 1$ again.

Indeed, the price elasticity of supply will always be equal to 1 at any point along a straight-line supply curve that passes through the origin. The reason is that for movements along any such line, both price and quantity always change in exactly the same proportion.

On the buyer's side of the market, two important polar cases are demand curves with infinite price elasticity and zero price elasticity. As the next two examples illustrate, analogous polar cases exist on the seller's side of the market.

EXAMPLE 4.4   Perfectly Inelastic Supply

What is the elasticity of supply of land within the borough limits of Manhattan?

Land in Manhattan sells in the market for a price, just like aluminum or corn or automobiles or any other product. And the demand for land in Manhattan is a downward-sloping function of its price. For all practical purposes, however, its supply is completely fixed. No matter whether its price is high or low, the same amount of it is available in the market. The supply curve of such a good is vertical, and its price elasticity is zero at every price. Supply curves like the one shown in Figure 4.16 are said to be **perfectly inelastic**.

perfectly inelastic supply supply is perfectly inelastic with respect to price if elasticity is zero

FIGURE 4.16

A Perfectly Inelastic Supply Curve.

Price elasticity of supply is zero at every point along a vertical supply curve.

EXAMPLE 4.5

Perfectly Elastic Supply

What is the elasticity of supply of lemonade?

Suppose that the ingredients required to bring a cup of lemonade to market and their respective costs are as follows.

Paper cup	2.0 cents
Lemon	3.8 cents
Sugar	2.0 cents
Water	0.2 cent
Ice	1.0 cent
Labor (30 seconds @ $6/hour)	5.0 cents

If these proportions remain the same no matter how many cups of lemonade are made, and the inputs can be purchased in any quantities at the stated prices, draw the supply curve of lemonade and compute its price elasticity.

Since each cup of lemonade costs exactly 14 cents to make, no matter how many cups are made, the marginal cost of lemonade is constant at 14 cents per cup. And since each point on a supply curve is equal to marginal cost (see Chapter 3, *Supply and Demand*), this means that the supply curve of lemonade is not upward-sloping but is instead a horizontal line at 14 cents per cup (Figure 4.17). The price elasticity of supply of lemonade is infinite.

FIGURE 4.17

A Perfectly Elastic Supply Curve.

The elasticity of supply is infinite at every point along a horizontal supply curve.

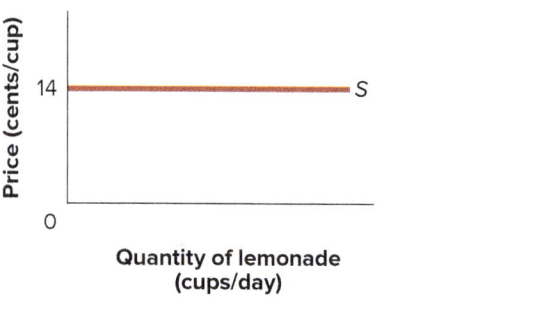

perfectly elastic supply
supply is perfectly elastic with respect to price if elasticity of supply is infinite

Whenever additional units of a good can be produced by using the same combination of inputs, purchased at the same prices, as have been used so far, the supply curve of that good will be horizontal. Such supply curves are said to be **perfectly elastic**.

DETERMINANTS OF SUPPLY ELASTICITY

The two preceding examples suggest some of the factors that govern the elasticity of supply of a good or service. The lemonade case was one whose production process was essentially like a cooking recipe. For such cases, we can exactly double our output by doubling each ingredient. If the price of each ingredient remains fixed, the marginal cost of production for such goods will be constant—and hence their horizontal supply curves.

The Manhattan land example is a contrast in the extreme. The inputs that were used to produce land in Manhattan—even if we knew what they were—could not be duplicated at any price.

The key to predicting how elastic the supply of a good will be with respect to price is to know the terms on which additional units of the inputs involved in producing that good can be acquired. In general, the more easily additional units of these inputs can be acquired, the higher price elasticity of supply will be. The following factors (among others) govern the ease with which additional inputs can be acquired by a producer.

Flexibility of Inputs

To the extent that production of a good requires inputs that are also useful for the production of other goods, it is relatively easy to lure additional inputs away from their current uses, making supply of that good relatively elastic with respect to price. Thus the fact that lemonade production requires labor with only minimal skills means that a large pool of workers could shift from other activities to lemonade production if a profitable opportunity arose. Brain surgery, by contrast, requires elaborately trained and specialized labor, which means that even a large price increase would not increase available supplies, except in the very long run.

Mobility of Inputs

If inputs can be easily transported from one site to another, an increase in the price of a product in one market will enable a producer in that market to summon inputs from other markets. For example, the supply of agricultural products is made more elastic with respect to price by the fact that thousands farmworkers are willing to migrate northward during the growing season. The supply of entertainment is similarly made more elastic by the willingness of entertainers to hit the road. Cirque performers, lounge singers, comedians, and dancers often spend a substantial fraction of their time away from home.

For most goods, the price elasticity of supply increases each time a new highway is built, or when the telecommunications network improves, or indeed when any other development makes it easier to find and transport inputs from one place to another.

Ability to Produce Substitute Inputs

The inputs required to produce finished diamond gemstones include raw diamond crystal, skilled labor, and elaborate cutting and polishing machinery. In time, the number of people with the requisite skills can be increased, as can the amount of specialized machinery. The number of raw diamond crystals buried in the earth is probably fixed in the same way that Manhattan land is fixed, but unlike Manhattan land, rising prices will encourage miners to spend the effort required to find a larger proportion of those crystals. Still, the supply of natural gemstone diamonds tends to be relatively inelastic because of the difficulty of augmenting the number of diamond crystals.

The day is close at hand, however, when gemstone makers will be able to produce synthetic diamond crystals that are indistinguishable from real ones. Indeed, there are already synthetic crystals that fool even highly experienced jewelers. The introduction of a perfect synthetic substitute for natural diamond crystals would increase the price elasticity of supply of diamonds (or, at any rate, the price elasticity of supply of gemstones that look and feel just like diamonds).

Time

Because it takes time for producers to switch from one activity to another, and because it takes time to build new machines and factories and train additional skilled workers, the price elasticity of supply will be higher for most goods in the long run than in the short run. In the short run, a manufacturer's inability to augment existing stocks of equipment and skilled labor may make it impossible to expand output beyond a certain limit. But if a shortage of managers was the bottleneck, new MBAs can be trained in only two years. Or if a shortage of legal staff is the problem, new lawyers can be trained in three years.

In the long run, firms can always buy new equipment, build new factories, and hire additional skilled workers.

The conditions that gave rise to the perfectly elastic supply curve for lemonade in the example we discussed earlier are satisfied for many other products in the long run. If a product can be copied (in the sense that any company can acquire the design and other technological information required to produce it), and if the inputs needed for its production are used in roughly fixed proportions and are available at fixed market prices, then the long-run supply curve for that product will be horizontal. But many products do not satisfy these conditions, and their supply curves remain steeply upward-sloping, even in the very long run.

The Economic Naturalist 4.3

Why are gasoline prices so much more volatile than car prices?

Automobile price changes in the United States usually occur just once a year, when manufacturers announce an increase of only a few percentage points. In contrast, gasoline prices often fluctuate wildly from day to day. As shown in Figure 4.18, for example, the highest daily gasoline prices in California's two largest cities were three times higher than the lowest daily prices in 2001 and early 2002. Why this enormous difference in volatility?

FIGURE 4.18

Gasoline Prices in Two California Cities.

Source: Oil Price Information Service, www.opisnet.com.

With respect to price volatility, at least two important features distinguish the gasoline market from the market for cars. One is that the short-run price elasticity of demand for gasoline is much smaller than the corresponding elasticity for cars. The other is that supply shifts are much more pronounced and frequent in the gasoline market than in the car market. (See Figure 4.19.)

Why are the two markets different in these ways? Consider first the difference in price elasticities of demand. The quantity of gasoline we demand

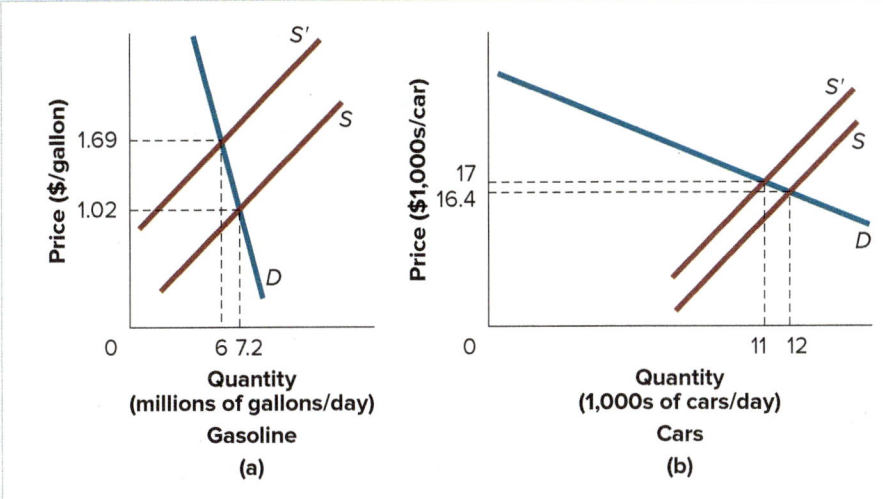

FIGURE 4.19

Greater Volatility in Gasoline Prices Than in Car Prices. Gasoline prices are more volatile because supply shifts are larger and more frequent in the gasoline market (a) than in the car market (b) and also because supply and demand are less elastic in the short run in the gasoline market.

depends largely on the kinds of cars we own and the amounts we drive them. In the short run, car ownership and commuting patterns are almost completely fixed, so even if the price of gasoline were to change sharply, the quantity we demand would not change by much. In contrast, if there were a sudden dramatic change in the price of cars, we could always postpone or accelerate our next car purchases.

To see why the supply curve in the gasoline market experiences larger and more frequent shifts than the supply curve in the car market, we need only examine the relative stability of the inputs employed by sellers in these two markets. Most of the inputs used in producing cars—steel, glass, rubber, plastics, electronic components, labor, and others—are reliably available to carmakers. In contrast, the key input used in making gasoline—crude oil—is subject to profound and unpredictable supply interruptions.

This is so in part because much of the world's supply of crude oil is controlled by the Organization of the Petroleum Exporting Countries (OPEC), which has sharply curtailed its oil shipments to the United States on several previous occasions. Even in the absence of formal OPEC action, however, large supply curtailments often occur in the oil market—for example, whenever producers fear that political instability might engulf the major oil-producing countries of the Middle East.

Note in Figure 4.18 the sharp spike in gasoline prices that occurred just after the terrorist attacks on the World Trade Center and Pentagon on September 11, 2001. Because many believed that the aim of these attacks was to provoke large-scale war between Muslim societies and the West, fears of an impending oil supply interruption were perfectly rational. Similar oil price spikes occurred in the early months of 2011, when political upheaval in several Middle Eastern countries threatened to disrupt oil supplies. Such fears alone can trigger a temporary supply interruption, even if war is avoided. The prospect of war creates the expectation of oil supply cutbacks that would cause higher prices in the future, which leads producers to withdraw some of their oil from current markets (in order to sell it at higher prices later). But once the fear of war recedes, the supply curve of gasoline reverts with equal speed to its earlier position. Given the low short-run price elasticity of demand for gasoline, that's all it takes to generate the considerable price volatility we see in this market.

Why are gasoline prices so much less stable than automobile prices?

Price volatility is also common in markets in which demand curves fluctuate sharply and supply curves are highly inelastic. One such market was California's unregulated market for wholesale electricity during the summer of 2000. The supply of electrical generating capacity was essentially fixed in the short run. And because air-conditioning accounts for a large share of demand, several spells of unusually warm weather caused demand to shift sharply to the right. Price at one point reached more than four times its highest level from the previous summer.

UNIQUE AND ESSENTIAL INPUTS: THE ULTIMATE SUPPLY BOTTLENECK

Fans of professional basketball are an enthusiastic bunch. Directly through their purchases of tickets and indirectly through their support of television advertisers, they spend literally billions of dollars each year on the sport. But these dollars are not distributed evenly across all teams. A disproportionate share of all revenues and product endorsement fees accrues to the people associated with consistently winning teams, and at the top of this pyramid generally stands the National Basketball Association's championship team.

Consider the task of trying to produce a championship team in the NBA. You would need inputs such as talented players, a shrewd and dedicated coach and assistants, trainers, physicians, an arena, practice facilities, means for transporting players to away games, a marketing staff, and so on. And whereas some of these inputs can be acquired at reasonable prices in the marketplace, many others cannot. Indeed, the most important input of all—highly talented players—is in extremely limited supply. This is so because the very definition of talented player is inescapably relative—simply put, such a player is one who is better than most others.

Given the huge payoff that accrues to the NBA championship team, it is no surprise that the bidding for the most talented players has become so intense. If there were a long list of players with the potential to boost a team's winning percentage substantially, the Golden State Warriors wouldn't have agreed to pay Steph Curry a salary of more than $48 million a year. But, of course, the supply of such players is extremely limited. There are many hungry organizations that would like nothing better than to claim the NBA championship each year, yet no matter how much each is willing to spend, only one can succeed. The supply of NBA championship teams is perfectly inelastic with respect to price even in the very long run.

Sports champions are by no means the only important product whose supply elasticity is constrained by the inability to reproduce unique and essential inputs. In the movie industry, for example, although the supply of movies starring Dwayne Johnson is not perfectly inelastic, there are only so many films he can make each year. Because his films consistently generate huge box office revenues, scores of film producers want to sign him for their projects. But because there isn't enough of him to go around, his salary per film typically exceeds $20 million.

In the long run, unique and essential inputs are the only truly significant supply bottleneck. If it were not for the inability to duplicate the services of such inputs, most goods and services would have extremely high price elasticities of supply in the long run.

SUMMARY

- The price elasticity of demand is a measure of how strongly buyers respond to changes in price. It is the percentage change in quantity demanded that occurs in response to a 1 percent change in price. The demand for a good is called elastic with respect to price if the absolute value of its price elasticity is more than 1, inelastic if its price elasticity is less than 1, and unit elastic if its price elasticity is equal to 1. *(LO1)*

- Goods such as salt, which occupy only a small share of the typical consumer's budget and have few or no good substitutes, tend to have low price elasticity of demand. Goods like new cars of a particular make and model, which occupy large budget shares and have many attractive substitutes, tend to have high price elasticity of demand. Price elasticity of demand is higher in the long run than in the short run because people often need time to adjust to price changes. *(LO1)*

- Long-run responses to price changes are shaped not only by individuals acting in isolation, but also by broader social and cultural forces. Elasticity estimates based on models that incorporate social contagion are substantially higher than those based on models that ignore it. *(LO2)*

- The price elasticity of demand at a point along a demand curve also can be expressed as the formula $\in = (\Delta Q/Q)/(\Delta P/P)$. Here, P and Q represent price and quantity at that point and ΔP and ΔQ represent small changes in price and quantity. For straight-line demand curves, this formula can also be expressed as $\in = (P/Q) \times (1/slope)$. These formulations tell us that price elasticity declines in absolute terms as we move down a straight-line demand curve. *(LO3)*

- A cut in price will increase total spending on a good if demand is elastic but reduce it if demand is inelastic. An increase in price will increase total spending on a good if demand is inelastic but reduce it if demand is elastic. Total expenditure on a good reaches a maximum when price elasticity of demand is equal to 1. *(LO4)*

- Analogous formulas are used to define the elasticity of demand for a good with respect to income and the prices of other goods. In each case, elasticity is the percentage change in quantity demanded divided by the corresponding percentage change in income or price. *(LO5)*

- Price elasticity of supply is defined as the percentage change in quantity supplied that occurs in response to a 1 percent change in price. The mathematical formula for the price elasticity of supply at any point is $(\Delta Q/Q)/(\Delta P/P)$, where P and Q are the price and quantity at that point, ΔP is a small change in the initial price, and ΔQ is the resulting change in quantity. This formula also can be expressed as $(P/Q) \times (1/slope)$, where $(1/slope)$ is the reciprocal of the slope of the supply curve. *(LO6)*

- The price elasticity of supply of a good depends on how difficult or costly it is to acquire additional units of the inputs involved in producing that good. In general, the more easily additional units of these inputs can be acquired, the higher price elasticity of supply will be. It is easier to expand production of a product if the inputs used to produce that product are similar to inputs used to produce other products, if inputs are relatively mobile, or if an acceptable substitute for existing inputs can be developed. And like the price elasticity of demand, the price elasticity of supply is greater in the long run than in the short run. *(LO6)*

KEY TERMS

cross-price elasticity of demand
elastic
income elasticity of demand
inelastic
perfectly elastic demand

perfectly elastic supply
perfectly inelastic demand
perfectly inelastic supply
price elasticity of demand
price elasticity of supply

social contagion
total expenditure (or total revenue)
unit elastic

REVIEW QUESTIONS

1. Why does a consumer's price elasticity of demand for a good depend on the fraction of the consumer's income spent on that good? *(LO1)*

2. Why does the price elasticity of demand for a good decline as we move down along a straight-line demand curve? *(LO3)*

3. Under what conditions will an increase in the price of a product lead to a reduction in total spending for that product? *(LO4)*

4. Why do economists pay little attention to the algebraic sign of the elasticity of demand for a good with respect to its own price, yet pay careful attention to the algebraic sign of the elasticity of demand for a good with respect to another good's price? *(LO5)*

5. Why is supply elasticity higher in the long run than in the short run? *(LO6)*

PROBLEMS

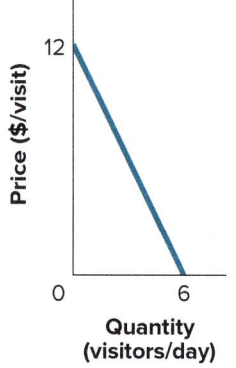

1. Is the demand for a particular brand of car, like a Chevrolet, likely to be more or less price-elastic than the demand for all cars? Explain. *(LO1)*

2. Imagine yourself the parent of a nonsmoking teenage daughter who's eligible to attend either of two high schools that are similar in every respect except one: The smoking rate is 80 percent at School A and only 10 percent at School B. If those who would become your daughter's close friends would be a random subset of the students at the school she attends, use the estimate from the study cited in Economic Naturalist 4.2 to compute how much more likely to become a smoker she would be if she attended School A? *(LO2)*

3. Calculate the price elasticity of demand (in absolute value) at points *A*, *B*, *C*, *D*, and *E* on the demand curve below. *(LO3)*

4. Suppose, while rummaging through your uncle's closet, you found the original painting of *Dogs Playing Poker*, a valuable piece of art. You decide to set up a display in your uncle's garage. The demand curve to see this valuable piece of art is as shown in the diagram. What price should you charge if your goal is to maximize your revenues from tickets sold? On a graph, show the inelastic and elastic regions of the demand curve. *(LO3, LO4)*

5. The schedule below shows the number of packs of bagels bought in Davis, California, each day at a variety of prices. *(LO3, LO4)*

Price of bagels ($/pack)	Number of packs purchased per day
6	0
5	3,000
4	6,000
3	9,000
2	12,000
1	15,000
0	18,000

a. Graph the daily demand curve for packs of bagels in Davis.

b. Calculate the price elasticity of demand at the point on the demand curve at which the price of bagels is $4 per pack.

c. If all bagel shops increased the price of bagels from $4 per pack to $5 per pack, what would happen to total revenues?

d. Calculate the price elasticity of demand at a point on the demand curve where the price of bagels is $1 per pack.

e. If bagel shops increased the price of bagels from $1 per pack to $2 per pack, what would happen to total revenues?

6.* At point *A* on the demand curve shown, by what percentage will a 1 percent increase in the price of the product affect total expenditure on the product? *(LO4)*

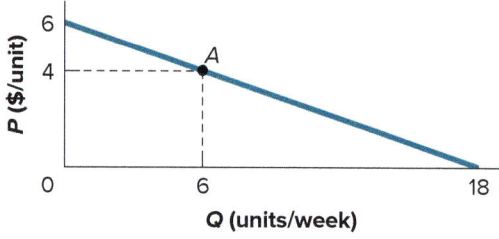

7.* Suppose that, in an attempt to induce citizens to conserve energy, the government enacted regulations requiring that all air conditioners be more efficient in their use of electricity. After this regulation was implemented, government officials were then surprised to discover that people used even more electricity than before. Using the concept of price elasticity, explain how this increase might have occurred. *(LO1)*

*Denotes more difficult problem.

8. A 2 percent increase in the price of milk causes a 4 percent reduction in the quantity demanded of chocolate syrup. What is the cross-price elasticity of demand for chocolate syrup with respect to the price of milk? Are the two goods complements or substitutes? *(LO5)*

9. What are the respective price elasticities of supply at *A* and *B* on the supply curve shown in the accompanying figure? *(LO6)*

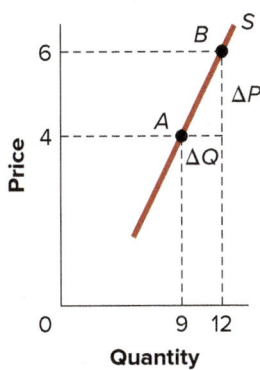

10. The price elasticity of supply for basmati rice (an aromatic strain of rice) is likely to be which of the following? *(LO6)*
    a. Higher in the long run than in the short run because farmers cannot easily change their decisions about how much basmati rice to plant once the crop has been planted.

b. High because consumers have many other kinds of rice and other staple foods to choose from.
c. Low in both the long run and the short run because rice farming requires only unskilled labor.
d. High in both the long run and the short run because the inputs required to produce basmati rice can easily be duplicated.

11. Suppose that the ingredients required to bring a slice of pizza to market and their respective costs are as listed in the table:

Paper plate	2 cents
Flour	8 cents
Tomato sauce	20 cents
Cheese	30 cents
Labor (3 minutes @ $12/hour)	60 cents

If these proportions remain the same no matter how many slices are made, and the inputs can be purchased in any quantities at the stated prices, draw the supply curve of pizza slices and compute its price elasticity. *(LO6)*

ANSWERS TO SELF-TESTS

4.1 In response to a 5 percent reduction in the price of ski passes, the quantity demanded increased by 20 percent. The price elasticity of demand for ski passes is thus (20 percent)/(5 percent) = 4, and that means that at the initial price of $400, the demand for ski passes is elastic with respect to price. *(LO1)*

4.2 At point *A* in the accompanying diagram, P/Q = 4/4 = 1. The slope of this demand curve is 20/5 = 4, so $\in$ = 1 × (1/slope) = 1/4. *(LO3)*

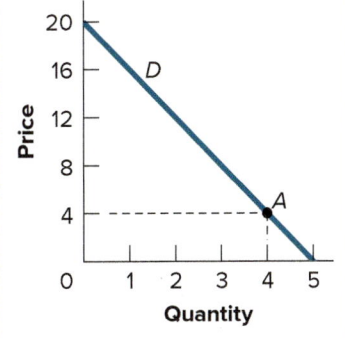

4.3 Income elasticity = Percentage change in quantity demanded/Percentage change in income = 5 percent/10 percent = 0.5. *(LO5)*

4.4 For the supply curve below, Q = 1 when P = 6, so elasticity of supply = $(P/Q) \times (1/\text{slope})$ = (6) × (1/2) = 3. *(LO6)*

The Midpoint Formula

Suppose you encounter a question like the following on a standardized test in economics:

> At a price of 3, quantity demanded of a good is 6, while at a price of 4, quantity demanded is 4. What is the price elasticity of demand for this good?

Let's attempt to answer this question by using the formula $\in = (\Delta Q/Q)/(\Delta P/P)$. In Figure 4A.1, we first plot the two price-quantity pairs given in the question and then draw the straight-line demand curve that connects them. From the graph, it is clear that $\Delta P = 1$ and $\Delta Q = 2$. But what values do we use for P and Q? If we use $P = 4$ and $Q = 4$ (point A), we get an elasticity of 2. But if we use $P = 3$ and $Q = 6$ (point B), we get an elasticity of 1. Thus, if we reckon price and quantity changes as proportions of their values at point A we get one answer, but if we compute them as proportions of their values at point B we get another. Neither of these answers is incorrect. The fact that they differ is merely a reflection of the fact that the elasticity of demand differs at every point along a straight-line demand curve.

FIGURE 4A.1

Two Points on a Demand Curve.

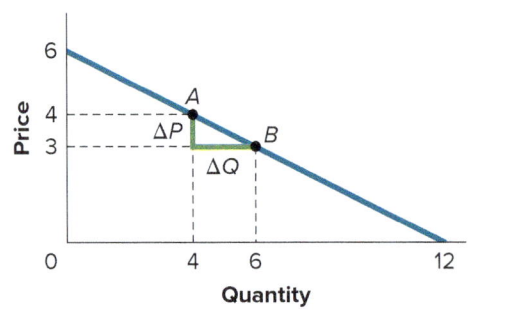

Strictly speaking, the original question ("What is the price elasticity of demand for this good?") was not well posed. To have elicited a uniquely correct answer, it should have been "What is the price elasticity of demand at point A?" or "What is the price elasticity of demand at point B?" Economists have nonetheless developed a convention, which we call the *midpoint formula*, for answering ambiguous questions like the one originally posed. If the two points in question are (Q_A, P_A) and (Q_B, P_B), this formula is given by

$$\in = \frac{\Delta Q/[(Q_A + Q_B)/2]}{\Delta P/[(P_A + P_B)/2]}. \tag{4A.1}$$

The midpoint formula thus sidesteps the question of which price–quantity pair to use by using averages of the new and old values. The formula reduces to

$$\in = \frac{\Delta Q/(Q_A + Q_B)}{\Delta P/(P_A + P_B)}. \tag{4A.2}$$

For the two points shown in Figure 4A.1, the midpoint formula yields $\in = [2/(4 + 6)]/[1/(4 + 3)] = 1.4$, which lies between the values for price elasticity at A and B.

We will not employ the midpoint formula again in this text. Hereafter, all questions concerning elasticity will employ the measure discussed in the text of this chapter, which is called *point elasticity*.

CHAPTER 5

Demand

Because of changes in the distribution of income, demand for premium wines has surged, while demand for low-priced wines has declined.

LEARNING OBJECTIVES

After reading this chapter, you should be able to:

LO1 Relate the law of demand to the *Cost-Benefit Principle*.

LO2 Discuss how individual wants are translated into demand using utility maximization.

LO3 Explain the reasoning behind the rational spending rule and apply it to consumer decision making to show how the rule is related to substitution and income effects.

LO4 Discuss the relationship between the individual demand curve and the market demand curve.

LO5 Define and calculate consumer surplus.

On the northern border of a large university in the East, a creek widens to form a picturesque lake, fondly remembered by generations of alumni as a popular recreation spot. Over the years, the lake had gradually silted in, and by the late 1980s, even paddling a canoe across it had become impossible. A generous alumnus then sponsored an effort to restore the lake. Heavy dredging equipment hauled out load after load of mud, and months later the lake was silt-free.

To mark the occasion, the university held a ceremony. Bands played, the president spoke, a chorus sang, and distinguished visitors applauded the donor's generosity. Hundreds of faculty and students turned out for the festivities. Spotting a good opportunity to promote their product, the proprietors of a local ice cream store set up a temporary stand at the water's edge, with a large sign: "Free Ice Cream."

Word spread. Soon scores of people were lined up waiting to try Vanilla Almond Delight, Hazelnut Cream, and Fudge Faire. The ice cream was plentiful, and because it was free, everyone could obviously afford it—or so it seemed. In fact, many people who wanted ice cream that day never got any. The reason, of course, was that they found waiting in a long line too steep a price to pay.

When a good or service is scarce, it must somehow be rationed among competing users. In most markets, monetary prices perform that task. But in the case of a stand offering free ice cream, waiting time becomes the effective rationing device. Having to stand in line is a cost, no less so than having to part with some money.

This example drives home the point that although the demand curve is usually described as a relationship between the quantity demanded of a good and its monetary price, the relationship is really a much more general one. At bottom, the demand curve is a relationship between the quantity demanded and *all* costs—monetary and nonmonetary—associated with acquiring a good.

law of demand people do less of what they want to do as the cost of doing it rises

Our task in this chapter will be to explore the demand side of the market in greater depth than was possible in Chapter 3, *Supply and Demand*. There we merely asked you to accept as an intuitively plausible claim that the quantity demanded of a good or service declines as its price rises. This relationship is known as the **law of demand**, and we'll see how it emerges as a simple consequence of the assumption that people spend their limited incomes in rational ways. In the process, we'll see more clearly the dual roles of income and substitution as factors that account for the law of demand. We'll also see how to generate market demand curves by adding the demand curves for individual buyers horizontally. Finally, we'll see how to use the demand curve to generate a measure of the total benefit that buyers reap from their participation in a market.

THE LAW OF DEMAND

With our discussion of the free ice cream offer in mind, let us restate the law of demand as follows:

Law of Demand: People do less of what they want to do as the cost of doing it rises.

By stating the law of demand this way, we can see it as a direct consequence of the Cost-Benefit Principle, which says that an activity should be pursued if (and only if) its benefits are at least as great as its costs. Recall that we measure the benefit of an activity by the highest price we'd be willing to pay to pursue it—namely, our reservation price for the activity. When the cost of an activity rises, it's more likely to exceed our reservation price, and we're therefore less likely to pursue that activity.

The law of demand applies to BMWs, cheap key rings, and "free" ice cream, not to mention manicures, medical care, and acid-free rain. It stresses that a "cost" is the sum of *all* the sacrifices—monetary and nonmonetary, implicit and explicit—we must make to engage in an activity.

THE ORIGINS OF DEMAND

How much are you willing to pay for the latest Beyoncé album? The answer will clearly depend on how you feel about her music. To her diehard fans, buying the new release might seem absolutely essential; they'd pay a steep price indeed. But those who don't like her music may be unwilling to buy it at any price.

Wants (also called "preferences" or "tastes") are clearly an important determinant of a consumer's reservation price for a good. But that raises the question of where wants come from. Many tastes—such as the taste for water on a hot day or for a comfortable place to sleep at night—are largely biological in origin. But many others are heavily shaped by culture, and even basic cravings may be socially molded. For example, people raised in southern India develop a taste for hot curry dishes, while those raised in France generally prefer milder foods.

Tastes for some items may remain stable for many years, but tastes for others may be highly volatile. Although books about the *Titanic* disaster have been continuously available since the vessel sank in spring 1912, not until the appearance of James Cameron's blockbuster film did these books begin to sell in large quantities. In spring 1998, 5 of the 15 books on *The New York Times* paperback bestseller list were about the *Titanic* itself or one of the actors in the film. Yet none of these books, or any other book about the *Titanic*, has made the bestseller list in the years since then. Still, echoes of the film continue to reverberate in the marketplace. In the years since its release, for example, demand for ocean cruises has grown sharply, and several television networks have introduced shows set on cruise ships.

Peer influence provides another example of how social forces often influence demand. Indeed, it is often the most important single determinant of demand. For instance, if our goal is to predict whether a young man will purchase an illegal recreational drug, knowing how much income he has is not very helpful. Knowing the prices of whiskey and other legal substitutes for illicit drugs also tells us little. Although these factors do influence purchase decisions, by themselves they are weak predictors. But if we know that most of the young man's best friends are heavy drug users, there's a reasonably good chance that he'll use drugs as well.

Another important way in which social forces shape demand is in the relatively common desire to consume goods and services that are recognized as the best of their kind. For instance, many people want to see LeBron James play basketball not just because of his skills on the court, but because he is widely regarded as one of the best basketball players of all time.

Consider, too, the decision of how much to spend on an interview suit. Employment counselors never tire of reminding us that making a good first impression is extremely important when you go for a job interview. At the very least, that means showing up in a suit that looks good. But looking good is a relative concept. If everyone else shows up in a $200 suit, you'll look good if you show up in a $300 suit. But you won't look as good in that same $300 suit if everyone else shows up in suits costing $1,000. The amount you'll choose to spend on an interview suit, then, clearly depends on how much others in your circle are spending.

NEEDS VERSUS WANTS

In everyday language, we distinguish between goods and services people need and those they merely want. For example, we might say that someone wants a ski vacation in Utah, but what he really needs is a few days off from his daily routine; or that someone wants a house with a view, but what she really needs is shelter from the elements. Likewise, because people need protein to survive, we might say that a severely malnourished person needs more protein. But it would strike us as odd to say that anyone—even a malnourished person—needs more prime filet of beef because health can be restored by consuming far less expensive sources of protein.

Economists like to emphasize that once we have achieved bare subsistence levels of consumption—the amount of food, shelter, and clothing required to maintain our health—we can abandon all reference to needs and speak only in terms of wants. This linguistic distinction helps us think more clearly about the true nature of our choices.

For instance, someone who says, "Californians don't have nearly as much water as they need" will tend to think differently about water shortages than someone who says, "Californians don't have nearly as much water as they want when the price of water is low." The first person is likely to focus on regulations to prevent people from watering their lawns, or on projects to capture additional runoff from the Sierra Nevada. The second person is more likely to focus on the artificially low price of water in California. Whereas remedies of the first sort are often costly and extremely difficult to implement, raising the price of water is both simple and effective.

The Economic Naturalist 5.1

Why does California experience chronic water shortages?

Some might respond that the state must serve the needs of a large population with a relatively low average annual rainfall. Yet other states, like New Mexico, have even less rainfall per person and do not experience water shortages nearly as often as California. California's problem exists because local governments sell water at extremely low prices, which encourages Californians to use water in ways

Why do farmers grow water-intensive crops like rice in an arid state like California?

that make no sense for a state with low rainfall. For instance, rice, which is well suited for conditions in high-rainfall states like South Carolina, requires extensive irrigation in California. But because California farmers can obtain water so cheaply, they plant and flood hundreds of thousands of acres of rice paddies each spring in the Central Valley. Two thousand tons of water are needed to produce one ton of rice, but many other grains can be produced with only half that amount. If the price of California water were higher, farmers would simply switch to other grains.

Likewise, cheap water encourages homeowners in Los Angeles and San Diego to plant water-intensive lawns and shrubs, like the ones common in the East and Midwest. By contrast, residents of cities like Santa Fe, New Mexico, where water prices are high, choose native plantings that require little or no watering.

TRANSLATING WANTS INTO DEMAND

It's a simple fact of life that although our resources are finite, our appetites for good things are boundless. Even if we had unlimited bank accounts, we'd quickly run out of the time and energy needed to do all the things we wanted to do. Our challenge is to use our limited resources to fulfill our desires to the greatest possible degree. That leaves us with a practical question: How should we allocate our incomes among the various goods and services that are available? To answer this question, it's helpful to begin by recognizing that the goods and services we buy are not ends in themselves, but rather means for satisfying our desires.

MEASURING WANTS: THE CONCEPT OF UTILITY

Economists use the concept of *utility* to represent the satisfaction people derive from their consumption activities. The assumption is that people try to allocate their incomes so as to maximize their satisfaction, a goal that is referred to as *utility maximization*.

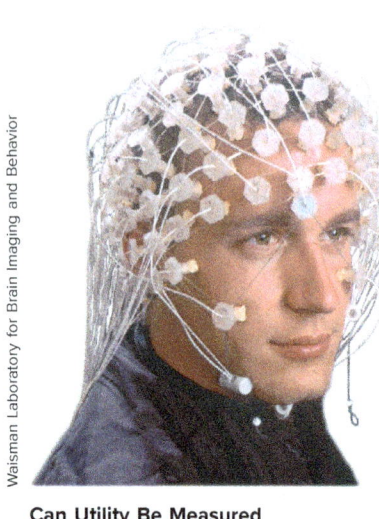

Waisman Laboratory for Brain Imaging and Behavior

Can Utility Be Measured Electronically?

Scientists have shown that higher levels of electrical activity on the brain's left side are strongly associated with higher levels of satisfaction.

Early economists imagined that the utility associated with different activities might someday be subject to precise measurement. The nineteenth-century British economist Jeremy Bentham, for example, wrote of a "utilometer," a device that could be used to measure the amount of utility provided by different consumption activities. Although no such device existed in Bentham's day, contemporary neuropsychologists now have equipment that can generate at least crude measures of satisfaction.

The accompanying photo, for example, shows a subject who is connected to an apparatus that measures the intensity of electrical waves emanating from different parts of his brain. University of Wisconsin psychologist Richard Davidson and his colleagues documented that subjects with relatively heavy brain-wave measures emanating from the left prefrontal cortex tend to be happier (as assessed by a variety of other measures) than subjects with relatively heavy brain-wave measures emanating from the right prefrontal cortex.

Jeremy Bentham would have been thrilled to learn that a device like the one pictured here might exist someday. His ideal utilometer would measure utility in utils, much as a thermometer measures temperature in degrees Fahrenheit or Celsius. It would assign a numerical utility value to every activity—watching a movie, eating a cheeseburger, and so on. Unfortunately, even sophisticated devices are far from capable of such fine-grained assessments.

For Bentham's intellectual enterprise, however, the absence of a real utilometer was of no practical significance. Even without such a machine, he could continue to envision the consumer as someone whose goal was to maximize the total utility she obtained from the goods she consumed. Bentham's "utility maximization model," as we'll see, affords important insights about how a rational consumer ought to spend her income.

To explore how the model works, we begin with a very simple problem, the one facing a consumer who reaches the front of the line at a free ice cream stand. How many cones of ice cream should this person, whom we'll call Sarah, ask for? Table 5.1 shows the relationship between the total number of ice cream cones Sarah eats per hour and the total utility, measured in utils per hour, she derives from them. Note that the measurements in the table are stated in terms of cones per hour and utils per hour. Why "per hour"? Because without an explicit time dimension, we would have no idea whether a given quantity was a lot or a little. Five ice cream cones in a lifetime isn't much, but five in an hour would be more than most of us would care to eat.

TABLE 5.1
Sarah's Total Utility from Ice Cream Consumption

Cone quantity (cones/hour)	Total utility (utils/hour)
0	0
1	50
2	90
3	120
4	140
5	150
6	140

As the entries in Table 5.1 show, Sarah's total utility increases with each cone she eats, up to the fifth cone. Eating five cones per hour makes her happier than eating four, which makes her happier than eating three, and so on. But beyond five cones per hour, consuming more ice cream actually makes Sarah less happy. Thus, the sixth cone reduces her total utility from 150 utils per hour to 140 utils per hour.

We can display the utility information in Table 5.1 graphically, as in Figure 5.1. Note in the graph that the more cones per hour Sarah eats, the more utils she gets—but again only up to the fifth cone. Once she moves beyond five, her total utility begins to decline. Sarah's happiness reaches a maximum of 150 utils when she eats five cones per hour. At that point she has no incentive to eat the sixth cone, even though it's absolutely free. Eating it would actually make her worse off.

Table 5.1 and Figure 5.1 illustrate another important aspect of the relationship between utility and consumption—namely, that the additional utility from additional units of consumption declines as total consumption increases. Thus, whereas one cone per hour is a *lot* better—by 50 utils—than zero, five cones per hour is just a *little* better than four (just 10 utils' worth).

FIGURE 5.1

Sarah's Total Utility from Ice Cream Consumption.

For most goods, utility rises at a diminishing rate with additional consumption.

TABLE 5.2
Sarah's Total and Marginal Utility from Ice Cream Consumption

Cone quantity (cones/hour)	Total utility (utils/hour)	Marginal utility (utils/cone)
0	0	—
		50
1	50	
		40
2	90	
		30
3	120	
		20
4	140	
		10
5	150	
		−10
6	140	

$$\text{Marginal utility} = \frac{\text{Change in utility}}{\text{Change in consumption}}$$

$$= \frac{90 \text{ utils} - 50 \text{ utils}}{2 \text{ cones} - 1 \text{ cone}}$$

$$= 40 \text{ utils/cone}$$

marginal utility the additional utility gained from consuming an additional unit of a good

    The term **marginal utility** denotes the amount by which total utility changes when consumption changes by one unit. In Table 5.2, the third column shows the marginal utility values that correspond to changes in Sarah's level of ice cream consumption. For example, the second entry in that column represents the increase in total utility (measured in utils per cone) when Sarah's consumption rises from one cone per hour to two. Note that the marginal utility entries in the third column are placed midway between the rows of the preceding columns. We do this to indicate that marginal utility corresponds to the movement from one consumption quantity to the next. Thus, we'd say that the marginal utility of moving from one to two cones per hour is 40 utils per cone.

    Because marginal utility is the change in utility that occurs as we move from one quantity to another, when we graph marginal utility, we normally adopt the convention of plotting each specific marginal utility value halfway between the two quantities to which it corresponds. Thus, in Figure 5.2, we plot the marginal utility value of 40 utils per cone midway between one cone per hour and two cones per hour, and so on. (In this example, the marginal utility graph is a downward-sloping straight line for the region shown, but this need not always be the case.)

law of diminishing marginal utility the tendency for the additional utility gained from consuming an additional unit of a good to diminish as consumption increases beyond some point

    The tendency for marginal utility to decline as consumption increases beyond some point is called the **law of diminishing marginal utility**. It holds not just for Sarah's consumption of ice cream in this illustration, but also for most other goods for most consumers. If we have one brownie or one Ferrari, we're happier than we are with none; if we have two, we'll be even happier—but not twice as happy—and so on. Though this pattern is called a law, there are exceptions. Indeed, some consumption activities even seem to exhibit *increasing* marginal utility. For example, an unfamiliar song may seem irritating the first time you hear it, but then gradually become more tolerable the next few times you hear it. Before long, you may discover that you *like* the song, and you may even find yourself singing it in the shower. Notwithstanding such exceptions, the law of diminishing marginal utility is a plausible characterization of the relationship between utility and consumption for many goods. Unless otherwise stated, we'll assume that it holds for the various goods we discuss.

    What will Sarah do when she gets to the front of the line? At that point, the opportunity cost of the time she spent waiting is a sunk cost and is hence irrelevant to her decision about how many cones to order. And since there is no monetary charge for the cones, the cost of ordering an additional one is zero. According to the Cost-Benefit

Cost-Benefit

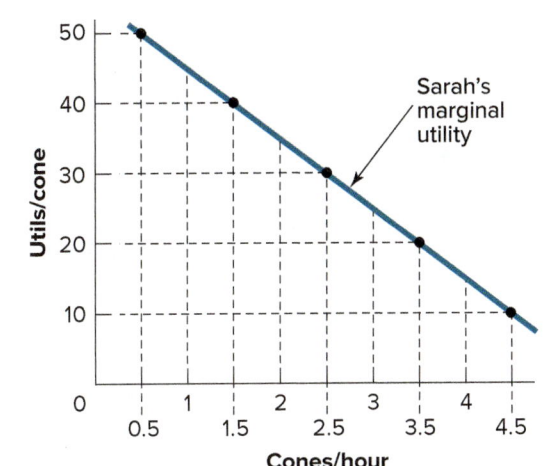

FIGURE 5.2
Diminishing Marginal Utility.
The more cones Sarah consumes each hour, the smaller her marginal utility will be. For Sarah, consumption of ice cream cones satisfies the law of diminishing marginal utility.

Principle, Sarah should therefore continue to order cones as long as the marginal benefit (here, the marginal utility she gets from an additional cone) is greater than or equal to zero. As we can see from the entries in Table 5.2, marginal utility is positive up to and including the fifth cone but becomes negative after five cones. Thus, as noted earlier, Sarah should order five cones.

ALLOCATING A FIXED INCOME BETWEEN TWO GOODS

Most of the time we face considerably more complex purchasing decisions than the one Sarah faced. For one thing, we generally must make decisions about many goods, not just a single one like ice cream. Another complication is that the cost of consuming additional units of each good will rarely be zero.

To see how to proceed in more complex cases, let's suppose Sarah must decide how to spend a fixed sum of money on two different goods, each with a positive price. Should she spend all of it on one of the goods or part of it on each? The law of diminishing marginal utility suggests that spending it all on a single good isn't a good strategy. Rather than devote more and more money to the purchase of a good we already consume in large quantities (and whose marginal utility is therefore relatively low), we generally do better to spend that money on other goods we don't have much of, whose marginal utility will likely be higher.

The simplest way to illustrate how economists think about the spending decisions of a utility-maximizing consumer is to work through a series of examples, beginning with the following.

EXAMPLE 5.1   **The Rational Spending Rule (Part 1)**

Is Sarah maximizing her utility from consuming chocolate and vanilla ice cream?

Chocolate ice cream sells for $2 per pint and vanilla sells for $1. Sarah has a budget of $400 per year to spend on ice cream, and her marginal utility from consuming each type varies with the amount consumed, as shown in Figure 5.3. If she is currently buying 200 pints of vanilla and 100 pints of chocolate each year, is she maximizing her utility?

Note first that with 200 pints per year of vanilla and 100 pints of chocolate, Sarah is spending $200 per year on each type of ice cream, for a total expenditure

FIGURE 5.3

Marginal Utility Curves for Two Flavors of Ice Cream (Part 1).

At Sarah's current consumption levels, her marginal utility of chocolate ice cream is 25 percent higher than her marginal utility of vanilla. But chocolate is twice as expensive as vanilla.

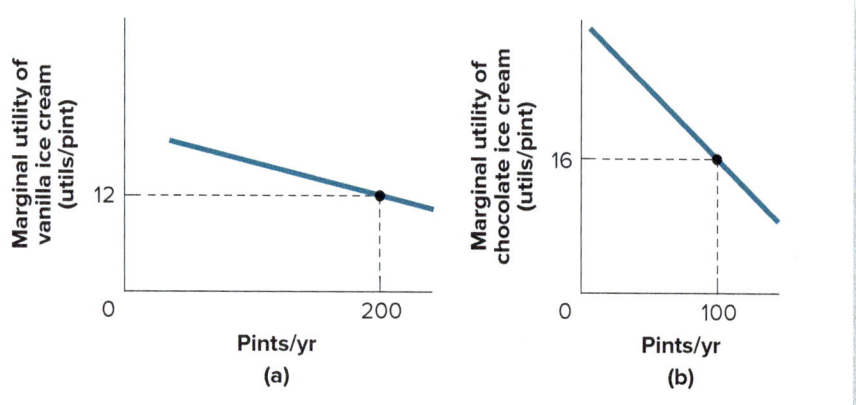

of $400 per year on ice cream, exactly the amount in her budget. By spending her money in this fashion, is she getting as much utility as possible? Note in Figure 5.3(b) that her marginal utility from chocolate ice cream is 16 utils per pint. Since chocolate costs $2 per pint, her current spending on chocolate is yielding additional utility at the rate of (16 utils/pint)/($2/pint) = 8 utils per dollar. Similarly, note in Figure 5.3(a) that Sarah's marginal utility for vanilla is 12 utils per pint. And since vanilla costs only $1 per pint, her current spending on vanilla is yielding (12 utils/pint)/($1/pint) = 12 utils per dollar. In other words, at her current rates of consumption of the two flavors, her spending yields higher marginal utility per dollar for vanilla than for chocolate. And this means that Sarah cannot possibly be maximizing her total utility.

To see why, note that if she spent $2 less on chocolate (that is, if she bought one pint less than before), she would lose about 16 utils;[1] but with the same $2, she could buy two additional pints of vanilla, which would boost her utility by about 24 utils,[2] for a net gain of about 8 utils. Under Sarah's current budget allocation, she is thus spending too little on vanilla and too much on chocolate.

In the next example, we'll see what happens if Sarah spends $100 per year less on chocolate and $100 per year more on vanilla.

EXAMPLE 5.2

The Rational Spending Rule (Part 2)

Is Sarah maximizing her utility from consuming chocolate and vanilla ice cream?

Sarah's total ice cream budget and the prices of the two flavors are the same as in the earlier example. If her marginal utility from consuming each type varies with the amount consumed, as shown in Figure 5.4, and if she's currently buying 300 pints of vanilla and 50 pints of chocolate each year, is she maximizing her utility?

[1]The actual reduction would be slightly larger than 16 utils because her marginal utility of chocolate rises slightly as she consumes less of it.
[2]The actual increase will be slightly smaller than 24 utils because her marginal utility of vanilla falls slightly as she buys more of it.

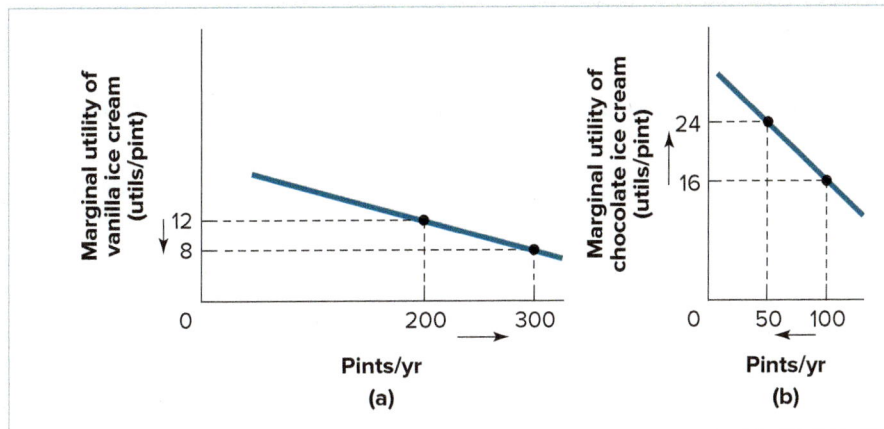

FIGURE 5.4

Marginal Utility Curves for Two Flavors of Ice Cream (Part 2).

When Sarah increases her consumption of vanilla (a), her marginal utility of vanilla falls. Conversely, when she reduces her consumption of chocolate (b), her marginal utility of chocolate rises.

Note first that the direction of Sarah's rearrangement of her spending makes sense in light of the original example, in which we saw that she was spending too much on chocolate and too little on vanilla. Spending $100 less on chocolate ice cream causes her marginal utility from that flavor to rise from 16 to 24 utils per pint [Figure 5.4(b)]. By the same token, spending $100 more on vanilla ice cream causes her marginal utility from that flavor to fall from 12 to 8 utils per pint [Figure 5.4(a)]. Both movements are a simple consequence of the law of diminishing marginal utility.

Since chocolate still costs $2 per pint, her spending on chocolate now yields additional utility at the rate of (24 utils/pint)/($2/pint) = 12 utils per dollar. Similarly, since vanilla still costs $1 per pint, her spending on vanilla now yields additional utility at the rate of only (8 utils/pint)/($1/pint) = 8 utils per dollar. So at her new rates of consumption of the two flavors, her spending yields higher marginal utility per dollar for chocolate than for vanilla—precisely the opposite of the ordering we saw in the original example.

Sarah has thus made too big an adjustment in her effort to remedy her original consumption imbalance. Starting from the new combination of flavors (300 pints per year of vanilla and 50 pints per year of chocolate), for example, if she then bought two fewer pints of vanilla (which would reduce her utility by about 16 utils) and used the $2 she saved to buy an additional pint of chocolate (which would boost her utility by about 24 utils), she would experience a net gain of about 8 utils. So, again, her current combination of the two flavors fails to maximize her total utility. This time, she is spending too little on chocolate and too much on vanilla.

 SELF-TEST 5.1

In the preceding examples, verify that the stated combination of flavors costs exactly the amount that Sarah has budgeted for ice cream.

What is Sarah's **optimal combination** of the two flavors? In other words, among all the combinations of vanilla and chocolate ice cream that Sarah can afford, which one provides the maximum possible total utility? The following example illustrates the condition that this optimal combination must satisfy.

optimal combination of goods the affordable combination that yields the highest total utility

EXAMPLE 5.3   The Rational Spending Rule (Part 3)

Is Sarah maximizing her utility from consuming chocolate and vanilla ice cream?

Sarah's total ice cream budget and the prices of the two flavors are the same as in the previous examples. If her marginal utility from consuming each type varies with the amounts consumed, as shown in Figure 5.5, and if she is currently buying 250 pints of vanilla and 75 pints of chocolate each year, is she maximizing her utility?

FIGURE 5.5

Marginal Utility Curves for Two Flavors of Ice Cream (Part 3).

At her current consumption levels, marginal utility per dollar is exactly the same for each flavor.

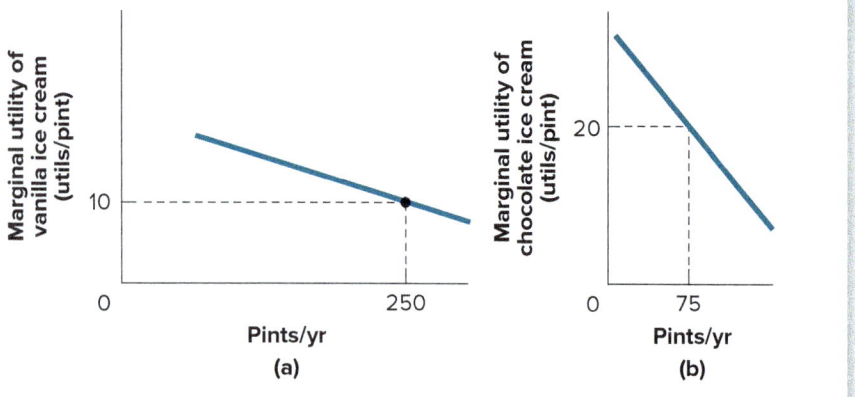

As you can easily verify, the combination of 250 pints per year of vanilla and 75 pints per year of chocolate again costs a total of $400, exactly the amount of Sarah's ice cream budget. Her marginal utility from chocolate is now 20 utils per pint [Figure 5.5(b)], and since chocolate still costs $2 per pint, her spending on chocolate now yields additional utility at the rate of (20 utils/pint)/($2/pint) = 10 utils per dollar. Sarah's marginal utility for vanilla is now 10 utils per pint [Figure 5.5(a)], and since vanilla still costs $1 per pint, her last dollar spent on vanilla now also yields (10 utils/pint)/($1/pint) = 10 utils per dollar. So at her new rates of consumption of the two flavors, her spending yields precisely the same marginal utility per dollar for each flavor. Thus, if she spent a little less on chocolate and a little more on vanilla (or vice versa), her total utility would not change at all. For example, if she bought two more pints of vanilla (which would increase her utility by 20 utils) and one fewer pint of chocolate (which would reduce her utility by 20 utils), both her total expenditure on ice cream and her total utility would remain the same as before. *When her marginal utility per dollar is the same for each flavor, it's impossible for Sarah to rearrange her spending to increase total utility.* Therefore, 250 pints of vanilla and 75 pints of chocolate per year form the optimal combination of the two flavors.

RECAP ↑

TRANSLATING WANTS INTO DEMAND

The Scarcity Principle challenges us to allocate our incomes among the various goods that are available so as to fulfill our desires to the greatest possible degree. The optimal combination of goods is the affordable combination that yields the highest total utility. For goods that are perfectly divisible, the rational spending rule tells us that the optimal combination is one for which the marginal utility per dollar is the same for each good. If this condition were not satisfied, the consumer could increase her utility by spending less on goods for which the marginal utility per dollar was lower and more on goods for which her marginal utility was higher.

Scarcity

THE RATIONAL SPENDING RULE

The examples we have worked through illustrate the **rational spending rule** for solving the problem of how to allocate a fixed budget across different goods. The optimal, or utility-maximizing, combination must satisfy this rule.

The Rational Spending Rule: Spending should be allocated across goods so that the marginal utility per dollar is the same for each good.

The rational spending rule can be expressed in the form of a simple formula. If we use MU_C to denote marginal utility from chocolate ice cream consumption (again measured in utils per pint) and P_C to denote the price of chocolate (measured in dollars per pint), then the ratio MU_C/P_C will represent the marginal utility per dollar spent on chocolate, measured in utils per dollar. Similarly, if we use MU_V to denote the marginal utility from vanilla ice cream consumption and P_V to denote the price of vanilla, then MU_V/P_V will represent the marginal utility per dollar spent on vanilla. The marginal utility per dollar will be exactly the same for the two types—and hence total utility will be maximized—when the following simple equation for the rational spending rule for two goods is satisfied

$$MU_C/P_C = MU_V/P_V.$$

The rational spending rule is easily generalized to apply to spending decisions regarding large numbers of goods. In its most general form, it says that the ratio of marginal utility to price must be the same for each good the consumer buys. If the ratio were higher for one good than for another, the consumer could always increase her total utility by buying more of the first good and less of the second.

Strictly speaking, the rational spending rule applies to goods that are perfectly divisible, such as milk or gasoline. Many other goods, such as bus rides and television sets, can be consumed only in whole-number amounts. In such cases, it may not be possible to satisfy the rational spending rule exactly. For example, when you buy one television set, your marginal utility per dollar spent on televisions may be somewhat higher than the corresponding ratio for other goods, yet if you bought a second set, the reverse might well be true. Your best alternative in such cases is to allocate each additional dollar you spend to the good for which your marginal utility per dollar is highest.

Notice that we have not chosen to classify the rational spending rule as one of the *Core Principles* of economics. We omit it from this list not because the rule is unimportant, but because it follows directly from the Cost-Benefit Principle. As we noted earlier, there is considerable advantage in keeping the list of Core Principles as small as possible.

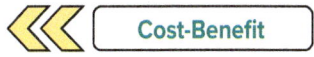

INCOME AND SUBSTITUTION EFFECTS REVISITED

In Chapter 3, *Supply and Demand*, we saw that the quantity of a good that consumers wish to purchase depends on its own price, on the prices of substitutes and complements, and on consumer incomes. We also saw that when the price of a good changes, the quantity of it demanded changes for two reasons: the substitution effect and the income effect. The substitution effect refers to the fact that when the price of a good goes up, substitutes for that good become relatively more attractive, causing some consumers to abandon the good for its substitutes.

The income effect refers to the fact that a price change makes the consumer either poorer or richer in real terms. Consider, for instance, the effect of a change in the price of one of the ice cream flavors in the preceding examples. At the original prices ($2 per pint for chocolate, $1 per pint for vanilla), Sarah's $400 annual ice cream budget enabled her to buy at most 200 pints per year of chocolate or 400 pints per year of vanilla. If the price of vanilla rose to $2 per pint, that would reduce not only the maximum amount of vanilla she could afford (from 400 to 200 pints per year), but also the maximum amount of chocolate she could afford in combination with any given amount of vanilla. For example, at the original price of $1 per pint for vanilla, Sarah could afford to buy 150 pints of chocolate while buying 100 pints of vanilla, but when the price of vanilla rises to $2, she can buy only

100 pints of chocolate while buying 100 pints of vanilla. As noted in Chapter 3, *Supply and Demand*, a reduction in real income shifts the demand curves for normal goods to the left.

The rational spending rule helps us see more clearly why a change in the price of one good affects demands for other goods. The rule requires that the ratio of marginal utility to price be the same for all goods. This means that if the price of one good goes up, the ratio of its current marginal utility to its new price will be lower than for other goods. Consumers can then increase their total utility by devoting smaller proportions of their incomes to that good and larger proportions to others.

EXAMPLE 5.4

Response to a Price Reduction

How should Sarah respond to a reduction in the price of chocolate ice cream?

Suppose that Sarah's total ice cream budget is still $400 per year and the prices of the two flavors are again $2 per pint for chocolate and $1 per pint for vanilla. Her marginal utility from consuming each type varies with the amounts consumed, as shown in Figure 5.6. As we showed in the previous example, she is currently buying 250 pints of vanilla and 75 pints of chocolate each year, which is the optimal combination for her at these prices. How should she reallocate her spending among the two flavors if the price of chocolate ice cream falls to $1 per pint?

FIGURE 5.6

Marginal Utility Curves for Two Flavors of Ice Cream (Part 4).

At the current combination of flavors, marginal utility per dollar is the same for each flavor. When the price of chocolate falls, marginal utility per dollar becomes higher for chocolate than for vanilla. To redress this imbalance, Sarah should buy more chocolate and less vanilla.

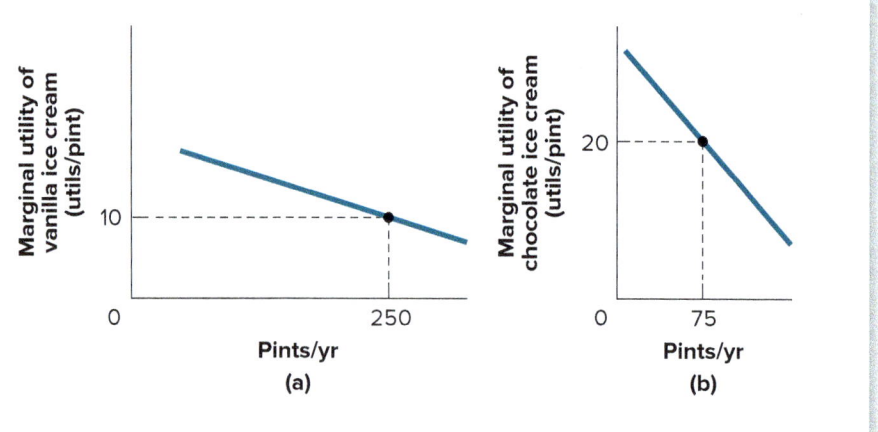

Because the quantities shown in Figure 5.6 constitute the optimal combination of the two flavors for Sarah at the original prices, they must exactly satisfy the rational spending rule:

$$MU_C/P_C = (20 \text{ utils/pint})/(\$2/\text{pint}) = 10 \text{ utils/dollar}$$
$$= MU_V/P_V = (10 \text{ utils/pint})/(\$1/\text{pint}).$$

When the price of chocolate falls to $1 per pint, the original quantities will no longer satisfy the rational spending rule because the marginal utility per dollar for chocolate will suddenly be twice what it was before:

$$MU_C/P_C = (20 \text{ utils/pint})/(\$1/\text{pint}) = 20 \text{ utils/dollar}$$
$$> MU_V/P_V = 10 \text{ utils/dollar}.$$

To redress this imbalance, Sarah must rearrange her spending on the two flavors in such a way as to increase the marginal utility per dollar for vanilla relative to the marginal utility per dollar for chocolate. And as we see in Figure 5.6, that will happen if she buys a larger quantity than before of chocolate and a smaller quantity than before of vanilla.

✔ **SELF-TEST 5.2**

John spends all of his income on two goods: food and shelter. The price of food is $5 per pound and the price of shelter is $10 per square yard. At his current consumption levels, his marginal utilities for the two goods are 20 utils per pound and 30 utils per square yard, respectively. Is John maximizing his utility? If not, how should he reallocate his spending?

In Chapter 1, *Thinking Like an Economist*, we saw that people often make bad decisions because they fail to appreciate the distinction between average and marginal costs and benefits. As the following example illustrates, this pitfall also arises when people attempt to apply the economist's model of utility maximization.

EXAMPLE 5.5   **Marginal vs. Average Utility**

Should Juan consume more apples?

Juan gets a total of 1,000 utils per week from his consumption of apples and a total of 400 utils per week from his consumption of oranges. The price of apples is $2 each, the price of oranges is $1 each, and he consumes 50 apples and 50 oranges each week. True or false: Juan should consume more apples and fewer oranges.

Juan spends $100 per week on apples and $50 on oranges. He thus averages (1,000 utils/week)/($100/week) = 10 utils per dollar from his consumption of apples and (400 utils/week)/($50/week) = 8 utils per dollar from his consumption of oranges. Many might be tempted to respond that because Juan's average utility per dollar for apples is higher than for oranges, he should consume more apples. But knowing only his *average* utility per dollar for each good doesn't enable us to say whether his current combination is optimal. To make that determination, we need to compare Juan's *marginal* utility per dollar for each good. The information given simply doesn't permit us to make that comparison.

APPLYING THE RATIONAL SPENDING RULE

The real payoff from learning the law of demand and the rational spending rule lies in using these abstract concepts to make sense of the world around you. To encourage you in your efforts to become an economic naturalist, we turn now to a sequence of Economic Naturalist examples in this vein.

Substitution at Work

In the first of these examples, we focus on the role of substitution. When the price of a good or service goes up, rational consumers generally turn to less expensive substitutes. Can't meet the payments on a new car? Then buy a used one, or rent an apartment on a bus or subway line. French restaurants too pricey? Then go out for Chinese, or eat at home more often. National Football League tickets too high? Watch the game on television, or read a book. Can't afford a book? Check one out of the library, or download some reading matter from the Internet. Once you begin to see substitution at work, you'll be amazed by the number and richness of the examples that confront you every day.

The Economic Naturalist 5.2

Why would Jeff Bezos live in a smaller house in Manhattan than in Medina, Washington?

Among his many residences, Amazon founder Jeff Bezos owns a 29,000-square-foot home in Medina, Washington. Bezos also owns a 20,000-square-foot apartment in Manhattan. Although both residences are enormous, Bezos's apartment in Manhattan is much smaller than his home in Medina. Bezos is one of the richest people in the world and could afford to buy an entire apartment building anywhere in Manhattan, so why would he buy a much smaller home there than Medina?

For people trying to decide how large a home to buy, the most obvious difference between Manhattan and Medina is the huge difference in housing prices. The cost of land alone is several times higher in Manhattan than in Medina, and construction costs are also much higher. So even though Bezos could *afford* to purchase a 29,000-square-foot home in Manhattan, housing prices are so high that he simply chooses to purchase a smaller home and spend his fortune in other ways.

But an even more important factor in Bezos's decision may have been the link between context and evaluation: A house seems small only if it is small relative to other houses in the same local environment. Because Manhattan prices are so high, others choose to build smaller houses there, too, so a 20,000-square-foot house in Manhattan is a larger dwelling, in relative terms, than a 29,000-square-foot house in Medina. The link between context and evaluation is closely related to the phenomenon of social contagion introduced in Chapter 4. We'll consider both in greater detail in Chapter 10, *An Introduction to Behavioral Economics*.

An especially vivid illustration of substitution occurred during the late 1970s, when fuel shortages brought on by interruptions in the supply of oil from the Middle East led to sharp increases in the price of gasoline and other fuels. In a variety of ways—some straightforward, others remarkably ingenious—consumers changed their behavior to economize on the use of energy. They formed car pools; switched to public transportation; bought four-cylinder cars; moved closer to work; took fewer trips; turned down their thermostats; installed insulation, storm windows, and solar heaters; and bought more efficient appliances. Many people even moved farther south to escape high winter heating bills.

As the next example points out, consumers not only abandon a good in favor of substitutes when it gets more expensive, but they also return to that good when prices return to their original levels.

The Economic Naturalist 5.3

Why did people turn to four-cylinder cars in the 1970s, only to shift back to six- and eight-cylinder cars in the 1990s?

In 1973, the price of gasoline was 38 cents per gallon. The following year the price shot up to 52 cents per gallon in the wake of a major disruption of oil supplies. A second disruption in 1979 drove the 1980 price to $1.19 per gallon. These sharp increases in the price of gasoline led to big increases in the demand for cars with four-cylinder engines, which delivered much better fuel economy than the six- and eight-cylinder cars most people had owned. After 1980, however, fuel supplies stabilized, and prices rose only slowly, reaching $1.40 per gallon by 1999. Yet despite the continued rise in the price of gasoline, the switch to smaller engines did not continue. By the late 1980s, the proportion of cars sold with six- and eight-cylinder engines began rising again. Why this reversal?

The key to explaining these patterns is to focus on changes in the **real price** of gasoline. When someone decides how big an automobile engine to choose, what matters is not the **nominal price** of gasoline, but the price of gasoline *relative* to all other goods. After all, for a consumer faced with a decision of whether to spend $1.40 for a gallon of gasoline, the important question is how much utility she could get from other things she could purchase with the same money. Even though the price of gasoline continued to rise slowly in nominal, or dollar, terms through the 1980s and 1990s, it declined sharply relative to the price of other goods. Indeed, in terms of real purchasing power, the 1999 price was actually slightly lower than the 1973 price. (That is, in 1999 $1.40 bought slightly fewer goods and services than 38 cents bought in 1973.) It is this decline in the real price of gasoline that accounts for the reversal of the trend toward smaller engines.

real price the dollar price of a good relative to the average dollar price of all other goods

nominal price the absolute price of a good in dollar terms

connect

▶ Visit your instructor's Connect course and access your eBook to view this video.

In 2004, gasoline prices yet again began to rise sharply in real terms, and by 2012, they had reached almost $5 per gallon in some parts of the country. Just as expected, the patterns of vehicle purchases began to shift almost immediately. Large SUVs, in high demand just months earlier, began selling at deep discounts. In 2006, Ford discontinued production of its largest SUV, the Excursion, followed shortly by General Motors' cancellation of its own biggest SUV, the Hummer H1. With long waiting lists for fuel-efficient cars such as the Toyota Prius, buyers not only seldom received discounts but frequently paid even more than the sticker price.

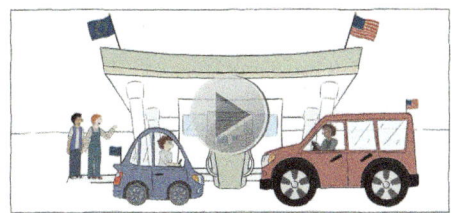

Why are smaller automobile engines more common in Europe than in the United States?

With the dramatic fall in real gasoline prices that began in 2012, sales for large SUVs and other light trucks again began to rise, accounting for more than 80 percent of new vehicles sold in the United States by 2022. More recently, higher gasoline prices in the wake of Russia's invasion of Ukraine, in combination with new government subsidies, have launched a significant shift toward electric vehicles.

As these movements attest, prices affect purchase decisions. Here's a closely related example of how taxes influence those decisions.

The Economic Naturalist 5.4

Why are automobile engines smaller in England than in the United States?

In England, the most popular model of BMW's 5-series car is the 516i, whereas in the United States it is the 530i. The engine in the 516i is almost 50 percent smaller than the engine in the 530i. Why this difference?

In both countries, BMWs appeal to professionals with roughly similar incomes, so the difference cannot be explained by differences in purchasing power. Rather, it is the direct result of the heavy tax the British levy on gasoline. With tax, a gallon of gasoline sells for more than two times the price in the United States. This difference encourages the British to choose smaller, more fuel-efficient engines.

The effect of higher gasoline taxes is also explained in part by the link between context and evaluation. Many motorists like fast cars, but what qualifies a car as fast is that it accelerates more briskly than other cars in the local environment. In the 1920s, a car would have seemed unbelievably fast to most American motorists if it could reach 60 mph eventually. But today's American cars don't qualify as fast unless they can reach that speed in under 5 seconds. The context is different in the UK, where high gasoline taxes have led motorists to buy cars with smaller engines. A BMW 516i would seem painfully sluggish in the United States, but the car's performance is deemed perfectly adequate in the UK.

Does the quantity of horsepower demanded depend on gasoline prices?

The preceding examples offer hints about the role of tax policy in efforts to mitigate the climate crisis, a subject to which we'll return in future chapters.

The Importance of Income Differences

The most obvious difference between the rich and the poor is that the rich have higher incomes. To explain why the wealthy generally buy larger houses than the poor, we need not assume that the wealthy feel more strongly about housing than the poor. A much simpler explanation is that the total utility from housing, as with most other goods, increases with the amount that one consumes.

As the next example illustrates, income influences the demand not only for housing and other goods, but also for quality of service.

The Economic Naturalist 5.5

Why are waiting lines longer in poorer neighborhoods?

As part of a recent promotional campaign, a Baskin-Robbins retailer offered free ice cream at two of its franchise stores. The first was located in a high-income neighborhood, the second in a low-income neighborhood. Why was the queue for free ice cream longer in the low-income neighborhood?

Residents of both neighborhoods must decide whether to stand in line for free ice cream or go to some other store and avoid the line by paying the usual price. If we make the plausible assumption that people with higher incomes are more willing than others to pay to avoid standing in line, we should expect to see shorter lines in the high-income neighborhood.

Why are lines longer in low-income neighborhoods?

Similar reasoning helps explain why lines are shorter in grocery stores that cater to high-income consumers. Keeping lines short at *any* grocery store means hiring more clerks, which means charging higher prices. High-income consumers are more likely than others to be willing to pay for shorter lines.

> **RECAP** ↑
>
> **THE RATIONAL SPENDING RULE**
>
> Application of the rational spending rule highlights the important roles of income and substitution in explaining differences in consumption patterns—among individuals, among communities, and across time. The rule also highlights the fact that real, as opposed to nominal, prices and income are what matter. The demand for a good falls when the real price of a substitute falls or the real price of a complement rises.

INDIVIDUAL AND MARKET DEMAND CURVES

If we know what each individual's demand curve for a good looks like, how can we use that information to construct the market demand curve for the good? We must add the individual demand curves together, a process that is straightforward but requires care.

HORIZONTAL ADDITION

Suppose that there are only two buyers—Raj and Zora—in the market for canned tuna and that their demand curves are as shown in Figure 5.7(a) and (b). To construct the market demand curve for canned tuna, we simply announce a sequence of prices and then add the quantity demanded by each buyer at each price. For example, at a price of 40 cents per can, Raj demands six cans per week (a) and Zora demands two cans per week (b), for a market demand of eight cans per week (c).

FIGURE 5.7

Individual and Market Demand Curves for Canned Tuna.

The quantity demanded at any price on the market demand curve (c) is the sum of the individual quantities demanded at that price, (a) and (b).

The process of adding individual demand curves to get the market demand curve is known as *horizontal addition*, a term used to emphasize that we are adding quantities, which are measured on the horizontal axes of individual demand curves.

 SELF-TEST 5.3

The buyers' side of the market for movie tickets consists of two consumers whose demands are as shown in the following diagram. Graph the market demand curve for this market.

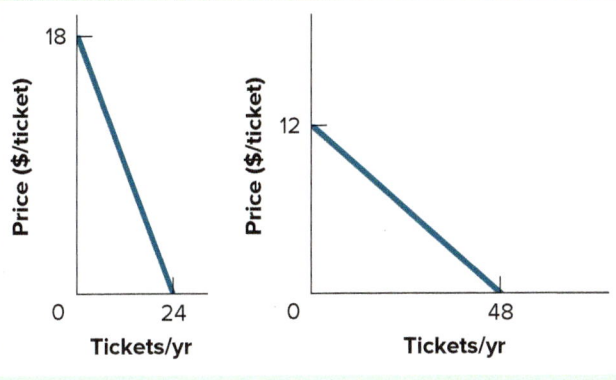

Figure 5.8 illustrates the special case in which each of 1,000 consumers in the market has the same demand curve (a). To get the market demand curve (b) in this case, we simply multiply each quantity on the representative individual demand curve by 1,000.

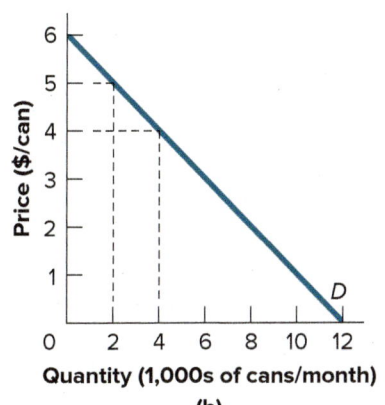

FIGURE 5.8

The Individual and Market Demand Curves When All Buyers Have Identical Demand Curves.

When individual demand curves are identical, we get the market demand curve (b) by multiplying each quantity on the individual demand curve (a) by the number of consumers in the market.

DEMAND AND CONSUMER SURPLUS

In Chapter 1, *Thinking Like an Economist*, we first encountered the concept of economic surplus, which in a buyer's case is the difference between the most she would have been willing to pay for a product and the amount she actually pays for it. The economic surplus received by buyers is often referred to as **consumer surplus**.

The term *consumer surplus* sometimes refers to the surplus received by a single buyer in a transaction. On other occasions, it's used to denote the total surplus received by all buyers in a market or collection of markets.

consumer surplus the difference between a buyer's reservation price for a product and the price actually paid

CALCULATING CONSUMER SURPLUS

For performing cost-benefit analysis, it's often important to be able to measure the total consumer surplus received by all buyers who participate in a given market. For example, a road linking a mountain village and a port city would create a new market for fresh fish in the mountain village; in deciding whether the road should be built, analysts would want to count as one of its benefits the gains that would be reaped by buyers in this new market.

To illustrate how economists actually measure consumer surplus, we'll consider a hypothetical market for a good with 11 potential buyers, each of whom can buy a maximum of one unit of the good each day. The first potential buyer's reservation price for the product is \$11; the second buyer's reservation price is \$10; the third buyer's reservation price is \$9; and so on. The demand curve for this market will have the staircase shape shown in Figure 5.9. We can think of this curve as the digital counterpart of traditional analog demand curves. (If the units shown on the horizontal axis were fine enough, this digital curve would be visually indistinguishable from its analog counterparts.)

Suppose the good whose demand curve is shown in Figure 5.9 were available at a price of \$6 per unit. How much total consumer surplus would buyers in this market reap? At a price of \$6, six units per day would be sold in this market. The buyer of the sixth unit would receive no economic surplus since his reservation price for that unit was exactly \$6, the same as its selling price. But the first five buyers would reap a surplus for their purchases. The buyer of the first unit, for example, would have been willing to pay as much as \$11 for it, but since she'd pay only \$6, she'd receive a surplus of exactly \$5. The buyer of the second unit, who would have been willing to pay as much as \$10, would receive a surplus of \$4. The surplus would be \$3 for the buyer of the third unit, \$2 for the buyer of the fourth unit, and \$1 for the buyer of the fifth unit.

If we add all the buyers' surpluses together, we get a total of \$15 of consumer surplus each day. That surplus corresponds to the shaded area shown in Figure 5.10.

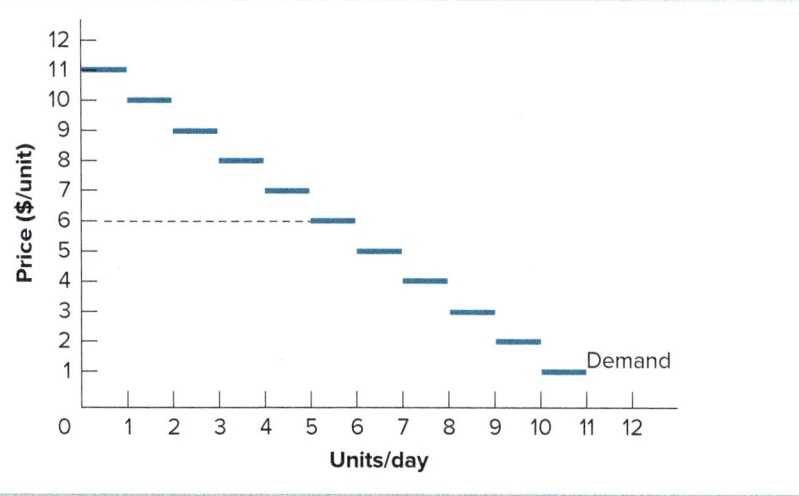

FIGURE 5.9

A Market with a "Digital" Demand Curve.

When a product can be sold only in whole-number amounts, its demand curve has the stair-step shape shown.

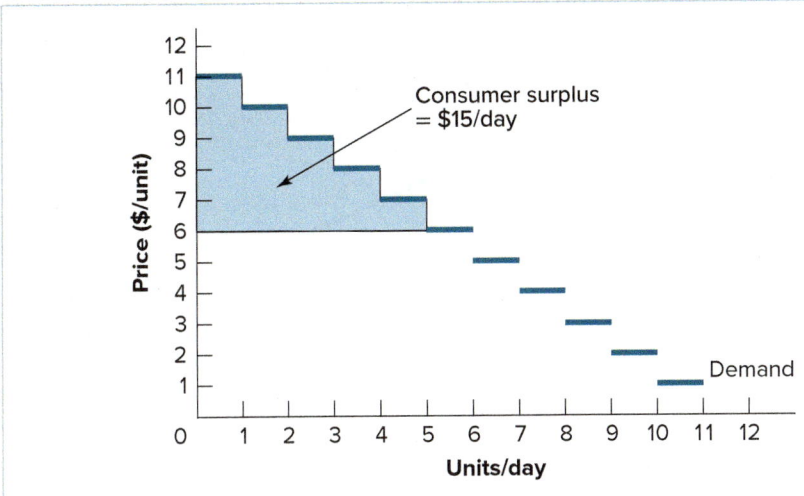

FIGURE 5.10

Consumer Surplus.

Consumer surplus (shaded region) is the cumulative difference between the most that buyers are willing to pay for each unit and the price they actually pay.

 SELF-TEST 5.4

Calculate consumer surplus for a demand curve like the one just described except that the buyers' reservation prices for each unit are $2 higher than before, as shown in the given graph.

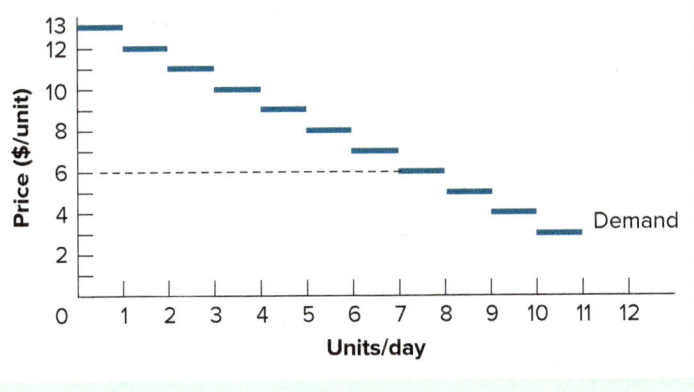

Now suppose we want to calculate consumer surplus in a market with a conventional straight-line demand curve. As the following example illustrates, this task is a simple extension of the method used for digital demand curves.

EXAMPLE 5.6   **Measuring Consumer Surplus**

How much do buyers benefit from their participation in the market for milk?

Consider the market for milk whose demand and supply curves are shown in Figure 5.11, which has an equilibrium price of $2 per gallon and an equilibrium quantity of 4,000 gallons per day. How much consumer surplus do the buyers in this market reap?

In Figure 5.11, note first that, as in Figure 5.10, the last unit exchanged each day generates no consumer surplus at all. Note also that for all milk sold up to

FIGURE 5.11

Supply and Demand in the Market for Milk.

For the supply and demand curves shown, the equilibrium price of milk is $2 per gallon and the equilibrium quantity is 4,000 gallons per day.

4,000 gallons per day, buyers receive consumer surplus, just as in Figure 5.10. For these buyers, consumer surplus is the cumulative difference between the most they'd be willing to pay for milk (as measured on the demand curve) and the price they actually pay.

Total consumer surplus received by buyers in the milk market is thus the shaded triangle between the demand curve and the market price in Figure 5.12. Note that this area is a right triangle whose vertical arm is $h = \$1$/gallon and whose horizontal arm is $b = 4{,}000$ gallons/day. And because the area of any triangle is equal to $(1/2)bh$, consumer surplus in this market is equal to

$$(1/2)(4{,}000 \text{ gallons/day})(\$1/\text{gallon}) = \$2{,}000/\text{day}.$$

FIGURE 5.12

Consumer Surplus in the Market for Milk.

Consumer surplus is the area of the shaded triangle ($2,000/day).

A useful way of thinking about consumer surplus is to ask what is the highest price consumers would pay, in the aggregate, for the right to continue participating in this milk market. The answer is $2,000 per day, since that's the amount by which their combined benefits exceed their combined costs.

As discussed in Chapter 3, *Supply and Demand*, the demand curve for a good can be interpreted either horizontally or vertically. The horizontal interpretation tells us, for each price, the total quantity that consumers wish to buy at that price. The vertical interpretation tells us, for each quantity, the most a buyer would be willing to pay for the good at that quantity. For the purpose of computing consumer surplus, we rely on the vertical interpretation of the demand curve. The value on the vertical axis that corresponds to each point along the demand curve corresponds to the marginal buyer's reservation price for the good. Consumer surplus is the cumulative sum of the differences between these reservation prices and the market price. It is the area bounded above by the demand curve and bounded below by the market price.

SUMMARY

- The rational consumer allocates income among different goods so that the marginal utility gained from the last dollar spent on each good is the same. This rational spending rule gives rise to the law of demand, which states that people do less of what they want to do as the cost of doing it rises. Here, "cost" refers to the sum of all monetary and nonmonetary sacrifices—explicit and implicit—that must be made in order to engage in the activity. *(LO1, LO2)*

- As the price of a good rises, people tend to choose less expensive alternatives. The ability to substitute one good for another is an important factor behind the law of demand. Because virtually every good or service has at least some substitutes, economists prefer to speak in terms of wants rather than needs. *(LO3)*

- For normal goods, the income effect is a second important reason that demand curves slope downward. When the price of such a good rises, not only does it become

less attractive relative to its substitutes, but the consumer also has less real purchasing power, and this, too, reduces the quantity demanded. *(LO3)*

- The demand curve is a schedule that shows the amounts of a good people want to buy at various prices. Demand curves can be used to summarize the price–quantity relationship for a single individual, but more commonly we employ them to summarize that relationship for an entire market. At any quantity along a demand curve, the corresponding price represents the amount by which the consumer (or consumers) would benefit from having an additional unit of the product. For this reason, the demand curve is sometimes described as a summary of the benefit side of the market. *(LO4)*

- Consumer surplus is a quantitative measure of the amount by which buyers benefit as a result of their ability to purchase goods at the market price. It is the area between the demand curve and the market price. *(LO5)*

KEY TERMS

consumer surplus
law of demand
law of diminishing marginal utility

marginal utility
nominal price
optimal combination of goods

rational spending rule
real price

REVIEW QUESTIONS

1. Why do economists prefer to speak of demands arising out of "wants" rather than "needs"? *(LO1)*

2. Explain why economists consider the concept of utility useful, even if psychologists cannot measure it precisely. *(LO2)*

3. Why does the law of diminishing marginal utility encourage people to spread their spending across many different types of goods? *(LO2)*

4. Explain why a good or service that is offered at a monetary price of zero is unlikely to be a truly "free" good from an economic perspective. *(LO3)*

5. Give an example of a good that you have consumed for which your marginal utility increased with the amount of it you consumed. *(LO3)*

PROBLEMS

1. Any consumer trying to decide whether to buy a given good or service will base the decision on their reservation price and the existing market price. When making this

decision, what does the buyer's reservation price measure? What does the market price measure? *(LO1)*

2. Which of the following factors would affect a buyer's reservation price for a given good or service: social influence, the price of the good, or the cost of producing the item? *(LO1)*

3. You are having lunch at an all-you-can-eat buffet. If you are rational, what should be your marginal utility from the last morsel of food you swallow? *(LO2)*

4. Kai's current marginal utility from consuming orange juice is 75 utils per ounce and her marginal utility from consuming coffee is 50 utils per ounce. If orange juice costs 25 cents per ounce and coffee costs 20 cents per ounce, is Kai maximizing her total utility from the two beverages? If so, explain how you know. If not, how should she rearrange her spending? *(LO2)*

5. Rohan's current marginal utility from consuming peanuts is 100 utils per ounce and his marginal utility from consuming cashews is 200 utils per ounce. If peanuts cost 10 cents per ounce and cashews cost 25 cents per ounce, is Rohan maximizing his total utility from the kinds of nuts? If so, explain how you know. If not, how should he rearrange his spending? *(LO2)*

6. Sienna gets a total of 20 utils per week from her consumption of pizza and a total of 40 utils per week from her consumption of yogurt. The price of pizza is $1 per slice, the price of yogurt is $1 per cup, and she consumes 10 slices of pizza and 20 cups of yogurt each week. True or false: Sienna is consuming the optimal combination of pizza and yogurt. *(LO2)*

7. Zander has a weekly allowance of $24, all of which he spends on pizza and movie rentals, whose prices are $6 per slice and $3 per rental, respectively. We assume that pizza slices and movie rentals are available only in whole-number amounts. *(LO2)*
   a. List all possible combinations of the two goods that Zander can purchase each week with his allowance.
   b. Zander's total utility is the sum of the utility he derives from pizza and movie rentals. If these utilities vary with the amounts consumed as shown in the table, and pizza slices and movie rentals are again consumable only in whole-number amounts, how many pizza slices and how many movie rentals should Zander consume each week?

8. Ishana lives in Princeton, New Jersey, and commutes by train each day to her job in New York City (20 round-trips per month). When the price of a round-trip goes up from $10 to $20, she responds by consuming exactly the same number of trips as before, while spending $200 per month less on restaurant meals. Does the fact that her quantity of train travel is completely unresponsive to the price increase imply that Ishana is not a rational consumer? *(LO3)*

9.* The buyers' side of the market for amusement park tickets consists of two consumers whose demands are as shown in the following diagram. *(LO4, LO5)*
   a. Graph the market demand curve for this market.
   b. Calculate the total consumer surplus in the amusement park market if tickets sell for $12 each.

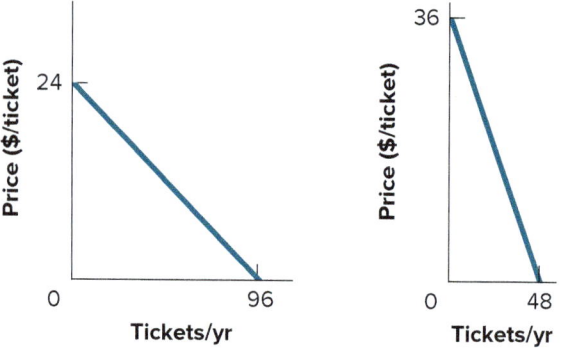

10. For the demand curve shown, find the total amount of consumer surplus that results in the gasoline market if gasoline sells for $2 per gallon. *(LO5)*

Pizza slices/week	Utils/week from pizza	Movie rentals/week	Utils/week from rentals
0	0	0	0
1	20	1	40
2	36	2	46
3	48	3	50
4	58	4	54
5	66	5	56
6	72	6	57
7	76	7	57
8	78	8	57

*Denotes more difficult problem.

ANSWERS TO SELF-TESTS

5.1 The combination of 300 pints per year of vanilla ($300) and 50 pints of chocolate ($100) costs a total of $400, which is exactly equal to Sarah's ice cream budget. *(LO2)*

5.2 The rational spending rule requires $MU_F/P_F = MU_S/P_S$ where MU_F and MU_S are Juan's marginal utilities from food and shelter and P_F and P_S are the prices of food and shelter, respectively. At Juan's original combination, $MU_F/P_F = 4$ utils per dollar and $MU_S/P_S = 3$ utils per dollar. Juan should thus spend more of his income on food and less on shelter. *(LO3)*

5.3 Adding the two individual demand curves, (a) and (b), horizontally yields the market demand curve (c). *(LO4)*

5.4 Consumer surplus is now the new shaded area, $28 per day. *(LO5)*

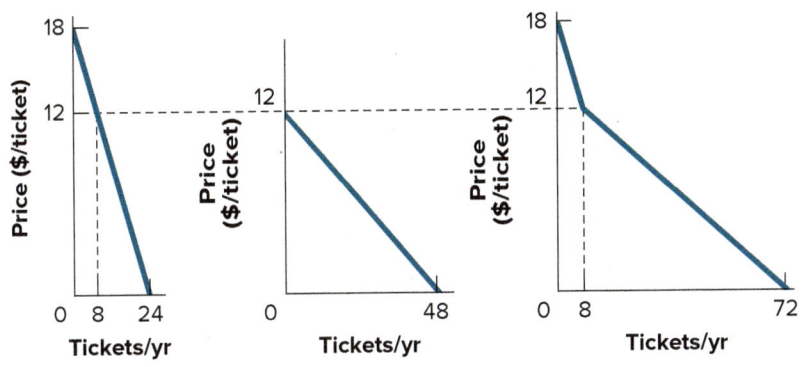

APPENDIX

Indifference Curves

In the main text of Chapter 5, *Demand*, we showed why the rational spending rule is a simple consequence of diminishing marginal utility. In this appendix, we introduce the concept of indifference curves to develop the same rule in another way.

As before, we begin with the assumption that consumers enter the marketplace with well-defined preferences. Taking prices as given, their task is to allocate their incomes to best serve these preferences.

There are two steps required to carry out this task. The first is to describe the various combinations of goods the consumer is *able* to buy. These combinations depend on her income level and on the prices of the goods she faces. The second step is to select from among the feasible combinations the particular one that she *prefers* to all others. This step will require some means of describing her preferences. We begin with the first step, a description of the set of possibilities.

THE BUDGET CONSTRAINT

As before, we keep the discussion simple by focusing on a consumer who spends her entire income on only two goods: chocolate and vanilla ice cream. A *bundle* of goods is the term used to describe a particular combination of the two types of ice cream, measured in pints per year. Thus, in Figure 5A.1, one bundle (bundle *A*) might consist of five pints per year of chocolate and seven pints per year of vanilla, while another (bundle *B*) consists of three pints per year of chocolate and eight pints per year of vanilla. For brevity's sake, we may use the notation (5, 7) to denote bundle *A* and (3, 8) to denote bundle *B*.

FIGURE 5A.1

Two Bundles of Goods.

A bundle is a specific combination of goods. Bundle *A* has five units of chocolate and seven units of vanilla. Bundle *B* has three units of chocolate and eight units of vanilla.

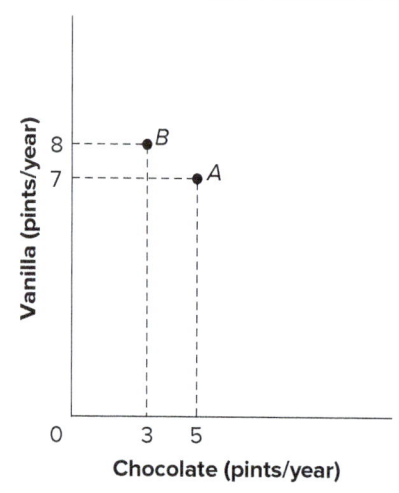

More generally, (C_0, V_0) will denote the bundle with C_0 pints per year of chocolate and V_0 pints per year of vanilla. By convention, the first number of the pair in any bundle represents the good measured along the horizontal axis.

Note that the units on both axes are *flows,* which means physical quantities per unit of time—in this case, pints per year. Consumption is always measured as a flow. It is important to keep track of the time dimension because, without it, there would be no way to evaluate whether a given quantity of consumption was large or small. (Again, suppose all you know is that your consumption of vanilla ice cream is four pints. If that's how much you eat each hour, it's a lot. But if that's all you eat in a decade, it's not very much.)

Suppose the consumer's income is $M = \$100$ per year, all of which she spends on some combination of vanilla and chocolate. (Note that income is also a flow.) Suppose further that the prices of chocolate and vanilla are $P_C = \$5$ per pint and $P_V = \$10$ per pint, respectively. If she spent her entire income on chocolate, she could buy $M/P_C = (\$100/\text{year}) \div (\$5/\text{pint}) = 20$ pints/year. That is, she could buy the bundle consisting of 20 pints per year of chocolate and 0 pints per year of vanilla, denoted $(20, 0)$. Alternatively, suppose she spent her entire income on vanilla. She would then get the bundle consisting of $M/P_V = (\$100/\text{year}) \div (\$10/\text{pint}) = 10$ pints per year of vanilla and 0 pints per year of chocolate, denoted $(0, 10)$.

In Figure 5A.2, these polar cases are labeled K and L, respectively. The consumer is also able to purchase any other bundle that lies along the straight line that joins points K and L. (Verify, for example, that the bundle $(12, 4)$ lies on this same line.) This line is called the *budget constraint* and is labeled B in the diagram.

Note that the slope of the budget constraint is its vertical intercept (the rise) divided by its horizontal intercept (the corresponding run)

$$-(10 \text{ pints/year})/(20 \text{ pints/year}) = -1/2.$$

The minus sign signifies that the budget line falls as it moves to the right—that it has a negative slope. More generally, if M denotes income and P_C and P_V denote the prices of chocolate and vanilla respectively, the horizontal and vertical intercepts will be given by (M/P_C) and (M/P_V), respectively. Thus, the general formula for the slope of the budget constraint is given by $-(M/P_V)/(M/P_C) = -P_C/P_V$, which is simply the negative of the price ratio of the two goods. Given their respective prices, it is the rate at which vanilla can be exchanged for chocolate. Thus, in Figure 5A.2, one pint of vanilla can be exchanged for two pints of chocolate. In the language of opportunity cost from Chapter 1, *Thinking Like an Economist*, we would say that the opportunity cost of an additional pint of chocolate is $P_C/P_V = 1/2$ pint of vanilla.

In addition to being able to buy any of the bundles along her budget constraint, the consumer is also able to purchase any bundle that lies within the *budget triangle* bounded by it and the two axes. D is one such bundle in Figure 5A.2. Bundle D costs \$65 per year,

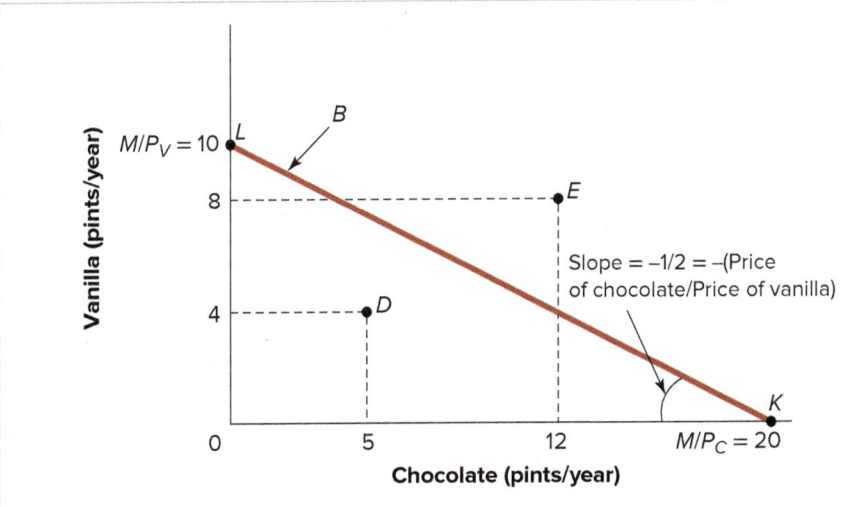

FIGURE 5A.2

The Budget Constraint.

The line B describes the set of all bundles the consumer can purchase for given values of income and prices. Its slope is the negative of the price of chocolate divided by the price of vanilla. In absolute value, this slope is the opportunity cost of an additional unit of chocolate: the number of pints of vanilla that must be sacrificed in order to purchase one additional pint of chocolate at market prices.

which is well below the consumer's ice cream budget of $100 per year. Bundles like E that lie outside the budget triangle are unaffordable. At a cost of $140 per year, E is simply beyond the consumer's reach.

If C and V denote the quantities of chocolate and vanilla, respectively, the budget constraint must satisfy the following equation

$$P_C C + P_V V = M, \qquad (5A.1)$$

which says simply that the consumer's yearly expenditure on chocolate ($P_C C$) plus her yearly expenditure on vanilla ($P_V V$) must add up to her yearly income (M). To express the budget constraint in the manner conventionally used to represent the formula for a straight line, we solve Equation 5A.1 for V in terms of C, which yields

$$V = M/P_V - (P_C/P_V)C. \qquad (5A.2)$$

Equation 5A.2 provides another way of seeing that the vertical intercept of the budget constraint is given by M/P_V, and its slope by $-(P_C/P_V)$. The equation for the budget constraint in Figure 5A.2 is $V = 10 - (1/2)C$.

BUDGET SHIFTS DUE TO INCOME OR PRICE CHANGES

Price Changes

The slope and position of the budget constraint are fully determined by the consumer's income and the prices of the respective goods. Change any one of these and we have a new budget constraint. Figure 5A.3 shows the effect of an increase in the price of chocolate from $P_{C1} = \$5$ per pint to $P_{C2} = \$10$ per pint. Since both her budget and the price of vanilla are unchanged, the vertical intercept of the consumer's budget constraint stays the same. The rise in the price of chocolate rotates the budget constraint inward about this intercept, as shown in the diagram.

FIGURE 5A.3

The Effect of a Rise in the Price of Chocolate.

When chocolate goes up in price, the vertical intercept of the budget constraint remains the same. The original budget constraint rotates inward about this intercept.

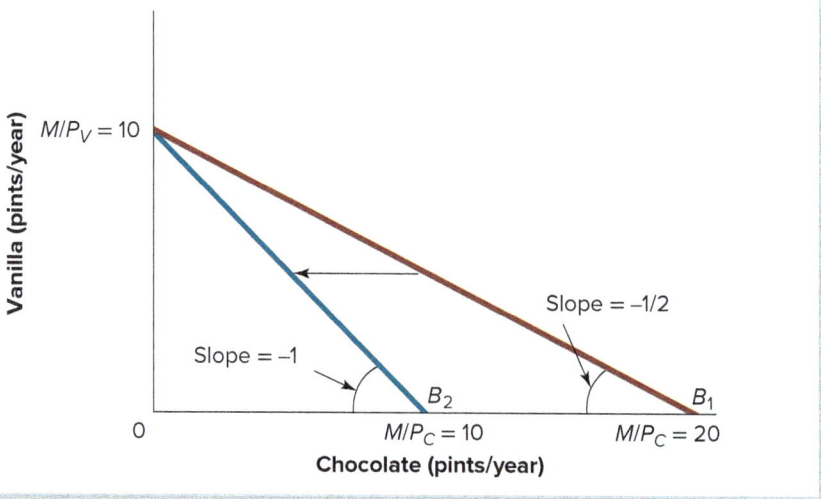

Note in Figure 5A.3 that even though the price of vanilla has not changed, the new budget constraint, B_2, curtails not only the amount of chocolate the consumer can buy but also the amount of vanilla.[1]

✅ **SELF-TEST 5A.1**

Show the effect on the budget constraint B_1 in Figure 5A.3 of a fall in the price of chocolate from $5 per pint to $4 per pint.

---

[1]The single exception to this statement involves the vertical intercept, (0, 10), which lies on both the original and the new budget constraints.

In Self-Test 5A.1, you saw that a fall in the price of chocolate again leaves the vertical intercept of the budget constraint unchanged. This time the budget constraint rotates outward. Note also in Self-Test 5A.1 that although the price of vanilla remains unchanged, the new budget constraint enables the consumer to buy bundles that contain not only more chocolate but also more vanilla than she could afford on the original budget constraint.

SELF-TEST 5A.2

Show the effect on the budget constraint B_1 in Figure 5A.3 of a rise in the price of vanilla from $10 per pint to $20 per pint.

Self-Test 5A.2 demonstrates that when the price of vanilla changes, the budget constraint rotates about its horizontal intercept. Note also that even though income and the price of chocolate remain the same, the new budget constraint curtails not only the amount of vanilla she can buy but also the amount of chocolate.

When we change the price of only one good, we necessarily change the slope of the budget constraint, $-P_C/P_V$. The same is true if we change both prices by different proportions. But as Self-Test 5A.3 will illustrate, changing both prices by exactly the same proportion gives rise to a new budget constraint with the same slope as before.

SELF-TEST 5A.3

Show the effect on the budget constraint B_1 in Figure 5A.3 of a rise in the price of vanilla from $10 per pint to $20 per pint and a rise in the price of chocolate from $5 per pint to $10 per pint.

Note from Self-Test 5A.3 that the effect of doubling the prices of both vanilla and chocolate is to shift the budget constraint inward and parallel to the original budget constraint. The important lesson of this exercise is that the slope of the budget constraint tells us only about *relative prices*, nothing about how high prices are in absolute terms. When the prices of vanilla and chocolate change in the same proportion, the opportunity cost of chocolate in terms of vanilla remains the same as before.

Income Changes
The effect of a change in income is much like the effect of an equal proportional change in all prices. Suppose, for example, that our hypothetical consumer's income is cut by half, from $100 per year to $50 per year. The horizontal intercept of her budget constraint will then fall from 20 pints per year to 10 pints per year and the vertical intercept from 10 pints per year to 5 pints per year, as shown in Figure 5A.4. Thus the new budget, B_2, is parallel to the old, B_1, each with a slope of $-1/2$. In terms of its effect on what the consumer can buy, cutting income by half is thus no different from doubling each price. Precisely the same budget constraint results from both changes.

SELF-TEST 5A.4

Show the effect on the budget constraint B_1 in Figure 5A.3 of an increase in income from $100 per year to $120 per year.

Self-Test 5A.4 illustrates that an increase in income shifts the budget constraint parallel outward. As in the case of an income reduction, the slope of the budget constraint remains the same.

FIGURE 5A.4

The Effect of Cutting Income by Half.

Both horizontal and vertical intercepts fall by half. The new budget constraint has the same slope as the old but is closer to the origin.

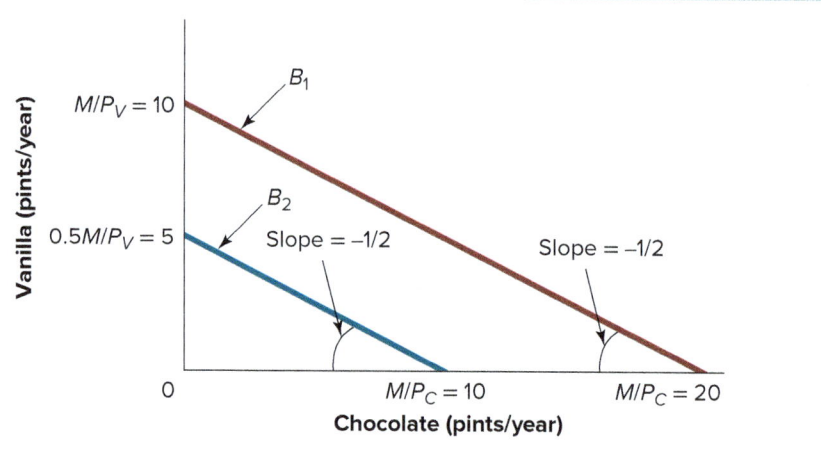

BUDGETS INVOLVING MORE THAN TWO GOODS

The examples discussed so far have all been ones in which the consumer is faced with the opportunity to buy only two different goods. Needless to say, not many consumers have such narrow options. In its most general form, the consumer budgeting problem can be posed as a choice between not two but N different goods, where N can be an indefinitely large number. With only two goods ($N = 2$), the budget constraint is a straight line, as we have just seen. With three goods ($N = 3$), it is a plane. When we have more than three goods, the budget constraint becomes what mathematicians call a *hyperplane,* or multidimensional plane. The only real difficulty is in representing this multidimensional case geometrically. We are just not very good at visualizing surfaces that have more than three dimensions.

The nineteenth-century economist Alfred Marshall proposed a disarmingly simple solution to this problem. It is to view the consumer's choice as being one between a particular good—call it X—and an amalgam of other goods denoted Y. This amalgam is called the *composite good.* We may think of the composite good as the amount of income the consumer has left over after buying the good X.

To illustrate how this concept is used, suppose the consumer has an income level of $\$M$ per year, and the price of X is given by P_X. The consumer's budget constraint may then be represented as a straight line in the X,Y plane, as shown in Figure 5A.5. For simplicity, the price of a unit of the composite good is taken to be one, so that if the consumer devotes none of his income to X, he will be able to buy M units of the composite good. All this means is that he will have $\$M$ available to spend on other goods if he buys no X. Alternatively, if he spends all his income on X, he will be able to purchase

FIGURE 5A.5

The Budget Constraint with the Composite Good.

The vertical axis measures the amount of money spent each month on all goods other than X.

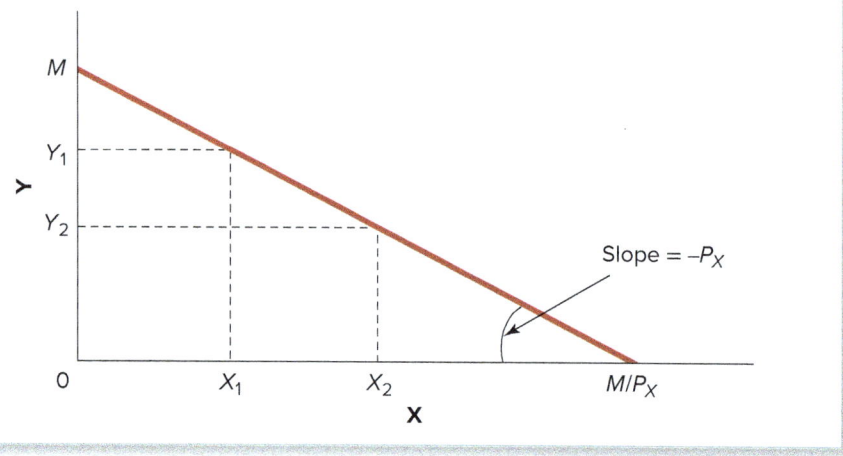

the bundle (M/P_X, 0). Since the price of Y is assumed to be one, the slope of the budget constraint is simply $-P_X$.

As before, the budget constraint summarizes the various combinations of bundles that are affordable. For example, the consumer can have X_1 units of X and Y_1 units of the composite good in Figure 5A.5, or X_2 and Y_2, or any other combination that lies on the budget constraint.

Summing up briefly, the budget constraint or opportunity set summarizes the combinations of bundles that the consumer is able to buy. Its position is determined jointly by income and prices. From the set of feasible bundles, the consumer's task is to pick the particular one she likes best. To identify this bundle, we need some means of summarizing the consumer's preferences over all possible bundles she might consume. To this task we now turn.

CONSUMER PREFERENCES

For simplicity, we again begin by considering a world with only two goods, chocolate and vanilla ice cream, and assume that a particular consumer is able to rank different bundles of goods in terms of their desirability or order of preference. Suppose this consumer currently has bundle A in Figure 5A.6, which has six pints per year of chocolate and four pints per year of vanilla. If we then take one pint per year of chocolate away from her, she is left with bundle D, which has only five pints per year of chocolate and the same four pints per year of vanilla. Let us suppose that this consumer feels worse off than before, as most people would, because although D has just as much vanilla as A, it has less chocolate. We can undo the damage by giving her some additional vanilla. If our goal is to compensate for exactly her loss, how much extra vanilla do we need to give her?

Suppose we start by giving her an additional half pint per year, which would move her to bundle E in Figure 5A.6. For some consumers, that might be enough to make up for the lost pint of chocolate, even though the total amount of ice cream at E (9.5 pints per year) is smaller than at A (10 pints per year). Indeed, consumers who *really* like vanilla

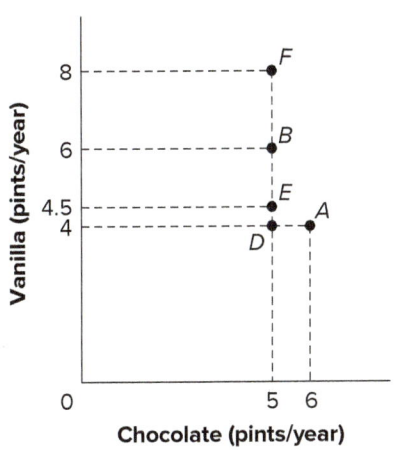

FIGURE 5A.6

Ranking Bundles.

This consumer will prefer A to D because A has more chocolate than D and just as much vanilla. She is assumed to prefer bundle A to bundle E and to prefer bundle F to bundle A. This means there must be a bundle between E and F (shown here as B) that she likes equally well as A. This consumer is said to be indifferent between A and B. If she moves from A to B, her gain of two pints per year of vanilla exactly compensates for her loss of one pint per year of chocolate. She will prefer F to B because F has more vanilla than B and just as much chocolate. For the same reason, she will prefer B to E and E to D.

FIGURE 5A.7

Equally Preferred Bundles.

This consumer is assumed to be indifferent between the bundles *A* and *C*. In moving from *A* to *C*, her gain of one pint per year of chocolate exactly compensates for her loss of one pint per year of vanilla. And since she was indifferent between *A* and *B*, she also must be indifferent between *B* and *C*.

might actually prefer *E* to *A*. But we'll assume that this particular consumer would still prefer *A* to *E*. So to compensate fully for her lost pint of chocolate, we would have to give her more than an additional half pint of vanilla. Suppose we gave her a *lot* more vanilla—say, an additional four pints per year. This would move her to bundle *F* in Figure 5A.6, and we'll assume that she regards the extra four pints per year of vanilla at *F* as more than enough to compensate for the lost pint of chocolate.

The fact that this particular consumer prefers *F* to *A* but prefers *A* to *E* tells us that the amount of extra vanilla needed to *exactly* compensate for the lost pint of chocolate must be between one-half pint per year (the amount of extra vanilla at *E*) and four pints per year (the amount of extra vanilla at *F*). Suppose, for the sake of discussion, that she would feel exactly compensated if we gave her an additional two pints of vanilla. This consumer would then be said to be indifferent between bundles *A* and *B* in Figure 5A.6. Alternatively, we could say that she likes the bundles *A* and *B* equally well, or that she regards these bundles as equivalent.

Now suppose that we again start at bundle *A* and pose a different question: How many pints of vanilla would this consumer be willing to sacrifice in order to obtain an additional pint of chocolate? This time let's suppose that her answer is exactly one pint. We have thus identified another point—call it *C*—that is equally preferred to *A*. In Figure 5A.7, *C* is shown as the bundle (7, 3). *C* is also equally preferred to *B* (since *C* is equally preferred to *A*, which is equally preferred to *B*).

If we continue to generate additional bundles that the consumer likes equally well as bundle *A*, the end result is an *indifference curve,* a set of bundles all of which the consumer views as equivalent to the original bundle *A*, and hence also equivalent to one another. This set is shown as the curve labeled IC_1 in Figure 5A.8. It is called an indifference curve because the consumer is indifferent among all the bundles that lie along it.

FIGURE 5A.8

An Indifference Curve.

An indifference curve, such as IC_1, is a set of bundles that the consumer prefers equally. Any bundle, such as *K*, that lies above an indifference curve is preferred to any bundle on the indifference curve. Any bundle on the indifference curve, in turn, is preferred to any bundle, such as *L*, that lies below the indifference curve.

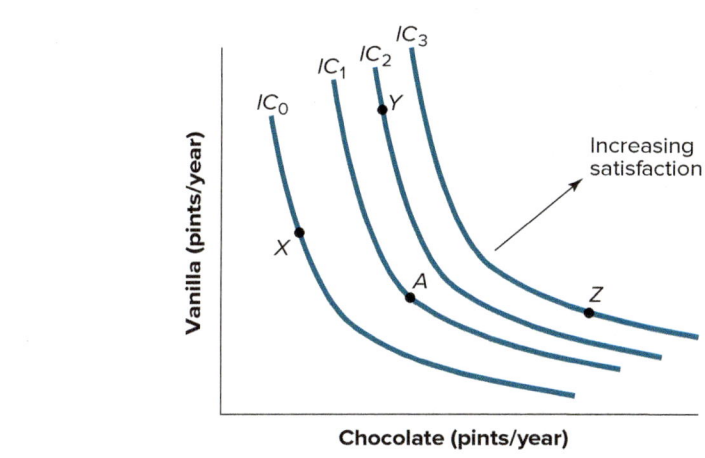

FIGURE 5A.9

Part of an Indifference Map.
The entire set of a consumer's indifference curves is called the consumer's indifference map. Bundles on any indifference curve are less preferred than bundles on a higher indifference curve and more preferred than bundles on a lower indifference curve. Thus, Z is preferred to Y, which is preferred to A, which is preferred to X.

An indifference curve also permits us to compare the satisfaction implicit in bundles that lie along it with those that lie either above or below it. It permits us, for example, to compare bundle C (7, 3) to a bundle like K (12, 2), which has less vanilla and more chocolate than C has. We know that C is equally preferred to N (12, 1) because both bundles lie along the same indifference curve. K, in turn, is preferred to N because it has just as much chocolate as N and one pint per year more vanilla. So if K is preferred to N, and N is just as attractive as C, then K must be preferred to C.

By analogous reasoning, we can say that bundle A is preferred to L. A and M are equivalent, and M is preferred to L since M has just as much chocolate as L and two pints per year more of vanilla. *In general, bundles that lie above an indifference curve are all preferred to the bundles that lie on it. Similarly, those that lie on an indifference curve are all preferred to those that lie below it.*

We can represent a useful summary of the consumer's preferences with an *indifference map,* an example of which is shown in Figure 5A.9. This indifference map shows just four of the infinitely many indifference curves that, taken together, yield a complete description of the consumer's preferences. As we move to the northeast on an indifference map, successive indifference curves represent higher levels of satisfaction. If we want to know how a consumer ranks any given pair of bundles, we simply compare the indifference curves on which they lie. The indifference map shown tells us, for example, that Z is preferred to Y because Z lies on a higher indifference curve (IC_3) than Y does (IC_2). By the same token, Y is preferred to A, and A is preferred to X.

TRADE-OFFS BETWEEN GOODS

An important property of a consumer's preferences is the rate at which she is willing to exchange, or "trade off," one good for another. This property is represented at any point on an indifference curve by the *marginal rate of substitution* (MRS), which is defined as the absolute value of the slope of the indifference curve at that point. In the left panel of Figure 5A.10, for example, the marginal rate of substitution at point T is given by the absolute value of the slope of the tangent to the indifference curve at T, which is the ratio $\Delta V_T / \Delta C_T$. (The notation ΔV_T means "small change in vanilla from the amount at point T.") If we take ΔC_T units of chocolate away from the consumer at point T, we have to give her ΔV_T additional units of vanilla to make her just as well off as before. If the marginal rate of substitution at T is 1.5, that means that the consumer must be given 1.5 pints per year of vanilla in order to make up for the loss of 1 pint per year of chocolate.

Whereas the slope of the budget constraint tells us the rate at which we can substitute vanilla for chocolate without changing total expenditure, the MRS tells us the rate at which we can substitute vanilla for chocolate without changing total satisfaction. Put another way, the slope of the budget constraint is the marginal cost of chocolate in terms of vanilla, while the MRS is the marginal benefit of chocolate in terms of vanilla.

FIGURE 5A.10

The Marginal Rate of Substitution.

The MRS at any point along an indifference curve is defined as the absolute value of the slope of the indifference curve at that point. It is the amount of vanilla the consumer is willing to give up to get another pint of chocolate.

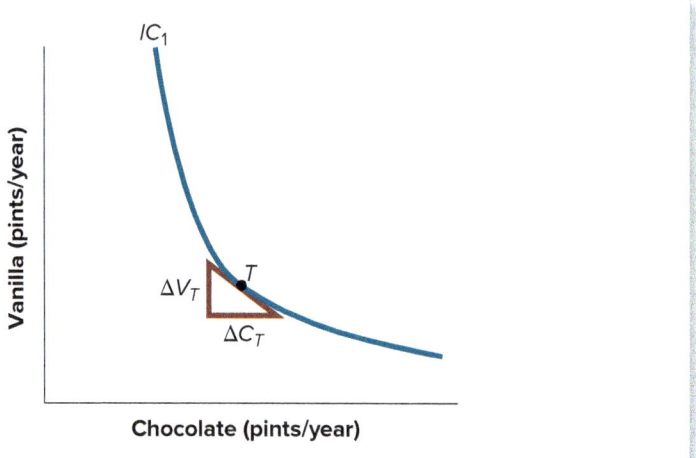

A common (but not universal) property of indifference curves is that the more a consumer has of one good, the more she must be given of that good before she will be willing to give up a unit of the other good. Stated differently, the MRS generally declines as we move downward to the right along an indifference curve. Indifference curves that exhibit diminishing marginal rates of substitution are thus convex—or bowed inward—when viewed from the origin. The indifference curves shown in Figures 5A.8, 5A.9, and 5A.10 all have this property, as does the curve shown in Figure 5A.11. This property is the indifference curve analog of the concept of diminishing marginal utility discussed in the main text of Chapter 5, *Demand*.

In Figure 5A.11, note that at bundle *A*, vanilla is relatively plentiful and the consumer would be willing to sacrifice three pints per year of it in order to obtain an additional pint of chocolate. Her MRS at *A* is 3. At *B*, the quantities of vanilla and chocolate are more balanced, and there she would be willing to give up only one pint per year to obtain an additional pint per year of chocolate. Her MRS at *B* is 1. Finally, note that vanilla is relatively scarce at *C*, where the consumer would need five additional pints per year of chocolate in return for giving up one pint per year of vanilla. Her MRS at *C* is 1/5.

Intuitively, diminishing MRS means that consumers like variety. We are usually willing to give up goods we already have a lot of in order to obtain more of those goods we now have only little of.

FIGURE 5A.11

Diminishing Marginal Rate of Substitution.

The more vanilla the consumer has, the more she is willing to give up to obtain an additional unit of chocolate. The marginal rates of substitution at bundles *A*, *B*, and *C* are 3, 1, and 1/5, respectively.

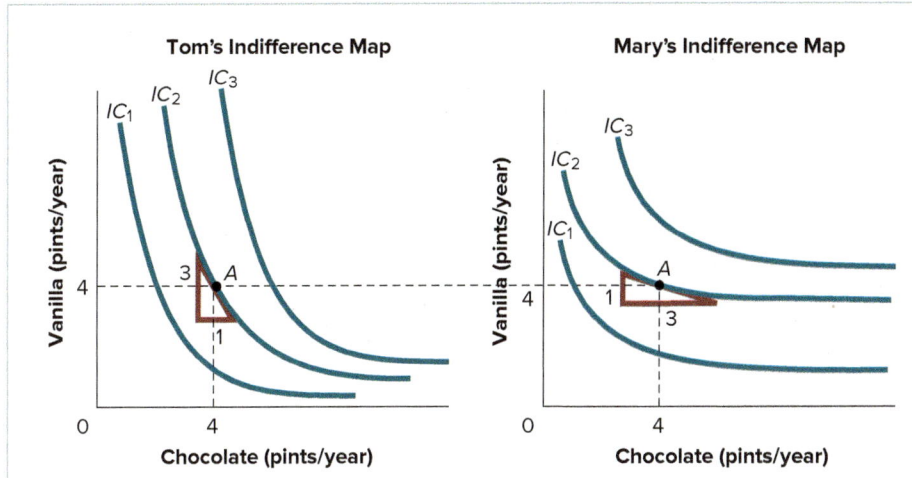

FIGURE 5A.12

People with Different Tastes.
Relatively speaking, Tom is a chocolate lover, Mary a vanilla lover. This difference shows up in the fact that at any given bundle, Tom's marginal rate of substitution of vanilla for chocolate is greater than Mary's. At bundle *A*, for example, Tom would give up three pints of vanilla to get another pint of chocolate, whereas Mary would give up three pints of chocolate to get another pint of vanilla.

USING INDIFFERENCE CURVES TO DESCRIBE PREFERENCES

To get a feel for how indifference maps describe a consumer's preferences, it is helpful to work through a simple example. Suppose that Tom and Mary like both chocolate and vanilla ice cream but that Tom's favorite flavor is chocolate while Mary's favorite is vanilla. This difference in their preferences is captured by the differing slopes of their indifference curves in Figure 5A.12. Note in the left panel, which shows Tom's indifference map, that he would be willing to exchange three pints of vanilla for one pint of chocolate at the bundle *A*. But at the corresponding bundle in the right panel, which shows Mary's indifference map, we see that Mary would trade three pints of chocolate to get another pint of vanilla. Their difference in preferences shows up clearly in this difference in their marginal rates of substitution of vanilla for chocolate.

THE BEST AFFORDABLE BUNDLE

We now have all the tools we need to determine how the consumer should allocate her income between two goods. The indifference map tells us how the various bundles are ranked in order of preference. The budget constraint, in turn, tells us which bundles are affordable. The consumer's task is to put the two together and choose the most preferred affordable bundle. (Recall from Chapter 1, *Thinking Like an Economist,* that we need not suppose that consumers think explicitly about budget constraints and indifference maps when deciding what to buy. It is sufficient that people make decisions *as if* they were thinking in these terms, just as experienced bicyclists ride as if they knew the relevant laws of physics.)

For the sake of concreteness, we again consider the choice between vanilla and chocolate ice cream that confronts a consumer with an income of $M = \$100$ per year facing prices of $P_V = \$10$ per pint and $P_C = \$5$ per pint. Figure 5A.13 shows this consumer's budget constraint and part of her indifference map. Of the five labeled bundles—*A, D, E, F,* and *G*—in the diagram, *G* is the most preferred because it lies on the highest indifference curve. *G*, however, is not affordable, nor is any other bundle that lies beyond the budget constraint. In general, the best affordable bundle will lie on the budget constraint, not inside it. (Any bundle inside the budget constraint would be less desirable than one just slightly to the northeast, which also would be affordable.)

Where, exactly, is the best affordable bundle located along the budget constraint? We know that it cannot be on an indifference curve that lies partly inside the budget constraint. On the indifference curve IC_1, for example, the only points that are even candidates for the best affordable bundle are the two that lie on the budget constraint, namely *A* and *E*. But *A* cannot be the best affordable bundle because it is equally preferred to *D*, which

The Best Affordable Bundle.

The best the consumer can do is to choose the bundle on the budget constraint that lies on the highest attainable indifference curve. Here, that is bundle *F*, which lies at a tangency between the indifference curve and the budget constraint.

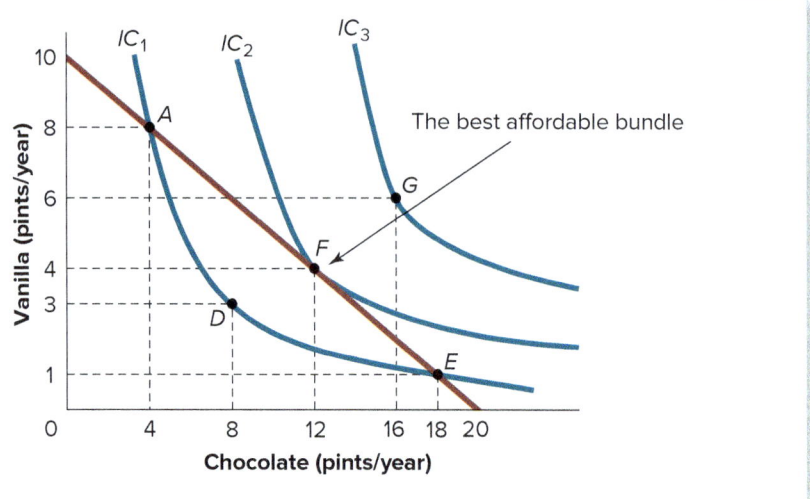

in turn is less desirable than *F*. So *A* also must be less desirable than *F*. For the same reason, *E* cannot be the best affordable bundle.

Since the best affordable bundle cannot lie on an indifference curve that lies partly inside the budget constraint, and since it must lie on the budget constraint itself, we know it has to lie on an indifference curve that intersects the budget constraint only once. In Figure 5A.13, that indifference curve is the one labeled IC_2, and the best affordable bundle is *F*, which lies at the point of tangency between IC_2 and the budget constraint. With an income of $100 per year and facing prices of $5 per pint for chocolate and $10 per pint of vanilla, the best this consumer can do is to buy 4 pints per year of vanilla and 12 pints per year of chocolate.

The choice of bundle *F* makes perfect sense on intuitive grounds. The consumer's goal, after all, is to reach the highest indifference curve she can, given her budget constraint. Her strategy is to keep moving to higher and higher indifference curves until she reaches the highest one that is still affordable. For indifference maps for which a tangency point exists, as in Figure 5A.13, the best bundle will always lie at the point of tangency. (See Problem 6 for an example in which a tangency does not exist.)

In Figure 5A.13, note that the marginal rate of substitution at *F* is exactly the same as the absolute value of the slope of the budget constraint. This will always be so when the best affordable bundle occurs at a point of tangency. The condition that must be satisfied in such cases is therefore

$$\text{MRS} = P_C/P_V. \tag{5A.3}$$

In the indifference curve framework, Equation 5A.3 is the counterpart to the rational spending rule developed in the main text of Chapter 5, *Demand*. The right-hand side of Equation 5A.3 represents the opportunity cost of chocolate in terms of vanilla. Thus, with $P_C = \$5$ per pint and $P_V = \$10$ per pint, the opportunity cost of an additional pint of chocolate is one-half pint of vanilla. The left-hand side of Equation 5A.3 is $|\Delta V/\Delta C|$, the absolute value of the slope of the indifference curve at the point of tangency. It is the amount of additional vanilla the consumer must be given in order to compensate her fully for the loss of one pint of chocolate. In the language of cost-benefit analysis discussed in Chapter 1, *Thinking Like an Economist*, the slope of the budget constraint represents the opportunity cost of chocolate in terms of vanilla, while the slope of the indifference curve represents the benefits of consuming chocolate as compared with consuming vanilla. Since the slope of the budget constraint is $-1/2$ in this example, the tangency condition tells us that one-half pint of vanilla would be required to compensate for the benefits given up with the loss of one pint of chocolate.

If the consumer were at some bundle on the budget line for which the two slopes were not the same, then it would always be possible for her to purchase a better bundle.

To see why, suppose she were at a point where the slope of the indifference curve (in absolute value) is less than the slope of the budget constraint, as at point E in Figure 5A.13. Suppose, for instance, that the MRS at E is only 1/4. This tells us that the consumer can be compensated for the loss of one pint of chocolate by being given an additional one-quarter pint of vanilla. But the slope of the budget constraint tells us that by giving up one pint of chocolate, he can purchase an additional one-half pint of vanilla. Since this is one-quarter pint more than he needs to remain equally satisfied, he will clearly be better off if he purchases more vanilla and less chocolate than at point E. The opportunity cost of an additional pint of vanilla is less than the benefit it confers.

 SELF-TEST 5A.5

Suppose that the marginal rate of substitution at point A in Figure 5A.13 is 1.0. Show that this means that the consumer will be better off if he purchases less vanilla and more chocolate than at A.

PROBLEMS

1. Suppose a consumer's income is $M = \$1,200$ per month, all of which he spends on some combination of rent and restaurant meals. If restaurant meals cost $12 each and if the monthly rent for an apartment is $3 per square foot, draw this consumer's budget constraint, with his monthly quantities of restaurant meals per month on the vertical axis and apartment size on the horizontal axis. Is the bundle (300 square feet/month, 50 meals/month) affordable?

2. Show what happens to the budget constraint in Problem 1 if the price of restaurant meals falls to $8. Is the bundle (300, 50) affordable?

3. What happens to the budget constraint in Problem 2 if the monthly rent for apartments falls to $2 per square foot? Is the bundle (300, 50) affordable?

4. When inflation happens, prices and incomes generally rise at about the same rate each year. What happens to the budget constraint from Problem 1 if the consumer's income rises by 10 percent and the prices of restaurant meals and apartment rents also rise by 10 percent? Has the consumer been harmed by inflation?

5. A consumer spends all his income on two goods, X and Y. Of the labeled points on his indifference map, indicate which ones are affordable and which ones are unaffordable. Indicate how the consumer ranks these bundles, ranging from most preferred to least preferred. Identify the best affordable bundle.

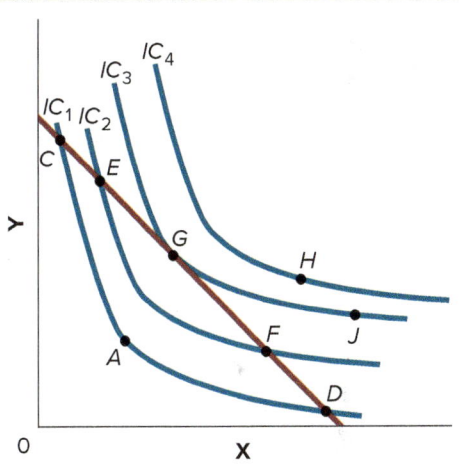

6. A consumer spends all his income on two goods, X and Y. His income and the prices of X and Y are such that his budget constraint is the line AF. Of the labeled points on his indifference map, indicate which is the best affordable bundle. (*Hint:* This problem does not have a tangency solution.)

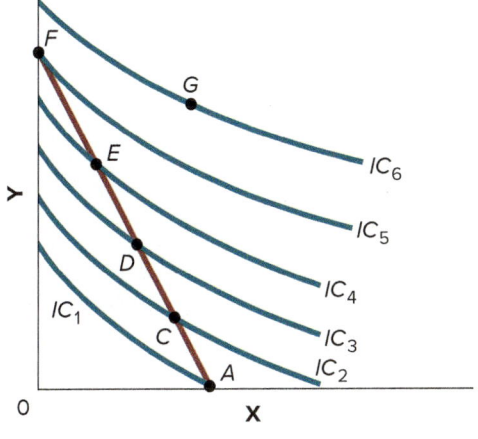

ANSWERS TO APPENDIX SELF-TESTS

5A.1

5A.2

5A.3

5A.4

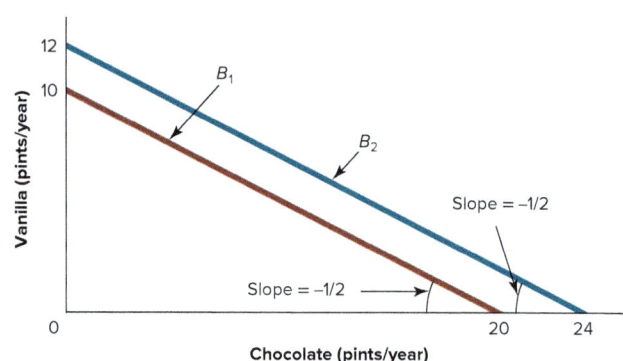

5A.5 At bundle *A*, the consumer is willing to give up one pint of vanilla in order to get an additional pint of chocolate. But at market prices it is necessary to give up only one-half pint of vanilla in order to buy an additional pint of chocolate. It follows that the consumer will be better off than at bundle *A* if he buys one pint less of vanilla and two pints more of chocolate.

CHAPTER 6

Perfectly Competitive Supply

Competitive markets never leave profit opportunities unexploited for long.

Emilio Ereza/Pixtal/age fotostock

LEARNING OBJECTIVES

After reading this chapter, you should be able to:

LO1 Explain how opportunity cost is related to the supply curve.

LO2 Discuss the relationship between the supply curve for an individual firm and the market supply curve for an industry.

LO3 Determine a perfectly competitive firm's profit-maximizing output level and profit in the short run and long run.

LO4 Match the determinants of supply with the factors that affect individual firms' costs and apply the theory of supply.

LO5 Define and calculate producer surplus.

Cars that took more than 50 hours to assemble in the 1970s are now built in less than 8 hours. Similar productivity growth has occurred in many other manufacturing industries. Yet in many service industries, productivity has grown only slowly, if at all. For example, the London Philharmonic Orchestra performs Beethoven's Fifth Symphony with no fewer musicians today than it did in 1850. And it still takes a barber about half an hour to cut someone's hair, just as it always has.

Given the spectacular growth in manufacturing workers' productivity, it's no surprise that their real wages have risen more than fivefold during the last century. But why have real wages for service workers risen just as much? If barbers and musicians are no more productive than they were at the turn of the century, why are they now paid five times as much?

An answer is suggested by the observation that the opportunity cost of pursuing any given occupation is the most one could have earned in some other occupation. Most people who become barbers or musicians could instead have chosen jobs in manufacturing. If workers in service industries were not paid roughly as much as they could have earned in other occupations, many of them would not have been willing to work in service industries in the first place.

Why are barbers paid five times as much now as in 1900, even though they can't cut hair any faster than they could then?

Cost-Benefit

The trajectories of wages in manufacturing and service industries illustrate the intimate link between the prices at which goods and services are offered for sale in the market and the opportunity cost of the resources required to produce them.

In Chapter 5, *Demand*, we saw that the demand curve is a schedule that tells how many units buyers wish to purchase at different prices. Our task here is to gain insight into the factors that shape the supply curve, the schedule that tells how many units suppliers wish to sell at different prices.

Although the demand side and the supply side of the market are different in several ways, many of these differences are superficial. Indeed, the behavior of both buyers and sellers is, in an important sense, fundamentally the same. After all, the two groups confront essentially similar questions—in the buyer's case, "Should I buy another unit?" and in the seller's, "Should I sell another unit?" What is more, buyers and sellers use the same criterion for answering these questions. Thus, a rational consumer will buy another unit if its benefit exceeds its cost and a rational seller will sell another unit if the cost of making it is less than the extra revenue he can get from selling it (the familiar Cost-Benefit Principle again).

THINKING ABOUT SUPPLY: THE IMPORTANCE OF OPPORTUNITY COST

Do you live in a state that requires refundable soft drink container deposits? If so, you've probably noticed that some people always redeem their own containers while other people pass up this opportunity, leaving their used containers to be recycled by others. Recycling used containers is a service and its production obeys the same logic that applies to the production of other goods and services. The following sequence of recycling examples shows how the supply curve for a good or service is rooted in the individual's choice of whether to produce it.

EXAMPLE 6.1

Opportunity Cost and Supply

How much time should Ushi spend recycling soft drink containers?

Ushi is trying to decide how to divide his time between his job as a dishwasher in the dining hall, which pays $6 an hour for as many hours as he chooses to work, and gathering soft drink containers to redeem for deposit, in which case his pay depends on both the deposit per container and the number of containers he finds. Earnings aside, Ushi is indifferent between the two tasks, and the number of containers he'll find depends, as shown in the following table, on the number of hours per day he searches:

Search time (hours/day)	Total number of containers found	Additional number of containers found
0	0	
		600
1	600	
		400
2	1,000	
		300
3	1,300	
		200
4	1,500	
		100
5	1,600	

If the containers may be redeemed for 2 cents each, how many hours should Ushi spend searching for containers?

For each additional hour Ushi spends searching for soft drink containers, he loses the $6 he could have earned as a dishwasher. This is his hourly opportunity cost of searching for soft drink containers. His benefit from each hour spent searching for containers is the number of additional containers he finds (shown in column 3 of the table) times the deposit he collects per container. Since he can redeem each container for 2 cents, his first hour spent collecting containers will yield earnings of 600($0.02) = $12, or $6 more than he could have earned as a dishwasher.

By the Cost-Benefit Principle, then, Ushi should spend his first hour of work each day searching for soft drink containers rather than washing dishes. A second hour searching for containers will yield 400 additional containers, for additional earnings of $8, so it too satisfies the cost-benefit test. A third hour spent searching yields 300 additional containers, for 300($0.02) = $6 of additional earnings. Since this is exactly what Ushi could have earned washing dishes, he's indifferent between spending his third hour of work each day on one task or the other. For the sake of discussion, however, we'll assume that he resolves ties in favor of searching for containers, in which case he'll spend three hours each day searching for containers.

Cost-Benefit

Using the data provided in Example 6.1, what is the lowest redemption price that would induce Ushi to spend at least one hour per day recycling? Since he'll find 600 containers in his first hour of search, a 1 cent deposit on each container would enable him to match his $6 per hour opportunity cost. More generally, if the redemption price is p, and the next hour spent searching yields ΔQ additional containers, then Ushi's additional earnings from searching the additional hour will be $p(\Delta Q)$. This means that the smallest redemption price that will lead Ushi to search another hour must satisfy the equation

$$p(\Delta Q) = \$6. \tag{6.1}$$

How high would the redemption price of containers have to be to induce Ushi to search for a second hour? Since he can find $\Delta Q = 400$ additional containers if he searches for a second hour, the smallest redemption price that will lead him to do so must satisfy $p(400) = \$6$, which solves for $p = 1.5$ cents.

 SELF-TEST 6.1

In the previous example, calculate the lowest container redemption prices that will lead Ushi to search a third, fourth, and fifth hour.

By searching for soft drink containers, Ushi becomes, in effect, a supplier of container-recycling services. In Self-Test 6.1, we saw that Ushi's reservation prices for his third, fourth, and fifth hours of container search are 2, 3, and 6 cents, respectively. Having calculated these reservation prices, we can now plot his supply curve of container-recycling services. This curve, which plots the redemption price per container on the vertical axis and the number of containers recycled each day on the horizontal axis, is shown in Figure 6.1. Ushi's individual supply curve of container-recycling services tells us the number of containers he is willing to recycle at various redemption prices.

The supply curve shown in Figure 6.1 is upward-sloping, just like those we saw in Chapter 3, *Supply and Demand*. There are exceptions to this general rule, but sellers of most goods will offer higher quantities at higher prices.

FIGURE 6.1

An Individual Supply Curve for Recycling Services.

When the deposit price increases, it becomes attractive to abandon alternative pursuits to spend more time searching for soft drink containers.

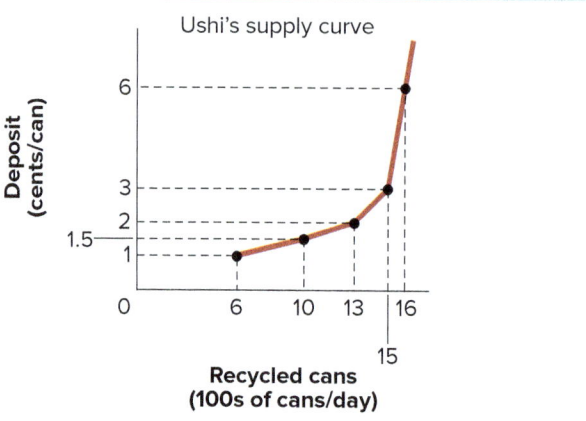

INDIVIDUAL AND MARKET SUPPLY CURVES

The relationship between the individual and market supply curves for a product is analogous to the relationship between the individual and market demand curves. The quantity that corresponds to a given price on the market demand curve is the sum of the quantities demanded at that price by all individual buyers in the market. Likewise, the quantity that corresponds to any given price on the market supply curve is the sum of the quantities supplied at that price by all individual sellers in the market.

Suppose, for example, that the supply side of the recycling-services market consists only of Ushi and his identical twin, Yoshi, whose individual supply curve is the same as Ushi's. To generate the market supply curve, we first put the individual supply curves side by side, as shown in Figure 6.2(a) and (b). We then announce a price, and for that price add the individual quantities supplied to obtain the total quantity supplied in the market. Thus, at a price of 3 cents per container, both Ushi and Yoshi wish to recycle 1,500 cans per day, so the total market supply at that price is 3,000 cans per day. Proceeding in like manner for a sequence of prices, we generate the market supply curve for recycling services shown in Figure 6.2(c). This is the same process of horizontal summation by which we generated market demand curves from individual demand curves in Chapter 5, *Demand*.

Alternatively, if there were many suppliers with individual supply curves identical to Ushi's, we could generate the market supply curve by simply multiplying each quantity value on the individual supply curve by the number of suppliers. For instance, Figure 6.3

FIGURE 6.2

The Market Supply Curve for Recycling Services.

To generate the market supply curve (c) from the individual supply curves (a) and (b), we add the individual supply curves horizontally.

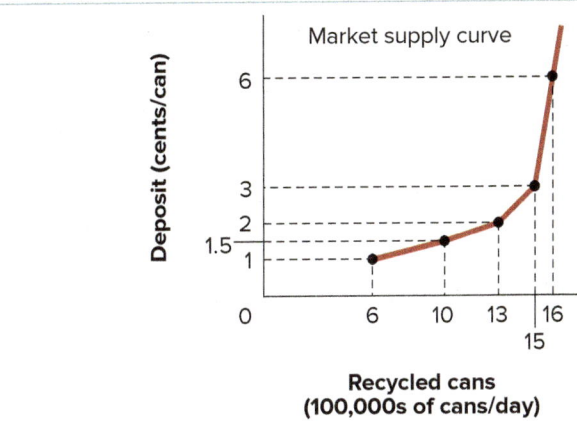

FIGURE 6.3

The Market Supply Curve with 1,000 Identical Sellers.

To generate the market supply curve for a market with 1,000 identical sellers, we simply multiply each quantity value on the individual supply curve by 1,000.

shows the supply curve for a market in which there are 1,000 suppliers with individual supply curves like Ushi's.

Why do individual supply curves tend to be upward-sloping? One explanation is suggested by the Principle of Increasing Opportunity Cost, or the Low-Hanging-Fruit Principle. Container recyclers will tend to be more productive if they always look first for the containers that are easiest to find–such as those in plain view in readily accessible locations. As the redemption price rises, it will pay to incur the additional cost of searching farther from the beaten path.

>> Increasing Opportunity Cost

If all individuals have identical upward-sloping supply curves, the market supply curve will be upward-sloping as well. But there is an important additional reason for the positive slope of market supply curves: Individual suppliers generally differ with respect to their opportunity costs of supplying the product. (The Principle of Increasing Opportunity Cost applies not only to each individual searcher, but also *across* individuals.) Thus, whereas people facing unattractive employment opportunities in other occupations may be willing to recycle soft drink containers even when the redemption price is low, those with more attractive options will recycle only if the redemption price is relatively high.

>> Increasing Opportunity Cost

In summary, then, the upward slope of the supply curve reflects the fact that costs tend to rise at the margin when producers expand production, partly because each individual exploits her most attractive opportunities first, but also because different potential sellers face different opportunity costs.

PROFIT-MAXIMIZING FIRMS IN PERFECTLY COMPETITIVE MARKETS

To explore the nature of the supply curve of a product more fully, we must say more about the goals of the organizations that supply the product and the kind of economic environment in which they operate. In virtually every economy, goods and services are produced by a variety of organizations that pursue a host of different motives. The Red Cross supplies blood because its organizers and donors want to help people in need; the local government fixes potholes because the mayor was elected on a promise to do so; karaoke singers perform because they like public attention; and car-wash employees are driven primarily by the hope of making enough money to pay their rent.

PROFIT MAXIMIZATION

Notwithstanding this rich variety of motives, *most* goods and services that are offered for sale in a market economy are sold by private firms whose main reason for existing is to earn **profit** for their owners. A firm's profit is the difference between the total revenue it receives from the sale of its product and all costs it incurs in producing it.

profit the total revenue a firm receives from the sale of its product minus all costs—explicit and implicit—incurred in producing it

profit-maximizing firm
a firm whose primary goal is
to maximize the difference
between its total revenues
and total costs

perfectly competitive market
a market in which no individual supplier has significant
influence on the market price
of the product

price taker a firm that has
no influence over the price at
which it sells its product

A **profit-maximizing firm** is one whose primary goal is to maximize the amount of profit it earns. The supply curves that economists use in standard supply and demand theory are based on the assumption that goods are sold by profit-maximizing firms in **perfectly competitive markets**, which are markets in which individual firms have no influence over the market prices of the products they sell. Because of their inability to influence market price, perfectly competitive firms are often described as **price takers**.

The following four conditions are characteristic of markets that are perfectly competitive:

1. *All firms sell the same standardized product.* Although this condition is almost never literally satisfied, it holds as a rough approximation for many markets. Thus, the markets for concrete building blocks of a given size, or for apples of a given variety, may be described in this way. This condition implies that buyers are willing to switch from one seller to another if by so doing they can obtain a lower price.

2. *The market has many buyers and sellers, each of which buys or sells only a small fraction of the total quantity exchanged.* This condition implies that individual buyers and sellers will be price takers, regarding the market price of the product as a fixed number beyond their control. For example, a single farmer's decision to plant fewer acres of wheat would have no appreciable impact on the market price of wheat, just as an individual consumer's decision to become a vegetarian would have no perceptible effect on the price of beef.

3. *Productive resources are mobile.* This condition implies that if a potential seller identifies a profitable business opportunity in a market, he or she will be able to obtain the labor, capital, and other productive resources necessary to enter that market. By the same token, sellers who are dissatisfied with the opportunities they confront in a given market are free to leave that market and employ their resources elsewhere.

4. *Buyers and sellers are well informed.* This condition implies that buyers and sellers are aware of the relevant opportunities available to them. If that were not so, buyers would be unable to seek out sellers who charge the lowest prices, and sellers would have no means of deploying their resources in the markets in which they would earn the most profit.

The market for wheat closely approximates a perfectly competitive market. The market for operating systems for desktop computers, however, does not. Roughly 80 percent of desktop operating systems are sold by Microsoft, giving the company enough influence in that market to have significant control over the price it charges. For example, if it were to raise the price of its latest edition of Windows by, say, 20 percent, some consumers might switch to macOS or Linux, and others might postpone their purchase; but many—perhaps even most—would continue with their plans to buy Windows.

By contrast, if an individual wheat farmer were to charge even a few cents more than the current market price for a bushel of wheat, he wouldn't be able to sell any of his wheat at all. And since he can sell as much wheat as he wishes at the market price, he has no motive to charge less.

THE DEMAND CURVE FACING A PERFECTLY COMPETITIVE FIRM

From the perspective of an individual firm in a perfectly competitive market, what does the demand curve for its product look like? Since it can sell as much or as little as it wishes at the prevailing market price, the demand curve for its product is perfectly elastic at the market price. Figure 6.4(a) shows the market demand and supply curves intersecting to determine a market price of P_0. Figure 6.4(b) shows the product demand curve, D_i, as seen by any individual firm in this market, a horizontal line at the market price level P_0.

imperfectly competitive firm (or **price setter**) a firm that has at least some control over the market price of its product

Many of the conclusions of the standard supply and demand model also hold for **imperfectly competitive firms** (or **price setters**)—those firms, like Microsoft, that have at least some ability to vary their own prices. But certain other conclusions do not, as we shall see when we examine the behavior of such firms more closely in Chapter 8, *Monopoly, Oligopoly, and Monopolistic Competition.*

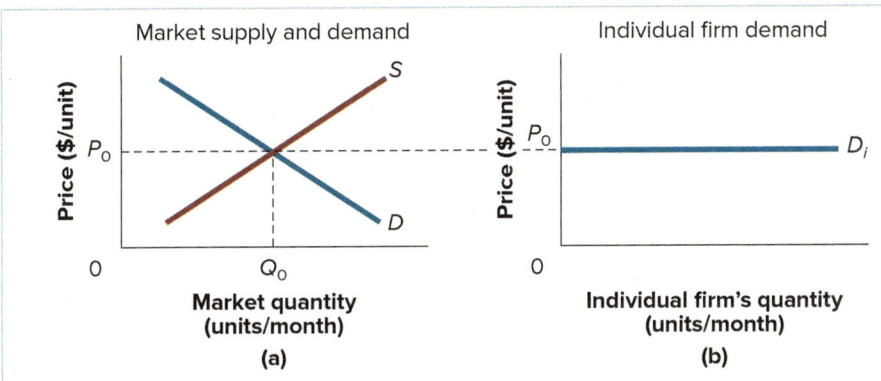

FIGURE 6.4

The Demand Curve Facing a Perfectly Competitive Firm.

The market demand and supply curves intersect to determine the market price of the product (a). The individual firm's demand curve, D_i (b), is a horizontal line at the market price.

Since a perfectly competitive firm has no control over the market price of its product, it needn't worry about choosing the level at which to set that price. As we've seen, the equilibrium market price in a competitive market comes from the intersection of the industry supply and demand curves. The challenge confronting the perfectly competitive firm is to choose its output level so that it makes as much profit as it can at that price. As we investigate how the competitive firm responds to this challenge, we'll see that some costs are more important than others.

PRODUCTION IN THE SHORT RUN

To gain a deeper understanding of the origins of the supply curve, it is helpful to consider a perfectly competitive firm confronting the decision of how much to produce. The firm in question is a small company that makes glass bottles. To keep things simple, suppose that the silica required for making bottles is available free of charge from a nearby desert and that the only costs incurred by the firm are the wages it pays its employees and the lease payment on its bottle-making machine. The employees and the machine are the firm's only two **factors of production**–inputs used to produce goods and services. In more complex examples, factors of production also might include land, structures, entrepreneurship, and possibly others, but for the moment we consider only labor and capital.

When we refer to the **short run**, we mean a period of time during which at least some of the firm's factors of production cannot be varied. For our bottle maker, we will assume that the number of employees can be varied on short notice but that the capacity of its bottle-making machine can be altered only with significant delay. For this firm, then, the short run is simply that period of time during which the firm cannot alter the capacity of its bottle-making machine. By contrast, when we speak of the **long run**, we refer to a time period of sufficient length that all the firm's factors of production are variable.

Table 6.1 shows how the company's bottle production depends on the number of hours its employees spend on the job each day. The output–employment relationship described in Table 6.1 exhibits a pattern that is common to many such relationships. Each time we add an additional unit of labor, output grows, but beyond some point the additional output that results from each additional unit of labor begins to diminish. Note in the right column, for example, that output gains begin to diminish with the third employee. Economists refer to this pattern as the **law of diminishing returns**, and it always refers to situations in which at least some factors of production are fixed.

Law of Diminishing Returns: When some factors of production are held fixed, increased production of the good eventually requires ever-larger increases in the variable factor.

Here, the **fixed factor** is the bottle-making machine, and the **variable factor** is labor. In the context of this example, the law of diminishing returns says simply that successive increases in the labor input eventually yield smaller and smaller increments in bottle output. (Strictly

factor of production an input used in the production of a good or service

short run a period of time sufficiently short that at least some of the firm's factors of production are fixed

long run a period of time of sufficient length that all the firm's factors of production are variable

law of diminishing returns a property of the relationship between the amount of a good or service produced and the amount of a variable factor required to produce it; the law says that when some factors of production are fixed, increased production of the good eventually requires ever-larger increases in the variable factor

fixed factor of production an input whose quantity cannot be altered in the short run

variable factor of production an input whose quantity can be altered in the short run

TABLE 6.1
Employment and Output for a Glass Bottle Maker

Total number of employees per day	Total number of bottles per day
0	0
1	80
2	200
3	260
4	300
5	330
6	350
7	362

speaking, the law ought to be called the law of *eventually* diminishing returns because output may initially grow at an increasing rate with additional units of the variable factor.)

Typically, returns from additional units of the variable input eventually diminish because of some form of congestion. For instance, in an office with three secretaries and only a single desktop computer, we would not expect to get three times as many letters typed per hour as in an office with only one secretary because only one person can use a computer at a time.

SOME IMPORTANT COST CONCEPTS

fixed cost the sum of all payments made to the firm's fixed factors of production

variable cost the sum of all payments made to the firm's variable factors of production

total cost the sum of all payments made to the firm's fixed and variable factors of production

For the bottle-making firm described in Table 6.1, suppose the lease payment for the company's bottle-making machine is $40 per day, which must be paid whether the company makes any bottles or not. This payment is both a **fixed cost** (since it does not depend on the number of bottles per day the firm makes) and, for the duration of the lease, a sunk cost. The first two columns of Table 6.2 reproduce the employment and output entries from Table 6.1, and the firm's fixed cost appears in column 3.

The company's payment to its employees is called **variable cost** because, unlike fixed cost, it varies with the number of bottles the company produces. The variable cost of producing 200 bottles per day, for example, is shown in column 4 of Table 6.2 as $24 per day. Column 5 shows the firm's **total cost**, which is the sum of its fixed and variable costs.

TABLE 6.2
Fixed, Variable, and Total Costs of Bottle Production

(1) Employees per day	(2) Bottles per day	(3) Fixed cost ($/day)	(4) Variable cost ($/day)	(5) Total cost ($/day)	(6) Marginal cost ($/bottle)
0	0	40	0	40	
					0.15
1	80	40	12	52	
					0.10
2	200	40	24	64	
					0.20
3	260	40	36	76	
					0.30
4	300	40	48	88	
					0.40
5	330	40	60	100	
					0.60
6	350	40	72	112	
					1.00
7	362	40	84	124	

Column 6, finally, shows the firm's **marginal cost**, a measure of how its total cost changes when its output changes. Specifically, marginal cost is defined as the change in total cost divided by the corresponding change in output. Note, for example, that when the firm expands production from 80 to 200 bottles per day, its total cost goes up by $12, which gives rise to the marginal cost entry of ($12/day)/(120 bottles/day) = $0.10 per bottle. To emphasize that marginal cost refers to the change in total cost when quantity changes, we place the marginal cost entries between the corresponding quantity rows of the table.

marginal cost the increase in total cost that results from carrying out one additional unit of an activity

CHOOSING OUTPUT TO MAXIMIZE PROFIT

In the following examples and exercises, we'll explore how the company's decision about how many bottles to produce depends on the price of bottles, the wage, and the cost of capital. Again, our starting assumption is that the firm's basic goal is to maximize the amount of profit it earns from the production and sale of bottles, where profit is the difference between its total revenue and its total cost:

$$\begin{aligned} \text{Profit} &= \text{Total revenue} - \text{Total cost} \\ &= \text{Total revenue} - \text{Variable cost} - \text{Fixed cost.} \end{aligned} \quad (6.2)$$

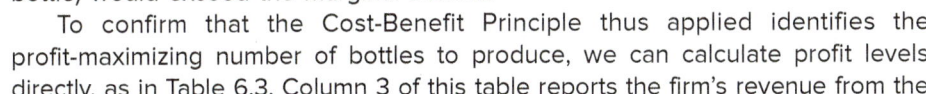

EXAMPLE 6.2   **The Profit-Maximizing Output Level**

If bottles sell for 35 cents each, how many bottles should the company described in Table 6.2 produce each day?

To answer this question, we need simply apply the Cost-Benefit Principle to the question "Should the firm expand its level of output?" If its goal is to maximize its profit, the answer to this question will be to expand as long as the marginal benefit from expanding is at least as great as the marginal cost. Since the perfectly competitive firm can sell as many bottles as it wishes at the market price of $0.35 per bottle, its marginal benefit from selling an additional bottle is $0.35. If we compare this marginal benefit with the marginal cost entries shown in column 6 of Table 6.2, we see that the firm should keep expanding until it reaches 300 bottles per day (four employees per day). To expand beyond that level, it would have to hire a fifth employee, and the resulting marginal cost ($0.40 per bottle) would exceed the marginal benefit.

Cost-Benefit

To confirm that the Cost-Benefit Principle thus applied identifies the profit-maximizing number of bottles to produce, we can calculate profit levels directly, as in Table 6.3. Column 3 of this table reports the firm's revenue from the

TABLE 6.3
Output, Revenue, Costs, and Profit

(1) Employees per day	(2) Output (bottles/day)	(3) Total revenue ($/day)	(4) Total cost ($/day)	(5) Profit ($/day)
0	0	0	40	−40
1	80	28	52	−24
2	200	70	64	6
3	260	91	76	15
4	300	105	88	17
5	330	115.50	100	15.50
6	350	122.50	112	10.50
7	362	126.70	124	2.70

sale of bottles, which is calculated as the product of the number of bottles produced per day and the price of $0.35 per bottle. Note, for example, that in the third row of that column, total revenue is (200 bottles/day)($0.35/bottle) = $70 per day. Column 5 reports the firm's total daily profit, which is just the difference between its total revenue (column 3) and its total cost (column 4). Note that the largest profit entry in column 5, $17 per day, occurs at an output of 300 bottles per day, just as suggested by our earlier application of the Cost-Benefit Principle.

As the Self-Test 6.2 demonstrates, an increase in the price of the product gives rise to an increase in the profit-maximizing level of output.

 SELF-TEST 6.2

How would the profit-maximizing level of bottle production change in Example 6.2 if bottles sell for 62 cents each?

The Self-Test 6.3 illustrates that a fall in the wage rate leads to a decline in marginal cost, which also causes an increase in the profit-maximizing level of output.

 SELF-TEST 6.3

How would the profit-maximizing level of bottle production change in Example 6.2 if bottles sell for 35 cents each, but wages fall to $6 per day?

Suppose that in the example the firm's fixed cost had been not $40 per day but $45 per day. How, if at all, would that have affected the firm's profit-maximizing level of output? The answer is not at all. Each entry in the profit column of Table 6.3 would have been $5 per day smaller than before, but the maximum profit entry still would have been 300 bottles per day.

 The observation that the profit-maximizing quantity does not depend on fixed costs is not an idiosyncrasy of this example. That it holds true in general is an immediate consequence of the Cost-Benefit Principle, which says that a firm should increase its output if, and only if, the *marginal* benefit exceeds the *marginal* cost. Neither the marginal benefit of expanding (which is the market price of bottles) nor the marginal cost of expanding is affected by a change in the firm's fixed cost.

When the law of diminishing returns applies (i.e., when some factors of production are fixed), marginal cost goes up as the firm expands production beyond some point. Under these circumstances, the firm's best option is to keep expanding output as long as marginal cost is less than price.

Note that if the bottle company's fixed cost had been any more than $57 per day, it would have made a loss at *every* possible level of output. As long as it still had to pay its fixed cost, however, its best bet would have been to continue producing 300 bottles per day. It's better, after all, to experience a smaller loss than a larger one. If a firm in that situation expected conditions to remain the same, though, it would want to get out of the bottle business as soon as its equipment lease expired.

A NOTE ON THE FIRM'S SHUTDOWN CONDITION

It might seem that a firm that can sell as much output as it wishes at a constant market price would *always* do best in the short run by producing and selling the output level for which price equals marginal cost. But there are exceptions to this rule. Suppose, for example, that the market price of the firm's product falls so low that its revenue from sales is smaller than its variable cost at all possible levels of output. The firm should then cease production for the time being. By shutting down, it will suffer a loss equal to its fixed costs. But by remaining open, it would suffer an even larger loss.

More formally, if P denotes the market price of the product and Q denotes the number of units produced and sold, then $P \times Q$ is the firm's total revenue from sales, and if we use VC to denote the firm's variable cost, the rule is that the firm should shut down in the short run if $P \times Q$ is less than VC for every level of Q:

Short-run shutdown condition: $P \times Q < VC$ for all levels of Q.   (6.3)

 SELF-TEST 6.4

Using the bottle company example, suppose bottles sold not for $0.35 but only $0.10. Calculate the profit corresponding to each level of output, as in Table 6.3, and verify that the firm's best option is to cease operations in the short run.

AVERAGE VARIABLE COST AND AVERAGE TOTAL COST

Suppose that the firm is unable to cover its variable cost at any level of output—that is, suppose that $P \times Q < VC$ for all levels of Q. It must then also be true that $P < VC/Q$ for all levels of Q, since we obtain the second inequality by simply dividing both sides of the first one by Q. VC/Q is the firm's **average variable cost (AVC)**—its variable cost divided by its output. The firm's short-run shutdown condition may thus be restated a second way: Discontinue operations in the short run if the product price is less than the minimum value of its average variable cost (*AVC*). Thus,

average variable cost (AVC) variable cost divided by total output

Short-run shutdown condition (alternate version): $P <$ minimum value of *AVC*.   (6.4)

As we'll see in the next section, this version of the shutdown condition often enables us to tell at a glance whether the firm should continue operations.

A related cost concept that facilitates assessment of the firm's profitability is **average total cost (ATC)**, which is total cost (*TC*) divided by output (*Q*): $ATC = TC/Q$. The firm's profit, again, is the difference between its total revenue ($P \times Q$) and its total cost. And since total cost is equal to average total cost times quantity, the firm's profit is also equal to $(P \times Q) - (ATC \times Q)$. A firm is said to be **profitable** if its revenue ($P \times Q$) exceeds its total cost ($ATC \times Q$). A firm can thus be profitable only if the price of its product (P) exceeds its *ATC* for some level of output.

average total cost (ATC) total cost divided by total output

profitable firm a firm whose total revenue exceeds its total cost

Keeping track of all these cost concepts may seem tedious. In the next section, however, we'll see that the payoff from doing so is that they enable us to recast the profit-maximization decision in a simple graphical framework.

A GRAPHICAL APPROACH TO PROFIT MAXIMIZATION

For the bottle-making firm we've been discussing, average variable cost and average total cost values are shown in columns 4 and 6 of Table 6.4. Using the entries in this table, we plot the firm's average total cost, average variable cost, and marginal cost curves in Figure 6.5. (Because marginal cost corresponds to the change in total cost as we move between two output levels, each marginal cost value in Table 6.4 is plotted at an output level midway between those in the adjacent rows.)

We call your attention to several features of the cost curves in Figure 6.5. Note, for example, that the upward-sloping portion of the marginal cost curve (*MC*) corresponds to the region of diminishing returns discussed earlier. Thus, as the firm moves beyond two employees per day (200 bottles per day), the increments to total output become

TABLE 6.4

Average Variable Cost and Average Total Cost of Bottle Production

(1) Employees per day	(2) Bottles per day	(3) Variable cost ($/day)	(4) Average variable cost ($/unit of output)	(5) Total cost ($/day)	(6) Average total cost ($/unit of output)	(7) Marginal cost ($/bottle)
0	0	0		40		
						0.15
1	80	12	0.15	52	0.65	
						0.10
2	200	24	0.12	64	0.32	
						0.20
3	260	36	0.138	76	0.292	
						0.30
4	300	48	0.16	88	0.293	
						0.40
5	330	60	0.182	100	0.303	
						0.60
6	350	72	0.206	112	0.32	
						1.00
7	362	84	0.232	124	0.343	

smaller with each additional employee, which means that the cost of producing additional bottles (*MC*) must be increasing in this region.

Note also that the definition of marginal cost implies that the marginal cost curve must intersect both the average variable cost curve (*AVC*) and the average total cost curve (*ATC*) at their respective minimum points. To see why, consider the logic that explains what happens to the average weight of children in a third-grade class when a new student joins the class. If the new (marginal) student is lighter than the previous average weight for the class, average weight will fall, but if the new student is heavier than the previous average, average weight will rise. By the same token, when marginal cost is below average total cost or average variable cost, the corresponding average cost must be falling, and vice versa. And this ensures that the marginal cost curve must pass through the minimum points of both average cost curves.

Seeing the bottle maker's *AVC* curve displayed graphically makes the question posed in Self-Test 6.4 much easier to answer. The question, recall, was whether the firm should shut down in the short run if the price per bottle was only $0.10. A glance at Figure 6.5 reveals that the firm should indeed shut down because this price lies below the minimum value of its *AVC* curve, making it impossible for the firm to cover its variable costs at any output level.

FIGURE 6.5

The Marginal, Average Variable, and Average Total Cost Curves for a Bottle Manufacturer.

The *MC* curve cuts both the *AVC* and *ATC* curves at their minimum points. The upward-sloping portion of the marginal cost curve corresponds to the region of diminishing returns.

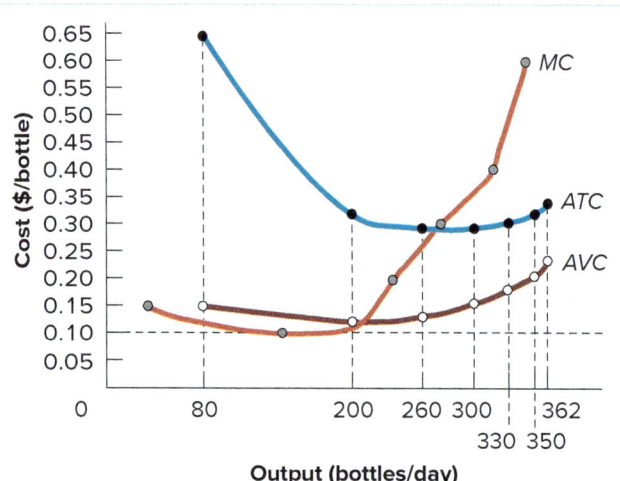

PRICE = MARGINAL COST: THE MAXIMUM-PROFIT CONDITION

So far, we've implicitly assumed that the bottle maker could employ workers only in whole-number amounts. Under these conditions, we saw that the profit-maximizing output level was one for which marginal cost was somewhat less than price (because adding yet another employee would have pushed marginal cost higher than price). In the next example, we'll see that when output and employment can be varied continuously, the maximum-profit condition is that price be equal to marginal cost.

EXAMPLE 6.3	The Graphical Approach to Profit Maximization

For the bottle maker whose cost curves are shown in Figure 6.6, find the profit-maximizing output level if bottles sell for $0.20 each. How much profit will this firm earn? What is the lowest price at which this firm would continue to operate in the short run?

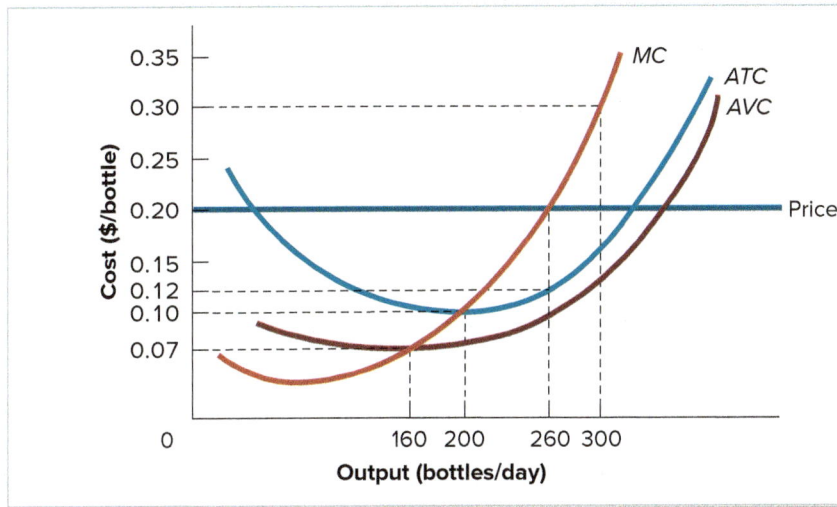

FIGURE 6.6

Price = Marginal Cost: The Perfectly Competitive Firm's Profit-Maximizing Supply Rule.

If price is greater than marginal cost, the firm can increase its profit by expanding production and sales. If price is less than marginal cost, the firm can increase its profit by producing and selling less output.

The Cost-Benefit Principle tells us that this firm should continue to expand as long as price is at least as great as marginal cost. In Figure 6.6 we see that if the firm follows this rule, it will produce 260 bottles per day, the quantity at which price and marginal cost are equal. To gain further confidence that 260 must be the profit-maximizing quantity when the price is $0.20 per bottle, first suppose that the firm had sold some amount less than that—say, only 200 bottles per day. Its benefit from expanding output by one bottle would then be the bottle's market price, here 20 cents. The cost of expanding output by one bottle is equal (by definition) to the firm's marginal cost, which at 200 bottles per day is only 10 cents (see Figure 6.6). So by selling the 201st bottle for 20 cents and producing it for an extra cost of only 10 cents, the firm will increase its profit by 20 − 10 = 10 cents per day. In a similar way, we can show that for *any* quantity less than the level at which price equals marginal cost, the seller can boost profit by expanding production.

Cost-Benefit

Conversely, suppose that the firm was currently selling more than 260 bottles per day—say, 300—at a price of 20 cents each. In Figure 6.6 we see that marginal cost at an output of 300 is 30 cents per bottle. If the firm then contracted its output by one bottle per day, it would cut its costs by 30 cents while losing only 20 cents in revenue. As a result, its profit would grow by 10 cents per day. The same argument can be made regarding any quantity larger than 260, so if the firm is currently selling an output at which price is less than marginal cost, it can always do better by producing and selling fewer bottles.

We've thus established that if the firm sold fewer than 260 bottles per day, it could earn more profit by expanding; and if it sold more than 260, it could earn more by contracting. It follows that at a market price of 20 cents per bottle, the seller maximizes its profit by selling 260 units per day, the quantity for which price and marginal cost are exactly the same.

At that quantity the firm will collect total revenue of $P \times Q =$ ($0.20/bottle) (260 bottles/day) = $52 per day. Note in Figure 6.6 that at 260 bottles per day the firm's average total cost is $ATC = $0.12 per bottle, which means that its total cost is $ATC \times Q = $($0.12/bottle)(260 bottles/day) = $31.20 per day. The firm's profit is the difference between its total revenue and its total cost, or $20.80 per day. Note, finally, that the minimum value of the firm's AVC curve is $0.07. So if the price of bottles fell below 7 cents each, the firm would shut down in the short run.

Another attractive feature of the graphical method of finding the profit-maximizing output level is that it permits us to calculate the firm's profit graphically. Thus, for the firm in the preceding example, daily profit is simply the difference between price and ATC times the number of units sold: ($0.20/bottle $-$ $0.12/bottle)(260 bottles/day) = $20.80 per day, which is the area of the shaded rectangle in Figure 6.7.

FIGURE 6.7

Measuring Profit Graphically.

Profit is equal to $(P - ATC) \times Q$, which is equal to the area of the shaded rectangle.

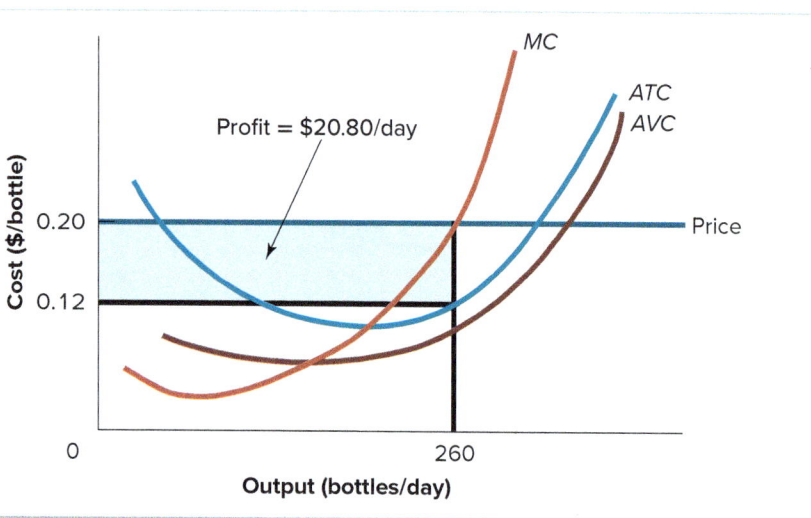

Not all firms are as fortunate as the one shown in Figure 6.7. Suppose, for example, that the price of bottles had been not 20 cents but only 8 cents. Since that price is greater than the minimum value of AVC (see Figure 6.8), the firm should continue to operate in the short run by producing the level of output for which price equals marginal cost (180 bottles per day). But because price is less than ATC at that level of output, the firm will now experience a loss, or negative profit, on its operations. This profit is calculated as $(P - ATC) \times Q =$ ($0.08/bottle $-$ $0.10/bottle) $\times$ (180 bottles/day) = $-$$3.60 per day, which is equal to the area of the shaded rectangle in Figure 6.8.

In Chapter 7, *Efficiency, Exchange, and the Invisible Hand in Action*, we'll see how firms move resources from one market to another in response to the incentives implicit in profits and losses. But such movements occur in the long run, and our focus here is on production decisions in the short run.

THE "LAW" OF SUPPLY

The law of demand tells us that consumers buy less of a product when its price rises. If there were an analogous law of supply, it would say that producers offer more of a product for sale when its price rises. Is there such a law? We know that supply curves are essentially marginal cost curves and that because of the law of diminishing returns,

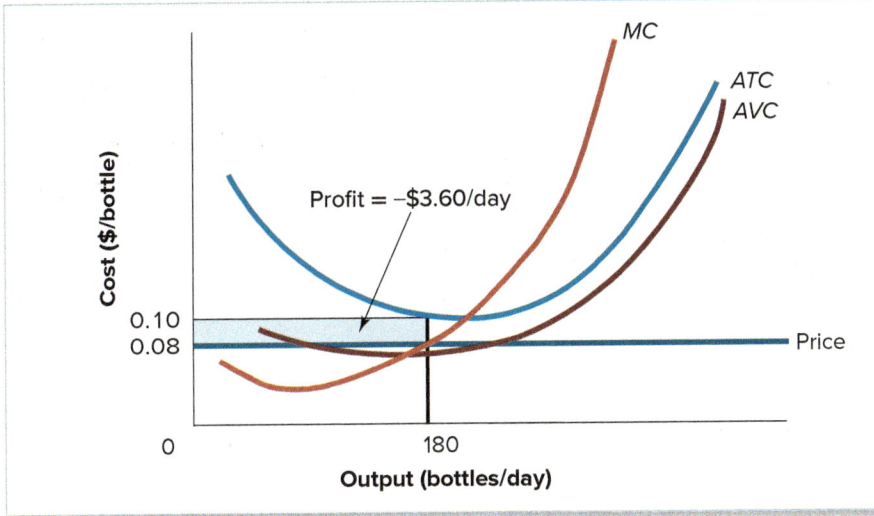

FIGURE 6.8

A Negative Profit.

When price is less than *ATC* at the profit-maximizing quantity, the firm experiences a loss, which is equal to the area of the shaded rectangle.

marginal cost curves are upward-sloping in the short run. And so there is indeed a law of supply that applies as stated in the short run.

In the long run, however, the law of diminishing returns does not apply. (Recall that it holds only if at least some factors of production are fixed.) Because firms can vary the amounts of *all* factors of production they use in the long run, they can often double their production by simply doubling the amount of each input they use. In such cases, costs would be exactly proportional to output and the firm's marginal cost curve in the long run would be horizontal, not upward-sloping. So for now we'll say only that the "law" of supply holds as stated in the short run but not necessarily in the long run. For both the long run and the short run, however, *the perfectly competitive firm's supply curve is its marginal cost curve.*[1]

Every quantity of output along the market supply curve represents the summation of all the quantities individual sellers offer at the corresponding price. So the correspondence between price and marginal cost exists for the market supply curve as well as for the individual supply curves that lie behind it. That is, *for every price-quantity pair along the market supply curve, price will be equal to each seller's marginal cost of production.*

This is why we sometimes say that the supply curve represents the cost side of the market, whereas the demand curve represents the benefit side of the market. At every point along a market demand curve, price represents what buyers would be willing to pay for an additional unit of the product—and this, in turn, is how we measure the amount by which they'd benefit by having an additional unit of the product. Likewise, at every point along a market supply curve, price measures what it would cost producers to expand production by one unit.

RECAP

PROFIT-MAXIMIZING FIRMS IN PERFECTLY COMPETITIVE MARKETS

The perfectly competitive firm faces a horizontal demand curve for its product, meaning that it can sell any quantity it wishes at the market price. In the short run, the firm's goal is to choose the level of output that maximizes its profits. It will accomplish this by choosing the output level for which its marginal cost is equal to the market price of its product, provided that price exceeds average variable cost. The perfectly competitive firm's supply curve is the portion of its marginal cost curve that lies above its average variable cost curve. At the profit-maximizing quantity, the firm's profit is the product of that quantity and the difference between price and average total cost.

---

[1]Again, this rule holds subject to the provision that total revenue exceed variable production cost at the output level for which price equals marginal cost.

DETERMINANTS OF SUPPLY REVISITED

What factors give rise to changes in supply? (Again, remember that a "change in supply" refers to a shift in the entire supply curve, as opposed to a movement along the curve, which we call a "change in the quantity supplied.") A seller will offer more units if the benefit of selling extra output goes up relative to the cost of producing it. And since the benefit of selling output in a perfectly competitive market is a fixed market price that is beyond the seller's control, our search for factors that influence supply naturally focuses on the cost side of the calculation. The preceding examples suggest why the following factors, among others, will affect the likelihood that a product will satisfy the cost-benefit test for a given supplier.

TECHNOLOGY

Perhaps the most important determinant of production cost is technology. Improvements in technology make it possible to produce additional units of output at lower cost. This shifts each individual supply curve downward (or, equivalently, to the right) and hence shifts the market supply curve downward as well. Over time, the introduction of more sophisticated machinery has resulted in dramatic increases in the number of goods produced per hour of effort expended. Every such development gives rise to a rightward shift in the market supply curve.

But how do we know technological change will reduce the cost of producing goods and services? Might not new equipment be so expensive that producers who used it would have higher costs than those who relied on earlier designs? If so, then rational producers simply would not use the new equipment. The only technological changes that rational producers will adopt are those that will reduce their cost of production.

INPUT PRICES

Whereas technological change generally (although not always) leads to gradual shifts in supply, changes in the prices of important inputs can give rise to large supply shifts literally overnight. As discussed in Chapter 4, *Elasticity,* for example, the price of crude oil, which is the most important input in the production of gasoline, often fluctuates sharply, and the resulting shifts in supply cause gasoline prices to exhibit corresponding fluctuations.

Similarly, when wage rates rise, the marginal cost of any business that employs labor also rises, shifting supply curves to the left (or, equivalently, upward). When interest rates fall, the opportunity cost of capital equipment also falls, causing supply to shift to the right.

THE NUMBER OF SUPPLIERS

Just as demand curves shift to the right when population grows, supply curves also shift to the right as the number of individual suppliers grows. For example, if container recyclers die or retire at a higher rate than new recyclers enter the industry, the supply curve for recycling services will shift to the left. Conversely, if a rise in the unemployment rate leads more people to recycle soft drink containers (by reducing the opportunity cost of time spent recycling), the supply curve of recycling services will shift to the right.

EXPECTATIONS

Expectations about future price movements can affect how much sellers choose to offer in the current market. Suppose, for example, that recyclers expect the future price of aluminum to be much higher than the current price because of growing use of aluminum components in cars. The rational recycler would then have an incentive to withhold aluminum from the market at today's lower price, thereby to have more available to sell at the higher future price. Conversely, if recyclers expected next year's price of aluminum to be lower than this year's, their incentive would be to offer more aluminum for sale in today's market.

CHANGES IN PRICES OF OTHER PRODUCTS

Apart from technological change, perhaps the most important determinant of supply is variation in the prices of other goods and services that sellers might produce. Prospectors, for example, search for those precious metals for which the surplus of benefits over costs is greatest. When the price of silver rises, many stop looking for gold and start looking for silver. Conversely, when the price of platinum falls, many platinum prospectors shift their attention to gold.

> **RECAP** ↑
>
> **THE DETERMINANTS OF SUPPLY**
>
> Among the relevant factors causing supply curves to shift are new technologies, changes in input prices, changes in the number of sellers, expectations of future price changes, and changes in the prices of other products that firms might produce.

► Visit your instructor's Connect course and access your eBook to view this video.

APPLYING THE THEORY OF SUPPLY

Whether the activity is producing new soft drink containers or recycling used ones, or indeed any other production activity at all, the same logic governs all supply decisions in perfectly competitive markets (and in any other setting in which sellers can sell as much as they wish to at a constant price): keep expanding output until marginal cost is equal to the price of the product. This logic helps us understand why recycling efforts are more intensive for some products than others.

Why are brown eggs more expensive than white ones?

The Economic Naturalist 6.1

When recycling is left to private market forces, why are many more aluminum beverage containers recycled than glass ones?

In both cases, recyclers gather containers until their marginal costs are equal to the containers' respective redemption prices. When recycling is left to market forces, the redemption price for a container is based on what companies can sell it (or the materials in it) for. Aluminum containers can be easily processed into scrap aluminum, which commands a high price, and this leads profit-seeking companies to offer a high redemption price for aluminum cans. By contrast, the glass from which glass containers are made has only limited resale value, primarily because the raw materials required to make new glass containers are so cheap. This difference leads profit-seeking companies to offer much lower redemption prices for glass containers than for aluminum ones.

The high redemption prices for aluminum cans induce many people to track down these cans, whereas the low redemption prices for glass containers lead most people to ignore them. If recycling is left completely to market forces, then we would expect to see aluminum soft drink containers quickly recycled, whereas glass containers would increasingly litter the landscape. This is in fact the pattern we do see in states without recycling laws. (More on how these laws work in a moment.) This pattern is a simple consequence of the fact that the supply curves of container-recycling services are upward-sloping.

In states that don't have beverage container deposit laws, why are aluminum cans more likely to be recycled than glass bottles?

The acquisition of valuable raw materials is only one of two important benefits from recycling. The second is that, by removing litter, recycling makes the environment more pleasant for everyone. As the next example suggests, this second benefit might easily justify the cost of recycling substantial numbers of glass containers.

EXAMPLE 6.4

Why the Optimal Amount of Pollution Isn't Zero

What is the socially optimal amount of recycling of glass containers?

Suppose that the 60,000 citizens of Burlington, Vermont, would collectively be willing to pay 6 cents for each glass container removed from their local environment. If the local market supply curve of glass container-recycling services is as shown in Figure 6.9, what is the socially optimal level of glass container recycling?

FIGURE 6.9

The Supply Curve of Container-Recycling Services for Burlington, Vermont.

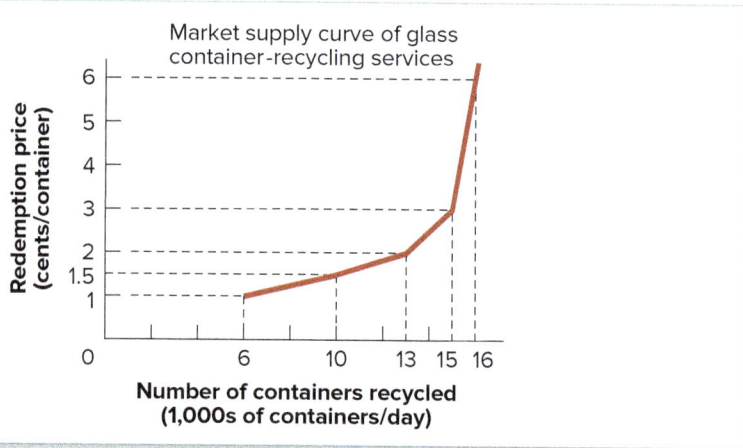

Suppose the citizens of Burlington authorize their city government to collect tax money to finance litter removal. If the benefit of each glass container removed, as measured by what residents are collectively willing to pay, is 6 cents, the government should offer to pay 6 cents for each glass container recycled. To maximize the total economic surplus from recycling, we should recycle that number of containers for which the marginal cost of recycling is equal to the 6-cent marginal benefit. Given the market supply curve shown, the optimal quantity is 16,000 containers per day, and that is how many will be redeemed when the government offers 6 cents per container.

Although 16,000 containers per day will be removed from the environment in the preceding example, others will remain. After all, some are discarded in remote locations, and a redemption price of 6 cents per container is simply not high enough to induce people to track them all down.

So why not offer an even higher price and get rid of *all* glass container litter? For the example given, the reason is that the marginal cost of removing the 16,001st glass container each day is greater than the benefit of removing it. Total economic surplus is largest when we remove litter only up to the point that the marginal benefit of litter removal is equal to its marginal cost, which occurs when 16,000 containers per day are recycled. To proceed past that point is actually wasteful.

Many people become upset when they hear economists say that the socially optimal amount of litter is greater than zero. In the minds of these people, the optimal amount of litter is *exactly* zero. But this position completely ignores the Scarcity Principle. Granted, there would be benefits from reducing litter further, but there also would be costs. Spending more on litter removal therefore means spending less on other useful things. No one would insist that the optimal amount of dirt in his own home is zero. (If someone does make this claim, ask him why he doesn't stay home all day vacuuming the dust that is accumulating in his absence.) If it doesn't pay to remove all the dust from your house, it doesn't pay to remove all the bottles from the environment. Precisely the same logic applies in each case.

 Scarcity ≫

If 16,000 containers per day is the optimal amount of litter removal, can we expect the individual spending decisions of private citizens to result in that amount of litter removal? Unfortunately we cannot. The problem is that anyone who paid for litter removal individually would bear the full cost of those services while reaping only a tiny fraction of the benefit. In Example 6.4, the 60,000 citizens of Burlington reaped a total benefit of 6 cents per container removed, which means a benefit of only $(6/60,000) = 0.0001$ cent per person! Someone who paid 6 cents for someone else to remove a container would thus be incurring a cost 60,000 times greater than his share of the resulting benefit.

Note that the incentive problem here is similar to the one discussed in Chapter 3, *Supply and Demand,* for the person deciding whether to be vaccinated against an illness. The problem was that the incentive to be vaccinated was too weak because, even though the patient bears the full cost of the vaccination, many of the resulting benefits accrue to others. Thus, an important part of the extra benefit from any one person being vaccinated is that others also become less likely to contract the illness.

The case of glass container litter is an example in which private market forces do not produce the best attainable outcome for society as a whole. Even people who carelessly toss containers on the ground, rather than recycle them, are often offended by the unsightly landscape to which their own actions contribute. Indeed, this is why they often support laws mandating adequate redemption prices for glass containers.

Activities that generate litter are a good illustration of the Equilibrium Principle described in Chapter 3, *Supply and Demand*. People who litter do so not because they don't care about the environment, but because their private incentives make littering misleadingly attractive. Recycling requires some effort, after all, yet no individual's recycling efforts have a noticeable effect on the quality of the environment. The soft drink container deposit laws enacted by numerous states were a simple way to bring individual interests more closely into balance with the interests of society as a whole. The vast majority of container litter disappeared almost overnight in states that enacted these laws.

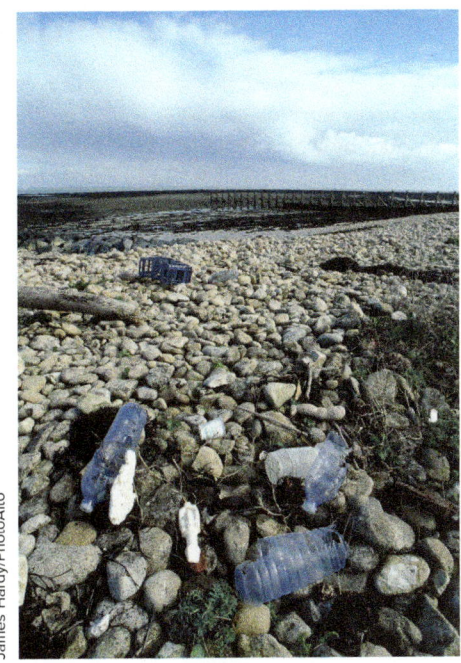

James Hardy/PhotoAlto

Is the socially optimal quantity of litter zero?

Equilibrium

✔ **SELF-TEST 6.5**

If the supply curve of glass container-recycling services is as shown in the diagram, and each of the city's 60,000 citizens would be willing to pay 0.00005 cent for each glass container removed from the landscape, at what level should the city government set the redemption price for glass containers, and how many will be recycled each day?

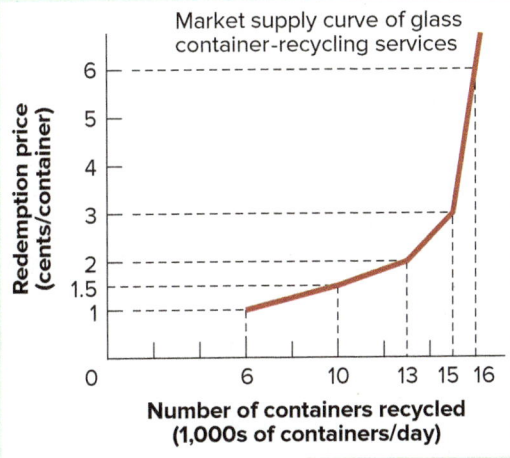

SUPPLY AND PRODUCER SURPLUS

producer surplus the amount by which price exceeds the seller's reservation price

The economic surplus received by a buyer is called *consumer surplus.* The analogous construct for a seller is **producer surplus**, the difference between the price a seller actually receives for the product and the lowest price for which she would have been willing to sell it (her reservation price, which in general will be her marginal cost).

As in the case of consumer surplus, the term *producer surplus* sometimes refers to the surplus received by a single seller in a transaction, while on other occasions it describes the total surplus received by all sellers in a market or collection of markets.

CALCULATING PRODUCER SURPLUS

In Chapter 5, *Demand*, we saw that consumer surplus in a market is the area bounded above by the demand curve and bounded below by the market price. Producer surplus in a market is calculated in an analogous way. As the following example illustrates, it is the area bounded above by the market price and bounded below by the market supply curve.

EXAMPLE 6.5   **Measuring Producer Surplus**

How much do sellers benefit from their participation in the market for milk?

Consider the market for milk, whose demand and supply curves are shown in Figure 6.10, which has an equilibrium price of $2 per gallon and an equilibrium quantity of 4,000 gallons per day. How much producer surplus do the sellers in this market reap?

FIGURE 6.10

Supply and Demand in the Market for Milk.

For the supply and demand curves shown, the equilibrium price of milk is $2 per gallon and the equilibrium quantity is 4,000 gallons per day.

In Figure 6.10, note first that for all milk sold up to 4,000 gallons per day, sellers receive a surplus equal to the difference between the market price of $2 per gallon and their reservation price as given by the supply curve. Total producer surplus received by buyers in the milk market is thus the shaded triangle between the supply curve and the market price in Figure 6.11. Note that this area is a right triangle whose vertical arm is h = $2/gallon and whose horizontal arm is b = 4,000 gallons/day. And since the area of any triangle is equal to (1/2)bh, producer surplus in this market is equal to

$$(1/2)(4,000 \text{ gallons/day})(\$2/\text{gallon}) = \$4,000/\text{day}.$$

Producer surplus in this example may be thought of as the highest price sellers would pay, in the aggregate, for the right to continue participating in the milk market. It is $4,000 per day since that's the amount by which their combined benefits exceed their combined costs.

FIGURE 6.11

Producer Surplus in the Market for Milk.

Producer surplus is the area of the shaded triangle ($4,000/day).

As discussed in Chapter 3, *Supply and Demand*, the supply curve for a good can be interpreted either horizontally or vertically. The horizontal interpretation tells us, for each price, the total quantity that producers wish to sell at that price. The vertical interpretation tells us, for each quantity, the smallest amount a seller would be willing to accept for the good. For the purpose of computing producer surplus, we rely on the vertical interpretation of the supply curve. The value on the vertical axis that corresponds to each point along the supply curve corresponds to the marginal seller's reservation price for the good, which is the marginal cost of producing it. Producer surplus is the cumulative sum of the differences between the market price and these reservation prices. It is the area bounded above by market price and bounded below by the supply curve.

SUMMARY

- The supply curve for a good or service is a schedule that, for any price, tells us the quantity that sellers wish to supply at that price. The prices at which goods and services are offered for sale in the market depend, in turn, on the opportunity cost of the resources required to produce them. *(LO1)*

- The demand curve facing a perfectly competitive firm is a horizontal line at the price for which industry supply and demand intersect. *(LO2)*

- Supply curves tend to be upward-sloping, at least in the short run, in part because of the *Principle of Increasing Opportunity Cost*. In general, rational producers will always take advantage of their best opportunities first, moving on to more difficult or costly opportunities only after their best ones have been exhausted. Reinforcing this tendency is the law of diminishing returns, which says that when some factors of production are held fixed, the amount of additional variable factors required to produce successive increments in output grows larger. The industry supply curve is the horizontal summation of the supply curves of individual firms in the industry. *(LO2, LO3)*

- For perfectly competitive markets—or, more generally, for markets in which individual sellers can sell whatever quantity they wish at a constant price—the seller's best option

is to sell that quantity of output for which price equals marginal cost, provided price exceeds the minimum value of average variable cost. The supply curve for the seller thus coincides with the portion of his marginal cost curve that exceeds average variable cost. This is why we sometimes say the supply curve represents the cost side of the market (in contrast to the demand curve, which represents the benefit side of the market). *(LO3)*

- Remember a "change in supply" means a shift in the entire supply curve, whereas a "change in quantity supplied" means a movement along the supply curve. Among the relevant factors causing supply curves to shift are new technologies, changes in input prices, changes in the number of sellers, expectations of future price changes, and changes in the prices of other products that firms might produce. You are now ready to apply the theory of supply. The logic that governs all supply decisions in perfectly competitive markets is as follows: keep expanding output until marginal cost is equal to the price of the product. *(LO4)*

- Producer surplus is a measure of the economic surplus reaped by a seller or sellers in a market. It is the cumulative sum of the differences between the market price and their reservation prices, which is the area bounded above by market price and bounded below by the supply curve. *(LO5)*

KEY TERMS

average total cost (*ATC*)	law of diminishing returns	profit-maximizing firm
average variable cost (*AVC*)	long run	profitable firm
factor of production	marginal cost	short run
fixed cost	perfectly competitive market	total cost
fixed factor of production	price taker	variable cost
imperfectly competitive firm	producer surplus	variable factor of production
(or price setter)	profit	

REVIEW QUESTIONS

1. Explain why you would expect supply curves to slope upward on the basis of the Principle of Increasing Opportunity Cost. *(LO1)*

2. True or false: The perfectly competitive firm should *always* produce the output level for which price equals marginal cost. *(LO3)*

3. Economists often stress that congestion helps account for the law of diminishing returns. With this in mind, explain why it would be impossible to feed all the people on Earth with food grown in a single flowerpot, even if unlimited water, labor, seed, fertilizer, sunlight, and other inputs were available. *(LO4)*

4. Which do you think is more likely to be a fixed factor of production for an ice cream producer during the next two months: its factory building or its workers who operate the machines? Explain. *(LO4)*

5. Why do we use the vertical interpretation of the supply curve when we measure producer surplus? *(LO5)*

PROBLEMS

1. Zoe is trying to decide how to divide her time between her job as a wedding photographer, which pays $27 per hour for as many hours as she chooses to work, and as a fossil collector, in which her pay depends on both the price of fossils and the number of fossils she finds. Earnings aside, Zoe is indifferent between the two tasks, and the number of fossils she can find depends on the number of hours a day she searches, as shown in the following table. *(LO1)*

Hours per day	Total fossils per day
1	5
2	9
3	12
4	14
5	15

a. Using this information, compute the lowest price that Zoe would accept per fossil in order to justify her spending more time collecting fossils and less time working as a wedding photographer.

b. Plot these points in a graph with price on the vertical axis and quantity per day on the horizontal. What is this curve called?

2. The supply curves for the only two firms in a competitive industry are given by, respectively, $P = 2Q_1$ and $P = 2 + Q_2$, where Q_1 is the output of firm 1 and Q_2 is the output of firm 2. What is the market supply curve for this industry? (*Hint:* Graph the two curves side by side; then add their respective quantities at a sample of different prices.) *(LO2)*

3. A price-taking firm makes air conditioners. The market price of one of its new air conditioners is $120. The firm's total cost information is given in the following table.

Air conditioners per day	Total cost ($ per day)
1	100
2	150
3	220
4	310
5	405
6	510
7	650
8	800

How many air conditioners should the firm produce per day if its goal is to maximize its profit? *(LO3)*

4. For the pizza seller whose marginal, average variable, and average total cost curves are shown in the

accompanying diagram, what is the profit-maximizing level of output and how much profit will this producer earn if the price of pizza is $2.50 per slice? *(LO3)*

5.* For the pizza seller whose marginal, average variable, and average total cost curves are shown in the accompanying diagram, what is the profit-maximizing level of output and how much profit will this producer earn if the price of pizza is $0.50 per slice? *(LO3)*

6.* For the pizza seller whose marginal, average variable, and average total cost curves are shown in the accompanying diagram (who is the same seller as in Problem 5), what is the profit-maximizing level of output and how much profit will this producer earn if the price of pizza is $1.18 per slice? *(LO3)*

7. Paducah Slugger Company makes baseball bats out of lumber supplied to it by Acme Sporting Goods, which pays Paducah $10 for each finished bat. Paducah's only factors of production are lathe operators and a small building with a lathe. The number of bats it produces per day depends on the number of employee-hours per day, as shown in the following table. *(LO3, LO4)*

Number of bats per day	Number of employee-hours per day
0	0
5	1
10	2
15	4
20	7
25	11
30	16
35	22

a. If the wage is $15 per hour and Paducah's daily fixed cost for the lathe and building is $60, what is the profit-maximizing quantity of bats?

b. What would be the profit-maximizing number of bats if the government imposed a tax of $10 per day on the company? (*Hint:* Think of this tax as equivalent to a $10 increase in fixed cost.)

c. What would be the profit-maximizing number of bats if the government imposed a tax of $2 per bat? (*Hint:* Think of this tax as equivalent to a $2-per-bat increase in marginal cost.)

d. Why do the taxes in parts b and c have such different effects?

8. The demand and supply curves for the pizza market are shown in the graph below. Calculate daily producer surplus. *(LO5)*

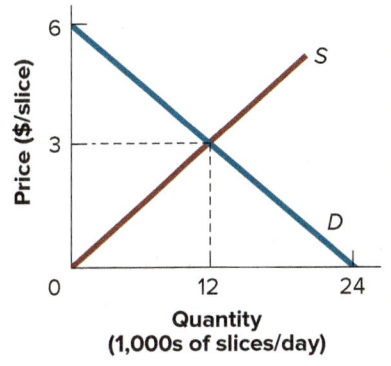

*Denotes more difficult problem.

ANSWERS TO SELF-TESTS

6.1 Since Ushi will find 300 containers if he searches a third hour, we find his reservation price for searching a third hour by solving $p(300) = \$6$ for $p = 2$ cents. His reservation prices for additional hours of search are calculated in an analogous way. *(LO1)*

Fourth hour: $p(200) = \$6$, so $p = 3$ cents.
Fifth hour: $p(100) = \$6$, so $p = 6$ cents.

6.2 If bottles sell for 62 cents each, the firm should continue to expand up to and including the sixth employee (350 bottles per day). *(LO3)*

6.3 The relevant costs are shown in the table below. With each variable and marginal cost entry half what it was in the original example, the firm should now hire six employees and produce 350 bottles per day. *(LO3)*

6.4 Because the firm makes its smallest loss when it hires zero employees, it should shut down in the short run. *(LO3)*

Employees per day	Output (bottles/ day)	Total revenue ($/day)	Total cost ($/day)	Profit ($/day)
0	0	0	40	−40
1	80	8	52	−44
2	200	20	64	−44
3	260	26	76	−50
4	300	30	88	−58
5	330	33	100	−67
6	350	35	112	−77
7	362	36.20	124	−87.80

6.5 The fact that each of the city's 60,000 residents is willing to pay 0.00005 cent for each bottle removed means that the collective benefit of each bottle removed is $(60,000)(0.00005) = 3$ cents. So the city should set the redemption price at 3 cents, and from the supply curve, we see that 15,000 bottles per day will be recycled at that price. *(LO4)*

Employees per day	Bottles per day	Fixed cost ($/day)	Variable cost ($/day)	Total cost ($/day)	Marginal cost ($/bottle)
0	0	40	0	40	
					0.075
1	80	40	6	46	
					0.05
2	200	40	12	52	
					0.10
3	260	40	18	58	
					0.167
4	300	40	24	64	
					0.20
5	330	40	30	70	
					0.30
6	350	40	36	76	
					0.50
7	362	40	42	82	

Efficiency, Exchange, and the Invisible Hand in Action

Robert Churchill/E+/Getty Images

Early suppliers of more fuel-efficient cars were able to charge premium prices for them, but that ability faded as other suppliers adopted similar technologies.

LEARNING OBJECTIVES

After reading this chapter, you should be able to:

LO1 Define and explain the differences between accounting profit, economic profit, and normal profit.

LO2 Explain the invisible hand theory and show how economic profit and economic loss affect the allocation of resources across industries.

LO3 Explain why economic profit, unlike economic rent, tends toward zero in the long run.

LO4 Identify whether the market equilibrium is socially efficient and why no opportunities for gain remain open to individuals when a market is in equilibrium.

LO5 Calculate total economic surplus and explain how it is affected by policies that prevent markets from reaching equilibrium.

T he restaurant market in Ithaca, New York, offered little variety in the 1970s: The city had only one Japanese, two Greek, four Italian, and three Chinese restaurants. Today, some 40 years later and with essentially the same population, Ithaca has one Sri Lankan, three Indian, one French, one Spanish, six Thai, two Korean, two Vietnamese, four Mexican, three Greek, seven Italian, two Caribbean, two Japanese, one Ethiopian, and nine Chinese restaurants. In some of the city's other markets, however, the range of available choices has narrowed. For example, several companies provided telephone answering services in 1972, but only one does so today.

Rare indeed is the marketplace in which the identities of the buyers and sellers remain static for extended periods. New businesses enter; established ones leave. There are more body-piercing studios in Ithaca now and fewer watch-repair shops; more marketing consultants and fewer intercity bus companies; and more appliances in stainless steel or black finishes, fewer in avocado or coppertone.

Driving these changes is the business owner's quest for profit. Businesses migrate to industries and locations in which profit opportunities abound and desert those whose

Why do most American cities now have more tattoo parlors and fewer watch-repair shops than in the 1980s?

prospects appear bleak. In perhaps the most widely quoted passage from his landmark treatise, *The Wealth of Nations,* Adam Smith wrote,

> It is not from the benevolence of the butcher, the brewer, or the baker that we expect our dinner, but from their regard of their own interest. We address ourselves not to their humanity, but to their self-love, and never talk to them of our necessities, but of their advantage.[1]

Smith went on to argue that although the entrepreneur "intends only his own gain," he is "led by an invisible hand to promote an end which was no part of his intention." As Smith saw it, even though self-interest is the prime mover of economic activity, the end result is an allocation of goods and services that serves society's collective interests remarkably well. If producers are offering "too much" of one product and "not enough" of another, profit opportunities stimulate entrepreneurs into action. All the while, the system exerts relentless pressure on producers to hold the price of each good close to its cost of production, and indeed to reduce that cost in any ways possible. The invisible hand, in short, is about all the good things that can happen because of the Incentive Principle.

Incentive

Our task in this chapter is to gain deeper insight into the nature of the forces that guide the invisible hand. What exactly does "profit" mean? How is it measured, and how does the quest for it serve society's ends? And if competition holds price close to the cost of production, why do so many entrepreneurs become fabulously wealthy? We will also discuss cases in which misunderstanding of Smith's theory results in costly errors, both in everyday decision making and in the realm of government policy.

THE CENTRAL ROLE OF ECONOMIC PROFIT

The economic theory of business behavior is built on the assumption that the firm's goal is to maximize its profit. So we must be clear at the outset about what, exactly, profit means.

THREE TYPES OF PROFIT

explicit costs the actual payments a firm makes to its factors of production and other suppliers

accounting profit the difference between a firm's total revenue and its explicit costs

implicit costs the opportunity costs of the resources supplied by the firm's owners

economic profit (or **excess profit**) the difference between a firm's total revenue and the sum of its explicit and implicit costs

The economist's understanding of profit is different from the accountant's, and the distinction between the two is important for understanding how the invisible hand works. Accountants define the annual profit of a business as the difference between the revenue it takes in and its **explicit costs** for the year, which are the actual payments the firm makes to its factors of production and other suppliers. Profit thus defined is called **accounting profit**:

$$\text{Accounting profit} = \text{Total revenue} - \text{Explicit costs.}$$

Accounting profit is the most familiar profit concept in everyday discourse. It is the one that companies use, for example, when they provide statements about their profits in press releases or annual reports.[2]

Economists, by contrast, define profit as the difference between the firm's total revenue and not just its explicit costs, but also its **implicit costs**, which are the opportunity costs of all the resources supplied by the firm's owners. Profit thus defined is called **economic profit** (or **excess profit**):

$$\text{Economic profit} = \text{Total revenue} - \text{Explicit costs} - \text{Implicit costs.}$$

[1]Adam Smith, *The Wealth of Nations* (New York: Everyman's Library, Book 1, 1910).
[2]For simplicity, this discussion ignores any costs associated with depreciation of the firm's capital equipment. Because the buildings and machines owned by a firm tend to wear out over time, the government allows the firm to consider a fraction of their value each year as a current cost of doing business. For example, a firm that employs a $1,000 machine with a 10-year life span might be allowed to record $100 as a current cost of doing business each year.

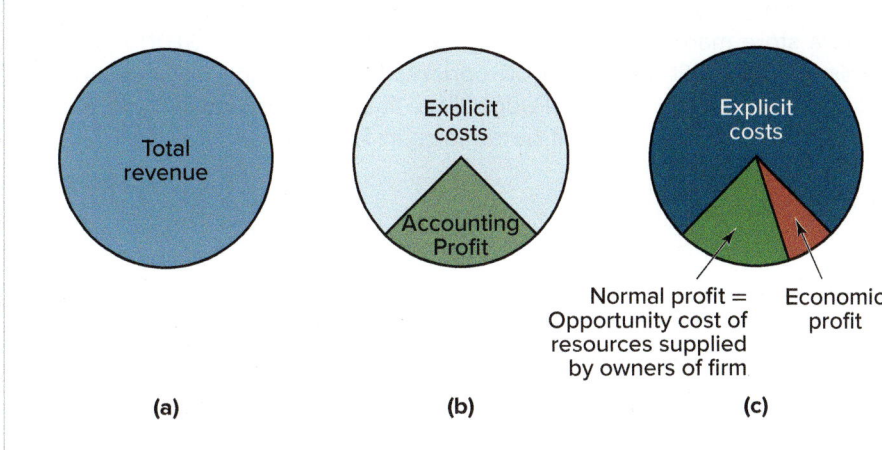

FIGURE 7.1

The Difference between Accounting Profit and Economic Profit.

Accounting profit (b) is the difference between total revenue and explicit costs. Normal profit (c) is the opportunity cost of all resources supplied by a firm's owners. Economic profit (c) is the difference between total revenue and all costs, explicit and implicit (also equal to the difference between accounting profit and normal profit).

To illustrate the difference between accounting profit and economic profit, consider a firm with $400,000 in total annual revenue whose only explicit costs are workers' salaries, totaling $250,000 per year. The owners of this firm have supplied machines and other capital equipment with a total resale value of $1 million. This firm's accounting profit then is $150,000, or the difference between its total revenue of $400,000 per year and its explicit costs of $250,000 per year.

To calculate the firm's economic profit, sometimes called its excess profit, we must first calculate the opportunity cost of the resources supplied by the firm's owners. Suppose the current annual interest rate on savings accounts is 10 percent. Had owners not invested in capital equipment, they could have earned an additional $100,000 per year interest by depositing their $1 million in a savings account. So the firm's economic profit is $400,000 per year − $250,000 per year − $100,000 per year = $50,000 per year.

Note that this economic profit is smaller than the accounting profit by exactly the amount of the firm's implicit costs–the $100,000 per year opportunity cost of the resources supplied by the firm's owners. This difference between a business's accounting profit and its economic profit is called its **normal profit**. Normal profit is simply the opportunity cost of the resources supplied to a business by its owners.

Figure 7.1 illustrates the difference between accounting and economic profit. A firm's total revenue is represented in Figure 7.1(a), while (b) and (c) show how this revenue is apportioned among the various cost and profit categories.

The following examples illustrate why the distinction between accounting and economic profit is so important.

normal profit the opportunity cost of the resources supplied by the firm's owners, equal to accounting profit minus economic profit

EXAMPLE 7.1   Accounting versus Economic Profit, Part 1

Should Pudge Buffet stay in the farming business?

Pudge Buffet is a corn farmer who lives near Lincoln, Nebraska. His payments for land and equipment rental and for other supplies come to $10,000 per year. The only input he supplies is his own labor, and he considers farming just as attractive as his only other employment opportunity, managing a retail store at a salary of $11,000 per year. Apart from the matter of pay, Pudge is indifferent between farming and being a manager. Corn sells for a constant price per bushel in an international market too large to be affected by changes in one farmer's corn production. Pudge's revenue from corn sales is $22,000 per year. What is his accounting profit? His economic profit? His normal profit? Should he remain a corn farmer?

As shown in Table 7.1, Pudge's accounting profit is $12,000 per year, the difference between his $22,000 annual revenue and his $10,000 yearly payment for land, equipment, and supplies. His economic profit is that amount less the opportunity cost of his labor. Since the latter is the $11,000 per year he could have earned as a store manager, he is making an economic profit of $1,000 per year. Finally, his normal profit is the $11,000 opportunity cost of the only resource he supplies, namely, his labor. Since Pudge likes the two jobs equally well, he will be better off by $1,000 per year if he remains in farming.

TABLE 7.1
Revenue, Cost, and Profit Summary

Total revenue ($/year)	Explicit costs ($/year)	Implicit costs ($/year)	Accounting profit (= total revenue − explicit costs) ($/year)	Economic profit (= total revenue − explicit costs − implicit costs) ($/year)	Normal profit (= implicit costs) ($/year)
22,000	10,000	11,000	12,000	1,000	11,000

 SELF-TEST 7.1

In Example 7.1, how will Pudge's economic profit change if his annual revenue from corn production is not $22,000, but $20,000? Should he continue to farm?

economic loss an economic profit that is less than zero

When revenue falls from $22,000 to $20,000, Pudge has an economic profit of −$1,000 per year. A negative economic profit is also called an **economic loss**. If Pudge expects to sustain an economic loss indefinitely, his best bet would be to abandon farming in favor of managing a retail store.

You might think that if Pudge could just save enough money to buy his own land and equipment, his best option would be to remain a farmer. But as the following example illustrates, that impression is based on a failure to perceive the difference between accounting profit and economic profit.

EXAMPLE 7.2   **Accounting versus Economic Profit, Part 2**

Does owning one's own land make a difference?

Let's build on Example 7.1 and Self-Test 7.1. Suppose Pudge's Uncle Warren, who owns the farmland Pudge has been renting, dies and leaves Pudge that parcel of land. If the land could be rented to some other farmer for $6,000 per year, should Pudge remain in farming?

As shown in Table 7.2, if Pudge continues to farm his own land, his accounting profit will be $16,000 per year, or $6,000 more than in Self-Test 7.1. But his economic profit will still be the same as before—that is, −$1,000 per year—

TABLE 7.2
Revenue, Cost, and Profit Summary

Total revenue ($/year)	Explicit costs ($/year)	Implicit costs ($/year)	Accounting profit (= total revenue − explicit costs) ($/year)	Economic profit (= total revenue − explicit costs − implicit costs) ($/year)	Normal profit (= implicit costs) ($/year)
20,000	4,000	17,000	16,000	−1,000	17,000

because Pudge must deduct the $6,000 per year opportunity cost of farming his own land, even though he no longer must make an explicit payment to his uncle for it. The normal profit from owning and operating his farm will be $17,000 per year—the opportunity cost of the land and labor he provides. But since Pudge earns an accounting profit of only $16,000, he will again do better to abandon farming for the managerial job.

Pudge obviously would be wealthier as an owner than he was as a renter. But the question of whether to remain a farmer is answered the same way whether Pudge rents his farmland or owns it. He should stay in farming only if that is the option that yields the highest economic profit.

RECAP ↑

THE CENTRAL ROLE OF ECONOMIC PROFIT

A firm's accounting profit is the difference between its revenue and the sum of all explicit costs it incurs. Economic profit is the difference between the firm's revenue and *all* costs it incurs—both explicit and implicit. Normal profit is the opportunity cost of the resources supplied by the owners of the firm. When a firm's accounting profit is exactly equal to the opportunity cost of the inputs supplied by the firm's owners, the firm's economic profit is zero. For a firm to remain in business in the long run, it must earn an economic profit greater than or equal to zero.

THE INVISIBLE HAND THEORY

TWO FUNCTIONS OF PRICE

In the free enterprise system, market prices serve two important and distinct functions. The first, the **rationing function of price**, is to distribute scarce goods among potential claimants, ensuring that those who get them are the ones who value them most. Thus, if three people want the only antique clock for sale at an auction, the clock goes home with the person who bids the most for it. The second function, the **allocative function of price**, is to direct productive resources to different sectors of the economy. Resources leave markets in which price cannot cover the cost of production and enter those in which price exceeds the cost of production.

Both the allocative and rationing functions of price underlie Adam Smith's celebrated **invisible hand theory** of the market. Recall that Smith thought the market system channeled the selfish interests of individual buyers and sellers so as to promote the greatest good for society. The carrot of economic profit and the stick of economic loss, he argued, were often the only forces necessary to ensure that existing supplies in any market would be allocated efficiently and that resources would be allocated across markets to produce the most efficient possible mix of goods and services.

rationing function of price changes in prices distribute scarce goods to those consumers who value them most highly

allocative function of price changes in prices direct resources away from overcrowded markets and toward markets that are underserved

invisible hand theory Adam Smith's theory that the actions of independent, self-interested buyers and sellers will often result in the most efficient allocation of resources

RESPONSES TO PROFITS AND LOSSES

To get a feel for how the invisible hand works, we begin by looking at how firms respond to economic profits and losses. If a firm is to remain in business in the long run, it must cover all its costs, both explicit and implicit. A firm's normal profit is just a cost of doing business. Thus, the owner of a firm that earns no more than a normal profit has managed only to recover the opportunity cost of the resources invested in the firm. By contrast, the owner of a firm that makes a positive economic profit earns more than the opportunity cost of the invested resources; she earns a normal profit and then some.

Naturally, everyone would be delighted to earn more than a normal profit, and no one wants to earn less. The result is that those markets in which firms are earning an

FIGURE 7.2

Economic Profit in the Short Run in the Corn Market.

At an equilibrium price of $2 per bushel (a), the typical farm earns an economic profit of $104,000 per year (b).

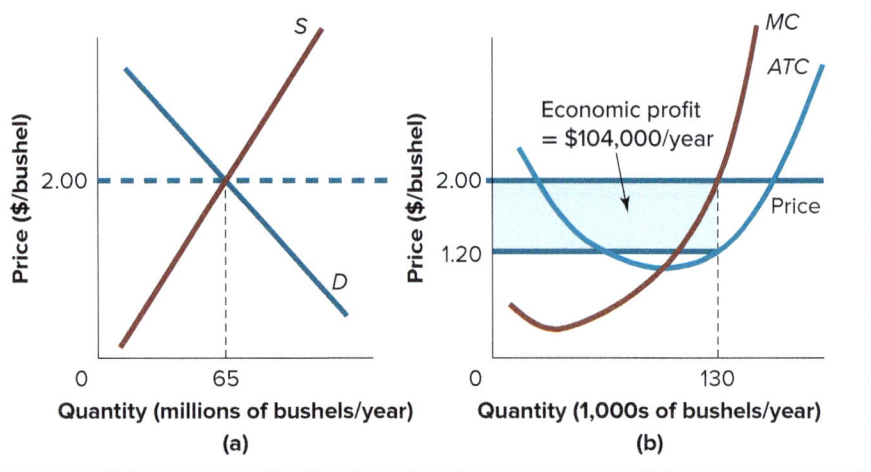

economic profit tend to attract additional resources, whereas markets in which firms are experiencing economic losses tend to lose resources.

To see how this happens, we'll examine the workings of the market for corn, whose short-run supply and demand curves are shown in Figure 7.2(a). Figure 7.2(b) depicts the marginal and average total cost curves for a representative farm. The equilibrium price of $2 per bushel is determined by the supply–demand intersection in (a). The representative farm whose *MC* and *ATC* curves are shown in (b) then maximizes its profit by producing the quantity for which price equals marginal cost, 130,000 bushels of corn per year.

Recall from Chapter 6, *Perfectly Competitive Supply,* that average total cost at any output level is the sum of all costs, explicit and implicit, divided by output. The difference between price and *ATC* is thus equal to the average amount of economic profit earned per unit sold. In Figure 7.2(b), that difference is $0.80 per unit. With 130,000 bushels per year sold, the representative farm earns an economic profit of $104,000 per year.

The existence of positive economic profit in the corn market means that producers in that market are earning more than their opportunity cost of farming. For simplicity, we assume that the inputs required to enter the corn market—land, labor, equipment, and the like—are available at constant prices and that anyone is free to enter this market if he or she chooses. The key point is that because price exceeds the opportunity cost of the resources required to enter the market, others *will* want to enter. And as they add their corn production to the amount already on offer, supply shifts to the right, causing the market equilibrium price to fall, as shown in Figure 7.3(a). At the new price of $1.50 per bushel, the representative farm now earns much less economic profit than before, only $50,400 per year [Figure 7.3(b)].

FIGURE 7.3

The Effect of Entry on Price and Economic Profit.

At the original price of $2 per bushel, existing farmers earned economic profit, prompting new farmers to enter. With entry, supply shifts right [from S to S′ in (a)] and equilibrium price falls, as does economic profit (b).

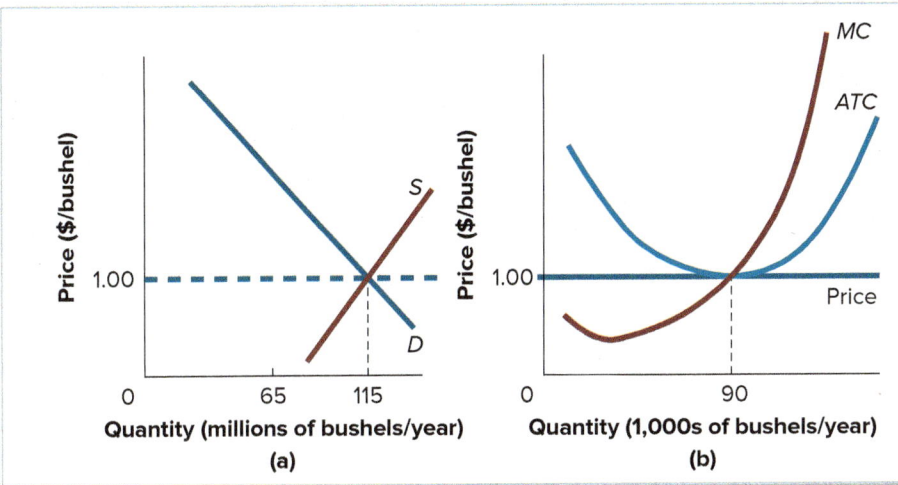

FIGURE 7.4

Equilibrium When Entry Ceases.

Further entry ceases once price falls to the minimum value of *ATC*. At that point, all firms earn a normal economic profit. Equivalently, each earns an economic profit of zero.

For simplicity, we assume that all farms employ the same standard production method, so that their *ATC* curves are identical. Entry will then continue until price falls all the way to the minimum value of *ATC*. (At any price higher than that, economic profit would still be positive, and entry would continue, driving price still lower.) Recall from Chapter 6, *Perfectly Competitive Supply,* that the short-run marginal cost curve intersects the *ATC* curve at the minimum point of the *ATC* curve. This means that once price reaches the minimum value of *ATC,* the profit-maximizing rule of setting price equal to marginal cost results in a quantity for which price and *ATC* are the same. And when that happens, economic profit for the representative farm will be exactly zero, as shown in Figure 7.4(b).

In the adjustment process just considered, the initial equilibrium price was above the minimum value of *ATC,* giving rise to positive economic profits. Suppose instead that the market demand curve for corn had intersected the short-run supply curve at a price below the minimum value of each firm's *ATC* curve, as shown in Figure 7.5(a). As long as this price is above the minimum value of average variable cost,[3] each farm will supply that quantity of corn for which price equals marginal cost, shown as 70,000 bushels per year in Figure 7.5(b). Note, however, that at that quantity, the farm's average total cost is $1.05 per bushel, or $0.30 more than the price for which it sells each bushel. As shown in (b), the farm thus sustains an economic loss of $21,000 per year.

FIGURE 7.5

A Short-Run Economic Loss in the Corn Market.

When price is below the minimum value of *ATC* (a), each farm sustains an economic loss (b).

---

[3]This qualification refers to the firm's shutdown condition, discussed in Chapter 6, *Perfectly Competitive Supply.*

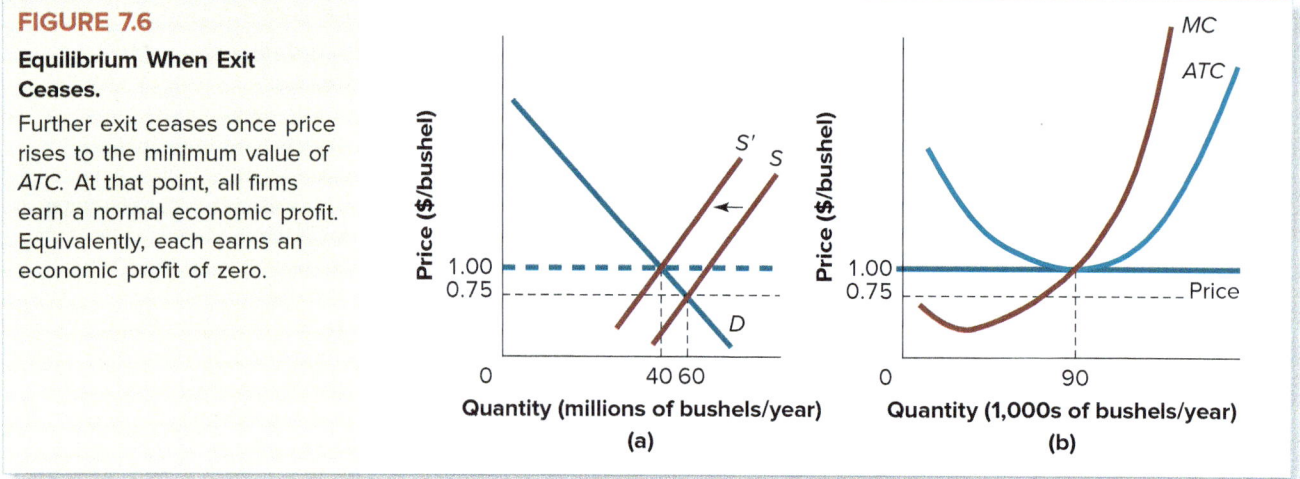

FIGURE 7.6

Equilibrium When Exit Ceases.

Further exit ceases once price rises to the minimum value of *ATC*. At that point, all firms earn a normal economic profit. Equivalently, each earns an economic profit of zero.

If the demand curve that led to the low price and resulting economic losses in Figure 7.5 is expected to persist, farmers will begin to abandon farming for other activities that promise better returns. This means that the supply curve for corn will shift to the left, resulting in higher prices and smaller losses. Exit from corn farming will continue, in fact, until price has again risen to $1 per bushel, at which point there will be no incentive for further exit. Once again we see a stable equilibrium in which price is $1 per bushel, as shown in Figure 7.6.

Given our simplifying assumptions that all corn farms employ a standardized production method and that inputs can be purchased in any quantities at fixed prices, the price of corn cannot remain above $1 per bushel (the minimum point on the *ATC* curve) in the long run. Any higher price would stimulate additional entry until price again fell to that level. Further, the price of corn cannot remain below $1 per bushel in the long run because any lower price would stimulate exit until the price of corn again rose to $1 per bushel.

The fact that firms are free to enter or leave an industry at any time ensures that, in the long run, all firms in the industry will tend to earn zero economic profit. Their *goal* is not to earn zero profit. Rather, the zero-profit tendency is a consequence of the price movements associated with entry and exit. As the Equilibrium Principle— also called the No-Cash-on-the-Table Principle (see Chapter 3, *Supply and Demand*)— predicts, when people confront an opportunity for gain, they are almost always quick to exploit it.

Equilibrium

What does the long-run supply curve look like in the corn market just discussed? This question is equivalent to asking, "What is the marginal cost of producing additional bushels of corn in the long run?" In general, adjustment in the long run may entail not just entry and exit of standardized firms but also the ability of firms to alter the mix of capital equipment and other fixed inputs they employ. Explicit consideration of this additional step would complicate the analysis considerably but would not alter the basic logic of the simpler account we present here, which assumes that all firms operate with the same standard mix of fixed inputs in the short run. Under this assumption, the long-run adjustment process consists exclusively of the entry and exit of firms that use a single standardized production method.

The fact that a new firm could enter or leave this corn market at any time means that corn production can always be augmented or reduced in the long run at a cost of $1 per bushel. And this, in turn, means that the long-run supply curve of corn will be a horizontal line at a price equal to the minimum value of the *ATC* curve, $1 per bushel. Since the long-run marginal cost (*LMC*) of producing corn is constant, so is the long-run average cost (*LAC*) and it, too, is $1 per bushel, as shown in Figure 7.7(a). Figure 7.7(b) shows the *MC* and *ATC* curves of a representative corn farm. At a price of $1 per bushel, this corn market is said to be in long-run equilibrium. The

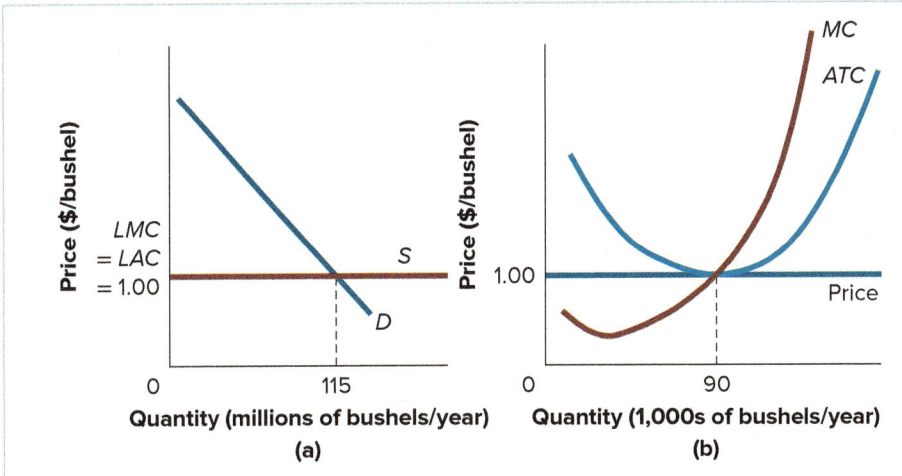

FIGURE 7.7

Long-Run Equilibrium in a Corn Market with Constant Long-Run Average Cost.

When each producer has the same *ATC* curve, the industry can supply as much or as little output as buyers wish to buy at a price equal to the minimum value of *ATC* (a). At that price, the representative producer (b) earns zero economic profit.

representative farm produces 90,000 bushels of corn each year, the quantity for which price equals its marginal cost. And since price is exactly equal to *ATC,* this farm also earns an economic profit of zero.

These observations call attention to two attractive features of the invisible hand theory. One is that the market outcome is efficient in the long run. Note, for example, that when the corn market is in long-run equilibrium, the value to buyers of the last unit of corn sold is $1 per bushel, which is exactly the same as the long-run marginal cost of producing it. Thus, there is no possible rearrangement of resources that would make some participants in this market better off without causing harm to some others. If farmers were to expand production, for example, the added costs incurred would exceed the added benefits; and if they were to contract production, the cost savings would be less than the benefits forgone.

A second attractive feature of long-run competitive equilibrium is the market outcome can be described as fair, in the sense that the price buyers must pay is no higher than the cost incurred by suppliers. That cost includes a normal profit, the opportunity cost of the resources supplied by owners of the firm.

We must emphasize that Smith's invisible hand theory does not mean that market allocation of resources is optimal in every way. It simply means that markets are efficient in the limited technical sense discussed in Chapter 6, *Perfectly Competitive Supply.* Thus, if the current allocation differs from the market equilibrium allocation, the invisible hand theory implies that we can reallocate resources in a way that makes some people better off without harming others.

The following example affords additional insight into how Smith's invisible hand works in practice.

EXAMPLE 7.3   Movement toward Equilibrium

What happens in a city with "too many" hairstylists and "too few" Pilates instructors?

At the initial equilibrium quantities and prices in the markets for haircuts and Pilates classes shown in Figure 7.8, all suppliers are currently earning zero economic profit. Now suppose that styles suddenly change in favor of longer hair and increased physical fitness. If the long-run marginal cost of altering current production levels is constant in both markets, describe how prices and quantities will change in each market, in both the short run and the long run. Are the new equilibrium quantities socially optimal?

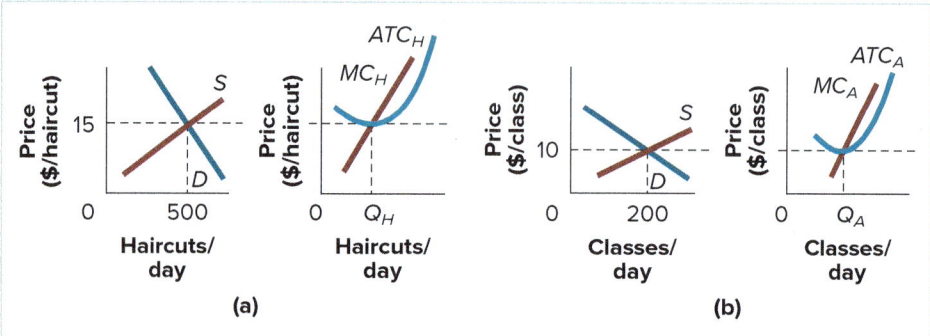

FIGURE 7.8

Initial Equilibrium in the Markets for (a) Haircuts and (b) Pilates Classes.

MC_H and ATC_H are the marginal cost and average total cost curves for a representative hairstylist, and MC_A and ATC_A are the marginal cost and average total cost curves for a representative Pilates instructor. Both markets are initially in long-run equilibrium, with sellers in each market earning zero economic profit.

The shift to longer hairstyles means a leftward shift in the demand for haircuts, while the increased emphasis on physical fitness implies a rightward shift in the demand curve for Pilates classes, as seen in Figure 7.9. As a result of these demand shifts, the new short-run equilibrium prices change. For the sake of illustration, these new prices are shown as $12 per haircut and $15 per Pilates class.

FIGURE 7.9

The Short-Run Effect of Demand Shifts in Two Markets.

(a) The decline in demand for haircuts causes the price of haircuts to fall from $15 to $12 in the short run.
(b) The increase in demand for Pilates classes causes the price of classes to rise from $10 to $15 in the short run.

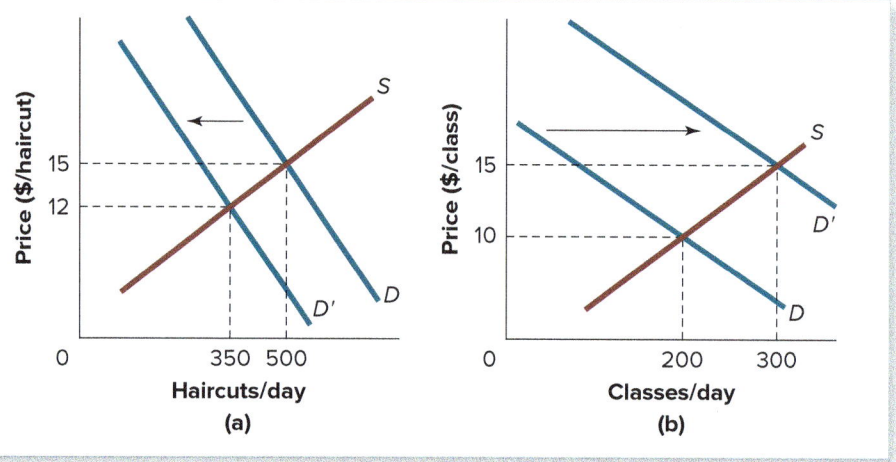

Because each producer was earning zero economic profit at the original equilibrium prices, hairstylists will experience economic losses and Pilates instructors will experience economic profits at the new prices, as seen in Figure 7.10.

Because the short-run equilibrium price of haircuts results in economic losses for hairstylists, some hairstylists will begin to leave that market in search of more favorable opportunities elsewhere. As a result, the short-run supply curve of haircuts will shift leftward, resulting in a higher equilibrium price. Exit of hairstylists will continue until the price of haircuts rises sufficiently to cover the long-run opportunity cost of providing them, which by assumption is $15.

By the same token, because the short-run equilibrium price of Pilates classes results in economic profits for instructors, outsiders will begin to enter that market, causing the short-run supply curve of classes to shift rightward. New instructors will continue to enter until the price of classes falls to the long-run opportunity cost of providing them. By assumption, that cost is $10. Once all adjustments have taken

FIGURE 7.10

Economic Profit and Loss in the Short Run.

The assumed demand shifts result in an economic loss for the representative hairstylist (a) and an economic profit for the representative Pilates instructor (b).

place, there will be fewer haircuts and more Pilates classes than before. But because marginal costs in both markets were assumed constant in the long run, the prices of the two goods will again be at their original levels.

It bears mention that those stylists who leave the hair-cutting market won't necessarily be the same people who enter the Pilates teaching market. Indeed, given the sheer number of occupations a former hairstylist might choose to pursue, the likelihood of such a switch is low. Movements of resources will typically involve several indirect steps. Thus, a former hairstylist might become a secretary, and a former postal worker might become a Pilates instructor.

We also note that the invisible hand theory says nothing about how long these adjustments might take. In some markets, especially labor markets, the required movements might take months or even years. But if the supply and demand curves remain stable, the markets will eventually reach equilibrium prices and quantities. And the new prices and quantities will be socially optimal in the same sense as before. Because the value to buyers of the last unit sold will be the same as the marginal cost of producing it, no additional transactions will be possible that benefit some without harming others.

THE IMPORTANCE OF FREE ENTRY AND EXIT

The allocative function of price cannot operate unless firms can enter new markets and leave existing ones at will. If new firms could not enter a market in which existing firms were making a large economic profit, economic profit would not tend to fall to zero over time, and price would not tend to gravitate toward the marginal cost of production.

Forces that inhibit firms from entering new markets are called **barriers to entry**. In the book publishing market, for example, the publisher of a book enjoys copyright protection granted by the government. Copyright law forbids other publishers from producing and selling their own editions of protected works. This barrier allows the price of a popular book to remain significantly above its cost of production for an extended period, all the while generating an economic profit for its publisher. (A copyright provides no *guarantee* of a profit, and indeed most new books actually generate an economic loss for their publishers.)

Barriers to entry may result from practical as well as legal constraints. Some economists, for example, have argued that the compelling advantages of product compatibility have created barriers to entry in the computer software market. Since roughly 80 percent of new desktop computers come with Microsoft's Windows operating system already installed, rival companies have difficulty selling other operating systems that may limit users' ability to exchange files with friends and colleagues. This fact, more than any other, explains Microsoft's spectacular profit history. But the share of computers equipped with

barrier to entry any force that prevents firms from entering a new market

Windows has been steadily falling, leading many economists to predict that Microsoft's profits will follow a similar trajectory.

No less important than the freedom to enter a market is the freedom to leave. When the airline industry was regulated by the federal government, air carriers were often required to serve specific markets, even though they were losing money in them. When firms discover that a market, once entered, is difficult or impossible to leave, they become reluctant to enter new markets. Barriers to exit thus become barriers to entry. Without reasonably free entry and exit, then, the implications of Adam Smith's invisible hand theory cannot be expected to hold.

All things considered, producers enjoy a high degree of freedom of entry in most U.S. markets. Because free entry is one of the defining characteristics of perfectly competitive markets, unless otherwise stated, we'll assume its existence.

RECAP

THE INVISIBLE HAND THEORY

In market economies, the allocative and rationing functions of prices guide resources to their most highly valued uses. Prices influence how much of each type of good gets produced (the allocative function). Firms enter industries in which prices are sufficiently high to sustain an economic profit and leave those in which low prices result in an economic loss. Prices also direct existing supplies of goods to the buyers who value them most (the rationing function).

Industries in which firms earn a positive economic profit tend to attract new firms, shifting industry supply to the right. Firms tend to leave industries in which they sustain an economic loss, shifting supply curves to the left. In each case, the supply movements continue until economic profit reaches zero. In long-run equilibrium, the value of the last unit produced to buyers is equal to its marginal cost of production, leaving no possibility for additional mutually beneficial transactions.

ECONOMIC RENT VERSUS ECONOMIC PROFIT

Microsoft cofounder Bill Gates is one of the wealthiest people on the planet, largely because the problem of compatibility prevents rival suppliers from competing effectively in the many software markets dominated by his company. Yet numerous people have become fabulously rich even in markets with no conspicuous barriers to entry. If market forces push economic profit toward zero, how can that happen?

The answer to this question hinges on the distinction between economic profit and **economic rent**. Most people think of rent as the payment they make to a landlord or the supplier of a dorm refrigerator, but the term *economic rent* has a different meaning. Economic rent is that portion of the payment for an input that is above the supplier's reservation price for that input. Suppose, for example, that a landowner's reservation price for an acre of land is $100 per year. That is, suppose he would be willing to lease it to a farmer as long as he received an annual payment of at least $100, but for less than that amount he would rather leave it fallow. If a farmer gives him an annual payment not of $100 but of $1,000, the landowner's economic rent from that payment will be $900 per year.

Economic profit is like economic rent in that it, too, may be seen as the difference between what someone is paid (the business owner's total revenue) and her reservation price for remaining in business (the sum of all her costs, explicit and implicit). But whereas competition pushes economic profit toward zero, it has no such effect on the economic rent for inputs that cannot be replicated easily. For example, although the lease payments for land may remain substantially above the landowner's reservation price, year in and year out, new land cannot come onto the market to reduce or eliminate the economic rent through competition. There is, after all, only so much land to be had.

As the following example illustrates, economic rent can accrue to people as well as land.

economic rent that part of the payment for a factor of production that exceeds the owner's reservation price, the price below which the owner would not supply the factor

EXAMPLE 7.4	Economic Rent

How much economic rent will a talented chef get?

A community has 100 restaurants, 99 of which employ chefs of normal ability at a salary of $30,000 per year, the same as the amount they could earn in other occupations that are equally attractive to them. But the 100th restaurant has an unusually talented chef. Because of her reputation, diners are willing to pay 50 percent more for the meals she cooks than for those prepared by ordinary chefs. Owners of the 99 restaurants with ordinary chefs each collect $300,000 per year in revenue, which is just enough to ensure that each earns exactly a normal profit. If the talented chef's opportunities outside the restaurant industry are the same as those of ordinary chefs, how much will she be paid by her employer at equilibrium? How much of her pay will be economic rent? How much economic profit will her employer earn?

Because diners are willing to pay 50 percent more for meals cooked by the talented chef, the owner who hires her will take in total receipts not of $300,000 per year but of $450,000. In the long run, competition should ensure that the talented chef's total pay each year will be $180,000 per year, the sum of the $30,000 that ordinary chefs get and the $150,000 in extra revenues for which she is solely responsible. Since the talented chef's reservation price is the amount she could earn outside the restaurant industry—by assumption, $30,000 per year, the same as for ordinary chefs—her economic rent is $150,000 per year. The economic profit of the owner who hires her will be exactly zero.

Since the talented chef's opportunities outside the restaurant industry are no better than an ordinary chef's, why is it necessary to pay the talented chef so much? Suppose her employer were to pay her only $60,000, which they both would consider a generous salary since it is twice what ordinary chefs earn. The employer would then earn an economic profit of $120,000 per year since his annual revenue would be $150,000 more than that of ordinary restaurants, but his costs would be only $30,000 more.

But this economic profit would create an opportunity for the owner of some other restaurant to bid the talented chef away. For example, if the owner of a competing restaurant were to hire the talented chef at a salary of $70,000, the chef would be $10,000 per year better off and the rival owner would earn an economic profit of $110,000 per year, rather than his current economic profit of zero. Furthermore, if the talented chef is the sole reason that a restaurant earns a positive economic profit, the bidding for that chef should continue as long as any economic profit remains. Some other owner will pay her $80,000, still another $90,000, and so on. Equilibrium will be reached only when the talented chef's salary has been bid up to the point that no further economic profit remains—in our example, at an annual paycheck of $180,000.

This bidding process assumes, of course, that the reason for the chef's superior performance is that she possesses some personal talent that cannot be copied. If instead it were the result of, say, training at a culinary institute in France, then her privileged position would erode over time, as other chefs sought similar training.

RECAP

ECONOMIC RENT VERSUS ECONOMIC PROFIT

Economic rent is the amount by which the payment to a factor of production exceeds the supplier's reservation price. Unlike economic profit, which is driven toward zero by competition, economic rent may persist for extended periods, especially in the case of factors with special talents that cannot easily be duplicated.

THE INVISIBLE HAND IN ACTION

To help develop your intuition about how the invisible hand works, we will examine how it helps us gain insight into patterns we observe in a wide variety of different contexts. In each case, the key idea we want you to focus on is that opportunities for private gain seldom remain unexploited for very long. Perhaps more than any other, this idea encapsulates the essence of that distinctive mindset known as "thinking like an economist."

The Invisible Hand at the Supermarket and on the Freeway

As the following example illustrates, the No-Cash-on-the-Table Principle refers not just to opportunities to earn economic profits in cash but also any other opportunity to achieve a more desirable outcome.

The Economic Naturalist 7.1

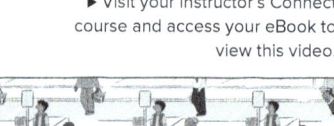

▶ Visit your instructor's Connect course and access your eBook to view this video.

Why do supermarket checkout lines all tend to be roughly the same length?

Why do supermarket checkout lines all tend to be roughly the same length?

Pay careful attention the next few times you go grocery shopping and you'll notice that the lines at all the checkout stations tend to be roughly the same length. Suppose you saw one line that was significantly shorter than the others as you wheeled your cart toward the checkout area. Which line would you choose? The shorter one, of course; because most shoppers would do the same, the short line seldom remains shorter for long.

 SELF-TEST 7.2

Use the No-Cash-on-the-Table Principle to explain why all lanes on a crowded, multilane freeway move at about the same speed.

The Invisible Hand and Cost-Saving Innovations

When economists speak of perfectly competitive firms, they have in mind businesses whose contribution to total market output is too small to have a perceptible impact on market price. As explained in Chapter 6, *Perfectly Competitive Supply*, such firms are often called price takers: they take the market price of their product as given and then produce that quantity of output for which marginal cost equals that price.

This characterization of the competitive firm gives the impression that the firm is essentially a passive actor in the marketplace. Yet for most firms, that is anything but the case. As the next example illustrates, even those firms that cannot hope to influence the market prices of their products have very powerful incentives to develop and introduce cost-saving innovations.

EXAMPLE 7.5   ## The Impact of Cost-Saving Innovations on Economic Profit

How do cost-saving innovations affect economic profit in the short run? In the long run?

Forty merchant marine companies operate supertankers that carry oil from the Middle East to the United States. The cost per trip, including a normal profit, is

$500,000. An engineer at one of these companies develops a more efficient propeller design that results in fuel savings of $20,000 per trip. How will this innovation affect the company's accounting and economic profits? Will these changes persist in the long run?

In the short run, the reduction in a single firm's costs will have no impact on the market price of transoceanic shipping services. The firm with the more efficient propeller will thus earn an economic profit of $20,000 per trip (since its total revenue will be the same as before, while its total cost will now be $20,000 per trip lower). As other firms learn about the new design, however, they will begin to adopt it, causing their individual supply curves to shift downward (since the marginal cost per trip at these firms will drop by $20,000). The shift in these individual supply curves will cause the market supply curve to shift, which in turn will result in a lower market price for shipping and a decline in economic profit at the firm where the innovation originated. When all firms have adopted the new, efficient design, the long-run supply curve for the industry will have shifted downward by $20,000 per trip and each company will again be earning only a normal profit. At that point, any firm that did *not* adopt the new propeller design would suffer an economic loss of $20,000 per trip.

The incentive to come up with cost-saving innovations in order to reap economic profit is one of the most powerful forces on the economic landscape. Its beauty, in terms of the invisible hand theory, is that competition among firms ensures that the resulting cost savings will be passed along to consumers in the long run.

THE DISTINCTION BETWEEN AN EQUILIBRIUM AND A SOCIAL OPTIMUM

The Equilibrium, or No-Cash-on-the-Table, Principle tells us that when a market reaches equilibrium, no further opportunities for mutually beneficial exchange are available to individuals. This principle implies that the market prices of resources will reflect their private economic values to the people who own them. As we'll see going forward, the same cannot be said of resources that are not owned by anyone, such as fish in international waters and the atmosphere that surrounds our planet.

The No-Cash-on-the-Table Principle is sometimes misunderstood to mean that there are *never* any valuable opportunities to exploit. For example, the story is told of two economists on their way to lunch when they spot what appears to be a $100 bill lying on the sidewalk. When the younger economist stoops to pick up the bill, his older colleague restrains him, saying, "That can't be a $100 bill." "Why not?" asks the younger colleague. "If it were, someone would have picked it up by now," the older economist replies.

The No-Cash-on-the-Table Principle means not that there *never* are any unexploited opportunities, but that there are none when the market is *in equilibrium*. Occasionally a $100 bill does lie on the sidewalk, and the person who first spots it and picks it up gains a windfall. Likewise, when a company's earnings prospects improve, *somebody* must be the first to recognize the opportunity, and that person can make a lot of money by purchasing the stock quickly.

Still, the No-Cash-on-the-Table Principle is important. It tells us, in effect, that there are only three ways to earn a big payoff: to work especially hard; to have some unusual skill, talent, or training; or simply to be lucky. The person who finds a big bill on the sidewalk is lucky, as are many of the investors whose stocks perform better than average. Other investors whose stocks do well achieve their gains through hard work or special talent. For example, the legendary investor Warren Buffett, whose portfolio has grown in value at almost three times the stock market average for the last 60 years, spends long hours studying annual financial reports and has a remarkably keen eye for the telling detail. Thousands of others work just as hard yet fail to beat the market averages.

It is important to stress, however, that a market being in equilibrium implies only that no additional opportunities are available *to individuals*. It does not imply that the resulting allocation is necessarily best from the point of view of society as a whole.

SMART FOR ONE, DUMB FOR ALL

As discussed in Chapter 1, *Thinking Like an Economist*, Adam Smith's profound insight was that the individual pursuit of self-interest often promotes the broader interests of society. But Smith also understood that the narrow interests of individuals are often in conflict with those of broader groups. In Chapter 3, *Supply and Demand*, we cited activities accompanied by harmful side effects, or externalities, to illustrate how the pursuit of narrow self-interest is often destructive, noting that behavior in such cases is often described as smart for one, dumb for all. The emission of greenhouse gases that damage climate stability is arguably the most consequential example under this heading. Ahead we'll focus more closely on these types of market failures along with policies for dealing with them.

As The Economic Naturalist 7.2 illustrates, conflicts between individual and collective interests also show up in more prosaic form.

The Economic Naturalist 7.2

Are there "too many" smart people working as corporate earnings forecasters?

Stock analysts use complex mathematical models to forecast corporate earnings. The more analysts invest in the development of these models, the more accurate the models become. Thus, the analyst whose model produces a reliable forecast sooner than others can reap a windfall by buying stocks whose prices are about to rise. Given the speed with which stock prices respond to new information, however, the results of even the second-fastest forecasting model may come too late to be of much use. Individual stock analysts thus face a powerful incentive to invest more and more money in their models, in the hope of generating the fastest forecast. Does this incentive result in the socially optimal level of investment in forecast models?

Beyond some point, increased speed of forecasting is of little benefit to society as a whole, whose interests suffer little when the price of a stock moves to its proper level a few hours more slowly. If *all* stock analysts spent less money on their forecasting models, *someone's* model would still produce the winning forecast, and the resources that might otherwise be devoted to fine-tuning the models could be put to more valued uses. Yet if any one individual spends less, he can be sure the winning forecast will not be his.

The invisible hand went awry in the situation just described because a side effect of one individual's investment in information gathering was to reduce the payoffs to similar investments by others.

Conspicuous examples of market failures notwithstanding, many of the most powerful forces at work in competitive markets are ones that promote society's interests. Consider, for example, the sheer volume of activity that is coordinated by market incentives. Throughout the dead of Ithaca winters, a food truck sits parked outside Cornell's dormitories all night, so that at 3 a.m. any student can take a few steps outside and purchase a fresh cup of coffee for a dollar. No one had to instruct the operator of that truck to be there or tell him where to buy paper cups or coffee beans or propane gas for his portable stove.

A store next to the Cornell campus will sell someone a new cartridge for her printer at a moment's notice, and a nearby shop will replace the brake pads on a student's bike while he waits. The meat counter at the Greenstar Coop offers fresh duck breasts on weekends, and a truck arrives each Friday morning at dawn carrying fresh seafood caught in the waters off the coast of Maine. On only a few hours' notice, several airlines stand ready to carry Ithacans to New York, Los Angeles, or Cedar Rapids, Iowa. All this activity and much more takes place without any central coordination at all, the result of a multitude of economic agents each striving to earn an economic profit.

In communist economies like the former Soviet Union, resources are allocated not by market incentives but by government planners. The question of whether central planning is more efficient than market incentives is no longer a hotly debated issue. Many formerly communist countries have now embraced markets enthusiastically while others have introduced market-like incentives in desperate attempts to revitalize their sluggish economies.

MARKET EQUILIBRIUM AND EFFICIENCY

Private markets cannot by themselves guarantee an income distribution that most people regard as fair. Nor can they ensure clean air, uncongested highways, or safe neighborhoods for all.

In virtually all successful societies, markets are supplemented by active political coordination in at least some instances. We will almost always achieve our goals more effectively if we know what tasks private markets can do well, and then allow them to perform those tasks. Unfortunately, the discovery that markets cannot solve *every* problem seems to have led some critics to conclude that markets cannot solve *any* problems. This misperception is a dangerous one because it has prompted attempts to prevent markets from doing even those tasks for which they are ideally suited.

We will explore why many tasks are best left to the market and the conditions under which unregulated markets generate the largest possible economic surplus. We also will discuss why attempts to interfere with market outcomes often lead to unintended and undesired consequences.

As noted in Chapter 3, *Supply and Demand*, the mere fact that markets coordinate the production of a large and complex list of goods and services is reason enough to marvel at them. But in the absence of pollution and other externalities like the ones discussed in the preceding section, economists make an even stronger claim—namely, that markets not only produce these goods, but also produce them as efficiently as possible.

The term **efficient**, as economists use it, has a narrow technical meaning. When we say that market equilibrium is efficient, we mean simply this: *If price and quantity take anything other than their equilibrium values, a transaction that will make at least some people better off without harming others can always be found.* This conception of efficiency is also known as **Pareto efficiency**, after Vilfredo Pareto, the nineteenth-century Italian economist who introduced it.

Why is market equilibrium efficient in this sense? The answer is that it is always possible to construct an exchange that helps some without harming others whenever a market is out of equilibrium. Suppose, for example, that the supply and demand curves for milk are as shown in Figure 7.11 and that the current price of milk is $1 per gallon. At that price, sellers offer only 2,000 gallons of milk a day. At that quantity, the marginal buyer values an extra gallon of milk at $2. This is the price that corresponds to 2,000 gallons a day on the

efficient (or **Pareto efficient**) a situation is efficient if no change is possible that will help some people without harming others

FIGURE 7.11

A Market in Which Price Is Below the Equilibrium Level.

In this market, milk is currently selling for $1 per gallon, $0.50 below the equilibrium price of $1.50 per gallon.

FIGURE 7.12

How Excess Demand Creates an Opportunity for a Surplus-Enhancing Transaction.

At a market price of $1 per gallon, the most intensely dissatisfied buyer is willing to pay $2 for an additional gallon, which a seller can produce at a cost of only $1. If this buyer pays the seller $1.25 for the extra gallon, the buyer gains an economic surplus of $0.75 and the seller gains an economic surplus of $0.25.

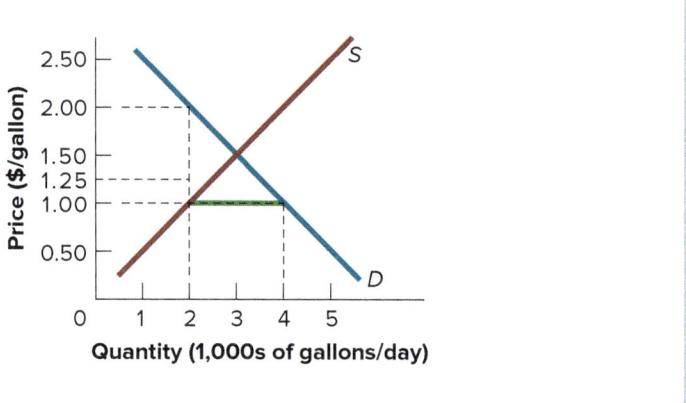

demand curve, which represents what the marginal buyer is willing to pay for an additional gallon (another application of the vertical interpretation of the demand curve). We also know that the cost of producing an extra gallon of milk is only $1. This is the price that corresponds to 2,000 gallons a day on the supply curve, which equals marginal cost (another application of the vertical interpretation of the supply curve).

Furthermore, a price of $1 per gallon leads to excess demand of 2,000 gallons per day, which means that many frustrated buyers cannot buy as much milk as they want at the going price. Now suppose a supplier sells an extra gallon of milk to the most eager of these buyers for $1.25, as in Figure 7.12. Since the extra gallon cost only $1 to produce, the seller is $0.25 better off than before. And since the most eager buyer values the extra gallon at $2, that buyer is $0.75 better off than before. In sum, the transaction creates an extra $1 of economic surplus out of thin air!

Note that none of the other buyers or sellers is harmed by this transaction. Thus, milk selling for only $1 per gallon cannot be efficient. As the following Self-Test 7.3 illustrates, there was nothing special about the price of $1 per gallon. Indeed, if milk sells for *any* price below $1.50 per gallon (the market equilibrium price), we can design a similar transaction, which means that selling milk for any price less than $1.50 per gallon cannot be efficient.

 SELF-TEST 7.3

In Figure 7.11, suppose that milk initially sells for 50 cents per gallon. Describe a transaction that will create additional economic surplus for both buyer and seller without causing harm to anyone else.

Furthermore, it is always possible to describe a transaction that will create additional surplus for both buyer and seller whenever the price lies *above* the market equilibrium level. Suppose, for example, that the current price is $2 per gallon in the milk market shown in Figure 7.13. At that price, we have excess supply of 2,000 gallons per day. Suppose the most dissatisfied producer sells a gallon of milk for $1.75 to the buyer who values it most highly. This buyer, who would have been willing to pay $2, will be $0.25 better off than before. Likewise the producer, who would have been willing to sell milk for as little as $1 per gallon (the marginal cost of production at 2,000 gallons per day), will be $0.75 better off than before. As when the price was $1 per gallon, the new transaction creates $1 of additional economic surplus without harming any other buyer or seller. Since we could design a similar surplus-enhancing transaction at any price above the equilibrium level, selling milk for more than $1.50 per gallon cannot be efficient.

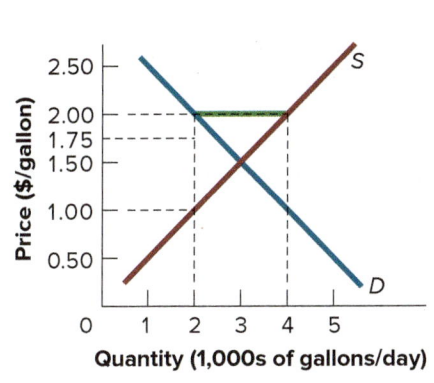

FIGURE 7.13

How Excess Supply Creates an Opportunity for a Surplus-Enhancing Transaction.

At a market price of $2 per gallon, dissatisfied sellers can produce an additional gallon of milk at a cost of only $1, which is $1 less than a buyer would be willing to pay for it. If the buyer pays the seller $1.75 for an extra gallon, the buyer gains an economic surplus of $0.25 and the seller gains an economic surplus of $0.75.

The vertical interpretations of the supply and demand curves thus make it clear why only the equilibrium price in a market can be efficient. When the price is either higher or lower than the equilibrium price, the quantity exchanged in the market will always be lower than the equilibrium quantity. If the price is below equilibrium, the quantity sold will be the amount that sellers offer. If the price is above equilibrium, the quantity sold will be the amount that buyers wish to buy. In either case, the vertical value on the demand curve at the quantity exchanged, which is the value of an extra unit to buyers, must be larger than the vertical value on the supply curve, which is the marginal cost of producing that unit.

So the market equilibrium price is the *only* price at which buyers and sellers cannot design a surplus-enhancing transaction. The market equilibrium price leads, in other words, to the largest possible total economic surplus. In this specific, limited sense, free markets are said to produce and distribute goods and services efficiently.

Actually, to claim that market equilibrium is always efficient even in this limited sense is an overstatement. The claim holds only if markets are perfectly competitive and if the demand and supply curves satisfy certain other restrictions. For example, market equilibrium will not be efficient if the individual marginal cost curves that add up to the market supply curve fail to include all relevant costs of producing the product. Thus, as we saw in Chapter 3, *Supply and Demand*, the true cost of expanding output will be higher than indicated by the market supply curve if production generates pollution that harms others. The equilibrium output will then be inefficiently large and the equilibrium price inefficiently low.

Likewise, market equilibrium will not be efficient if the individual demand curves that make up the market demand curve do not capture all the relevant benefits of buying additional units of the product. For instance, if a homeowner's willingness to pay for ornamental shrubs is based only on the enjoyment she herself gains from them, and not on any benefits that may accrue to her neighbors, the market demand curve for shrubs will understate their value to the neighborhood. The equilibrium quantity of ornamental shrubs will be inefficiently small and the market price for shrubs will be inefficiently low.

We will take up such market imperfections in greater detail in later chapters. For now, we will confine our attention to perfectly competitive markets whose demand curves capture all relevant benefits and whose supply curves capture all relevant costs. For such goods, market equilibrium will always be efficient in the limited sense described earlier.

Efficiency Is Not the Only Goal

The fact that market equilibrium maximizes economic surplus is an attractive feature, to be sure. Bear in mind, however, that "efficient" does not mean the same thing as "good." For example, the market for milk may be in equilibrium at a price of $1.50 per gallon, yet many poor families may be unable to afford milk for their children at that price. Still others may not even have a place for their children to sleep.

Markets may be highly efficient at producing what people demand, but those demands depend heavily on how much income specific individuals have. Nothing in the invisible hand theory suggests that the distribution of income that results from market exchange will satisfy ordinary norms of fairness. And if the distribution of purchasing power isn't fair, there's no compelling reason to approve of the resulting pattern of goods and services served up by competitive markets.

Most of us could agree, for example, that the world would be a better one if all people had enough income to feed their families adequately. The claim that equilibrium in the market for milk is efficient means simply that *taking people's incomes as given*, the resulting allocation of milk cannot be altered so as to help some people without at the same time harming others.

To this a critic of the market system might respond: So what? As such critics rightly point out, imposing costs on others may be justified if doing so will help those with sufficiently important unmet demands. For example, most people would prefer to fund homeless shelters with their tax dollars rather than let homeless people freeze to death. Arguing in these terms, American policymakers responded to rapid increases in the price of oil in the late 1970s by imposing price controls on home heating oil. Many of us might agree that if the alternative had been to take no action at all, price controls might have been justified in the name of social justice.

The economist's concept of market efficiency makes clear that there *must* be a better alternative policy. Price controls on oil prevent the market from reaching equilibrium, and as we've seen, that means forgoing transactions that would benefit some people without harming others.

Why Efficiency Should Be the First Goal

Efficiency is important not because it is a desirable end in itself, but because it enables us to achieve all our other goals to the fullest possible extent. It is always possible to generate additional economic surplus when a market is out of equilibrium. To gain additional economic surplus is to gain more of the resources we need to do the things we want to do.

RECAP

EQUILIBRIUM, SOCIAL OPTIMUM, AND EFFICIENCY

- A market in equilibrium is one in which no additional opportunities for gain remain available to individual buyers or sellers. The No-Cash-on-the-Table Principle describes powerful forces that help push markets toward equilibrium. But even if all markets are in equilibrium, the resulting allocation of resources need not be socially optimal. Equilibrium will be socially optimal only if markets are perfectly competitive and if the costs and benefits to individual participants in the market are the same as those experienced by society as a whole.
- A market in equilibrium is said to be efficient, or Pareto efficient, meaning that no reallocation is possible that will benefit some people without harming others.
- When a market is not in equilibrium—because price is either above the equilibrium level or below it—the quantity exchanged is always less than the equilibrium level. At such a quantity, a transaction can always be made in which both buyer and seller benefit from the exchange of an additional unit of output.
- Total economic surplus in a market is maximized when exchange occurs at the equilibrium price. But the fact that equilibrium is "efficient" in this sense does not mean that it is "good." All markets can be in equilibrium, yet many people may lack sufficient income to buy even basic goods and services. Still, permitting markets to reach equilibrium is important because, when economic surplus is maximized, it is possible to pursue every goal more fully.

THE COST OF PREVENTING PRICE ADJUSTMENTS

PRICE CEILINGS

During 1979, an interruption in oil supplies from the Middle East caused the price of home heating oil to rise by more than 100 percent. Concern about the hardship this sudden price increase would impose on poor families in northern states led the government to impose a price ceiling in the market for home heating oil. This price ceiling prohibited sellers from charging more than a specified amount for heating oil.

The following example illustrates why imposing a price ceiling on heating oil, though well intended, was a bad idea.

EXAMPLE 7.6   A Price Ceiling on Heating Oil

How much waste does a price ceiling on heating oil cause?

Suppose the demand and supply curves for home heating oil are as shown in Figure 7.14, in which the equilibrium price is $1.40 per gallon. Suppose that, at that price, many poor families cannot heat their homes adequately. Out of concern for the poor, legislators pass a law setting the maximum price at $1 per gallon. How much lost economic surplus does this policy cost society?

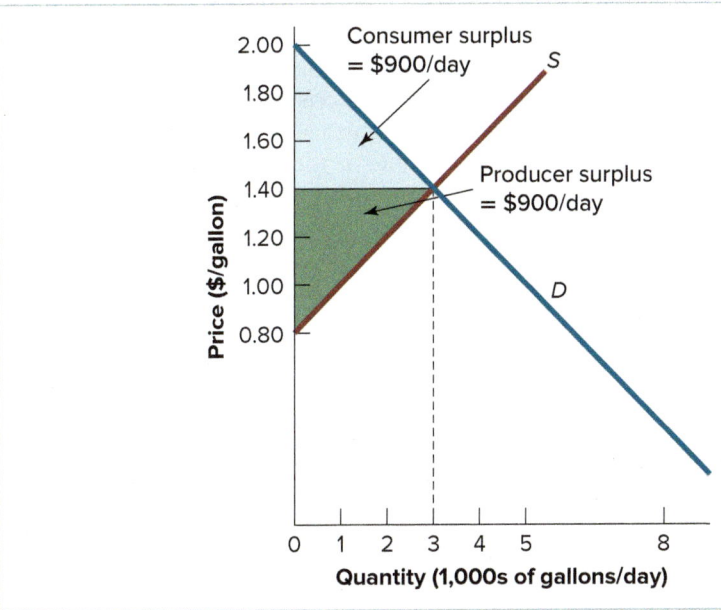

FIGURE 7.14

Economic Surplus in an Unregulated Market for Home Heating Oil.

For the supply and demand curves shown, the equilibrium price of home heating oil is $1.40 per gallon and the equilibrium quantity is 3,000 gallons per day. Consumer surplus is the area of the upper shaded triangle ($900 per day). Producer surplus is the area of the lower shaded triangle (also $900 per day).

First, let's calculate total economic surplus without price controls. If this market is not regulated, 3,000 gallons per day will be sold at a price of $1.40 per gallon. In Figure 7.14, the economic surplus received by buyers is the area of the upper shaded triangle. Since the height of this triangle is $0.60 per gallon and its base is 3,000 gallons per day, its area is equal to (1/2)(3,000 gallons/day)($0.60/gallon) = $900 per day. The economic surplus received by producers is the area of the lower shaded triangle. This triangle also has an area of $900 per day, so total economic surplus in this market will be $1,800 per day.

If the price of heating oil is prevented from rising above $1 per gallon, only 1,000 gallons per day will be sold and the total economic surplus will be reduced by the area of the lined triangle shown in Figure 7.15. Since the height of this

FIGURE 7.15

The Waste Caused by Price Controls.

By limiting output in the home heating oil market to 1,000 gallons per day, price controls cause a loss in economic surplus of $800 per day (area of the lined triangle).

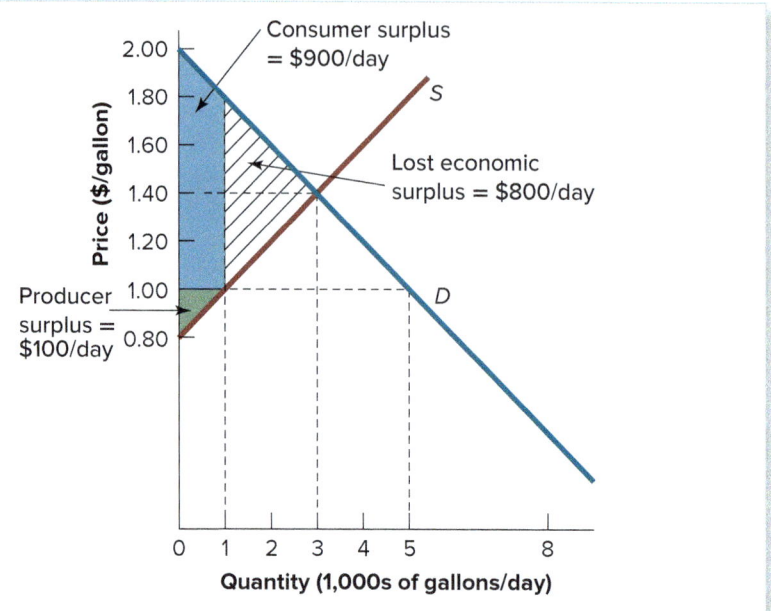

triangle is $0.80 per gallon and its base is 2,000 gallons per day, its area is (1/2)(2,000 gallons/day)($0.80/gallon) = $800 per day. Producer surplus falls from $900 per day in the unregulated market to the area of the lower shaded triangle, or (1/2)(1,000 gallons/day)($0.20/gallon) = $100 per day, which is a loss of $800 per day. Thus, the loss in total economic surplus is equal to the loss in producer surplus, which means that the new consumer surplus must be the same as the original consumer surplus. To verify this, note that consumer surplus with the price ceiling is the area of the upper shaded figure, which is again $900 per day. (*Hint:* To compute this area, first split the figure into a rectangle and a triangle.) By preventing the home heating oil market from reaching equilibrium, price controls waste $800 of producer surplus per day without creating any additional surplus for consumers!

 SELF-TEST 7.4

In Example 7.6, by how much would total economic surplus have been reduced if the price ceiling had been set not at $1 but at $1.20 per gallon?

For several reasons, the reduction in total economic surplus shown in Figure 7.15 is a conservative estimate of the waste caused by attempts to hold price below its equilibrium level. For one thing, the analysis assumes that each of the 1,000 gallons per day that are sold in this market will end up in the hands of the consumers who value them most—in the diagram, those whose reservation prices are above $1.80 per gallon. But since any buyer whose reservation price is above $1 per gallon will want to buy at the ceiling price, much of the oil actually sold is likely to go to buyers whose reservation prices are below $1.80. Suppose, for example, that a buyer whose reservation price was $1.50 per gallon made it into the line outside a heating oil supplier just ahead of a buyer whose reservation price was $1.90 per gallon. If each buyer had a 20-gallon tank to fill, and if the first buyer got the last of the day's available oil, then total surplus would be smaller by $8 that day than if the oil had gone to the second buyer.

A second reason that the reduction in surplus shown in Figure 7.15 is likely to be an underestimate is that shortages typically prompt buyers to take costly actions to enhance their chances of being served. For example, if the heating oil distributor begins selling its

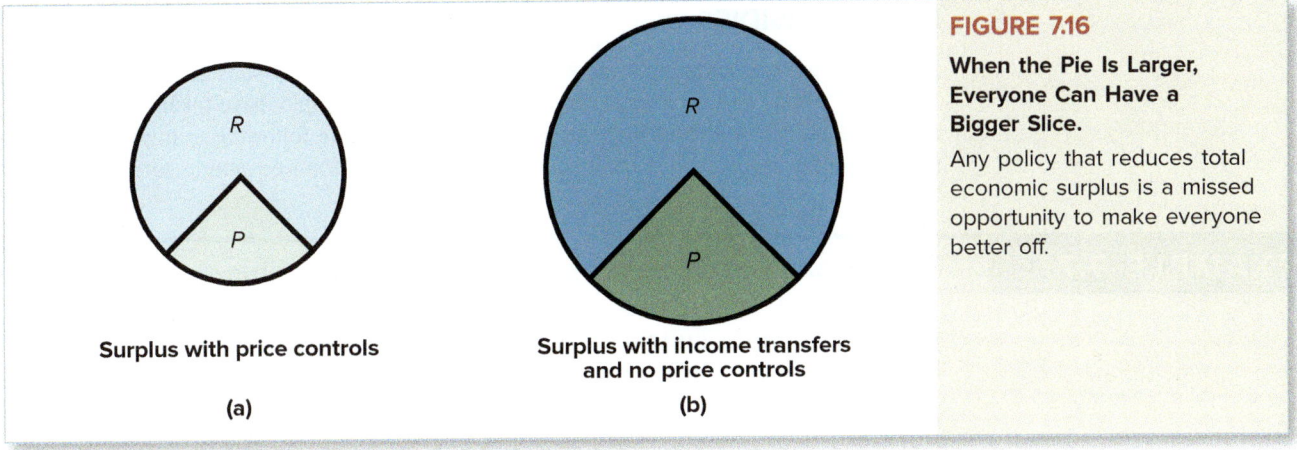

FIGURE 7.16

When the Pie Is Larger, Everyone Can Have a Bigger Slice.

Any policy that reduces total economic surplus is a missed opportunity to make everyone better off.

Surplus with price controls

(a)

Surplus with income transfers and no price controls

(b)

available supplies at 6:00 a.m., many buyers may arrive several hours early to ensure a place near the front of the line. Yet when all buyers incur the cost of arriving earlier, no one gets any more oil than before.

Notwithstanding the fact that price ceilings reduce total economic surplus, their defenders might argue that controls are justified because they enable at least some low-income families to buy heating oil at affordable prices. Yes, but the same objective could have been accomplished in a much less costly way—namely, by giving the poor more income with which to buy heating oil.

It may seem natural to wonder whether the poor, who have limited political power, can really hope to receive income transfers that would enable them to heat their homes. On reflection, the answer to this question would seem to be yes, *if the alternative is to impose price controls that would be even more costly than the income transfers.* After all, the price ceiling as implemented ends up costing heating oil sellers $800 per day in lost economic surplus. So they ought to be willing to pay some amount less than $800 a day in additional taxes in order to escape the burden of controls. The additional tax revenue could finance income transfers that would be far more beneficial to the poor than price controls.

This point is so important, and so often misunderstood by voters and policymakers, that we will emphasize it by putting it another way. Think of the economic surplus from a market as a pie to be divided among the various market participants. Figure 7.16(a) represents the $1,000 per day of total economic surplus available to participants in the home heating oil market when the government limits the price of oil to $1 per gallon. We divided this pie into two slices, labeled *R* and *P,* to denote the surpluses received by rich and poor participants. Figure 7.16(b) represents the $1,800 per day of total economic surplus available when the price of home heating oil is free to reach its equilibrium level. This pie is divided among rich and poor participants in the same proportion as the pie in the left panel.

The important point to notice is this: *Because the pie on the right side is larger, both rich and poor participants in the home heating oil market can get a bigger slice of the pie than they would have had under price controls.* Rather than tinker with the market price of oil, it is in everyone's interest to simply transfer additional income to the poor.

With the Incentive Principle in mind, supporters of price controls may object that income transfers to the poor might weaken people's incentive to work, and thus might prove extremely costly in the long run. Difficult issues do indeed arise in the design of programs for transferring income to the poor—issues we will consider in some detail in later chapters. But for now, suffice it to say that ways exist to transfer income without undermining work incentives significantly. One such method is the Earned Income Tax Credit, a program that supplements the wages of low-income workers. Given such programs, transferring income to the poor will always be more efficient than trying to boost their living standard through price controls.

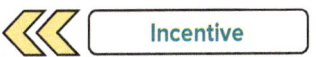

Incentive

PRICE SUBSIDIES

Sometimes governments try to assist low-income consumers by subsidizing the prices of "essential" goods and services. France and Russia, for example, have taken this approach at various points by subsidizing the price of bread. As the following example illustrates, such subsidies are like price ceilings in that they reduce total economic surplus.

EXAMPLE 7.7   **The Impact of Subsidies on Economic Surplus**

By how much do subsidies reduce total economic surplus in the market for bread?

A small island nation imports bread for its population at the world price of $2 per loaf. If the domestic demand curve for bread is as shown in Figure 7.17, by how much will total economic surplus decline in this market if the government provides a $1-per-loaf subsidy?

FIGURE 7.17

Economic Surplus in a Bread Market without Subsidy.

For the demand curve shown, consumer surplus (area of the shaded triangle) is $4,000,000 per month. This amount is equal to total economic surplus in the domestic bread market since no bread is produced domestically.

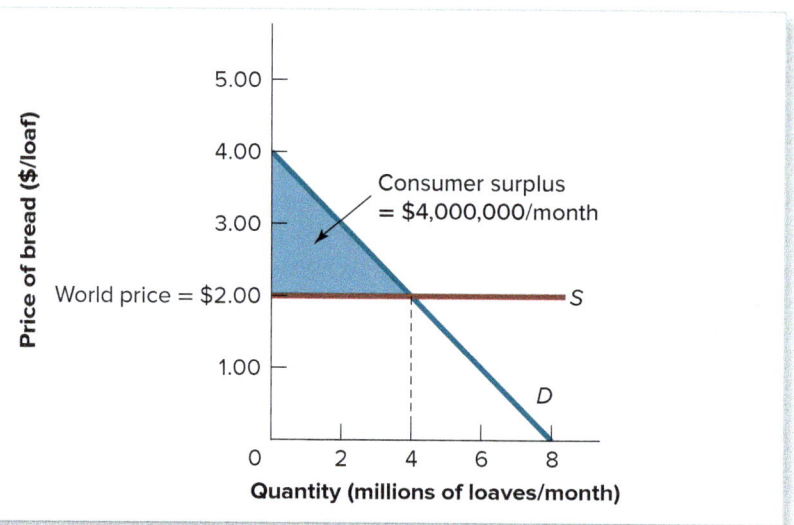

With no subsidy, the equilibrium price of bread in this market would be the world price of $2 per loaf and the equilibrium quantity would be 4,000,000 loaves per month. The shaded triangle in Figure 7.17 represents consumer economic surplus for buyers in the domestic bread market. The height of this triangle is $2 per loaf, and its base is 4,000,000 loaves per month, so its area is equal to (1/2)(4,000,000 loaves/month)($2/loaf) = $4,000,000 per month. Because the country can import as much bread as it wishes at the world price of $2 per loaf, supply is perfectly elastic in this market. Because the marginal cost of each loaf of bread to sellers is exactly the same as the price buyers pay, producer surplus in this market is zero. So total economic surplus is exactly equal to consumer surplus, which, again, is $4,000,000 per month.

Now suppose that the government administers its $1 per loaf subsidy program by purchasing bread in the world market at $2 per loaf and reselling it in the domestic market for only $1 per loaf. At the new lower price, buyers will now consume not 4,000,000 loaves per month but 6,000,000. Consumer surplus for buyers in the bread market is now the area of the larger shaded triangle in Figure 7.18: (1/2)($3/loaf)(6,000,000 loaves/month) = $9,000,000 per month, or $5,000,000 per month more than before. The catch is that the subsidy wasn't free. Its cost, which must be borne by taxpayers, is ($1/loaf)(6,000,000 loaves/month) = $6,000,000 per month. So even though consumer surplus in the bread

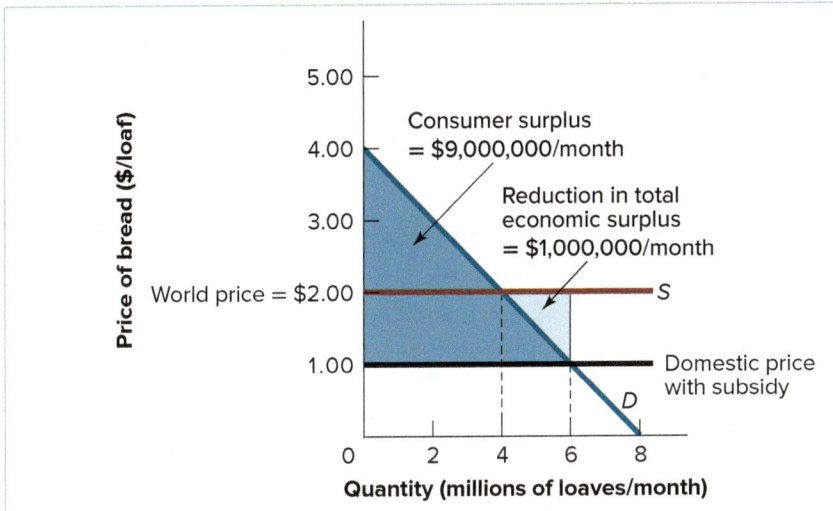

FIGURE 7.18

The Reduction in Economic Surplus from a Subsidy.
Since the marginal cost of bread is $2 per loaf, total economic surplus is maximized at 4,000,000 loaves per month, the quantity for which the marginal buyer's reservation price is equal to marginal cost. The reduction in economic surplus from consuming an additional 2,000,000 loaves per month is $1,000,000 per month, the area of the smaller shaded triangle.

market is larger than before, the net effect of the subsidy program is actually to reduce total economic surplus by $1,000,000 per month.

Another way to see why the subsidy reduces total economic surplus by that amount is to note that total economic surplus is maximized at 4,000,000 loaves per month, the quantity for which the marginal buyer's reservation price is equal to marginal cost, and that the subsidy induces additional consumption of 2,000,000 loaves per month. Each additional loaf has a marginal cost of $2 but is worth less than that to the buyer (as indicated by the fact that the vertical coordinate of the demand curve lies below $2 for consumption beyond 4,000,000). As consumption expands from 4,000,000 to 6,000,000 loaves per month, the cumulative difference between the marginal cost of bread and its value to buyers is the area of the smaller shaded triangle in Figure 7.18, which is $1,000,000 per month.

This reduction in economic surplus constitutes pure waste—no different, from the perspective of participants in this market, than if they had siphoned that much cash out of their bank accounts each month and thrown it into a bonfire.

 SELF-TEST 7.5

How much total economic surplus would have been lost if the bread subsidy, as illustrated in Example 7.7, had been set at $0.50 per loaf instead of $1?

Compared to a bread subsidy, a much better policy would be to give low-income people some additional income and then let them buy bread on the open market. Subsidy advocates who complain that taxpayers would be unwilling to give low-income people income transfers must be asked to explain why people would be willing to tolerate subsidies, which are *more* costly than income transfers. Logically, if voters are willing to support subsidies, they should be even more eager to support income transfers to low-income persons.

This is not to say that the poor reap no benefit at all from bread subsidies. Because they get to buy bread at lower prices and because the subsidy program is financed by taxes collected primarily from middle- and upper-income families, poor families probably come out ahead on balance. *The point is that for the same expense, we could do much more to help the poor.* Their problem is that they have too little income. The simplest and best solution is not to try to peg the prices of the goods they and others buy below equilibrium levels, but rather to give them some additional money.

RECAP ↑

THE COST OF PREVENTING PRICE ADJUSTMENTS

In an effort to help low-income consumers, governments often impose price ceilings and provide price subsidies that make housing and other basic goods more affordable. These policies prevent markets from reaching equilibrium and typically reduce total economic surplus.

SUMMARY

- Accounting profit is the difference between a firm's revenue and its explicit expenses. It differs from economic profit, which is the difference between revenue and the sum of the firm's explicit and implicit costs. Normal profit is the difference between accounting profit and economic profit. It is the opportunity cost of the resources supplied to a business by its owners. *(LO1)*

- The quest for economic profit is the invisible hand that drives resource allocation in market economies. Markets in which businesses earn an economic profit tend to attract additional resources, whereas markets in which businesses experience an economic loss tend to lose resources. If new firms enter a market with economic profits, that market's supply curve shifts to the right, causing a reduction in the price of the product. Prices will continue to fall until economic profits are eliminated. By contrast, the departure of firms from markets with economic losses causes the supply curve in such markets to shift left, increasing the price of the product. Prices will continue to rise until economic losses are eliminated. In the long run, market forces drive economic profits and losses toward zero. *(LO2, LO3)*

- Economic rent is the portion of the payment for an input that exceeds the reservation price for that input. If a professional basketball player who is willing to play for as little as $100,000 per year is paid $15 million, he earns an economic rent of $14,900,000 per year. Whereas the invisible hand drives economic profit toward zero over the long run, economic rent can persist indefinitely because replicating the services of players like Steph Curry is impossible. Talented individuals who are responsible for the superior performance of a business will tend to capture the resulting financial gains as economic rents. *(LO3)*

- The benefit of an investment to an individual sometimes differs from its benefit to society as a whole. Such conflicting incentives may give rise to behavior that is smart for one but dumb for all. Despite such exceptions, the invisible hand of the market works remarkably well much of the time. One of the market system's most important contributions to social well-being is the pressure it creates to adopt cost-saving innovations. Competition among firms ensures that the resulting cost savings get passed along to consumers in the long run. *(LO4)*

- When the supply and demand curves for a product capture all the relevant costs and benefits of producing that product, then market equilibrium for that product will be efficient. In such a market, if price and quantity do not equal their equilibrium values, a transaction can be found that will make at least some people better off without harming others. *(LO4)*

- When market supply and demand curves reflect the underlying costs and benefits to society of the production of a good or service, the quest for economic profit ensures not only that existing supplies are allocated efficiently among individual buyers, but also that resources are allocated across markets in the most efficient way possible. In any allocation other than the one generated by the market, resources could be rearranged to benefit some people without harming others. *(LO4)*

- The No-Cash-on-the-Table Principle implies that if someone owns a valuable resource, the market price of that resource will typically reflect its economic value. The implication of this principle is not that lucrative opportunities never exist, but rather that such opportunities cannot exist when markets are in equilibrium. *(LO4)*

- Total economic surplus is a measure of the amount by which participants in a market benefit by participating in it. It is the sum of total consumer surplus and total producer surplus in the market. One of the attractive properties of market equilibrium is that it maximizes the value of total economic surplus. *(LO5)*

- Efficiency should not be equated with social justice. If we believe that the distribution of income among people is unjust, we won't like the results produced by the intersection of the supply and demand curves based on that income distribution, even though those results are efficient. *(LO5)*

- Even so, we should always strive for efficiency because it enables us to achieve all our other goals to the fullest possible extent. Whenever a market is out of equilibrium, the economic pie can be made larger. And with a larger pie, everyone can have a larger slice. *(LO5)*

- Regulations or policies that prevent markets from reaching equilibrium—such as price ceilings and price subsidies—are often defended on the grounds that they help the poor. But such schemes reduce economic surplus, meaning that we can find alternatives under which both rich and poor would be better off. The main difficulty of the poor is that they have too little income. Rather than trying to control the prices of the goods they buy, we could do better by enacting policies that raise the incomes of the poor and then letting prices seek their equilibrium levels. Those who complain that the poor lack the political power to obtain such income transfers must explain why the poor have the power to impose regulations that are far more costly than income transfers. *(LO5)*

KEY TERMS

accounting profit
allocative function of price
barrier to entry
economic loss
economic profit (or excess profit)

economic rent
efficient (or Pareto efficient)
explicit costs
implicit costs
invisible hand theory

normal profit
rationing function of price

REVIEW QUESTIONS

1. How can a business owner who earns $10 million per year from her business credibly claim to earn zero economic profit? *(LO1)*

2. Why do most cities in the United States now have more radios but fewer radio-repair shops than they did in 1960? *(LO2)*

3. Why do market forces drive economic profit but not economic rent toward zero? *(LO3)*

4. Why do economists emphasize efficiency as an important goal of public policy? *(LO4)*

5. You are a senator considering how to vote on a policy that would increase the economic surplus of workers by $100 million per year but reduce the economic surplus of retirees by $1 million per year. What additional measure might you combine with the policy to ensure that the overall result is a better outcome for everyone? *(LO5)*

PROBLEMS

1. Explain why the following statements are true or false. *(LO1, LO2, LO3, LO4)*
   a. The economic maxim "There's no cash on the table" means that there are never any unexploited economic opportunities.
   b. Firms in competitive environments make no accounting profit when the market is in long-run equilibrium.
   c. Firms that can introduce cost-saving innovations can make an economic profit in the short run.

2. Jaime owns and manages a café in Collegetown whose annual revenue is $5,000. Annual expenses are as follows: *(LO1, LO2)*

Labor	$2,000
Food and drink	500
Electricity	100
Vehicle lease	150
Rent	500
Interest on loan for equipment	1,000

a. Calculate Jaime's annual accounting profit.

b. Jaime could earn $1,000 per year as a recycler of aluminum cans. However, she prefers to run the café. In fact, she would be willing to pay up to $275 per year to run the café rather than to recycle. Is the café making an economic profit? Should Jaime stay in the café business? Explain.

c. Suppose the café's revenues and expenses remain the same, but recyclers' earnings rise to $1,100 per year. Is the café still making an economic profit? Explain.

d. Suppose Jaime had not gotten a $10,000 loan at an annual interest rate of 10 percent to buy equipment, but instead had invested $10,000 of her own money in equipment. How would your answer to parts a and b change?

e. If Jaime can earn $1,000 a year as a recycler, and she likes recycling just as well as running the café, how much additional revenue would the café have to collect each year to earn a normal profit?

3. The city of New Orleans has 200 advertising companies, 199 of which employ designers of normal ability at a salary of $100,000 a year. The companies that employ normal designers each collect $500,000 in revenue a year, which is just enough to ensure that each earns exactly a normal profit. The 200th company, however, employs Janus, an unusually talented designer. Because of Janus's talent, this company collects $1,000,000 in revenue a year. *(LO3)*

a. How much will Janus earn? What proportion of her annual salary will be economic rent?

b. Why won't the advertising company for which Janus works be able to earn an economic profit?

4. Unskilled workers in a poor cotton-growing region must choose between working in a factory for $6,000 a year and being a tenant cotton farmer. One farmer can work a 120-acre farm, which rents for $10,000 a year. Such farms yield $20,000 worth of cotton each year. The total nonlabor cost of producing and marketing the cotton is $5,000 a year. A local politician whose motto is "Working people come first" has promised that if she is elected, her administration will fund a fertilizer, irrigation, and marketing scheme that will triple cotton yields on tenant farms at no charge to tenant farmers. *(LO3)*

a. If the market price of cotton would be unaffected by this policy and no new jobs would be created in the cotton-growing industry, how would the project affect the incomes of tenant farmers in the short run? In the long run?

b. Who would reap the benefit of the scheme in the long run? How much would they gain each year?

5. Suppose the weekly demand and supply curves for used DVDs in Lincoln, Nebraska, are as shown in the diagram. Calculate the following: *(LO5)*

a. The weekly consumer surplus.

b. The weekly producer surplus.

c. The maximum weekly amount that producers and consumers in Lincoln would be willing to pay to be able to buy and sell used DVDs in any given week (total economic surplus).

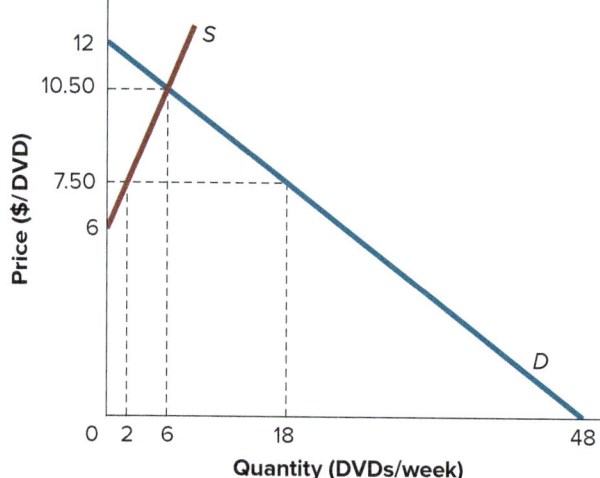

6. Refer to Problem 5. Suppose a coalition of students from Lincoln High School succeeds in persuading the local government to impose a price ceiling of $7.50 on used DVDs, on the grounds that local suppliers are taking advantage of teenagers by charging exorbitant prices. *(LO5)*

a. Calculate the weekly shortage of used DVDs that will result from this policy.

b. Calculate the total economic surplus lost every week as a result of the price ceiling.

7.* The government of Islandia, a small island nation, imports heating oil at a price of $2 per gallon and makes it available to citizens at a price of $1 per gallon. If Islandians' demand curve for heating oil is given by $P = 6 - Q$, where P is the price per gallon in dollars and Q is the quantity in millions of gallons per year, how much economic surplus is lost as a result of the government's policy? *(LO5)*

8.* Refer to Problem 7. Suppose each of the 1 million Islandian households has the same demand curve for heating oil. *(LO5)*

a. What is the household demand curve?

b. How much consumer surplus would each household lose if it had to pay $2 per gallon instead of $1 per gallon for heating oil, assuming there were no other changes in the household budget?

c. With the money saved by not subsidizing oil, by how much could the Islandian government afford to cut each family's annual taxes?

d. If the government abandoned its oil subsidy and implemented the tax cut, by how much would each family be better off?

*Denotes more difficult problem.

ANSWERS TO SELF-TESTS

7.1 As shown in the table below, Pudge's accounting profit is now $10,000, the difference between his $20,000 annual revenue and his $10,000-per-year payment for land, equipment, and supplies. His economic profit is that amount minus the opportunity cost of his labor—again, the $11,000 per year he could have earned as a store manager. So Pudge is now earning a negative economic profit, −$1,000 per year. As before, his normal profit is the $11,000-per-year opportunity cost of his labor. Although an accountant would say Pudge is making an annual profit of $10,000, that amount is less than a normal profit for his activity. An economist would therefore say that he is making an economic loss of $1,000 per year. Since Pudge likes the two jobs equally well, he will be better off by $1,000 per year if he leaves farming to become a manager. *(LO1)*

Total revenue ($/year)	Explicit costs ($/year)	Implicit costs ($/year)	Accounting profit (= total revenue − explicit costs) ($/year)	Economic profit (= total revenue − explicit costs − implicit costs) ($/year)	Normal profit (= implicit costs) ($/year)
20,000	10,000	11,000	10,000	−1,000	11,000

7.2 If each lane did not move at about the same pace, any driver in a slower lane could reduce his travel time by simply switching to a faster one. People will exploit these opportunities until each lane moves at about the same pace. *(LO3)*

7.3 At a price of 50 cents per gallon, there is excess demand of 4,000 gallons per day, as shown in the given figure. Suppose a seller produces an extra gallon of milk (marginal cost = 50 cents) and sells it to the buyer who values it most (reservation price = $2.50) for $1.50. Both buyer and seller will gain additional economic surplus of $1, and no other buyers or sellers will be hurt by the transaction. *(LO4)*

7.4 As shown in the accompanying diagram, the new loss in total economic surplus is $200 per day. *(LO5)*

7.5 With a $0.50-per-loaf subsidy, the new domestic price becomes $1.50 per loaf. The new lost surplus is the area of the small shaded triangle in the given diagram: (1/2)($0.50/loaf)(1,000,000 loaves/month) = $250,000 per month. *(LO5)*

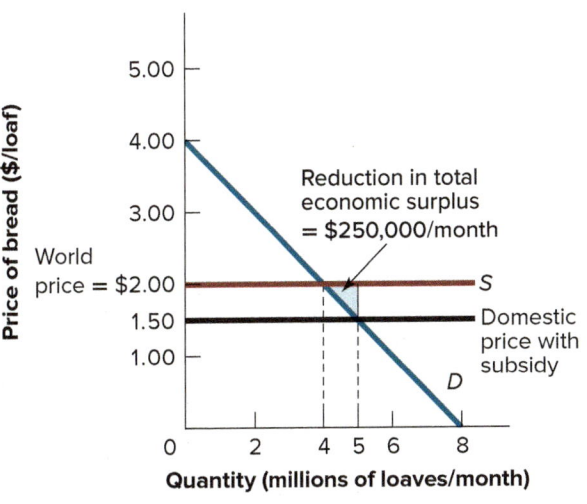

CHAPTER 8

Monopoly, Oligopoly, and Monopolistic Competition

Monopoly sellers almost always offer discount prices to buyers who are willing to mail in a rebate coupon or endure some other type of inconvenience.

Mim Friday/Alamy Stock Photo

Some years ago, fantasy game enthusiasts around the country became obsessed with the game of Magic: The Gathering. To play, you need a deck of Magic cards, available only from the creators of the game. But unlike ordinary playing cards, which can be bought in most stores for only a dollar or two, a deck of Magic cards sells for many times that. And because Magic cards cost no more to manufacture than ordinary playing cards, their producer earns an enormous economic profit.

In a perfectly competitive market, entrepreneurs would see this economic profit as cash on the table. It would entice them to offer Magic cards at slightly lower prices so that, eventually, the cards would sell for roughly their cost of production, just as ordinary playing cards do. But Magic cards have been on the market for decades now, and that hasn't happened. The reason is that the cards are copyrighted, which means the government has granted the creators of the game an exclusive license to sell them.

imperfectly competitive firm (or **price setter**) a firm that has at least some control over the market price of its product

The holder of a copyright is an example of an **imperfectly competitive firm**, or **price setter**—that is, a firm with at least some latitude to set its own price. The competitive firm, by contrast, is a price taker, a firm with no influence over the price of its product.

Our focus in this chapter will be on the ways in which markets served by imperfectly competitive firms differ from those served by perfectly competitive firms. One salient difference is the imperfectly competitive firm's ability, under certain circumstances, to charge more than its cost of production. But if the producer of Magic cards could charge any price it wished, why does it charge only $10? Why not $100, or even $1,000? We'll see that even though such a company may be the only seller of its product, its pricing freedom is far from absolute. We'll also see how some imperfectly competitive firms manage to earn an economic profit, even in the long run, and even without government protections like copyright. And we'll explore why Adam Smith's invisible hand is less evident in a world served by imperfectly competitive firms.

PERFECT AND IMPERFECT COMPETITION

The perfectly competitive market is an ideal; the actual markets we encounter in everyday life differ from the ideal in varying degrees. Economics texts usually distinguish among three types of imperfectly competitive market structures. The classifications are somewhat arbitrary, but they are quite useful in analyzing real-world markets.

DIFFERENT FORMS OF IMPERFECT COMPETITION

pure monopoly the only supplier of a unique product with no close substitutes

Farthest from the perfectly competitive ideal is the **pure monopoly**, a market in which a single firm is the lone seller of a unique product. The producer of Magic cards is a pure monopolist, as are many providers of electric power. If the residents of Miami don't buy their electricity from Florida Power and Light Company, they simply do without. In between these two extremes are many different types of imperfect competition. We focus on two of them here: monopolistic competition and oligopoly.

Monopolistic Competition

monopolistic competition an industry structure in which a large number of firms produce slightly differentiated products that are reasonably close substitutes for one another

Recall from Chapter 6, *Perfectly Competitive Supply,* that in a perfectly competitive industry, a large number of firms typically sell products that are essentially perfect substitutes for one another. In contrast, **monopolistic competition** is an industry structure in which a large number of rival firms sell products that are close, but not quite perfect, substitutes. Rival products may be highly similar in many respects, but there are always at least some features that differentiate one product from another in the eyes of some consumers. Monopolistic competition has in common with perfect competition the feature that there are no significant barriers preventing firms from entering or leaving the market.

Local gasoline retailing is an example of a monopolistically competitive industry. The gas sold by different stations may be nearly identical in chemical terms, but a station's particular location is a feature that matters for many consumers. Convenience stores are another example. Although most of the products found on any given store's shelves are also carried by most other stores, the product lists of different stores are not identical. Some offer sim cards and lottery tickets, for example, while others offer foam coolers and flashlights. And even more so than in the case of gasoline retailing, location is an important differentiating feature of convenience stores.

Recall that if a perfectly competitive firm were to charge even just slightly more than the prevailing market price for its product, it would not sell any output at all. Things are different for the monopolistically competitive firm. The fact that its offering is not a perfect substitute for those of its rivals means that it can charge a slightly higher price than they do and not lose all its customers.

But that does not mean that monopolistically competitive firms can expect to earn positive economic profits in the long run. On the contrary, because new firms are able to enter freely, a monopolistically competitive industry is essentially the same as a perfectly competitive industry in this respect. If existing monopolistically competitive firms were earning positive economic profits at prevailing prices, new firms would have an incentive to enter the industry. Downward pressure on prices would then result as the larger number of firms competed for a limited pool of potential customers.[1] As long as positive economic profits remained, entry would continue and prices would be driven ever lower. Conversely, if firms in a monopolistically competitive industry were initially suffering economic losses, some firms would begin leaving the industry. As long as economic losses remained, exit and the resulting upward pressure on prices would continue. So in long-run equilibrium, monopolistically competitive firms are in this respect essentially like perfectly competitive firms: All expect to earn zero economic profit.

Although monopolistically competitive firms have some latitude to vary the prices of their product in the short run, pricing is not the most important strategic decision they confront. A far more important issue is how to differentiate their products from those of existing rivals. Should a product be made to resemble a rival's product as closely as possible? Or should the aim be to make it as different as possible? Or should the firm strive for something in between? We'll consider these questions in Chapter 9, *Games and Strategic Behavior*, where we'll focus on this type of strategic decision making.

Oligopoly

Further along the continuum between perfect competition and pure monopoly lies **oligopoly**, a structure in which the entire market is supplied by a small number of large firms. Cost advantages associated with large size are one of the primary reasons for pure monopoly, as we will discuss presently. Oligopoly is also typically a consequence of cost advantages that prevent small firms from being able to compete effectively.

oligopoly an industry structure in which a small number of large firms produce products that are either close or perfect substitutes

In some cases, oligopolists sell undifferentiated products. In the market for wireless phone service, for example, the offerings of AT&T, Verizon, and T-Mobile are very similar. The cement industry is another example of an oligopoly selling an essentially undifferentiated product. The most important strategic decisions facing firms in such cases are more likely to involve pricing and advertising than specific features of their product. Here, too, we leave a more detailed discussion of such decisions to Chapter 9, *Games and Strategic Behavior*.

In other cases, such as the automobile and tobacco industries, oligopolists are more like monopolistic competitors than pure monopolists, in the sense that differences in their product features have significant effects on consumer demand. Many long-time Ford buyers, for example, would not even consider buying a Chevrolet, and very few smokers ever switch from Camels to Marlboros. As with oligopolists who produce undifferentiated products, pricing and advertising are important strategic decisions for firms in these industries, but so, too, are those related to specific product features.

Because cost advantages associated with large size are usually so important in oligopolies, there is no presumption that entry and exit will push economic profit to zero. Consider, for example, an oligopoly served by two firms, each of which currently earns an economic profit. Should a new firm enter this market? Possibly, but it also might be that a third firm large enough to achieve the cost advantages of the two incumbents would

[1] See Edward Chamberlin, *The Theory of Monopolistic Competition* (Cambridge, MA: Harvard University Press, 1st ed. 1933, 8th ed. 1962); and Joan Robinson, *The Economics of Imperfect Competition* (London: Macmillan, 1st ed. 1933, 2nd ed. 1969).

effectively flood the market, driving price so low that all three firms would suffer economic losses. There is no guarantee, however, that an oligopolist will earn a positive economic profit.

As we'll see in the next section, the essential characteristic that differentiates imperfectly competitive firms from perfectly competitive firms is the same in each of the three cases. So for the duration of this chapter, we'll use the term *monopolist* to refer to any of the three types of imperfectly competitive firms. In the next chapter, we'll consider the strategic decisions confronting oligopolists and monopolistically competitive firms in greater detail.

THE ESSENTIAL DIFFERENCE BETWEEN PERFECTLY AND IMPERFECTLY COMPETITIVE FIRMS

In advanced economics courses, professors generally devote much attention to the analysis of subtle differences in the behavior of different types of imperfectly competitive firms. Far more important for our purposes, however, will be to focus on the single, common feature that differentiates all imperfectly competitive firms from their perfectly competitive counterparts—namely, that *whereas the perfectly competitive firm faces a perfectly elastic demand curve for its product, the imperfectly competitive firm faces a downward-sloping demand curve.*

In the perfectly competitive industry, the supply and demand curves intersect to determine an equilibrium market price. At that price, the perfectly competitive firm can sell as many units as it wishes. It has no incentive to charge more than the market price because it won't sell anything if it does so. Nor does it have any incentive to charge less than the market price because it can sell as many units as it wants to at the market price. The perfectly competitive firm's demand curve is thus a horizontal line at the market price, as we saw in previous chapters.

By contrast, if a local gasoline retailer—an imperfect competitor—charges a few pennies more than its rivals for a gallon of gas, some of its customers may desert it. But others will remain, perhaps because they are willing to pay a little extra to continue stopping at their most convenient location. An imperfectly competitive firm thus faces a negatively sloped demand curve. Figure 8.1 summarizes this contrast between the demand curves facing perfectly competitive and imperfectly competitive firms.

If the BP station at State and Meadow Streets raised its gasoline prices by 3 cents per gallon, would all its customers shop elsewhere?

FIGURE 8.1

The Demand Curves Facing Perfectly and Imperfectly Competitive Firms.

(a) The demand curve confronting a perfectly competitive firm is perfectly elastic at the market price. (b) The demand curve confronting an imperfectly competitive firm is downward-sloping.

> *RECAP*↑
>
> **PERFECT AND IMPERFECT COMPETITION**
>
> Monopolistic competition is the industry structure in which a large number of small firms offer products that are similar in many respects, yet not perfect substitutes in the eyes of at least some consumers. Monopolistically competitive industries resemble perfectly competitive industries, in that entry and exit cause economic profits to tend toward zero in the long run.
>
> Oligopoly is the industry structure in which a small number of large firms supply the entire market. Cost advantages associated with large-scale operations tend to be important. Oligopolists may produce either standardized products or differentiated products.
>
> In contrast to each form of imperfect competition, in which all firms face downward-sloping demand curves, perfectly competitive firms face demand curves that are horizontal at the prevailing market price.

FIVE SOURCES OF MARKET POWER

Firms that confront downward-sloping demand curves are said to enjoy **market power**, a term that refers to their ability to set the prices of their products. A common misconception is that a firm with market power can sell any quantity at any price it wishes. It cannot. All it can do is pick a price-quantity combination on its demand curve. If the firm chooses to raise its price, it must settle for reduced sales.

market power a firm's ability to raise the price of a good without losing all its sales

Why do some firms have market power while others don't? Market power often carries with it the ability to charge a price above the cost of production, so such power tends to arise from factors that limit competition. In practice, the following five factors often confer such power: exclusive control over inputs, patents and copyrights, government licenses or franchises, economies of scale, and network economies.

EXCLUSIVE CONTROL OVER IMPORTANT INPUTS

If a single firm controls an input essential to the production of a given product, that firm will have market power. For example, to the extent that some U.S. tenants are willing to pay a premium for office space in the country's tallest building, One World Trade Center, the owner of that building has market power.

PATENTS AND COPYRIGHTS

Patents give the inventors or developers of new products the exclusive right to sell those products for a specified period of time. By insulating sellers from competition for an interval, patents enable innovators to charge higher prices to recoup their product's development costs. Pharmaceutical companies, for example, spend millions of dollars on research in the hope of discovering new drug therapies for serious illnesses. The drugs they discover are insulated from competition for an interval—currently 20 years in the United States—by government patents. For the life of the patent, only the patent holder may legally sell the drug. This protection enables the patent holder to set a price above the marginal cost of production to recoup the cost of the research on the drug. In the same way, copyrights protect the authors of movies, software, music, books, and other published works.

GOVERNMENT LICENSES OR FRANCHISES

Yosemite Hospitality, LLC has an exclusive license from the U.S. government to run the lodging and concession operations at Yosemite National Park. One of the government's goals in granting this monopoly was to preserve the wilderness character of the area to the greatest degree possible. And indeed, the inns and cabins offered by Yosemite Hospitality, LLC blend nicely with the valley's scenery. No garish neon signs mar the national park as they do in places where rivals compete for the tourist's dollars.

ECONOMIES OF SCALE AND NATURAL MONOPOLIES

constant returns to scale a production process is said to have constant returns to scale if, when all inputs are changed by a given proportion, output changes by the same proportion

When a firm doubles all its factors of production, what happens to its output? If output exactly doubles, the firm's production process is said to exhibit **constant returns to scale**. If output more than doubles, the production process is said to exhibit **increasing returns to scale**, or **economies of scale**. When production is subject to economies of scale, the average cost of production declines as the number of units produced increases. For example, in the generation of electricity, the use of larger generators lowers the unit cost of production. The markets for such products tend to be served by a single seller, or perhaps only a few sellers, because having a large number of sellers would result in significantly higher costs. A monopoly that results from economies of scale is called a **natural monopoly**.

increasing returns to scale (or **economies of scale**) a production process is said to have increasing returns to scale if, when all inputs are changed by a given proportion, output changes by more than that proportion

NETWORK ECONOMIES

natural monopoly a monopoly that results from economies of scale (increasing returns to scale)

Although most of us don't care what brand of a product like dental floss others use, many other products become more valuable to us as more people use them. In the case of social media, for instance, the more people use a particular social media platform, the more valuable it becomes. After all, the goal of social media is to connect with others. With over 1 billion active monthly users, posts on Instagram, for example, have the potential to be seen by large numbers of people. If, instead, Instagram had only a handful of users, none of whom you knew, the value of posting would be much smaller. Indeed, if many of your friends stopped using Instagram, you might follow suit.

A similar network economy helps account for the dominant position of Microsoft's Windows operating system, which, as noted earlier, is currently installed in roughly 80 percent of all desktop computers. Because Microsoft's initial sales advantage gave software developers a strong incentive to write for the Windows format, the inventory of available software in the Windows format is now vastly larger than that for any competing operating system. And although general-purpose software such as word processors and spreadsheets continues to be available for multiple operating systems, specialized professional software and games usually appear first—and often only—in the Windows format. This software gap and the desire to achieve compatibility for file sharing gave people a good reason for choosing Windows, even if, as in the case of many Apple users, they believed a competing system was otherwise superior. But, again, network dominance need not be permanent, as witnessed by Apple's dramatic resurgence in recent years.

By far the most important and enduring of these sources of market power are economies of scale and network economies. Lured by economic profit, firms almost always find substitutes for exclusive inputs. If there's enough profit to be had by renting out space in this country's tallest building, some real estate developer will eventually build one taller than One World Trade Center in New York. Likewise, firms can often evade patent laws by making slight changes in the design of products. Patent protection is only temporary, in any case. Finally, governments grant very few franchises each year. But economies of scale are both widespread and enduring, even if not completely insurmountable.

Firmly entrenched network economies can be as persistent a source of natural monopoly as economies of scale. Indeed, network economies are essentially similar to economies of scale. When network economies are of value to the consumer, a product's quality increases as the number of users increases, so we can say that any given quality level can be produced at lower cost as sales volume increases. Thus network economies may be viewed as just another form of economies of scale in production, and that's how we'll treat them here.

ECONOMIES OF SCALE AND THE IMPORTANCE OF START-UP COSTS

As we saw in Chapter 6, *Perfectly Competitive Supply*, variable costs are those that vary with the level of output produced, while fixed costs are independent of output. Suppose, for example, that a firm produces output by employing one fixed input, capital, and one variable input, labor. Its payment to capital would then be a fixed cost, and its payment to labor a variable cost. Strictly speaking, there are no fixed costs in the long run because all inputs can be varied. But as a practical matter, start-up costs often loom large for the duration of a product's useful life. Most of the costs involved in the production of computer software, for example, are start-up costs of this sort, one-time costs incurred in writing and testing the software. Once those tasks are done, additional copies of the software can be produced at a very low marginal cost. A good such as software, whose production entails large fixed start-up costs and low variable costs, will be subject to significant economies of scale. Because, by definition, fixed costs don't increase as output increases, the average total cost of production for such goods will decline sharply as output increases.

To illustrate, consider a production process for which total cost is given by the equation $TC = F + M \times Q$, where F is fixed cost, M is marginal cost (assumed constant in this illustration), and Q is the level of output produced. For the production process with this simple total cost function, variable cost is simply $M \times Q$, the product of marginal cost and quantity. Average total cost (ATC), TC/Q, is equal to $F/Q + M$. As Q increases, average cost declines steadily because the fixed costs are spread out over more and more units of output.

Figure 8.2 shows the total production cost (a) and average total cost (b) for a firm with the total cost curve $TC = F + M \times Q$ and the corresponding average total cost curve $ATC = F/Q + M$. The average total cost curve (b) shows the decline in per-unit cost as output grows. Though average total cost is always higher than marginal cost for this firm, the difference between the two diminishes as output grows. At extremely high levels of output, average total cost becomes very close to marginal cost (M). Because the firm is spreading out its fixed cost over an extremely large volume of output, fixed cost per unit becomes almost insignificant.

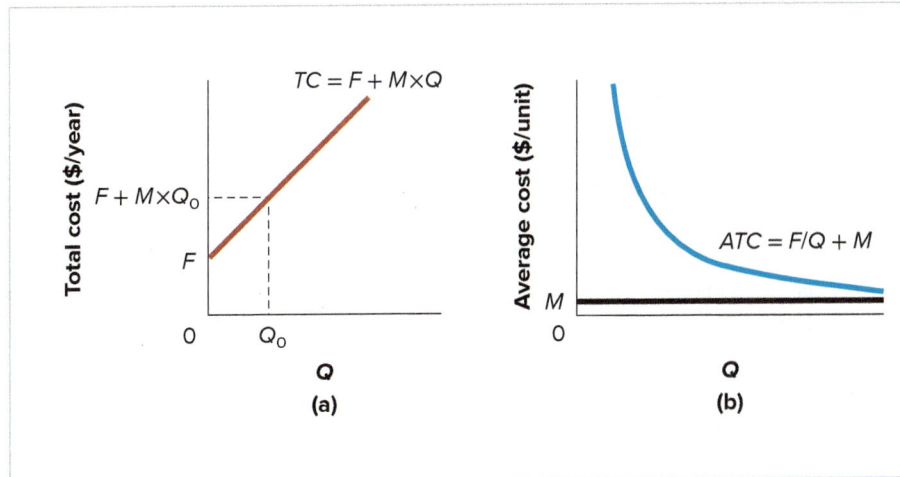

FIGURE 8.2

Total and Average Total Costs for a Production Process with Economies of Scale.

For a firm whose total cost curve of producing Q units of output per year is $TC = F + M \times Q$, total cost (a) rises at a constant rate as output grows, while average total cost (b) declines. Average total cost is always higher than marginal cost for this firm, but the difference becomes less significant at high output levels.

As the following examples illustrate, the importance of economies of scale depends on how large fixed cost is in relation to marginal cost.

EXAMPLE 8.1

Economies of Scale—Small Fixed Cost

Two video game producers, Nintendo and Sony Computer Entertainment, each have fixed costs of $200,000 and marginal costs of $0.80 per game. If Nintendo produces 1 million units per year and Sony produces 1.2 million, how much lower will Sony's average total production cost be?

Table 8.1 summarizes the relevant cost categories for the two firms. Note in the bottom row that Sony enjoys only a 3-cent average cost advantage over Nintendo. Even though Nintendo produces 20 percent fewer copies of its video game than Sony, it does not suffer a significant cost disadvantage because fixed cost is a relatively small part of total production cost.

TABLE 8.1
Costs for Two Video Game Producers (a)

	Nintendo	Sony Computer Entertainment
Annual production	1,000,000	1,200,000
Fixed cost	$200,000	$200,000
Variable cost	$800,000	$960,000
Total cost	$1,000,000	$1,160,000
Average total cost per game	$1.00	$0.97

In the next example, note how the picture changes when fixed cost looms large relative to marginal cost.

EXAMPLE 8.2

Economies of Scale—Large Fixed Cost

Two video game producers, Nintendo and Sony Computer Entertainment, each have fixed costs of $10,000,000 and marginal costs of $0.20 per video game. If Nintendo produces 1 million units per year and Sony produces 1.2 million, how much lower will Sony's average total cost be?

The relevant cost categories for the two firms are now summarized in Table 8.2. The bottom row shows that Sony enjoys a $1.67 average total cost advantage over Nintendo, substantially larger than in the previous example.

TABLE 8.2
Costs for Two Video Game Producers (b)

	Nintendo	Sony Computer Entertainment
Annual production	1,000,000	1,200,000
Fixed cost	$10,000,000	$10,000,000
Variable cost	$200,000	$240,000
Total cost	$10,200,000	$10,240,000
Average total cost per game	$10.20	$8.53

If the video games the two firms produce are essentially similar, the fact that Sony can charge significantly lower prices and still cover its costs should enable it to attract customers away from Nintendo. As more and more of the market goes to Sony, its cost advantage will become self-reinforcing. Table 8.3 shows how a shift of 500,000 units from Nintendo to Sony would cause Nintendo's average total cost to rise to $20.20 per unit, while Sony's average total cost would fall to $6.08 per unit. The fact that a firm cannot long survive at such a severe disadvantage explains why the video game market is served now by only a small number of firms.

TABLE 8.3
Costs for Two Video Game Producers (c)

	Nintendo	Sony Computer Entertainment
Annual production	500,000	1,700,000
Fixed cost	$10,000,000	$10,000,000
Variable cost	$100,000	$340,000
Total cost	$10,100,000	$10,340,000
Average total cost per game	$20.20	$6.08

 SELF-TEST 8.1

How big will Sony's unit cost advantage be if it sells 2,000,000 units per year, while Nintendo sells only 200,000?

An important worldwide economic trend during recent decades is that an increasing share of the value embodied in the goods and services we buy stems from fixed investment in research and development. For example, in 1984 some 80 percent of the cost of a computer was in its hardware (which has relatively high marginal cost); the remaining 20 percent was in its software. But by 1990 those proportions were reversed. Fixed cost now accounts for about 85 percent of total costs in the computer software industry, whose products are included in a growing share of ordinary manufactured goods.

The Economic Naturalist 8.1

Why does Intel sell more microprocessors used in personal computers than any other chipmaker?

The fixed investment required to produce a new leading-edge microprocessor runs upward of several billion dollars. But once the chip has been designed and the manufacturing facility built, the low marginal cost of producing each chip means that average cost will fall steadily with the number of chips produced. This cost pattern explains why Intel dominated the market for microprocessors for so many years. But the company's once commanding share of that market has eroded in recent years with the rise of smartphones and tablets as alternatives to Windows personal computers. Although economies of scale are the most durable of the five sources that confer monopoly power, changing technology can disrupt even the most dominant firms.

As fixed cost becomes more and more important, the perfectly competitive pattern of many small firms, each producing only a small share of its industry's total output, becomes less common. For this reason, we must develop a clear sense of how the behavior of firms with market power differs from that of the perfectly competitive firm.

> **RECAP ↑**
>
> ### ECONOMIES OF SCALE AND THE IMPORTANCE OF START-UP COSTS
>
> Research, design, engineering, and other fixed costs account for an increasingly large share of all costs required to bring products successfully to market. For products with large fixed costs, marginal cost is lower, often substantially, than average total cost, and average total cost declines, often sharply, as output grows. This cost pattern explains why many industries are dominated by either a single firm or a small number of firms.

PROFIT MAXIMIZATION FOR THE MONOPOLIST

Cost-Benefit ⟫

Regardless of whether a firm is a price taker or a price setter, economists assume that its basic goal is to maximize its profit. In both cases, the firm expands output as long as the benefit of doing so exceeds the cost. Further, the calculation of marginal cost is also the same for the monopolist as for the perfectly competitive firm.

The profit-maximizing decision for a monopolist differs from that of a perfectly competitive firm when we look at the benefits of expanding output. For both the perfectly competitive firm and the monopolist, the marginal benefit of expanding output is the additional revenue the firm will receive if it sells one additional unit of output. In both cases, this marginal benefit is called the firm's **marginal revenue**. For the perfectly competitive firm, marginal revenue is exactly equal to the market price of the product. If that price is $6, for example, then the marginal benefit of selling an extra unit is exactly $6.

marginal revenue the change in a firm's total revenue that results from a one-unit change in output

MARGINAL REVENUE FOR THE MONOPOLIST

The situation is different for a monopolist. *To a monopolist, the marginal benefit of selling an additional unit is strictly less than the market price.* As the following discussion will make clear, the reason is that while the perfectly competitive firm can sell as many units as it wishes at the market price, the monopolist can sell an additional unit only if it cuts the price—and it must do so not just for the additional unit but for the units it is currently selling.

Suppose, for example, that a monopolist with the demand curve shown in Figure 8.3 is currently selling 2 units of output at a price of $6 per unit. What would be its marginal revenue from selling an additional unit?

FIGURE 8.3

The Monopolist's Benefit from Selling an Additional Unit.

The monopolist shown receives $12 per week in total revenue by selling 2 units per week at a price of $6 each. This monopolist could earn $15 per week by selling 3 units per week at a price of $5 each. In that case, the benefit from selling the third unit would be $15 − $12 = $3, less than its selling price of $5.

This monopolist's total revenue from the sale of 2 units per week is ($6 per unit) (2 units per week) = $12 per week. Its total revenue from the sale of 3 units per week would be $15 per week. The difference–$3 per week–is the marginal revenue from the sale of the third unit each week. Note that this amount is not only smaller than the original price ($6) but smaller than the new price ($5) as well.

 SELF-TEST 8.2

Calculate marginal revenue for the monopolist in Figure 8.3 as it expands output from 3 to 4 units per week, and then from 4 to 5 units per week.

For the monopolist whose demand curve is shown in Figure 8.3, a sequence of increases in output–from 2 to 3, from 3 to 4, and from 4 to 5–will yield marginal revenue of $3, $1, and −$1, respectively. We display these results in tabular form in Table 8.4.

TABLE 8.4
Marginal Revenue for a Monopolist ($ per unit)

Quantity	Marginal revenue
2	
	3
3	
	1
4	
	−1
5	

Note in the table that the marginal revenue values are displayed between the two quantity figures to which they correspond. For example, when the firm expanded its output from 2 units per week to 3, its marginal revenue was $3 per unit. Strictly speaking, this marginal revenue corresponds to neither quantity but to the movement between those quantities, hence its placement in the table. Likewise, in moving from 3 to 4 units per week, the firm earned marginal revenue of $1 per unit, so that figure is placed midway between the quantities of 3 and 4, and so on.

To graph marginal revenue as a function of quantity, we would plot the marginal revenue for the movement from 2 to 3 units of output per week ($3) at a quantity value of 2.5, because 2.5 lies midway between 2 and 3. Similarly, we would plot the marginal revenue for the movement from 3 to 4 units per week ($1) at a quantity of 3.5 units per week, and the marginal revenue for the movement from 4 to 5 units per week (−$1) at a quantity of 4.5. The resulting marginal revenue curve, *MR,* is shown in Figure 8.4.

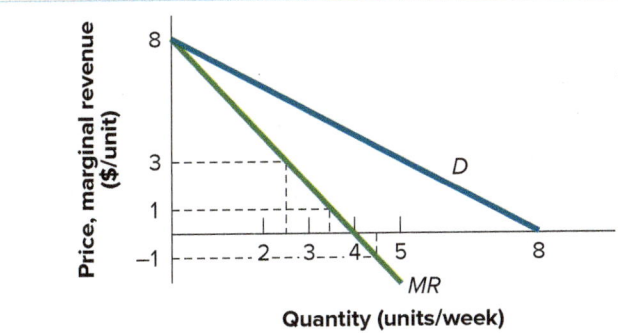

FIGURE 8.4

Marginal Revenue in Graphical Form.

Because a monopolist must cut price to sell an extra unit, not only for the extra unit sold but also for all existing units, marginal revenue from the sale of the extra unit is less than its selling price.

FIGURE 8.5

The Marginal Revenue Curve for a Monopolist with a Straight-Line Demand Curve.

For a monopolist with the demand curve shown, the corresponding marginal revenue curve has the same vertical intercept as the demand curve, and a horizontal intercept only half as large as that of the demand curve.

More generally, consider a monopolist with a straight-line demand curve whose vertical intercept is a and whose horizontal intercept is Q_0, as shown in Figure 8.5. This monopolist's marginal revenue curve also will have a vertical intercept of a, and it will be twice as steep as the demand curve. Thus, its horizontal intercept will be not Q_0, but $Q_0/2$, as shown in Figure 8.5.

Marginal revenue curves also can be expressed algebraically. If the formula for the monopolist's demand curve is $P = a - bQ$, then the formula for its marginal revenue curve will be $MR = a - 2bQ$. If you have had calculus, this relationship is easy to derive,[2] but even without calculus you can verify it by working through a few numerical examples. First, translate the formula for the demand curve into a diagram, and then construct the corresponding marginal revenue curve graphically. Reading from the graph, write the formula for that marginal revenue curve.

THE MONOPOLIST'S PROFIT-MAXIMIZING DECISION RULE

Having derived the monopolist's marginal revenue curve, we're now in a position to describe how the monopolist chooses the output level that maximizes profit. As in the case of the perfectly competitive firm, the Cost-Benefit Principle says that the monopolist should continue to expand output as long as the gain from doing so exceeds the cost. At the current level of output, the benefit from expanding output is the marginal revenue value that corresponds to that output level. The cost of expanding output is the marginal cost at that level of output. Whenever marginal revenue exceeds marginal cost, the firm should expand. Conversely, whenever marginal revenue falls short of marginal cost, the firm should reduce its output. *Profit is maximized at the level of output for which marginal revenue precisely equals marginal cost.*

When the monopolist's profit-maximizing rule is stated in this way, we can see that the perfectly competitive firm's rule is actually a special case of the monopolist's rule. When the perfectly competitive firm expands output by one unit, its marginal revenue exactly equals the product's market price (because the perfectly competitive firm can expand sales by a unit without having to cut the price of existing units). So when the perfectly competitive firm equates price with marginal cost, it is also equating marginal revenue with marginal cost. *Thus, the only significant difference between the two cases concerns the calculation of marginal revenue.*

EXAMPLE 8.3

Marginal Revenue

What is the monopolist's profit-maximizing output level?

Consider a monopolist with the demand and marginal cost curves shown in Figure 8.6. If this firm is currently producing 12 units per week, should it expand or contract production? What is the profit-maximizing level of output?

---

[2]For those who have had an introductory course in calculus, marginal revenue can be expressed as the derivative of total revenue with respect to output. If $P = a - bQ$, then total revenue will be given by $TR = PQ = aQ - bQ_2$, which means that $MR = dTR/dQ = a - 2bQ$.

FIGURE 8.6

The Demand and Marginal Cost Curves for a Monopolist.
At the current output level of 12 units per week, price equals marginal cost. Because the monopolist's price is always greater than marginal revenue, marginal revenue must be less than marginal cost, which means this monopolist should produce less.

In Figure 8.7, we begin by constructing the marginal revenue curve that corresponds to the monopolist's demand curve. It has the same vertical intercept as the demand curve, and its horizontal intercept is half as large. Note that the monopolist's marginal revenue at 12 units per week is zero, which is clearly less than its marginal cost of $3 per unit. This monopolist will therefore earn a higher profit by contracting production until marginal revenue equals marginal cost, which occurs at an output level of 8 units per week. At this profit-maximizing output level, the firm will charge $4 per unit, the price that corresponds to 8 units per week on the demand curve.

FIGURE 8.7

The Monopolist's Profit-Maximizing Output Level.
This monopolist maximizes profit by selling 8 units per week, the output level at which marginal revenue equals marginal cost. The profit-maximizing price is $4 per unit, the price that corresponds to the profit-maximizing quantity on the demand curve.

 SELF-TEST 8.3

For the monopolist with the demand and marginal cost curves shown, find the profit-maximizing price and level of output.

BEING A MONOPOLIST DOESN'T GUARANTEE AN ECONOMIC PROFIT

The fact that the profit-maximizing price for a monopolist will always be greater than marginal cost provides no assurance that the monopolist will earn an economic profit. Consider, for example, the local cable Internet service provider whose demand, marginal revenue, marginal cost, and average total cost curves are shown in Figure 8.8(a). This monopolist maximizes its monthly profit by providing 70,000 households per month with cable Internet at price of $45 per household. At that quantity, $MR = MC$, yet price is $10 per household less than the company's average total cost of $55 per household. As a result, the company sustains an economic loss of $10 per household served, or a total loss of ($10 per household)(70,000 households per month) = $700,000 per month.

The monopolist in Figure 8.8(a) suffered a loss because its profit-maximizing price was lower than its *ATC*. If the monopolist's profit-maximizing price exceeds its average total cost, however, the company will, of course, earn an economic profit. Consider, for example, the local cable Internet provider shown in Figure 8.8(b). This firm has the same demand, marginal revenue, and marginal cost curves as the firm shown in Figure 8.8(a). But because the firm in (b) has lower fixed costs, its *ATC* curve is lower at every level of output than the *ATC* curve in (a). At the profit-maximizing price of $45 per household, the firm in Figure 8.8(b) earns an economic profit of $10 per household, for a total economic profit of $700,000 per month.

FIGURE 8.8

Even a Monopolist May Suffer an Economic Loss.

The monopolist in (a) maximizes its profit by providing cable Internet service to 70,000 households per month but suffers an economic loss of $700,000 per month in the process. Because the profit-maximizing price of the monopolist in (b) exceeds *ATC*, this monopolist earns an economic profit.

(a)

(b)

RECAP ↑

PROFIT MAXIMIZATION FOR THE MONOPOLIST

Both the perfectly competitive firm and the monopolist maximize profit by choosing the output level at which marginal revenue equals marginal cost. But whereas marginal revenue equals the market price for the perfectly competitive firm, it is always less than the market price for the monopolist. A monopolist will earn an economic profit only if price exceeds average total cost at the profit-maximizing level of output.

WHY THE INVISIBLE HAND BREAKS DOWN UNDER MONOPOLY

In our discussion of equilibrium in perfectly competitive markets in Chapter 7, *Efficiency, Exchange, and the Invisible Hand in Action,* we saw conditions under which the self-serving pursuits of consumers and firms were consistent with the broader interests of society as a whole. Let's explore whether the same conclusion holds true for the case of imperfectly competitive firms.

Consider the monopolist in Figures 8.6 and 8.7. Is this firm's profit-maximizing output level efficient from society's point of view? For any given level of output, the corresponding price on the demand curve indicates the amount buyers would be willing to pay for an additional unit of output. When the monopolist is producing 8 units per week, the marginal benefit to society of an additional unit of output is thus $4 (see Figure 8.7). And since the marginal cost of an additional unit at that output level is only $2 (again, see Figure 8.7), society would gain a net benefit of $2 per unit if the monopolist were to expand production by 1 unit above the profit-maximizing level. Because this economic surplus is not realized, the profit-maximizing monopolist is socially inefficient.

Recall that the existence of inefficiency means that the economic pie is smaller than it might be. If that is so, why doesn't the monopolist simply expand production? The answer is that the monopolist would gladly do so, if only there were some way to maintain the price of existing units and cut the price of only the extra units. As a practical matter, however, that is not always possible.

Now, let's look at this situation from a different angle. For the market served by this monopolist, what *is* the socially efficient level of output?

At any output level, the cost to society of an additional unit of output is the same as the cost to the monopolist, namely, the amount shown on the monopolist's marginal cost curve. The marginal benefit *to society* (not to the monopolist) of an extra unit of output is simply the amount people are willing to pay for it, which is the amount shown on the monopolist's demand curve. To achieve social efficiency, the monopolist should expand production until the marginal benefit to society equals the marginal cost, which in this case occurs at a level of 12 units per week. Social efficiency is thus achieved at the output level at which the market demand curve intersects the monopolist's marginal cost curve.

The fact that marginal revenue is less than price for the monopolist results in a **deadweight loss**. For the monopolist just discussed, the size of this deadweight loss is equal to the area of the pale blue triangle in Figure 8.9, which is (1/2)($2 per unit) (4 units per week) = $4 per week. That is the amount by which total economic surplus is reduced because the monopolist produces too little.

deadweight loss the loss of consumer and producer surplus caused by disparity between price and marginal cost

For a monopolist, profit maximization occurs when marginal cost equals marginal revenue. Since the monopolist's marginal revenue is always less than price, the monopolist's profit-maximizing output level is always below the socially efficient level. Under perfect competition, by contrast, profit maximization occurs when marginal cost equals the market price—the same criterion that must be satisfied for social efficiency. This difference explains why the invisible hand of the market is less evident in monopoly markets than in perfectly competitive markets.

If perfect competition is socially efficient and monopoly is not, why isn't monopoly against the law? Congress has, in fact, tried to limit the extent of monopoly through antitrust laws. But even the most enthusiastic proponents of those laws recognize the limited usefulness of the legislative approach since the alternatives to monopoly often entail problems of their own.

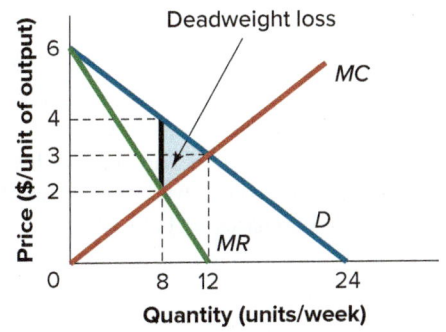

FIGURE 8.9

The Deadweight Loss from Monopoly.

A loss in economic surplus results because the profit-maximizing level of output (8 units per week) is less than the socially optimal level of output (12 units per week). This deadweight loss is the area of the pale blue triangle, $4 per week.

Suppose, for example, that a monopoly results from a patent that prevents all but one firm from manufacturing some highly valued product. Would society be better off without patents? Probably not because eliminating such protection would discourage innovation. Virtually all successful industrial nations grant some form of patent protection, which gives firms a chance to recover the research and development costs without which new products would seldom reach the market.

Or suppose that the market in question is a natural monopoly—one that, because of economies of scale, is most cheaply served by a single firm. Would society do better to require this market to be served by many small firms, each with significantly higher average costs of production? Such a requirement would merely replace one form of inefficiency with another.

In short, we live in an imperfect world. Monopoly is socially inefficient, and that, needless to say, is bad. But the alternatives to monopoly aren't perfect either.

> *RECAP* ↑
>
> **WHY THE INVISIBLE HAND BREAKS DOWN UNDER MONOPOLY**
>
> The monopolist maximizes profit at the output level for which marginal revenue equals marginal cost. Because its profit-maximizing price exceeds marginal revenue, and hence also marginal cost, the benefit to society of the last unit produced (the market price) must be greater than the cost of the last unit produced (the marginal cost). So the output level for an industry served by a profit-maximizing monopolist is smaller than the socially optimal level of output.

USING DISCOUNTS TO EXPAND THE MARKET

The source of inefficiency in monopoly markets is the fact that the benefit to the monopolist of expanding output is less than the corresponding benefit to society. From the monopolist's point of view, the price reduction the firm must grant existing buyers to expand output is a loss. But from the point of view of those buyers, each dollar of price reduction is a gain—one dollar more in their pockets.

Note the tension in this situation, which is similar to the tension that exists in all other situations in which the economic pie is smaller than it might otherwise be. As the Efficiency Principle reminds us, when the economic pie grows larger, everyone can have a larger slice. To say that monopoly is inefficient means that steps could be taken to make some people better off without harming others. If people have a healthy regard for their own self-interest, why doesn't someone take those steps? Why, for example, doesn't the monopolist from the earlier examples sell 8 units of output at a price of $4, and then once those buyers are out the door, cut the price for more price-sensitive buyers?

PRICE DISCRIMINATION DEFINED

price discrimination the practice of charging different buyers different prices for essentially the same good or service

Sometimes the monopolist does precisely that. Charging different buyers different prices for the same good or service is a practice known as **price discrimination**. Examples of price discrimination include seniors' and children's discounts on movie tickets, supersaver discounts on air travel, and rebate coupons on retail merchandise.

Attempts at price discrimination seem to work effectively in some markets, but not in others. Buyers are not stupid, after all; if the monopolist periodically offered a 50 percent discount on the $8 list price, those who were paying $8 might anticipate the next price cut and postpone their purchases to take advantage of it. In some markets, however, buyers may not know, or simply may not take the trouble to find out, how the price they pay compares to the prices paid by other buyers. Alternatively, the monopolist may be in a position to prevent some groups from buying at the discount prices made available to others. In such cases, the monopolist can price-discriminate effectively.

The Economic Naturalist 8.2

Why do many movie theaters offer discount tickets to students?

Whenever a firm offers a discount, the goal is to target that discount to buyers who would not purchase the product without it. People with low incomes generally have lower reservation prices for movie tickets than people with high incomes. Because students generally have lower disposable incomes than working adults, theater owners can expand their audiences by charging lower prices to students than to adults. Student discounts are one practical way of doing so. Offering student discounts also entails no risk of some people buying the product at a low price and then reselling it to others at a higher price.

Why do students pay lower ticket prices at many movie theaters?

HOW PRICE DISCRIMINATION AFFECTS OUTPUT

In the following examples, we'll see how the ability to price-discriminate affects the monopolist's profit-maximizing level of output. First we'll consider a baseline case in which the monopolist must charge the same price to every buyer.

EXAMPLE 8.4	Profit Maximization and Opportunity Cost

How many manuscripts should Preeti edit?

Preeti supplements her income as a teaching assistant by editing term papers for undergraduates. There are eight students per week for whom she might edit, each with a reservation price as given in the following table.

Student	Reservation price
A	$40
B	38
C	36
D	34
E	32
F	30
G	28
H	26

Preeti is a profit maximizer. If the opportunity cost of her time to edit each paper is $29 and she must charge the same price to each student, how many papers should she edit? How much economic profit will she make? How much accounting profit?

Table 8.5 summarizes Preeti's total and marginal revenue at various output levels. To generate the amounts in column 3, we simply multiplied the corresponding reservation price by the number of students whose reservation prices were at least that high. For example, to edit 4 papers per week (for students A, B, C, and D), Preeti must charge a price no higher than D's reservation price ($34). So her total revenue when she edits 4 papers per week is (4)($34) = $136 per week. Preeti should keep expanding the number of students she serves as long as her marginal revenue exceeds the opportunity cost of her time. Marginal revenue, or the difference in total revenue that results from adding another student, is shown in column 4 of Table 8.5.

TABLE 8.5
Total and Marginal Revenue from Editing

(1) Student	(2) Reservation price ($ per paper)	(3) Total revenue ($ per week)	(4) Marginal revenue ($ per paper)
			40
A	40	40	
			36
B	38	76	
			32
C	36	108	
			28
D	34	136	
			24
E	32	160	
			20
F	30	180	
			16
G	28	196	
			12
H	26	208	

Note that if Preeti were editing 2 papers per week, her marginal revenue from editing a third paper would be $32. Since that amount exceeds her $29 opportunity cost, she should take on the third paper. But since the marginal revenue of taking on a fourth paper would be only $28, Preeti should stop at 3 papers per week. The total opportunity cost of the time required to edit the 3 papers is (3)($29) = $87, so Preeti's economic profit is $108 − $87 = $21 per week. Since Preeti incurs no explicit costs, her accounting profit will be $108 per week.

EXAMPLE 8.5 **Social Efficiency**

What is the socially efficient number of papers for Preeti to edit?

Again, suppose that Preeti's opportunity cost of editing is $29 per paper and that she could edit as many as 8 papers per week for students whose reservation prices are again as listed in the following table.

Student	Reservation price
A	$40
B	38
C	36
D	34
E	32
F	30
G	28
H	26

What is the socially efficient number of papers for Preeti to edit? If she must charge the same price to each student, what will her economic and accounting profits be if she edits the socially efficient number of papers?

Students *A* to *F* are willing to pay more than Preeti's opportunity cost, so serving these students is socially efficient. But students *G* and *H* are unwilling to pay at least $29 for Preeti's services. The socially efficient outcome, therefore, is for Preeti to edit 6 papers per week. To attract that number, she must charge a price no higher than $30 per paper. Her total revenue will be (6)($30) = $180 per week, slightly more than her total opportunity cost of (6)($29) = $174 per week. Her economic profit will thus be only $6 per week. Again, because Preeti incurs no explicit costs, her accounting profit will be the same as her total revenue, $180 per week.

EXAMPLE 8.6　　Price Discrimination

If Preeti can price-discriminate, how many papers should she edit?

Suppose Preeti is a shrewd judge of human nature. After a moment's conversation with a student, she can discern that student's reservation price. The reservation prices of her potential customers are again as given in the following table. If Preeti confronts the same market as before, but can charge students their respective reservation prices, how many papers should she edit, and how much economic and accounting profit will she make?

Student	Reservation price
A	$40
B	38
C	36
D	34
E	32
F	30
G	28
H	26

Preeti will edit papers for students *A* to *F* and charge each exactly his or her reservation price. Because students *G* and *H* have reservation prices below $29, Preeti will not edit their papers. Preeti's total revenue will be $40 + $38 + $36 + $34 + $32 + $30 = $210 per week, which is also her accounting profit. Her total opportunity cost of editing 6 papers is (6)($29) = $174 per week, so her economic profit will be $210 − $174 = $36 per week, $30 per week more than when she edited 6 papers but was constrained to charge each customer the same price.

perfectly discriminating monopolist a firm that charges each buyer exactly his or her reservation price

A monopolist who can charge each buyer exactly his or her reservation price is called a **perfectly discriminating monopolist**. Notice that, when Preeti was discriminating among customers in this way, her profit-maximizing level of output was exactly the same as the socially efficient level of output: 6 papers per week. With a perfectly discriminating monopoly, there is no loss of efficiency. All buyers who are willing to pay a price high enough to cover marginal cost will be served.

Note that although total economic surplus is maximized by a perfectly discriminating monopolist, consumers would have little reason to celebrate if they found themselves dealing with such a firm. After all, consumer surplus is exactly zero for the perfectly discriminating monopolist. In this instance, total economic surplus and producer surplus are one and the same.

In practice, of course, perfect price discrimination can never occur because no seller knows each and every buyer's precise reservation price. But even if some sellers did know, practical difficulties would stand in the way of their charging a separate price to each buyer. For example, in many markets the seller could not prevent buyers who bought at low prices from reselling to other buyers at higher prices, capturing some of the seller's business in the process. Despite these difficulties, price discrimination is widespread. But it is generally *imperfect price discrimination*—that is, price discrimination in which at least some buyers are charged less than their reservation prices.

THE HURDLE METHOD OF PRICE DISCRIMINATION

The profit-maximizing seller's goal is to charge each buyer the highest price that buyer is willing to pay. Two primary obstacles prevent sellers from achieving this goal. First, sellers don't know exactly how much each buyer is willing to pay. And second, they need some means of excluding those who are willing to pay a high price from buying at a low price. These are formidable problems, which no seller can hope to solve completely.

hurdle method of price discrimination the practice by which a seller offers a discount to all buyers who overcome some obstacle

One common method by which sellers achieve a crude solution to both problems is to require buyers to overcome some obstacle to be eligible for a discount price. This method is called the **hurdle method of price discrimination**. For example, the seller might sell a product at a standard list price and offer a rebate to any buyer who takes the trouble to mail in a rebate coupon.

The hurdle method solves both of the seller's problems, provided that buyers with low reservation prices are more willing than others to jump the hurdle. Because a decision to jump the hurdle must satisfy the Cost-Benefit Principle, such a link seems to exist. As noted earlier, buyers with low incomes are more likely than others to have low reservation prices (at least in the case of normal goods). Because of the low opportunity cost of their time, they are more likely than others to take the trouble to send in rebate coupons. Rebate coupons thus target a discount toward those buyers whose reservation prices are low and who therefore might not buy the product otherwise.

perfect hurdle a threshold that completely segregates buyers whose reservation prices lie above it from others whose reservation prices lie below it, imposing no cost on those who jump the hurdle

A **perfect hurdle** is one that separates buyers precisely according to their reservation prices, and in the process imposes no cost on those who jump the hurdle. With a perfect hurdle, the highest reservation price among buyers who jump the hurdle will be lower than the lowest reservation price among buyers who choose not to jump the hurdle. In practice, perfect hurdles do not exist. Some buyers will always jump the hurdle, even though their reservation prices are high. And hurdles will always exclude at least some buyers with low reservation prices. Even so, many commonly used hurdles do a remarkably good job of targeting discounts to buyers with low reservation prices. In the example that follows, we will assume for convenience that the seller is using a perfect hurdle.

EXAMPLE 8.7	Perfect Hurdle

How much should Preeti charge for editing if she uses a perfect hurdle?

Suppose Preeti again has the opportunity to edit as many as 8 papers per week for the students whose reservation prices are as given in the following table. This time she can offer a rebate coupon that gives a discount to any student who takes the trouble to mail it back to her. Suppose further that students whose reservation prices are at least $36 never mail in the rebate coupons, while those whose reservation prices are below $36 always do so.

Student	Reservation price
A	$40
B	38
C	36
D	34
E	32
F	30
G	28
H	26

If Preeti's opportunity cost of editing each paper is again $29, what should her list price be, and what amount should she offer as a rebate? Will her economic profit be larger or smaller than when she lacked the discount option?

The rebate coupon allows Preeti to divide her original market into two submarkets in which she can charge two different prices. The first submarket consists of students A, B, and C, whose reservation prices are at least $36 and who therefore will not bother to mail in a rebate coupon. The second submarket consists of students D through H, whose lower reservation prices indicate a willingness to use rebate coupons.

In each submarket, Preeti must charge the same price to every buyer, just like an ordinary monopolist. She should therefore keep expanding output in each submarket as long as marginal revenue in that market exceeds her marginal cost. The relevant data for the two submarkets are displayed in Table 8.6.

On the basis of the entries in column 4 for the list price submarket, we see that Preeti should serve all three students (A, B, and C) since marginal revenue for each exceeds $29. Her profit-maximizing price in the list price submarket is $36, the highest price she can charge in that market and still sell her services to students A, B, and C. For the discount price submarket, marginal revenue exceeds $29 only for the first two students (D and E). So the profit-maximizing price in this submarket is $32, the highest price Preeti can charge and still sell her services to D and E. (A discount price of $32 means that students who mail in the coupon will receive a rebate of $4 on the $36 list price.)

Note that the rebate offer enables Preeti to serve a total of five students per week, compared to only three without the offer. Preeti's combined total revenue for the two markets is (3)($36) + 2($32) = $172 per week. Since her opportunity cost is $29 per paper, or a total of (5)($29) = $145 per week, her economic profit is $172 per week − $145 per week = $27 per week, $6 more than when she edited 3 papers and did not offer the rebate.

TABLE 8.6
Price Discrimination with a Perfect Hurdle

(1) Student	(2) Reservation price ($ per paper)	(3) Total revenue ($ per week)	(4) Marginal revenue ($ per paper)
List Price Submarket			
			40
A	40	40	
			36
B	38	76	
			32
C	36	108	
Discount Price Submarket			
			34
D	34	34	
			30
E	32	64	
			26
F	30	90	
			22
G	28	112	
			18
H	26	130	

 SELF-TEST 8.4

In Example 8.7, how much should Preeti charge in each submarket if she knows that only those students whose reservation prices are below $34 will use rebate coupons?

IS PRICE DISCRIMINATION A BAD THING?

We are so conditioned to think of discrimination as bad that we may be tempted to conclude that price discrimination must run counter to the public interest. In Example 8.7, however, both consumer surplus and producer surplus were actually enhanced by the monopolist's use of the hurdle method of price discrimination. To show this, let's compare consumer and producer surplus when Preeti employs the hurdle method to the corresponding values when she charges the same price to all buyers.

When Preeti had to charge the same price to every customer, she edited only the papers of students A, B, and C, each of whom paid a price of $36. We can tell at a glance that the total surplus must be larger under the hurdle method because not only are students A, B, and C served at the same price ($36), but also students D and E are now served at a price of $32.

To confirm this intuition, we can calculate the exact amount of the surplus. For any student who hires Preeti to edit her paper, consumer surplus is the difference between her reservation price and the price actually paid. In both the single price and discount price examples, student A's consumer surplus is thus $40 − $36 = $4; student B's consumer surplus is $38 − $36 = $2; and student C's consumer surplus is $36 − $36 = 0. Total consumer surplus in the list price submarket is thus $4 + $2 = $6 per week, which is the same as total consumer surplus in the original situation. But now the discount price submarket generates additional consumer surplus. Specifically, student D receives $2 per week of consumer surplus since this student's reservation price of $34 is $2 more than the discount price of $32. So total consumer surplus is now $6 + $2 = $8 per week, or $2 per week more than before.

Preeti's producer surplus also increases under the hurdle method. For each paper she edits, her producer surplus is the price she charges minus her reservation price ($29). In the single-price case, Preeti's surplus was (3)($36 − $29) = $21 per week. When she offers a rebate coupon, she earns the same producer surplus as before from students A, B, and C and an additional (2)($32 − $29) = $6 per week from students D and E. Total producer surplus with the discount is thus $21 + $6 = $27 per week. Adding that amount to the total consumer surplus of $8 per week, we get a total economic surplus of $35 per week with the rebate coupons, $8 per week more than without the rebate.

Note, however, that even with the rebate, the final outcome is not socially efficient because Preeti does not serve student F, even though this student's reservation price of $30 exceeds her opportunity cost of $29. Although the hurdle method is not perfectly efficient, it's still more efficient than charging a single price to all buyers.

EXAMPLES OF PRICE DISCRIMINATION

Once you grasp the principle behind the hurdle method of price discrimination, you'll begin to see examples of it all around you. Next time you visit a grocery, hardware, or appliance store, for instance, notice how many different product promotions include cash rebates. Temporary sales are another illustration of the hurdle method. Most of the time, retailers sell most of their merchandise at the "regular" price but periodically offer special sales at a significant discount. The hurdle in this instance is taking the trouble to find out when and where the sales occur and then making a purchase during that period. This technique works because buyers who care most about price (mainly, those with low reservation prices) are more likely to monitor advertisements carefully and buy only during sale periods.

To give another example, book publishers typically launch a new book in hardcover at a price from $20 to $30, and a year later they bring out a paperback edition priced between $5 and $15. In this instance, the hurdle involves having to wait the extra year and accepting a slight reduction in the quality of the finished product. People who are strongly concerned about price end up waiting for the paperback edition, while those with high reservation prices usually spring for the hardback.

Or take the example of automobile producers, who typically offer several different models with different trim and accessories. Although GM's actual cost of producing a Cadillac may be only $2,000 more than its cost of producing a Chevrolet, the Cadillac's selling price may be $10,000 to $15,000 higher than the Chevrolet's. Buyers with low reservation prices purchase the Chevrolet, while those with high reservation prices are more likely to choose the Cadillac.

Commercial air carriers have perfected the hurdle method to an extent matched by almost no other seller. Their supersaver fares are often less than half their regular coach fares. To be eligible for these discounts, travelers must purchase their tickets 7 to 21 days in advance and their journey must include a Saturday night stayover. Vacation travelers can more easily satisfy these restrictions than business travelers, whose schedules often change at the last moment and whose trips seldom involve Saturday stayovers. And—no surprise—the business traveler's reservation price tends to be much higher than the vacation traveler's.

Many sellers employ not just one hurdle but several by offering deeper discounts to buyers who jump successively more difficult hurdles. For example, movie studios initially release their major films to first-run theaters at premium prices and then, several months later, on DVD and video-on-demand platforms like iTunes. Still later they make the films available through subscription television providers like HBO and Netflix, and finally permit them to be shown on network television. Each successive hurdle involves waiting a little longer and, in the case of the televised versions, accepting lower quality. These hurdles are remarkably effective in segregating moviegoers according to their reservation prices.

Recall that the efficiency loss from single-price monopoly occurs because, to the monopolist, the benefit of expanding output is smaller than the benefit to society as a whole. The hurdle method of price discrimination reduces this loss by giving the monopolist a practical means of cutting prices for price-sensitive buyers only. In general, the more finely the monopolist can partition a market using the hurdle method, the smaller the efficiency loss. Hurdles are not perfect, however, and some degree of efficiency will inevitably be lost.

The Economic Naturalist 8.3

▶ Visit your instructor's Connect course and access your eBook to view this video.

Why might an appliance retailer hammer dents into the sides of its stoves and refrigerators?

Why might an appliance retailer instruct its clerks to hammer dents into the sides of its stoves and refrigerators?

The "Scratch 'n' Dent Sale" is another example of how retailers use quality differentials to segregate buyers according to their reservation prices. Many stores hold an annual sale in which they display appliances with minor scratches and blemishes in the parking lot at deep discounts. People who don't care much about price are unlikely to turn out for these events, but those with very low reservation prices often get up early to be first in line. Indeed, these sales have proven so popular that it might even be in a retailer's interest to put dents in some of its sale items deliberately.

RECAP

USING DISCOUNTS TO EXPAND THE MARKET

A price-discriminating monopolist is one who charges different prices to different buyers for essentially the same good or service. A common method of price discrimination is the hurdle method, which involves granting a discount to buyers who jump over a hurdle such as mailing in a rebate coupon. An effective hurdle is one that is more easily cleared by buyers with low reservation prices than by buyers with high reservation prices. Such a hurdle enables the monopolist to expand output and thereby reduce the deadweight loss from monopoly pricing.

PUBLIC POLICY TOWARD NATURAL MONOPOLY

Monopoly is problematic not only because of the loss in efficiency associated with restricted output, but also because the monopolist earns an economic profit at the buyer's expense. Many people are understandably uncomfortable about having to purchase from the sole provider of any good or service. For this reason, voters in many societies have empowered government to adopt policies aimed at controlling natural monopolists.

There are several ways to achieve this aim. A government may assume ownership and control of a natural monopoly, or it may merely attempt to regulate the prices it charges. In some cases, government solicits competitive bids from private firms to produce natural monopoly services. In still other cases, governments attempt to dissolve natural monopolies into smaller entities that compete with one another. But many of these policies create economic problems of their own. In each case, the practical challenge is to come up with the solution that yields the greatest surplus of benefits over costs. Natural monopoly may be inefficient and unfair, but, as noted earlier, the alternatives to natural monopoly are far from perfect.

STATE OWNERSHIP AND MANAGEMENT

Natural monopoly is inefficient because the monopolist's profit-maximizing price is greater than its marginal cost. But even if the natural monopolist *wanted* to set price equal to marginal cost, it could not do so and hope to remain in business. After all, the defining feature of a natural monopoly is economies of scale in production, which means that marginal cost will always be less than average total cost. Setting price equal to marginal cost would fail to cover average total cost, which implies an economic loss.

Consider the case of a local cable Internet provider. Once an area has been wired for cable Internet, the marginal cost of adding an additional subscriber is very low. For the sake of efficiency, all subscribers should pay a price equal to that marginal cost. Yet a cable company that priced in this manner would never be able to recover the fixed cost of setting up the network. This same problem applies not just to Internet providers but to all other natural monopolies. Even if such firms wanted to set price equal to marginal cost (which, of course, they do not since they will earn more by setting marginal revenue equal to marginal cost), they cannot do so without suffering an economic loss.

One way to attack the efficiency and fairness problems is for the government to take over the industry, set price equal to marginal cost, and then absorb the resulting losses out of general tax revenues. This approach has been followed with good results in the state-owned electric utility industry in France, whose efficient pricing methods have set the standard for electricity pricing worldwide.

But state ownership and efficient management do not always go hand in hand. Granted, the state-owned natural monopoly is free to charge marginal cost, while the private natural monopoly is not. Yet the Incentive Principle directs our attention to the fact that private natural monopolies often face a much stronger incentive to cut costs than their government-owned counterparts. When the private monopolist figures out a way to cut $1 from the cost of production, its profit goes up by $1. But when the government manager of a state-owned monopoly cuts $1 from the cost of production, the government typically cuts the monopoly's budget by $1. Think back to your last visit to the Department of Motor Vehicles. Did it strike you as an efficiently managed organization?

Incentive

Whether the efficiency that is gained by being able to set price equal to marginal cost outweighs the inefficiency that results from a weakened incentive to cut costs is an empirical question.

STATE REGULATION OF PRIVATE MONOPOLIES

In the United States, the most common method of curbing monopoly profits is for government to regulate the natural monopoly rather than own it. Most states, for example, take this approach with electric utilities, natural gas providers, local telephone companies, and cable Internet providers. The standard procedure in these cases is called **cost-plus regulation**: Government regulators gather data on the monopolist's explicit costs of production and then permit the monopolist to set prices that cover those costs, plus a markup to ensure a normal return on the firm's investment.

cost-plus regulation a method of regulation under which the regulated firm is permitted to charge prices that cover explicit costs of production plus a markup to cover the opportunity cost of resources provided by the firm's owners

While it may sound reasonable, cost-plus regulation has several pitfalls. First, it generates costly administrative proceedings in which regulators and firms quarrel over which of the firm's expenditures can properly be included in the costs it is allowed to recover. This question is difficult to answer even in theory. Consider a firm like AT&T, whose local telephone service is subject to cost-plus regulation but whose other products and services are unregulated. Many AT&T employees, from the president on down, are involved in both regulated and unregulated activities. How should their salaries be allocated between the two? The company has a strong incentive to argue for greater allocation to the regulated activities, which allows it to capture more revenue from captive customers in the local telephone market.

A second problem with cost-plus regulation is that it blunts the firm's incentive to adopt cost-saving innovations because when it does, regulators require the firm to cut its rates. The firm gets to keep its cost savings in the current period, which is a stronger incentive to cut costs than the one facing a government-owned monopoly. But the incentive to cut costs would be stronger still if the firm could retain its cost savings indefinitely. Furthermore, in cases in which regulators set rates by allowing the monopolist to add a fixed markup to costs incurred, the regulated monopolist may actually have an incentive to *increase* costs rather than reduce them. Outrageous though the thought may be, the monopolist may earn a higher profit by installing gold-plated faucets in the company restrooms.

Finally, cost-plus regulation does not solve the natural monopolist's basic problem: the inability to set price equal to marginal cost without losing money. Although these are all serious problems, governments seem to be in no hurry to abandon cost-plus regulation.

EXCLUSIVE CONTRACTING FOR NATURAL MONOPOLY

One of the most promising methods for dealing with natural monopoly is for the government to invite private firms to bid for the natural monopolist's market. The government specifies in detail the service it wants—cable Internet, fire protection, garbage collection—and firms submit bids describing how much they will charge for the service. The low bidder wins the contract.

The incentive to cut costs under such an arrangement is every bit as powerful as that facing ordinary competitive firms. Competition among bidders should also eliminate any concerns about the fairness of monopoly profits. And if the government is willing to provide a cash subsidy to the winning bidder, exclusive contracting even allows the monopolist to set price equal to marginal cost.

Contracting has been employed with good results in municipal fire protection and garbage collection. Communities that employ private companies to provide these services often spend only half as much as adjacent communities served by municipal fire and sanitation departments.

Despite these attractive features, however, exclusive contracting is not without problems, especially when the service to be provided is complex or requires a large fixed investment in capital equipment. In such cases, contract specifications may be so detailed and complicated that they become tantamount to regulating the firm directly. And in cases involving a large fixed investment—electric power generation and distribution, for example—officials face the question of how to transfer the assets if a new firm wins the contract. The winning firm naturally wants to acquire the assets as cheaply as possible, but the retiring firm is entitled to a fair price for them. What, in such cases, is a fair price?

Fire protection and garbage collection are simple enough that the costs of contracting out these functions are not prohibitive. But in other cases, such costs might easily outweigh any savings made possible by exclusive contracting.

VIGOROUS ENFORCEMENT OF ANTITRUST LAWS

The nineteenth century witnessed the accumulation of massive private fortunes, the likes of which had never been seen in the industrialized world. Public sentiment ran high against the so-called robber barons of the period—the Carnegies, Rockefellers, Mellons, and others. In 1890, Congress passed the Sherman Act, which declared illegal any conspiracy "to monopolize, or attempt to monopolize . . . any part of the trade or commerce among the several States." And in 1914, Congress passed the Clayton Act, whose aim was to prevent corporations from acquiring shares in a competitor if the transaction would "substantially lessen competition or create a monopoly."

Antitrust laws have helped prevent the formation of cartels, or coalitions of firms that collude to raise prices above competitive levels. But they also have caused some harm. For example, federal antitrust officials spent more than a decade trying to break up IBM Corporation in the belief that it had achieved an unhealthy dominance in the computer industry. That view was proved comically wrong by IBM's subsequent failure to foresee and profit from the rise of the personal computer. By breaking up large companies and discouraging mergers between companies in the same industry, antitrust laws may help promote competition, but they also may prevent companies from achieving economies of scale.

A final possibility is simply to ignore the problem of natural monopoly: to let the monopolist choose the quantity to produce and sell it at whatever price the market will bear. The obvious objections to this policy are the two we began with, namely, that a natural monopoly is not only inefficient but also unfair. But just as the hurdle method of price discrimination mitigates efficiency losses, it also lessens the concern about taking unfair advantage of buyers.

Consider first the source of the natural monopolist's economic profit. This firm, recall, is one with economies of scale, which means that its average production cost declines as output increases. Efficiency requires that price be set at marginal cost, but because the natural monopolist's marginal cost is lower than its average cost, it cannot charge all buyers the marginal cost without suffering an economic loss.

The depth and prevalence of discount pricing suggest that whatever economic profit a natural monopolist earns generally will not come out of the discount buyer's pocket. Although discount prices are higher than the monopolist's marginal cost of production, in most cases they are lower than the average cost. Thus, the monopolist's economic profit, if any, must come from buyers who pay list price. And since those buyers have the option, in most cases, of jumping a hurdle and paying a discount price, their contribution, if not completely voluntary, is at least not strongly coerced.

So much for the source of the monopolist's economic profit. What about its disposition? Who gets it? A significant chunk goes to the federal government via the corporate income tax. The remainder is paid out to shareholders, some of whom are wealthy, others not. Shareholders pay additional income taxes to federal, state, and local governments, and their spending out of what remains is subject to sales taxes in most states. Disbursements to shareholders also help fund charitable contributions. In the end, two-thirds or more of a monopolist's profit may support spending on the public's behalf.

Both the source of the monopolist's economic profit (the list-price buyer) and the disposition of that profit (largely, to fund public services) cast doubt on the claim that monopoly profit constitutes a social injustice on any grand scale. Nevertheless, the hurdle method of differential pricing cannot completely eliminate the fairness and efficiency problems that result from monopoly pricing. In the end, then, we are left with a choice among imperfect alternatives. As the Cost-Benefit Principle emphasizes, the best choice is the one for which the balance of benefits over costs is largest. But which choice that is will depend on the circumstances at hand.

RECAP

PUBLIC POLICY TOWARD NATURAL MONOPOLY

The natural monopolist sets price above marginal cost, resulting in too little output from society's point of view (the efficiency problem). The natural monopolist also may earn an economic profit at buyers' expense (the fairness problem). Policies for dealing with the efficiency and fairness problems include state ownership and management, state regulation, exclusive contracting, and vigorous enforcement of antitrust laws. Each of these remedies entails problems of its own.

SUMMARY

- Our concern in this chapter was the conduct and performance of the imperfectly competitive firm, a firm that has at least some latitude to set its own price. Economists often distinguish among three different types of imperfectly competitive firms: the pure monopolist, the lone seller of a product in a given market; the oligopolist, one of only a few sellers of a given product; and the monopolistic competitor, one of a relatively large number of firms that sell similar though slightly differentiated products. *(LO1)*

- Although advanced courses in economics devote much attention to differences in behavior among these three types of firms, our focus was on the common feature that differentiates them from perfectly competitive firms. Whereas the perfectly competitive firm faces an infinitely elastic demand curve for its product, the imperfectly competitive firm faces a downward-sloping demand curve. For convenience, we use the term *monopolist* to refer to any of the three types of imperfectly competitive firms. *(LO1)*

- Monopolists are sometimes said to enjoy market power, a term that refers to their power to set the price of their product. Market power stems from exclusive control over important inputs, from economies of scale, from patents and government licenses or franchises, and from network economies. The most important and enduring of these five sources of market power are economies of scale and network economies. *(LO2)*

- Research, design, engineering, and other fixed costs account for an increasingly large share of all costs required to bring products successfully to market. For products with large fixed costs, marginal cost is lower, often substantially, than average total cost, and average total cost declines, often sharply, as output grows. This cost pattern explains why many industries are dominated by either a single firm or a small number of firms. *(LO3)*

- Unlike the perfectly competitive firm, for which marginal revenue exactly equals market price, the monopolist realizes a marginal revenue that is always less than its price.

This shortfall reflects the fact that to sell more output, the monopolist must cut the price not only to additional buyers but to existing buyers as well. For the monopolist with a straight-line demand curve, the marginal revenue curve has the same vertical intercept and a horizontal intercept that is half as large as the intercept for the demand curve. *(LO4)*

- Whereas the perfectly competitive firm maximizes profit by producing at the level at which marginal cost equals the market price, the monopolist maximizes profit by equating marginal cost with marginal revenue, which is significantly lower than the market price. The result is an output level that is best for the monopolist but smaller than the level that would be best for society as a whole. At the profit-maximizing level of output, the benefit of an extra unit of output (the market price) is greater than its cost (the marginal cost). At the socially efficient level of output, where the monopolist's marginal cost curve intersects the demand curve, the benefit and cost of an extra unit are the same. *(LO4, LO5)*

- Both the monopolist and its potential customers can do better if the monopolist can grant discounts to price-sensitive buyers. The extreme example is the perfectly discriminating monopolist, who charges each buyer exactly his or her reservation price. Such producers are socially efficient because they sell to every buyer whose reservation price is at least as high as the marginal cost. *(LO6)*

- The various policies that governments employ to mitigate concerns about fairness and efficiency losses arising from natural monopoly include state ownership and management of natural monopolies, state regulation, private contracting, and vigorous enforcement of antitrust laws. Each of these remedies entails costs as well as benefits. In some cases, a combination of policies will produce a better outcome than simply allowing natural monopolists to do as they please. But in other cases, a hands-off policy may be the best available option. *(LO7)*

KEY TERMS

constant returns to scale
cost-plus regulation
deadweight loss
hurdle method of price
 discrimination
imperfectly competitive firm
 (or price setter)

increasing returns to scale
 (or economies of scale)
marginal revenue
market power
monopolistic competition
natural monopoly
oligopoly

perfect hurdle
perfectly discriminating
 monopolist
price discrimination
pure monopoly

REVIEW QUESTIONS

1. What important characteristic do all three types of imperfectly competitive firms share? *(LO1)*

2. True or false: A firm with market power can sell whatever quantity it wishes at whatever price it chooses. *(LO2)*

3. Why do most successful industrial societies offer patents and copyright protection, even though these protections enable sellers to charge higher prices? *(LO2)*

4. Why is marginal revenue always less than price for a monopolist but equal to price for a perfectly competitive firm? *(LO4)*

5. True or false: Because a natural monopolist charges a price greater than marginal cost, it necessarily earns a positive economic profit. *(LO4)*

PROBLEMS

1. State whether the following statements are true or false, and explain why. *(LO1, LO2)*
   a. In a perfectly competitive industry, the industry demand curve is horizontal, whereas for a monopoly it is downward-sloping.
   b. Perfectly competitive firms have no control over the price they charge for their product.
   c. For a natural monopoly, average cost declines as the number of units produced increases over the relevant output range.

2. Two car manufacturers, Nissan and Honda, have fixed costs of $1 billion and marginal costs of $20,000 per car. If Nissan produces 50,000 cars per year and Honda produces 200,000, calculate the average production cost for each company. On the basis of these costs, which company's market share do you think will grow in relative terms? *(LO3)*

3. A single-price, profit-maximizing monopolist *(LO4)*
   a. causes excess demand, or shortages, by selling too few units of a good or service.
   b. chooses the output level at which marginal revenue begins to increase.
   c. always charges a price above the marginal cost of production.
   d. also maximizes marginal revenue.
   e. none of the above statements is true.

4. If a monopolist could perfectly price-discriminate *(LO4, LO5)*
   a. the marginal revenue curve and the demand curve would coincide.
   b. the marginal revenue curve and the marginal cost curve would coincide.
   c. every consumer would pay a different price.
   d. marginal revenue would become negative at some output level.
   e. the resulting pattern of exchange would still be socially inefficient.

5. What is the socially desirable price for a natural monopoly to charge? Why will a natural monopoly that attempts to charge the socially desirable price invariably suffer an economic loss? *(LO5, LO7)*

6. Explain why price discrimination and the existence of slightly different variants of the same product tend to go hand in hand. Give an example from your own experience. *(LO6)*

7. TotsPoses Inc., a profit-maximizing business, is the only photography business in town that specializes in portraits of small children. George, who owns and runs TotsPoses, expects to encounter an average of eight customers per day, each with a reservation price shown in the following table. Assume George has no fixed costs, and his cost of producing each portrait is $12. *(LO4, LO5, LO6)*

Customer	Reservation price ($ per photo)
1	50
2	46
3	42
4	38
5	34
6	30
7	26
8	22

   a. How much should George charge if he must charge a single price to all customers? At this price, how many portraits will George produce each day? What will be his economic profit?
   b. How much consumer surplus is generated each day at this price?
   c. What is the socially efficient number of portraits?
   d. George is very experienced in the business and knows the reservation price of each of his customers. If he is allowed to charge any price he likes to

any consumer, how many portraits will he produce each day and how much economic profit will he earn?

e. In this case, how much consumer surplus is generated each day?

8. Refer back to Problem 7 and answer the following questions. *(LO5, LO6)*

a. Suppose George is permitted to charge two prices. He knows that customers with a reservation price above $30 never bother with coupons, whereas those with a reservation price of $30 or less always use them. At what level should George set the list price of a portrait? At what level should he set the discount price? How many photo portraits will he sell at each price?

b. In this case, what is George's economic profit and how much consumer surplus is generated each day?

9. Serena is a single-price, profit-maximizing monopolist in the sale of her own patented perfume, whose demand and marginal cost curves are as shown. *(LO4, LO5, LO6)*

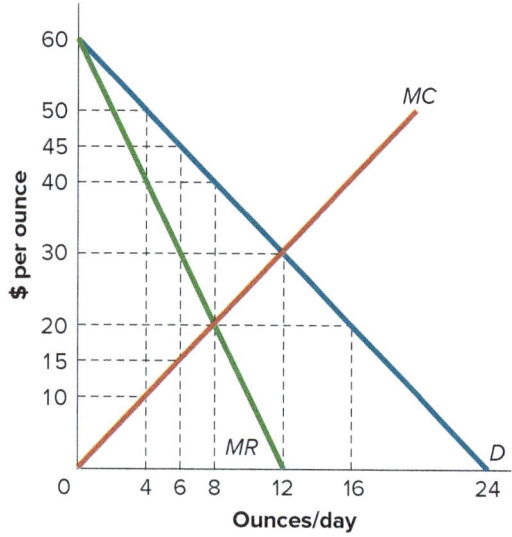

a. Relative to the consumer surplus that would result at the socially optimal quantity and price, how much consumer surplus is lost from her selling at the monopolist's profit-maximizing quantity and price?

b. How much total surplus would result if Serena could act as a perfectly price-discriminating monopolist?

10. Jada is a second-grader who sells lemonade on a street corner in your neighborhood. Each cup of lemonade costs Jada 20 cents to produce; she has no fixed costs. The reservation prices for the 10 people who walk by Jada's lemonade stand each day are listed in the following table.

Person	Reservation price
A	$1.00
B	$0.90
C	$0.80
D	$0.70
E	$0.60
F	$0.50
G	$0.40
H	$0.30
I	$0.20
J	$0.10

Jada knows the distribution of reservation prices (that is, she knows that one person is willing to pay $1, another $0.90, and so on), but she does not know any specific individual's reservation price. *(LO4, LO5, LO6)*

a. Calculate the marginal revenue of selling an additional cup of lemonade. (Start by figuring out the price Jada would charge if she produced only one cup of lemonade, and calculate the total revenue; then find the price Jada would charge if she sold two cups of lemonade; and so on.)

b. What is Jada's profit-maximizing price?

c. At that price, what are Jada's economic profit and total consumer surplus?

d. What price should Jada charge if she wants to maximize total economic surplus?

e. Now suppose Jada can tell the reservation price of each person. What price would she charge each person if she wanted to maximize profit? Compare her profit to the total surplus calculated in part d.

ANSWERS TO SELF-TESTS

8.1 The relevant cost figures are shown in the following table, which shows that Sony's unit-cost advantage is now $50.20 - $5.20 = $45.00. *(LO3)*

	Nintendo	Sony Computer Entertainment
Annual production	200,000	2,000,000
Fixed cost	$10,000,000	$10,000,000
Variable cost	$40,000	$400,000
Total cost	$10,040,000	$10,400,000
Average total cost per game	$50.20	$5.20

8.2 When the monopolist expands from 3 to 4 units per week, total revenue rises from $15 to $16 per week, which means that the marginal revenue from the sale of the fourth unit is only $1 per week. When the monopolist expands from 4 to 5 units per week, total revenue drops from $16 to $15 per week, which means that the marginal revenue from the sale of the fifth unit is actually negative, or −$1 per week. *(LO4)*

8.3 The profit-maximizing price and quantity are $P^* = $6/unit and $Q^* = 2$ units/week. *(LO4)*

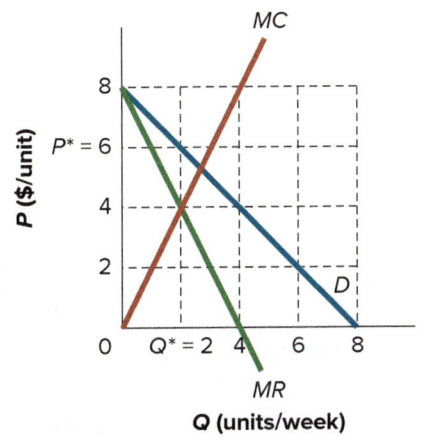

8.4 As column 4 in the following table shows, Preeti should again serve students *A*, *B*, and *C* in the list price submarket (at a price of $36) and only student *E* in the discount submarket (at a price of $32). *(LO6)*

(1) Student	(2) Reservation price ($ per paper)	(3) Total revenue ($ per week)	(4) Marginal revenue ($ per paper)
List Price Submarket			
			40
A	40	40	
			36
B	38	76	
			32
C	36	108	
			28
D	34	136	
Discount Price Submarket			
			32
E	32	32	
			28
F	30	60	
			24
G	28	84	
			20
H	26	104	

APPENDIX

The Algebra of Monopoly Profit Maximization

I n the text of this chapter, we developed the profit-maximization analysis for monopoly in a geometric framework. In this brief appendix, we show how this analysis can be done in an algebraic framework. The advantage of the algebraic framework is that it greatly simplifies computing the numerical values of the profit-maximizing prices and quantities.

EXAMPLE 8A.1 — Profit-Maximizing Price and Quantity

Find the profit-maximizing price and quantity for a monopolist with the demand curve $P = 15 - 2Q$ and the marginal cost curve $MC = Q$, where P is the product price in dollars per unit and Q is the quantity in units of output per week.

The first step is to find the equation for the marginal revenue curve associated with the monopolist's demand curve. Recall that in the case of a straight-line demand curve, the associated marginal revenue curve has the same vertical intercept as the demand curve and twice the slope of the demand curve. So the equation for this monopolist's marginal revenue curve is $MR = 15 - 4Q$. Letting Q^* denote the profit-maximizing output level, setting $MR = MC$ then yields:

$$15 - 4Q^* = Q^*,$$

which solves for $Q^* = 3$. The profit-maximizing price, P^*, is then found by substituting $Q^* = 3$ into the demand equation:

$$P^* = 15 - 2Q^* = 15 - 6 = 9.$$

Thus, the profit-maximizing price and quantity are $9 per unit and 3 units per week, respectively.

 SELF-TEST 8A.1

Find the profit-maximizing price and level of output for a monopolist with the demand curve $P = 12 - Q$ and the marginal cost curve $MC = 2Q$, where P is the price of the product in dollars per unit and Q is output in units per week.

PROBLEMS

connect

1. Suppose that the University of Michigan Cinema is a local monopoly whose demand curve for adult tickets on Saturday night is $P = 12 - 2Q$, where P is the price of a ticket in dollars and Q is the number of tickets sold in hundreds. The demand for children's tickets on Sunday afternoon is $P = 8 - 3Q$, and for adult tickets on Sunday afternoon, $P = 10 - 4Q$. On both Saturday night and Sunday afternoon, the marginal cost of an additional patron, child or adult, is $2. *(LO4)*
   a. What is the marginal revenue curve in each of the three submarkets?
   b. What price should the cinema charge in each of the three markets if its goal is to maximize profit?

2. Suppose you are a monopolist in the market for a specific video game. Your demand curve is given by $P = 80 - Q/2$; your marginal cost curve is $MC = Q$. Your fixed costs equal $400. *(LO4, LO5)*
   a. Graph the demand and marginal cost curves.
   b. Derive and graph the marginal revenue curve.
   c. Calculate and indicate on the graph the equilibrium price and quantity.
   d. What is your profit?
   e. What is the level of consumer surplus?

ANSWER TO APPENDIX SELF-TEST

8A.1 For the demand curve $P = 12 - Q$, the corresponding marginal revenue curve is $MR = 12 - 2Q$. Equating MR and MC, we solve the equation $12 - 2Q = 2Q$ for $Q = 3$. Substituting $Q = 3$ into the demand equation, we solve for the profit-maximizing price, $P = 12 - 3 = 9$. *(LO4)*

CHAPTER 9

Games and Strategic Behavior

Visual blight often results from the fact that the ability of a merchant's sign to attract attention depends on the size and brightness of other merchants' signs.

LEARNING OBJECTIVES

After reading this chapter, you should be able to:

LO1 Describe the three basic elements of a game, how the possible payoffs are summarized, and the effect of dominant and dominated strategy choices.

LO2 Identify and explain the prisoner's dilemma and how it applies to real-world situations.

LO3 Explain games in which the timing of players' choices matters.

LO4 Discuss strategies that enable players to solve commitment problems through material or psychological incentives.

At a Christmas Eve dinner party in 1997, actor Robert DeNiro pulled aside singer Tony Bennett for a moment. "Hey, Tony—there's a film I want you in," DeNiro said. He was referring to the project that became the 1999 Warner Brothers hit comedy *Analyze This*, in which the troubled head of a crime family, played by DeNiro, seeks the counsel of a psychotherapist, played by Billy Crystal. In the script, both the mob boss and his therapist are big fans of Bennett's music.

Bennett heard nothing further about the project for almost a year. Then his son and financial manager, Danny Bennett, got a phone call from Warner Brothers, in which the studio offered Tony $15,000 to sing "Got the World on a String" in the movie's final scene. As Danny described the conversation, "They made a fatal mistake. They told me they had already shot the film. So I'm like: 'Hey, they shot the whole film around Tony being the end gag and they're offering me $15,000?'"[1]

[1]As quoted by Geraldine Fabrikant, "Talking Money with Tony Bennett," *The New York Times,* May 2, 1999, Money & Business, p. 1.

Warner Brothers wound up paying $200,000 for Bennett's performance.

In business negotiations, as in life, timing can be everything. If executives at Warner Brothers had thought the problem through carefully, they would have negotiated with Bennett *before* shooting the movie. At that point, Bennett would have realized that the script could be rewritten if he asked too high a fee. By waiting, studio executives left themselves with no attractive option other than to pay Bennett's price.

The payoff to many actions depends not only on the actions themselves, but also on when they're taken and how they relate to actions taken by others. In previous chapters, economic decision makers confronted an environment that was essentially fixed. This chapter will focus on cases in which people must consider the effect of their behavior on others. For example, an imperfectly competitive firm will want to weigh the likely responses of rivals when deciding whether to cut prices or to increase its advertising budget. Interdependencies of this sort are the rule rather than the exception in economic and social life. To make sense of the world we live in, then, we must take these interdependencies into account.

Our focus in Chapter 8, *Monopoly, Oligopoly, and Monopolistic Competition*, was on the pure monopolist. In this chapter, we'll explore how a few simple principles from the theory of games can help us better understand the behavior of oligopolists and monopolistic competitors—the two types of imperfectly competitive firms for which strategic interdependencies are most important. Along the way, we'll also see how the same principles enable us to answer a variety of interesting questions drawn from everyday social interaction.

USING GAME THEORY TO ANALYZE STRATEGIC DECISIONS

In chess, tennis, or any other game, the payoff to a given move depends on what your opponent does in response. In choosing your move, therefore, you must anticipate your opponent's responses, how you might respond, and what further moves your own response might elicit. Economists and other behavioral scientists have devised the theory of games to analyze situations in which the payoffs to different actors depend on the actions their opponents take.

THE THREE ELEMENTS OF A GAME

basic elements of a game the players, the strategies available to each player, and the payoffs each player receives for each possible combination of strategies

A game has three **basic elements**: the players, the list of possible actions (or strategies) available to each player, and the payoffs the players receive for each possible combination of strategies. We'll use a series of examples to illustrate how these elements combine to form the basis of a theory of behavior.

The first example focuses on an important strategic decision confronting two oligopolists who produce an undifferentiated product and must decide how much to spend on advertising.

EXAMPLE 9.1	The Cost of Advertising

Should United Airlines spend more money on advertising?

Suppose that United Airlines and American Airlines are the only air carriers that serve the Chicago–St. Louis market. Each currently earns an economic profit of $6,000 per flight on this route. If United increases its advertising spending in this market by $1,000 per flight, and American spends no more on advertising than it does now, United's profit will rise to $8,000 per flight and American's will fall to $2,000. If both spend $1,000 more on advertising, each will earn an economic profit of $5,500 per flight. These payoffs are symmetric so that if United spends the same amount on advertising while American increases its spending by $1,000, United's economic profit will fall to $2,000 per flight and American's will rise to $8,000. The payoff structure is also common knowledge—that is, each company knows what the relevant payoffs will be for both parties under each of the possible combinations of choices. If each must decide independently whether to increase spending on advertising, what should United do?

TABLE 9.1
The Payoff Matrix for an Advertising Game

	American's Choices	
	Raise ad spending	Leave ad spending the same
United's Choices Raise ad spending	$5,500 for United $5,500 for American	$8,000 for United $2,000 for American
Leave ad spending the same	$2,000 for United $8,000 for American	$6,000 for United $6,000 for American

Both airlines do better if both leave ad spending the same than if both raise spending. Yet if one holds spending the same, the other always does better to raise spending.

Think of this situation as a game. What are its three elements? The players are the two airlines. Each airline must choose one of two strategies: to raise ad spending by $1,000 or leave it the same. The payoffs are the economic profits that correspond to the four possible scenarios resulting from their choices. One way to summarize the relevant information about this game is to display the players, strategies, and payoffs in the form of a simple table called a **payoff matrix** (see Table 9.1).

Confronted with the payoff matrix in Table 9.1, what should United Airlines do? The essence of strategic thinking is to begin by looking at the situation from the other party's point of view. Suppose United assumes that American will raise its spending on advertising (the left column in Table 9.1). In that case, United's best bet would be to follow suit (the top row in Table 9.1). Why is the top row United's best response when American chooses the left column? United's economic profits, given in the upper-left cell of Table 9.1, will be $5,500, compared to only $2,000 if it keeps spending the same (see the lower-left cell).

Alternatively, suppose United assumes that American will keep ad spending the same (that is, that American will choose the right column in Table 9.1). In that case, United would still do better to increase spending because it would earn $8,000 (the upper-right cell), compared to only $6,000 if it keeps spending the same (the lower-right cell). In this particular game, no matter which strategy American chooses, United will earn a higher economic profit by increasing its spending on advertising. And since this game is perfectly symmetric, a similar conclusion holds for American: No matter which strategy United chooses, American will do better by increasing its spending on ads.

When one player has a strategy that yields a higher payoff no matter which choice the other player makes, that player is said to have a **dominant strategy**. Not all games involve dominant strategies, but both players in this game have one, and that is to increase spending on ads. For both players, to leave ad spending the same is a **dominated strategy**—one that leads to a lower payoff than an alternative choice, regardless of the other player's choice.

Notice, however, that when each player chooses the dominant strategy, the resulting payoffs are smaller than if each had left spending unchanged. When United and American increase their spending on ads, each earns only $5,500 in economic profits, compared to the $6,000 each would have earned without the increase.

payoff matrix a table that describes the payoffs in a game for each possible combination of strategies

dominant strategy one that yields a higher payoff no matter what the other players in a game choose

dominated strategy any other strategy available to a player who has a dominant strategy

NASH EQUILIBRIUM

Nash equilibrium any combination of strategy choices in which each player's choice is his or her best choice, given the other players' choices

A game is said to be in equilibrium if each player's strategy is the best he or she can choose, given the other players' choices. This definition of equilibrium is sometimes called a **Nash equilibrium**, after the mathematician John Nash, who developed the concept in the early 1950s. Nash was awarded the Nobel Prize in Economics in 1994 for his contributions to game theory.[2] When a game is in equilibrium, no player has any incentive to deviate from his current strategy.

If each player in a game has a dominant strategy, as in Example 9.1, equilibrium occurs when each player follows that strategy. But even in games in which not every player has a dominant strategy, we can often identify an equilibrium outcome. Consider, for instance, the following variation on the advertising game as illustrated in Example 9.2.

EXAMPLE 9.2	Nash Equilibrium

Should American Airlines spend more money on advertising?

Suppose United Airlines and American Airlines are the only carriers that serve the Chicago–St. Louis market. Their payoff matrix for advertising decisions is shown in Table 9.2. Does United have a dominant strategy? Does American? If each firm does the best it can, given the incentives facing the other, what will be the outcome of this game?

In this game, no matter what United does, American will do better to raise its ad spending, so raising the advertising budget is a dominant strategy for American. United, however, does not have a dominant strategy. If American raises its spending, United will do better to leave its spending unchanged; but if American does not raise spending, United will do better to spend more. Even though United doesn't have a dominant strategy, we can employ the Incentive Principle to predict

TABLE 9.2
Equilibrium When One Player Lacks a Dominant Strategy

American's Choices

United's Choices	Raise ad spending	Leave ad spending the same
Raise ad spending	$3,000 for United $4,000 for American	$8,000 for United $3,000 for American
Leave ad spending the same	$4,000 for United $5,000 for American	$5,000 for United $2,000 for American

In this game, United lacks a dominant strategy, but American's dominant strategy is to raise its ad spending. Because United can predict that American will choose the left column, United will do best to leave its ad spending the same. Equilibrium occurs in the lower-left cell.

---

[2]Nash was awarded the Nobel Prize in Economics in 1994 for his contributions to game theory. His life was also the subject of the Academy Award–winning film *A Beautiful Mind*.

what is likely to happen in this game. United's managers are assumed to know what the payoff matrix is, so they can predict that American will spend more on ads since that is American's dominant strategy. Thus the best strategy for United, given the prediction that American will spend more on ads, is to keep its own spending unchanged. If both players do the best they can, taking account of the incentives each faces, this game will end in the lower-left cell of the payoff matrix: American will raise its spending on ads and United will not.

Note that the choices corresponding to the lower-left cell in Table 9.2 satisfy the definition of a Nash equilibrium. If United found itself in that cell, its alternative would be to raise its ad spending, a move that would reduce its payoff from $4,000 to $3,000. So United has no incentive to abandon the lower-left cell. Similarly, if American found itself in the lower-left cell of Table 9.2, its alternative would be to leave ad spending the same, a move that would reduce its payoff from $5,000 to $2,000. So American also has no incentive to abandon the lower-left cell. The lower-left cell of Table 9.2 is a Nash equilibrium—a combination of strategies for which each player's choice is the best available option, given the choice made by the other player.

 SELF-TEST 9.1

What should United and American do if their payoff matrix is modified as follows?

American

		Raise ad spending	Leave spending the same
United	Raise ad spending	$3,000 for United $8,000 for American	$4,000 for United $5,000 for American
	Leave spending the same	$8,000 for United $4,000 for American	$5,000 for United $2,000 for American

RECAP ↑

USING GAME THEORY TO ANALYZE STRATEGIC DECISIONS

The three elements of any game are the players, the list of strategies from which they can choose, and the payoffs to each combination of strategies. This information can be summarized in a payoff matrix.

Equilibrium in a game occurs when each player's strategy choice yields the highest payoff available, given the strategies chosen by other players. Such a combination of strategies is called a Nash equilibrium.

THE PRISONER'S DILEMMA

The first advertising example we discussed belongs to an important class of games called the **prisoner's dilemma**. In the prisoner's dilemma, when each player chooses a dominant strategy, the result is unattractive to the group of players as a whole.

prisoner's dilemma a game in which each player has a dominant strategy, and when each plays it, the resulting payoffs are smaller than if each had played a dominated strategy

THE ORIGINAL PRISONER'S DILEMMA

The next example recounts the original scenario from which the prisoner's dilemma drew its name.

| EXAMPLE 9.3 | Prisoner's Dilemma |

Should the prisoners confess?

Two prisoners, Horace and Jasper, are being held in separate cells for a serious crime that they did in fact commit. The prosecutor, however, has enough hard evidence to convict them of only a minor offense, for which the penalty is a year in jail. Each prisoner is told that if one confesses while the other remains silent, the confessor will be cleared of the crime, and the other will spend 20 years in prison. If both confess, they will get an intermediate sentence of 5 years. These payoffs are summarized in Table 9.3. The two prisoners are not allowed to communicate with one another. Do they have a dominant strategy? If so, what is it?

In this game, the dominant strategy for each prisoner is to confess. No matter what Jasper does, Horace will get a lighter sentence by speaking out. If Jasper confesses, Horace will get 5 years (upper-left cell) instead of 20 (lower-left cell). If Jasper remains silent, Horace will go free (upper-right cell) instead of spending a year in jail (lower-right cell). Because the payoffs are perfectly symmetric, Jasper will also do better to confess, no matter what Horace does. The difficulty is that when each follows his dominant strategy and confesses, both will do worse than if each had shown restraint. When both confess, they each get 5 years (upper-left cell), instead of the 1 year they would have gotten by remaining silent (lower-right cell). Hence the name of this game, the prisoner's dilemma.

TABLE 9.3
The Payoff Matrix for a Prisoner's Dilemma

The payoffs describe the lengths of prison sentences the two will receive under different combinations of choices.

✔ SELF-TEST 9.2

GM and Chrysler must both decide whether to invest in a new process. Games 1 and 2 show how their profits (in millions of dollars) depend on the decisions they might make. Which of these games is a prisoner's dilemma?

Game 1

Chrysler

		Don't invest	Invest
GM	Don't invest	10 for each	4 for GM 12 for Chrysler
	Invest	12 for GM 4 for Chrysler	5 for each

Game 2

Chrysler

		Don't invest	Invest
GM	Don't invest	4 for GM 12 for Chrysler	5 for each
	Invest	10 for each	12 for GM 4 for Chrysler

The prisoner's dilemma is one of the most powerful metaphors in all of human behavioral science. Countless social and economic interactions have payoff structures analogous to the one confronted by the two prisoners. Some of those interactions occur between only two players, as in the examples just discussed; many others involve larger groups. Games of the latter sort are called *multiplayer prisoner's dilemmas*. But regardless of the number of players involved, the common thread is one of conflict between the narrow self-interest of individuals and the broader interests of larger communities.

THE ECONOMICS OF CARTELS

A **cartel** is any coalition of firms that conspires to restrict production for the purpose of earning an economic profit. As we will see in the next example, the problem confronting oligopolists who are trying to form a cartel is a classic illustration of the prisoner's dilemma.

cartel a coalition of firms that agree to restrict output for the purpose of earning an economic profit

The Economic Naturalist 9.1

Why are cartel agreements notoriously unstable?

Consider a market for bottled water served by two oligopolists, Aqua-pure and Mountain Spring. Each firm can draw water free of charge from a mineral spring located on its own land. Customers supply their own bottles. Rather than compete with one another, the two firms decide to join together by selling water at the price a profit-maximizing pure monopolist would charge. Under their agreement (which constitutes a cartel), each firm would produce and sell half the quantity of water demanded by the market at the monopoly price (see Figure 9.1). The agreement isn't legally enforceable, however, which means that each firm has the option of charging less than the agreed price. If one firm sells water for less than the other firm, it will capture the entire quantity demanded by the market at the lower price.

Why is this agreement likely to collapse?

Since the marginal cost of mineral water is zero, the profit-maximizing quantity for a monopolist with the demand curve shown in Figure 9.1 is

Why is it so difficult for companies to enforce agreements against price cutting?

FIGURE 9.1

The Market Demand for Mineral Water.

Faced with the demand curve shown, a monopolist with zero marginal cost would produce 1,000 bottles per day (the quantity at which marginal revenue equals zero) and sell them at a price of $1.00 per bottle.

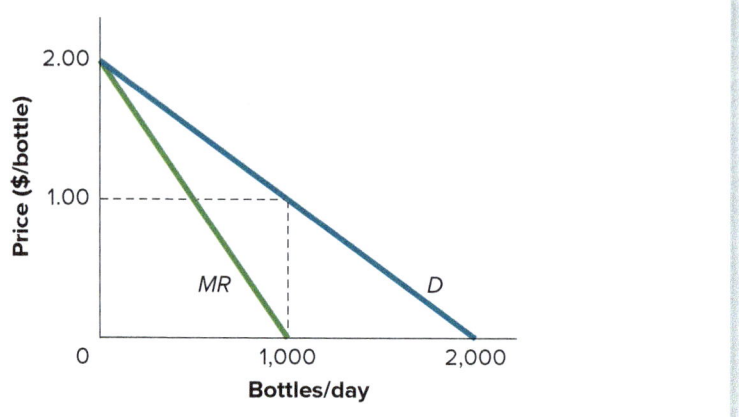

1,000 bottles per day, the quantity for which marginal revenue equals marginal cost. At that quantity, the monopoly price is $1 per bottle. If the firms abide by their agreement, each will sell half the market total, or 500 bottles per day, at a price of $1 per bottle, for an economic profit of $500 per day.

But suppose Aquapure reduced its price to 90 cents per bottle. By underselling Mountain Spring, it would capture the entire quantity demanded by the market, which, as shown in Figure 9.2, is 1,100 bottles per day. Aquapure's economic profit would rise from $500 per day to ($0.90 per bottle)(1,100 bottles per day) = $990 per day—almost twice as much as before. In the process, Mountain Spring's economic profit would fall from $500 per day to zero. Rather than see its economic profit disappear, Mountain Spring would match Aquapure's price cut, recapturing its original 50 percent share of the market. But when each firm charges $0.90 per bottle and sells 550 bottles per day, each earns an economic profit of ($0.90 per bottle)(550 bottles per day) = $495 per day, or $5 less per day than before.

Suppose we view the cartel agreement as an economic game in which the two available strategies are to sell for $1 per bottle or to sell for $0.90 per bottle. The payoffs are the economic profits that result from these strategies. Table 9.4 shows the payoff matrix for this game. Each firm's dominant strategy is to sell at the lower price, yet in following that strategy, each earns a lower profit than if each had sold at the higher price.

The game does not end with both firms charging $0.90 per bottle. Each firm knows that if it cuts the price a little further, it can recapture the entire market

FIGURE 9.2

The Temptation to Violate a Cartel Agreement.

By cutting its price from $1 per bottle to 90 cents per bottle, Aquapure can sell the entire market quantity demanded at that price, 1,100 bottles per day, rather than half the monopoly quantity of 1,000 bottles per day.

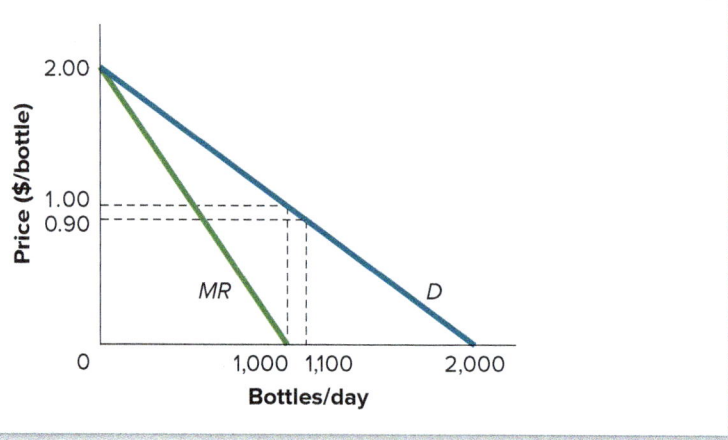

TABLE 9.4
The Payoff Matrix for a Cartel Agreement

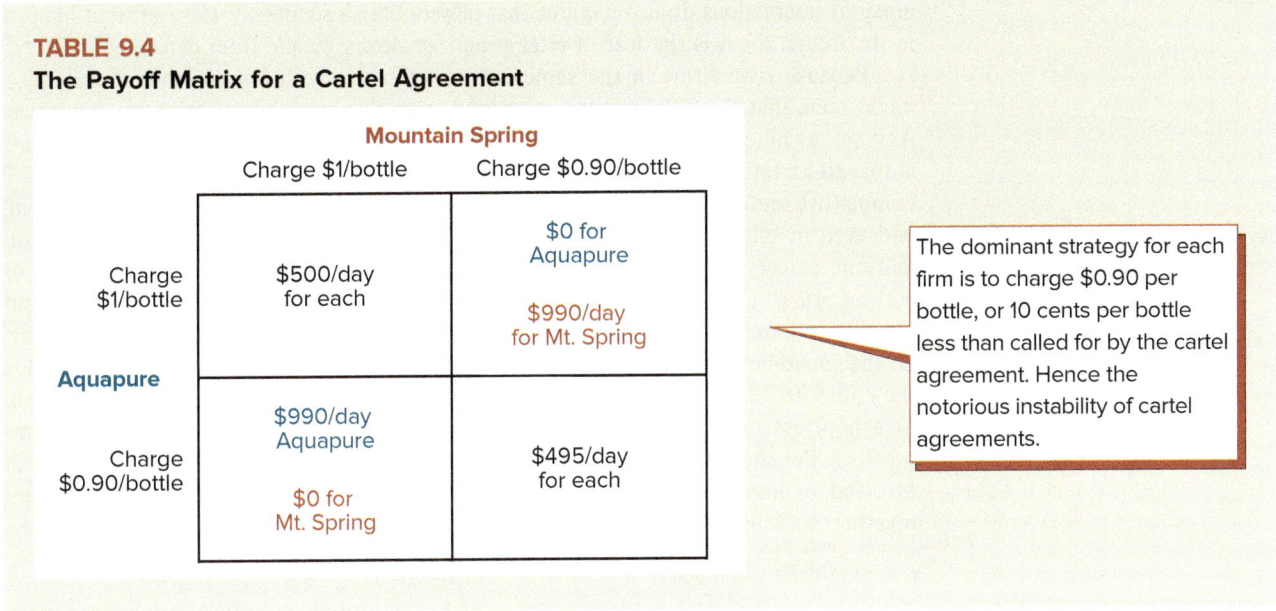

The dominant strategy for each firm is to charge $0.90 per bottle, or 10 cents per bottle less than called for by the cartel agreement. Hence the notorious instability of cartel agreements.

and, in the process, earn a substantially higher economic profit. At every step, the rival firm will match any price cut, until the price falls all the way to the marginal cost—in this example, zero.

Cartel agreements confront participants with the economic incentives inherent in the prisoner's dilemma, which explains why such agreements have historically been so unstable. Usually a cartel involves not just two firms, but several; an arrangement that can make retaliation against price cutters extremely difficult. In many cases, discovering which parties have broken the agreement is difficult. For example, the Organization of the Petroleum Exporting Countries (OPEC), a cartel of oil producers formed in the 1970s to restrict oil production, has no practical way to prevent member countries from secretly pumping oil offshore in the dead of night.

TIT-FOR-TAT AND THE REPEATED PRISONER'S DILEMMA

When all players cooperate in a prisoner's dilemma, each gets a higher payoff than when all defect. So people who confront prisoner's dilemmas will be on the lookout for ways to create incentives for mutual cooperation. What they need is some way to penalize players who defect. When players interact with one another only once, this turns out to be difficult. But when they expect to interact repeatedly, new possibilities emerge.

A **repeated prisoner's dilemma** is a standard prisoner's dilemma that confronts the same players not just once but many times. Experimental research on repeated prisoner's dilemmas in the 1960s identified a simple strategy that proves remarkably effective at limiting defection. The strategy is called **tit-for-tat**, and here's how it works: The first time you interact with someone, you cooperate. In each subsequent interaction, you simply do what that person did in the previous interaction. Thus, if your partner defected on your first interaction, you'd then defect on your next interaction with her. If she then cooperates, your move next time will be to cooperate as well.

On the basis of elaborate computer simulations, University of Michigan political scientist Robert Axelrod showed that tit-for-tat was a remarkably effective strategy, even when pitted against a host of ingenious counterstrategies that had been designed for the explicit purpose of trying to exploit it. The success of tit-for-tat requires a reasonably stable set of players, each of whom can remember what other players have done in

repeated prisoner's dilemma a standard prisoner's dilemma that confronts the same players repeatedly

tit-for-tat a strategy for the repeated prisoner's dilemma in which players cooperate on the first move and then mimic their partner's last move on each successive move previous interactions. It also requires that players have a significant stake in what happens in the future, for it is the fear of retaliation that deters people from defecting.

Because rival firms in the same industry interact with one another repeatedly, it might seem that the tit-for-tat strategy would ensure widespread collusion to raise prices. And yet, as noted earlier, cartel agreements are notoriously unsuccessful. One difficulty is that tit-for-tat's effectiveness depends on there being only two players in the game. In competitive and monopolistically competitive industries, there are generally many firms, and even in oligopolies there are often several. When there are more than two firms and one defects now, how do the cooperators selectively punish the defector later? By cutting price? That will penalize everyone, not just the defector. Even if there are only two firms in an industry, these firms realize that other firms may enter their industry. So the would-be cartel members have to worry not only about each other, but also about the entire list of firms that might decide to compete with them. Each firm may see this as a hopeless task and decide to defect now, hoping to reap at least some economic profit in the short run. What seems clear, in any event, is that the practical problems involved in implementing tit-for-tat have made it difficult to hold cartel agreements together for long.

The Economic Naturalist 9.2

How did Congress unwittingly solve the television advertising dilemma confronting cigarette producers?

In 1970, Congress enacted a law making cigarette advertising on television illegal after January 1, 1971. As evidenced by the steadily declining proportion of Americans who smoke, this law seems to have achieved its stated purpose of protecting citizens against a proven health hazard. But the law also had an unintended effect, which was to increase the economic profit of cigarette makers, at least in the short run. In the year before the law's passage, manufacturers spent more than $300 million on advertising—about $60 million more than they spent during the year after the law was enacted. Much of the saving in advertising expenditures in 1971 was reflected in higher cigarette profits at year-end. But if eliminating television advertising made companies more profitable, why didn't the manufacturers eliminate the ads on their own?

When an imperfectly competitive firm advertises its product, its demand curve shifts rightward for two reasons. First, people who have never used that type of product learn about it, and some buy it. Second, people who consume a different brand of the product may switch brands. The first effect boosts sales industrywide; the second merely redistributes existing sales among brands.

Although advertising produces both effects in the cigarette industry, its primary effect is brand switching. Thus, the decision of whether to advertise confronts the individual firm with a prisoner's dilemma. Table 9.5 shows the payoffs facing a pair of cigarette producers trying to decide whether to advertise. If both firms advertise on TV (upper-left cell), each earns a profit of only $10 million per year, compared to a profit of $20 million per year for each if neither advertises (lower-right cell). Clearly, both will benefit if neither advertises.

Yet note the powerful incentive that confronts each firm. RJR (the R.J. Reynolds Tobacco Company) sees that if Philip Morris doesn't advertise, RJR can earn higher profits by advertising ($35 million per

Why were cigarette manufacturers happy when Congress made it illegal for them to advertise on television?

TABLE 9.5
Profits from Cigarette Advertising as a Prisoner's Dilemma

	Philip Morris	
	Advertise on TV	Don't advertise on TV
RJR — Advertise on TV	$10 million/yr for each	$35 million/yr for RJR $5 million/yr for Philip Morris
RJR — Don't advertise on TV	$5 million/yr for RJR $35 million/yr for Philip Morris	$20 million/yr for each

In many industries, the primary effect of advertising is to encourage consumers to switch brands. In such industries, the dominant strategy is to advertise heavily (upper-left cell), even though firms as a group would do better by not advertising (lower-right cell).

year) than by not advertising ($20 million per year). RJR also sees that if Philip Morris does advertise, RJR will again earn more by advertising ($10 million per year) than by not advertising ($5 million per year). Thus, RJR's dominant strategy is to advertise. And because the payoffs are symmetric, Philip Morris's dominant strategy is also to advertise. So when each firm behaves rationally from its own point of view, the two together do worse than if they had both shown restraint. The congressional ad ban forced cigarette manufacturers to do what they could not have accomplished on their own.

As The Economic Naturalist 9.3 example makes clear, understanding the prisoner's dilemma can help the economic naturalist make sense of human behavior not only in the world of business but also in other domains of life as well.

The Economic Naturalist 9.3

Why do people shout at parties?

Whenever large numbers of people gather for conversation in a closed space, the ambient noise level rises sharply. After attending such gatherings, people often complain of sore throats and hoarse voices. If everyone spoke at a normal volume at parties, the overall noise level would be lower, and people would hear just as well. So why do people shout?

The problem involves the difference between individual incentives and group incentives. Suppose everyone starts by speaking at a normal level. But because of the crowded conditions, conversation partners have difficulty hearing one another, even when no one is shouting. The natural solution, from the point of the individual, is to simply raise one's voice a bit. But that is also the natural solution for everyone else. And when everyone speaks more loudly, the ambient noise level rises so that no one hears any better than before.

▶ Visit your instructor's Connect course and access your eBook to view this video.

Why do people shout at parties?

No matter what others do, the individual will do better by speaking more loudly. Doing so is a dominant strategy for everyone, in fact. Yet when everyone follows the dominant strategy, the result is worse (no one can hear well) than if everyone had continued to speak normally. While shouting is wasteful, individuals acting alone have no better option. If anyone were to speak softly while others shout, that person wouldn't be heard. No one wants to go home with raw vocal cords, but people apparently prefer that cost to the alternative of not being heard at all.

By now it should be clear that the prisoner's dilemma is a powerful metaphor for describing why markets don't always deliver the best outcomes possible. As Example 9.4 illustrates, it helps explain the origins of the climate crisis.

EXAMPLE 9.4   Choosing a Production Process

Will firms voluntarily incur costs to adopt cleaner production methods?

Suppose that firms in a perfectly competitive industry must choose between a clean but more expensive production process and a dirty but less expensive one. Although the clean process is $1 per unit more costly, it is worthwhile from a societal standpoint because it reduces the external damage from pollution by $2 per unit.

If all firms adopted the dirty process, each would earn zero economic profit and the resulting pollution level would be high. In that case, the market price would be too low to enable any single firm that adopted the clean process to cover its higher costs. It would suffer an economic loss and eventually be forced out of business.

Firms would also earn zero profit if they all used the clean process, since prices would rise to cover firms' higher costs. The problem is that any one of them could then earn a huge profit by switching back to the dirty process, which would enable it to earn $1 per unit of economic profit on as much as it could produce and sell.

As discussed in Chapter 7, in any competitive market, a firm's primary goal is to maximize its profit. After all, any firm that failed to do so would quickly be driven out of business by its competitors. For any given level of profit, however, let's assume, plausibly, that firm owners prefer lower pollution levels. The implied rankings of selected combinations of profit levels and pollution levels would then be as shown in Table 9.6.

TABLE 9.6
Ranking of Combination of Profit Levels and Pollution Levels

Economic Profit	Pollution Level	Ranking
Very High	Low	1
Zero	Low	2
Zero	High	3
Negative	High	4

These rankings give rise to what game theorists call a *multiparty prisoner's dilemma*. We can represent it with a conventional 2 x 2 payoff matrix in which we designate one player as Firm A and the other as "All Other Firms." The implied players' rankings of the four combinations of strategy choices are then as shown in Table 9.7.

TABLE 9.7
A Multiparty Prisoner's Dilemma

	All Other Firms	
	Clean process	Dirty process
Firm A — Clean process	Second Best for All Other Firms	Worst for Firm A Best for All Other Firms
Firm A — Dirty process	Best for Firm A Worst for All Other Firms	Third Best for All Other Firms

Each player has a dominant strategy, and when each chooses it, each gets a worse result than if each had chosen its dominated strategy.

Note that if other firms adopt the clean process, Firm A would get its second-best outcome if it too adopts the clean process. In this case, all firms would earn zero economic profit and pollution would be low. On the other hand, if Firm A adopts the dirty process while all others use the clean one, Firm A would get its most preferred outcome since it would earn an enormous profit and pollution would still be low (since Firm A's use of the dirty production process would have only a negligible impact on overall pollution).

Alternatively, if all others adopt the dirty process, Firm A would get its least preferred outcome by adopting the clean process. In this case, Firm A's profit would be negative and overall pollution would be high. If instead Firm A and all others adopt the dirty process, Firm A would get its third-best outcome since its profit would be zero and pollution would be high.

Firm A thus has a dominant strategy, which is to adopt the dirty process. Since the payoffs in Table 9.7 are symmetric, the dirty process is also a dominant strategy choice for other firms. And when all players adopt their dominant strategies in this game, all end up in the lower right cell of Table 9.7, which is a worse outcome than if all firms had adopted the clean process. This game thus satisfies the criteria that define a prisoner's dilemma.

Payoff structures analogous to this one capture in a nutshell the forces that spawned the climate crisis. Firms pollute not because they like to but because competitive pressure makes it difficult to survive without doing so.

RECAP ↑

THE PRISONER'S DILEMMA

The prisoner's dilemma is a game in which each player has a dominant strategy, and in which the payoff to each player when each chooses that strategy is smaller than if each had chosen a dominated strategy. Incentives analogous to those found in the prisoner's dilemma help explain a broad range of behavior in business and everyday life—among them excessive spending on advertising and cartel instability. The tit-for-tat strategy can help sustain cooperation in two-player repeated prisoner's dilemmas but tends to be ineffective in multiplayer repeated prisoner's dilemmas.

GAMES IN WHICH TIMING MATTERS

In the games discussed so far, players were assumed to choose their strategies simultaneously, and which player moved first didn't matter. For example, in the prisoner's dilemma, self-interested players would follow their dominant strategies even if they knew in advance what strategies their opponents had chosen. But in other situations, such as the negotiations between Warner Brothers and Tony Bennett described at the beginning of this chapter, timing is of the essence.

We begin with an example of a game whose outcome cannot be predicted if both players move simultaneously, but whose outcome is clear if one player has the opportunity to move before the other.

EXAMPLE 9.5 | **The Importance of Timing**

Should Ford build a hybrid Mustang?

The Ford Mustang and the Chevrolet Camaro compete for a limited pool of domestic sports car enthusiasts. Each company knows that the other is considering whether to bring out a hybrid version of its car. If both companies bring out hybrids, each will earn $60 million in profit. If neither brings out a hybrid, each company will earn $50 million. If Chevrolet introduces a hybrid and Ford does not, Chevrolet will earn $80 million and Ford will earn $70 million. If Ford brings out a hybrid and Chevrolet does not, Ford will earn $80 million and Chevrolet will earn $70 million. Does either firm have a dominant strategy in this situation? What will happen in this game if Ford gets to choose first, with Chevrolet choosing after having seen Ford's choice?

When both companies must make their decisions simultaneously, the payoff matrix for the example looks like Table 9.8.

The logic of the profit figures in Table 9.8 is that although consumers generally like the idea of a hybrid sports car (hence the higher profits when both companies bring out hybrids than when neither does), the companies will have to compete more heavily with one another if both offer the same type of car (and

---

TABLE 9.8
The Advantage of Being Different

	Ford Mustang	
	Offer hybrid	Don't offer hybrid
Offer hybrid	$60 million for Chevrolet $60 million for Ford	$80 million for Chevrolet $70 million for Ford
Chevrolet Camaro **Don't offer hybrid**	$70 million for Chevrolet $80 million for Ford	$50 million for Chevrolet $50 million for Ford

Profits are higher when each company offers a different type of car than the other (upper-right and lower-left cells). Customers generally prefer hybrid cars (upper-left cell) to nonhybrids (lower-right cell).

hence the lower profits when both offer the same type of car than when each offers a different type).

In the payoff matrix in Table 9.8, neither company has a dominant strategy. The best outcome for Ford is to offer a hybrid Mustang while Chevrolet does not offer a hybrid Camaro (lower-left cell). The best outcome for Chevrolet is to offer a hybrid Camaro while Ford does not offer a hybrid Mustang (upper-right cell). Both the lower-left and upper-right cells are Nash equilibria of this game because if the companies found themselves in either of these cells, neither would unilaterally want to change its position. Thus, in the upper-right cell, Chevrolet wouldn't want to change (that cell is, after all, the best possible outcome for Chevrolet), and neither would Ford (since switching to a hybrid would reduce its profit from $70 million to $60 million). But without being told more, we simply cannot predict where the two companies will end up.

If one side can move before the other, however, the incentives for action become instantly clearer. For games in which timing matters, a **decision tree**, or **game tree**, is a more useful way of representing the payoffs than a traditional payoff matrix. This type of diagram describes the possible moves in the sequence in which they may occur, and lists the final payoffs for each possible combination of moves.

If Ford has the first move, the decision tree for the game is shown in Figure 9.3. At *A*, Ford begins the game by deciding whether to offer a hybrid. If it chooses to offer one, Chevrolet must then make its own choice at *B*. If Ford does not offer a hybrid, Chevrolet will make its choice at *C*. In either case, once Chevrolet makes its choice, the game is over.

In thinking strategically about this game, the key for Ford is to put itself in Chevrolet's shoes and imagine how Chevrolet would react to the various choices it might confront. In general, it will make sense for Ford to assume that Chevrolet will respond in a self-interested way—that is, by choosing the available option that offers the highest profit for Chevrolet. Ford knows that if it chooses to offer a hybrid, Chevy's best option at *B* will be not to offer a hybrid (since Chevy's profit is $10 million higher at *E* than at *D*). Ford also knows that if it chooses not to offer a hybrid, Chevy's best option at *C* will be to offer one (since Chevy's profit is

decision tree (or **game tree**) a diagram that describes the possible moves in a game in sequence and lists the payoffs that correspond to each possible combination of moves

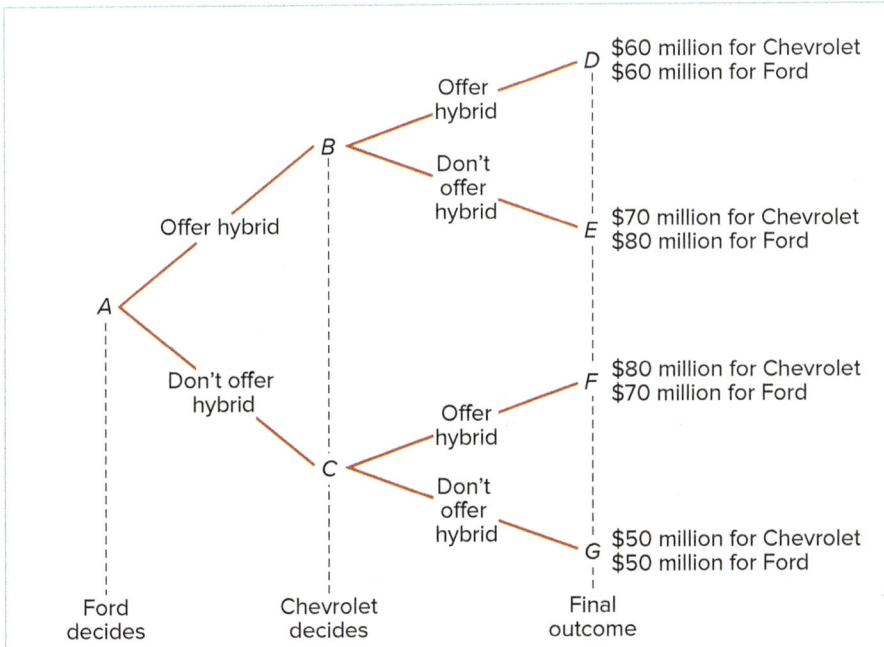

FIGURE 9.3

Decision Tree for Hybrid Example.

This decision tree shows the possible moves and payoffs for the game in the hybrid example, in the sequence in which they may occur.

- *A* — Ford decides
  - Offer hybrid → *B* (Chevrolet decides)
    - Offer hybrid → *D*: $60 million for Chevrolet / $60 million for Ford
    - Don't offer hybrid → *E*: $70 million for Chevrolet / $80 million for Ford
  - Don't offer hybrid → *C* (Chevrolet decides)
    - Offer hybrid → *F*: $80 million for Chevrolet / $70 million for Ford
    - Don't offer hybrid → *G*: $50 million for Chevrolet / $50 million for Ford

Ford decides   Chevrolet decides   Final outcome

$30 million higher at *F* than at *G*). Ford thus knows that if it offers a hybrid, it will end up at *E,* where it will earn $80 million, whereas if it does not offer a hybrid, it will end up at *F,* where it will earn only $70 million. So when Ford has the first move in this game, its best strategy is to offer a hybrid. And Chevrolet then follows by choosing not to offer one.

Note that, in this game, the company that moves first has a considerable advantage. By moving first, Ford is able to earn $80 million compared to Chevrolet's $70 million. In general, being the first company to introduce a desirable product innovation is highly profitable. This undoubtedly explains the real-world battle between Ford and Chevrolet to introduce the first hybrid versions of their cars.

CREDIBLE THREATS AND PROMISES

credible threat a threat to take an action that is in the threatener's interest to carry out

Could Chevrolet have deterred Ford from offering a hybrid by threatening to offer a hybrid of its own, no matter what Ford did? The problem with this strategy is such a threat would not have been credible. In the language of game theory, a **credible threat** is one that will be in the threatener's interest to carry out when the time comes to act. As the Incentive Principle suggests, people are likely to be skeptical of any threat if they know there will be no incentive to follow through when the time comes. The problem here is that Ford knows that it would not be in Chevrolet's interest to carry out its threat in the event that Ford offered a hybrid. After all, once Ford has already offered the hybrid, Chevy's best option is to offer a nonhybrid.

The concept of a credible threat figured prominently in the negotiations between Warner Brothers' managers and Tony Bennett over the matter of Mr. Bennett's fee for performing in *Analyze This*. Once most of the film had been shot, managers knew they couldn't threaten credibly to refuse Mr. Bennett's salary demand because at that point adapting the film to another singer would have been extremely costly. In contrast, a similar threat made before production of the movie had begun would have been credible.

credible promise a promise to take an action that is in the promiser's interest to keep

Just as in some games credible threats are impossible to make, in others **credible promises** are impossible. A credible promise is one that is in the interests of the promiser to keep when the time comes to act. In the following example, both players suffer because of the inability to make a credible promise.

EXAMPLE 9.6 | **A Credible Promise**

Should the business owner open a remote office?

The owner of a thriving business wants to start up an office in a distant city. If she hires someone to manage the new office, she can afford to pay a weekly salary of $1,000—a premium of $500 over what the manager would otherwise be able to earn—and still earn a weekly economic profit of $1,000 for herself. The owner's concern is that she won't be able to monitor the manager's behavior. The owner knows that by managing the remote office dishonestly, the manager can boost his take-home pay to $1,500 while causing the owner an economic loss of $500 per week. If the owner believes that all managers are selfish income-maximizers, will she open the new office?

The decision tree for the remote-office game is shown in Figure 9.4. At *A*, the managerial candidate promises to manage honestly, which brings the owner to *B*, where she must decide whether to open the new office. If she opens it, they reach *C*, where the manager must decide whether to manage honestly. If the manager's only goal is to make as much money as he can, he will manage dishonestly (bottom branch at *C*) because, that way, he will earn $500 more than by managing honestly (top branch at *C*).

So if the owner opens the new office, she will end up with an economic loss of $500. If she had not opened the office (bottom branch at *B*), she would have realized an economic profit of zero. Because zero is better than −$500, the owner will choose not to open the remote office. In the end, the opportunity cost of the manager's inability to make a credible promise is $1,500: the manager's forgone $500 salary premium and the owner's forgone $1,000 return.

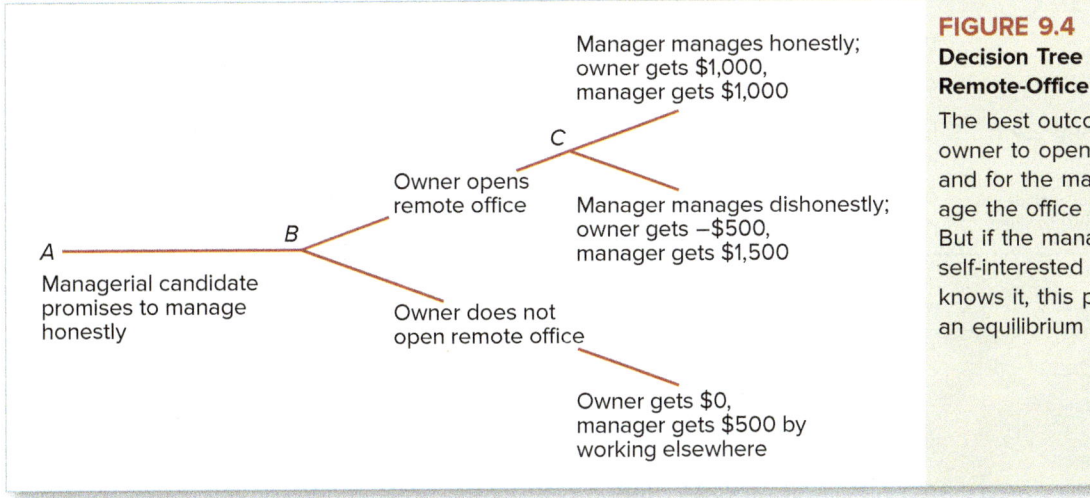

Manager manages honestly; owner gets $1,000, manager gets $1,000

Owner opens remote office

Manager manages dishonestly; owner gets −$500, manager gets $1,500

A
Managerial candidate promises to manage honestly

B

Owner does not open remote office

Owner gets $0, manager gets $500 by working elsewhere

FIGURE 9.4

Decision Tree for the Remote-Office Game.

The best outcome is for the owner to open the office at *B* and for the manager to manage the office honestly at *C*. But if the manager is purely self-interested and the owner knows it, this path will not be an equilibrium outcome.

✔ SELF-TEST 9.3

Smith and Jones are playing a game in which Smith has the first move at *A* in the decision tree shown. Once Smith has chosen either the top or bottom branch at *A*, Jones, who can see what Smith has chosen, must choose the top or bottom branch at *B* or *C*. If the payoffs at the end of each branch are as shown, what is the equilibrium outcome of this game? If before Smith chose, Jones could make a credible commitment to choose either the top or bottom branch when his turn came, what would he do?

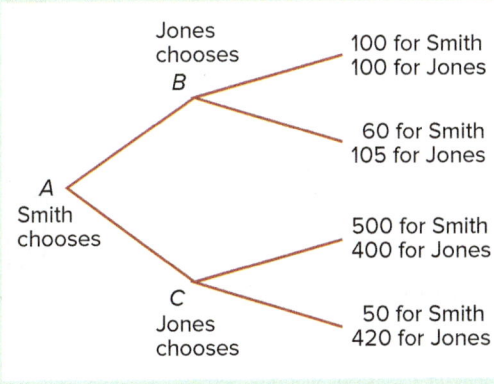

Jones chooses *B*

100 for Smith
100 for Jones

60 for Smith
105 for Jones

A
Smith chooses

500 for Smith
400 for Jones

C
Jones chooses

50 for Smith
420 for Jones

MONOPOLISTIC COMPETITION WHEN LOCATION MATTERS

In many sequential games, the player who gets to move first enjoys a strategic advantage. That was the case, for instance, in the decision of whether to produce a hybrid sports car in Example 9.5. In that example, the first mover did better because he was able to exploit the knowledge that both firms do better if each one's product is different from the other's rather than similar to it. But that won't always be true. When the feature that differentiates one seller's product from another's is temporal or spatial location, the firm with the last move in a game sometimes enjoys the upper hand, as The Economic Naturalist 9.4 illustrates.

The Economic Naturalist 9.4

Why do we often see convenience stores located on adjacent street corners?

▶ Visit your instructor's Connect course and access your eBook to view this video.

Why do we often see convenience stores located on adjacent street corners?

In many cities, it's common to see convenience stores located in clusters, followed by long stretches with no stores at all. If the stores were more spread out, almost all consumers would enjoy a shorter walk to the nearest convenience store. Why do stores tend to cluster in this fashion?

In Figure 9.5, suppose that when the convenience store located at *A* first opened, it was the closest store for the 1,200 shoppers who live in identical apartment houses evenly distributed along the road between *A* and the freeway mile to the east.[3] Those who live to the east of the freeway shop elsewhere because they cannot cross the freeway. Those who live to the west of the store at *A* shop either at *A* or at some other store still further to the west, whichever is closer. In this setting, why might a profit-maximizing entrepreneur planning to open a new store between *A* and the freeway choose to locate at *B* rather than at some intermediate location such as *C*?

It turns out that a store located at *C* would, in fact, minimize the distance that shoppers living between *A* and the freeway would have to walk to reach the nearest store. If there were a store at *C*, no shopper on this stretch of

---

FIGURE 9.5
The Curious Tendency of Monopolistic Competitors to Cluster.

As a group, consumers would enjoy a shorter walk if the store at *B* were instead located at *C*, or even at *D*. But a second store will attract more customers by locating at *B*.

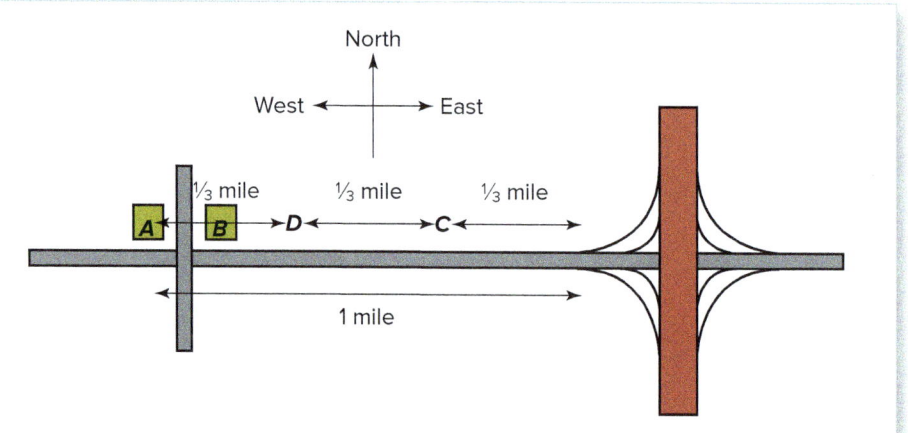

---

[3]"Evenly distributed" means that the number of shoppers who live on any segment of the road between *A* and the freeway is exactly proportional to the length of that segment. For example, the number who live along a segment one-tenth of a mile in length would be $1/10 \times 1,200 = 120$.

road would have to walk more than 1/3 of a mile to reach the nearest store. The 800 people who live between point *D* (which is halfway between *A* and *C*) and the freeway would shop at *C*, while the 400 who live between *D* and *A* would shop at *A*.

Despite the fact that *C* is the most attractive location for a new store from the perspective of consumers, it is not the most advantageous for the store's owner. The reason is that the owner's profit depends on how many people choose to shop at his store, not on how far they have to walk to get there. Given that consumers shop at the store closest to where they live, the best option from the entrepreneur's perspective is to locate his store at *B*, on the street corner just east of *A*. That way, his store will be closer to all 1,200 people who live between *A* and the freeway. It is this logic that often helps explain the clustering of convenience stores, gas stations, and other monopolistically competitive firms whose most important differentiating feature is geographic location.

The insight that helped answer the question posed in The Economic Naturalist 9.4 comes from economist Harold Hotelling.[4] Hotelling employed this insight to explain why two hot dog vendors on a stretch of beach almost invariably locate next to one another midway between the endpoints of the beach.

For many oligopolistic or monopolistically competitive firms, an important dimension of product differentiation is location in time rather than in physical space. The timing of flight departures for different airlines in the New York–Los Angeles market is one example. The timing of film showings by different local movie theaters is another. In these cases, too, we often see product clustering. Thus, in the New York–Los Angeles market, both United and American have flights throughout the afternoon departing exactly on the hour. And in many local movie markets, the first evening showing starts at 7:15 p.m. in dozens of different theaters.

In other examples, the differentiating features that matter most might be said to describe the product's location in a more abstract "product space." With soft drinks, for example, we might array different products according to their degrees of sweetness or carbonation. Here, too, it is common to see rival products that lie very close to one another, such as Coca-Cola and Pepsi. Clustering occurs in these cases for the reasons analogous to those discussed by Hotelling in his classic paper.

> *RECAP* ↑
>
> **GAMES IN WHICH TIMING MATTERS**
>
> The outcomes in many games depend on the timing of each player's move. For such games, the payoffs are best summarized by a decision tree rather than a payoff matrix. Sometimes the second mover does best to offer a product that differs markedly from existing products. Other times, the second mover does best to mimic existing products closely.

COMMITMENT PROBLEMS

Games like the one in Self-Test 9.3, as well as the prisoner's dilemma, the cartel game, and the remote-office game, confront players with a **commitment problem**—a situation in which they have difficulty achieving the desired outcome because they cannot make credible threats or promises. If both players in the original prisoner's dilemma could make a binding promise

commitment problem a situation in which people cannot achieve their goals because of an inability to make credible threats or promises

---

[4]Harold Hotelling, "Stability and Competition," *Economic Journal* 39, no. 1 (1929), pp. 41–57.

to remain silent, both would be assured of a shorter sentence, hence the logic of the underworld code of *Omerta*, under which the family of anyone who provides evidence against a fellow mob member is killed. A similar logic explains the adoption of military-arms-control agreements, in which opponents sign an enforceable pledge to curtail weapons spending.

The commitment problem in the remote-office game could be solved if the managerial candidate could find some way of committing himself to manage honestly if hired. The candidate needs a **commitment device**—something that provides the candidate with an incentive to keep his promise.

commitment device a way of changing incentives so as to make otherwise empty threats or promises credible

Business owners are well aware of commitment problems in the workplace and have adopted a variety of commitment devices to solve them. Consider, for example, the problem confronting the owner of a restaurant. She wants her table staff to provide good service so that customers will enjoy their meals and come back in the future. Because good service is valuable to her, she would be willing to pay servers extra for it. For their part, servers would be willing to provide good service in return for the extra pay. The problem is that the owner cannot always monitor whether the servers do provide good service. Her concern is that having been paid extra for it, the servers may slack off when she isn't looking. Unless the owner can find some way to solve this problem, she will not pay extra; the servers will not provide good service; and she, they, and the diners will suffer. A better outcome for all concerned would be for the servers to find some way to commit themselves to good service.

Restaurateurs in many countries have tried to solve this commitment problem by encouraging diners to leave tips at the end of their meals. The attraction of this solution is that the diner is *always* in a good position to monitor service quality. The diner should be happy to reward good service with a generous tip because doing so will help ensure good service in the future. And the server has a strong incentive to provide good service because he knows that the size of his tip may depend on it.

The various commitment devices just discussed—the underworld code of *Omerta*, military-arms-control agreements, the tip for the server—all work because they change the incentives facing the decision makers. But as the next example illustrates, changing incentives in precisely the desired way is not always practical.

EXAMPLE 9.7   Changing Incentives

Will leaving a tip at an out-of-town restaurant affect the quality of service you receive?

Will Sylvester leave a tip when dining on the road?

Sylvester has just finished a $100 steak dinner at a restaurant that is 500 miles from where he lives. The server provided good service. If Sylvester cares only about himself, will he leave a tip?

Once the server has provided good service, there is no way for her to take it back if the diner fails to leave a tip. In restaurants patronized by local diners, failure to tip is not a problem because the server can simply provide poor service the next time a nontipper comes in. But the server lacks that leverage with out-of-town diners. Having already received good service, Sylvester must choose between paying $100 and paying $120 for his meal. If he is an essentially selfish person, the former choice may be a compelling one.

SELF-TEST 9.4

A traveler dines at a restaurant far from home. Both he and the server are rational and self-interested in the narrow sense. The server must first choose between providing good service and bad service, whereupon the diner must choose whether or not to leave a tip. The payoffs for their interaction are as summarized on the accompanying game tree. What is the most the diner would be willing to pay for the right to make a binding commitment (visible to the server) to leave a tip at the end of the meal in the event of having received good service?

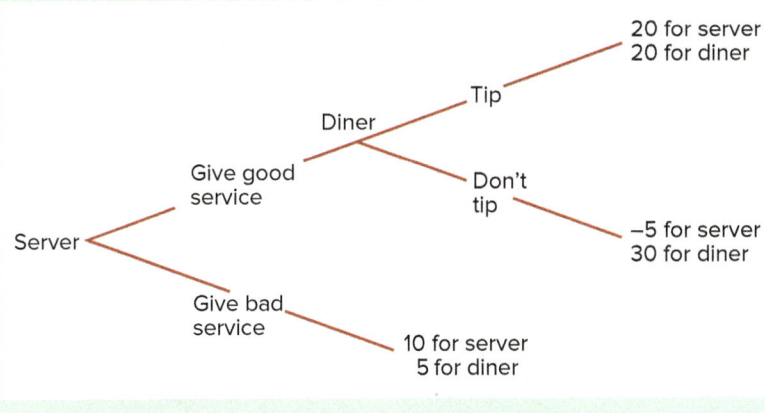

SOLVING COMMITMENT PROBLEMS WITH PSYCHOLOGICAL INCENTIVES

In all the games we have discussed so far, players were assumed to care only about obtaining the best possible outcome for themselves. Thus, each player's goal was to get the highest monetary payoff, the shortest jail sentence, the best chance to be heard, and so on. The irony, in most of these games, is that players do not attain the best outcomes. Better outcomes can sometimes be achieved by altering the material incentives selfish players face, but not always.

If altering the relevant material incentives is not possible, commitment problems can sometimes be solved by altering people's psychological incentives. As the next example illustrates, in a society in which people are strongly conditioned to develop moral sentiments—feelings of guilt when they harm others, feelings of sympathy for their trading partners, feelings of outrage when they are treated unjustly—commitment problems arise less often than in more narrowly self-interested societies.

EXAMPLE 9.8	The Impact of Moral Sentiments

In a moral society, will the business owner open a remote office?

Consider again the owner of the thriving business who is trying to decide whether to open an office in a distant city. Suppose the society in which she lives is one in which all citizens have been strongly conditioned to behave honestly. Will she open the remote office?

Suppose, for instance, that the managerial candidate would suffer guilt pangs if he embezzled money from the owner. Most people would be reluctant to assign a monetary value to guilty feelings. But for the sake of discussion, let's suppose that those feelings are so unpleasant that the manager would be willing to pay at least $10,000 to avoid them. On this assumption, the manager's payoff if he manages dishonestly will be not $1,500, but $1,500 − $10,000 = −$8,500. The new decision tree is shown in Figure 9.6.

In this case, the best choice for the owner at *B* will be to open the remote office because she knows that at *C* the manager's best choice will be to manage honestly. The irony, of course, is that the honest manager in this example ends up richer than the selfish manager in the previous example, who earned only a normal salary.

FIGURE 9.6
The Remote-Office Game with an Honest Manager.
If the owner can identify a managerial candidate who would choose to manage honestly at *C*, she will hire that candidate at *B* and open the remote office.

Manager manages honestly; owner gets $1,000, manager gets $1,000

Owner opens remote office

Manager manages dishonestly; owner gets −$500, manager gets −$8,500

Managerial candidate promises to manage honestly

Owner does not open remote office

Owner gets $0, manager gets $500 by working elsewhere

Are People Fundamentally Selfish?

As Example 9.8 suggests, the assumption that people are self-interested in the narrow sense of the term does not always capture the full range of motives that govern choice in strategic settings. Think, for example, about the last time you had a meal at an out-of-town restaurant. Did you leave a tip? If so, your behavior was quite normal. Researchers have found that tipping rates in restaurants patronized mostly by out-of-town diners are essentially the same as in restaurants patronized mostly by local diners.

Indeed, there are many exceptions to the outcomes predicted on the basis of the assumption that people are self-interested in the narrowest sense of the term. People who have been treated unjustly often seek revenge even at ruinous cost to themselves. Every day, people walk away from profitable transactions whose terms they believe to be "unfair." In these and countless other ways, people do not seem to be pursuing self-interest narrowly defined. And if motives beyond narrow self-interest are significant, we must take them into account in attempting to predict and explain human behavior.

Preferences as Solutions to Commitment Problems

Economists tend to view preferences as ends in themselves. Taking them as given, they calculate what actions will best serve those preferences. This approach to the study of behavior is widely used by other social scientists, and by game theorists, military strategists, philosophers, and others. In its standard form, it assumes purely self-interested preferences for present and future consumption goods of various sorts, leisure pursuits, and so on. Concerns about fairness, guilt, honor, sympathy, and the like typically play no role.

Yet such concerns clearly affect the choices people make in strategic interactions. Sympathy for one's trading partner can make a businessperson trustworthy even when material incentives favor cheating. A sense of justice can prompt a person to incur the costs of retaliation, even when incurring those costs will not undo the original injury.

Preferences can clearly shape behavior in these ways; however, this alone does not solve commitment problems. The solution to such problems requires not only that a person *have* certain preferences, but also that others have some way of *discerning* them. Unless the business owner can identify the trustworthy employee, that employee cannot land a job whose pay is predicated on trust. And unless the predator can identify a potential victim whose character will motivate retaliation, that person is likely to become a victim.

From among those with whom we might engage in ventures requiring trust, can we identify reliable partners? If people could make *perfectly* accurate character judgments, they could always steer clear of dishonest persons. That people continue to be victimized at least occasionally by dishonest persons suggests that perfectly reliable character judgments are either impossible to make or prohibitively expensive.

Vigilance in the choice of trading partners is an essential element in solving (or avoiding) commitment problems, for if there is an advantage in being honest and being perceived as such, there is an even greater advantage in only *appearing* to be honest. After all, a liar who appears trustworthy will have better opportunities than one who glances about furtively, sweats profusely, and has difficulty making eye contact. Indeed, he will have the same opportunities as an honest person but will get higher payoffs because he will exploit them to the fullest.

In the end, the question of whether people can make reasonably accurate character judgments is an empirical one. Experimental studies have shown that even on the basis of brief encounters involving strangers, subjects are adept at predicting who will cooperate and who will defect in prisoner's dilemma games. For example, in one experiment in which only 26 percent of subjects defected, the accuracy rate of predicted defections was more than 56 percent. One might expect that predictions regarding those we know well would be even more accurate.

Do you know someone who would return an envelope containing $1,000 in cash to you if you lost it at a crowded concert? If so, then you accept the claim that personal character can help people solve commitment problems. As long as honest individuals can identify at least some others who are honest, and can interact selectively with them, honest individuals can prosper in a competitive environment.

RECAP ↑

COMMITMENT PROBLEMS AND THE EFFECTS OF PSYCHOLOGICAL INCENTIVES

- Commitment problems arise when the inability to make credible threats and promises prevents people from achieving desired outcomes. Such problems can sometimes be solved by employing commitment devices—ways of changing incentives to facilitate making credible threats or promises.
- Most applications of the theory of games assume that players are self-interested in the narrow sense of the term. In practice, however, many choices—such as leaving tips in out-of-town restaurants—appear inconsistent with this assumption.
- The fact that people seem driven by a more complex range of motives makes behavior more difficult to predict, but also creates new ways of solving commitment problems. Psychological incentives often can serve as commitment devices when changing players' material incentives is impractical. For example, people who are able to identify honest trading partners, and interact selectively with them, are able to solve commitment problems that arise from lack of trust.

SUMMARY

- Economists use the theory of games to analyze situations in which the payoffs of one's actions depend on the actions taken by others. Games have three basic elements: the players; the list of possible actions, or strategies, from which each player can choose; and the payoffs the players receive for those strategies. The payoff matrix is the most useful way to summarize this information in games in which the timing of the players' moves is not decisive. In games in which timing matters, a decision tree provides a much more useful summary of the information. *(LO1, LO3)*

- Equilibrium in a game occurs when each player's strategy choice yields the highest payoff available, given the strategies chosen by the other. *(LO1)*

- A dominant strategy is one that yields a higher payoff regardless of the strategy chosen by the other player. In some games such as the prisoner's dilemma, each player has a dominant strategy. Equilibrium occurs in such games when each player chooses his or her dominant strategy. In other games, not all players have a dominant strategy. *(LO1, LO2)*

- Equilibrium outcomes are often unattractive from the perspective of players as a group. The prisoner's dilemma has this feature because it is each prisoner's dominant strategy to confess, yet each spends more time in jail if both confess than if both remain silent. The incentive structure of this game helps explain such disparate social dilemmas as excessive advertising, cartels, and failure to reap the potential benefits of interactions requiring trust. *(LO2)*

- Individuals often can resolve these dilemmas if they can make binding commitments to behave in certain ways. Some commitments—such as those involved in military-arms-control agreements—are achieved by altering the material incentives confronting the players. Other commitments can be achieved by relying on psychological incentives to counteract material payoffs. Moral sentiments such as guilt, sympathy, and a sense of justice often foster better outcomes than can be achieved by narrowly self-interested players. For this type of commitment to work, the relevant moral sentiments must be discernible by one's potential trading partners. *(LO4)*

KEY TERMS

basic elements of a game
cartel
commitment device
commitment problem
credible promise

credible threat
decision tree (or game tree)
dominant strategy
dominated strategy
Nash equilibrium

payoff matrix
prisoner's dilemma
repeated prisoner's dilemma
tit-for-tat

REVIEW QUESTIONS

1. Identify the three basic elements of a game. *(LO1)*

2. How is your incentive to defect in a prisoner's dilemma altered if you learn that you will play the game not just once but rather indefinitely many times with the same partner? *(LO2)*

3. Explain why a cartel is an example of a prisoner's dilemma. *(LO2)*

4. Why did Warner Brothers make a mistake by waiting until the filming of *Analyze This* was almost finished before negotiating with Tony Bennett to perform in the final scene? *(LO3)*

5. Suppose General Motors is trying to hire a small firm to manufacture the door handles for Buick sedans. The task requires an investment in expensive capital equipment that cannot be used for any other purpose. Why might the president of the small firm refuse to undertake this venture without a long-term contract fixing the price of the door handles? *(LO3)*

6. Describe the commitment problem that narrowly self-interested diners and servers would confront at restaurants located on interstate highways. Given that in such restaurants tipping does seem to ensure reasonably good service, do you think people are always selfish in the narrowest sense? *(LO4)*

PROBLEMS

1. Consider the following game, called matching pennies, which you are playing with a friend. Each of you has a penny hidden in your hand, facing either heads up or tails up (you know which way the one in your hand is facing). On the count of "three," you simultaneously show your pennies to each other. If the face-up side of your coin matches the face-up side of your friend's coin, you get to keep the two pennies. If the faces do not match, your friend gets to keep the pennies. *(LO1)*

   a. Who are the players in this game? What are each player's strategies? Construct a payoff matrix for the game.

   b. Does either player have a dominant strategy? If so, what?

   c. Is there an equilibrium? If so, what?

2. Consider the following game. Harry has four quarters. He can offer Sally from one to four of them. If she accepts his offer, she keeps the quarters Harry offered her and Harry keeps the others. If Sally declines Harry's offer, they both get nothing ($0). They play the game only once, and each cares only about the amount of money he or she ends up with. *(LO1, LO3)*

   a. Who are the players? What are each player's strategies? Construct a decision tree for this game.

   b. Given their goal, what is the optimal choice for each player?

3. Blackadder and Baldrick are rational, self-interested criminals imprisoned in separate cells in a dark medieval dungeon. They face the prisoner's dilemma displayed in the matrix.

   Assume that Blackadder is willing to pay $1,000 for each year by which he can reduce his sentence below 20 years. A corrupt jailer tells Blackadder that before he decides whether to confess or deny the crime, she can tell him Baldrick's decision. How much is this information worth to Blackadder? *(LO2)*

| | **Blackadder** | |
	Confess	Deny
Baldrick Confess	5 years for each	0 for Baldrick / 20 years for Blackadder
Baldrick Deny	20 years for Baldrick / 0 for Blackadder	1 year for each

4. In studying for your economics final, Sam is concerned about only two things: his grade and the amount of time he spends studying. A good grade will give him a benefit of 20; an average grade, a benefit of 5; and a poor grade, a benefit of 0. By studying a lot, Sam will incur a cost of 10; by studying a little, a cost of 6. Moreover, if Sam studies a lot and all other students study a little, he will get a good grade and they will get poor ones. But if they study a lot and he studies a little, they will get good grades and he will get a poor one. Finally, if Sam and all other students study the same amount of time, everyone will get average grades. Other students share Sam's preferences regarding grades and study time. *(LO2)*

   a. Model this situation as a two-person prisoner's dilemma in which the strategies are to study a little and to study a lot, and the players are Sam and all other students. Construct a payoff matrix in which the payoffs account for both the cost and benefit of studying.

   b. What is the equilibrium outcome in this game? Which outcome would everyone (both the other students and Sam) prefer?

5. Newfoundland's fishing industry has recently declined sharply due to overfishing, even though fishing companies were supposedly bound by a quota agreement. If all companies had abided by the agreement, yields could have been maintained at high levels. *(LO2)*

   a. Model this situation as a prisoner's dilemma in which the players are Company A and Company B, and the strategies are to keep the quota and break the quota. Suppose that if both companies keep the quota, then each receives a payoff of $100, and if both break the quota, then each receives a payoff of $0. On the other hand, if one company breaks the quota and the other keeps the quota, then the company that breaks the quota receives a payoff of $150 and the company that keeps the quota receives a payoff of −$50. Construct the corresponding payoff matrix, and explain why overfishing is inevitable in the absence of effective enforcement of the quota agreement.

   b. Provide another environmental example of a prisoner's dilemma.

   c. In many potential prisoner's dilemmas, a way out of the dilemma for a would-be cooperator is to make reliable character judgments about the trustworthiness of potential partners. Explain why this solution is not available in many situations involving degradation of the environment.

6. Two airplane manufacturers are considering the production of a new product, a 150-passenger jet. Both are deciding whether to enter the market and produce the new planes. The payoff matrix is as follows (payoff values are in millions of dollars).

Airbus

	Produce	Don't produce
Produce	−5 for each	100 for Boeing 0 for Airbus
Don't produce	0 for Boeing 100 for Airbus	0 for each

Boeing (row player label)

The implication of these payoffs is that the market demand is large enough to support only one manufacturer. If both firms enter, both will sustain a loss. *(LO2)*

a. Identify two possible equilibrium outcomes in this game.

b. Consider the effect of a subsidy. Suppose the European Union decides to subsidize the European producer, Airbus, with a check for $25 million if it enters the market. Revise the payoff matrix to account for this subsidy. What is the new equilibrium outcome?

c. Compare the two outcomes (pre- and post-subsidy). What qualitative effect does the subsidy have?

7. Jill and Jack both have two pails that can be used to carry water down a hill. Each makes only one trip down the hill, and each pail of water can be sold for $6. Carrying the pails of water down requires considerable effort. Both Jill and Jack would be willing to pay $3 each to avoid carrying one pail down the hill and an additional $4 to avoid carrying a second pail down the hill. *(LO2)*

a. Given market prices, how many pails of water will each child fetch from the top of the hill?

b. Jill and Jack's parents are worried that the two children don't cooperate enough with one another. Suppose they make Jill and Jack share equally their revenues from selling the water. Given that both are self-interested, construct the payoff matrix for the decisions Jill and Jack face regarding the number of pails of water each should carry. What is the equilibrium outcome?

8. The owner of a thriving business wants to open a new office in a distant city. If they can hire someone who will manage the new office honestly, they can afford to pay that person a weekly salary of $2,000 ($1,000 more than the manager would be able to earn elsewhere) and still earn an economic profit of $800. The owner's concern is that they will not be able to monitor the manager's behavior and that the manager would therefore be in a position to embezzle money from the business. The owner knows that if the remote office is managed

dishonestly, the manager can earn $3,100, which results in an economic loss of $600 per week. *(LO3)*

a. If the owner believes that all managers are narrowly self-interested income maximizers, will they open the new office?

b. Suppose the owner knows that a managerial candidate is a genuinely honest person who condemns dishonest behavior and who would be willing to pay up to $15,000 to avoid the guilt they would feel if they were dishonest. Will the owner open the remote office?

9. Consider the following "dating game," which has two players, A and B, and two strategies, to buy a movie ticket or a baseball ticket. The payoffs, given in points, are as shown in the matrix below. Note that the highest payoffs occur when both A and B attend the same event.

B

	Buy movie ticket	Buy baseball ticket
Buy movie ticket	2 for A 3 for B	0 for A 0 for B
Buy baseball ticket	1 for A 1 for B	3 for A 2 for B

A (row player label)

Assume that players A and B buy their tickets separately and simultaneously. Each must decide what to do knowing the available choices and payoffs but not what the other has actually chosen. Each player believes the other to be rational and self-interested. *(LO1, LO2, LO3)*

a. Does either player have a dominant strategy?

b. How many potential equilibria are there? (*Hint:* To see whether a given combination of strategies is an equilibrium, ask whether either player could get a higher payoff by changing his or her strategy.)

c. Is this game a prisoner's dilemma? Explain.

d. Suppose player A gets to buy his or her ticket first. Player B does not observe A's choice but knows that A chose first. Player A knows that player B knows he or she chose first. What is the equilibrium outcome?

e. Suppose the situation is similar to part d, except that player B chooses first. What is the equilibrium outcome?

10. Imagine yourself sitting in your car in a campus parking lot that is currently full, waiting for someone to pull out so that you can park your car. Somebody pulls out, but at the same moment a driver who has just arrived overtakes you in an obvious attempt to park in the vacated spot before you can. Suppose this driver would be willing to

pay up to $10 to park in that spot and up to $30 to avoid getting into an argument with you. (That is, the benefit of parking is $10 and the cost of an argument is $30.) At the same time he guesses, accurately, that you too would be willing to pay up to $30 to avoid a confrontation and up to $10 to park in the vacant spot. *(LO3, LO4)*

a. Model this situation as a two-stage decision tree in which his bid to take the space is the opening move and your strategies are (1) to protest and (2) not to protest. If you protest (initiate an argument), the rules of the game specify that he has to let you take the space. Show the payoffs at the end of each branch of the tree.

b. What is the equilibrium outcome?

c. What would be the advantage of being able to communicate credibly to the other driver that your *failure* to protest would be a significant psychological cost to you (for example, maybe a cost of $25)?

ANSWERS TO SELF-TESTS

9.1 No matter what American does, United will do better to leave ad spending the same. No matter what United does, American will do better to raise ad spending. So each player will play its dominant strategy: American will raise its ad spending and United will leave its ad spending the same. *(LO1)*

American's Choice

	Raise ad spending	Leave ad spending the same
Raise ad spending **United's Choice**	United gets $3,000 American gets $8,000	United gets $4,000 American gets $5,000
Leave ad spending the same	United gets $8,000 American gets $4,000	United gets $5,000 American gets $2,000

9.2 In game 1, no matter what Chrysler does, GM will do better to invest, and no matter what GM does, Chrysler will do better to invest. Each has a dominant strategy, but in following it, each does worse than if it had not invested. So game 1 is a prisoner's dilemma. In game 2, no matter what Chrysler does, GM again will do better to invest; but no matter what GM does, Chrysler will do better *not* to invest. Each has a dominant strategy, and in following it, each gets a payoff of 10—which is 5 more than if each had played its dominated strategy. So game 2 is not a prisoner's dilemma. *(LO2)*

9.3 Smith assumes that Jones will choose the branch that maximizes his payoff, which is the bottom branch at either *B* or *C*. So Jones will choose the bottom branch when his turn comes, no matter what Smith chooses. Since Smith will do better (60) on the bottom branch at *B* than on the bottom branch at *C* (50), Smith will choose the top branch at *A*. So equilibrium in this game is for Smith to choose the top branch at *A* and Jones to choose the bottom branch at *B*. Smith gets 60 and Jones gets 105.

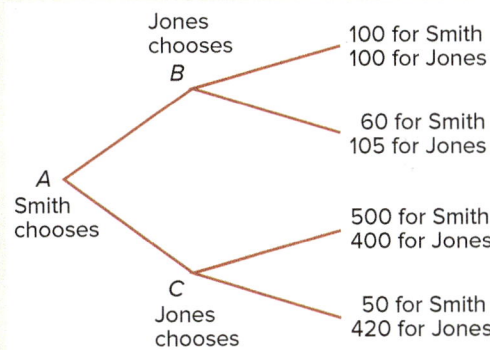

If Jones could make a credible commitment to choose the top branch no matter what, both would do better. Smith would choose the bottom branch at *A* and Jones would choose the top branch at *C*, giving Smith 500 and Jones 400. *(LO3)*

9.4 The equilibrium of this game in the absence of a commitment to tip is that the server will give bad service because if she provides good service, she knows that the diner's best option will be not to tip, which leaves the server worse off than if she had provided good service. Since the diner gets an outcome of 20 if he can commit to leaving a tip (15 more than he would get in the absence of such a commitment), he would be willing to pay up to 15 for the right to commit. *(LO4)*

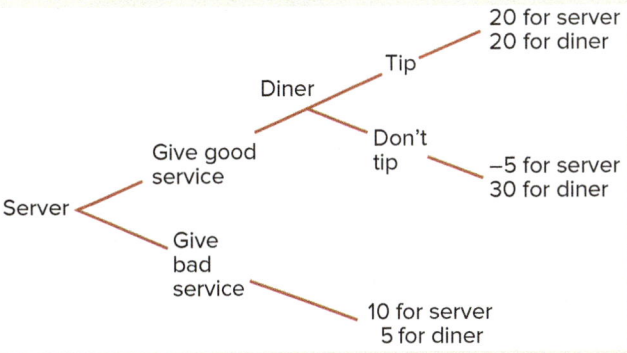

CHAPTER 10

An Introduction to Behavioral Economics

Behavioral economics introduces more realistic assumptions about human motivation and cognition.

Hayden Frank

LO1 Describe and illustrate numerous rules of thumb people employ when making decisions using incomplete information and explain how reliance on these rules sometimes leads to poor choices.

LO2 Explain how misinterpretation of contextual clues can lead to poor choices.

LO3 Describe situations in which impulse-control problems prevent people from executing rationally conceived economic plans.

LO4 Describe the phenomenon of loss aversion and explain how it often creates a powerful bias in favor of the status quo.

LO5 Explain how relaxing the assumption that people are narrowly self-interested alters the predictions of traditional economic models.

LO6 Describe how concerns about relative position often create conflicts between the interests of individuals and those of the broader community.

LO7 List examples of laws and regulations that appear motivated by the behavioral tendencies described in this chapter.

U ntil the 1980s, traditional economic models almost invariably assumed a decision maker who was narrowly self-interested, well informed, highly disciplined, possessed of sufficient cognitive capacity to solve relatively simple optimization problems, and unconcerned with relative position. This mythical individual was often called **homo economicus** for short.

During the intervening years, theoretical and empirical developments in economics and psychology have challenged each of these core assumptions. The challenges fall into three broad categories: (1) we often make systematic cognitive errors that prevent us from

homo economicus the narrowly self-interested, well-informed, highly disciplined, and cognitively formidable actor often assumed in traditional economic models

satisficing a decision-making strategy that aims for adequate results because optimal results may necessitate excessive expenditure of resources

Cost-Benefit

fungibility the property of an entity whose individual units are interchangeable, as money in separate accounts

Richard Thaler, who was awarded the Nobel Prize in Economics in 2017 for his pioneering work in behavioral economics.

discovering which choices will best promote our interests; (2) even when we can discern which choices would be best, we often have difficulty summoning the willpower to execute them; and (3) we often pursue goals different from those attributed to homo economicus. In this chapter, we will consider each of these challenges in turn.

The late Nobel laureate Herbert Simon (1984) was the first to impress upon economists that human beings are incapable of behaving like the rational beings portrayed in standard rational choice models. Simon, a pioneer in the field of artificial intelligence, stumbled upon this realization in the process of trying to instruct a computer to "reason" about a problem. He discovered that when we ourselves confront a puzzle, we rarely reach a solution in a neat, linear fashion. Rather, we search in a haphazard way for potentially relevant facts and information and usually quit once our understanding reaches a certain threshold. Our conclusions are often inconsistent, sometimes even flatly incorrect. But much of the time, we come up with serviceable, if imperfect, solutions. In Simon's terms, we are "**satisficers**," not maximizers. We move on once we feel we've got a solution that is "good enough."

Subsequent economists have taken Simon's lead and developed a very sophisticated literature on decision making under incomplete information. We now realize that when information is costly to gather and cognitive processing ability is limited, it is not even rational to make fully informed choices of the sort portrayed in traditional models. Paradoxically, it is irrational to be completely well informed! When information is costly, the benefit from gathering more of it—from being able to make a very good decision rather than just a good one—may simply not justify the added cost. Thus, the literature on decision making under incomplete information, far from being a challenge to the traditional model, has actually bolstered our confidence in it. (More on these issues in Chapter 12, *The Economics of Information.*)

But there is another offshoot of Simon's work, one that is less friendly to traditional models. This research, which has been strongly influenced by the economist Richard Thaler and the cognitive psychologists Daniel Kahneman and the late Amos Tversky, demonstrates that even with transparently simple problems, people often violate the most fundamental axioms of rational choice. One of the most cherished tenets of the rational choice model, for example, is that wealth is fungible, or freely movable across categories. **Fungibility** implies, among other things, that our total wealth, not the amount we have in any particular account, determines what we buy. But Tversky and Kahneman provided a vivid experimental demonstration to the contrary.[1] They asked one group of people to imagine that, having earlier purchased tickets for $10, they arrive at the theater to discover they have lost them. Members of a second group were asked to picture themselves arriving just before the performance to buy their tickets when they find that they have each lost $10 from their wallets. People in both groups were then asked whether they would continue with their plans to attend the performance. In the rational choice model, the forces governing this decision are exactly the same for both groups. Losing a $10 ticket should have precisely the same effect as losing a $10 bill. And yet, in repeated trials, most people in the lost-ticket group said they would not attend the performance, while an overwhelming majority—88 percent—in the lost-bill group say they would.

Richard Thaler developed a theory of mental accounting to explain this anomaly.[2] He began by noting that people apparently organize their spending into separate "mental accounts" for food, housing, entertainment, general expenses, and so on. People who lose their tickets act as if they debit $10 from their mental entertainment accounts, while those who lose a $10 bill debit that amount from their general expense account. For people in the former group, the loss makes the apparent cost of seeing the show rise from $10 to $20, whereas for those in the second it remains $10. The rational choice model makes clear that the second group's assessment is the correct one. And on reflection, most people do, in fact, agree that losing a ticket is no better reason not to see the performance than losing a $10 bill.

Working with numerous collaborators, Thaler, Kahneman, and Tversky identified a large catalog of systematic departures from rational choice, many of which stem from the

[1]Amos Tversky and Daniel Kahneman, "Judgment under Uncertainty: Heuristics and Biases," *Science* 185 (1974), pp. 1124–1131.
[2]Richard Thaler, "Mental Accounting and Consumer Choice," *Marketing Science* 4, no. 3 (Summer 1985), pp. 199–214.

Carsten Rehder/AFP/Getty Images

application of **judgmental and decision heuristics**, or rules of thumb. Next, we describe some of the heuristics they identified.

JUDGMENTAL HEURISTICS OR RULES OF THUMB

AVAILABILITY

We often estimate the frequency of an event, or class of events, by the ease with which we can summon relevant examples from memory.[3] The more easily we can recall examples, the more likely we judge an event to be. This rule of thumb is called the **availability heuristic**. On balance, it is an effective strategy since it is generally easier to recall examples of things that happen frequently. The problem is that frequency is not the only factor that influences ease of recall. If people are asked, for example, whether there are more murders than suicides in New York State each year, most answer confidently in the affirmative, yet there are always more suicides than murders. Murders are easier to recall not because they are more frequent, but because they are more salient.

EXAMPLE 10.1   Availability Heuristic

Which category of words is more common in the English language: those that begin with "r" or those that have "r" as their third letter?

Using the availability heuristic, most people react by trying to summon examples in each category. And since most people find it easier to think of examples of words starting with "r," the availability heuristic leads them to answer that such words occur more frequently. Yet English words with "r" in the third slot are actually far more numerous. The availability heuristic fails here because frequency isn't the only thing that governs ease of recall. We store words in memory in multiple ways—by their meanings, by the sounds they make, by the images they evoke, by their first letters, and by numerous other features. But virtually no one stores words in memory by the identity of their third letter, which is why words with "r" in that slot are harder to recall.

REPRESENTATIVENESS

Another common rule of thumb is to assume that the likelihood of something belonging to a given category is directly related to the degree to which it shares characteristics thought to be representative of membership in that category.[4] For example, because librarians are stereotypically viewed as introverted while salespersons are viewed as gregarious, the **representativeness heuristic** suggests that a given shy person is more likely to be a librarian than a salesperson. But this reasoning leads us astray when we fail to account for other factors that influence the relevant probabilities. Suppose the popular stereotypes are accurate—that, say, 90 percent of all librarians are shy, as compared with only 20 percent of salespeople. Would it then be safe to conclude that a given shy person is more likely to be a librarian than a salesperson? Not necessarily. Suppose, conservatively, that there are 90 salespeople in the population for every 10 librarians (the true ratio is more than 1,000 to 1). Under the assumed proportions of shy persons in each group, there would then be 9 shy librarians in the population for every 18 shy salespeople. And in that case, any given shy person would actually be twice as likely to be a salesperson than to be a librarian!

---

[3]Amos Tversky and Daniel Kahneman, "The Framing of Decisions and the Psychology of Choice," *Science* 211 (1981), pp. 453–458.
[4]Daniel Kahneman and Amos Tversky, "Subjective Probability: A Judgment of Representativeness," *Cognitive Psychology* 3, no. 3 (1972), pp. 430–454.

EXAMPLE 10.2 Representativeness Heuristic

Only two moving companies, United and North American, provide local delivery service in a small western city. United operates 80 percent of the vans, North American the remaining 20 percent. On a dark and rainy night, a pedestrian is run over and killed by a moving van. The lone witness to the incident testifies that the van was owned by North American. The law states that a company shall be held liable for damages only if it can be shown that the probability that the company was the guilty party is at least half. An independent laboratory hired by the court finds that under dark and rainy conditions, the witness is able to identify the owner of a moving van with 60 percent accuracy. What is the probability that a North American van ran over the pedestrian?

Out of every 100 moving vans in the area, 80 are United's and 20 are North American's. Of the 80 United vans, the witness incorrectly identifies 32 (or 40 percent of them) as belonging to North American. Of the 20 North American trucks, the witness correctly identifies 12 as belonging to North American. Thus the probability that a van identified as North American's actually is North American's is 12/(32 + 12) = 3/11. So North American will not be held liable.

 SELF-TEST 10.1

A witness testifies that the taxicab that struck and injured Smith in a dark alley was green. On investigation, the attorney for Green Taxi Company discovers that the witness identifies the correct color of a taxi in a dark alley 80 percent of the time. There are two taxi companies in town, Green and Blue. Green operates 15 percent of all local taxis. The law says that Green Taxi Company is liable for Smith's injuries if and only if the probability that it caused them is greater than 0.5. Is Green liable?

REGRESSION TO THE MEAN

regression to the mean
the phenomenon that unusual events are likely to be followed by more nearly normal ones

Another common judgment error is to ignore a phenomenon known to statisticians as **regression to the mean**. The idea is that if our first measurement of something is far from its average value, a second measurement will tend to be closer to its average value. Suppose, for example, that you draw a ball from an urn containing balls numbered from 1 to 100 and get a ball numbered 85. Would you then be surprised that if you drew a second ball from that same urn, the number on it would be smaller than 85? Since the urn contains 84 balls with smaller numbers and only 15 with higher ones, it is in fact very likely that your second ball will have a smaller number. Errors often occur when people fail to take this phenomenon into account.

Suppose, for example, that you are a manager choosing whether to adopt a supportive stance toward your employees—by praising them when they perform well—or a critical stance—by criticizing them when they perform poorly. To help you decide, you do an experiment in which you adopt a critical stance toward employees who have performed unusually poorly and a supportive stance toward those who have performed unusually well. On the basis of this experiment, you decide that the critical stance works better. Why might this inference have been misleading?

When you praise an employee, it will often be after that employee has turned in an unusually good performance. Similarly, when you are critical of an employee, it will often be after that employ has performed unusually poorly. Quite apart from any direct effects of praise or blame, subsequent performances in both cases are likely to be more nearly normal. This could lead you to conclude that praise caused worse performance and that criticism caused better performance. Independent experimental work suggests that this conclusion would be erroneous. Supportive management styles, it appears, are more likely than critical styles to bring out the best in employees.

The Economic Naturalist 10.1

Why did the American Olympic swimmer Shirley Babashoff, who set one world record and six national records at the 1976 Olympics, refuse to appear on the cover of *Sports Illustrated*?

AP Images

Invitations to appear on the cover of the magazine typically come, as in Babashoff's case, in the wake of outstanding athletic performances. Many athletes believed that appearing on the cover of *Sports Illustrated* made them subject to the *Sports Illustrated* jinx, which doomed them to subpar performance during the ensuing months. But this perception was a statistical illusion. As the psychologist Tom Gilovich explained, "It does not take much statistical sophistication to see how regression effects may be responsible for the belief in the *Sports Illustrated* jinx. Athletes' performances at different times are imperfectly correlated. Thus, due to regression alone, we can expect an extraordinary good performance to be followed, on the average, by a somewhat less extraordinary performance. Athletes appear on the cover of *Sports Illustrated* when they are newsworthy—i.e., when their performance is extraordinary. Thus, an athlete's superior performance in the weeks preceding a cover story is very likely to be followed by somewhat poorer performance in the weeks after. Those who believe in the jinx . . . are mistaken, not in what they observe, but in how they interpret what they see. Many athletes do suffer deterioration in their performance after being pictured on the cover of *Sports Illustrated*, and the mistake lies in citing a jinx, rather than citing regression as the proper interpretation of this phenomenon."[5]

 SELF-TEST 10.2

Following an unusual increase in burglaries in a New York City neighborhood, the chief of police assigned additional officers to patrol the neighborhood. In the following month, the number of burglaries declined significantly. Does this mean the increased patrols were effective?

ANCHORING AND ADJUSTMENT

Another common judgmental heuristic is called **anchoring and adjustment**. It holds that when we try to estimate something, we often begin with a tentative initial estimate, called the anchor, which we then adjust in the light of whatever additional information is available. A common bias pattern observed in anchoring and adjustment is that the anchors are sometimes of questionable relevance, and the adjustments people make are often insufficient.

Suppose, for example, that a professor who stands 6′4″ asks his students to estimate his height. They may often anchor on the average height for men—about 5′10″ in the United States—and then adjust that value upward because their visual assessment indicates

anchoring and adjustment an estimation technique that begins with an initial approximation (the anchor), which is then modified in accordance with additional available information (the adjustment)

[5]Thomas Gilovich, *How We Know What Isn't So: The Fallibility of Human Reason in Everyday Life* (New York: Free Press, 1991).

that their professor is significantly taller than average. Typically, however, their adjustments will fall short. In most cases, the average of their estimates of the professor's height in this example will be two or three inches shorter than his actual height.

A particularly vivid example of this potential bias comes from an experiment in which American students were asked to estimate the percentage of African countries belonging to the United Nations. Most had no idea what the true percentage was. Before even hearing the question, subjects in two groups were asked to perform the ostensibly unrelated task of spinning a wheel that could stop on any number from 1 to 100. In the first group, the wheel was rigged to stop on 65, while in the second it was rigged to stop on 10. Students in both groups surely knew that the number on which the spinning wheel stopped bore no relation to the true percentage of African nations in the UN. Yet the average estimate of the group whose wheel stopped on 65 was 45 percent, while the average estimate of the group whose wheel stopped on 10 was only 25.[6]

> **RECAP ↑**
>
> **JUDGMENTAL HEURISTICS AND RULES OF THUMB**
>
> According to the *availability heuristic*, we often estimate the frequency of an event by the ease with which we can recall relevant examples. Errors often result because frequency is only imperfectly correlated with ease of recall.
>
> The *representative heuristic* holds that the likelihood of something belonging to a given category is directly related to the degree to which it resembles stereotypical members of that category. Here, too, errors often result because other factors also influence the relevant probabilities.
>
> The tendency to ignore *regression to the mean*—the idea that extreme events are likely to be followed by more nearly normal ones—is yet another source of judgmental errors.
>
> *Anchoring and adjustment* holds that when we try to estimate something, we often begin with a tentative anchor, which we then adjust in the light of additional information. The anchors that people employ are often of questionable relevance, and the corresponding adjustments are often insufficient.

MISINTERPRETATION OF CONTEXTUAL CLUES

Another important class of judgment errors stems from misinterpretation of common contextual cues.

THE PSYCHOPHYSICS OF PERCEPTION

As psychologists have long understood, our assessments are almost always heavily shaped by the local environmental context. Consider a couple driving with their 10-year-old daughter to visit her grandparents. They are 10 miles from their destination when she asks, "Are we almost there yet?" If those 10 miles remain on a 120-mile journey, her parents will reassure her that they're nearly there. But if the same 10 miles remain on a 12-mile journey they will answer differently: "No, honey, we've still got quite a way to go." Similarly, in the year 1920, if your car could reach a speed of 60 miles per hour eventually, it would have seemed blazingly fast. But unless a car could reach 60 mph in under 6 seconds today, many motorists would think it sluggish.

Every assessment of this sort rests on an explicit or implicit frame of reference. According to a relationship known as the **Weber-Fechner law** of psychophysics, our

Weber-Fechner law the relationship according to which the perceived change in any stimulus varies according to the size of the change measured as a proportion of the original stimulus

---

[6]Amos Tversky and Daniel Kahneman, "Judgment under Uncertainty: Heuristics and Biases," *Science* 185 (1974), pp. 1124–1131.

perception of the change in any stimulus varies according to the size of the change measured as a proportion of the original stimulus. In some contexts, there is nothing problematic about reckoning importance in proportional terms. But in other contexts, it can lead us astray. Real estate developers, for example, often exploit people's tendency to think in percentage terms by bundling additional features into the prices of their houses for sale. Buyers might be reluctant to spend $5,000 for a jacuzzi for a house they already owned, but might see the same expense as far less daunting if it meant paying $250,000 for a new house instead of $245,000.[7]

THE DIFFICULTY OF ACTUALLY DECIDING

In the tale of Buridan's ass, a starving donkey stands equidistant from two identical bales of hay. But because his attraction to each bale is exactly equal, he is unable to decide which bale to approach and therefore dies of hunger. Although it is difficult to imagine such indecision causing a human to die of hunger, the fact remains that many people experience significant anxiety when forced to decide between two options that are roughly equally attractive. If the options were, in fact, equally attractive, it would of course not matter which one was chosen. But the anxiety some people experience in such situations leads them to violate basic predictions of traditional economic models.

Suppose you were faced with a choice between the two apartments labeled A and B in Figure 10.1. The attraction of A is that it's close to campus, but the downside is that its rent is fairly high. In contrast, B's rent is much more reasonable, but unfortunately it happens to be much farther from campus. By suitable manipulation of the rent/distance values, it should be possible to describe pairs of apartments like A and B such that a given individual would be essentially indifferent between them. The interesting thing, however, is that this doesn't mean that she would find it easy to choose. On the contrary, many people experience significant anxiety when confronted with such choices.

Now suppose we gather a large group of subjects and manipulate the distance/rent values of A and B so that when forced to choose, half the subjects choose A and the remaining half choose B. What do you think would have happened if we had asked that same group of subjects to choose among three apartments—the same A and B as before plus a new option at C, as shown in Figure 10.2. According to traditional rational choice theory, the apartment at C is an irrelevant option, since it is worse along both dimensions than B. And, in fact, when C is added to the set of options, no one chooses it.

Yet the presence of the option at C has a profound effect on the observed pattern of choices between A and B. This time many more subjects choose B, and many fewer choose A.[8] The apparent explanation of the shift is that subjects find it easy to choose B over C, and that invests option B with a halo that leads subjects to favor it when confronted with the anxiety-inducing choice between A and B.

Experienced salespersons may exploit this pattern when dealing with people who have difficulty choosing among hard-to-compare alternatives. To close the deal, it may be enough to expose the client to a new option that is worse along every dimension than one of the original options.

As the preceding examples illustrate, cognitive errors often lead to departures from the predictions of standard rational choice models. We call such examples "departures from rational choice with regret," the idea being that once people are made aware of the cognitive errors they have made, they seem motivated to avoid those errors in the future.

Many proponents of traditional economic models appear reluctant to amend those models to take account of systematic cognitive errors. Some argue, for example, that in competitive environments, the penalties associated with such errors will reduce their frequency, enabling us to safely neglect them. Yet the mere fact that people make

FIGURE 10.1

The Trade-Off between Rent and Convenience

FIGURE 10.2

An Irrelevant Alternative

▶ Visit your instructor's Connect course and access your eBook to view this video.

Why do real estate agents often show clients two nearly identical houses, even though one is both cheaper and in better condition than the other?

---

[7]For more examples along similar lines, see Richard Thaler, "Toward a Positive Theory of Consumer Choice," *Journal of Economic Behavior and Organization* 1 (1980), pp. 39–60.
[8]Amos Tversky and Itamar Simonson, "Context-Dependent Preferences," *Management Science* 39, no. 10 (October 1993), pp. 1179–1189.

systematic cognitive errors does not imply that reliance on heuristics is maladaptive in any global sense. The important question is whether following some alternative strategy would lead to better results on average. Rules like the availability heuristic are extremely easy to apply and work well much of the time. The costs of an occasional wrong decision must be weighed against the obvious advantages of reliance on simple decision and judgment rules.

In any event, there is clear evidence that systematic cognitive errors exist and are widespread. Absent clear evidence that reliance on heuristics is a losing strategy on balance, there is a strong methodological case for taking explicit account of cognitive errors in descriptive models of individual behavior. A plausible case can also be made that by becoming more aware of the circumstances that are likely to elicit cognitive errors, we can learn to commit those errors less frequently.

> ### RECAP ↑
>
> #### MISINTERPRETATION OF CONTEXTUAL CLUES
>
> Almost every human judgment requires an explicit or implicit frame of reference. The *Weber-Fechner law* holds that perceptions of the change in any stimulus vary according to the size of the change as a proportion of the original stimulus. This reckoning leads many to say, for example, that they would drive across town to save $10 on a $20 radio but not to save $10 on a $1,000 computer. Yet if the benefit of driving across town exceeds the cost of driving across town for the radio, the same must be true for the computer (since the benefit is $10 in both cases and the cost of driving is the same in both cases).
>
> Other choice anomalies arise because people often have difficulty choosing between two alternatives whose characteristics are difficult to compare. When confronted by such choices, the addition of a third alternative that is worse than the first of the original alternatives on every dimension often has the effect of tilting choice heavily in favor of the first alternative. According to traditional models, the addition of such an alternative should have no effect on the choice between the other two.

IMPULSE-CONTROL PROBLEMS

Another troubling feature of traditional economic models is that they appear to rule out the possibility that people might regret having chosen behaviors whose consequences were perfectly predictable at the outset. Yet such expressions of regret are common. Many people wake up wishing they had drunk less the night before, but few wake up wishing they had drunk more.

It is likewise a puzzle within traditional economic models that people often incur great expense and inconvenience to prevent behaviors they would otherwise freely choose. For example, the model has difficulty explaining why some people would pay thousands of dollars to attend weight-loss camps that will feed them only 1,500 calories per day.

Welfare analysis based on the traditional models assigns considerable importance, as it should, to people's own judgments about what makes them better off. In this framework, it is not clear how one could ever conclude that a risk freely chosen by a well-informed person was a wrong choice. By itself, the fact that the choice led to a bad outcome is clearly not decisive. If someone is unlucky enough to be killed crossing the street, for example, we would not conclude that crossing streets is a generally bad idea.

Compelling evidence from psychology suggests, however, that expressions of regret may often be genuine, that people might sensibly impose constraints on their own behavior, and that risks freely chosen by well-informed people may not be optimal from their own point of view. Much of this evidence concerns behavior in the realm of intertemporal choice.

The rational choice model says that people will discount future costs and benefits in such a way that the choice between two rewards that are separated by a fixed time interval will be the same no matter when the choice is made.[9] Consider, for example, the pair of choices A and B:

A: $100 tomorrow vs. $110 a week from tomorrow.
B: $100 after 52 weeks vs. $110 after 53 weeks.

Both pairs of rewards are separated by exactly one week. If future receipts are discounted as assumed in traditional models, people will always make the same choice under alternative A as they do under alternative B. Since the larger payoff comes a week later in each case, the cost of choosing the smaller, but earlier, payoff is the same in each case—namely, the $10 forgone by doing so. When people confront such choices in practice, however, there is a pronounced tendency to choose differently under the two scenarios: Most pick the $100 option in A, whereas most choose the $110 option in B.

Researchers who have studied intertemporal choices experimentally have amassed substantial evidence that perceived future costs and benefits fall much more sharply with delay than assumed in traditional models.[10] One consequence is that preference reversals of the kind just observed occur frequently. The classic reversal involves choosing the larger, later reward when both alternatives occur with substantial delay, then switching to the smaller, earlier reward when its availability becomes imminent. This reversal shows up in The Economic Naturalist 10.2.

The Economic Naturalist 10.2

Why would people pay thousands of dollars to attend a weight-loss camp that will feed them only 1,500 calories per day?

Viewed within the framework of conventional rational choice models, it would be puzzling indeed that people would spend large sums to be prevented from eating food that they were free to refrain from eating on their own. But if people tend to discount future costs and benefits sharply, the answer is clear: They really want to eat less, but they know that if tempting foods are readily available, they will lack the willpower to do so. The weight-loss camp solves this problem by making tempting foods less available.

The tendency to discount future costs and benefits excessively gives rise to a variety of familiar impulse-control problems and, in turn, to a variety of strategies for solving them. Anticipating their temptation to overeat, people often try to limit the quantities of sweets, salted nuts, and other delicacies they keep on hand. Anticipating their temptation to spend cash in their checking accounts, people enroll in payroll-deduction savings plans. Foreseeing the difficulty of putting down a good mystery novel in midstream, many people know better than to start one on the evening before an important meeting. Reformed

---

[9]This is known as "exponential discounting."
[10]According to psychologists, people tend to discount future costs and benefits hyperbolically, not exponentially. Two of the most important earlier papers on this issue are Shin-Ho Chung and Richard Herrnstein, "Choice and Delay of Reinforcement," *Journal of the Experimental Analysis of Behavior* 10 (1967), pp. 67–74; George Ainslie, "Specious Reward: A Behavioral Theory of Impulsiveness and Impulse Control," *Psychological Bulletin* 82 (July 1975), pp. 463–496. See also Jon Elster, "Don't Burn Your Bridge before You Come to It: Seven Types of Ambiguity in Precommitment," Texas Law Review Symposium on Precommitment Theory, Bioethics, and Constitutional Law, September 2002; Thomas Schelling, "The Intimate Contest for Self-Command," *The Public Interest,* Summer 1980, pp. 94–118; R. Thaler and H. Shefrin, "An Economic Theory of Self-Control," *Journal of Political Economy* 89 (1981), pp. 392–405; Gordon Winston, "Addiction and Backsliding: A Theory of Compulsive Consumption," *Journal of Economic Behavior and Organization* 1 (1980), pp. 295–394. For a comprehensive review of work discussing the economic applications of the hyperbolic discounting model, see Shane Frederick, George Loewenstein, and Ted O'Donoghue, "Time Discounting and Time Preference: A Critical Review," *Journal of Economic Literature* 40, no. 2 (June 2002), pp. 351–401.

smokers seek the company of nonsmokers when they first try to kick the habit and are more likely than others to favor laws that limit smoking in public places. The recovering alcoholic avoids cocktail lounges.

Effective as these bootstrap methods of self-control may often be, they are far from perfect. Many people continue to express regret about having overeaten, having drunk and smoked too much, having saved too little, having stayed up too late, having watched too much television, and so on. Traditional economic models urge us to dismiss these expressions as sour grapes. But behavioral evidence suggests that these same expressions are often coherent. In each case, the actor chose an inferior option when a better one was available and later feels genuinely sorry about it. As with behaviors that stem from systematic cognitive errors, those that stem from impulse-control problems may be described as "departures from rational choice with regret."

In view of the obvious difficulties to which excessive discounting gives rise, it might seem puzzling that this particular feature of human motivation is so widespread. As with cognitive errors that stem from reliance on judgmental heuristics, however, here too it is important to stress that a behavioral tendency leading to bad outcomes some of the time does not imply that it is maladaptive in a global sense. Heavy discounting of future events forcefully directs our attention to immediate costs and benefits. If forced to choose between a motivational structure that gave heavy weight to current payoffs and an alternative that gave relatively greater weight to future payoffs, it is easy to imagine why evolutionary forces might have favored the former. After all, in highly competitive and uncertain environments, immediate threats to survival were numerous, and there must always have been compelling advantages in directing most of our energies toward meeting them.

In any case, there is clear evidence here, too, that excessive discounting exists and is widespread. Whether or not this motivational structure is disadvantageous on balance, there is a persuasive case for taking explicit account of it if our aim is to predict how people will behave under real-world conditions.

We also note that societies around the world have adopted a variety of policies that are most easily understood as attempts to mitigate the consequences of impulse-control problems. These include the treatment of so-called crimes of passion; prohibitions against gambling, addictive drugs, and prostitution; entrapment laws; and sanctions against adultery. Programs that aim to stimulate savings can also be viewed as a response to impulse-control problems that make it difficult to execute rational savings plans.

RECAP

IMPULSE-CONTROL PROBLEMS

Although many traditional economic models rule out the possibility that people might regret having chosen behaviors whose consequences were perfectly predictable, such regrets are common.

Compelling evidence from psychology suggests that expressions of regret may often be genuine, that people often have difficulty waiting for a larger, better reward when an inferior reward is available immediately. Traditional models also have difficulty explaining why people might pay large sums to attend a weight-loss camp that will dramatically constrain their daily caloric intake. But if people tend to discount future costs and benefits excessively, they know that if tempting foods are readily available, they may lack the willpower to avoid them. Without taking explicit account of self-control problems, it is difficult to predict how people will behave under real-world conditions.

Some of the most important developments in economics in recent decades have entailed revisions to traditional assumptions about the nature of people's preferences. We focus next on three major changes—the introduction of asymmetries in the way people evaluate alternatives involving gains and losses, the relaxation of the assumption that people are self-interested in the narrow sense, and the introduction of concerns about relative position.

LOSS AVERSION AND STATUS QUO BIAS ——————

Traditional economic models hold that the extra satisfaction from gaining a dollar should be roughly equal to the reduction in satisfaction from losing a dollar. In practice, however, people's behavior suggests that losses often weigh much more heavily than gains.

An illustration of this tendency comes in the form of experiments designed to probe the difference in the value people assign to an object they already own versus the value they assign to one they have an opportunity to buy. In one experiment involving 44 subjects, half of participants were chosen at random to receive a coffee mug that they were free to keep or sell as they chose. The other half of the participants did not receive a mug. Participants were then given an opportunity to examine the mugs carefully—their own if they'd been given one, a neighboring subject's if they hadn't.

Subjects were then told to submit bids reflecting how much they'd be willing to pay for a mug if they didn't already have one or how much they'd be willing to accept for selling the mug they already had. In repeated rounds of this experiment, researchers used these bids to determine the prices at which the number of mugs offered would be equal to the number of mugs demanded. Those equilibrium prices varied between $4.25 and $4.75.

The researchers used the term *mug lovers* to describe the half of all subjects who happened to like the mugs most among all participants and *mug haters* to describe those who liked the mugs least. The fact that the mugs had been distributed at random implied that half of them, on average, would have ended up in the hands of mug lovers and the other half in the hands of mug haters. Thus, the apparent prediction of traditional economic models was that approximately half of the mugs—which is to say, 11 mugs on average—should be exchanged at the market-clearing prices. But the actual number of observed trades was dramatically smaller—only slightly more than two mugs changed hands, on average.

The apparent explanation was that the mere fact of owning a mug caused people to assign much greater value to it. The median price at which mug owners were willing to sell their mugs was $5.25, for example, more than twice the amount the median non-owner was willing to pay.[11]

This asymmetry in valuations is often called **loss aversion**. Similar experiments involving the exchange of modestly priced objects suggest that someone who possesses an object values it about twice as high, on average, as someone who does not possess it.

But there is evidence that when the things at stake are significantly more important, loss aversion becomes even more pronounced. In another experiment by Richard Thaler, subjects were asked to imagine that there was a 1 in 1,000 chance they had been exposed to an invariably fatal disease.[12] How much would they be willing to pay for the only available dose of an antidote that would save their lives? Their median response to this question was $2,000. A second group of subjects was asked how much they would have to be paid to be willing to volunteer to be exposed to that same disease if there was no available antidote. This time the median response was close to $500,000—more than 250 times higher than in the first case.

Note that in both cases, subjects are being asked how much they value a one-in-a-thousand reduction in their probability of dying. If people treated gains and losses symmetrically, their answers to the two questions would be roughly the same. But in the first case, they were being asked to buy an increase in their survival prospects (a gain), and in the second case, they were asked to sell a health benefit they already owned (a loss). People do not treat gains and losses symmetrically, and it appears that loss aversion becomes much more pronounced when the objects in question are more important.

Because every change in policy generates winners and losers, loss aversion has important implications for public policy. When the total benefits from a change in policy exceed the total cost, it will sometimes be practical for the winners to compensate the losers so that everyone comes out ahead. But when large numbers of people are involved, compensation often becomes impractical. And in such cases, resistance from those who stand to lose from the policy change often overwhelms the support of those who stand to gain,

loss aversion the tendency to experience losses as more painful than the pleasures that result from gains of the same magnitude

[11]Daniel Kahneman, Jack L. Knetsch, and Richard H. Thaler, "Anomalies: The Endowment Effect, Loss Aversion, and Status Quo Bias," *The Journal of Economic Perspectives* 5, no. 1 (Winter 1991), pp. 193–206.
[12]Michael Lewis, "The Economist Who Realized How Crazy We Are," *Bloomberg View,* May 29, 2015.

status quo bias the general resistance to change, often stemming from *loss aversion*

even when the total benefits substantially exceed the total costs. Loss aversion is thus an important source of what has been called **status quo bias** in the domain of public policy. The difficulty of enacting policy changes is encapsulated in the fabled *iron law of politics*: The losers always cry louder than the winners sing.

Is status quo bias a bad thing? It might seem reasonable to wonder whether the best posture for cost-benefit analysts might be to simply accept at face value the inflated weights that people assign to losses. In other words, perhaps the widespread resistance to change that we observe in practice should be interpreted to mean that change often does more harm than good.

Weighing against this interpretation, however, is evidence that people's initial estimates of how painful losses will be often fail to take into account the remarkable human tendency to adapt to altered circumstances. Many people say, for example, that they would prefer to be killed in an accident than to survive as a paraplegic. And most people who have become paralyzed have indeed experienced the transition as devastating. But what psychologists were surprised to discover was that paraplegics adapt more quickly and completely than they ever would have thought possible. According to one study, the post-accident happiness levels of paralyzed accident victims were significantly lower than they had been before their accidents but not statistically different from those of a control group.[13] Parting with a possession, similarly, is likely to be far more aversive at first than it is after a period of adaptation to living without it.

There are thus reasonable grounds for believing that steps to counteract status quo bias will often serve community interests. Behavioral economists have begun to explore such steps. One effective way to mitigate status quo bias is to focus more carefully on how different alternatives are presented to people. Suppose, for example, that policymakers want to encourage citizens to save a larger proportion of their incomes. Researchers have discovered that an effective and relatively painless way to accomplish that goal is to make participation in employer payroll-deduction savings the default option. Historically, most employers required their employees to take an active step in setting up a payroll-deduction savings plan. But researchers persuaded a sample of firms to make enrollment in the plan automatic, allowing those who didn't want to participate to take the active step of opting out. An influential study by Brigitte Madrian and Dennis Shea found that when participation became the status quo, savings plan enrollments shot up dramatically—in one case, a jump from less than 50 percent participation to 86 percent of all first-year employees.[14] Similar experiments have demonstrated the power of default options to alter behavior in other domains, ranging from the kinds of insurance people buy to their willingness to be organ donors.

The Economic Naturalist 10.3

Why was Obamacare difficult to enact and harder still to repeal?

The Obama administration's strategy for reforming the American health care system was heavily shaped by its understanding of status quo bias. Most other developed countries guarantee universal health care coverage either by having the government hire health care providers directly (as in the UK) or by having the government reimburse private health care providers for their services (as in France and Canada). But in the United States, most people received health insurance provided by their employers. Although there are sound policy reasons to favor the approach used elsewhere (where health systems deliver care at about half the cost as in the United States), government officials realized that many citizens had grown accustomed to employer-sponsored insurance and would

[13]Philip Brinkman, Dan Coates, and Ronnie Janoff-Bulman, "Lottery Winners and Accident Victims: Is Happiness Relative?" *Journal of Personality and Social Psychology* 36, no. 8 (1978), pp. 917–927.
[14]Brigitte C. Madrian and Dennis F. Shea, "The Power of Suggestion: Inertia in 401(k) Participation and Savings Behavior," *Quarterly Journal of Economics* 116, no. 4 (2001), pp. 1149–1187.

resist attempts to require them to abandon it for a different approach. So the Affordable Care Act as passed in 2010 left the employer-provided insurance system intact, supplementing it with private market exchanges through which people without employer-provided insurance could purchase health insurance at affordable rates. Despite this compromise, the legislative effort to enact the Affordable Care Act was extremely contentious, and it passed by the slimmest of margins.

Once the act was implemented, it came under relentless attack from Republicans in the House of Representatives, who voted scores of times to repeal it. But to the surprise of no one familiar with loss aversion and status quo bias, these efforts also met stiff resistance. Obamacare had boosted the number of Americans with health insurance by more than 20 million, and estimates by the nonpartisan Congressional Budget Office suggested that repeal would reduce that number by a similar amount.

In short, once the Affordable Care Act was enacted into law, the conditions it brought about became the new status quo. So even as loss aversion helps explain why passage of the Affordable Care Act was so difficult in the first place, it also explains why it was so difficult to repeal once it became law.

RECAP

LOSS AVERSION AND STATUS QUO BIAS

Widespread behavioral evidence suggests that people tend to weigh losses much more heavily than gains. The minimum price for which people would be willing to sell objects they already own is substantially higher than the price they would be willing to pay to acquire those same objects if they do not already own them.

This asymmetry is often called *loss aversion*. In experiments involving low-priced items, the difference between willingness to accept and willingness to pay is often on the order of two to one. But the ratio can be dramatically higher for high-valued items, such as conditions related to health and safety.

Because every change in policy generates winners and losers, loss aversion implies a large bias in favor of the status quo in public policy decisions. Evidence suggests that this bias often has harmful consequences since people's initial estimates of how painful losses will be often fail to take into account their ability to adapt to altered circumstances.

The strategic use of default options has proven to be an effective way to mitigate *status quo bias*. For example, making participation in employer payroll-deduction savings plans the default option has been shown to significantly reduce the tendency to save too little.

BEYOND NARROW SELF-INTEREST

Most traditional economic models exclude other-regarding motives. They concede, for example, that homo economicus might volunteer in a United Way campaign in order to reap the benefits of an expanded network of business or social contacts, but insist that he would never make anonymous donations to charity. Yet charitable donations, many of them completely anonymous, totaled more than $425 billion a year in the United States in 2018.[15] Traditional models acknowledge that homo economicus might tip in a local restaurant to ensure good

[15] https://givingusa.org/giving-usa-2019-americans-gave-427-71-billion-to-charity-in-2018-amid-complex-year-for-charitable-giving.

service on his next visit, but predict that he would not tip when dining alone in a restaurant far from home. Yet tipping rates are essentially the same in these two situations.[16] Traditional models also concede that homo economicus might go to the polls in a local ward election, in which a single vote might be decisive, but predict universal abstention in presidential elections. Yet tens of millions of people regularly vote in presidential elections. In short, traditional self-interest models are simple and elegant, but they also predict incorrectly much of the time.

THE PRESENT-AIM STANDARD OF RATIONALITY

The most widely employed alternative to the self-interest model is the present-aim model, which holds that people are efficient in the pursuit of whatever objectives they happen to hold at the moment of action.[17] The obvious appeal of the present-aim model is that it enables us to accommodate the plurality of goals that many people actually seem to hold, thus permitting us to account for behaviors that are anomalous within the self-interest framework. Someone donates anonymously to charity not because she hopes to receive indirect material benefits, but because she gets a warm glow from helping others in need. Someone tips in a restaurant away from home not to ensure good service on his next visit, but because he feels sympathy for the server's interests. Someone votes in a presidential election not because his vote might tip the balance, but because he feels it is his civic duty to do so. And so on.

But the present-aim model's flexibility also turns out to be a significant liability. The problem is that virtually any bizarre behavior can be "explained" after the fact simply by assuming a sufficiently strong taste for it. We call this the "crankcase-oil problem": If someone drinks a gallon of used crankcase oil from his car, then writhes in agony and dies, a present-aim theorist has a ready explanation—the man must have *really* liked crankcase oil. Proponents of traditional models thus have sound reasons for their methodological skepticism about the present-aim model. As they correctly point out, a model that can explain virtually everything is not really a scientific model at all.

We are confronted, then, with a choice between two flawed alternatives. The self-interest standard of rationality generates testable predictions about behavior, but these predictions often turn out to be flatly incorrect. The **present-aim standard of rationality** accommodates a much broader range of observed behavior but remains vulnerable to the charge of excessive flexibility. In addition to these two, we consider a third standard, one that is significantly more flexible than the self-interest standard, but also one whose flexibility sidesteps the most serious objections to the present-aim standard.

THE ADAPTIVE RATIONALITY STANDARD[18]

Like both the self-interest and present-aim standards, the **adaptive rationality standard** assumes that people choose efficient means to achieve their ends. But unlike the other conceptions, which take goals as given, adaptive rationality regards goals as objects of choice themselves and, as such, subject to a similar efficiency requirement.

By what criterion might we evaluate the efficiency of an individual's choice of goals? Since the problem that plagues the present-aim standard is excessive flexibility, the efficiency standard we employ for evaluating alternatives to this model should be both objective and strict. On both counts, Charles Darwin's theory of natural selection, enriched to allow for the influence of cultural and other environmental forces during development, is an attractive candidate. In this framework, the design criterion for a goal or taste is the same as for an arm or a leg or an eye—namely, the extent to which it assists the individual in the struggle to acquire the resources required for survival and reproduction. If it works better than the available alternatives, selection pressure will favor it. Otherwise,

present-aim standard of rationality a variant of the rational choice model that permits greater flexibility in assumptions about preferences

adaptive rationality standard a variant of the rational choice model that permits additional preferences to be added if they can be shown not to handicap resource acquisition in competitive environments

---

[16]O. Bodvarsson and W. Gibson, "Gratuities and Customer Appraisal of Service: Evidence from Minnesota Restaurants," *Journal of Socio-Economics* 23, no. 3 (1994), pp. 287–302.
[17]Derek Parfit, *Reasons and Persons* (Oxford: Clarendon Press, 1984).
[18]The discussion that follows draws heavily on Robert H. Frank, "If *Homo Economicus* Could Choose His Own Utility Function, Would He Want One with a Conscience?" *American Economic Review* 77 (September 1987), pp. 593–604; Robert H. Frank, *Passions within Reason* (New York: Norton, 1988).

selection pressure will work against it. Our proposal, in brief, is that analysts be free to add a preference to the individual's list of concerns, but only upon showing that an individual motivated by that preference need not be handicapped in the competition to acquire the resources needed for survival and reproduction.

This standard passes the simple test of ruling out a taste for drinking crankcase oil. Indeed, it might seem such a stringent standard as to rule out any conception of rationality other than narrow self-interest. After all, if natural selection favors the traits and behaviors that maximize individual reproductive fitness, and if we *define* behaviors that enhance personal fitness as selfish, then self-interest becomes the only viable human motive by definition. This tautology was a central message of much of the sociobiological literature of the 1970s and 1980s.

On a closer look, however, the issues are less simple. For there are many situations in which individuals whose only goal is self-interest are likely to fare worse than others who pursue a richer mix of goals. Such is the case, for example, when individuals confront commitment problems, of which the one-shot prisoner's dilemma, discussed in Chapter 9, *Games and Strategic Behavior*, provides a clear illustration. If both players in this game cooperate, each does better than if both defect, and yet each gets a higher payoff by defecting no matter which strategy the other player chooses. If both players could commit themselves to a strategy of mutual cooperation, they would have a clear incentive to do so. Yet mere promises issued by narrowly self-interested persons would not seem to suffice, for each person would have no incentive to keep such a promise.

Suppose, however, that some people have a (perhaps context-specific) taste for cooperating in one-shot prisoner's dilemmas. If two players knew one another to have this taste, they could interact selectively, thereby reaping the gains of mutual cooperation. It is important to stress that merely having the taste is by itself insufficient to solve the problem. One must also be able to communicate its presence credibly to others and be able to identify its presence in them.

Can the presence of a taste for cooperation be reliably discerned by outsiders? Some experiments suggest that subjects are surprisingly accurate at predicting who would cooperate and who would defect in one-shot prisoner's dilemmas played with near strangers.[19] In these experiments, the base rate of cooperation was 73.7 percent and the base rate of defection only 26.3 percent. If subjects randomly guessed that a player would cooperate, they would thus have been accurate 73.7 percent of the time and a random prediction of defection accurate only 26.3 percent of the time. The actual accuracy rates for these two kinds of prediction were 80.7 percent and 56.8 percent, respectively. The likelihood of such high accuracy rates occurring by chance is less than 1 in 1,000.

Subjects in this experiment were strangers at the outset and were able to interact with one another for only 30 minutes before making their predictions. It is plausible to suppose that predictions would be considerably more accurate for people we have known for a long time.

For example, consider a thought experiment based on the following scenario:

> An individual has a gallon jug of unwanted pesticide. To protect the environment, the law requires that unused pesticide be turned in to a government disposal facility located 30 minutes' drive from her home. She knows, however, that she could simply pour the pesticide down her basement drain with no chance of being caught and punished. She also knows that her one gallon of pesticide, by itself, will cause only negligible harm to her if disposed of in this fashion. (But the harm would of course be far from negligible if everyone disposed of unwanted pesticide in this way.)

Can you think of anyone who you feel certain would dispose of the pesticide properly? Most people say they can. Usually they have in mind friends they have known for a long

---

[19]Robert H. Frank, Thomas Gilovich, and Dennis Regan, "The Evolution of One-Shot Cooperation," *Ethology and Sociobiology* 14 (July 1993), pp. 247–256.

time. If you feel you can identify such a person, then you, too, accept the central premise of the adaptive rationality account—namely, that it is possible to identify unselfish motives in at least some other people.

The presence of such motives, coupled with the ability of outsiders to discern them, makes it possible to solve a broad range of important commitment problems. Knowing this, even a rational, self-interested individual would have every reason to choose preferences that were not narrowly self-interested. Of course, people do not choose their preferences in any literal sense. The point is that if moral sentiments can be reliably discerned by others, then the complex interaction of genes and culture that yields human preferences can sustain preferences that lead people to subordinate narrow self-interest to the pursuit of other goals.

For example, although homo economicus might want to deter a potential aggressor by threatening to retaliate, his threat would not be credible if the cost of retaliation exceeded the value of what he stood to recover. By contrast, someone known to care strongly about honor for its own sake could credibly threaten to retaliate even in such cases. Such a person would thus be much less vulnerable to aggression than someone believed to be narrowly self-interested.

Similarly, although homo economicus might want to deter a one-sided offer from a potential trading partner by threatening to reject it, his threat would not be credible if his incentives clearly favored accepting the offer. By contrast, someone known to care strongly about equity for its own sake could credibly threaten to refuse such offers. Such a person would thus be a more effective bargainer than someone believed to be narrowly self-interested.

A second potential pathway whereby moral sentiments might be adaptive at the individual level is by helping people solve a variety of impulse-control problems.[20] Consider, for example, the repeated prisoner's dilemma. As Rapoport, Axelrod, and others have shown, the tit-for-tat strategy fares well against alternative strategies in the repeated prisoner's dilemma.[21] Self-interested persons thus have good reasons to play tit-for-tat, yet to do so they must first solve an impulse-control problem. Playing tit-for-tat means cooperating on the first interaction, which in turn implies a lower payoff on that move than could have been had by defecting. The reward for playing tit-for-tat lies in the prospect of a string of mutually beneficial interactions in the future. The rational choice model holds that if the benefits of future cooperation, suitably discounted, outweigh the current costs, people will cooperate. But because the gain from defecting comes now, whereas its cost comes in the future, the decision maker confronts a classic impulse-control problem. (For more information on game theory, see Chapter 9, *Games and Strategic Behavior.*)

The moral sentiment of sympathy, which figured so prominently in Adam Smith's early writings, helps to solve this problem. Someone who feels sympathy for the interests of her trading partner faces an additional cost of defecting, one that occurs at the same time as the gain from defecting. Because of this cost, the person who sympathizes with her trading partners is less likely to defect and is thus more likely to reap the long-run gains of cooperation.

Moral sentiments and other non-self-interested motives figure prominently in economic and social life. Traditional economic models often ignore such motives, implicitly viewing the behaviors they provoke as irrational. But it is more descriptive to call them "departures from traditional rational choice models without regret" because, when people are told that they are behaving irrationally under the self-interest standard, they typically do not seem to want to alter their behavior. The attraction of the adaptive rationality standard is that it provides a methodologically rigorous framework within which to expand the narrow range of motives considered in traditional models. In the same fashion, it provides a coherent framework within which to take explicit account of systematic cognitive errors and impulse-control problems.

[20]Robert H. Frank, *Passions within Reason* (New York: Norton, 1988).
[21]In tit-for-tat, each player cooperates on the first move, and on each successive move does whatever her partner did on the previous move. See Anatol Rapoport and A. Chammah, *Prisoner's Dilemma* (Ann Arbor: University of Michigan Press, 1965); Robert Axelrod, *The Evolution of Cooperation* (New York: Basic Books, 1984).

CONCERNS ABOUT FAIRNESS

Additional evidence for the claim that narrow self-interest is not the only important human motive comes from an elegant experiment known as the **ultimatum bargaining game**.[22] The game is played by two players, "Proposer" and "Responder." It begins with Proposer being given a sum of money (say, $100) that he must then propose how to divide between himself and Responder. Responder then has two options: (1) he can accept, in which case each party gets the amount proposed, or (2) he can refuse, in which each party gets zero and the $100 goes back to the experimenter.

If both players cared only about their own absolute incomes, as assumed by economic orthodoxy, Proposer should propose $99 for himself and $1 for Responder (only whole-dollar amounts are allowed). And Responder will then accept this one-sided offer because he will reason that getting $1 is better than nothing.

Yet in scores of experiments performed in many different countries, this is almost never what happens. Thus, in one typical study in which the total amount to be divided was $10, the average amount offered by Proposer was $4.71, and in more than 80 percent of all cases Proposer offered exactly $5, a 50-50 split.[23] When Responders in this same study were asked to report the minimum amounts they would accept, their average response was $2.59. These experiments suggest clearly that laboratory subjects care not only about how much money they get but also about how it is apportioned in relative terms.[24] Most people seem predisposed to reject offers whose terms they find sufficiently "unfair."

A large literature has emerged in recent years, much of it based on laboratory experiments, showing that concerns about fairness influence numerous similar economic choices. As in the laboratory, so in life. Believing their current contracts to be unfair, workers are often willing to go on strike, even when they know it may cost them their jobs. Customers often refuse to patronize merchants whose terms they believe to be inequitable, even when it will be more costly or less convenient to buy from alternative suppliers.[25]

Material incentives clearly matter. Ultimately, however, the law can do only so much to constrain individual behavior. To achieve a well-ordered society, we must rely at least in part on people's willingness to subordinate personal interests for the common good. Although the adaptive rationality standard embraces the possibility of voluntary self-restraint in such cases, the self-interest standard all but denies that possibility.

It is troubling, therefore, that at least some evidence suggests that exposure to self-interest models tends to inhibit self-restraint. For example, one study found that economics majors were more than twice as likely as non-majors to defect when playing one-shot prisoner's dilemmas with strangers, a difference that was not merely a reflection of the fact that people who chose to major in economics were more opportunistic to begin with.[26] The same study also found that academic economists were more than twice as likely as the members of other disciplines to report giving no money at all to any private charity.[27]

ultimatum bargaining game
a game in which the first player has the power to confront the second player with a take-it-or-leave-it offer

---

[22]Werner Guth, Rolf Schmittberger, and Bernd Schwarze, "An Experimental Analysis of Ultimatum Bargaining," *Journal of Economic Behavior and Organization* 3 (1982), pp. 367–388.

[23]See Table 1 in Daniel Kahneman, Jack Knetsch, and Richard Thaler, "Perceptions of Unfairness: Constraints on Wealthseeking," *American Economic Review* 76 (September 1986), pp. 728–741.

[24]For evidence in favor of this interpretation, see especially Lawrence M. Kahn and J. Keith Murnighan, "A General Experiment on Bargaining in Demand Games with Outside Options," *American Economic Review* 83 (December 1993), pp. 1260–1280.

[25]For an engaging survey of relevant evidence, see Chapters 14 and 15 of Richard Thaler, *Misbehaving* (New York: Norton, 2015).

[26]Robert H. Frank, Thomas Gilovich, and Dennis Regan, "Does Studying Economics Inhibit Cooperation?" *Journal of Economic Perspectives* 7 (Spring 1993), pp. 159–171. We found, for example, that the difference in defection rates grew larger the longer a student had studied economics. Questionnaire responses also indicated that first-year college students in their first microeconomics course were more likely at the end of the term to expect opportunistic behavior from others than they were at the beginning.

[27]For more information on the issue of whether exposure to the self-interest model inhibits cooperation, see Gerald Marwell and Ruth Ames, "Economists Free Ride, Does Anyone Else?" *Journal of Public Economics* 15 (1981), pp. 295–310; John Carter and Michael Irons, "Are Economists Different, and If So, Why?" *Journal of Economic Perspectives* 5 (Spring 1991); Antony Yezer, Robert Goldfarb, and Paul Poppen, "Does Studying Economics Discourage Cooperation? Watch What We Do, Not What We Say," *Journal of Economic Perspectives,* Spring 1996; Robert H. Frank, Thomas Gilovich, and Dennis Regan, "Do Economists Make Bad Citizens?" *Journal of Economic Perspectives,* Spring 1996.

These findings suggest that our choice among standards of rationality may be important not just for our attempts to predict and explain behavior, but also because of its potential impact on our willingness to engage in self-restraint. If so, we have even greater reason to reconsider the welfare implications of traditional economic models.

RECAP↑

BEYOND NARROW SELF-INTEREST

Self-interest is without doubt an important human motive. But predictions based on the assumption that it is the only important motive fall short. Most people vote in presidential elections despite the negligible possibility that their votes will tip the balance. Most people leave tips even in restaurants they never expect to visit again. And people donate billions of dollars to charity each year, much of it anonymously.

The *present-aim model of rational choice* asserts that people often behave unselfishly because they get a warm glow from doing so. That enables the present-aim model to accommodate many behaviors that the narrow self-interest model cannot. But that flexibility also turns out to be a significant liability since virtually any bizarre behavior can be "explained" after the fact simply by assuming a sufficiently strong taste for it. For this reason, critics object that the present-aim model doesn't make any testable predictions.

Like both the self-interest and present-aim standards, the *adaptive rationality standard* assumes that people choose efficient means to achieve their ends. But unlike the other conceptions, which take goals as given, adaptive rationality regards goals as objects of choice themselves and, as such, subject to a similar efficiency requirement. Analysts are free to add a preference to the individual's list, but only upon showing that the preference not compromise efforts to acquire the resources needed for survival in competitive environments. Certain unselfish motives qualify under this standard because they help people solve important commitment problems, such as the one-shot prisoner's dilemma. If two players had reason to believe one another to be trustworthy, they could interact selectively, thereby reaping the gains of mutual cooperation. But merely being trustworthy is not enough. One must also be able to communicate one's trustworthiness to others credibly and be able to identify its presence in them. Experimental evidence suggests that these conditions are often met.

Additional evidence for the claim that narrow self-interest is not the only important human motive comes from experiments showing that people reject transactions that would have benefited them if they believe the terms of those transactions to be unfair.

CONCERNS ABOUT RELATIVE POSITION

Many traditional economic models assume that well-being depends on current and future levels of absolute consumption. Considerable evidence suggests, however, that well-being depends as much or more on current and future levels of relative consumption.[28] The adaptive rationality standard holds that a taste for relative consumption can be introduced into the utility function if being thus motivated need not compromise resource acquisition in competitive environments. If people known to care about relative consumption are indeed better bargainers than those thought to care only about absolute consumption, this test is met.

---

[28]The points developed in this section are developed in greater detail in Robert H. Frank, "The Demand for Unobservable and Other Nonpositional Goods," *American Economic Review 75* (March 1985), pp. 101–116; Robert H. Frank, *Choosing the Right Pond* (New York: Oxford University Press, 1985).

The following thought experiment provides an intuitive test of whether relative consumption matters:

Which world would you choose?

World A: You and your family live in a neighborhood with 4,000-square-foot houses, and all other neighborhoods have 6,000-square-foot houses.

World B: You and your family live in a neighborhood with 3,000-square-foot houses, and all other neighborhoods have 2,000-square-foot houses.

If the satisfaction provided by a house depended only on its absolute features, World A would be the unambiguously better choice. Yet significantly more than half of respondents faced with this question choose World B. Some of the minority who choose World A seem to do so out of concern that they *shouldn't* care about others' houses. Even so, few among them seem puzzled that others might choose differently. The point is not that World B is the uniquely correct choice here. But if our goal is to predict people's actual choices, the traditional assumption that only absolute consumption matters is often misleading.

In some domains, however, the traditional assumption serves reasonably well. Consider a second thought experiment, one with exactly the same structure as the one for house size:

Which world would you choose?

World A: You have a 2 in 100,000 chance of dying on the job this year, and others have a 1 in 100,000 chance.

World B: You have a 4 in 100,000 chance of dying, and others have a 6 in 100,000 chance.

As before, this choice is between absolute advantage (World A) and relative advantage (World B). When people face that choice in the domain of housing, most choose relative advantage. But when their choice involves safety, almost everyone opts for absolute advantage.

The late British economist Fred Hirsch coined the term **positional good** to describe things that derive their value primarily from their relative scarcity rather than from their absolute characteristics. "The value of my education," he wrote, "depends on how much the man ahead of me in the job line has."[29] In what follows, we use Hirsch's term to mean a good whose value depends relatively heavily on how it compares with other goods in the same category. For people who chose relative over absolute advantage in the first thought experiment, housing would thus be a positional good.

Similarly, we use the term **nonpositional good** to describe one whose value depends relatively little on how it compares with other goods in the same category. For people who chose absolute advantage in the second thought experiment, workplace safety would be a nonpositional good.

To call housing positional is not to say that only the relative attributes of a house matter. Someone who chose World B in the first thought experiment, for example, might well have preferred to live in a world in which her neighborhood had 3,500-square-foot houses and others had houses of 3,000 square feet.

Similarly, choosing a world with high absolute safety doesn't mean that relative safety levels are of no concern. Most people choosing World A would almost certainly notice that their jobs were much more dangerous than others'. But if their only recourse were to move to World B, where their own absolute risk of death would double, they would decline.

Caring more about relative consumption in some domains than in others distorts people's spending decisions. It leads to what we call *positional arms races*—patterns of escalating expenditure focused on positional goods. The resulting dynamic is exactly analogous to the one that drives military arms races. In both cases, wasteful spending occurs only because some categories of expenditure are more context-sensitive than others.

Military arms races occur only because relative differences in spending on weapons have more important consequences than relative differences in nonmilitary spending. If,

positional good a good whose value depends relatively heavily on how it compares with other goods in the same category

nonpositional good a good whose value does not depend heavily on how it compares with other goods in the same category

[29]Fred Hirsch, *Social Limits to Growth* (Cambridge, MA: Harvard University Press, 1976).

to the contrary, spending less than a rival nation spent on toasters and television sets had more serious consequences than spending less on bombs, we would expect expenditure imbalances of precisely the opposite sort: Countries would spend ever less on armaments in a quest to gain relative advantage in the domain of nonmilitary spending. That is of course not what we see. Military arms races are a consequence, pure and simple, of relative spending on armaments being more important—because it contributes so heavily to the outcome of military conflict.

Similar distortions appear to occur in domestic consumption patterns. Because relative spending matters more, by definition, for positional goods than for nonpositional goods, people often end up spending too much on the former and too little on the latter. To see how the dynamic unfolds, consider a worker's choice between two jobs that offer different levels of risk to safety. Both because safety devices are costly and because workers prefer safe jobs to risky ones, employers who want to attract workers to riskier jobs can and must pay higher wages. Choosing additional safety on the job therefore comes at the expense of having less income to spend on other things. Choosing a riskier job would enable a worker to buy a nicer house. If she has children, that option might look doubly attractive since she knows that in almost every jurisdiction, better schools are those located in more expensive neighborhoods.

So let's imagine that she chooses the higher-paying but riskier job. The same logic would also lead similarly situated workers to make the same choice. And if they too chose riskier jobs to be able to afford houses in better school districts, their increased bidding would serve only to bid up the prices of those houses. Half of all children would still attend bottom-half schools, the same as if no one had sacrificed safety for higher wages. All will have sold their safety in pursuit of a goal that none achieves.

Since Adam Smith's day, classical economic theory has held that well-informed workers in competitive markets will sensibly navigate this trade-off between income and safety. They will accept additional risk in return for higher pay only if the satisfaction from having what they can buy with the extra income is greater than the corresponding loss in satisfaction from reduced safety. According to proponents of this view, regulations that mandate higher safety levels harm workers by forcing them to buy safety they value at less than its cost.

But why, then, does virtually every country in the world regulate workplace safety?[30] (Even the poorest countries have at least rudimentary safety requirements.) Classical economic theory doesn't have a good answer. It portrays such regulations as either anomalous, or else needed because workers are uninformed, or because markets aren't competitive enough. Yet we regulate many safety risks that workers clearly understand. Most coal miners, for example, know their work entails risk of black lung disease since their fathers and grandfathers died of it.

Nor is imperfect competition the problem. Most safety regulations, after all, have their greatest impact in precisely those markets that most closely approximate the competitive ideal. They have little effect on engineers in Silicon Valley or on investment bankers on Wall Street, whose conditions of employment are substantially safer than required by the Occupational Safety and Health Administration. It's the employers who compete most fiercely with one another to attract the workers they need, such as fast-food restaurants and manufacturing firms that employ unskilled labor, that seldom go long without a visit from a safety inspector.

Analogous reasoning suggests that individual incentives are misleadingly high for many other things we might sell for money—our leisure time, future job security, and a host of other environmental amenities. The problem is not that we exchange these items for money, but that our incentives lead us to sell them too cheaply. In the case of workplace safety, the solution is not to ban risk, but to make it less attractive to individuals. As concerns the length of the workweek, the best solution is not strict limits on hours worked, but rather a change in incentives (such as overtime laws) that make long hours less attractive.

---

[30]Scott Coulter, "Advancing Safety around the World," *Occupational Health and Safety,* February 1, 2009.

One rationale for policy measures to stimulate additional savings is that impulse-control problems often prevent people from adhering to rationally chosen savings plans. But savings shortfalls also stem from a second source, one that is difficult to address by unilateral action. The following thought experiment illustrates the basic problem:

If you were society's median earner, which of these two worlds would you prefer?

World A. You save enough to support a comfortable standard of living in retirement, but your children attend a school whose students score in bottom 20 percent on standardized tests in reading and math.

World B. You save too little to support a comfortable standard of living in retirement, but your children attend a school whose students score in the 50th percentile on those tests.

Because the concept of a "good" school is inescapably relative, this thought experiment captures an essential element of the savings decision confronting most middle-income families. If others bid for houses in better school districts, failure to do likewise will often consign one's children to inferior schools. But as noted earlier, no matter how much each family spends, half of all children must attend schools in the bottom half. The choice posed by the thought experiment is one that most parents would prefer to avoid. But when forced to choose, most say they would pick the second option.

Like workplace safety decisions, savings decisions are thus also examples of the collective action problem inherent in a military arms race. Each nation knows that it would be better if all spent less on arms. Yet if others keep spending, it is simply too dangerous not to follow suit. Curtailing an arms race thus requires an enforceable agreement. Similarly, unless all families can bind themselves to save more, those who do so unilaterally will pay the price of having to send their children to inferior schools. In these observations lie the seeds of a possible answer to the question posed in The Economic Naturalist 10.4.

The Economic Naturalist 10.4

Why have attempts to privatize Social Security proved so politically unpopular in the United States?

Since its inception during the Great Depression, the Social Security system has required universal participation. People's labor earnings are subject to the payroll tax, which is then used to finance pension payments for older Americans in retirement. Early in his second term in office, President George W. Bush promoted a proposal to privatize Social Security. Under this proposal, people would be free to decide for themselves how much to save each month and how much to spend. To the president's surprise, however, this proposal proved deeply unpopular. Why didn't most people welcome the additional freedom that privatization would have offered?

As discussed, if parents had complete access to their retirement savings accounts, some would undoubtedly withdraw money from those accounts in order to bid for houses in better school districts. Rather than see their own children fall behind, many other parents would feel compelled to follow suit. But the increased bidding would serve only to drive up the prices of the houses in better school districts, even as many parents would end up with inadequate savings to support themselves in retirement. Mandatory participation in the Social Security system solves this dilemma. The money paid in payroll taxes, which is unavailable to bid for houses in better school districts, remains available to finance pension payments to retirees.

Positional concerns also appear to alter the distribution between public and private spending. Public goods are fundamentally different from private goods: When some people spend more on houses or wedding celebrations, for example, others may feel pressure to follow suit, but the same dynamic does not occur for public goods, which are available on essentially equal terms to all citizens. Because public goods do not lend themselves to interpersonal comparisons, they are nonpositional almost by definition.

In any event, there is little question that levels of public investment have not kept pace in recent decades. For example, engineers report record maintenance backlogs not only in the nation's roads and bridges, but also in airports, schools, drinking water, and sewage systems.[31] And in the face of these backlogs, proposals to launch significant new infrastructure initiatives, such as high-speed rail service or a smart electric grid, have consistently failed in Congress. More troubling, we have not yet launched the investments required to confront the climate crisis, by far the biggest challenge facing the planet.

In short, substantial evidence suggests that most people would be happier if a larger share of national income were spent on nonpositional goods, including long-neglected public investment. Such misallocations tend to be stubborn, however, because they stem largely from the kinds of collective-action problems we earlier described as "departures from rational choice without regret." Just as the practice of standing at concerts persists because it is rational for each individual to continue standing when others are doing so, spending imbalances that arise from collective-action problems cannot be remedied by individual action. People must turn to the political system in search of effective ways to act collectively.

In contrast, welfare losses that arise from cognitive errors can be attacked at the individual level. Once people realize that it's irrational to take sunk costs into account, for example, they may become both motivated to—and able to—alter their choices unilaterally. That's why we earlier described choices that are driven by cognitive errors as "departures from rational choice with regret."

As noted, many of the tax and regulatory policies already in effect, such as workplace safety laws and pollution taxes, are most plausibly interpreted as positional arms control agreements.

RECAP ↑

CONCERNS ABOUT RELATIVE POSITION

Evidence suggests that well-being depends not only on absolute levels of current and future consumption but also on the corresponding levels of relative consumption.

Adding a taste for relative consumption alters many of the predictions and prescriptions of traditional economic models. Traditional models hold, for example, that the optimal amount of workplace safety will be provided in competitive labor markets. Critics respond that because labor markets are not effectively competitive, safety regulation is needed to prevent employers from exploiting workers. The puzzle for both camps is why safety regulations are most binding in those labor markets that, on traditional measures, are the most highly competitive.

Models that incorporate concerns about relative position address this puzzle by noting that by accepting riskier jobs, parents can use their higher pay to bid for housing in better school districts. But because school quality is an inherently relative concept, when other parents follow suit, the collective effect of their efforts is merely to bid up the prices of houses in better school districts. As before, half of all children end up attending bottom-half schools.

Workers confronting these incentives might well prefer an alternative state of the world in which all enjoyed greater safety, even at the expense of all having lower wages. Analogous reasoning suggests that individual incentives are misleadingly high for many other things we might sell for money—our leisure time, future job security, and a host of other environmental amenities. The problem is not that we exchange these items for money, but rather that we tend to sell them too cheaply.

---

[31] *2017 Infrastructure Report Card: D+*, www.infrastructurereportcard.org.

SUMMARY

- Because it is costly to gather and analyze information, it often makes sense to employ rules of thumb when making complex assessments and decisions. Although the rules that most of us use appear to work reasonably well under a broad range of circumstance, they sometimes lead to error. *(LO1)*

- Behavioral economists have identified numerous systematic errors that are associated with the availability and representativeness heuristics. Anchoring and adjustment can also lead to biased assessments, as can failure to take account of regression to the mean or the tendency for extreme events to be followed by more nearly normal ones. It is also common for people to misinterpret contextual cues in their assessments and choices, as, for example, by reckoning the importance of a price reduction not by its absolute magnitude, but by its fraction of the original price. *(LO1, LO2)*

- Traditional economic models typically rule out the possibility that people might regret having chosen behaviors whose consequences were perfectly predictable, yet such expressions of regret appear genuine. Evidence suggests that people tend to discount future costs and benefits excessively leading them to choose imminent, though inferior, rewards instead of substantially larger rewards that require waiting. *(LO3)*

- Although traditional models assume that the reduction in happiness from a very small decline in wealth should be approximately the same as the gain in happiness from a similar gain in wealth, evidence suggests that losses weigh much more heavily than gains. Called loss aversion, this asymmetry in valuations is approximately two to one for minor changes, but can be substantially larger when important changes are at stake. Because every change in policy generates winners and losers, loss aversion implies a large bias in favor of the status quo in public policy decisions. Evidence suggests that this bias often has harmful consequences since people's initial estimates of how painful losses will be often fail to take into account their ability to adapt to altered circumstances. *(LO4)*

- Self-interest is not the only important human motive, as evidenced by the fact that most people vote in presidential elections whose outcomes their votes won't influence. The present-aim model of rational choice broadens the narrow self-interest model by asserting that people often behave unselfishly because they get a warm glow from doing so. Methodologists object that the present-aim approach is not really a testable theory since it can "explain" virtually any bizarre behavior simply by assuming a suitably strong taste for it. *(LO5)*

- The *adaptive rationality approach* also permits a broader conception of human motivation, but unlike the present-aim approach, permits new motives to be added only if they can be plausibly shown not to handicap people in their quest to survive in competitive environments. Certain unselfish motives qualify under this standard because they help people solve important commitment problems, such as the one-shot prisoner's dilemmas. *(LO5)*

- Additional evidence for the claim that narrow self-interest is not the only important human motive comes from experiments showing that when people believe the terms of a transaction to be unfair, they often reject it, even if the transaction would have increased their wealth in absolute terms. *(LO5)*

- Many traditional models assume that well-being depends only on absolute levels of current and future consumption. But evidence suggests that it also depends heavily on the corresponding levels of relative consumption. Adding concerns about relative position alters many of the predictions and prescriptions of traditional economic models. When well-being depends only on absolute levels of consumption and certain other conditions are met, traditional models hold that individual incentives produce socially optimal patterns of spending. But when reward depends on relative position, individual incentives often result in mutually offsetting, and hence partially wasteful spending patterns. *(LO6)*

- The findings of behavioral economists in recent decades have contributed to our understanding of laws and other institutions. Societies around the world, for example, have adopted a variety of policies that are most easily understood as attempts to mitigate the consequences of impulse-control problems. These include special treatment of so-called crimes of passion; prohibitions against gambling, addictive drugs, and prostitution; entrapment laws; sanctions against adultery; and programs to stimulate savings. *(LO7)*

- Many other widely adopted laws, norms, and regulations are parsimoniously interpreted as attempts to mitigate collective action problems caused by concerns about relative position. These include workplace safety regulation, limitations on work hours, and programs to stimulate savings, all of which reduce individual incentives to engage in mutually offsetting patterns of spending. *(LO7)*

KEY TERMS

adaptive rationality standard
anchoring and adjustment
availability heuristic
fungibility
homo economicus
judgmental and decision
   heuristics

loss aversion
nonpositional good
positional good
present-aim standard of
   rationality
regression to the mean

representativeness
   heuristic
satisficing
status quo bias
ultimatum bargaining game
Weber-Fechner law

REVIEW QUESTIONS

1. How does the representativeness heuristic explain why people might think, mistakenly, that a randomly chosen shy person is more likely to be a librarian than a sales-person? *(LO1)*

2. Explain why thinking of costs or benefits in proportional terms might lead to suboptimal choices. *(LO2)*

3. Explain why traditional economic models find it difficult to explain why people would pay to attend weight-loss camps that restrict their daily calorie intake. *(LO3)*

4. How does loss aversion help explain why attempts to repeal the Affordable Care Act have met such strong resistance? *(LO4)*

5. Cite two examples of behavior that appear to contradict the assumption that people are narrowly self-interested. *(LO5)*

PROBLEMS

1. Only two moving companies, United and North American, provide local delivery service in a small western city. United operates 20 percent of the trucks, North American the remaining 80 percent. On a dark and rainy night, a pedestrian is run over and killed by a moving van. The lone witness to the incident testifies that the van was owned by United. An independent laboratory hired by the court finds that under dark and rainy conditions, the witness is able to identify the owner of a moving van with 90 percent accuracy. What is the probability that the van that struck the witness was owned by United? *(LO1)*

2. Kaela, a tennis player, has been struggling to develop a more consistent serve. She made the following remark to her partner during the second set of a recent match: "I feel like I'm making progress. I haven't double-faulted once today." She then served two double faults, which caused her to say, "Every time I say I haven't double-faulted, I immediately start to." Kaela's perception may have been influenced by *(LO1)*
   a. the sunk cost effect.
   b. regression to the mean.
   c. the availability heuristic.
   d. More than one of the above are correct.
   e. None of the above.

3. Studies have shown that in the New York City subways crime rates fall in the years following increased police patrols. Does this pattern suggest that the increased patrols are the cause of the crime reductions? *(LO1)*

4. Dalgliesh the detective fancies himself a shrewd judge of human nature. In careful tests, it has been discovered that he is right 80 percent of the time when he says that a suspect is lying. Dalgliesh says that Jones is lying. The polygraph expert, who is right 100 percent of the time, says that 40 percent of the subjects interviewed by Dalgliesh are telling the truth. What is the probability that Jones is lying? *(LO1)*

5. Shobhana is a gourmet. She makes it a point never to visit a restaurant a second time unless she has been served a superb meal on her first visit. She is puzzled at how seldom the quality of her second meal is as high as the first. Should she be? *(LO1)*

6. Maria will drive across town to take advantage of a 40 percent off sale on a $40 blouse but will not do so to take advantage of a 10 percent off sale on a $1,000 stereo. Assuming that her alternative is to pay list price for both products at the department store next to her home, is her behavior rational? *(LO2)*

7. Soo-Jin has said she would be willing to drive across town in order to save $10 on the purchase price of a $20 waffle maker. If Soo-Jin is rational, this implies that she *(LO2)*
   a. believes that the opportunity cost of the trip is not more than $10.
   b. should also drive across town to save $10 on a $500 television set.
   c. should not drive across town to save $10 on a $500 television set.
   d. should drive across town only if the savings on a $500 television set is at least $250.
   e. More than one of these is correct.

8. Marco is having difficulty choosing between two tennis racquets, A and B. As shown in the diagram, A has more power than B, but less control. According to the rational choice model, how will the availability of a third alternative—racquet C—influence Marco's final decision? If Marco behaves like most ordinary decision makers in this situation, how will the addition of C to his choice set matter? *(LO2)*

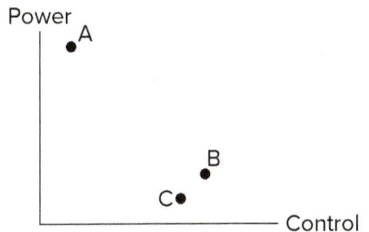

9. In the fall, Crusoe puts 50 coconuts from his harvest into a cave just before a family of bears goes in to hibernate. As a result, he is unable to get the coconuts out before the bears emerge the following spring. Coconuts spoil at the same rate no matter where he stores them, and yet he continues this practice each year. Why might he do this? *(LO3, LO5)*

10. When students in a large class were surveyed about how much they would be willing to pay for a coffee mug with their university's logo on it, their median willingness to pay was $5. At random, half of the students in this class were then given such a coffee mug, and each of the remaining students were given $5 in cash. Students who got mugs were then offered an opportunity to sell them to students who had not gotten one. According to standard economic models, how many mugs would be expected to change hands? How, if at all, would a behavioral economist's prediction differ? *(LO4)*

11. Describe the advantages and disadvantages of electing a political leader who is known to favor harsh military reprisals against foreign aggression, even when such reprisals are highly injurious to our own national interests. *(LO5)*

12. Explain why rational voters whose happiness depends on relative consumption might favor laws that require them to save a certain portion of each year's earnings for retirement. *(LO6, LO7)*

ANSWERS TO SELF-TESTS

10.1 For every 100 taxis in a dark alley, 15 will be green, 85 blue. The witness will identify $0.8(15) = 12$ of the green taxis as green, the remaining 3 green taxis as blue; he will identify $0.8(85) = 68$ of the blue taxis as blue, the remaining 17 blue taxis as green. The probability that the cab in question was green, given that the witness said it was, is thus equal to $12/(12 + 17) = 0.413$ and as this is less than half, the Green Taxi Company should not be held liable. *(LO1)*

10.2 Regression to the mean suggests that a month with an unusually high number of burglaries is likely to be followed by a month in which the number of burglaries is more nearly normal. So the increased patrols were not necessarily the cause of the observed reduction in burglaries. *(LO1)*

CHAPTER 11

Externalities, Property Rights, and the Environment

When costs or benefits accrue to people not directly involved in transactions, market allocations are often inefficient.

Ginosphotos/Getty Images

LEARNING OBJECTIVES

After reading this chapter, you should be able to:

LO1 Define negative and positive externalities and analyze their effect on resource allocation.

LO2 Explain and discuss the Coase theorem.

LO3 Explain how the effects of externalities can be remedied and discuss why the optimal amount of an externality is almost never zero.

LO4 Illustrate the tragedy of the commons and show how private ownership is a way of preventing it.

LO5 Define positional externalities and their effects and show how they can be remedied.

LO6 Compare and contrast the ways in which taxes and tradable permits reduce pollution.

A droll television ad for a British brand of pipe tobacco opens with a distinguished-looking gentleman sitting quietly on a park bench, smoking his pipe and reading a book of poetry. Before him lies a pond, unrippled except for a mother duck swimming peacefully with her ducklings. Suddenly a raucous group of teenage boys bursts onto the scene with a remote-controlled toy warship. Yelling and laughing, they launch their boat and maneuver it in aggressive pursuit of the terrified ducks.

Interrupted from his reverie, the gentleman looks up from his book and draws calmly on his pipe as he surveys the scene before him. He then reaches into his bag, pulls out a remote control of his own, and begins manipulating the joystick. The scene shifts underwater, where a miniature submarine rises from the depths of the pond. Once the boys' boat is in the sub's sights, the gentleman pushes a button on his remote control. Seconds later, the boat is blown to smithereens by a torpedo. The scene fades to a close-up of the tobacco company's label.

EXTERNAL COSTS AND BENEFITS

external cost (or **negative externality**) a cost of an activity that falls on people other than those who pursue the activity

external benefit (or **positive externality**) a benefit of an activity received by people other than those who pursue the activity

externality an external cost or benefit of an activity

External costs (or **negative externality**) and **external benefits** (or **positive externality**)—**externalities**, for short—are activities that generate costs or benefits that accrue to people not directly involved in those activities. These effects are generally unintended. From the pipe smoker's point of view, the noise generated by the marauding boys was an external cost. Had others been disturbed by the boys' rowdiness, they may well have regarded the pipe smoker's retaliatory gesture as an external benefit.

This chapter focuses on how externalities affect the allocation of resources. Adam Smith's theory of the invisible hand applies to an ideal marketplace in which externalities do not exist. In such situations, Smith argued, the self-interested actions of individuals would lead to socially efficient outcomes. We will see that when the parties affected by externalities can easily negotiate with one another, the invisible hand will still produce an efficient outcome.

But in many cases, such as the scene depicted in the tobacco ad, negotiation is impractical. In those cases, the self-serving actions of individuals won't lead to efficient outcomes. The need to deal with externalities and other collective-action problems is one of the most important rationales for the existence of government along with a variety of other forms of collective action.

HOW EXTERNALITIES AFFECT RESOURCE ALLOCATION

The following examples illustrate the ways in which externalities distort the allocation of resources.

EXAMPLE 11.1 **Positive Externalities**

Does the honeybee keeper face the right incentives? (Part I)

Phoebe earns her living as a keeper of honeybees. Her neighbors on all sides grow apples. Because bees pollinate apple trees as they forage for nectar, the more hives Phoebe keeps, the larger the harvests will be in the surrounding orchards. If Phoebe takes only her own costs and benefits into account in deciding how many hives to keep, will she keep the socially optimal number of hives?

Phoebe's hives constitute an external benefit, or a positive externality, for the orchard owners. If she takes only her own personal costs and benefits into account, she will add hives only until the added revenue she gets from the last hive just equals the cost of adding it. But because the orchard owners also benefit from additional hives, the total benefit of adding another hive at that point will be greater than its cost. Phoebe, then, will keep too few hives.

As we will discuss later in the chapter, problems like the one in Example 11.1 have several possible solutions. One is for orchard owners to pay beekeepers for keeping additional hives. But such solutions often require complex negotiations between the affected parties. For the moment, we assume that such negotiations are not practical.

EXAMPLE 11.2 **Negative Externalities**

Does the honeybee keeper face the right incentives? (Part 2)

As in Example 11.1, Phoebe earns her living as a keeper of honeybees. Now her neighbors are not apple growers but an elementary school and a nursing home. The more hives Phoebe keeps, the more students and nursing home residents will be stung by bees. If Phoebe takes only her own costs and benefits into account in deciding how many hives to keep, will she keep the socially optimal number of hives?

For the students and nursing home residents, Phoebe's hives constitute an external cost, or a negative externality. If she considers only her own costs and benefits in deciding how many hives to keep, she will continue to add hives until the added revenue from the last hive is just enough to cover its cost. But since Phoebe's neighbors also incur costs when she adds a hive, the benefit of the last hive at that point will be smaller than its cost. Phoebe, in other words, will keep too many hives.

Every activity involves costs and benefits. When all the relevant costs and benefits of an activity accrue directly to the person who carries it out—that is, when the activity generates no externalities—the level of the activity that is best for the individual will be best for society as a whole. But when an activity generates externalities, be they positive or negative, individual self-interest does not produce the best allocation of resources. Individuals who consider only their own costs and benefits will tend to engage too much in activities that generate negative externalities and too little in activities that generate positive externalities. When an activity generates both positive and negative externalities, private and social interests will coincide only in the unlikely event that the opposing effects offset one another exactly.

HOW DO EXTERNALITIES AFFECT SUPPLY AND DEMAND?

The effects of externalities on resource allocation can be shown in a supply and demand diagram. Consider first the case of negative externalities. Figure 11.1(a) depicts the supply (Private *MC*) and demand curves for a product whose production involves no external costs or benefits. Imagine, say, that the energy that powers the factories in this market comes from nonpolluting hydroelectric generators. The resulting equilibrium price and quantity in the market for this product will then be socially optimal: the value to buyers of the last unit of the product consumed (as measured on the demand curve) will be exactly equal to the marginal cost of producing it (as measured on the supply curve), leaving no further possible gains from exchange (see Chapter 3, *Supply and Demand*, and Chapter 7, *Efficiency, Exchange, and the Invisible Hand in Action*).

But now suppose that a protracted drought has eliminated hydroelectric power generation, forcing factories to rely instead on electric power produced by coal-burning

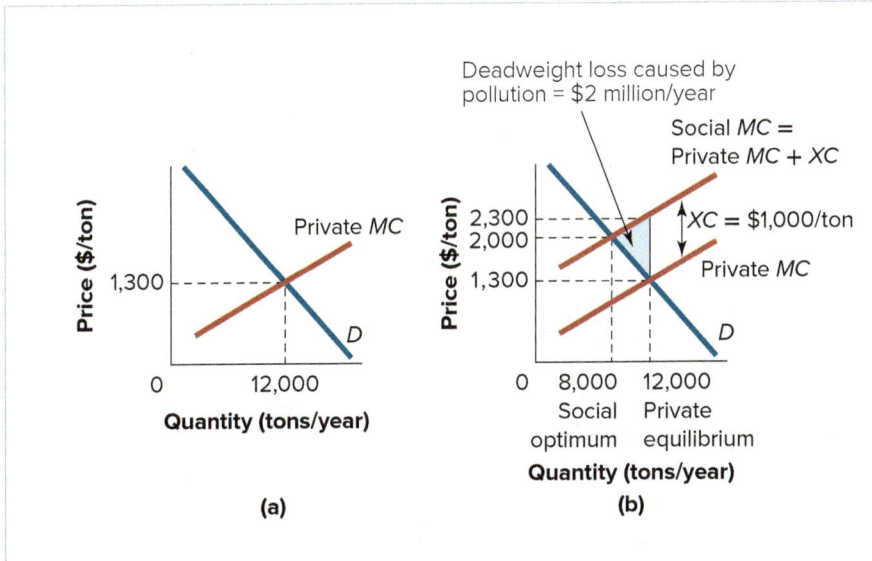

(a)

(b)

FIGURE 11.1

How External Costs Affect Resource Allocation.

(a) When a market has no external costs or benefits, the resulting equilibrium quantity and price are socially optimal. (b) By contrast, when production of a good is accompanied by an external cost, the market equilibrium price ($1,300 per ton) is too low and the market equilibrium quantity (12,000 tons per year) is too high. The deadweight loss from the negative externality is the area of the blue-shaded triangle, $2 million per year.

generators. Now each unit of output produced is accompanied by an external pollution cost of *XC,* as shown in Figure 11.1(b). Since the external pollution cost falls not on firm owners but on others who live downwind from their factories, Private *MC* is still the supply curve for this product, and its demand curve is again as before, so the equilibrium price and quantity will be exactly the same as in Figure 11.1(a). But this time the private market equilibrium is not socially optimal. As before, the market equilibrium level of output is 12,000 tons per year, the output level at which the demand curve (*D*) intersects Private *MC.* Note, however, that at that output level, the value to consumers of the last unit of output produced is only $1,300 per ton, while the true cost of producing that last unit (including the external cost) is $2,300 per ton.

This means that society could gain additional economic surplus by producing fewer units of the product. Indeed, the same conclusion will continue to hold whenever the current output exceeds 8,000 tons per year, the output level at which the demand curve intersects Social *MC.* Social *MC,* which includes all relevant marginal costs of producing the product, is constructed by adding the external pollution cost, *XC,* to every value along Private *MC.* The socially optimal level of output of the good occurs where Social *MC* intersects the demand curve. As shown in Figure 11.1(b), it is 8,000 tons per year. This is the level of output that exhausts all possibilities from exchange. At that quantity, the marginal benefit of the product, as measured by what buyers are willing to pay for it, is exactly equal to the marginal cost of producing it, which is the private marginal cost *MC* plus the marginal pollution cost *XC.* The market equilibrium quantity thus will be higher than the socially optimal quantity for a good whose production generates external costs.

By how much does the presence of pollution reduce total economic surplus from its maximum value, which occurs at an output level of 8,000 tons per year in Figure 11.1(b)? Note in the diagram that as output expands past 8,000, the marginal cost of each successive unit (as measured on the Social *MC* curve) is greater than the marginal benefit of that unit (as measured on the demand curve). Expanding output from 8,000 tons per year to the private equilibrium level, 12,000 tons per year, thus entails a cumulative reduction in total economic surplus equal to the area of the blue-shaded triangle in Figure 11.1(b), or $2 million per year. The deadweight loss from pollution is $2 million per year in this market.

What about a good whose production generates external benefits? In Figure 11.2, Private demand is the demand curve for a product whose production generates an external benefit of *XB* per unit. The market equilibrium quantity of this good, Q_{pvt}, is the output level at which Private demand intersects the supply curve of the product (*MC*). This time, market equilibrium quantity is smaller than the socially optimal level of output, denoted Q_{soc}. Q_{soc} is the output level at which *MC* intersects the socially optimal demand curve (the curve labeled Social demand in Figure 11.2), which is constructed by adding the external benefit, *XB,* to every value along Private demand. Note that the private market equilibrium again fails to exhaust all possible gains from exchange. Thus, at Q_{pvt}, the marginal cost of producing an additional unit of output is only MB_{pvt}, which is smaller than the marginal benefit of an additional unit by the amount *XB.* The market equilibrium quantity thus will be lower than the socially optimal quantity for a good whose production generates external benefits.

In comparison with the maximum attainable total economic surplus in this market, how much does the total economic surplus associated with the private equilibrium fall short? In Figure 11.2, note that at Q_{pvt}, the marginal benefit of the product (as measured on the curve labeled Social demand) is *XB* units larger than its marginal cost (as measured on *MC*). Total economic surplus will continue to increase by successively smaller increments as output grows from Q_{pvt} to Q_{soc}, the socially optimal quantity. The total deadweight loss associated with the positive externality is thus the area of the blue-shaded triangle in Figure 11.2.

If the production of a product generates a positive externality, why do we say that this product causes a reduction in total economic surplus? To say that there is a deadweight loss in this market does not mean that the positive externality causes harm. Rather, it means that failure to take the positive externality into account makes the economic surplus associated with private equilibrium smaller than it could have been. Failure to reap an economic benefit is the same thing as sustaining an economic loss.

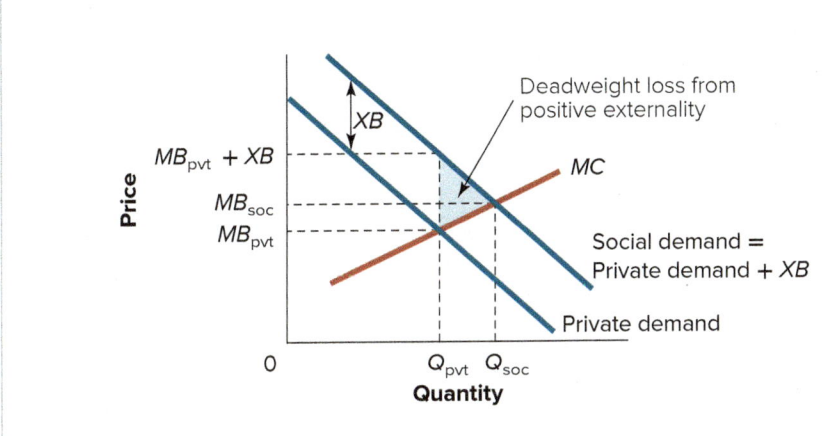

FIGURE 11.2

A Good Whose Production Generates a Positive Externality for Consumers.

For such goods, the market equilibrium quantity, Q_{pvt}, is smaller than the socially optimal quantity, Q_{soc}, because individual buyers are willing to pay only for the benefits they reap from directly consuming the product. The deadweight loss from the positive externality is the area of the blue-shaded triangle.

To summarize, whether externalities are positive or negative, they distort the allocation of resources in otherwise efficient markets. When externalities are present, the individual pursuit of self-interest will not result in the largest possible economic surplus. This outcome is thus inefficient by definition.

THE COASE THEOREM

To say that a situation is inefficient means that it can be rearranged in a way that would make at least some people better off without harming others. Such situations, we have seen, are a source of creative tension. The existence of inefficiency, after all, means that there is cash on the table, which usually triggers a race to see who can capture it. For example, we saw that because monopoly pricing results in an inefficiently low output level, the potential for gain gave monopolists an incentive to make discounts available to price-sensitive buyers. As the next examples illustrate, the inefficiencies that result from externalities create similar incentives for remedial action.

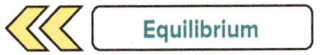

Equilibrium

EXAMPLE 11.3	Inefficiencies That Result from Externalities

Will Abercrombie dump toxins in the river? (Part I)

Abercrombie's factory produces a toxic waste by-product. If Abercrombie dumps it in the river, he causes damage to Fitch, a fisherman located downstream. The toxins are short-lived and cause no damage to anyone other than Fitch. At a cost, Abercrombie can filter out the toxins, in which case Fitch will suffer no damage at all. The relevant gains and losses for the two individuals are listed in Table 11.1.

TABLE 11.1
Costs and Benefits of Eliminating Toxic Waste (Part I)

	With filter	Without filter
Gains to Abercrombie	$100/day	$130/day
Gains to Fitch	$100/day	$ 50/day

If the law does not penalize Abercrombie for dumping toxins in the river, and if Abercrombie and Fitch cannot communicate with one another, will Abercrombie operate with or without a filter? Is that choice socially efficient?

Abercrombie has an incentive to operate without a filter since he earns $30 per day more than if he operates with a filter. But the outcome when he does so is socially inefficient. Thus, when Abercrombie operates without a filter, the total daily gain to both parties is only $130 + $50 = $180, compared to $100 + $100 = $200 if Abercrombie had operated with a filter. The daily cost of the filter to Abercrombie is only $130 − $100 = $30, which is smaller than its daily benefit to Fitch of $100 − $50 = $50. The fact that Abercrombie does not install the filter implies a squandered daily surplus of $20.

| EXAMPLE 11.4 | Negotiating Efficient Solutions to Externalities |

Will Abercrombie dump toxins in the river? (Part 2)

Suppose the costs and benefits of using the filter are as in the previous example except that Abercrombie and Fitch can now communicate with one another at no cost. Even though the law does not require him to do so, will Abercrombie use a filter?

This time, Abercrombie will use a filter. Recall from Chapter 7, *Efficiency, Exchange, and the Invisible Hand*, the observation that when the economic pie grows larger, everyone can have a larger slice (the *Efficiency Principle*). Because use of a filter would result in the largest possible economic surplus, it would enable both Abercrombie and Fitch to have a larger net gain than before. Fitch thus has an incentive to *pay* Abercrombie to use a filter. Suppose, for instance, that Fitch offers Abercrombie $40 per day to compensate him for operating with a filter. Both Abercrombie and Fitch will then be exactly $10 per day better off than before, for a total daily net gain of $20.

 SELF-TEST 11.1

In Example 11.4, what is the largest whole-dollar amount by which Fitch could compensate Abercrombie for operating with a filter and still be better off than before?

Ronald Coase, a professor at the University of Chicago Law School, was the first to see clearly that if people can negotiate with one another at no cost over the right to perform activities that cause externalities, they will always arrive at an efficient solution. This insight, which is often called the **Coase theorem**, is a profoundly important idea, for which Coase (rhymes with "rose") was awarded the 1991 Nobel Prize in Economics.

Why, you might ask, should Fitch pay Abercrombie to filter out toxins that would not be there in the first place if not for Abercrombie's factory? The rhetorical force of this question is undeniable. Yet Coase points out that externalities are reciprocal in nature. The toxins do harm Fitch, to be sure, but preventing Abercrombie from emitting them would penalize Abercrombie, by exactly $30 per day. Why should Fitch necessarily have the right to harm Abercrombie? Indeed, as the next example illustrates, even if Fitch had that right, he would exercise it only if filtering the toxins proved the most efficient outcome.

Coase theorem if, at no cost, people can negotiate the purchase and sale of the right to perform activities that cause externalities, they can always arrive at efficient solutions to the problems caused by externalities

EXAMPLE 11.5	Social Efficiency

Will Abercrombie dump toxins in the river? (Part 3)

Suppose the law says that Abercrombie may *not* dump toxins in the river unless he has Fitch's permission. If the relevant costs and benefits of filtering the toxins are as shown in Table 11.2, and if Abercrombie and Fitch can negotiate with one another at no cost, will Abercrombie filter out the toxins?

TABLE 11.2
Costs and Benefits of Eliminating Toxic Waste (Part 3)

	With filter	Without filter
Gains to Abercrombie	$100/day	$150/day
Gains to Fitch	$100/day	$70/day

Note that this time, the most efficient outcome is for Abercrombie to operate without a filter because the total daily surplus in that case will be $220 as compared to only $200 with a filter. Under the law, however, Fitch has the right to insist that Abercrombie use a filter. We might expect him to exercise that right since his own gain would rise from $70 to $100 per day if he did so. But because this outcome would be socially inefficient, we know that each party can do better.

Suppose, for example, that Abercrombie gives Fitch $40 per day in return for Fitch's permission to operate without a filter. Each would then have a net daily gain of $110, which is $10 better for each of them than if Fitch had insisted that Abercrombie use a filter. Abercrombie's pollution harms Fitch, sure enough. But failure to allow the pollution would have caused even greater harm to Abercrombie.

The Coase theorem tells us that regardless of whether the law holds polluters liable for damages, the affected parties will achieve efficient solutions to externalities if they can negotiate costlessly with one another. Note carefully that this does not imply that affected parties will be indifferent about whether the law holds polluters responsible for damages. If polluters are liable, they will end up with lower incomes and those who are injured by pollutants will end up with higher incomes than if the law does not hold polluters liable—even though the same efficient production methods would be adopted in each case. When polluters are held liable, they must remove the pollution at their own expense. When they are not held liable, those who are injured by pollution must pay polluters to cut back.

Externalities are hardly rare and isolated occurrences. On the contrary, finding examples of actions that are altogether free of them is difficult. And because externalities can distort the allocation of resources, it is important to recognize them and deal intelligently with them. Consider the following example of an externality that arises because of shared living arrangements.

| EXAMPLE 11.6 | **Cost-Benefit Principle—Shared Living Expenses** |

Will Adriana and Sofia share an apartment?

Adriana and Sofia can live together in a two-bedroom apartment for $1,000 per month, or separately in 2 one-bedroom apartments, each for $600 per month. If the rent paid were the same for both alternatives, the two women would be indifferent between living together or separately, except for one problem: Adriana often has friends over late at night when Sofia is trying to sleep. Adriana would pay up to $250 per month for this privilege. Sofia, for her part, would pay up to $150 per month to consistently get a good night's sleep. Should they live together or separately?

Adriana and Sofia should live together only if the benefit of doing so exceeds the cost. The benefit of living together is the reduction in their rent. Since 2 one-bedroom apartments would cost a total of $1,200 per month, compared to $1,000 for a two-bedroom unit, their benefit from living together is $200 per month. Their cost of living together is the least costly accommodation they can make to Adriana's objectionable habits. Adriana would be willing to pay up to $250 per month to avoid changing her behavior, so the $200 rent saving is too small to persuade her to change. But Sofia is willing to put up with Adriana's behavior for a compensation payment of only $150 per month. Since that amount is smaller than the total saving in rent, the least costly solution to the problem is for Sofia to live with Adriana and simply put up with her behavior.

 Cost-Benefit ⟩⟩

Table 11.3 summarizes the relevant costs and benefits of this shared living arrangement. The Cost-Benefit Principle tells us that Adriana and Sofia should live together if and only if the benefit of living together exceeds the cost. The cost of the shared living arrangement is not the sum of all possible costs but the least

TABLE 11.3
The Gain in Surplus from Shared Living Arrangements

Benefits of Shared Living		
Total cost of separate apartments	**Total cost of shared apartment**	**Rent savings from sharing**
2 × $600/month $1,200/month	$1,000/month	$200/month

Costs of Shared Living			
Problem	**Adriana's cost of solving problem**	**Sofia's cost of solving problem**	**Least costly solution to the problem**
Adriana inviting friends over late at night	Limiting when her friends come over: $250/month	Tolerating the noise at night: $150/month	Sofia tolerates the noise made by Adriana's friends: $150/month

Gain in Surplus from Shared Living		
Rent savings ($200/month)	— Least costly accommodation to shared living problems ($150/month)	= Gain in surplus: ($50/month)

costly accommodation to the problem (or problems) of shared living. Since the $200 per month saving in rent exceeds the least costly accommodation to the noise problem, Adriana and Sofia can reap a total gain in economic surplus of $50 per month by sharing their living quarters.

Some people might conclude that Adriana and Sofia should not live together because if the two share the rent equally, Sofia would end up paying $500 per month—which when added to the $150 cost of putting up with Adriana's behavior comes to $50 more than the cost of living alone. As persuasive as that argument may sound, however, it is mistaken. The source of the error, as the following example illustrates, is the assumption that the two must share the rent equally.

EXAMPLE 11.7   Cost-Benefit Principle—Paying Unequal Rent Amounts

What is the highest rent Sofia would be willing to pay for the two-bedroom apartment?

In Example 11.6, Sofia's alternative is to live alone, which would mean paying $600 per month, her reservation price for a living arrangement in which she is not woken up by Adriana's friends. Since the most she would be willing to pay to avoid this problem is $150 per month, the highest monthly rent she would be willing to pay for the shared apartment is $600 − $150 = $450. If she pays that amount, Adriana will have to pay the difference, namely, $550 per month, which is clearly a better alternative for Adriana than paying $600 to live alone.

EXAMPLE 11.8   Cost-Benefit Principle—Splitting Economic Surplus

How much should Adriana and Sofia pay if they agree to split their economic surplus equally?

As we saw in Table 11.3, the total rent saving from the shared apartment is $200, and since the least costly solution to the problem is $150, the monthly gain in economic surplus is $50. We know from Example 11.7 that Adriana's reservation price for living together is $600 per month and Sofia's is $450. So if the two women want to split the $50 monthly surplus equally, each should pay $25 less than her reservation price. Adriana's monthly rent will thus be $575 and Sofia's, $425. The result is that each is $25 per month better off than if she had lived alone.

> ✔ **SELF-TEST 11.2**
>
> As in Examples 11.6 and 11.7, Adriana and Sofia can live together in a two-bedroom apartment for $1,000 per month or separately in 2 one-bedroom apartments, each for $600 per month. Adriana would pay up to $250 per month rather than moderate her social habits, and Sofia would pay up to $150 per month to consistently get a good night's sleep. Now, suppose Sofia would also be willing to pay up to $60 per month to avoid the loss of privacy that comes with a shared living space. Should the two women live together?

REMEDIES FOR EXTERNALITIES

LAWS AND REGULATIONS

We have seen that efficient solutions to externalities can be found whenever the affected parties can negotiate with one another at no cost. But negotiation is not always practical. A motorist with a noisy muffler imposes costs on others, yet they cannot flag him down and offer him a compensation payment to fix his muffler. In recognition of this difficulty, most governments simply require that cars have working mufflers. Indeed, the explicit or implicit purpose of a large share—perhaps the lion's share—of laws is to solve problems caused by externalities. The goal of such laws is to help people achieve the solutions they might have reached had they been able to negotiate with one another.

When negotiation is costless, the task of adjustment generally falls on the party who can accomplish it at the lowest cost. For instance, in our examples, Sofia put up with Adriana's annoying habits because doing so was less costly than asking Adriana to change her habits. Many municipal noise ordinances also place the burden of adjustment on those who can accomplish it at the lowest cost. Consider, for example, the restrictions on loud party music, which often take effect at a later hour on weekends than on weekdays. This pattern reflects both the fact that the gains from loud music tend to be larger on weekends and the fact that such music is more likely to disturb people on weekdays. By setting the noise curfew at different hours on different days of the week, the law places the burden on partygoers during the week and on sleepers during the weekend. Similar logic explains why noise ordinances allow motorists to honk their horns in most neighborhoods, but not in the immediate vicinity of a hospital.

The list of laws and regulations that may be fruitfully viewed as solutions to externalities is a long one. When a motorist drives his car at high speed, he endangers not just his own life and property, but also the lives and property of others. Speed limits, no-passing zones, right-of-way rules, and a host of other traffic laws may be seen as reasoned attempts to limit the harm one party inflicts on another. Many jurisdictions even have laws requiring that motorists install snow tires on their cars by the first of November. These laws promote not just safety, but also the smooth flow of traffic: If one motorist can't get up a snow-covered hill, he delays not only himself, but also the motorists behind him.

Similar reasoning helps us understand the logic of zoning laws that restrict the kinds of activities that take place in various parts of cities. Because many residents place a high value on living in an uncongested neighborhood, some cities have enacted zoning laws specifying minimum lot sizes. In places like Manhattan, where a shortage of land encourages developers to build very large and tall buildings, zoning laws limit both a building's height and the proportion of a lot it may occupy. Such restrictions recognize that the taller a building is, and the greater the proportion of its lot that it occupies, the more it blocks sunlight from reaching surrounding properties. The desire to control external costs also helps explain why many cities establish separate zones for business and residential activity. Even within business districts, many cities limit certain kinds of commercial activity. For example, in an effort to revitalize the Times Square neighborhood, New York City enacted a zoning law banning adult bookstores and pornographic movie theaters from the area.

Limitations on the discharge of pollutants into the environment are perhaps the clearest examples of laws aimed at solving problems caused by externalities. The details of these laws reflect the principle of placing the burden of adjustment on those who can accomplish it at least cost. The discharge of toxic wastes into rivers, for example, tends to be most strictly regulated on those waterways whose commercial fishing or recreational uses are most highly valued. On other waterways, the burden of adjustment is likely to fall more heavily on fishermen, recreational boaters, and swimmers. Similarly, air-quality regulations tend to be strictest in the most heavily populated regions of the country, where the marginal benefit of pollution reduction is the greatest.

The following examples suggest additional ways in which Coase's insights about how societies deal with externalities provide rich fodder for the economic naturalist.

The Economic Naturalist 11.1

What is the purpose of free speech laws?

The First Amendment's protection of free speech and the pattern of exceptions to that protection are another illustration of how legal remedies are used to solve the problems caused by externalities. The First Amendment acknowledges the decisive value of open communication, as well as the practical difficulty of identifying and regulating acts of speech that cause more harm than good. Yet there are some important exceptions. The Supreme Court has ruled, for instance, that the First Amendment does not allow someone to yell "fire" in a crowded theater if there is no fire, nor does it allow someone to advocate the violent overthrow of the government. In those instances, the external benefits of free speech are far too small to justify the external costs.

Why does the U.S. Constitution protect the right of free speech?

The Economic Naturalist 11.2

Why do many states have laws requiring students to be vaccinated against childhood illnesses?

Proof of immunization against chickenpox, diphtheria, measles, mumps, pertussis, polio, rubella, and tetanus is now universally required for entry into American public schools. Most states also require immunization against hepatitis B (43 states). Why these requirements?

Vaccinating children against childhood illnesses can entail a small but potentially serious risk (though the supposed link between vaccinations and autism has been thoroughly debunked). On the other hand, it can protect children against dangerous diseases. For an individual family, the decision to vaccinate involves weighing the benefits of vaccination against its potential risks and cost. The problem is that this calculation ignores the fact that a family's decision to become vaccinated benefits not just the family, but also everyone else in the community because the family would be far less likely to contract the illness and pass it on to others.

Relegating the vaccination decision to individuals would result in a suboptimally low vaccination rate because many families would fail to take adequate account of the benefit that becoming vaccinated would have on others. It is for this reason that most states require vaccinations against specific childhood illnesses.

Even these laws, however, allow parents to apply for exemptions on religious or philosophical grounds. Communities vary in the extent to which parents avail themselves of these

Why are vaccinations against many childhood illnesses required by law?

exemptions. In Colorado, for example, Boulder County heads the list of parents who opt to exempt their children from taking the pertussis vaccine, where only 84.1 percent of public school children have an up-to-date pertussis vaccination compared to 89.9 percent statewide. Not surprisingly, the incidence of whooping cough is much higher in Boulder (37.4 cases per year per 100,000 people) than in the state as a whole (22.4 cases per year per 100,000 people).[1]

THE OPTIMAL AMOUNT OF NEGATIVE EXTERNALITIES IS NOT ZERO

Curbing pollution and other negative externalities entails both costs and benefits. As we saw in Chapter 6, *Perfectly Competitive Supply*, when we analyzed how many cans should be recycled, the best policy is to curtail pollution until the cost of further abatement just equals the marginal benefit. In general, the marginal cost of abatement rises with the amount of pollution eliminated. (Following the Low-Hanging-Fruit Principle, polluters use the cheapest cleanup methods first and then turn to more expensive ones.) And the law of diminishing marginal utility suggests that beyond some point, the marginal benefit of pollution reduction tends to fall as more pollution is removed. As a result, the marginal cost and marginal benefit curves almost always intersect at less than the maximum amount of pollution reduction.

The intersection of the two curves marks the socially optimal level of pollution reduction. If pollution is curtailed by any less than that amount, society will gain more than it will lose by pushing the cleanup effort a little further. But if regulators push beyond the point at which the marginal cost and benefit curves intersect, society will incur costs that exceed the benefits. The existence of a socially optimal level of pollution reduction implies the existence of a socially optimal level of pollution, and that level will almost always be greater than zero.

Because people have been conditioned to think of pollution as bad, many cringe when they hear the phrase "socially optimal level of pollution." How can any positive level of pollution be socially optimal? *But to speak of a socially optimal level of pollution is not the same as saying that pollution is good.* It is merely to recognize that society has an interest in cleaning up the environment, but only up to a certain point. The underlying idea is no different from the idea of an optimal level of dirt in an apartment. After all, even if you spent the whole day, every day, vacuuming your apartment, there would be *some* dirt left in it. And because you have better things to do than vacuum all day, you probably tolerate substantially more than the minimal amount of dirt. A dirty apartment is not good, nor is pollution in the air you breathe. But in both cases, the cleanup effort should be expanded only until the marginal benefit equals the marginal cost.

COMPENSATORY TAXES AND SUBSIDIES

As noted, when transaction costs prohibit negotiation among affected parties, negative externalities lead to excessive output levels because activities that produce negative externalities are misleadingly attractive to those who engage in them. One solution to this problem, proposed by the British economist A. C. Pigou, is to make such activities less attractive by taxing them. Figure 11.3(a) reproduces Figure 11.1's portrayal of a market in which each unit of output generates an external cost of *XC* equal to $1,000 per ton. Because producers fail to take this external cost into account, the private equilibrium is 12,000 tons per year, or 4,000 tons per year more than the socially optimal level of 8,000 tons per year.

Figure 11.3(b) portrays that same market after the imposition of a tax of $1,000 per unit of output. This tax has the effect of raising each producer's marginal cost curve by $1,000, so the industry supply curve shifts upward by $1,000 at every quantity. Note that the resulting private equilibrium output, 8,000 tons per year, is now exactly equal to the socially optimal output. Although many critics insist that taxes always reduce economic efficiency, here we have an example of a tax that actually makes the economy *more*

[1]From the Colorado School and Childcare Immunization Data 2016–2017 (www.cohealthdata.dphe.state.co.us/Data/Details/1) and the Colorado Department of Public Health and Environment (www.colorado.gov/pacific/cdphe/colorado-health-indicators).

FIGURE 11.3

Taxing a Negative Externality.

(a) Negative externalities lead to an equilibrium with more than the socially optimal level of output.
(b) Imposing a tax equal to the external cost leads to an equilibrium in which the output level is socially optimal. The tax makes the economy more efficient because it leads producers to take account of a relevant cost that they would otherwise ignore.

efficient. The tax has that effect because it forces producers to take explicit account of the fact that each additional unit of output they produce imposes an external cost of $1,000 on the rest of society.

Similar reasoning suggests that a subsidy to producers can serve to counteract misallocations that result from positive externalities. Figure 11.4(a) portrays a market in which each unit of output generates an external benefit $XB = \$6$ per ton. In this market, the socially optimal output level occurs at the intersection of the supply curve (MC) and the

FIGURE 11.4

Subsidizing a Positive Externality.

(a) Positive externalities lead to an equilibrium with less than the socially optimal level of output. (b) Paying producers a subsidy equal to the external benefit of the activity leads to an equilibrium in which the output level is socially optimal. The subsidy makes the economy more efficient because it leads producers to take account of a relevant benefit that they would otherwise ignore.

Social demand curve, which is constructed by adding $XB = \$6$ per ton to the height of Private demand at each level of output. The socially optimal level of output is thus 1,600 tons per year. But private equilibrium in this market will occur at the intersection of Private demand and *MC,* which means that the equilibrium output, 1,200 tons per year, falls short of the social optimum by 400 tons per year.

Figure 11.4(b) shows the effect of paying a subsidy to producers of $6 per ton, the amount of the external benefit. In the presence of this subsidy, the new private equilibrium is 1,600 tons per year, exactly the socially optimal level. The subsidy makes the economy more efficient because it induces producers to take account of a relevant benefit that they otherwise would have ignored.

The Economic Naturalist 11.3

Why does the government subsidize private property owners to plant trees on their hillsides?

Societies use laws not only to discourage activities that generate negative externalities, but also to encourage activities that generate positive externalities. The planting of trees on hillsides, for example, benefits not just the landowner, but also his neighbors by limiting the danger of flooding. In recognition of this fact, many jurisdictions subsidize the planting of trees. Similarly, Congress budgets millions of dollars each year in support of basic research—an implicit acknowledgment of the positive externalities associated with the generation of new knowledge.

Why does the government subsidize scientific research?

RECAP ↑

EXTERNAL COSTS AND BENEFITS

Externalities occur when the costs or benefits of an activity accrue to people other than those directly involved in the activity. The Coase theorem says that when affected parties can negotiate with one another without cost, activities will be pursued at efficient levels, even in the presence of positive or negative externalities. But when negotiation is prohibitively costly, inefficient behavior generally results. Activities that generate negative externalities are pursued to excess, while those that generate positive externalities are pursued too little. Laws and regulations, including taxes and subsidies, are often adopted in an effort to alter inefficient behavior that results from externalities.

PROPERTY RIGHTS AND THE TRAGEDY OF THE COMMONS

People who grow up in industrialized nations tend to take the institution of private property for granted. Our intuitive sense is that people have the right to own any property they acquire by lawful means and to do with that property as they see fit. In reality, however, property laws are considerably more complex in terms of the rights they confer and the obligations they impose.

THE PROBLEM OF UNPRICED RESOURCES

To understand the laws that govern the use of property, let's begin by asking why societies created the institution of private property in the first place. The following examples, which show what happens to property that nobody owns, suggest an answer.

EXAMPLE 11.9   Individual Income

How many steers will villagers send onto the commons?

A village has five residents, each of whom has accumulated savings of $100. Each villager can use the money to buy a government bond that pays 13 percent interest per year or to buy a year-old steer, send it onto the commons to graze, and sell it after 1 year. The price the villager will get for the 2-year-old steer depends on the amount of weight it gains while grazing on the commons, which in turn depends on the number of steers sent onto the commons, as shown in Table 11.4.

TABLE 11.4
The Relationship between Herd Size and Steer Price

Number of steers on the commons	Price per 2-year-old steer ($)	Income per steer ($/year)
1	126	26
2	119	19
3	116	16
4	113	13
5	111	11

The price of a 2-year-old steer declines with the number of steers grazing on the commons because the more steers, the less grass available to each. The villagers make their investment decisions one at a time, and the results are public. If each villager decides how to invest individually, how many steers will be sent onto the commons, and what will be the village's total income?

If a villager buys a $100 government bond, he'll earn $13 of interest income at the end of 1 year. Thus, he should send a steer onto the commons if and only if that steer will command a price of at least $113 as a 2-year-old. When each villager chooses in this self-interested way, we can expect four villagers to send a steer onto the commons. (Actually, the fourth villager would be indifferent between investing in a steer or buying a bond since he would earn $13 either way. For the sake of discussion, we'll assume that in the case of a tie, people choose to be cattle owners.) The fifth villager, seeing that he would earn only $11 by sending a fifth steer onto the commons, will choose instead to buy a government bond. As a result of these decisions, the total village income will be $65 per year—$13 for the one bondholder and 4($13) = $52 for the four cattle owners.

Has Adam Smith's invisible hand produced the most efficient allocation of these villagers' resources? We can tell at a glance that it has not, since their total village income is only $65—precisely the same as it would have been had the possibility of cattle raising not existed. The source of the difficulty will become evident in the following example.

EXAMPLE 11.10   Maximizing Total Group Income

What is the socially optimal number of steers to send onto the commons?

Suppose the five villagers in the previous example confront the same investment opportunities as before, except that this time they are free to make their decisions as a group rather than individually. How many steers will they send onto the commons, and what will be their total village income?

This time the villagers' goal is to maximize the income received by the group as a whole. When decisions are made from this perspective, the criterion is to send a steer onto the commons only if its marginal contribution to village income is at least $13, the amount that could be earned from a government bond. As the entries in column 5 indicate, the first steer clearly meets this criterion since it contributes $26 to total village income. But the second steer does not. Sending that steer onto the commons raises the village's income from cattle raising from $26 to $38, a gain of just $12. The $100 required to buy the second steer would thus have been better invested in a government bond. Worse, the collective return from sending a third steer is only $10; from a fourth, only $4; and from a fifth, only $3.

TABLE 11.5
Marginal Income and the Socially Optimal Herd Size

(1) Number of steers on the commons	(2) Price per 2-year-old steer ($)	(3) Income per steer ($/year)	(4) Total village income ($/year)	(5) Marginal income ($/year)
				26
1	126	26	26	
				12
2	119	19	38	
				10
3	116	16	48	
				4
4	113	13	52	
				3
5	111	11	55	

In sum, when investment decisions are made with the goal of maximizing total village income, the best choice is to buy four government bonds and send only a single steer onto the commons. The resulting village income will be $78: $26 from sending the single steer and $52 from the four government bonds. That amount is $13 more than the total income that resulted when villagers made their investment decisions individually. Once again, the reward from moving from an inefficient allocation to an efficient one is that the economic pie grows larger. And when the pie grows larger, everyone can get a larger slice. For instance, if the villagers agree to pool their income and share it equally, each will get $15.60, or $2.60 more than before.

 SELF-TEST 11.3

How would your answers to Examples 11.9 and 11.10 change if the interest rate were 11 percent per year rather than 13 percent?

Why do the villagers in Examples 11.9 and 11.10 do better when they make their investment decisions collectively? The answer is that when individuals decide alone, they ignore the fact that sending another steer onto the commons will cause existing steers to gain less weight. Their failure to consider this effect makes the return from sending another steer seem misleadingly high to them.

The grazing land on the commons is a valuable economic resource. When no one **tragedy of the commons** owns it, no one has any incentive to take the opportunity cost of using it into account. the tendency for a resource And when that happens, people will tend to use it until its marginal benefit is zero. This that has no price to be used problem, and others similar to it, are known as the **tragedy of the commons**. The essential until its marginal benefit falls cause of the tragedy of the commons is the fact that one person's use of commonly held to zero property imposes an external cost on others by making the property less valuable. The tragedy of the commons also provides a vivid illustration of the Equilibrium Principle. Each individual villager behaves rationally by sending an additional steer onto the commons, yet the overall outcome falls far short of the attainable ideal.

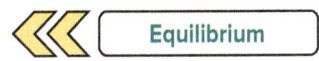
Equilibrium

THE EFFECT OF PRIVATE OWNERSHIP

As the following example illustrates, one solution to the tragedy of the commons is to place the village grazing land under private ownership.

EXAMPLE 11.11   Private Ownership

How much will the right to control the village commons sell for?

Suppose the five villagers face the same investment opportunities as before, except that this time they decide to auction off the right to use the commons to the highest bidder. Assuming that villagers can borrow as well as lend at an annual interest rate of 13 percent, what price will the right to use the commons fetch? How will the owner of that property right use it, and what will be the resulting village income?

To answer these questions, simply ask yourself what you would do if you had complete control over how the grazing land were used. As we saw earlier, the most profitable way to use this land is to send only a single steer to graze on it. If you do so, you will earn a total of $26 per year. Since the opportunity cost of the $100 you spent on the single yearling steer is the $13 in interest you could have earned from a bond, your economic profit from sending a single steer onto the commons will be $13 per year, provided you can use the land for free. But you cannot; to finance your purchase of the property right, you must borrow money (since you used your $100 savings to buy a year-old steer).

What is the most you would be willing to pay for the right to use the commons? Its use generates an income of $26 per year—or $13 more than the opportunity cost of your investment in the steer—so the most you would pay is $100 (since that amount used to purchase a bond that pays 13 percent interest would also generate income of $13 per year). If the land were sold at auction, $100 is precisely the amount you would have to pay. Your annual earnings from the land would be exactly enough to pay the $13 interest on your loan and cover the opportunity cost of not having put your savings into a bond.

Note that when the right to use the land is auctioned to the highest bidder, the village achieves a more efficient allocation of its resources because the owner has a strong incentive to take the opportunity cost of more intensive grazing fully into account. Total village income in this case will again be $78. If the annual interest on the $100 proceeds from selling the land rights is shared equally among the five villagers, each will again have an annual investment income of $15.60.

The logic of economic surplus maximization helps explain why the most economically successful nations have all been ones with well-developed private property laws. Property that belongs to everyone belongs, in effect, to no one. Not only is its potential economic value never fully realized; it usually ends up being of no value at all.

Bear in mind, however, that in most countries the owners of private property are not free to do *precisely* as they wish with it. For example, local zoning laws may give the owner of a residential building lot the right to build a three-story house but not a taller one. Here, too, the logic of economic surplus maximization applies, for a fully informed and rational legislature would define property rights so as to create the largest possible total economic surplus. In practice, of course, such ideal legislatures never really exist. Yet the essence of politics is the cutting of deals that make people better off. If a legislator could propose a change in the property laws that would enlarge the total economic surplus, she could also propose a scheme that would give each of her constituents a larger slice, thus enhancing her chances for reelection.

As an economic naturalist, challenge yourself to use this framework when thinking about the various restrictions you encounter in private property laws: zoning laws that constrain what you can build and what types of activities you can conduct on your land; traffic laws that constrain what you can do with your car; employment and environmental laws that constrain how you can operate your business. Your understanding of these and countless other laws will be enhanced by the insight that everyone can gain when the private property laws are defined so as to create the largest total economic surplus.

WHEN PRIVATE OWNERSHIP IS IMPRACTICAL

Don't be misled into thinking that the law provides an *ideal* resolution of all problems associated with externalities and the tragedy of the commons. Defining and enforcing efficient property rights entail costs, after all, and sometimes, as in the following examples, the costs outweigh the gains.

The Economic Naturalist 11.4

Why do blackberries in public parks get picked too soon?

Wild blackberries grow profusely at the edge of a wooded area in a crowded city park. The blackberries will taste best if left to ripen fully, but they still taste reasonably good if picked and eaten a few days early. Will the blackberries be left to ripen fully?

▶ Visit your instructor's Connect course and access your eBook to view this video.

Why do blackberries in public parks get picked before they're completely ripe?

Obviously, the costs of defining and enforcing the property rights to blackberries growing in a public park are larger than the potential gains, so the blackberries will remain common property. That means that whoever picks them first gets them. Even though everyone would benefit if people waited until the berries were fully ripe, everyone knows that those who wait are likely to end up with no berries at all. And that means that the berries will be eaten too soon.

The Economic Naturalist 11.5

Why are shared milkshakes drunk too quickly?

Why are shared milkshakes consumed too quickly?

Sara and Susan are identical twins who have been given a chocolate milkshake to share. If each has a straw and each knows that the other is self-interested, will the twins consume the milkshake at an optimal rate?

Because drinking a milkshake too quickly chills the taste buds, the twins will enjoy their shake more if they drink it slowly. Yet each knows that the other will drink any part of the milkshake she doesn't finish herself. The result is that each will consume the shake at a faster rate than she would if she had half a shake all to herself.

Here are some further examples in which the tragedy of the commons is not easily solved by defining private ownership rights.

Harvesting Timber on Remote Public Land

On remote public lands, enforcing restrictions against cutting down trees may be impractical. Each tree cutter knows that a tree that is not harvested this year will be bigger, and hence more valuable, next year. But he also knows that if he doesn't cut the tree down this year, someone else might do so. In contrast, private companies that grow trees on their own land have no incentive to harvest timber prematurely and a strong incentive to prevent outsiders from doing so.

Harvesting Whales in International Waters

Each individual whaler knows that harvesting an extra whale reduces the breeding population, and hence the size of the future whale population. But the whaler also knows that any whale that is not harvested today may be taken by some other whaler. The solution would be to define and enforce property rights to whales. But the oceans are vast, and the behavior of whalers is hard to monitor. And even if their behavior could be monitored, the concept of national sovereignty would make the international enforcement of property rights problematic.

More generally, the animal species that are most severely threatened with extinction tend to be those that are economically valuable to humans but that are not privately owned by anyone. This is the situation confronting whales as well as elephants. Contrast this with the situation confronting chickens, which are also economically valuable to humans but which, unlike whales, are governed by traditional laws of private property. This difference explains why no one worries that Colonel Sanders might threaten the extinction of chickens.

Controlling Emissions of Greenhouse Gases

The atmosphere surrounding the planet is perhaps the most important current example of the tragedy of the commons. As we saw in Example 9.4 in Chapter 9, reducing emissions is costly, and the harm caused by any single firm's emissions is negligible. Any firm that reduced its own emissions while others didn't would thus confront significant risk of bankruptcy. Economists are in near unanimous agreement that the best response to this externality would be to levy taxes that reflect our best estimates of the damage done by additional emissions, a topic to which we'll return shortly.

As the world's population continues to grow, the absence of an effective system of international property rights will become an economic problem of increasing significance.

RECAP

PROPERTY RIGHTS AND THE TRAGEDY OF THE COMMONS

When a valuable resource has a price of zero, people will continue to exploit it as long as its marginal benefit remains positive. The tragedy of the commons describes situations in which valuable resources are squandered because users are not charged for them. In many cases, an efficient remedy is to define and enforce rights to the use of valuable property. But this solution is difficult to implement for resources such as the oceans and the atmosphere because no single government has the authority to enforce property rights for these resources.

POSITIONAL EXTERNALITIES

Former tennis champion Steffi Graf received more than $1.6 million in tournament winnings in 1992; her endorsement and exhibition earnings totaled several times that amount. By any reasonable measure, the quality of her play was outstanding, yet she consistently lost to archrival Monica Seles. But in April 1993, Seles was stabbed in the back by a deranged fan and forced to withdraw from the tour. In the ensuing months, Graf's tournament winnings accumulated at almost double her 1992 pace, despite little change in the quality of her play.

PAYOFFS THAT DEPEND ON RELATIVE PERFORMANCE

In professional tennis and a host of other competitive situations, the rewards people receive typically depend not only on how they perform in absolute terms but also on how they perform relative to their closest rivals. In these situations, competitors have an incentive to take actions that will increase their odds of winning. For example, tennis players can increase their chances of winning by hiring personal fitness trainers and sports psychologists to travel with them on the tour. Yet the simple mathematics of competition tells us that the sum of all individual payoffs from such investments will be larger than the collective payoff. In any tennis match, for example, each contestant will get a sizable payoff from money spent on fitness trainers and sports psychologists, yet each match will have exactly one winner and one loser, no matter how much players spend. The overall gain to tennis spectators is likely to be small, and the overall gain to players as a group must be zero. To the extent that each contestant's payoff depends on his or her relative performance, then, the incentive to undertake such investments will be excessive, from a collective point of view.

Consider the following example.

The Economic Naturalist 11.6

Why do football players take anabolic steroids?

The offensive linemen of many National Football League teams currently average more than 330 pounds. In the 1970s, by contrast, offensive linemen in the league averaged barely 280 pounds, and the all-decade linemen of the 1940s averaged only 229 pounds. One reason that today's players are so much heavier is that players' salaries have escalated sharply over the last several decades, which has intensified competition for the positions. Size and strength are the two cardinal virtues of an offensive lineman, and other things being equal, the job will go to the larger and stronger of two rivals.

Size and strength, in turn, can be enhanced by the consumption of anabolic steroids. But if all players consume these substances, the rank ordering of players by size and strength—and hence the question of who lands the jobs—will be largely unaffected. And because the consumption of anabolic steroids entails potentially serious long-term health consequences, football players as a group are clearly worse off if they consume these drugs. So why do football players take steroids?

The problem here is that contestants for starting berths on the offensive line confront a prisoner's dilemma, like the ones analyzed in Chapter 9, *Games and Strategic Behavior*. Consider two closely matched rivals—Smith and Jones—who are competing for a single position. If neither takes steroids, each has a 50 percent chance of winning the job and a starting salary of $1 million per year. If both take steroids, each again has a 50 percent chance of winning the job. But if one takes steroids and the other doesn't, the first is sure to win the job. The loser ends up selling insurance for $60,000 per year. Neither likes the fact that the drugs may have adverse health consequences, but each would be willing to take that risk in return for a shot at the big salary. Given these choices, the two competitors face a payoff matrix like the one shown in Table 11.6.

Why do so many football players take steroids?

TABLE 11.6
Payoff Matrix for Steroid Consumption

		Jones	
		Don't take steroids	Take steroids
Smith	Don't take steroids	Second best for each	Best for Jones Worst for Smith
	Take steroids	Best for Smith Worst for Jones	Third best for each

Clearly, the dominant strategy for both Smith and Jones is to take steroids. Yet when they do, each gets only the third-best outcome, whereas they could have gotten the second-best outcome by not taking the drugs—hence the attraction of rules that forbid the consumption of anabolic steroids.

POSITIONAL ARMS RACES AND POSITIONAL ARMS CONTROL AGREEMENTS

The steroid problem is an example of a **positional externality**. Whenever the payoffs to one contestant depend at least in part on how he or she performs relative to a rival, any step that improves one side's relative position must necessarily worsen the other's. The shouting-at-parties example discussed in Chapter 9, *Games and Strategic Behavior*, is another instance of a positional externality. Just as the invisible hand of the market is weakened by the presence of standard externalities, it is also weakened by positional externalities.

We have seen that positional externalities often lead contestants to engage in an escalating series of mutually offsetting investments in performance enhancement. We call such spending patterns **positional arms races**.

Because positional arms races produce inefficient outcomes, people have an incentive to curtail them. Steps taken to reduce positional arms races, such as blue laws and rules against anabolic steroids, may therefore be thought of as **positional arms control agreements**.

Once you become aware of positional arms races, you will begin to see them almost everywhere. You can hone your skills as an economic naturalist by asking these questions about every competitive situation you observe: What form do the investments in performance enhancement take? What steps have contestants taken to limit these investments? Sometimes positional arms control agreements are achieved by the imposition of formal rules or by the signing of legal contracts. Some examples of this type of agreement follow.

Campaign Spending Limits

In the United States, presidential candidates routinely spend hundreds of millions of dollars on advertising. Yet if both candidates double their spending on ads, each one's odds of winning will remain essentially the same. Recognition of this pattern led Congress to adopt strict spending limits for presidential candidates. (That those regulations have proved difficult to enforce does not call into question the logic behind the legislation.)

positional externality this occurs when an increase in one person's performance reduces the expected reward of another's in situations in which reward depends on relative performance

positional arms race a series of mutually offsetting investments in performance enhancement that is stimulated by a positional externality

positional arms control agreement an agreement in which contestants attempt to limit mutually offsetting investments in performance enhancement

Roster Limits

Major League Baseball permits franchises to have only 25 players on the roster during the regular season. The National Football League sets its roster limit at 53; the National Basketball Association at 12. Why these limits? In their absence, any team could increase its chance of winning by simply adding players. Inevitably, other teams would follow suit. On the plausible assumption that, beyond some point, larger rosters do not add much to the entertainment value for fans, roster limits are a sensible way to deliver sports entertainment at a more reasonable cost.

Arbitration Agreements

In the business world, contracting parties often sign a binding agreement that commits them to arbitration in the event of a dispute. By doing so, they sacrifice the option of pursuing their interests as fully as they might wish to later, but they also insulate themselves from costly legal battles. Other parties in the legal system may sometimes take steps to limit spending on litigation. For example, a federal judge in South Dakota announced—presumably to the approval of litigants—that he would read only the first 15 pages of any brief submitted to his court.

Mandatory Starting Dates for Kindergarten

A child who is a year or so older than most of her kindergarten classmates is likely to perform better, in relative terms, than if she had entered school with children her own age. And since most parents are aware that admission to prestigious universities and eligibility for top jobs upon graduation depend largely on *relative* academic performance, many are tempted to keep their children out of kindergarten a year longer than necessary. Yet there is no social advantage in holding *all* children back an extra year since their relative performance would essentially be unaffected. In most jurisdictions, therefore, the law requires children who reach their fifth birthday before December 1 of a given year to start kindergarten the same year.

SOCIAL NORMS AS POSITIONAL ARMS CONTROL AGREEMENTS

In some cases, social norms may take the place of formal agreements to curtail positional arms races. Some familiar examples follow.

Is being on fashion's cutting edge more valuable now than in the 1950s?

Nerd Norms

Some students care more—in the short run, at least—about the grades they get than how much they actually learn. When such students are graded on the curve—that is, on the basis of their performance relative to other students—a positional arms race ensues because if all students were to double the amount of time they studied, the distribution of grades would remain essentially the same. Students who find themselves in this situation are often quick to embrace "nerd norms," which brand as social misfits those who "study too hard."

Fashion Norms

Social norms regarding dress and fashion often change quickly because of positional competition. Consider, for instance, the person who wishes to be on the cutting edge of fashion. In some American social circles during the 1950s, that goal could be accomplished by having pierced ears. But as more and more people adopted the practice, it ceased to communicate avant-garde status. At the same time, those who wanted to make a conservative fashion statement gradually became freer to have their ears pierced.

For a period during the 1960s and 1970s, one could be on fashion's cutting edge by wearing two earrings in one earlobe. But by the 1990s multiple ear piercings had lost much of their social significance, the threshold of cutting-edge status having been raised to upward of a dozen piercings of each ear or a smaller number of piercings of the nose, eyebrows, or other body parts. A similar escalation has taken place in the number, size, and placement of tattoos.

The increase in the required number of tattoos or body piercings has not changed the value of avant-garde fashion status to those who desire it. Being on the outer limits of fashion has much the same meaning now as it once did. To the extent that there are costs associated with body piercings, tattoos, and other steps required to achieve avant-garde status, the current fashions are wasteful compared to earlier ones. In this sense, the erosion of social norms against tattoos and body piercings has produced a social loss. Of course, the costs associated with this loss are small in most cases. Yet since each body piercing entails a small risk of infection, the costs will continue to rise with the number of piercings. And once those costs reach a certain threshold, support may mobilize on behalf of social norms that discourage these activities.

Norms of Taste

Similar cycles occur with respect to behaviors considered to be in bad taste. In the 1950s, for example, prevailing norms prevented major national magazines from accepting ads that featured nude photographs. Naturally, advertisers had a powerful incentive to chip away at such norms in an effort to capture the reader's limited attention. And indeed, taboos against nude photographs have eroded in the same way as with those against body piercings and tattoos.

Consider, for instance, the evolution of perfume ads. First came the nude silhouette; then, increasingly well-lit and detailed nude photographs; and more recently, photographs of what appear to be group sex acts. Each innovation achieved just the desired effect: capturing the reader's instant and rapt attention. Inevitably, however, other advertisers followed suit, causing a shift in our sense of what is considered attention-grabbing. Photographs that once would have shocked readers now often draw little more than a bored glance.

Opinions differ, of course, about whether this change is an improvement. Many believe that the earlier, stricter norms were ill-advised, the legacy of a more prudish and repressive era. Yet even people who take that view are likely to believe that *some* kinds of photographic material ought not to be used in magazine advertisements. Obviously, what is acceptable will differ from person to person, and each person's threshold of discomfort will depend in part on current standards. But as advertisers continue to break new ground in their struggle to capture attention, the point may come when people begin to mobilize in favor of stricter standards of "public decency." Such a campaign would provide yet another case of a positional arms control agreement.

Norms against Vanity

Cosmetic and reconstructive surgery has produced dramatic benefits for many people, enabling badly disfigured accident victims to recover a normal appearance. It also has eliminated the extreme self-consciousness felt by people born with strikingly unusual features. Such surgery, however, is by no means confined to the conspicuously disfigured. Increasingly, "normal" people are seeking surgical improvements to their appearance. For example, in the United States, over 18 million cosmetic procedures were performed in 2019, and demand has continued to grow. Once a carefully guarded secret, these procedures are now offered as prizes in Southern California charity raffles.

In individual cases, cosmetic surgery may be just as beneficial as reconstructive surgery is for accident victims. Buoyed by the confidence of having a straight nose or a wrinkle-free complexion, patients sometimes go on to achieve much more than they ever thought possible. But the growing use of cosmetic surgery also has had an unintended side effect: It has altered the standards of normal appearance. A nose that once would have seemed only slightly larger than average may now seem jarringly big. The same person who once would have looked like an average 55-year-old may now look nearly 70. And someone who once would have tolerated slightly thinning hair or an average amount of cellulite may now feel compelled to undergo hair transplantation or liposuction. Because such procedures shift people's frame of reference, their payoffs to individuals are misleadingly large. From a social perspective, therefore, reliance on them is likely to be excessive.

Legal sanctions against cosmetic surgery are difficult to imagine. But some communities have embraced powerful social norms against cosmetic surgery, heaping scorn and ridicule on the consumers of face-lifts and tummy tucks. In individual cases, such norms may seem cruel. Yet without them, many more people might feel compelled to bear the risk and expense of cosmetic surgery.

> ## RECAP ↻
>
> ### POSITIONAL EXTERNALITIES
>
> Positional externalities occur when an increase in one person's performance reduces the expected reward of another person in situations in which reward depends on relative performance. Positional arms races are a series of mutually offsetting investments in performance enhancement that are stimulated by a positional externality. Positional arms control agreements are sometimes enacted in an attempt to limit positional arms races. In some cases, social norms can act as positional arms control agreements.

USING PRICE INCENTIVES IN ENVIRONMENTAL REGULATION

As we have seen, goods whose production generates negative externalities, such as atmospheric pollution, tend to be overproduced whenever negotiation among private parties is costly. Suppose we decide, as a society, that the best attainable outcome would be to have half as much pollution as would occur under completely unregulated conditions. In that case, how should the cleanup effort be distributed among those firms that currently discharge pollution into the environment?

The most efficient—and hence best—distribution of effort is the one for which each polluter's marginal cost of abatement is exactly the same. To see why, imagine that under current arrangements, the cost to one firm of removing a ton of pollution from the air is larger than the cost to another firm. Society could then achieve the same total reduction in pollution at lower cost by having the first firm discharge one ton more into the air and the second firm one ton less.

Unfortunately, government regulators seldom have detailed information on how the cost of reducing pollution varies from one firm to another. Many pollution laws therefore require all polluters simply to cut back their emissions by the same proportion or to meet the same absolute emissions standards. If different polluters have different marginal costs of pollution abatement, however, these approaches will not be efficient.

TAXING POLLUTION

Fortunately, alternative policies can distribute the cleanup more efficiently, even if the government lacks detailed information about how much it costs different firms to curtail pollution. One method is to tax pollution and allow firms to decide for themselves how much pollution to emit. The following example illustrates the logic of this approach.

EXAMPLE 11.12   ### Taxing Pollution

What is the least costly way to cut pollution by half?

Two firms, Sludge Oil and Northwest Lumber, each have access to five production processes, each of which has a different cost and produces a different amount of pollution. The daily costs of the processes and the number of tons of smoke emitted are as shown in Table 11.7. Pollution is currently unregulated, and negotiation between the firms and those who are harmed by pollution is impossible, which means that each firm uses process *A*, the least costly of the five. Each firm emits 4 tons of pollution per day, for a total of 8 tons of pollution per day.

TABLE 11.7
Costs and Emissions for Different Production Processes

Process (smoke)	A (4 tons/day)	B (3 tons/day)	C (2 tons/day)	D (1 ton/day)	E (0 tons/day)
Cost to Sludge Oil ($/day)	100	200	600	1,300	2,300
Cost to Northwest Lumber ($/day)	300	320	380	480	700

The government is considering two options for reducing total emissions by half. One is to require each firm to curtail its emissions by half. The other is to set a tax of $T per ton of smoke emitted each day. How large must T be to curtail emissions by half? What would be the total cost to society under each alternative?

If each firm is required to cut pollution by half, each must switch from process A to process C. The result will be 2 tons per day of pollution for each firm. The cost of the switch for Sludge Oil will be $600 per day − $100 per day = $500 per day. The cost to Northwest Lumber will be $380 per day − $300 per day = $80 per day, for a total cost of $580 per day.

Consider now how each firm would react to a tax of $T per ton of pollution. If a firm can cut pollution by 1 ton per day, it will save $T per day in tax payments. Whenever the cost of cutting a ton of pollution is less than $T, then each firm has an incentive to switch to a cleaner process. For example, if the tax were set at $40 per ton, Sludge Oil would stick with process A because switching to process B would cost $100 per day extra but would save only $40 per day in taxes. Northwest Lumber, however, would switch to process B because the $40 saving in taxes would be more than enough to cover the $20 cost of switching.

The problem is that a $40 per day tax on each ton of pollution results in a reduction of only 1 ton per day, 3 short of the 4-ton target. Suppose instead that the government imposed a tax of $101 per ton. Sludge Oil would then adopt process B because the $100 extra daily cost of doing so would be less than the $101 saved in taxes. Northwest Lumber would adopt process D because, for every process up to and including D, the cost of switching to the next process would be less than the resulting tax saving.

Overall, then, a tax of $101 per ton would result in the desired pollution reduction of 4 tons per day. The total cost of the reduction would be only $280 per day ($100 per day for Sludge Oil and $180 per day for Northwest Lumber), or $300 per day less than when each firm was required to cut its pollution by half. (The taxes paid by the firms do not constitute a cost of pollution reduction because the money can be used to reduce whatever taxes would otherwise need to be levied on citizens.)

 SELF-TEST 11.4

In Example 11.12, if the tax were $61 per ton of pollution emitted each day, which production processes would the two firms adopt?

The advantage of the tax approach is that it concentrates pollution reduction in the hands of the firms that can accomplish it at least cost. Requiring each firm to cut emissions by the same proportion ignores the fact that some firms can reduce pollution much more cheaply than others. Note that under the tax approach, the cost of the last ton of smoke removed is the same for each firm, so the efficiency condition is satisfied.

One problem with the tax approach is that unless the government has detailed knowledge about each firm's cost of reducing pollution, it cannot know how high to set the pollution tax.

A tax that is too low will result in too much pollution, while a tax that is too high will result in too little. Of course, the government could start by setting a low tax rate and gradually increase the rate until pollution is reduced to the target level. But because firms often incur substantial sunk costs when they switch from one process to another, that approach might be even more wasteful than requiring all firms to cut their emissions by the same proportion.

AUCTIONING POLLUTION PERMITS

Another alternative is to establish a target level for pollution and then auction off permits to emit that level. The virtues of this approach are illustrated in the following example.

EXAMPLE 11.13   Pollution Permits

How much will pollution permits sell for?

Two firms, Sludge Oil and Northwest Lumber, again have access to the production processes described earlier (which are reproduced in Table 11.8). The government's goal is to cut the current level of pollution, 8 tons per day, by half. To do so, the government auctions off four permits, each of which entitles the bearer to emit 1 ton of smoke per day. No smoke may be emitted without a permit. What price will the pollution permits fetch at auction, how many permits will each firm buy, and what will be the total cost of the resulting pollution reduction?

TABLE 11.8
Costs and Emissions for Different Production Processes

Process (smoke)	A (4 tons/day)	B (3 tons/day)	C (2 tons/day)	D (1 ton/day)	E (0 tons/day)
Cost to Sludge Oil ($/day)	100	200	600	1,300	2,300
Cost to Northwest Lumber ($/day)	300	320	380	480	700

If Sludge Oil has no permits, it must use process *E*, which costs $2,300 per day to operate. If it had one permit, it could use process *D*, which would save it $1,000 per day. Thus, the most Sludge Oil would be willing to pay for a single 1-ton pollution permit is $1,000 per day. With a second permit, Sludge Oil could switch to process *C* and save another $700 per day; with a third permit, it could switch to process *B* and save another $400; and with a fourth permit, it could switch to process *A* and save another $100. Using similar reasoning, we can see that Northwest Lumber would pay up to $220 for one permit, up to $100 for a second, up to $60 for a third, and up to $20 for a fourth.

Suppose the government starts the auction at a price of $90. Sludge Oil will then demand four permits and Northwest Lumber will demand two, for a total demand of six permits. Since the government wishes to sell only four permits, it will keep raising the price until the two firms together demand a total of only four permits. Once the price reaches $101, Sludge Oil will demand three permits and Northwest Lumber will demand only one, for a total quantity demanded of four permits. Compared to the unregulated alternative, in which each firm used process *A*, the daily cost of the auction solution is $280: Sludge Oil spends $100 switching from process *A* to process *B*, and Northwest Lumber spends $180 switching from *A* to *D*. This total is $300 less than the cost of requiring each firm to reduce its emissions by half. (Again, the permit fees paid by the firms do not constitute a cost of cleanup because the money can be used to reduce taxes that would otherwise have to be collected.)

The auction method has the same virtue as the tax method: It concentrates pollution reduction in the hands of those firms that can accomplish it at the lowest cost. But the auction method has other attractive features that the tax approach does not. First, it does not induce firms to commit themselves to costly investments that they will have to abandon if the cleanup falls short of the target level. And second, it allows private citizens a direct voice in determining where the emission level will be set. For example, any group that believes the pollution target is too lenient could raise money to buy permits at auction. By keeping those permits locked away in a safe, the group could ensure that they will not be used to emit pollution.

Several decades ago, when economists first proposed the auctioning of pollution permits, reactions of outrage were widely reported in the press. Most of those reactions amounted to the charge that the proposal would "permit rich firms to pollute to their hearts' content." Such an assertion betrays a total misunderstanding of the forces that generate pollution. Firms pollute not because they *want* to pollute but because dirty production processes are cheaper than clean ones. Society's only real interest is in keeping the total amount of pollution from becoming excessive, not in *who* actually does the polluting. And in any event, the firms that do most of the polluting under an auction system will not be rich firms, but those for whom pollution reduction is most costly.

Economists have argued patiently against these misinformed objections to the auction system, and their efforts have finally borne fruit. The sale of pollution permits is now common in several parts of the United States, and there is growing interest in the approach in other countries.

The problem of acid rain is an instructive case in point. Electric power plants in the Midwest had long burned high-sulfur coal, in the process discharging large quantities of sulfur dioxide (SO_2) from their smokestacks. Prevailing winds carried these emissions eastward, where they precipitated out over New York State and New England as acid rain, killing large quantities of trees and fish.

Beginning in the 1960s, economists advocated addressing this problem by requiring firms to acquire marketable permits for each ton of SO_2 they emitted. But as discussed earlier, economists' proposals, despite their compelling logic, languished in Congress for more than three decades. Only with the passage of amendments to the Clean Air Act in 1995 did Congress require the establishment of a market for permits for discharging SO_2.

As economists had predicted, the permit system worked spectacularly well. Acid rain caused by SO_2 emissions quickly plummeted, and at about one-sixth the cost that more complex regulatory approaches would have entailed.[2] Once people have to pay for their emissions, they quickly find ingenious ways of reducing them.

CLIMATE CHANGE AND CARBON TAXES

Growing concentrations of carbon dioxide (CO_2) in the atmosphere are widely recognized as a principal contributor to global warming. Concerns about the consequences of climate change have led to proposals to tax CO_2 emissions or require marketable permits for them. Critics of these proposals emphasize that forecasts involving climate change are highly uncertain, a fact they view as arguing for inaction. But uncertainty is a two-edged sword. Climate researchers themselves readily concede that estimates based on their models are extremely uncertain. But that means that although the actual outcome might be much better than their median forecast, it might also be significantly worse.

The Paris Agreement, which was adopted by representatives from nearly every nation on December 12, 2015, seeks to limit global warming to 2°C (3.6°F) by the end of the twenty-first century. But even the current increase of roughly 1.1°C (2°F) over pre-industrial times has led to dramatically increased frequency and severity of droughts, floods, storms, wildfires, and heat emergencies. The most respected climate change models estimate that average temperature will rise by far more than the Paris targets if we take no action.

A 2019 study published in *Nature Geoscience*, for example, demonstrated that increased concentrations of greenhouse gases could eventually result in the complete disappearance of clouds in Earth's atmosphere.[3] If that were to happen, the authors estimated, the

[2]See the United States Environmental Protection Agency, www.epa.gov/airmarkets.
[3]Tapio Schneider, Colleen M. Kaul, and Kyle G. Pressel, "Possible Climate Transitions from Breakup of Stratocumulus Decks under Greenhouse Warming," *Nature Geoscience* 12 (2019), pp. 163–167.

effect would be to add an additional 8°C (14.4°F) of warming beyond that attributable to other known greenhouse gas effects. Because an increase even far short of that magnitude could end life on Earth as we know it, it seems hardly an overstatement to call global climate change the most serious threat we've ever faced.

Again, the inherent uncertainty of climate estimates doesn't counsel inaction. Few would recommend, for example, that we disband the military simply because adversaries might not invade. In the climate arena, the only remaining uncertainty is how much worse things will get. To decide whether mitigation measures make sense, we must weigh their cost against the damage they would prevent.

An influential 1922 study published in *Nature* estimated what's called the social cost of carbon (SCC) at $185/ton.[4] SCC is an estimate of the additional current and future damage that will be caused by the emission of an additional ton of CO_2. Under any carbon tax, the prices of goods would rise in proportion to their carbon footprints. A tax of $185 per ton, for example, would raise the price of gasoline by about $1.60 a gallon, roughly similar to the increase that occurred shortly after Russia invaded Ukraine in 2022. As American motorists saw then, a sudden price increase of that magnitude could indeed be painful.

But if phased in gradually, adaptation to a carbon tax would cause much less difficulty. Facing steadily increasing fuel prices, for example, manufacturers would scramble to develop more fuel-efficient vehicles. Many Europeans now pay $4 a gallon more for gas than Americans do. But precisely because of that fact, European automakers have pioneered development of many of the world's most fuel-efficient cars. Europeans actually spend less on gas than Americans do and seem no less satisfied with their automobiles.

If a family traded in its aging Ford Explorer (15 mpg) for a Kia Niro wagon (49 mpg), it would spend considerably less on gas than before the imposition of a carbon tax, even if it drove just as much. If it bought an electric vehicle, its energy costs would be lower still. Phasing the tax in slowly would give people time to adjust. People would also move closer to work, form carpools, choose less distant vacation destinations, and so on. If the tax were revenue-neutral, monthly rebate checks would further ease the burden of higher gas prices.

In 2009 the U.S. House of Representatives passed an energy bill that included a comprehensive carbon cap and trade system, the functional equivalent of a carbon tax. But the bill couldn't win Senate approval. Of course, that doesn't mean change is permanently out of reach. For example, climate advocates won narrow majorities in both state legislature chambers and won the governorship in Virginia for the first time in November 2019. The Virginia Clean Economy Act, which was signed into law in February 2020, ranks among the most ambitious renewable energy measures enacted by any state.

Critics often object that no single country's imposition of a carbon tax would solve the problem. They're correct that for the tax approach to work, virtually all countries must adopt it. Greenhouse gas emissions are a global problem that can't be solved by reducing only one country's emissions.

The good news is that only a few of the world's largest industrial economies could create incentives for more widespread adoption of the tax approach to work by assuming a leadership role. Suppose, for example, that the United States and the European Union, which together accounted for more than 44 percent of global CO_2 emissions in 2021, enacted a significant carbon tax (which for countries in the EU would mean increasing the modest carbon taxes they have already adopted). World Trade Organization officials would then permit them to levy what are called Border Carbon Adjustments on any imported products that had not been subject to carbon taxation in their countries of origin. That would mean that if China did not impose a carbon tax domestically, the United States and the EU could levy one on any imported Chinese products.

Rather than let the United States and EU collect the revenue from a Border Carbon Adjustment, it would of course be in China's interest to levy a carbon tax of its own. Because the United States and the EU together comprise the world's most lucrative export market, their taking the lead on a carbon tax would virtually guarantee that most other countries would follow suit.

---

[4]Kevin Rennert et al., "Comprehensive Evidence Implies a Higher Social Cost of CO_2," *Nature* 610 (September 1, 2022), pp. 687–692.

A dispassionate application of the Cost-Benefit Principle comes down decisively in favor of carbon taxation. The American failure to have adopted this measure is a vivid illustration of how status quo bias and our tendency to discount future events excessively (see Chapter 10, *An Introduction to Behavioral Economics*) can lead to suboptimal policy choices. Moreover, America's five largest trading partners already have adopted either carbon taxes (Canada, Germany, Japan, and Mexico) or a comprehensive emissions trading system (China).

Cost-Benefit

RECAP↑

USING PRICE INCENTIVES IN ENVIRONMENTAL REGULATION

An efficient program for reducing pollution is one for which the marginal cost of abatement is the same for all polluters. Taxing pollution has this desirable property, as does the auction of pollution permits. The auction method has the advantage that regulators can achieve a desired abatement target without having detailed knowledge of the abatement technologies available to polluters.

Climate scientists warn that increasing atmospheric concentrations of greenhouse gases threatens to cause catastrophic global warming. That risk could be averted by imposition of a carbon tax or equivalent carbon permit system.

SUMMARY

- Externalities are the costs and benefits of activities that accrue to people who are not directly involved in those activities. When all parties affected by externalities can negotiate with one another at no cost, the invisible hand of the market will produce an efficient allocation of resources. *(LO1)*

- According to the Coase theorem, the allocation of resources is efficient in such cases because the parties affected by externalities can compensate others for taking remedial action. *(LO2)*

- Negotiation over externalities is often impractical, however. In these cases, the self-serving actions of individuals typically will not lead to an efficient outcome. The attempt to forge solutions to the problems caused by externalities is one of the most important rationales for collective action. Sometimes collective action takes the form of laws and government regulations that alter the incentives facing those who generate, or are affected by, externalities. Such remedies work best when they place the burden of accommodation on the parties who can accomplish it at the lowest cost. Traffic laws, zoning laws, environmental protection laws, and free speech laws are examples. *(LO3)*

- Curbing pollution and other negative externalities entails costs as well as benefits. The optimal amount of pollution reduction is the amount for which the marginal benefit of further reduction just equals the marginal cost. In general, this formula implies that the socially optimal level of pollution, or of any other negative externality, is greater than zero. *(LO3)*

- When grazing land and other valuable resources are owned in common, no one has an incentive to take into account the opportunity cost of using those resources. This problem is known as the tragedy of the commons. Defining and enforcing private rights governing the use of valuable resources is often an effective solution to the tragedy of the commons. Not surprisingly, most economically successful nations have well-developed institutions of private property. Property that belongs to everyone belongs, in effect, to no one. Not only is its potential economic value never fully realized; it usually ends up having no value at all. *(LO4)*

- The difficulty of enforcing property rights in certain situations explains a variety of inefficient outcomes such as the excessive harvest of whales in international waters and the premature harvest of timber on remote public lands. The excessive pollution of seas that are bordered by many countries also results from a lack of enforceable property rights. *(LO4)*

- Situations in which people's rewards depend on how well they perform in relation to their rivals give rise to positional externalities. In these situations, any step that improves one side's relative position necessarily worsens the other's. Positional externalities tend to spawn positional arms races—escalating patterns of mutually offsetting investments in performance enhancement. Collective measures to curb positional arms races are known as positional arms control agreements. These collective actions may take the form of formal regulations or rules such as rules against anabolic steroids in sports, campaign spending limits, and binding arbitration agreements. Informal social norms can also curtail positional arms races. *(LO5)*

- An understanding of the forces that give rise to environmental pollution can help identify those policy measures that will achieve a desired reduction in pollution at the lowest possible cost. Both the taxing of pollution and the sale of transferable permits promote this goal. Each distributes the cost of the environmental cleanup effort so that the marginal cost of pollution abatement is the same for all polluters. *(LO6)*

KEY TERMS

Coase theorem
external benefit
  (or positive externality)
external cost (or negative externality)

externality
positional arms control
  agreement
positional arms race

positional externality
tragedy of the commons

REVIEW QUESTIONS

1. If Congress could declare illegal any activity that imposes external costs on others, would such legislation be advisable? *(LO2)*

2. What incentive problem explains why the freeways in cities like Los Angeles suffer from excessive congestion? *(LO3)*

3. How would you explain to a friend why the optimal amount of freeway congestion is not zero? *(LO3)*

4. Why might it be easier to reduce pollution levels in the Great Salt Lake, which is located solely in the state of Utah, than in Lake Erie, which is bordered by several states and Canada? *(LO4)*

5. Explain why the wearing of high-heeled shoes might be viewed as the result of a positional externality. *(LO5)*

6. Why do economists believe that pollution taxes and tradable pollution permits are a more efficient way to curb pollution than laws mandating across-the-board cutbacks? *(LO6)*

PROBLEMS

1. For each of the goods listed below, discuss whether the good is likely to entail an external cost or an external benefit. In addition, discuss whether the market is likely to provide more or less than the socially optimal quantity of the good. *(LO1)*
   a. Vaccinations.
   b. Cigarettes.
   c. Antibiotics.

2. Suppose the law says that Jones may *not* emit smoke from his factory unless he gets permission from Smith, who lives downwind. The relevant costs and benefits of filtering the smoke from Jones's production process are as shown in the following table. If Jones and Smith can negotiate with one another at no cost, will Jones emit smoke? *(LO2)*

	Jones emits smoke	Jones does not emit smoke
Surplus for Jones	$200	$160
Surplus for Smith	$400	$420

3. John and Karl can live together in a two-bedroom apartment for $900 per month, or each can rent a single-bedroom apartment for $550 per month. Aside from the rent, the two would be indifferent between living together and living separately, except for one problem: John leaves dirty dishes in the sink every night. Karl would be willing to pay up to $175 per month to avoid John's dirty dishes. John, for his part, would be willing to pay up to $225 to be able to continue his sloppiness. *(LO2)*
   a. Should John and Karl live together? If they do, will there be dirty dishes in the sink? Explain.
   b. What if John would be willing to pay up to $30 per month to avoid giving up his privacy by sharing quarters with Karl? Should John and Karl live together?

4. Khatia and Gwendolyn are neighbors in an apartment complex. Khatia is a concert pianist, and Gwendolyn is a poet working on an epic poem. Khatia rehearses her concert pieces on the baby grand piano in her front room, which is directly above Gwendolyn's study. The following matrix shows the monthly payoffs to Khatia and Gwendolyn when Khatia's front room is and is not soundproofed. The soundproofing will be effective only if it is installed in Khatia's apartment. *(LO2)*

	Soundproofed	Not soundproofed
Gains to Khatia	$100/month	$150/month
Gains to Gwendolyn	$120/month	$ 80/month

   a. If Khatia has the legal right to make any amount of noise she wants and she and Gwendolyn can negotiate with one another at no cost, will Khatia install and maintain soundproofing? Explain. Is her choice socially efficient?

b. If Gwendolyn has the legal right to peace and quiet and can negotiate with Khatia at no cost, will Khatia install and maintain soundproofing? Explain. Is her choice socially efficient?

c. Does the attainment of an efficient outcome depend on whether Khatia has the legal right to make noise, or Gwendolyn the legal right to peace and quiet?

5. Refer to Problem 4. Khatia decides to buy a full-size grand piano. The new payoff matrix is as follows: *(LO2)*

	Soundproofed	Not soundproofed
Gains to Khatia	$100/month	$150/month
Gains to Gwendolyn	$120/month	$ 60/month

a. If Gwendolyn has the legal right to peace and quiet and Khatia and Gwendolyn can negotiate at no cost, will Khatia install and maintain soundproofing? Explain. Is this outcome socially efficient?

b. Suppose that Khatia has the legal right to make as much noise as she likes and that negotiating an agreement with Khatia costs $15 per month. Will Khatia install and maintain soundproofing? Explain. Is this outcome socially efficient?

c. Suppose Gwendolyn has the legal right to peace and quiet, and it costs $15 per month for Gwendolyn and Khatia to negotiate any agreement. (Compensation for noise damage can be paid without incurring negotiation cost.) Will Khatia install and maintain soundproofing? Is this outcome socially efficient?

d. Why does the attainment of a socially efficient outcome now depend on whether Khatia has the legal right to make noise?

6. Phoebe keeps a bee farm next door to an apple orchard. She chooses her optimal number of beehives by selecting the honey output level at which her private marginal benefit from beekeeping equals her private marginal cost. *(LO3)*

a. Assume that Phoebe's private marginal benefit and marginal cost curves from beekeeping are normally shaped. Draw a diagram of them.

b. Phoebe's bees help pollinate the blossoms in the apple orchard, increasing the fruit yield. Show the social marginal benefit from Phoebe's beekeeping in your diagram.

c. Phoebe's bees are Africanized killer bees that aggressively sting anyone who steps into their flight path. Phoebe, fortunately, is naturally immune to the bees' venom. Show the social marginal cost curve from Phoebe's beekeeping in your diagram.

d. Indicate the socially optimal quantity of beehives in your diagram. Is it higher or lower than the privately optimal quantity? Explain.

7. Suppose the supply curve of motorized scooter rentals in Golden Gate Park is given by $P = 5 + 0.1Q$, where

P is the daily rent per unit in dollars and Q is the volume of units rented in hundreds per day. The demand curve for motorized scooters is $20 - 0.2Q$. *(LO3)*

a. If each motorized scooter imposes $6 per day in traffic costs on others, by how much will the equilibrium number of motorized scooters rented exceed the socially optimal number?

b. How would the imposition of a tax of $6 per unit on each daily motorized scooter rental affect efficiency in this market?

8.* A village has six residents, each of whom has accumulated savings of $100. Each villager can use this money either to buy a government bond that pays 15 percent interest per year or to buy a year-old llama, send it onto the commons to graze, and sell it after 1 year. The price the villager gets for the 2-year-old llama depends on the quality of the fleece it grows while grazing on the commons. That in turn depends on the animal's access to grazing, which depends on the number of llamas sent to the commons, as shown in the following table:

Number of llamas on the commons	Price per 2-year-old llama ($)
1	122
2	118
3	116
4	114
5	112
6	109

The villagers make their investment decisions one after another, and their decisions are public. *(LO4)*

a. If each villager decides individually how to invest, how many llamas will be sent onto the commons, and what will be the resulting village income?

b. What is the socially optimal number of llamas for this village? Why is that different from the actual number? What would village income be if the socially optimal number of llamas were sent onto the commons?

c. The village committee votes to auction the right to graze llamas on the commons to the highest bidder. Assuming villagers can both borrow and lend at 15 percent annual interest, how much will the right sell for at auction? How will the new owner use the right, and what will be the resulting village income?

9. Two firms, Sludge Oil and Northwest Lumber, have access to five production processes, each one of which has a different cost and gives off a different amount of pollution. The daily costs of the processes and the corresponding number of tons of smoke emitted are as shown in the following table: *(LO6)*

*Denotes more difficult problem.

Process (smoke)	*A* (4 tons/day)	*B* (3 tons/day)	*C* (2 tons/day)	*D* (1 ton/day)	*E* (0 tons/day)
Cost to Sludge Oil ($/day)	50	70	120	200	500
Cost to Northwest Lumber ($/day)	100	180	500	1,000	2,000

a. If pollution is unregulated, which process will each firm use, and what will be the total daily smoke emission?

b. The City Council wants to curb smoke emissions by 50 percent. To accomplish this, it requires each firm to curb its emissions by 50 percent. What will be the total cost to society of this policy?

c. The City Council again wants to curb emissions by half. This time, it sets a tax of $$T$ per day on each ton of smoke emitted. How large will T have to be to effect the desired reduction? What is the total cost to society of this policy?

10. Refer to Problem 9. Instead of taxing pollution, the City Council decides to auction off four permits, each of which entitles the bearer to emit 1 ton of smoke per day. No smoke may be emitted without a permit. Suppose the government conducts the auction by starting at $1 and asking how many permits each firm wants to buy at that price. If the total is more than four, it then raises the price by $1 and asks again, and so on, until the total quantity of demanded permits falls to four. How much will each permit sell for in this auction? How many permits will each firm buy? What will be the total cost to society of this reduction in pollution? *(LO6)*

ANSWERS TO SELF-TESTS

11.1 Since Fitch gains $50 per day when Abercrombie operates with a filter, he could pay Abercrombie as much as $49 per day and still come out ahead. *(LO2)*

11.2 If the two were to live together, the most efficient way to resolve the problem would be as before, for Sofia to tolerate sometimes being woken up by Adriana's friends. But on top of that cost, which is $150, Sofia would also bear a $60 cost from the loss of her privacy. The total cost of their living together would thus be $210 per month. Since that amount is greater than the $200 saving in rent, the two should live separately. *(LO2)*

11.3 The income figures from the different levels of investment in cattle would remain as before, as shown in the table. What is different is the opportunity cost of investing in each steer, which is now $11 per year instead of $13. Column 5 of the table shows that the socially optimal number of steers is now 2 instead of 1. And if individuals still favor holding cattle, all other

things being equal, they will now send 5 steers onto the commons instead of 4, as shown in column 3. *(LO4)*

(1) Number of steers on the commons	(2) Price per 2-year-old steer ($)	(3) Income per steer ($/year)	(4) Total village income ($/year)	(5) Marginal income ($/year)
				26
1	126	26	26	
				12
2	119	19	38	
				10
3	116	16	48	
				4
4	113	13	52	
				3
5	111	11	55	

11.4 With a tax of $61 per ton each day, Sludge Oil would adopt process *A* and Northwest Lumber would adopt process *C*. *(LO6)*

Process (smoke)	*A* (4 tons/day)	*B* (3 tons/day)	*C* (2 tons/day)	*D* (1 ton/day)	*E* (0 tons/day)
Cost to Sludge Oil ($/day)	100	200	600	1,300	2,300
Cost to Northwest Lumber ($/day)	300	320	380	480	700

CHAPTER 12

The Economics of Information

Matching the right buyers with the right sellers creates economic value that is just as real as the value created by the actual production of goods and services.

LEARNING OBJECTIVES

After reading this chapter, you should be able to:

LO1 Explain how middlemen add value to market transactions.

LO2 Use the concept of rational search to find the optimal amount of information market participants should obtain.

LO3 Define asymmetric information and describe how it influences buying and selling decisions.

LO4 Discuss how incomplete information leads to statistical discrimination.

LO5 Understand why people purchase insurance and how the problems of adverse selection and moral hazard affect insurance markets.

Years ago, a naive young economist spent a week in Kashmir on a houseboat on scenic Dal Lake, outside the capital city of Srinagar. Kashmir is renowned for its woodcarvings, and one afternoon a man in a gondola stopped by to show the economist some of his wooden bowls. When the economist expressed interest in one of them, the woodcarver quoted a price of 200 rupees. The economist had lived in that part of Asia long enough to realize that the price was more than the woodcarver expected to get, so he made a counteroffer of 100 rupees.

The woodcarver appeared to take offense, saying that he couldn't possibly part with the bowl for less than 175 rupees. Suspecting that the woodcarver was merely feigning anger, the young economist held firm. The woodcarver appeared to become even angrier, but quickly retreated to 150 rupees. The economist politely restated his unwillingness to pay more than 100 rupees. The woodcarver then tried 125 rupees, and again the economist replied that 100 was his final offer. Finally, they struck a deal at 100 rupees, and with cash in hand, the woodcarver left in a huff.

Pleased with his purchase, the economist showed it to the houseboat's owner later that evening. "It's a lovely bowl," he agreed, and asked how much the economist had paid for it. The economist told him, expecting praise for his negotiating prowess. The host's failed attempt at suppressing a laugh was the economist's first clue that he had paid too much. When asked how much such a bowl would normally sell for, the houseboat owner was reluctant to respond. But the economist pressed him, and the host speculated that the seller had probably hoped for 30 rupees at most.

Adam Smith's invisible hand theory presumes that buyers are fully informed about the myriad ways in which they might spend their money—what goods and services are available, what prices they sell for, how long they last, how frequently they break down, and so on. But, of course, no one is ever really *fully* informed about anything. And sometimes, as in the transaction with the woodcarver, people are completely ignorant of even the most basic information. Still, life goes on, and most people muddle through somehow.

Consumers employ a variety of strategies for gathering information, some of which are better than others. They read *Consumer Reports*, talk to family and friends, visit stores, kick the tires on used cars, and so on. But one of the most important aspects of choosing intelligently without having complete information is having at least some idea of the extent of one's ignorance. Someone once said that there are two kinds of consumers in the world: those who don't know what they're doing and those who don't know that they don't know what they're doing. As in the case of the wooden bowl, the people in the second category are the ones who are most likely to choose foolishly.

Basic economic principles can help you identify those situations in which additional information is most likely to prove helpful. In this chapter, we will explore what those principles tell us about how much information to acquire and how to make the best use of limited information.

HOW THE MIDDLEMAN ADDS VALUE

One of the most common problems consumers confront is the need to choose among different versions of a product whose many complex features they don't fully understand. As the following example illustrates, in such cases consumers can sometimes rely on the knowledge of others.

EXAMPLE 12.1	Consumer Choice

How should a consumer decide which pair of skis to buy?

You need a new pair of skis, but the technology has changed considerably since you bought your last pair and you don't know which of the current brands and models would be best for you. Skis R Us has the largest selection, so you go there and ask for advice. The salesperson appears to be well informed; after asking about your experience level and how aggressively you ski, she recommends the Rossignol Experience 77. You buy a pair for $600 and then head back to your apartment and show them to your roommate, who says that you could have bought them on the Internet for only $400. How do you feel about your purchase? Are the different prices charged by the two suppliers related to the services they offer? Were the extra services you got by shopping at Skis R Us worth the extra $200?

Internet retailers can sell for less because their costs are much lower than those of full-service retail stores. Those stores, after all, must hire knowledgeable salespeople, put their merchandise on display, rent space in expensive shopping malls, and so on. Internet retailers and mail-order houses, by contrast, typically employ unskilled telephone clerks, and they store their merchandise in cheap warehouses. If you're a consumer who doesn't know which is the right product for you, the extra expense of shopping at a specialty retailer is likely to be a good investment. Spending $600 on the right skis is smarter than spending $400 on the wrong ones.

Many people believe that wholesalers, retailers, and other agents who assist manufacturers in the sale of their products play a far less important role than the one played by those who actually make the products. In this view, the production worker is the ultimate source of economic value added. Sales agents are often disparaged as mere middlemen, parasites on the efforts of others who do the real work.

On a superficial level, this view might seem to be supported by the fact that many people go to great lengths to avoid paying for the services of sales agents. Many manufacturers cater to them by offering consumers a chance to "buy direct" and sidestep the middleman's commission. But on closer examination, we can see that the economic role of sales agents is essentially the same as that of production workers. Consider this example.

EXAMPLE 12.2 — The Economic Role of Sales Agents

How does better information affect economic surplus?

Ellis has just inherited a rare Babe Ruth baseball card issued during the great slugger's rookie year. He'd like to keep the card but has reluctantly decided to sell it to pay some overdue bills. His reservation price for the card is $300, but he is hoping to get significantly more for it. He has two ways of selling it: He can place a classified ad in the local newspaper for $5 or he can list the card on eBay. If he sells the card on eBay, the fee will be 5 percent of the winning bid.

Because Ellis lives in a small town with few potential buyers of rare baseball cards, the local buyer with the highest reservation price is willing to pay $400 at most. If Ellis lists the card on eBay, however, a much larger number of potential buyers will see it. If the two eBay shoppers who are willing to pay the most for Ellis's card have reservation prices of $900 and $800, respectively, by how much will the total economic surplus be larger if Ellis sells his card on eBay? (For the sake of simplicity, assume that the eBay commission and the classified ad fee equal the respective costs of providing those services.)

In an eBay auction, each bidder reports his or her reservation price for an item. When the auction closes, the bidder with the highest reservation price wins, and the price he or she pays is the reservation price of the second-highest bidder. So in this example, the Babe Ruth baseball card will sell for $800 if Ellis lists it on eBay. Net of the $40 eBay commission, Ellis will receive a payment of $760, or $460 more than his reservation price for the card. Ellis's economic surplus will thus be $460. The winning bidder's surplus will be $900 − $800 = $100, so the total surplus from selling the card on eBay will be $560.

If Ellis instead advertises the card in the local newspaper and sells it to the local buyer whose reservation price is $400, then Ellis's surplus (net of the newspaper's $5 fee) will be only $95 and the buyer's surplus will be $0. Thus, total economic surplus will be $560 − $95 = $465 larger if Ellis sells the card on eBay than if he lists it in the local newspaper.

eBay provides a service by making information available to people who can make good use of it. A real increase in economic surplus results when an item ends up in the hands of someone who values it more highly than the person who otherwise would have bought it. That increase is just as valuable as the increase in surplus that results from manufacturing cars, growing corn, or any other productive activity.

In recent years, another important type of middleman has emerged: apps and online marketplaces that connect buyers and sellers who might not otherwise be able to find one another. Consider ride-share services like Uber and Lyft. These companies provide real-time information that enables drivers and riders to find one another. These companies also provide information through ratings systems so that both drivers and riders can feel confident they will have a positive interaction. As evidenced by their massive popularity, these and other digital middlemen like Craigslist, Etsy, and eBay have been tremendously beneficial to both buyers and sellers and have helped spur the growth of the gig economy.

RECAP ↑

HOW THE MIDDLEMAN ADDS VALUE

In a world of incomplete information, sales agents and other middlemen add genuine economic value by increasing the extent to which goods and services find their way to the consumers who value them most. For example, when a sales agent causes a good to be purchased by a person who values it by $20,000 more than the person who would have bought it in the absence of a sales agent, that agent augments total economic surplus by $20,000, an achievement on a par with the production of a $20,000 car. Many apps and digital marketplaces now serve a similar function.

THE OPTIMAL AMOUNT OF INFORMATION

Increasing Opportunity Cost ⟫

Without a doubt, having more information is better than having less. But information is generally costly to acquire. In most situations, the value of additional information will decline beyond some point. And because of the Low-Hanging-Fruit Principle, people tend to gather information from the cheapest sources first before turning to more costly ones. Typically, then, the marginal benefit of information will decline, and its marginal cost will rise, as the amount of information gathered increases.

THE COST-BENEFIT TEST

Cost-Benefit ⟫

Information gathering is an activity like any other. The Cost-Benefit Principle tells us that a rational consumer will continue to gather information as long as its marginal benefit exceeds its marginal cost. Suppose, for the sake of discussion, that analysts had devised a scale that permits us to measure units of information, as on the horizontal axis of Figure 12.1. If the relevant marginal cost and marginal benefit curves are as shown in the diagram, a rational consumer will acquire I^* units of information, the amount for which the marginal benefit of information equals its marginal cost.

Another way to think about Figure 12.1 is that it shows the optimal level of ignorance. When the cost of acquiring information exceeds its benefits, acquiring additional information simply doesn't pay. If information could be acquired at no cost, decision makers would, of course, be glad to have it. But when the cost of acquiring the information exceeds the gain in value from the decision it will facilitate, people are better off to remain ignorant.

free-rider problem an incentive problem in which too little of a good or service is produced because nonpayers cannot be excluded from using it

THE FREE-RIDER PROBLEM

Does the invisible hand ensure that the optimal amount of advice will be made available to consumers in the marketplace? The next example suggests one reason why it might not.

FIGURE 12.1

The Optimal Amount of Information.

For the marginal cost and benefit curves shown, the optimal amount of information is I^*. Beyond that point, information costs more to acquire than it is worth.

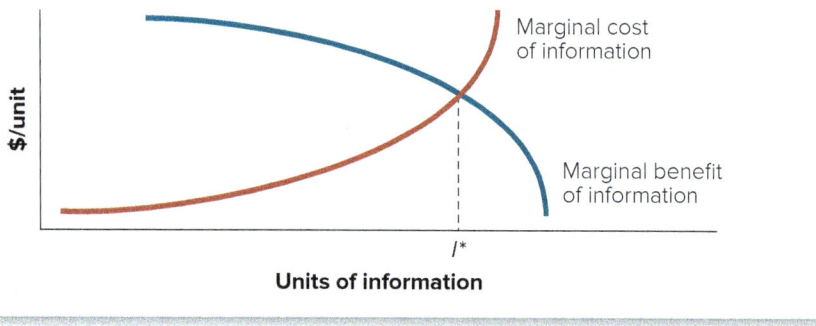

The Economic Naturalist 12.1

Why is finding a knowledgeable salesclerk often difficult?

People can choose for themselves whether to bear the extra cost of retail shopping. Those who value advice and convenience can pay slightly higher prices, while those who know what they want can buy for less from a mail-order house. True or false: It follows that private incentives lead to the optimal amount of retail service.

The market would provide the optimal level of retail service except for one practical problem, namely, that consumers can make use of the services offered by retail stores without paying for them. After benefiting from the advice of informed salespersons and after inspecting the merchandise, the consumer can return home and buy the same item from an Internet retailer or mail-order house. Not all consumers do so, of course. But the fact that customers can benefit from the information provided by retail stores without paying for it is an example of the **free-rider problem**, an incentive problem that results in too little of a good or service being produced. Because retail stores have difficulty recovering the cost of providing information, private incentives are likely to yield less than the socially optimal level of retail service. So the statement above is false.

Why are there so few knowledgeable salesclerks?

The Economic Naturalist 12.2

Why did Rivergate Books, the last bookstore in Lambertville, New Jersey, go out of business?

Small independent bookstores often manage to survive competition from large chains like Barnes & Noble by offering more personalized service. Janet Holbrooke, the proprietor of Rivergate Books, followed this strategy successfully for more than a decade before closing her doors in 1999. What finally led her to quit?

Holbrooke, a retired English teacher, said that many of her customers had experimented with Barnes & Noble when the large chain opened an outlet nearby, but that most had remained loyal because they valued the more personal service her clerks were able to provide. Customers also were drawn in by special events such as readings and book signings by authors. But during one of these events, Holbrooke saw that her store's days were numbered. She had invited Gerald Stern, a National Book Award–winning poet, to do a reading, but despite a good turnout for the event, few attendees purchased books. When she overheard a woman in the book-signing line say that she'd brought her book to the event after having purchased it from Amazon.com, Holbrooke realized it was a losing battle.

Why are so many independent booksellers going out of business?

 SELF-TEST 12.1

Apart from its possible contribution to free-rider problems, how is increased access to the Internet likely to affect total economic surplus?

TWO GUIDELINES FOR RATIONAL SEARCH

Cost-Benefit

In practice, of course, the exact value of additional information is difficult to know, so the amount of time and effort one should invest in acquiring it is not always obvious. But as the following examples suggest, the Cost-Benefit Principle provides a strong conceptual framework for thinking about this problem.

EXAMPLE 12.3

Searching for an Apartment

Should a person living in Paris, Texas, spend more or less time searching for an apartment than someone living in Paris, France?

Suppose that rents for one-bedroom apartments in Paris, Texas, vary between $500 and $700 per month, with an average rent of $600 per month. Rents for similar one-bedroom apartments in Paris, France, vary between $2,000 and $3,000 per month, with an average rent of $2,500. In which city should a rational person expect to spend a longer time searching for an apartment?

In both cities, visiting additional apartments entails a cost, largely the opportunity cost of one's time. In both cities, the more apartments someone visits, the more likely it is that he or she will find one near the lower end of the rent distribution. But because rents are higher and are spread over a broader range in Paris, France, the expected saving from further time spent searching will be greater there than in Paris, Texas. A rational person will expect to spend more time searching for an apartment in France.

This example illustrates the principle that spending additional search time is more likely to be worthwhile for expensive items than for cheap ones. For example, one should spend more time searching for a good price on a diamond engagement ring than for a good price on a stone made of cubic zirconium; more time searching for a low fare to Sydney, Australia, than for a low fare to Sidney, New York; and more time searching for a car than for a bicycle. By extension, hiring an agent—someone who can assist with a search—is more likely to be a good investment in searching for something expensive than for something cheap. For example, people typically engage real estate agents to help them find a house, but they seldom hire agents to help them buy a gallon of milk.

EXAMPLE 12.4

The Cost of Searching

Who should expect to search longer for a good price on a used piano?

Both Mateo and Samuel are shopping for a used upright piano. To examine a piano listed in the classified ads, they must travel to the home of the piano's current owner. If Mateo has a car and Samuel does not and both are rational, which one should expect to examine fewer pianos before making his purchase?

The benefits of examining an additional piano are the same in both cases, namely, a better chance of finding a good instrument for a low price. But because it is more costly for Samuel to examine pianos, he should expect to examine fewer of them than Mateo.

The preceding example makes the point that when searching becomes more costly, we should expect to do less of it. And as a result, the prices we expect to pay will be higher when the cost of a search is higher.

THE GAMBLE INHERENT IN SEARCH

Suppose you are in the market for a one-bedroom apartment and have found one that rents for $900 per month. Should you rent it or search further in hopes of finding a cheaper apartment? Even in a large market with many vacant apartments, there is no guarantee that searching further will turn up a cheaper or better apartment. Searching further entails a cost, which might outweigh the gain. In general, someone who engages in further search must accept certain costs in return for unknown benefits. Thus, further search invariably carries an element of risk.

In thinking about whether to take any gamble, a helpful first step is to compute its expected value–the average amount you would win (or lose) if you played that gamble an infinite number of times. To calculate the **expected value of a gamble** with more than one outcome, we first multiply each outcome by its corresponding probability of occurring, and then add. For example, suppose you win $1 if a coin flip comes up heads and lose $1 if it comes up tails. Since 1/2 is the probability of heads (and also the probability of tails), the expected value of this gamble is $(1/2)(\$1) + (1/2)(-\$1) = 0$. A gamble with an expected value of zero is called a **fair gamble**. If you played this gamble a large number of times, you wouldn't expect to make money, but you also wouldn't expect to lose money.

A **better-than-fair gamble** is one with a positive expected value. (For instance, a coin flip in which you win $2 for heads and lose $1 for tails is a better-than-fair gamble.) A **risk-neutral person** is someone who would accept any gamble that is fair or better. A **risk-averse person** is someone who would refuse to take any fair gamble.

expected value of a gamble the sum of the possible outcomes of the gamble multiplied by their respective probabilities

fair gamble a gamble whose expected value is zero

better-than-fair gamble a gamble whose expected value is positive

risk-neutral person someone who would accept any gamble that is fair or better

risk-averse person someone who would refuse any fair gamble

> ✔ **SELF-TEST 12.2**
>
> Consider a gamble in which you win $4 if you flip a fair coin and it comes up heads and lose $2 if it comes up tails. What is the expected value of this gamble? Would a risk-neutral person accept it?

In the next example, we apply these concepts to the decision of whether to search further for an apartment.

EXAMPLE 12.5   The Gamble in the Search

Should you search further for an apartment?

You have arrived in San Francisco for a one-month summer visit and are searching for a one-bedroom sublet for the month. There are only two kinds of one-bedroom apartments in the neighborhood in which you wish to live, identical in every respect except that one rents for $2,400 and the other for $2,300. Of the vacant apartments in this neighborhood, 80 percent are of the first type and 20 percent are of the second type. The only way you can discover the rent for a vacant apartment is to visit it in person. The first apartment you visit is one that rents for $2,400. If you are risk-neutral and your opportunity cost of visiting an additional apartment is $15, should you visit another apartment or rent the one you've found?

If you visit one more apartment, you have a 20 percent chance of it being one that rents for $2,300 and an 80 percent chance of it being one that rents for $2,400. If the former, you'll save $100 in rent, but if the latter, you'll face the same rent as before. Since the cost of a visit is $15, visiting another apartment is a gamble with a 20 percent chance to win $100 − $15 = $85 and an 80 percent chance of losing $15 (which means "winning" −$15). The expected value of this gamble is thus $(0.20)(\$85) + (0.80)(-\$15) = \$5$. Visiting another apartment is a better-than-fair gamble, and since you are risk-neutral, you should take it.

> ✅ **SELF-TEST 12.3**
>
> Refer to Example 12.5. Suppose you visit another apartment and discover it, too, is one that rents for $2,400. If you are risk-neutral, should you visit a third apartment?

THE COMMITMENT PROBLEM WHEN SEARCH IS COSTLY

When most people search for an apartment, they want a place to live not for just a month, but for a year or more. Most landlords, for their part, are also looking for long-term tenants. Similarly, few people accept a full-time job in their chosen field unless they expect to hold the job for several years. Firms, too, generally prefer employees who will stay for extended periods. Finally, when most people search for mates, they are looking for someone with whom to settle down.

Because in all these cases search is costly, examining every possible option will never make sense. Apartment hunters don't visit every vacant apartment, nor do landlords interview every possible tenant. Job seekers don't visit every employer, nor do employers interview every job seeker. And not even the most determined searcher can manage to date every eligible mate. In these and other cases, people are rational to end their searches, even though they know a more attractive option surely exists out there somewhere.

But herein lies a difficulty. What happens when, by chance, a more attractive option comes along after the search has ceased? Few people would rent an apartment if they thought the landlord would kick them out the moment another tenant came along who was willing to pay higher rent. Few landlords would be willing to rent to a tenant if they expected her to move out the moment she discovers a cheaper apartment. Employers, job seekers, and people who are looking for mates would have similar reservations about entering relationships that could be terminated once a better option happened to come along.

This potential difficulty in maintaining stable matches between partners in ongoing relationships would not arise in a world of perfect information. In such a world, everyone would end up in the best possible relationship, so no one would be tempted to renege. But when information is costly and the search must be limited, there will always be the potential for existing relationships to dissolve.

In most contexts, people solve this problem not by conducting an exhaustive search (which is usually impossible, in any event) but by committing themselves to remain in a relationship once a mutual agreement has been reached to terminate the search. Thus, landlords and tenants sign a lease that binds them to one another for a specified period, usually one year. Employees and firms enter into employment contracts, either formal or informal, under which each promises to honor his obligations to the other, except under extreme circumstances. And in most countries a marriage contract penalizes those who abandon their spouses. Entering into such commitments limits the freedom to pursue one's own interests. Yet most people freely accept such restrictions because they know the alternative is failure to solve the search problem.

> **RECAP** ↑
>
> ### THE OPTIMAL AMOUNT OF INFORMATION
>
> Additional information creates value, but it's also costly to acquire. A rational consumer will continue to acquire information until its marginal benefit equals its marginal cost. Beyond that point, it's rational to remain uninformed.
>
> Markets for information do not always function perfectly. Free-rider problems often hinder retailers' efforts to provide information to consumers.
>
> Search inevitably entails an element of risk because costs must be incurred without any assurance that search will prove fruitful. A rational consumer can minimize this risk by concentrating search efforts on goods for which the variation in price or quality is relatively high and on those for which the cost of search is relatively low.

ASYMMETRIC INFORMATION

One of the most common information problems occurs when the participants in a potential exchange are not equally well informed about the product or service that's offered for sale. For instance, the owner of a used car may know that the car is in excellent mechanical condition, but potential buyers cannot know that merely by inspecting it or taking it for a test drive. Economists use the term **asymmetric information** to describe situations in which buyers and sellers are not equally well informed about the characteristics of products or services. In these situations, sellers are typically much better informed than buyers, but sometimes the reverse will be true.

The problem of asymmetric information can easily prevent exchanges that would benefit both parties. Here is a classic example.

asymmetric information situations in which buyers and sellers are not equally well informed about the characteristics of goods and services for sale in the marketplace

---

EXAMPLE 12.6   Asymmetric Information

Will Katie sell her car to Samir?

Katie's 2014 Mazda Miata has 70,000 miles on the odometer, but most of these are highway miles driven during weekend trips to see her boyfriend in Toronto. (Highway driving causes less wear and tear on a car than city driving.) Moreover, Katie has maintained the car precisely according to the manufacturer's specifications. In short, she knows her car to be in excellent condition. Because she is about to start graduate school in Boston, however, Katie wants to sell the car. On average, 2014 Miatas sell for a price of $12,000, but because Katie knows her car to be in excellent condition, her reservation price for it is $14,000.

Samir wants to buy a used Miata. He would be willing to pay $16,000 for one that is in excellent condition but only $13,000 for one that is not in excellent condition. Samir has no way of telling whether Katie's Miata is in excellent condition. (He could hire a mechanic to examine the car, but doing so is expensive, and many problems cannot be detected even by a mechanic.) Will Samir buy Katie's car? Is this outcome efficient?

Because Katie's car looks no different from other 2014 Miatas, Samir will not pay $14,000 for it. After all, for only $12,000, he can buy some other 2014 Miata that's in just as good condition, *as far as he can tell*. Samir therefore will buy someone else's Miata, and Katie's will go unsold. This outcome is not efficient. If Samir had bought Katie's Miata for, say, $14,500, his surplus would have been $1,500 and Katie's another $500. Instead, Samir ends up buying a Miata that is in average condition (or worse), and his surplus is only $1,000. Katie gets no economic surplus at all.

THE LEMONS MODEL

We can't be sure, of course, that the Miata Samir ends up buying will be in worse condition than Katie's—since *someone* might have a car in perfect condition that must be sold even if the owner cannot get what it is really worth. Even so, the economic incentives created by asymmetric information suggest that most used cars that are put up for sale will be of lower-than-average quality. One reason is that people who mistreat their cars, or whose cars were never very good to begin with, are more likely than others to want to sell them. Buyers know from experience that cars for sale on the used car market are more likely to be "lemons" than cars that are not for sale. This realization causes them to lower their reservation prices for a used car.

But that's not the end of the story. Once used car prices have fallen, the owners of cars that are in good condition have an even stronger incentive to hold onto them. That causes the average quality of the cars offered for sale on the used car market to decline still further. Berkeley economist George Akerlof, a Nobel laureate, was the first to explain the logic behind this downward spiral.[1] Economists use the term **lemons model** to describe Akerlof's explanation of how asymmetric information affects the average quality of the used goods offered for sale.

The next example suggests that the lemons model has important practical implications for consumer choice.

lemons model George Akerlof's explanation of how asymmetric information tends to reduce the average quality of goods offered for sale

---

EXAMPLE 12.7

The Lemons Model in Action

Should you buy your aunt's car?

You want to buy a used Honda Accord. Your Aunt Germaine buys a new car every four years, and she has a four-year-old Accord that she's about to trade in. You believe her report that the car is in good condition, and she's willing to sell it to you for $16,000, which is the current blue book value for four-year-old Accords. (The blue book value of a car is the average price for which cars of that age and model sell in the used car market.) Should you buy your aunt's Honda?

Akerlof's lemons model tells us that cars for sale in the used car market will be of lower average quality than cars of the same vintage that are not for sale. If you believe your aunt's claim that her car is in good condition, then being able to buy it for its blue book value is definitely a good deal for you, since the blue book price is the equilibrium price for a car that is of lower quality than your aunt's.

The following two examples illustrate the conditions under which asymmetric information about product quality results in a market in which *only* lemons are offered for sale.

EXAMPLE 12.8

The Naive Buyer (Part 1)

How much will a naive buyer pay for a used car?

Consider a world with only two kinds of cars: good ones and lemons. An owner knows with certainty which type of car she has, but potential buyers cannot distinguish between the two types. Ten percent of all new cars produced are lemons. Good used cars are worth $16,000 to their owners, but lemons are worth only $12,000. Consider a naive consumer who believes that the used cars currently for sale have the same quality distribution as new cars (i.e., 90 percent good, 10 percent lemons). If this consumer is risk-neutral, how much would he be willing to pay for a used car?

Buying a car of unknown quality is a gamble, but a risk-neutral buyer would be willing to take the gamble provided it is fair. If the buyer can't tell the difference between a good car and a lemon, the probability that he will end up with a lemon is simply the proportion of lemons among the cars from which he chooses. The buyer believes he has a 90 percent chance of getting a good car and a 10 percent chance of getting a lemon. Given the prices he is willing to pay for the two types of car, his expected value of the car he buys will thus be 0.90($16,000) + 0.10($12,000) = $15,600. And since he is risk-neutral, that is his reservation price for a used car.

---

[1]George Akerlof, "The Market for Lemons," *Quarterly Journal of Economics* 84 (1970), pp. 488–500.

✅ **SELF-TEST 12.4**

How would your answer to the question posed in Example 12.8 differ if the proportion of new cars that are lemons had been 20 percent?

EXAMPLE 12.9　　**The Naive Buyer (Part 2)**

Who will sell a used car for what the naive buyer is willing to pay?

Continuing with the previous example: If you were the owner of a good used car, what would it be worth to you? Would you sell it to a naive buyer? What if you owned a lemon?

Since you know your car is good, it is worth $16,000 to you, by assumption. But a naive buyer would be willing to pay only $15,600, so neither you nor any other owner of a good car would be willing to sell to that buyer. If you had a lemon, of course, you'd be happy to sell it to a naive buyer, since the $15,600 the buyer is willing to pay is $3,600 more than the lemon would be worth to you. So the only used cars for sale will be lemons. In time, buyers will revise their naively optimistic beliefs about the quality of the cars for sale on the used car market. In the end, all used cars will sell for a price of $12,000, and all will be lemons.

In practice, of course, the mere fact that a car is for sale does not guarantee that it is a lemon because the owner of a good car will sometimes be forced to sell it, even at a price that does not reflect its condition. The logic of the lemons model explains this owner's frustration. The first thing sellers in this situation want a prospective buyer to know is the reason they are selling their cars. For example, classified ads often announce, "Just had a baby, must sell my 2015 Corvette" or "Transferred to Germany, must sell my 2016 Toyota Camry." Anytime you pay the blue book price for a used car that is for sale for some reason unrelated to its condition, you are beating the market.

▶ Visit your instructor's Connect course and access your eBook to view this video.

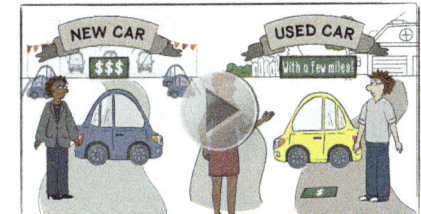

Why do "almost new" used cars sell for so much less than brand-new ones?

THE CREDIBILITY PROBLEM IN TRADING

Why can't someone with a high-quality used car simply *tell* the buyer about the car's condition? The difficulty is that buyers' and sellers' interests tend to conflict. Sellers of used cars, for example, have an economic incentive to overstate the quality of their products. Buyers, for their part, have an incentive to understate the amount they are willing to pay for used cars and other products (in the hope of bargaining for a lower price). Potential employees may be tempted to overstate their qualifications for a job. And people searching for mates have been known to engage in deception.

That isn't to say that most people *consciously* misrepresent the truth in communicating with their potential trading partners. But people do tend to interpret ambiguous information in ways that promote their own interests. Thus, 92 percent of factory employees surveyed in one study rated themselves as more productive than the average factory worker. Psychologists call this phenomenon the "Lake Wobegon effect," after Garrison Keillor's mythical Minnesota homestead, where "all the children are above average."

Notwithstanding the natural tendency to exaggerate, the parties to a potential exchange can often gain if they can find some means to communicate their knowledge truthfully. In general, however, mere statements of relevant information will not suffice. People have long since learned to discount the used car salesman's inflated claims about the cars he's trying to unload. But as the next example illustrates, though communication between potential adversaries may be difficult, it's not impossible.

EXAMPLE 12.10   Credible Signals

How can a used car seller signal high-quality credibly?

Katie knows her Miata to be in excellent condition, and Samir would be willing to pay considerably more than her reservation price if he could be confident of getting such a car. What kind of signal about the car's quality would Samir find credible?

Again, the potential conflict between Samir's and Katie's interests suggests that mere statements about the car's quality may not be persuasive. But suppose Katie offers a warranty, under which she agrees to remedy any defects the car develops over the next six months. Katie can afford to extend such an offer because she knows her car is unlikely to need expensive repairs. In contrast, the person who knows his car has a cracked engine block would never extend such an offer. The warranty is a credible signal that the car is in good condition. It enables Samir to buy the car with confidence, to both his and Katie's benefit.

The Costly-to-Fake Principle

costly-to-fake principle
to communicate information credibly to a potential rival, a signal must be costly or difficult to fake

The preceding examples illustrate the **costly-to-fake principle**, which holds that if parties whose interests potentially conflict are to communicate credibly with one another, the signals they send must be costly or difficult to fake. If the seller of a defective car could offer an extensive warranty just as easily as the seller of a good car, a warranty offer would communicate nothing about the car's quality. But warranties entail costs that are significantly higher for defective cars than for good cars—hence their credibility as a signal of product quality.

To the extent that sellers have an incentive to portray a product in the most flattering light possible, their interests conflict with those of buyers, who want the most accurate assessment of product quality possible. Note that in the following example, the costly-to-fake principle applies to a producer's statement about the quality of a product.

The Economic Naturalist 12.3

Why do firms insert the phrase "As advertised on TV" when they advertise their products in magazines and social media?

Company *A* sponsors an expensive national television advertising campaign on behalf of its surround sound speakers, claiming it has the clearest sound and the best repair record of any surround sound speakers in the market. Company *B* makes similar claims in a sales brochure but does not advertise its product on television. If you had no additional information to go on, which company's claim would you find more credible? Why do you suppose Company *A* mentions its TV ads when it advertises its surround sound speakers in print and social media?

Accustomed as we are to discounting advertisers' inflated claims, the information given might seem to provide no real basis for a choice between the two products. On closer examination, however, we see that a company's decision to advertise its product on national television constitutes a credible signal about the product's quality. The cost of a national television campaign can run well into the millions of dollars, a sum a company would be foolish to spend on an inferior product.

For example, the going rate for 30-second ad slots for the 2020 Super Bowl was $5.6 million. National TV ads can attract potential buyers'

Why should buyers care whether a product is advertised on TV?

attention and persuade a small fraction of them to try a product. But these huge investments pay off only if the resulting initial sales generate other new business—either repeat sales to people who tried the product and liked it or sales to others who heard about the product from a friend.

Because ads cannot persuade buyers that a bad product is a good one, a company that spends millions of dollars advertising a bad product is wasting its money. An expensive national advertising campaign is therefore a credible signal that the producer *thinks* its product is a good one. Of course, the ads don't guarantee that a product *is* a winner, but in an uncertain world, they provide one more piece of information. Note, however, that the relevant information lies in the expenditure on the advertising campaign, not in what the ads themselves say.

These observations may explain why some companies mention their television ads in their print ads. Advertisers understand the costly-to-fake principle and hope that consumers will understand it as well.

As The Economic Naturalist 12.4 illustrates, the costly-to-fake principle is also well known to many employers.

The Economic Naturalist 12.4

Why do many companies care so much about elite educational credentials?

Microsoft is looking for a hard-working, smart person for an entry-level managerial position in a new technical products division. Two candidates, Eva and Donna, seem alike in every respect but one: Eva graduated with the highest honors from MIT, while Donna graduated with a C+ average from Somerville College. Whom should Microsoft hire?

If you want to persuade prospective employers that you are both hardworking and intelligent, there is perhaps no more credible signal than to have graduated with distinction from a highly selective educational institution. Most people would like potential employers to think of them as hardworking and intelligent. But unless you actually have both those qualities, graduating with the highest honors from a school like MIT will be extremely difficult. The fact that Donna graduated from a much less selective institution and earned only a C+ average is not proof positive that she is not diligent and talented, but companies are forced to play the percentages. In this case, the odds strongly favor Eva.

Conspicuous Consumption as a Signal of Ability

Some individuals of high ability are not highly paid. (Remember the best elementary school teacher you ever had.) And some people—such as the multibillionaire investor Warren Buffett—earn a lot, yet spend very little. But such cases run counter to general tendencies. In competitive markets, the people with the most ability tend to receive the highest salaries. And as suggested by the Cost-Benefit Principle, the more someone earns, the more he or she is likely to spend on high-quality goods and services. As the following example suggests, these tendencies often lead us to infer a person's ability from the amount and quality of the goods he or she consumes.

 Cost-Benefit

The Economic Naturalist 12.5

Why do many clients seem to prefer lawyers who wear expensive suits?

If you were on trial for a serious crime, which lawyer would you hire?

You've been unjustly accused of a serious crime and are looking for an attorney. Your choice is between two lawyers who appear identical in all respects except for the things they buy. One of them wears a cheap polyester suit and arrives at the courthouse in a 10-year-old rust-eaten Dodge Caliber. The other wears an impeccably tailored suit and drives a new BMW 750i. If this were the *only* information available to you at the time you choose, which lawyer would you hire?

The correlation between salary and the abilities buyers value most is particularly strong in the legal profession. A lawyer whose clients usually prevail in court will be much more in demand than one whose clients generally lose, and their fees will reflect the difference. The fact that one of the lawyers consumes much more than the other doesn't *prove* that he is the better lawyer, but if that is the only information you have, you can ill afford to ignore it.

If the less able lawyer loses business because of the suits he wears and the car he drives, why doesn't he simply buy better suits and a more expensive car? His choice is between saving for retirement or spending more on his car and clothing. In one sense, he cannot afford to buy a more expensive car, but in another sense, he cannot afford *not* to. If his current car is discouraging potential clients from hiring him, buying a better one may simply be a prudent investment. But because *all* lawyers have an incentive to make such investments, their effects tend to be mutually offsetting.

When all is said and done, the things people consume will continue to convey relevant information about their respective ability levels. The costly-to-fake principle tells us that the BMW 750i is an effective signal precisely because the lawyer of low ability cannot afford one, no matter how little he saves for retirement. Yet from a social perspective, the resulting spending pattern is inefficient, for the same reason that other positional arms races are inefficient. (We discussed positional arms races in Chapter 11, *Externalities, Property Rights, and the Environment.*) Society would be better off if everyone spent less and saved more for retirement.

The problem of conspicuous consumption as an ability signal doesn't arise with equal force in every environment. In small towns, where people tend to know one another well, a lawyer who tries to impress people by spending beyond her means is likely to succeed only in demonstrating how foolish she is. Thus, the wardrobe a professional person "needs" in towns like Dubuque, Iowa, or Athens, Ohio, costs less than half as much as the wardrobe the same person would need in Manhattan or Los Angeles.

> **RECAP**
>
> **ASYMMETRIC INFORMATION**
>
> - Asymmetric information describes situations in which not all parties to a potential exchange are equally well informed. In the typical case, the seller of a product will know more about its quality than the potential buyers. Such asymmetries often stand in the way of mutually beneficial exchange in the markets for high-quality goods because buyers' inability to identify high quality makes them unwilling to pay a commensurate price.
> - Information asymmetries and other communication problems between potential exchange partners can often be solved through the use of signals that are costly or difficult to fake. Product warranties are such a signal because the seller of a low-quality product would find them too costly to offer.

STATISTICAL DISCRIMINATION

In a competitive market with perfect information, the buyer of a service would pay the seller's cost of providing the service. In many markets, however, the seller does not know the exact cost of serving each individual buyer.

In such cases, the missing information has an economic value. If the seller can come up with even a rough estimate of the missing information, she can improve her position. As The Economic Naturalist 12.6 illustrates, firms often do so by imputing characteristics to individuals on the basis of the groups to which they belong.

The Economic Naturalist 12.6

Why do males under 25 years of age pay more than other drivers for auto insurance?

Gerald is 23 years old and is an extremely careful and competent driver. He has never had an accident, or even a moving traffic violation. His twin sister Geraldine has had two accidents, one of them serious, in the last three years and has accumulated three speeding tickets during that same period. Why does Gerald pay $1,600 per year for auto insurance, while Geraldine pays only $1,400?

The expected cost to an insurance company of insuring any given driver depends on the probability that the driver will be involved in an accident. No one knows what that probability is for any given driver, but insurance companies can estimate rather precisely the proportion of drivers in specific groups who will be involved in an accident in any given year. Males under 25 are much more likely than older males and females of any age to become involved in auto accidents. Gerald pays more than his sister because even those males under 25 who have never had an accident are more likely to have one than females the same age who have had several accidents.

Why do young males pay so much more for auto insurance?

Of course, females who have had two accidents and accumulated several tickets in the last three years are more likely to have an accident than a female with a spotless driving record. The insurance company knows that and has increased Geraldine's premium accordingly. Yet it is still less than her brother's premium. That doesn't mean that Gerald is in fact more likely to have an accident than Geraldine. Indeed, given the twins' respective driving skills, Geraldine clearly poses the higher risk. But because insurance companies lack such detailed information, they are forced to set rates according to the information they possess.

To remain in business, an insurance company must collect enough money from premiums to cover the cost of the claims it pays out, plus whatever administrative expenses it incurs. Consider an insurance company that charges lower rates for young males with clean driving records than for females with blemished ones. Given that the former group is more likely to have accidents than the latter, the company cannot break even unless it charges females more, and males less, than the respective costs of insuring them. But if it does so, rival insurance companies will see cash on the table: They can offer females slightly lower rates and lure them away from the first company. The first company will end up with only young male policyholders and thus will suffer an economic loss at the low rates it charges. That is why, in equilibrium, young males with clean driving records pay higher insurance rates than young females with blemished records.

statistical discrimination
the practice of making judgments about the quality of people, goods, or services based on the characteristics of the groups to which they belong

The insurance industry's policy of charging high rates to young male drivers is an example of **statistical discrimination**. Other examples include the common practice of paying higher salaries to people with college degrees than to people without them and the policy of favoring college applicants with high SAT scores. Statistical discrimination occurs whenever people or products are judged on the basis of the groups to which they belong.

Competition promotes statistical discrimination, even though everyone knows that the characteristics of specific individuals can differ markedly from those of the group to which they belong. For example, insurance companies know perfectly well that *some* young males are careful and competent drivers. But unless they can identify *which* males are the better drivers, competitive pressure forces them to act on their knowledge that, as a group, young males are more likely than others to generate insurance claims.

Similarly, employers know that many people with only a high school diploma are more productive than the average college graduate. But because employers usually cannot tell in advance who those people are, competitive pressure leads them to offer higher wages to college graduates, who are more productive, on average, than high school graduates. Universities, too, realize that many applicants with low SAT scores will earn higher grades than applicants with high scores. But if two applicants look equally promising except for their SAT scores, competition forces universities to favor the applicant with higher scores since, on average, that applicant will perform better than the other.

Statistical discrimination is the *result* of observable differences in group characteristics, not the cause of those differences. Young males, for example, do not generate more insurance claims because of statistical discrimination. Rather, statistical discrimination occurs because insurance companies know that young males generate more claims. Nor does statistical discrimination cause young males to pay insurance rates that are high in relation to the claims they generate. Among any group of young male drivers, some are careful and competent, and others are not. Statistical discrimination means the more able males will pay high rates relative to the volume of claims they generate, but it also means the less able male drivers will pay low rates relative to the claims they generate. On average, the group's rates will be appropriate to the claims its members generate.

Still, these observations do little to ease the frustration of the young male who knows himself to be a careful and competent driver, or the high school graduate who knows herself to be a highly productive employee. Competitive forces provide firms an incentive to identify such individuals and treat them more favorably whenever practical. When firms succeed in this effort, however, they have often discovered some other relevant information on group differences. For example, many insurance companies offer lower rates to young males who belong to the National Honor Society or make the dean's list at school. Members of those groups generate fewer claims, on average, than other young males. But even these groups include risky drivers, and the fact that companies offer discounts to their members means that all other young males must pay higher rates.

DISAPPEARING POLITICAL DISCOURSE

An intriguing illustration of statistical discrimination arises when a politician decides what to say about controversial public issues. Politicians have an interest in supporting the positions they genuinely believe in, but they also have an interest in winning reelection. As The Economic Naturalist 12.7 and 12.8 illustrate, the two motives often conflict, especially when a politician's statements about one subject convey information about her beliefs on other subjects.

The Economic Naturalist 12.7

Why do opponents of the death penalty often remain silent?

Quite apart from the question of whether execution of convicted criminals is morally legitimate, there are important practical arguments against capital punishment. For one thing, it is extremely expensive relative to the alternative of life without parole. Execution is costly because of judicial safeguards against execution of innocent persons. In each capital case prosecuted in the United States, these safeguards consume thousands of person-hours from attorneys and other officers of the court, at a cost that runs well into the millions of dollars.[2] Such efforts notwithstanding, the record is replete with examples of executed persons who are later shown to be innocent. Another argument against capital punishment is that many statistical studies find that it does not deter people from committing capital crimes. Though many political leaders in both parties find these and other arguments against capital punishment compelling, few politicians voice their opposition to capital punishment publicly. Why not?

A possible answer to this puzzle is suggested by the theory of statistical discrimination. Voters in both parties are concerned about crime and want to elect politicians who take the problem seriously. Suppose there are two kinds of politicians: some who in their heart of hearts take the crime issue seriously and others who merely pay lip service to it. Suppose also that voters classify politicians in a second way: those who publicly favor the death penalty or remain silent and those who publicly oppose it. Some politicians will oppose the death penalty for the reasons just discussed, but others will oppose it because they are simply reluctant to punish criminals—perhaps because they believe that crime is ultimately more society's fault than the criminal's. (Politicians in the latter category are the ones voters think of as being "not serious about crime"; they are the ones many voters want to get rid of.) These two possible motives for opposing the death penalty suggest that the proportion of death penalty opponents who take the crime issue seriously, in the public's view, will be somewhat smaller than the corresponding proportion among proponents of the death penalty. For the sake of discussion, imagine that 95 percent of politicians who favor the death penalty and only 80 percent of politicians who oppose the death penalty are "serious about crime."

If you are a voter who cares about crime, how will your views about a politician be affected by hearing that he opposes the death penalty? If you knew nothing about that politician to begin with, your best guess on hearing his opposition to the death penalty would be that there is an 80 percent chance that he is serious about crime. Had he instead voiced support for the death penalty, your best guess would be that there is a 95 percent chance that he is serious about crime. And since voters are looking for politicians who are serious about crime, the mere act of speaking out against the death penalty will entail a small loss of political support even for those politicians who are extremely serious about crime.

Knowing this tendency on the part of voters, some politicians who are only marginally opposed to the death penalty may prefer to keep their views to themselves. As a result, the composition of the group that speaks out publicly against the death penalty will change slightly so that it is more heavily weighted with people reluctant to punish criminals in any way. Suppose, for example, that the proportion of death penalty opponents who are serious about crime falls from 80 to 60 percent. Now the political cost of speaking out against the death penalty rises, leading still more opponents to remain silent. Once the dust settles, very few opponents of capital punishment will risk stating their views publicly. In their desire to convince voters that they are tough on crime, some may even become outspoken proponents of the death penalty. In the end, public discourse will strongly favor capital punishment. But that is no reason to conclude that most leaders—or even most voters—genuinely favor it.

---

[2]See Philip J. Cook and Donna B. Slawson, "The Costs of Processing Murder Cases in North Carolina," The Sanford Institute of Public Policy, Duke University, Durham, NC, 1993.

disappearing political discourse the theory that people who support a position may remain silent because speaking out would create a risk of being misunderstood

The economist Glenn Loury was the first to call attention to the phenomenon described in the preceding example. We call it the problem of **disappearing political discourse**. Once you understand it, you will begin to notice examples not just in the political sphere but in everyday discourse as well.

The Economic Naturalist 12.8

Why do proponents of legalized drugs remain silent?

That addictive drugs like heroin, cocaine, and methamphetamines cause enormous harm is not a matter of dispute. The clear intent of laws that ban commerce in these drugs is to prevent that harm. But the laws also entail costs. By making the drugs illegal, they substantially increase their price, leading many addicts to commit crimes to pay for drugs. The high incomes of many illicit-drug dealers also divert people from legitimate careers and result in turf battles that often have devastating consequences for both participants and bystanders. If these drugs were legal, drug-related crime would vanish completely. Drug use would also rise, how significantly we do not know. In short, it's at least *conceivable* that legalizing addictive drugs might be sound public policy. Why, then, do virtually no politicians publicly favor such a policy?

Many politicians may simply believe that legalizing drugs is a bad idea. Theoretically, legalization could lead to such a steep rise in drug consumption that the cost of the policy might far outweigh its benefits. This concern, however, is not supported by experience in countries such as England and the Netherlands, which have tried limited forms of legalization. A second explanation is that politicians who favor legalization are reluctant to speak out for fear that others will misinterpret them. Suppose that some people favor legalization based on careful analysis of the costs and benefits, while other proponents are merely crazy. If the proportion of crazies is higher among supporters than among opponents of legalization, someone who speaks out in favor of legalization may cause those who do not know her to increase their estimate of the likelihood she is crazy. This possibility deters some proponents from speaking out, which raises the proportion of crazies among the remaining public supporters of legalization—and so on in a downward spiral, until most of the remaining public supporters really are crazy.

The disappearing political discourse problem helps explain why the United States had difficulty reestablishing normal diplomatic relations with China, which were severed in the wake of the communist revolution. One could oppose communist expansionism and yet still favor normalized relations with China on the grounds that war is less likely when antagonists communicate openly. In the Cold War environment, however, American politicians were under enormous pressure to demonstrate their steadfast opposition to communism at every opportunity. Fearing that support for the normalization of relations with China would be misinterpreted as a sign of softness toward communism, many supporters of the policy remained silent. Not until Richard Nixon—whose anticommunist credentials no one could question—was elected president were diplomatic relations with China finally reopened.

The problem of disappearing discourse also helps explain the impoverished state of public debate on issues such as the reform of Social Security, Medicare, and other entitlement programs.

INSURANCE

Hurricanes, fires, car accidents, and illnesses are largely unforeseeable events. Since most people are risk-averse, they often purchase insurance to help guard against the possibility of facing the enormous expenses associated with such events.

To see how this works, consider David. Most of the time, he is healthy, but he knows there's a chance he could face a serious illness. In particular, suppose there's a 75 percent chance David won't have any health care expenses all year, but there's a 25 percent chance he'll face a serious illness and will have to pay $16,000 in medical bills. David's annual health care expenses are thus a gamble with an expected value of $(0.75)(\$0) + (0.25)(\$16,000) = \$4,000$. This means that if David is risk-averse, he'd rather pay $4,000 each year than face a 25 percent chance of paying $16,000. In fact, David might be willing to pay substantially more than $4,000 to avoid this risk.

▶ Visit your instructor's Connect course and access your eBook to view this video.

This is exactly where insurance steps in. Suppose David is willing to pay $4,500 a year to avoid the risk of having to pay $16,000 in medical bills. An insurance company can charge David $4,500 a year in exchange for the promise of paying his medical expenses should he face a serious illness. This arrangement makes David better off because he no longer faces a 25 percent chance of having to pay $16,000 in medical bills should he fall ill, and it's beneficial for the insurance company, since it gets $4,500 a year from David, but expects to pay out only $4,000. This extra $500 paid to the insurance company can go toward the cost of administering the insurance plan. And, unlike David, the insurance company doesn't mind

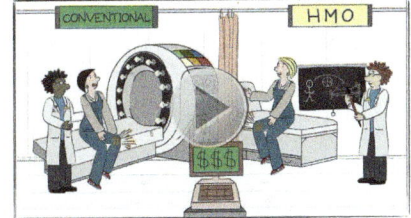

Why might a patient be more likely to receive an expensive magnetic resonance imaging (MRI) exam for a sore knee if covered under a conventional health insurance plan rather than a Health Maintenance Organization (HMO) plan?

the risk associated with David's health care costs because the company has lots of other customers just like him, some of whom will have good years and others of whom will have bad years, so that, on average, the company pays only $4,000 a year for each customer.

Despite these obvious benefits, insurance markets often do not function as well as we would like. As we discuss next, the problem of incomplete information again plays a role.

ADVERSE SELECTION

One of the most pernicious problems in insurance markets relates to asymmetric information. To remain in business, an insurance company must set premiums that are high enough to pay for the expenses it has promised to cover. Thus, for example, health insurance companies determine premiums based on the expected medical expenses of the average person. The problem is that individuals often have more information about the likelihood that they will need insurance than do the companies providing the insurance. For example, David's health insurance company might not know that he has a family history of diabetes. This means that the premiums set by insurance companies are a better deal for high-risk individuals than for low-risk individuals, and as a result, high-risk individuals are more likely to buy insurance than low-risk individuals. This pattern is

adverse selection the pattern in which insurance tends to be purchased disproportionately by those who are most costly for companies to insure

moral hazard the tendency of people to expend less effort protecting those goods that are insured against theft or damage

known as **adverse selection**. Because of it, insurance companies raise their premiums, which makes buying insurance even less attractive to low-risk individuals, which raises still further the average risk level of those who remain insured. In some cases, only those individuals faced with extreme risks may continue to find insurance an attractive purchase.

MORAL HAZARD

Moral hazard is another problem that makes buying insurance less attractive for the average person. This problem refers to the fact that some people take fewer precautions when they know they are insured. Someone whose car is insured, for example, may take less care to prevent it from being damaged or stolen. Driving cautiously and searching for safe parking spaces require effort, after all, and if the losses from failing to engage in these precautions are covered by insurance, some people will become less vigilant.

Insurance companies help many of their potential clients soften the consequences of problems like moral hazard and adverse selection by offering policies with deductible provisions. Under the terms of an automobile collision insurance policy with, say, a $1,000 deductible provision, the insurance company covers only those collision repair costs in excess of $1,000. For example, if you have an accident in which $3,000 in damage occurs, the insurance company covers only $2,000, and you pay the remaining $1,000.

How does the availability of such policies mitigate the negative effects of adverse selection and moral hazard? Because policies with high deductibles are cheaper for insurance companies to provide, they sell for lower prices. The lower prices represent a much better bargain, however, for those drivers who are least likely to file insurance claims since those drivers are least likely to incur any uncovered repair costs. Policies with deductible provisions also confront careless drivers with more of the extra costs for which they are responsible, giving them additional incentives to take precautions.

These policies benefit insurance buyers in another way. Because the holder of a policy with a deductible provision will not file a claim at all if the damage to his car in an accident is less than the deductible threshold, insurance companies require fewer resources to process and investigate claims, savings that get passed along in the form of lower premiums.

THE PROBLEM WITH HEALTH CARE PROVISION
THROUGH PRIVATE INSURANCE

It is troubling, but perhaps not surprising, that access to medical care is extremely limited in many of the world's poorest nations. After all, citizens of those nations lack enough income to buy adequate food, shelter, and many other basic goods and services. What *is* surprising, however, is that almost 50 million Americans had no health coverage of any kind when President Barack Obama took office in 2009. In a country as wealthy as the United States, why was this the case?

The answer to that question is rooted in the fact that the United States was almost alone among the world's nations in its reliance on unregulated private insurance markets to orchestrate the delivery of health care to its citizens. Unregulated private insurance markets are a deeply flawed mechanism for providing access to health care because of the adverse-selection problem. As previously discussed, if insurance companies set their rates based on the expected medical expenses of the average person, its policy will seem like a bargain to potential customers who know themselves to be in bad health. At the same time, its policies will seem overpriced to those who know themselves to be in excellent health. The upshot is that a disproportionate share of the customers it attracts will have below-average health status, which means its initial premiums will be too low to cover its costs. To stay in business, it will have to raise its rates. But then potential customers in good health will find its policies even less attractive. A downward spiral often ensues, with the end result that insurance becomes unaffordable for most people.

Reliance upon unregulated private health insurance markets in the United States was essentially a historical accident, a consequence of the fact that many labor unions managed to negotiate employer-provided health insurance as part of their compensation packages during the rapidly growing economy of the immediate post–WWII years. Under government policy, employer expenditures for health insurance were nontaxable.

Employer-provided insurance was thus much cheaper for employees than private insurance purchased individually with income on which they had already been taxed. That incentive induced nonunion employers to join their union counterparts in offering employer-provided health insurance. And as long as health care spending was a fairly small share of total income, coverage was broad and the system functioned reasonably well.

An important policy detail was that eligibility for the tax exemption was conditional on insurance being made available to all employees irrespective of preexisting medical conditions. Given the high cost of treating individuals with chronic medical problems, private insurance companies are generally reluctant to issue policies to people with serious health problems. But by covering large groups of employees, only a small percentage of whom would be likely to have serious health problems during any year, insurance companies could issue these policies without taking unacceptable risks. Indeed, the large new employer-provided insurance market was sufficiently lucrative that most insurance companies were eager to participate in it.

Although the employer-provided group insurance approach helped keep the adverse-selection problem at bay for many years, this approach began to unravel as medical costs continued to rise relative to all other goods and services. With health insurance premiums taking a bigger and bigger bite out of workers' paychecks and heightened competition forcing companies to look for new ways to cut costs, some began offering higher wages in lieu of employer-provided health coverage. Younger, healthier workers—for whom medical expenses are normally small—found these offers increasingly tempting.

Parents who didn't buy health insurance for their families were once viewed as irresponsible, but this stigma lost some of its sting as the number of uninsured grew. As more and more people took jobs without health coverage, going without insurance became more socially acceptable. Making matters worse was the changing composition of the pool of the insured. As more healthy families took jobs without coverage, those left tended to be sicker and more costly to treat, forcing premiums to rise still more rapidly. In short, because of adverse selection, our health insurance system was caught in a long-term death spiral.

THE AFFORDABLE CARE ACT OF 2010

Passed by Congress and signed into law by President Obama in March 2010, the Affordable Care Act (ACA) was the government's first serious attempt to halt that death spiral. It contained three main provisions, each one of which was essential for reform to succeed. First, it required insurance companies to offer coverage to everyone on roughly equal terms, irrespective of preexisting medical conditions. Without this provision, the economic imperative of every private insurance company would have been to take every step possible to deny coverage to anyone expected to incur significant medical expenses. Any insurance system that couldn't cover those who most need care would clearly be unacceptable.

Because insurance companies cannot cover their costs if they insure only the least healthy people, it was also necessary for the ACA to include a mandate requiring everyone to buy health insurance. Without a mandate, healthy individuals would face strong incentives to go without health insurance until they got sick, since they would then be able to buy affordable insurance from companies that were forbidden to charge high rates based on preexisting conditions.

The third major feature of the ACA was to provide for subsidies to low-income families. You can't require people to buy insurance if they can't afford it. With health care costs already high and rapidly rising, it was essential to include some provision to ease the burden on those who are unable to pay.

The act contained numerous other provisions, many of which were designed to slow the rate of health care costs by requiring more streamlined medical record keeping and supporting research on the questions of which treatments were most effective. But the essence of the act lies in its three main provisions—nondiscrimination on the basis of preexisting conditions, the mandate, and subsidies for low-income families. Without any one of these provisions, the decline in the percentage of Americans with health coverage would have surely continued.

In tax legislation enacted in late 2017, Congress included a measure repealing the ACA's mandate requiring that everyone purchase health insurance. Perhaps not surprisingly, between 2017 and 2018, the share of Americans without health insurance increased from 7.9 percent to 8.5 percent, suggesting that without further legislative action, the health care industry's long-term death spiral may be poised to resume.

RECAP

INSURANCE

Risk-averse people will purchase insurance to guard themselves against the risk of unanticipated and costly events like hurricanes, car accidents, and illness. Adverse selection drives up the cost of insurance because individuals who are the most expensive for companies to insure have the greatest incentive to purchase insurance. Moral hazard also drives up insurance premiums because people have less incentive to protect items that have been insured against theft or damage. In the United States, the problem of adverse selection has left large numbers of Americans without health care coverage and has led to ongoing efforts to reform our health care system.

Mounting insurance premiums have caused many people in good health to do without health coverage, resulting in higher premiums for those who remain insured. The Affordable Care Act of 2010 was enacted in an attempt to remedy market failures that exist in attempts to provide health care access through unregulated private insurance contracts. In the wake of congressional repeal of the ACA's mandate provision in late 2017, the proportion of Americans without health insurance is on the rise again.

SUMMARY

- Retailers and other sales agents are important sources of information. To the extent that they enable consumers to find the right products and services, they add economic value. In that sense they are no less productive than the workers who manufacture goods or perform services directly. Unfortunately, the free-rider problem often prevents firms from offering useful product information. *(LO1)*

- Virtually every market exchange takes place on the basis of less-than-complete information. More information is beneficial both to buyers and to sellers, but information is costly to acquire. The rational individual therefore acquires information only up to the point at which its marginal benefit equals its marginal cost. Beyond that point, one is rational to remain ignorant. *(LO2)*

- Several principles govern the rational search for information. Searching more intensively makes sense when the cost of a search is low, when quality is highly variable, or when prices vary widely. Further search is always a gamble. A risk-neutral person will search whenever the expected gains outweigh the expected costs. A rational search will always terminate before all possible options have been investigated. Thus, in a search for a partner in an ongoing bilateral relationship, there is always the possibility that a better partner will turn up after the search is over. In most contexts, people deal with this problem by entering into contracts that commit them to their partners once they have mutually agreed to terminate the search. *(LO2)*

- Many potentially beneficial transactions are prevented from taking place by asymmetric information—the fact that one party lacks information that the other has. For example, the owner of a used car knows whether it is in good condition, but potential buyers do not. Even though a buyer may be willing to pay more for a good car than the owner of such a car would require, the fact that the buyer cannot be sure she is getting a good car often discourages the sale. More generally, asymmetric information often prevents sellers from supplying the same quality level that consumers would be willing to pay for. *(LO3)*

- Both buyers and sellers often can gain by finding ways of communicating what they know to one another. But because of the potential conflict between the interests of buyers and sellers, mere statements about the relevant information may not be credible. For a signal between potential trading partners to be credible, it must be costly to fake. For instance, the owner of a high-quality used car can credibly signal the car's quality by offering a warranty—an offer that the seller of a low-quality car could not afford to make. *(LO3)*

- Firms and consumers often try to estimate missing information by making use of what they know about the groups to which people or things belong. For example, insurance firms estimate the risk of insuring individual young male drivers on the basis of the accident rates for young males as a group. This practice is known as statistical discrimination. Statistical discrimination helps explain the phenomenon of disappearing political discourse, which occurs when opponents of a practice such as the death penalty remain silent when the issue is discussed publicly. *(LO4)*

- Risk-averse people will purchase insurance to guard themselves against the risk of unanticipated and costly events like hurricanes, car accidents, and illness. Adverse selection drives up the cost of insurance because individuals who are the most expensive for companies to insure have the great-

est incentive to purchase insurance. In some cases, adverse selection can lead insurance to become so costly that few choose to purchase it. Moral hazard also drives up insurance premiums because people have less incentive to protect items that have been insured against theft or damage. In the United States, the problem of adverse selection has left large numbers of Americans without health care coverage and has led to ongoing efforts to reform our health care system. *(LO5)*

KEY TERMS

adverse selection
asymmetric information
better-than-fair gamble
costly-to-fake principle
disappearing political discourse

expected value of a gamble
fair gamble
free-rider problem
lemons model
moral hazard

risk-averse person
risk-neutral person
statistical discrimination

REVIEW QUESTIONS

1. Explain why a gallery owner who sells a painting might actually create more economic surplus than the artist who painted it. *(LO1)*

2. Can it be rational for a consumer to buy a Chevrolet without having first taken test drives in competing models built by Ford, Chrysler, Honda, Toyota, and others? *(LO2)*

3. Explain why used cars offered for sale are different, on average, from used cars not offered for sale. *(LO3)*

4. Explain why the used car market would be likely to function more efficiently in a community in which

moral norms of honesty are strong than in a community in which such norms are weak. *(LO3)*

5. Explain why banks are generally more willing to lend money to someone who is employed than to someone who is unemployed. *(LO4)*

6. Disability insurance pays a portion of an individual's wages should a nonwork–related injury or illness prevent that person from being able to work. Explain why disability insurance premiums might be lower if everyone were required to purchase disability insurance. *(LO5)*

PROBLEMS

1. Carlos is risk-neutral and has an ancient farmhouse with great character for sale in Slaterville Springs. His reservation price for the house is $130,000. The only possible local buyer is Whitney, whose reservation price for the house is $150,000. The only other houses on the market are modern ranch houses that sell for $125,000, which is exactly equal to each potential buyer's reservation price for such a house. Suppose that if Carlos does not hire a realtor, Whitney will learn from her neighbor that Carlos's house is for sale and will buy it for $140,000. However, if Carlos hires a realtor, he knows that the realtor will put him in touch with an enthusiast for old farmhouses who is willing to pay up to $300,000 for the house. Carlos also knows that if he and this person negotiate, they will agree on a price of $250,000. If realtors charge a commission of 5 percent of the selling price and all realtors have opportunity costs of $2,000 for negotiating a sale, will Carlos hire a realtor? If so, how will total economic surplus be affected? *(LO1)*

2. Makenna and Sienna are computer programmers in Nashville who are planning to move to Seattle. Each owns a house that has just been appraised for $300,000. But whereas Makenna's house is one of hundreds of highly similar houses in a large, well-known suburban development, Sienna's is the only one that was built from her architect's design. Who will benefit more by hiring a realtor to assist in selling her house, Makenna or Sienna? *(LO1)*

3. Brokers who sell stocks over the Internet can serve many more customers than those who transact business by mail or over the phone. How will the expansion of Internet access affect the average incomes of stockbrokers who continue to do business in the traditional way? *(LO2)*

4. Whose income do you predict will be more affected by the expansion of Internet access: *(LO2)*
   a. Stockbrokers or lawyers?
   b. Doctors or pharmacists?
   c. Bookstore owners or the owners of galleries that sell original oil paintings?

5. Kendall, a retired accountant, and Kadence, a government manager, are 63-year-old identical twins who collect

antique pottery. Each has an annual income of $100,000 (Kendall's from a pension, Kadence's from salary). One buys most of her pottery at local auctions, and the other buys most of hers from a local dealer. Which sister is more likely to buy at an auction, and does she pay more or less than her sister who buys from the local dealer? *(LO2)*

6. How will growing Internet access affect the number of film actors and musicians who have active fan clubs? *(LO2)*

7. Consumers know that some fraction x of all new cars produced and sold in the market are defective. The defective ones cannot be identified except by those who own them. Cars do not depreciate with use. Consumers are risk-neutral and value nondefective cars at $30,000 each. New cars sell for $15,000 and used ones for $7,500. What is the fraction x? *(LO3)*

8. State whether the following are true or false, and briefly explain why: *(LO3)*
   a. Companies spend billions of dollars advertising their products on network TV primarily because the content of their advertisements persuades consumers that the advertised products are of high quality.
   b. You may not get the optimal level of advice from a retail shop when you go in to buy a lamp for your bike because of the free-rider problem.
   c. If you need a lawyer, and all your legal expenses are covered by insurance, you should *always* choose the best-dressed lawyer with the most expensive car and the most ostentatiously furnished office.
   d. The benefit of searching for a spouse is affected by the size of the community you live in.

9. For each pair of occupations listed, identify the one for which the kind of car a person drives is more likely to be a good indication of how good they are at their job. *(LO3)*
   a. Elementary school teacher, real estate agent.
   b. Dentist, municipal government administrator.
   c. Engineer in the private sector, engineer in the military.

10. Female heads of state (e.g., Israel's Golda Meir, India's Indira Gandhi, Britain's Margaret Thatcher) have often been described as more bellicose in foreign policy matters than the average male head of state. Using Loury's theory of disappearing political discourse, suggest an explanation for this pattern. *(LO4)*

11. Anika knows there's a 2 percent chance that her house will be destroyed by fire next year, which would require $250,000 to rebuild (and if her house is not destroyed, she won't have to pay anything). If Anika is risk-averse, will she pay $5,000 a year for an insurance policy that covers the full cost of rebuilding her house should it be destroyed by fire? Might she pay $5,200? What about $5,400? *(LO5)*

12. Suppose people cannot tell for sure whether they will fall ill in any given year. High-risk people correctly perceive that their chance of falling ill in a year is 30 percent, and low-risk people correctly perceive that their chance of falling ill is 10 percent. Both high-risk people and low-risk people have to pay $10,000 in medical expenses if they fall ill, and nothing if they remain healthy. *(LO5)*
   a. What are the expected annual medical expenses of a high-risk person?
   b. What are the expected annual medical expenses of a low-risk person?
   c. Suppose insurance companies cannot tell whether someone is high-risk or low-risk. They only know that half of all people are high-risk, and half of all people are low-risk. So, they offer a health insurance policy that costs $2,000 per year in exchange for covering all of a person's medical expenses should they fall ill. If high risk-people and low-risk people are risk-neutral, then who will purchase this insurance policy? Will the insurance company be able to stay in business if it continues to charge $2,000 per year? Briefly explain.

ANSWERS TO SELF-TESTS

12.1 An Internet search is a cheap way to acquire information about many goods and services, so the effect of increased Internet access will be a downward shift in the supply curve of information. In equilibrium, people will acquire more information, and the goods and services they buy will more closely resemble those they would have chosen in an ideal world with perfect information. These effects will cause total economic surplus to grow. Some of these gains, however, might be offset if the Internet makes the free-rider problem more serious. *(LO2)*

12.2 The probability of getting heads is 0.5, the same as the probability of getting tails. Thus, the expected value of this gamble is $(0.5)(\$4) + (0.5)(-\$2) = \$1$.

Since the gamble is better than fair, a risk-neutral person would accept it. *(LO2)*

12.3 Since you still have a 20 percent chance of finding a cheaper apartment if you make another visit, the expected outcome of the gamble is again $5, and you should search again. The bad outcome of any previous search is a sunk cost and should not influence your decision about whether to search again. *(LO2)*

12.4 The expected value of a new car will now be $(0.8) \times (\$16,000) + (0.2)(\$12,000) = \$15,200$. Any risk-neutral consumer who believed that the quality distribution of used cars for sale was the same as the quality distribution of new cars off the assembly line would be willing to pay $15,200 for a used car. *(LO3)*

CHAPTER 13

Labor Markets, Poverty, and Income Distribution

The growing concentration of income among top earners has led to dramatic changes in consumption patterns.

Franck Boston/franckito/123RF

LEARNING OBJECTIVES

After reading this chapter, you should be able to:

LO1 Explain the relationship between wages and the marginal productivity of workers.

LO2 Analyze how wages and employment are determined in competitive labor markets.

LO3 Compare and contrast the various hypotheses economists have proposed to explain earnings differences.

LO4 Recall recent trends in U.S. income inequality and philosophical justifications for income redistribution.

LO5 Describe and analyze some of the methods used to reduce poverty in the United States.

By only the slimmest of margins, Serena Williams won her first professional singles title at the Open Gaz de France in 1999. She then went on to become one of the most highly decorated and highly paid female tennis players of all time, earning more than $450 million in prize money and endorsement fees before her retirement in 2022. The runner-up from that 1999 tournament, French player Amélie Mauresmo, was herself one of the most talented players of her era. And although she nearly beat Williams in 1999 and went on to win numerous major tournaments, she received nowhere near Williams's level of recognition or pay.

Many physicians in France are likewise every bit as talented and hardworking as those in the United States. But while American orthopedists earn an average annual income of over $550,000, their French counterparts earn less than $300,000.

Why do some people earn so much more than others? No other single question in economics has stimulated nearly as much interest and discussion. American citizenship, of course, is neither necessary nor sufficient for receiving high income. Many of the wealthiest people in the world come from extremely poor countries, and many Americans are homeless and malnourished.

Why do small differences in performance sometimes translate into enormous differences in pay?

Our aim in this chapter will be to employ simple economic principles in an attempt to explain why different people earn different salaries. We'll first discuss the human capital model, which emphasizes the importance of differences in personal characteristics. Next, we'll focus on why people with similar personal characteristics often earn sharply different incomes. Among the factors we'll consider are labor unions, discrimination, the effect of nonwage conditions of employment, and winner-take-all markets. Finally, we'll explore whether income inequality is something society should be concerned about, and if so, whether practical remedies for it exist. As we'll see, government programs to redistribute income have costs as well as benefits. As always, policymakers must compare an imperfect status quo with the practical consequences of imperfect government remedies.

THE ECONOMIC VALUE OF WORK

In some respects, the sale of human labor is profoundly different from the sale of other goods and services. For example, although someone may legally relinquish all future rights to the use of her television set by selling it, the law does not permit people to sell themselves into slavery. The law does, however, permit employers to "rent" our services. And in many ways the rental market for labor services functions much like the market for most other goods and services. Each specific category of labor has a demand curve and a supply curve. These curves intersect to determine both the equilibrium wage and the equilibrium quantity of employment for each category of labor.

What is more, shifts in the relevant demand and supply curves produce changes analogous to those produced by shifts in the demand and supply curves for other goods and services. For instance, an increase in the demand for a specific category of labor will generally increase both the equilibrium wage and the equilibrium quantity of employment in that category. By the same token, an increase in the supply of labor to a given occupation will tend to increase the level of employment and lower the wage rate in that occupation.

As in our discussions of other markets, our strategy for investigating how the labor market works will be to go through a series of examples that shed light on different parts of the picture. In the first example, we focus on how the Equilibrium Principle helps us understand how wages will differ among workers with different levels of productive ability.

Equilibrium

EXAMPLE 13.1   **Productive Ability and the Equilibrium Principle**

How much will the potters earn?

Mackintosh Pottery Works is one of numerous identical companies that hire potters who mold clay into pots. These companies sell the pots for $1.10 each to a finishing company that glazes and fires them and then sells them in the retail marketplace. Clay, which is available free of charge in unlimited quantities, is the only input used by the potters. Rennie and Laura are currently the only two potters who work for Mackintosh, whose only cost other than potters' salaries is a 10-cent handling cost for each pot it delivers to the finisher. Rennie delivers 100 pots per week and Laura delivers 120. If the labor market for potters is perfectly competitive, how much will each be paid?

We begin with the assumption that Rennie and Laura have decided to work full-time as potters, so our focus is not on how much they'll work but on how much they'll be paid. After taking handling costs into account, the value of the pots that Rennie delivers is $100 per week, and that is the amount Mackintosh will pay him. To pay him less would risk having him bid away by a competitor. For example, if Mackintosh paid Rennie only $90 per week, the company would then enjoy an economic profit of $10 per week as a result of hiring him. Seeing this cash on the table, a rival firm could then offer Rennie $91, thus earning an additional economic profit of $9 per week by bidding him away from Mackintosh. So under the bidding pressure from rival employers, Mackintosh will have difficulty keeping Rennie if it pays him less than $100 per week. And the company would suffer an economic loss if it paid him more than $100 per week. Similarly, the value of the pots delivered each week by Laura is $120, and this will be her competitive equilibrium wage.

In Example 13.1, the number of pots each potter delivered each week was that potter's **marginal product of labor (*MPL*)**. More generally, a worker's marginal product is the extra output the firm gets as a result of hiring that worker. When we multiply a worker's marginal product by the net price for which each unit of the product sells, we get the **value of the marginal product of labor (*VMPL*)**. (In Example 13.1, the "net price" of each pot was $1.00–the difference between the $1.10 sale price and the $0.10 handling charge.) The general rule in competitive labor markets is that *a worker's pay in long-run equilibrium will be equal to his or her* VMPL–*the net contribution he or she makes to the employer's revenue.* Employers would be delighted to pay workers less than their respective *VMPL*s, to be sure. But if labor markets are truly competitive, they cannot get away with doing so for long.

In the pottery example, each worker's *VMPL* was independent of the number of other workers employed by the firm. In such cases, we cannot predict how many workers a firm will hire. Mackintosh could break even with 2 potters, with 10, or even with 1,000 or more. In many other situations, however, we can predict exactly how many workers a firm will hire. Consider the following example.

marginal product of labor (*MPL*) the additional output a firm gets by employing one additional unit of labor

value of the marginal product of labor (*VMPL*) the dollar value of the additional output a firm gets by employing one additional unit of labor

EXAMPLE 13.2   Hiring

How many workers should Adirondack hire?

Adirondack Woodworking Company hires workers in a competitive labor market at a wage of $350 per week to make kitchen cutting boards from scrap wood that is available free of charge. If the boards sell for $20 each and the company's weekly output varies with the number of workers hired as shown in Table 13.1, how many workers should Adirondack hire?

In the pottery example, our focus was on wage differences for employees whose productive abilities differed. In contrast, we assume here that all workers are equally productive and the firm faces a fixed market wage for each. The fact that the marginal product of labor declines with the number of workers hired is a consequence of the law of diminishing returns. (As discussed in Chapter 6, *Perfectly Competitive Supply*, this law says that when a firm's capital or other productive inputs are held fixed in the short run, adding workers beyond some point results in ever smaller increases in output.) Column 3 of the table reports

TABLE 13.1

Employment and Productivity in a Woodworking Company (when cutting boards sell for $20 each)

(1) Number of workers	(2) Total number of cutting boards/week	(3) MPL (extra cutting boards/week)	(4) VMPL ($/week)
0	0		
		30	600
1	30		
		25	500
2	55		
		21	420
3	76		
		18	360
4	94		
		14	280
5	108		

the marginal product for each additional worker, and column 4 reports the value of each successive worker's marginal product—the number of cutting boards he or she adds times the selling price of $20. Adirondack should keep hiring as long as the next worker's *VMPL* is at least $350 per week (the market wage). The first four workers have *VMPL*s larger than $350, so Adirondack should hire them. But since hiring the fifth worker would add only $280 to weekly revenue, Adirondack should not hire that worker.

Note the similarity between the perfectly competitive firm's decision about how many workers to hire and the perfectly competitive firm's output decision we considered in Chapter 6, *Perfectly Competitive Supply*. When labor is the only variable factor of production, the two decisions are essentially the same. Because of the unique correspondence between the firm's total output and the total number of workers it hires, deciding how many workers to hire is the same as deciding how much output to supply.

The worker's attractiveness to the employer depends not only on how many cutting boards he or she produces, but also on the price of cutting boards and on the wage rate. For example, because *VMPL* rises when product price rises, an increase in product price will lead employers to hire more workers. Employers also will increase hiring when the wage rate falls.

 SELF-TEST 13.1

In the woodworking example, how many workers should Adirondack hire if the price of cutting boards rises to $26?

 SELF-TEST 13.2

In the woodworking example, how many workers should Adirondack hire if the wage rate falls to $275 per week?

RECAP ↑

THE ECONOMIC VALUE OF WORK

In competitive labor markets, employers face pressure to pay each worker the value of his or her marginal product. When a firm can hire as many workers as it wishes at a given market wage, it should expand employment as long as the value of marginal product of labor exceeds the market wage.

THE EQUILIBRIUM WAGE AND EMPLOYMENT LEVELS

As we saw in Chapter 3, *Supply and Demand,* the equilibrium price and quantity in any competitive market occur at the intersection of the relevant supply and demand curves. The same is true in competitive markets for labor.

THE DEMAND CURVE FOR LABOR

An employer's reservation price for a worker is the most the employer could pay without suffering a decline in profit. As discussed, this reservation price for the employer in a perfectly competitive labor market is simply the value of the worker's marginal product ($VMPL$). Because of the law of diminishing returns, we know that the marginal product of labor, and hence $VMPL$, declines in the short run as the quantity of labor rises. The individual employer's demand curve for labor in any particular occupation–say, computer programmers–may thus be shown, as in Figure 13.1, as a downward-sloping function of the wage rate. Suppose firm 1 [Figure 13.1(a)] and firm 2 [Figure 13.1(b)] are the only two firms that employ programmers in a given community. The demand for programmers in that community will then be the horizontal sum of the individual firm demands [Figure 13.1(c)].

THE SUPPLY CURVE OF LABOR

What does the supply curve of labor for a specific occupation look like? Will more labor be offered at high wage rates than at low wage rates? An equivalent way to pose the same question is to ask whether consumers will wish to consume less leisure at high wage rates than at low wage rates. By themselves, the principles of economic theory do not provide an answer to this question because a change in the wage rate exerts two opposing effects on the quantity of leisure demanded. One is the substitution effect, which says that at a higher wage, leisure is more expensive, leading consumers to consume less of it. The second is the income effect, which says that at a higher wage, consumers have more purchasing power, leading them to consume more leisure. Which of these two opposing effects dominates is an empirical question.

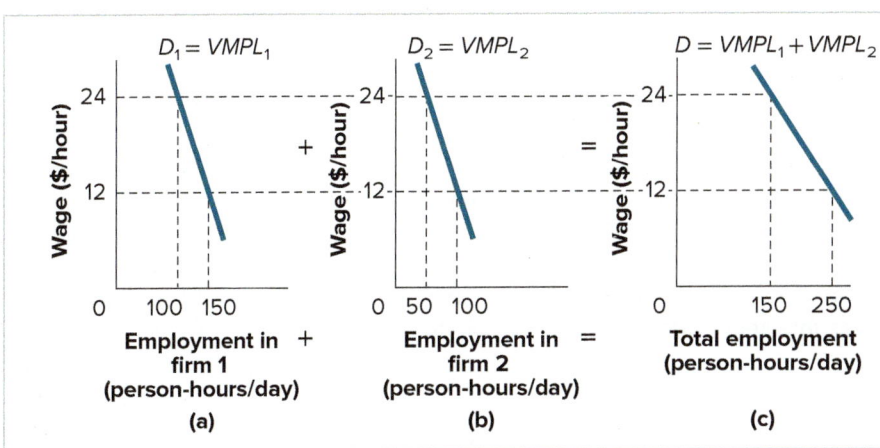

FIGURE 13.1

The Occupational Demand for Labor.

If firm 1 and firm 2 are the only firms that employ labor in a given occupation, we generate the demand curve for labor in that occupation by adding the individual demand curves horizontally.

FIGURE 13.2

The Effect of an Increase in the Demand for Computer Programmers.

An increase in the demand for programmers from D_1 to D_2 results in an increase in the equilibrium level of employment (from L_1 to L_2) and an increase in the equilibrium wage (from W_1 to W_2).

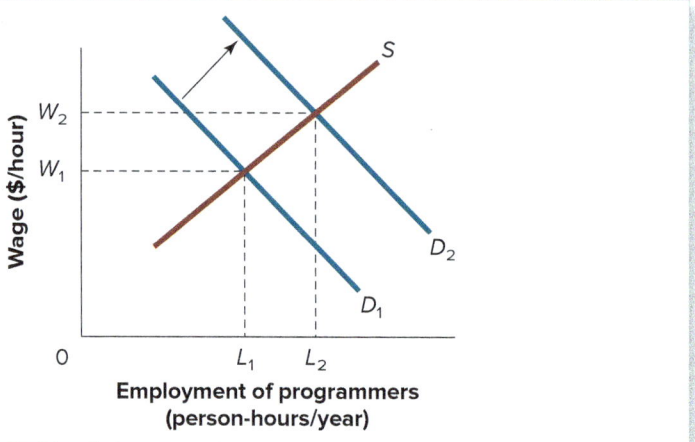

For the economy as a whole during the past several centuries, the workweek has been declining and real wages have been rising. This pattern might seem to suggest that the supply curve of labor is downward-sloping, and for the economy as a whole it may be. There is also evidence that individual workers may sometimes work fewer hours when wage rates are high than when they are low. A study of taxicab drivers in New York City, for example, found that drivers quit earlier on rainy days (when the effective wage is high because of high demand for cab rides) than on sunny days (when the effective wage is lower).[1]

These observations notwithstanding, the supply of labor *to any particular occupation* is almost surely upward-sloping because wage differences among occupations influence occupational choice. It is no accident, for example, that many more people are choosing jobs as computer programmers now than in 1970. Wages of programmers have risen sharply during the past several decades, which has led many people to forsake other career paths in favor of programming. Curve *S* in Figure 13.2 represents the supply curve of computer programmers. Its positive slope is typical of the supply curves for most individual occupations.

MARKET SHIFTS

As more tasks have become computerized in recent decades, the demand for programmers has grown, as shown by the shift from D_1 to D_2 in Figure 13.2. Equilibrium in the market for computer programmers occurs at the intersection of the relevant supply and demand curves. The increase in demand has led to an increase in the equilibrium level of programmers from L_1 to L_2 and a rise in the equilibrium wage from W_1 to W_2.

As discussed in Chapter 7, *Efficiency, Exchange, and the Invisible Hand in Action*, the market for stocks and other financial assets reaches equilibrium very quickly in the wake of shifts in the underlying supply and demand curves. Labor markets, by contrast, are often much slower to adjust. When the demand for workers in a given profession increases, shortages may remain for months or even years, depending on how long it takes people to acquire the skills and training needed to enter the profession.

RECAP

EQUILIBRIUM IN THE LABOR MARKET

The demand for labor in a perfectly competitive labor market is the horizontal sum of each employer's value of the marginal product of labor (*VMPL*) curve. The supply curve of labor for any particular occupation is upward-sloping, even though the supply curve of labor for the economy as a whole may be vertical or even downward-sloping. In each labor market, the demand and supply curves intersect to determine the equilibrium wage and level of employment.

[1]L. Babcock, C. Camerer, G. Loewenstein, and R. Thaler, "Labor Supply of New York City Cab Drivers: One Day at a Time," *Quarterly Journal of Economics* 111 (1997), pp. 408–41.

EXPLAINING DIFFERENCES IN EARNINGS

▶ Visit your instructor's Connect course and access your eBook to view this video.

The theory of competitive labor markets tells us that differences in pay reflect differences in the corresponding *VMPL*s. Recall that in Example 13.1, Laura earned 20 percent more than Rennie because she made 20 percent more pots each week than he did. This difference in productivity may have resulted from an underlying difference in talent or training, or perhaps Laura simply worked harder than Rennie.

Yet often we see large salary differences even among people who appear equally talented and hardworking. Why, for instance, do lawyers earn so much more than those plumbers who are just as smart as they are and work just as hard? And why do surgeons earn so much more than general practitioners? These wage differences might seem to violate the No-Cash-on-the-Table Principle, which says that only differences in talent, luck, or hard work can account for long-run differences in earnings. For example, if plumbers could earn more by becoming lawyers, why don't they just switch occupations? Similarly, if general practitioners could boost their incomes by becoming surgeons, why didn't they become surgeons in the first place?

Why do female models earn so much more than male models?

Equilibrium

HUMAN CAPITAL THEORY

Answers to these questions are suggested by **human capital theory**, which holds that an individual's *VMPL* is proportional to their stock of **human capital**—an amalgam of factors such as education, experience, training, intelligence, energy, work habits, trustworthiness, and initiative. According to this theory, some occupations pay better than others because they require larger stocks of human capital. For example, a general practitioner could become a surgeon, but only by extending her formal education by several more years. An even larger investment in additional education is required for a plumber to become a lawyer.

Differences in demand can result in some kinds of human capital being more valuable than others. Consider again the increase in demand for computer programmers that has been occurring for the past several decades. During that same time period, the demand for the services of tax accountants has fallen as more and more taxpayers have used tax-preparation software in lieu of hiring accountants to help them with their taxes. Both occupations require demanding technical training, but the training received by computer programmers now yields a higher return in the labor market.

human capital theory a theory of pay determination that says a worker's wage will be proportional to their stock of human capital

human capital an amalgam of factors such as education, training, experience, intelligence, energy, work habits, trustworthiness, and initiative that affect the value of a worker's marginal product

LABOR UNIONS

Two workers with the same amount of human capital may earn different wages if one of them belongs to a **labor union** and the other does not. A labor union is an organization through which workers bargain collectively with employers for better wages and working conditions.

Many economists believe that unions affect labor markets in much the same way that cartels affect product markets. To illustrate, consider a simple economy with two labor markets, neither of which is unionized initially. Suppose the total supply of labor to the two markets is fixed at $S_0 = 200$ workers per day, and that the demand curves are as shown by $VMPL_1$ and $VMPL_2$ in Figure 13.3(a) and (b). The sum of the two demand curves, $VMPL_1 + VMPL_2$ [Figure 13.3(c)], intersects the supply curve to determine an equilibrium wage of $18 per hour. At that wage, firms in market 1 hire 125 workers per day [Figure 13.3(a)] and firms in market 2 hire 75 [Figure 13.3(b)].

Now suppose workers in market 1 form a union and refuse to work for less than $24 per hour. Because demand curves for labor are downward-sloping, employers of unionized workers reduce employment from 125 workers per day to 100 [Figure 13.4(a)]. The 25 displaced workers in the unionized market would, of course, be delighted to find other jobs in that market at $24 per hour. But they cannot, and so they are forced to seek employment in the nonunionized market. The result is an excess supply of 25 workers in the nonunion market at the original wage of $18 per hour. In time, wages in that market

labor union a group of workers who bargain collectively with employers for better wages and working conditions

FIGURE 13.3

An Economy with Two Nonunionized Labor Markets.

Supply and demand intersect to determine a market wage of $18 per hour (c). At that wage, employers in market 1 hire 125 workers per day and employers in market 2 hire 75 workers per day. The *VMPL* is $18 in each market.

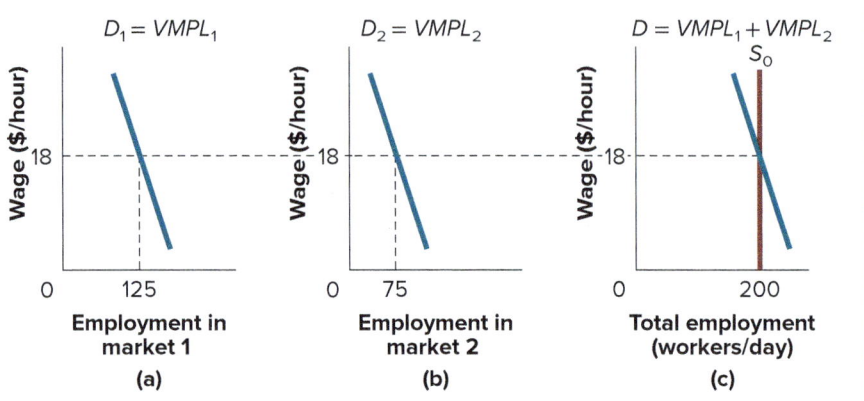

decline to $W_N = \$12$ per hour, the level at which 100 workers can find jobs in the nonunionized market [Figure 13.4(b)].

It might seem that the gains of the unionized workers are exactly offset by the losses of nonunionized workers. On closer inspection, however, we see that pegging the union wage above the equilibrium level actually reduces the value of total output. If labor were allocated efficiently between the two markets, the value of the marginal product of labor would have to be the same in each. Otherwise, the total value of output could be increased by moving workers from the low-*VMPL* market to the high-*VMPL* market. With the wage set initially at $18 per hour in both markets, the condition for efficient allocation was met because the *VMPL* was $18 per hour in both markets. But because the collective bargaining process drives wages (and hence *VMPLs*) in the two markets apart, the value of total output is no longer maximized. To verify this claim, note that if a worker is taken out of the nonunionized market, the reduction in the value of output there will be only $12 per hour, which is less than the $24-per-hour gain in the value of output when that same worker is added to the unionized market.

FIGURE 13.4

The Effect of a Union Wage above the Equilibrium Wage.

When the unionized wage is pegged at $W_U = \$24$/hour (a), 25 workers are discharged. When these workers seek employment in the nonunionized market, the wage in that market falls to $W_N = \$12$/hour (b).

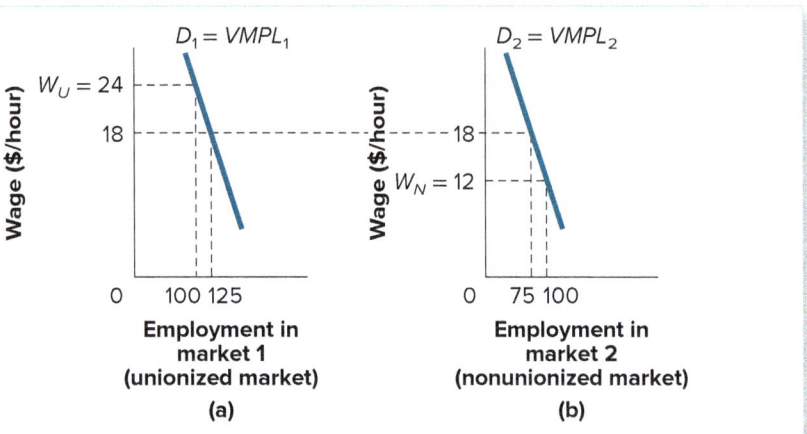

✅ **SELF-TEST 13.3**

In Figure 13.4, by how much would the value of total output be increased if the wage rate were $18 per hour in each market?

Wages paid to workers in a unionized firm are sometimes 50 percent or more above the wages paid to their nonunionized counterparts. To the alert economic naturalist, this difference prompts the following question:

The Economic Naturalist 13.1

If unionized firms have to pay more, how do they manage to survive in the face of competition from their nonunionized counterparts?

In fact, nonunionized firms sometimes do drive unionized firms out of business, as when the American textile industry moved to the South in the late nineteenth and early twentieth centuries to escape the burden of high union wages in New England. Even so, unionized and nonunionized firms often manage to compete head-to-head for extended periods. If their costs are significantly higher, how do the unionized firms manage to survive?

The observed pay differential actually overstates the difference between the labor costs of the two types of firm. Because the higher union wage attracts an excess supply of workers, unionized employers can adopt more stringent hiring requirements than their nonunionized counterparts. As a result, unionized workers tend to be more experienced and skilled than nonunionized workers. Studies estimate that the union wage premium for workers with the same amount of human capital is only about 10 percent.

Another factor is that unions may actually boost the productivity of workers with any given amount of human capital, perhaps by improving communication between management and workers. Similarly, the implementation of formal grievance procedures, in combination with higher pay, may boost morale among unionized workers, leading to higher productivity. Labor turnover is also significantly lower in unionized firms, which reduces hiring and training costs. Studies suggest that union productivity may be sufficiently high to compensate for the premium in union wages. So even though wages are higher in unionized firms, these firms may not have significantly higher labor costs per unit of output than their nonunionized counterparts.

How do firms that employ higher-paid union labor remain competitive?

In 2019, 10.3 percent of American workers belonged to a labor union, less than one-third of the union membership rate during the 1950s. Because the union wage premium is small and applies to only a small fraction of the labor force, union membership in the United States is probably not an important explanation for why workers with similar qualifications often earn sharply different incomes.

COMPENSATING WAGE DIFFERENTIALS

If people are paid the value of what they produce, why do garbage collectors earn more than lifeguards? Picking up the trash is important, to be sure, but is it more valuable than saving the life of a drowning child? Similarly, we need not question the value of a timely plumbing repair to wonder why plumbers get paid more than fourth-grade teachers. Is replacing faucet washers really more valuable than educating children? As the next example illustrates, the wage for a particular job depends not only on the value of what workers produce, but also on how attractive they find its working conditions.

The Economic Naturalist 13.2

Why do some ad copywriters earn more than others?

You plan to pursue a career in advertising and have two job offers: one to write ad copy for the American Cancer Society, the other to write copy for Camel cigarette ads aimed at the youth market. Except for the subject matter of the ads, working conditions are identical in the two jobs. If each job paid $30,000 per year and offered the same prospects for advancement, which would you choose?

When this question was recently posed to a sample of graduating seniors at Cornell University, almost 90 percent of them chose the American Cancer Society job. When asked how much more they would have to be paid to induce them to switch to the Camel cigarettes job, their median response was a premium of $15,000 per year. As this sample suggests, employers who offer jobs with less attractive working conditions cannot hope to fill them unless they also offer higher salaries.

Other things being equal, jobs with attractive working conditions will pay less than jobs with less attractive conditions. Wage differences associated with differences in working conditions are known as **compensating wage differentials**. Economists have identified compensating differentials for a host of specific working conditions. Studies have found, for example, that safe jobs tend to pay less than otherwise similar jobs that entail greater risks to health and safety. Studies also have found that wages vary in accord with the attractiveness of the work schedule. For instance, working night shifts commands a wage premium, and teachers must accept lower wages in part because many of those with children value having hours that coincide with the school calendar.

Do tobacco company CEOs get paid extra for testifying that cigarette smoking does not cause cancer?

compensating wage differential a difference in the wage rate—negative or positive—that reflects the attractiveness of a job's working conditions

employer discrimination an arbitrary preference by an employer for one group of workers over another

DISCRIMINATION IN THE LABOR MARKET

Women and minorities continue to receive lower wage rates, on average, than white males with similar measures of human capital. This pattern poses a profound challenge to standard theories of competitive labor markets, which hold that competitive pressures will eliminate wage differentials not based on differences in productivity. Defenders of standard theories attribute the wage gap to unmeasured differences in human capital. Many critics of these theories reject the idea that labor markets are effectively competitive, and instead attribute the gap to various forms of discrimination.

Discrimination by Employers

Employer discrimination is the term used to describe wage differentials that arise from an arbitrary preference by an employer for one group of workers over another. An example occurs if two labor force groups, such as males and females, are equally productive, on average, yet some employers ("discriminators") prefer hiring males and are willing to pay higher wages to do so.

Most consumers are not willing to pay more for a product produced by males than for an identical one produced by females (if indeed they even *know* which type of worker produced the product). If product price is unaffected by the composition of the workforce that produces the product, a firm's profit will be smaller the more males it employs because males cost more yet are no more productive (on the assumption that discrimination is the cause of the wage gap). Thus, the most profitable firms will be ones that employ only females.

Arbitrary wage gaps are an apparent violation of the No-Cash-on-the-Table Principle. The initial wage differential provides an opportunity for employers who hire mostly females to grow at the expense of their rivals. Because such firms make an economic profit on the

Equilibrium

sale of each unit of output, their incentive is to expand as rapidly as they possibly can. And to do that, they would naturally want to continue hiring only the cheaper females.

But as profit-seeking firms continue to pursue this strategy, the supply of females at the lower wage rate will run out. The short-run solution is to offer females a slightly higher wage. But this strategy works only if other firms do not pursue it. Once they too start offering a higher wage, females will again be in short supply. The only stable outcome occurs when the wage of females reaches parity with the wage of males. The wage for both males and females will thus settle at the common value of their *VMPL*.

Any employer who wants to voice a preference for hiring males must now do so by paying males a wage in excess of *VMPL*. Employers can discriminate against females if they wish, but only if they are willing to pay premium wages to males out of their own profits. Not even the harshest critics of the competitive model seem willing to impute such behavior to the owners of capitalist enterprises.

For this reason, if employer discrimination arises in an imperfectly competitive market, we would expect it to disappear if the market suddenly becomes more competitive. Consistent with this prediction, there is evidence that increased competition in the banking industry resulting from deregulation in the mid-1970s to the mid-1980s reduced both the male–female wage gap and the Black–white wage gap for workers in this industry.[2]

Discrimination by Others

If employer discrimination is not the primary explanation of the wage gap, what is? In some instances, **customer discrimination** may provide a plausible explanation. For example, if people believe that juries and clients are less likely to take female or minority attorneys seriously, members of these groups will face a reduced incentive to attend law school, and law firms will face a reduced incentive to hire those who do.

Another possible source of persistent wage gaps is discrimination and socialization within the family. For example, families may provide less education for their female children, or they may socialize them to believe that lofty career ambitions are not appropriate.

customer discrimination
the willingness of consumers to pay more for a product produced by members of a favored group, even if the quality of the product is unaffected

Other Sources of the Wage Gap

Part of the wage gap may be explained by compensating wage differentials that spring from differences in preferences for other nonwage elements of the compensation package. Jobs that involve exposure to physical risk, for example, command higher wages, and if men are relatively more willing to accept such risks, they will earn more than females with otherwise identical stocks of human capital. (The same difference would result if employers felt constrained by social norms not to assign female employees to risky jobs.)

Elements of human capital that are difficult to measure also may help explain earnings differentials. For example, productivity is influenced not only by the quantity of education an individual has, which is easy to measure, but also by its quality, which is much harder to measure. Part of the Black–white differential in wages may thus be due to the fact that schools in Black neighborhoods have not been as good, on average, as those in white neighborhoods.

Differences in the courses people take in college appear to have similar implications for differences in productivity. For instance, students in math, engineering, or business—male or female—tend to earn significantly higher salaries than those who concentrate in the humanities. The fact that males are disproportionately represented in the former group gives rise to a male wage premium that is unrelated to employer discrimination.

As economists have grown more sophisticated in their efforts to measure human capital and other factors that influence individual wage rates, unexplained wage differentials by sex and race have grown steadily smaller, and have even disappeared altogether. Many studies, however, continue to find significant unexplained differentials by race and sex. Debate about discrimination in the workplace will continue until the causes of these differentials are more fully understood.

[2]R. Levine, A. Levkov, and Y. Rubinstein, "Bank Deregulation and Racial Inequality in America," *Critical Finance Review* 3, no. 1 (2014), pp. 1–48; S. Black and P. Strahan, "The Division of Spoils: Rent Sharing and Discrimination in a Regulated Industry," *American Economic Review* 91 (2001), pp. 814–31.

WINNER-TAKE-ALL MARKETS

Differences in human capital do much to explain observed differences in earnings. Yet earnings differentials have also grown sharply in many occupations within which the distribution of human capital among workers seems essentially unchanged. Consider the following example.

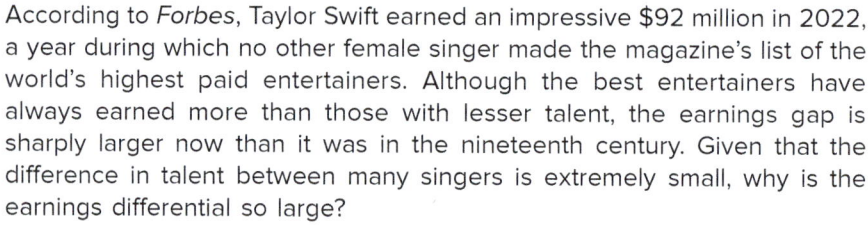

The Economic Naturalist 13.3

Why does Taylor Swift earn many millions more than singers with only slightly less talent?

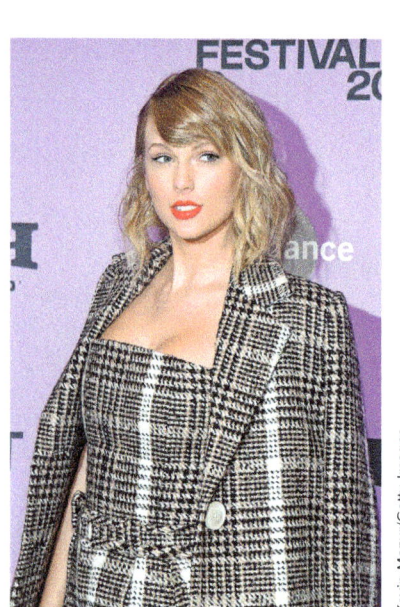

Why does Taylor Swift earn so much more than singers with only slightly less talent?

According to *Forbes*, Taylor Swift earned an impressive $92 million in 2022, a year during which no other female singer made the magazine's list of the world's highest paid entertainers. Although the best entertainers have always earned more than those with lesser talent, the earnings gap is sharply larger now than it was in the nineteenth century. Given that the difference in talent between many singers is extremely small, why is the earnings differential so large?

The answer lies in a fundamental change in the way we consume most of our music. In the nineteenth century, virtually all professional musicians delivered their services in concert halls in front of live audiences. (In 1900, the state of Iowa alone had more than 1,300 concert halls!) Audiences of that day would have been delighted to listen to the world's best performer, but no one singer could hope to perform in more than a tiny fraction of the world's concert halls. Today, in contrast, most of the music we hear comes in recorded form, which enables the most popular singers to be literally everywhere at once. As soon as the master recording has been made, the latest Taylor Swift song can be saved as an MP3 or other audio file format at the same low cost as that of a slightly less-talented singer.

Tens of millions of buyers worldwide are willing to pay a few cents extra to hear the most popular performers. Thus, small differences in talent are amplified into massive earnings differentials, leading top singers to earn millions of dollars each year (most of which constitute economic rents, as discussed in Chapter 7, *Efficiency, Exchange, and the Invisible Hand in Action*), while slightly less-talented singers earn far less.

Kevin Mazur/Getty Images

winner-take-all labor market one in which small differences in human capital translate into large differences in pay

The market for singers is an example of a **winner-take-all market**, one in which small differences in ability or other dimensions of human capital translate into large differences in pay. Such markets have long been familiar in entertainment and professional sports. But as technology has enabled the most talented individuals to serve broader markets, the winner-take-all reward structure has become an increasingly important feature of modern economic life, permeating such diverse fields as law, journalism, consulting, medicine, investment banking, corporate management, publishing, design, fashion, and even the hallowed halls of academe.

Contrary to what the name seems to imply, a winner-take-all market does not mean a market with literally only one winner. Indeed, hundreds of professional musicians earn multimillion-dollar annual salaries. Yet tens of thousands of others, many of them nearly as good, struggle to pay their bills.

The fact that small differences in human capital often give rise to extremely large differences in pay might seem to contradict human capital theory. Note, however, that the winner-take-all reward pattern is completely consistent with the competitive labor market theory's claim that individuals are paid in accordance with the contributions they make to the employer's net revenue. The leverage of technology often amplifies small perfor-mance differentials into very large ones.

> *RECAP*
>
> **EXPLAINING DIFFERENCES IN EARNINGS AMONG PEOPLE**
>
> Earnings differ among people in part because of differences in their human capital, an amalgam of personal characteristics that affect productivity. But pay often differs substantially between two people with the same amount of human capital. This can happen for many reasons: One may belong to a labor union while the other does not, one may work in a job with less pleas-ant conditions, one may be the victim of discrimination, or one may work in an arena in which technology or other factors provide greater leverage to human capital.

RECENT TRENDS IN INEQUALITY

In the United States, as in most other market economies, a majority of citizens receive most of their income from the sale of their own labor. An attractive feature of the free-market system is that it rewards initiative, effort, and risk taking. The harder, longer, and more effectively a person works, the more she will be paid.

Yet relying on the marketplace to distribute income also entails an important draw-back: Those who do well often end up with vastly more money than they can spend, while those who fail often cannot afford even basic goods and services. Hundreds of thousands of American families are homeless, and still larger numbers go to bed hungry each night. Many distinguished philosophers have argued that such poverty in the midst of plenty is impossible to justify on moral grounds. It is thus troubling that income inequality has been growing rapidly in recent decades.

The period from the end of World War II until the early 1970s was one of balanced income growth in the United States. During that period, incomes grew at almost 3 percent a year for rich, middle-class, and poor Americans alike. In the ensuing years, however, the pattern of income growth has been dramatically different.

In the first column of Table 13.2, for example, notice that families at the 20th percentile of the income distribution saw their real incomes increase by less than 20 percent over the entire 41-year period between 1980 and 2021 (a growth rate of less than half of 1 percent per year). The third column of the table indicates that the real incomes of families at the 60th percentile grew by about one-third over the same span (a growth rate of slightly more than seven-tenths of 1 percent per year). In contrast, families at the

TABLE 13.2

Income Received by Families at Selected Income Percentiles, 1980–2021 (2021 dollars)

Year	20th Percentile	40th Percentile	60th Percentile	80th Percentile	95th Percentile
2021	28,007	55,000	89,744	149,131	286,304
2010	24,906	47,322	76,587	124,568	224,761
2000	28,272	52,064	82,315	129,002	229,113
1990	25,202	47,707	72,985	111,303	191,028
1980	23,475	44,025	67,494	98,824	159,038

Source: www.census.gov/library/publications/2022/demo/p60-276.html.

80th percentile saw their real incomes grow by more than one-third between 1980 and 2021, while for families at the 95th percentile, real incomes jumped by more than 80 percent. Even for these families, however, income growth rates were low relative to those of the immediate post–World War II decades.

The only people whose incomes have grown substantially faster than in that earlier period are those at the very pinnacle of the income ladder. Real earnings of the top one-tenth of 1 percent of U.S. earners, for example, have risen more than four-fold since 1980, and those even higher up have taken home paychecks that might have seemed unimaginable just a few decades ago. The CEOs of America's largest companies, who earned roughly 30 times as much as the average worker in 1980, earned 324 times as much in 2021.

It's important to emphasize that being near the bottom of the income distribution in one year does not necessarily mean being stranded there forever. On the contrary, people in the United States have always experienced a high degree of economic mobility by international standards. Many CEOs now earning multimillion-dollar paychecks, for example, were struggling young graduate students in 1980, and were hence among those classified in the bottom 20 percent of the income distribution for that year in Table 13.2. We must bear in mind, too, that not all economic mobility is upward. Many blue-collar workers, for instance, had higher real incomes in 1980 than they do today.

On balance, then, the entries in Table 13.2 tell an important story. In contrast to the economy 40 years ago, those near the top of the income ladder today are prospering as never before, while those farther down have seen their living standards grow much more slowly.

IS INCOME INEQUALITY A MORAL PROBLEM?

The late John Rawls, a moral philosopher at Harvard University, constructed a cogent ethical critique of the marginal productivity system, one based heavily on the economic theory of choice itself.[3] In thinking about what constitutes a just distribution of income, Rawls asked us to imagine ourselves meeting to choose the rules for distributing income. The meeting takes place behind a "veil of ignorance," which conceals from participants any knowledge of what talents and abilities each has. Because no individual knows whether he is smart or dull, strong or weak, fast or slow, no one knows which rules of distribution would work to his own advantage.

Rawls argued that the rules people would choose in such a state of ignorance would necessarily be fair; and if the rules are fair, the income distribution to which they give rise will also be fair.

What sort of rules would people choose from behind a veil of ignorance? If the national income were a fixed amount, most people would probably give everyone an equal share. That scenario is likely, Rawls argued, because most people are strongly risk-averse. Since an unequal income distribution would involve not only a chance of doing well, but a chance of doing poorly, most people would prefer to eliminate the risk by choosing an equal distribution. Imagine, for example, that you and two friends have been told that an anonymous benefactor donated $300,000 to divide among you. How would you split it? If you are like most people, you would propose an equal division, or $100,000 for each of you.

Yet the attraction of equality is far from absolute. Indeed, the goal of absolute equality is quickly trumped by other concerns when we make the rules for distributing wealth in modern market economies. Wealth, after all, generally doesn't come from anonymous benefactors; we must produce it. In a large economy, if each person were guaranteed an equal amount of income, few would invest in education or the development of special talents; and as the next example illustrates, the incentive to work would be sharply reduced.

---

[3]John Rawls, *A Theory of Justice* (Cambridge, MA: Harvard University Press, 1971).

EXAMPLE 13.3   Income Sharing

Does income sharing affect labor supply?

Sue is offered a job reshelving books in the University of Montana library from noon until 1 p.m. each Friday. Her reservation wage for this task is $10 per hour. If the library director offers Sue $100 per hour, how much economic surplus will she enjoy as a result of accepting the job? Now suppose the library director announces that the earnings from the job will be divided equally among the 400 students who live in Sue's dormitory. Will Sue still accept?

When the $100 per hour is paid directly to Sue, she accepts the job and enjoys an economic surplus of $100 − $10 = $90. If the $100 were divided equally among the 400 residents of Sue's dorm, however, each resident's share would be only 25 cents. Accepting the job would thus mean a negative surplus for Sue of $0.25 − $10 = −$9.75, so she will not accept the job.

 SELF-TEST 13.4

What is the largest dorm population for which Sue would accept the job on a pay-sharing basis?

In a country without rewards for hard work and risk taking, national income would be dramatically smaller than in a country with such rewards. Of course, material rewards for effort and risk taking necessarily lead to inequality. Rawls argued, however, that people would be willing to accept a certain degree of inequality as long as these rewards produced a sufficiently large increase in the total amount of output available for distribution.

But how much inequality would people accept? Much less than the amount produced by purely competitive markets, Rawls argued. The idea is that behind the veil of ignorance, each person would fear ending up in a disadvantaged position, so each would choose rules that would produce a more equal distribution of income than exists under the marginal productivity system. And since such choices *define* the just distribution of income, he argued, fairness requires at least some attempt to reduce the inequality produced by the market system.

> **RECAP** ↑
>
> **TRENDS IN INEQUALITY AND IS INCOME INEQUALITY A MORAL PROBLEM?**
>
> - From 1945 until the mid-1970s, incomes grew at almost 3 percent a year for rich, middle-class, and poor families alike. In contrast, most of the income growth since the mid-1970s has been concentrated among top earners.
> - John Rawls argued that the degree of inequality typical of unregulated market systems is unfair because people would favor substantially less inequality if they chose distributional rules from behind a veil of ignorance.

METHODS OF INCOME REDISTRIBUTION ——————

Although we as a society have an interest in limiting income inequality, programs for reducing it are often fraught with practical difficulties. The challenge is to find ways to raise the incomes of those who cannot fend for themselves, without at the same time undermining their incentive to work, and without using scarce resources to subsidize those who are not poor. Of course, some people simply cannot work, or cannot find work that pays enough to live on. In a world of perfect information, the government could make generous cash payments to those people, and withhold support from those who can fend for themselves. In practice, however, the two groups are often hard to distinguish from each other. And so we must choose among imperfect alternative measures.

WELFARE PAYMENTS AND IN-KIND TRANSFERS

in-kind transfer a payment made not in the form of cash, but in the form of a good or service

Cash transfers and in-kind transfers are at the forefront of antipoverty efforts around the globe. **In-kind transfers** are direct transfers of goods or services to low-income individuals or families, such as the Supplemental Nutrition Assistance Program (also known as SNAP or food stamps), public housing, subsidized school lunches, and Medicaid.

From the mid-1960s until 1996, the most important federal program of cash transfers was Aid to Families with Dependent Children (AFDC), which provided cash payments to poor single-parent households. A sharp rise in AFDC caseloads in the early 1990s raised concerns among many lawmakers that AFDC recipients had become dependent on welfare and were trapped in a "cycle of poverty." Critics of the program also argued that AFDC undermined family stability because in many states a poor mother became ineligible for benefits if her husband or other able-bodied adult male lived with her and her children. This provision confronted many long-term unemployed fathers with an agonizing choice: They could leave their families, making them eligible for public assistance, or they could remain, making them ineligible. Even fathers who deeply loved their families understandably chose to leave.

Personal Responsibility and Work Opportunity Reconciliation Act the 1996 federal law that transferred responsibility for welfare programs from the federal level to the state level and placed a five-year lifetime limit on payment of TANF benefits to any given recipient

Concern about work incentives led Congress to pass the **Personal Responsibility and Work Opportunity Reconciliation Act** in 1996, which abolished the AFDC program and replaced it with Temporary Assistance for Needy Families (TANF). Under the new law, the federal government makes lump-sum cash grants to the states, which then have broad discretion in determining TANF benefit levels and eligibility requirements. In addition, the new law set a five-year lifetime limit on the receipt of TANF benefits.

Supporters of the Personal Responsibility and Work Reconciliation Act argue that it has already reduced the nation's welfare rolls considerably and that it will encourage greater self-reliance over the long run. Skeptics fear that the five-year lifetime limit on benefits may eventually impose severe hardships on the poor, especially poor children, if overall economic conditions deteriorate. Indeed, debate continues about the extent to which the observed increases in poverty rates during the economic downturns of 2001 and 2008–2009 were attributable to the Personal Responsibility and Work Opportunity Reconciliation Act. What is clear, however, is that the new law has not eliminated the need to discover efficient ways of providing assistance to low-income families.

MEANS-TESTED BENEFIT PROGRAMS

means-tested a benefit program whose benefit level declines as the recipient earns additional income

Many welfare programs, including TANF, are **means-tested**, which means that the more income a family has, the smaller are the benefits it receives under these programs. The purpose of means testing is to avoid paying benefits to those who don't really need them. But because of the way welfare programs are administered, means testing often has a pernicious effect on work incentives.

Consider, for example, an unemployed participant in four welfare programs: food stamps, rent stamps, energy stamps, and day care stamps. Each program gives him $100 worth of stamps per month, which he is then free to spend on food, rent, energy, and day care. If he gets a job, his benefits in each program are reduced by 50 cents for each dollar he earns. Thus, if he accepts a job that pays $50 weekly, he'll lose $25 in weekly benefits from each of the four welfare programs, for a total benefit reduction of $100 per week. Taking the job thus leaves him $50 per week worse off than before. Low-income persons need no formal training in economics to realize that seeking gainful employment does not pay under these circumstances.

What is more, means-tested programs of cash and in-kind transfers are extremely costly to administer. If the government were to eliminate all existing welfare and social service agencies that are involved in these programs, the resulting savings would be enough to lift every poor person out of poverty. One proposal to do precisely this is the negative income tax.

THE NEGATIVE INCOME TAX

Under the **negative income tax (NIT)**, every man, woman, and child—rich or poor—would receive a substantial income tax credit, say $5,000 per year. A person who earns no income would receive this credit in cash. People who earn income would receive the same initial credit, and their income would continue to be taxed at some rate less than 100 percent.

The negative income tax would do much less than current programs to weaken work incentives because, unlike current programs, it would ensure that someone who earned an extra dollar would keep at least a portion of it. And because the program would be administered by the existing Internal Revenue Service, administrative costs would be far lower than under the current welfare system.

Despite these advantages, however, the negative income tax is by no means a perfect solution to the income-transfer problem. Although the incentive problem under the program would be less severe than under current welfare programs, it would remain a serious difficulty. To see why, note that if the negative income tax were the *sole* means of insulating people against poverty, the payment to people with no earned income would need to be at least as large as the government's official **poverty threshold**.

The poverty threshold is the annual income level below which a family is officially classified as "poor" by the government. The threshold is based on government estimates of the cost of the so-called economy food plan, the least costly of four nutritionally adequate food plans designed by the Department of Agriculture. The department's 1955 Household Food Consumption Survey found that families of three or more people spent approximately one-third of their after-tax income on food, so the government pegs the poverty threshold at three times the cost of the economy food plan. In 2023, that threshold was approximately $28,000 for an urban family of four.

For a family of four living in a city, $28,000 a year is scarcely enough to make ends meet. But suppose a group of, say, 10 families were to pool their negative tax payments and move to the mountains of northern New Mexico. With a total of $280,000 per year to spend, plus the fruits of their efforts at gardening and animal husbandry, such a group could live very nicely indeed.

Once a small number of experimental groups demonstrated the feasibility of quitting their jobs and living well on the negative income tax, others would surely follow suit. But two practical difficulties would ensue. First, as more and more people left their jobs to live at government expense, the program would eventually become prohibitively costly. And second, the political cost of the program would almost surely force supporters to abandon it long before that point. Reports of people living lives of leisure at taxpayers' expense would be sure to appear on the nightly news. People who work hard at their jobs all day long would wonder why their tax dollars were being used to support those who are capable of holding paying jobs, yet choose not to work. If the resulting political backlash did not completely eliminate the negative income tax program, it would force policymakers to cut back the payment so that members of rural communes could no longer afford to live comfortably. And that would mean the payment would no longer support an urban family. This difficulty has led policymakers to focus on other ways to increase the incomes of the working poor.

MINIMUM WAGES

The United States and many other industrialized countries have sought to ease the burden of low-wage workers by enacting minimum wage legislation—laws that prohibit employers from paying workers less than a specified hourly wage. The federal minimum wage in the United States is currently set at $7.25 per hour, and several states have set minimum wage

negative income tax (NIT) a system under which the government would grant every citizen a cash payment each year, financed by an additional tax on earned income

poverty threshold the level of income below which the federal government classifies a family as poor

FIGURE 13.5

The Effect of Minimum Wage Legislation on Employment.

If minimum wage legislation requires employers to pay more than the equilibrium wage, the result will be a decline in employment for low-wage workers.

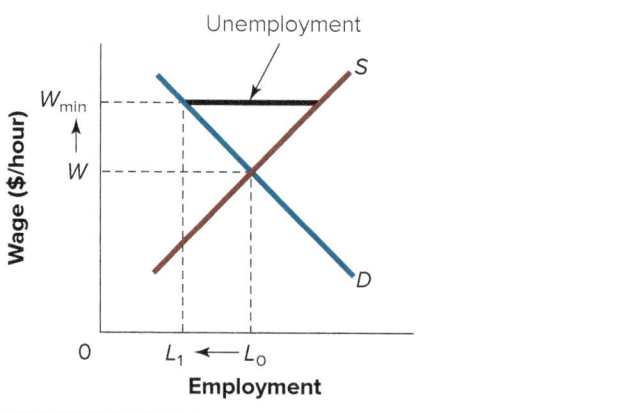

levels significantly higher. For example, the minimum wage in the state of Washington was $17.00 per hour for 2023.

How does a minimum wage affect the market for low-wage labor? In Figure 13.5, note that when the law prevents employers from paying less than W_{min}, employers hire fewer workers (a decline from L_0 to L_1). Unemployment results: The L_1 workers who keep their jobs earn more than before, but the $L_0 - L_1$ workers who lose their jobs earn nothing. Whether workers together earn more or less than before depends on the elasticity of demand for labor. If elasticity of demand is less than 1, workers as a group will earn more than before. If it is more than 1, workers as a group will earn less.

At one point, economists were almost unanimous in their opposition to minimum wage laws, arguing that those laws reduce total economic surplus, as do other regulations that prevent markets from reaching equilibrium. Some economists, however, have softened their opposition to minimum wage laws, citing studies that have failed to show significant reductions in employment following increases in minimum wage levels. But as we saw in Chapter 7, *Efficiency, Exchange, and the Invisible Hand in Action,* any policy that prevents a market from reaching equilibrium causes a reduction in total economic surplus—which means society ought to be able to find a more effective policy for helping low-wage workers.

THE EARNED-INCOME TAX CREDIT

earned-income tax credit (EITC) a policy under which low-income workers receive credits on their federal income tax

One such policy is the **earned-income tax credit (EITC)**, which gives low-wage workers a credit on their federal income tax each year. The EITC was enacted into law in 1975, and in the years since has drawn praise from both liberals and conservatives. The program is essentially a wage subsidy in the form of a credit against the amount a family owes in federal income taxes. For example, in 2019, a married couple with two children under the age of 18 and a total annual earnings of $24,000 could have received an annual tax credit of approximately $5,800 under this program. That is, the program would have reduced the annual federal income tax payment of this family by roughly that amount. Families who earned more would have received smaller tax credit, with no credit at all for families of four earning more than $56,000. Families whose tax credit exceeds the amount of tax owed actually receive a check from the government for the difference. The EITC is thus essentially the same as a negative income tax, except that eligibility for the program is confined to people who work.

Like both the negative income tax and the minimum wage, the EITC puts extra income into the hands of workers who are employed at low wage levels. But unlike the minimum wage, the earned-income tax credit creates no incentive for employers to lay off low-wage workers.

The following examples illustrate how switching from a minimum wage to an earned-income tax credit can produce gains for both employers and workers.

EXAMPLE 13.4	Surplus in an Unregulated Labor Market

By how much will a minimum wage reduce total economic surplus?

Suppose the demand and supply curves for unskilled labor in the Tallahassee labor market are as shown in Figure 13.6. By how much will the imposition of a minimum wage at $7 per hour reduce total economic surplus? By how much do worker surplus and employer surplus change as a result of adopting the minimum wage?

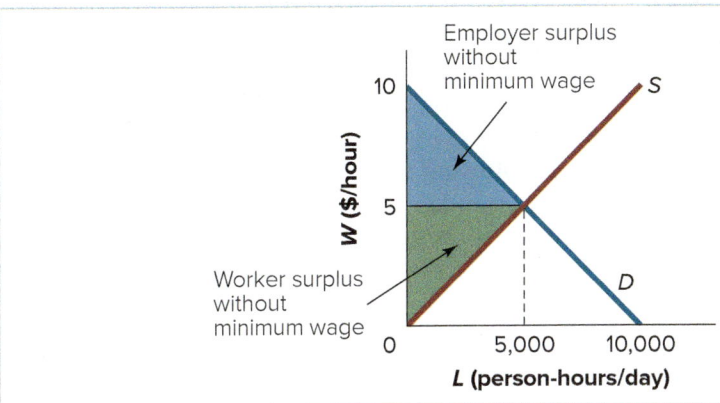

FIGURE 13.6

Worker and Employer Surplus in an Unregulated Labor Market.

For the demand and supply curves shown, worker surplus is the area of the lower shaded triangle, $12,500 per day, the same as employer surplus (upper shaded triangle).

In the absence of a minimum wage, the equilibrium wage for Tallahassee would be $5 per hour, and employment would be 5,000 person-hours per day. Both employers and workers would enjoy economic surplus equal to the area of the shaded triangles in Figure 13.6, $12,500 per day.

With a minimum wage set at $7 per hour, employer surplus is the area of the crosshatched triangle in Figure 13.7, $4,500 per day, and worker surplus is the area of the green-shaded figure, $16,500 per day. The minimum wage thus reduces employer surplus by $8,000 per day and increases worker surplus by $4,000 per day. The net reduction in surplus is the area of the blue-shaded triangle shown in Figure 13.7, $4,000 per day.

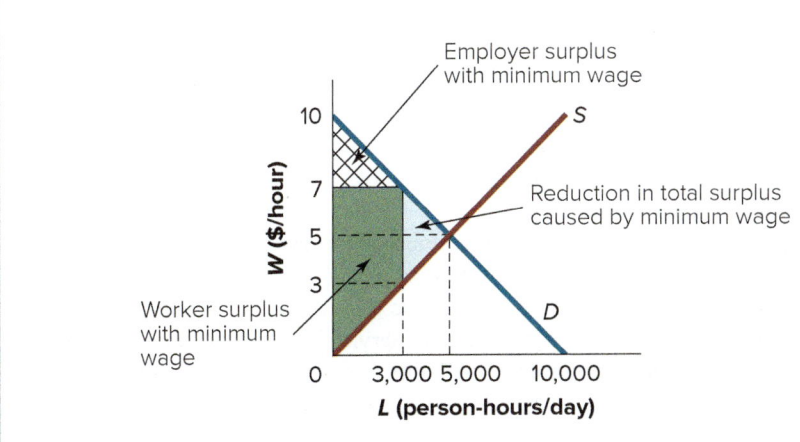

FIGURE 13.7

The Effect of a Minimum Wage on Economic Surplus.

A minimum wage of $7 per hour reduces employment in this market by 2,000 person-hours per day, for a reduction in total economic surplus of $4,000 per day (area of the blue-shaded triangle). Employer surplus falls to $4,500 per day (area of crosshatched triangle), while worker surplus rises to $16,500 per day (green-shaded area).

SELF-TEST 13.5

In the previous minimum wage example, by how much would total economic surplus have been reduced by the $7 minimum wage if labor demand in Tallahassee had been perfectly inelastic at 5,000 person-hours per day?

The following example illustrates the central message of the Efficiency Principle, which is that if the economic pie can be made larger, everyone can have a larger slice.

EXAMPLE 13.5

The Efficiency Principle in Action

Suppose that, instead of imposing a minimum wage' the government enacts an earned-income tax credit program. How much would it cost the government each day to provide an earned-income tax credit under which workers as a group receive the same economic surplus as they do under the $7 per hour minimum wage? (Assume for simplicity that the earned-income tax credit has no effect on labor supply.)

With an earned-income tax credit in lieu of a minimum wage, employment will be 5,000 person-hours per day at $5 per hour, just as in the unregulated market. Since worker surplus in the unregulated market was $4,000 per day less than under the minimum wage, the government would have to offer a tax credit worth $0.80 per hour for each of the 5,000 person-hours of employment to restore worker surplus to the level obtained under the $7 minimum wage. With an EITC of that amount in effect, worker surplus would be the same as under the $7 minimum wage. If the EITC were financed by a $4,000 tax on employers, employer surplus would be $4,000 greater than under the $7 minimum wage.

We stress that our point is not that the minimum wage produces no gains for low-income workers, but rather that it is possible to provide even larger gains for these workers if we avoid policies that try to prevent labor markets from reaching equilibrium.

PUBLIC EMPLOYMENT FOR THE POOR

The main shortcoming of the EITC is that it does nothing for the unemployed poor. The negative income tax lacks that shortcoming but may substantially weaken work incentives. There is yet another method of transferring income to the poor that avoids both shortcomings. Government-sponsored jobs could pay wages to the unemployed poor for useful work. With public service employment, the specter of people living lives of leisure at public expense simply does not arise.

But public service employment has difficulties of its own. Evidence shows that if government jobs pay the same wages as private jobs, many people will leave their private jobs in favor of government jobs, apparently because they view government jobs as being more secure. Such a migration would make public service employment extremely expensive. Other worrisome possibilities are that such jobs might involve make-work tasks, and that they would prompt an expansion in government bureaucracy.

Acting alone, government-sponsored jobs for the poor, the EITC, or the negative income tax cannot solve the income-transfer problem. But a combination of these programs might do so.

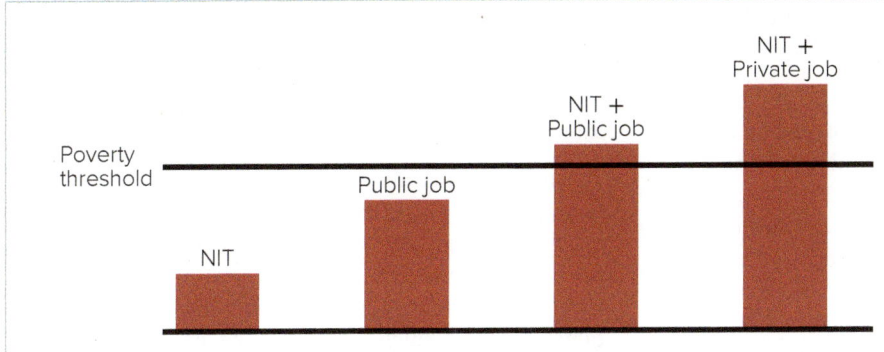

Ariel Skelley/Blend Images/the Agency Collection/Getty Images

FIGURE 13.8

Income by Source in a Combination NIT–Jobs Program.

Together, a small negative income tax and a public job at below minimum wage would provide a family enough income to escape poverty, without weakening work incentives significantly.

A COMBINATION OF METHODS

Consider a negative income tax whose cash grant is far too small for anyone to live on, but that is supplemented if necessary by a public service job at below minimum wage. Keeping the wage in public service jobs well below the minimum wage would eliminate the risk of a large-scale exodus from private jobs. And while living well on either the negative income tax or the public service wage would be impossible, the two programs together could lift people out of poverty (see Figure 13.8).

To prevent an expansion of the bureaucracy, the government could solicit bids from private management companies to oversee the public service employment program. The fear that this program would inevitably become a make-work project is allayed by evidence that unskilled workers can, with proper supervision, perform many valuable tasks that would not otherwise be performed in the private sector. They can, for example, do landscaping and maintenance in public parks, provide transportation for older adults and people with disabilities, fill potholes in city streets and replace burned-out street lamps, transplant seedlings in erosion control projects, remove graffiti from public places and paint government buildings, recycle newspapers and containers, staff day care centers, and so on.

Can unskilled workers perform useful public service jobs?

This combination of a small negative income tax payment and public service employment at a subminimum wage would not be cheap. But the direct costs of existing welfare programs are also large, and the indirect costs, in the form of perverse work incentives and misguided attempts to control prices, are even larger. In economic terms, dealing intelligently with the income-transfer problem may in fact prove relatively inexpensive, once society recognizes the enormous opportunity cost of failing to deal intelligently with it.

RECAP

METHODS OF INCOME REDISTRIBUTION

Minimum wage laws reduce total economic surplus by contracting employment. The earned-income tax credit boosts the incomes of the working poor without that drawback, but neither policy provides benefits for those who are not employed.

Other instruments in the battle against poverty include in-kind transfers such as food stamps, subsidized school lunches, Medicaid, and public housing as well as cash transfers such as Temporary Assistance for Needy Families. Because benefits under most of these programs are means-tested, beneficiaries often experience a net decline in income when they accept paid employment.

The negative income tax is an expanded version of the earned-income tax credit that includes those who are not employed. Combining this program with access to public service jobs would enable government to ensure adequate living standards for the poor without significantly undermining work incentives.

SUMMARY

- A worker's long-run equilibrium pay in a competitive labor market will be equal to the value of her marginal product of labor (*VMPL*)—the market value of whatever goods and services she produces for her employer. The law of diminishing returns says that when a firm's capital and other productive inputs are held fixed in the short run, adding workers beyond some point results in ever smaller increases in output. Firms that purchase labor in competitive labor markets face a constant wage, and they will hire labor up to the point at which *VMPL* equals the market wage. *(LO1, LO2)*

- Human capital theory says that an individual's *VMPL* is proportional to his stock of human capital—an amalgam of education, experience, training, intelligence, and other factors that influence productivity. According to this theory, some occupations pay better than others simply because they require larger stocks of human capital. *(LO3)*

- Wages often differ between individuals whose stocks of human capital appear nearly the same, as when one belongs to a labor union and the other does not. Compensating wage differentials—wage differences associated with differences in working conditions—are another important explanation for why individuals with similar human capital might earn different salaries. They help explain why garbage collectors earn more than lifeguards and, more generally, why individuals with a given stock of human capital tend to earn more in jobs that have less-attractive working conditions. *(LO3)*

- Many firms pay members of certain groups—notably Blacks and females—less than they pay white males who seem to have similar personal characteristics. If such wage gaps are the result of employer discrimination, their existence implies profit opportunities for firms that do not discriminate. Several other factors, including discrimination by customers and institutions other than firms, may explain at least part of the observed wage gaps. *(LO3)*

- Technologies that allow the most productive individuals to serve broader markets can translate even small differences in human capital into enormous differences in pay. Such technologies give rise to winner-take-all markets, which have long been common in sports and entertainment, and which are becoming common in other professions. *(LO3)*

- Although incomes grew at almost 3 percent a year for all income classes during the three decades following World War II, the lion's share of income growth in the years since has been concentrated among top earners. *(LO4)*

- Philosophers have argued that at least some income redistribution is justified in the name of fairness, because if people chose society's distributional rules without knowing their own personal circumstances, most would favor less inequality than would be produced by market outcomes. *(LO4)*

- Policies and programs for reducing poverty include minimum wage laws, the earned-income tax credit, food stamps, subsidized school lunches, Medicaid, public housing, and Temporary Assistance for Needy Families. Of these, all but the earned-income tax credit fail to maximize total economic surplus, either by interfering with work incentives or by preventing markets from reaching equilibrium. *(LO5)*

- The negative income tax works much like the earned-income tax credit, except that it includes those who are not employed. A combination of a small negative income tax and access to public service jobs at subminimum wages could ensure adequate living standards for the poor without significantly undermining work incentives. *(LO5)*

KEY TERMS

compensating wage differential
customer discrimination
earned-income tax credit (EITC)
employer discrimination
human capital
human capital theory

in-kind transfer
labor union
marginal product of labor (*MPL*)
means-tested
negative income tax (NIT)

Personal Responsibility and Work Reconciliation Act
poverty threshold
value of the marginal product of labor (*VMPL*)
winner-take-all labor market

REVIEW QUESTIONS

1. Why is the supply curve of labor for any specific occupation likely to be upward-sloping, even if, for the economy as a whole, people work fewer hours when wage rates increase? *(LO2)*

2. True or false: If the human capital possessed by two workers is nearly the same, their wage rates will be nearly the same. Explain. *(LO3)*

3. How might recent changes in income inequality be related to the proliferation of technologies that enable the most productive individuals to serve broader markets? *(LO3, LO4)*

4. Mention two self-interested reasons that a top earner might favor policies to redistribute income. *(LO4)*

5. Why is exclusive reliance on the negative income tax unlikely to constitute a long-term solution to the poverty problem? *(LO5)*

PROBLEMS

1. Mountain Breeze supplies air filters to the retail market and hires workers to assemble the components. An air filter sells for $26, and Mountain Breeze can buy the components for each filter for $1. Sandra and Bobby are two workers for Mountain Breeze. Sandra can assemble 60 air filters per month and Bobby can assemble 70. If the labor market is perfectly competitive, how much will Sandra and Bobby be paid? *(LO1)*

2. Acme Incorporated supplies rocket ships to the retail market and hires workers to assemble the components. A rocket ship sells for $35,000, and Acme can buy the components for each rocket ship for $25,000. Wiley and Sam are two workers for Acme. Sam can assemble 1/5 of a rocket ship per month and Wiley can assemble 1/10. If the labor market is perfectly competitive and rocket components are Acme's only other cost, how much will Sam and Wiley be paid? *(LO1)*

3. Stone Incorporated owns a clothing factory and hires workers in a competitive labor market to stitch cut denim fabric into jeans. The fabric required to make each pair of jeans costs $5. The company's weekly output of finished jeans varies with the number of workers hired, as shown in the following table: *(LO2, LO3)*

Number of workers	Jeans (pairs/week)
0	0
1	25
2	45
3	60
4	72
5	80
6	85

a. If the jeans sell for $35 a pair and the competitive market wage is $250 per week, how many workers should Stone hire? How many pairs of jeans will the company produce each week?

b. Suppose the Clothing Workers Union now sets a weekly minimum acceptable wage of $230 per week. All the workers Stone hires belong to the union. How does the minimum wage affect Stone's decision about how many workers to hire?

c. If the minimum wage set by the union had been $400 per week, how would the minimum wage affect Stone's decision about how many workers to hire?

d. If Stone again faces a market wage of $250 per week but the price of jeans rises to $45, how many workers will the company now hire?

4. Carolyn owns a soda factory and hires workers in a competitive labor market to bottle the soda. Her company's weekly output of bottled soda varies with the number of workers hired, as shown in the following table: *(LO2, LO3)*

Number of workers	Cases/week
0	0
1	200
2	360
3	480
4	560
5	600

a. If each case sells for $10 more than the cost of the materials used in producing it and the competitive market wage is $1,000 per week, how many workers should Carolyn hire? How many cases will be produced per week?

b. Suppose the Soda Bottlers Union now sets a weekly minimum acceptable wage of $1,500 per week. All the workers Carolyn hires belong to the union. How does the minimum wage affect Carolyn's decision about how many workers to hire?

c. If the wage is again $1,000 per week but the price of soda rises to $15 per case, how many workers will Carolyn now hire?

5. Malik, a high school senior, is offered a job walking his neighbor's dog for an hour each Friday afternoon. His reservation wage for this task is $6. *(LO4)*

a. If Malik's neighbor offers him $15 per hour, how much economic surplus will Malik enjoy each week as a result of accepting this job?

b. Now suppose that Malik's parents announce that he will have to split his earnings evenly with his two younger siblings. Will Malik still accept the job?

c. Explain how your answers to parts a and b illustrate one of the incentive problems inherent in income redistribution programs.

6. Jones, who is currently unemployed, is a participant in three means-tested welfare programs: food stamps, rent stamps, and day care stamps. Each program grants him $150 per month in stamps, which can be used like cash to purchase the good or service they cover. *(LO5)*

a. If benefits in each program are reduced by 30 cents for each additional dollar Jones earns in the labor market, how will Jones's economic position change if he accepts a job paying $120 per week?

b. In light of your answer to part a, explain why means testing for welfare recipients has undesirable effects on work incentives.

7. Suppose the equilibrium wage for unskilled workers in New Jersey is $16 per hour. How will the wages and employment of unskilled workers in New Jersey change if the state legislature raises the minimum wage from $8.85 per hour to $15 per hour? *(LO5)*

8.* Suppose the demand and supply curves for unskilled labor in the Corvallis labor market are as shown in the accompanying figure. *(LO5)*

a. By how much will the imposition of a minimum wage at $12 per hour reduce total economic surplus? Calculate the amounts by which employer surplus and worker surplus change as a result of the minimum wage.

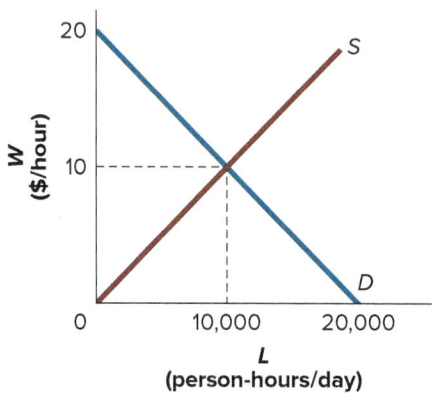

b. How much would it cost the government each day to provide an earned-income tax credit under which workers as a group receive the same economic surplus as they do under the $12-per-hour minimum wage? (Assume for simplicity that the earned-income tax credit has no effect on labor supply.)

9.* Suppose employers and workers are risk-neutral, and Congress is about to enact the $12-per-hour minimum wage described in Problem 8. Congressional staff economists have urged legislators to consider adopting an earned-income tax credit instead. Suppose neither workers nor employers would support that proposal unless the expected value of each party's economic surplus would be at least as great as under the minimum wage. Describe an earned-income tax credit (and a tax that would raise enough money to pay for it) that would receive unanimous support from both workers and employers. *(LO5)*

ANSWERS TO SELF-TESTS

13.1 At a price of $26 per cutting board, the fifth worker has a *VMPL* of $364 per week, so Adirondack should hire five workers. *(LO1)*

13.2 Since the *VMPL* of each worker exceeds $275, Adirondack should hire five workers. *(LO1)*

13.3 When the wage rate is $18 per hour in each market, 25 fewer workers will be employed in the nonunionized market and 25 more in the unionized market. The loss in output from removing 25 workers from the nonunionized market is the sum of the *VMPL*s of those workers, which is the shaded area in the right panel of the figure below. This area is $375 per hour. *(Hint:* To calculate this area, first break the figure into a rectangle and a triangle.) The gain in output from adding 25 workers to the unionized market is the shaded area in the left panel, which is $525 per hour. The net increase in output is thus $525 − $375 = $150 per hour. *(LO3)*

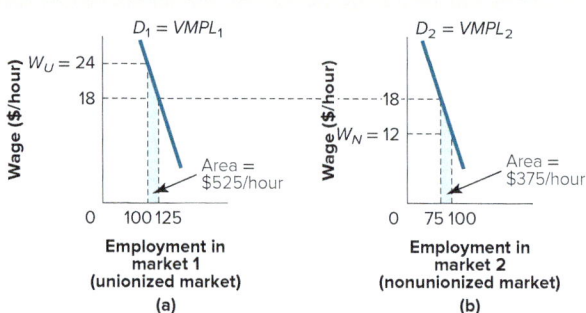

13.4 Since Sue's reservation wage is $10 per hour, she must be paid at least that amount before she will accept the job. The largest dorm population for which she will accept is thus 10 residents since her share in that case would be exactly $10 per hour. *(LO4)*

13.5 With perfectly inelastic demand, employment would remain at 5,000 person-hours per day, so the minimum wage would cause no reduction in economic surplus. *(LO5)*

*Denotes more difficult problem.

CHAPTER 14

Public Goods and Tax Policy

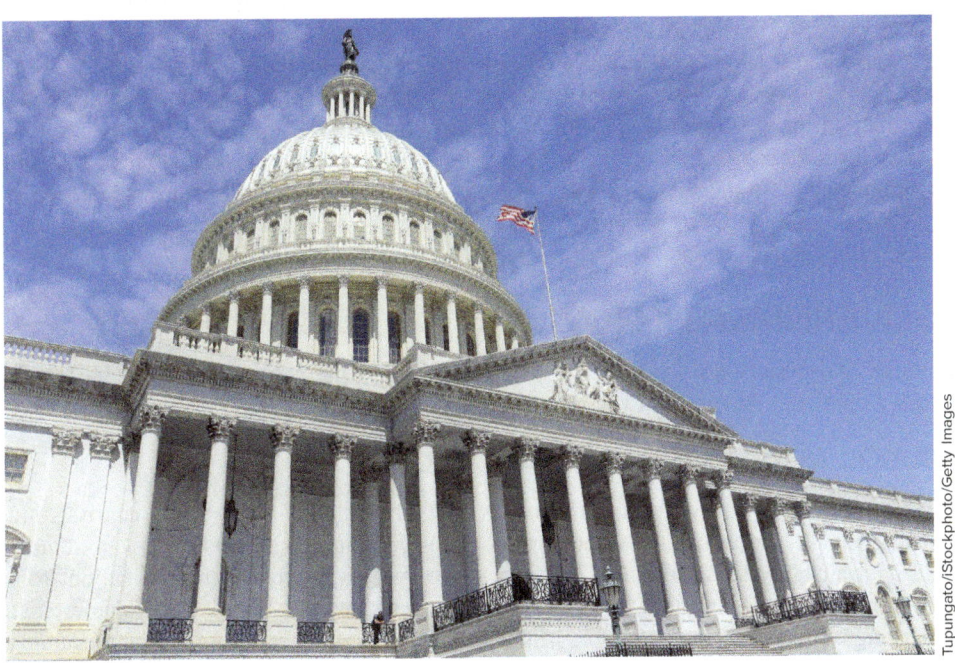

Government is imperfect. But markets are also imperfect, and all successful societies rely on a mix of government and private production to meet their economic demands.

Tupungato/iStockphoto/Getty Images

LEARNING OBJECTIVES

After reading this chapter, you should be able to:

LO1 Use the concepts of rivalry and excludability to distinguish among private goods, public goods, collective goods, and commons goods.

LO2 Show how economic concepts can be used to find the optimal quantity of a public good and describe the ways in which private firms can supply public goods.

LO3 Analyze the types of efficiencies and inefficiencies that are associated with the provision of public goods.

LO4 Explain why the maintenance of climate stability is an important public good and evaluate the case for using taxation as a means of funding climate mitigation.

LO5 Describe a cognitive illusion that leads many wealthy voters to oppose higher top tax rates.

LO6 Describe how international data on the determinants of human flourishing inform the debate on how extensive the government's role should be.

I n the face of living standards that had stagnated perilously close to subsistence levels for many thousands of years, Adam Smith was prescient to foresee market exchange as the source of the explosive growth in income and wealth that began during his lifetime and has continued ever since.

Yet he also understood that the pursuit of narrow self-interest didn't always serve society's ends. In his *The Theory of Moral Sentiments*, published almost two decades before *The Wealth of Nations*, he argued that markets could not function in the absence of institutional arrangements that discouraged people from harming one another. As he saw it, the creation and nurturing of important components of that institutional foundation, including social norms and moral sentiments, rested largely in private hands. But he viewed other components, including the enforcement of laws and property rights, as responsibilities of government.

Smith also recognized that important goods and services, such as national defense, were impractical to provide by profit-seeking companies. And unlike many of his modern disciples, he saw taxation of the wealthy as a practical way—sometimes the only way—to help pay for them.

In the centuries since Smith wrote, economists have focused increasingly on externalities, both positive and negative, as important sources of market failure. As discussed in earlier chapters, actions with spillover effects create conflicts between individual and collective interests that span a broad range. At one end, they may be trivial, as when a person stands, blocking the view of someone behind. But they can also pose existential threats, as when greenhouse gas emissions threaten the ecosystems that sustain life on our planet.

In Chapter 11, we saw that people can sometimes work out private solutions to misallocations caused by externalities. But as Ronald Coase emphasized throughout his long career, practical barriers to negotiation often preclude such solutions. The threat posed by climate change, in particular, cannot be parried unless powerful actors refrain from taking actions from which they currently receive enormous private benefits. In such cases, government intervention can sometimes be the only practical remedy. With a changing climate inflicting ever more frequent and severe damage, the role of government is now arguably more important than at any previous moment in history.

Our task in this chapter will be to explore that role. We'll first consider the properties that define public goods and discuss how cost-benefit analysis can help determine the optimal levels of their provision. We'll discuss a variety of mechanisms that have enabled public goods to be provided by entities other than governments. But we'll also see why government provision is often more efficient than other options.

For such cases, we'll consider the question of how best to pay for public goods, focusing on the economic case for taxing negative externalities. We'll see that the scale of public investment required to parry the threat posed by climate change suggests that the maintenance of climate stability might aptly be described as the ultimate public good.

We'll conclude by examining proposals for how best to pay for those measures and other public goods.

GOVERNMENT PROVISION OF PUBLIC GOODS

public good a good or service that, to at least some degree, is both nonrival and nonexcludable

One of the primary tasks of government is to provide what economists call **public goods** such as national defense and the criminal justice system.

PUBLIC GOODS VERSUS PRIVATE GOODS

nonrival good a good whose consumption by one person does not diminish its availability for others

Public goods are those goods or services that are, in varying degrees, **nonrival** and **nonexcludable**. A nonrival good is one whose consumption by one person does not diminish its availability for others. For example, if the military prevents a hostile nation from invading your city, your enjoyment of that protection does not diminish its value to your neighbors. A good is nonexcludable if it is difficult to exclude nonpayers from consuming it. For instance, even if your neighbors don't pay their share of the cost of maintaining an army, they will still enjoy its protection.

nonexcludable good a good that is difficult, or costly, to exclude nonpayers from consuming

Another example of a nonrival and nonexcludable good is an over-the-air broadcast of *The Late Show with Stephen Colbert*. The fact that you tune in one evening does not make the program any less available to others, and once the broadcast has been beamed out over the airwaves, it is difficult to prevent anyone from tuning in. Similarly, if the City of New York puts on a fireworks display in New York harbor to celebrate a special occasion, it cannot charge admission because the harbor may be viewed from many different locations in the city. And the fact that additional persons view the display does not in any way diminish its value to other potential viewers.

In contrast, the typical private good is diminished one-for-one by any individual's consumption of it. For instance, when you eat a cheeseburger, it is no longer available for anyone else. Moreover, people can be easily prevented from consuming cheeseburgers they don't pay for.

> ✅ **SELF-TEST 14.1**
>
> Which of the following, if any, is nonrival?
>
> a.   The website of the Bureau of Labor Statistics at 3 a.m.
> b.   The World Cup soccer championship game watched in person.
> c.   The World Cup soccer championship game watched on television.

Goods that are both highly nonexcludable and nonrival are often called **pure public goods**. Two reasons favor government provision of such goods. First, for-profit private companies would have obvious difficulty recovering their cost of production. Many people might be willing to pay enough to cover the cost of producing the good, but if it is nonexcludable, the company cannot easily charge for it (an example of the free-rider problem discussed in Chapter 12, *The Economics of Information*). And second, if the marginal cost of serving additional users is zero once the good has been produced, then charging for the good would be inefficient, even if there were some practical way to do so. This inefficiency often characterizes the provision of **collective goods**—nonrival goods for which it is possible to exclude nonpayers. Subscription video streaming services like Netflix are an example. People who don't pay to get Netflix don't get to watch programs shown only on Netflix, a restriction that excludes many viewers who would have benefited from watching. Because the marginal cost to society of their tuning in is essentially zero, excluding these viewers is wasteful.

A **pure private good** is one from which nonpayers can easily be excluded and for which one person's consumption creates a one-for-one reduction in the good's availability for others. The theory of perfectly competitive supply developed in the chapter on perfectly competitive supply applies to pure private goods, of which basic agricultural products are perhaps the best examples. A **pure commons good** is a rival good that is also nonexcludable, so-called because goods with this combination of properties almost always result in a tragedy of the commons (see Chapter 11, *Externalities, Property Rights, and the Environment*). Fish in ocean waters are an example.

The classification scheme defined by the nonrival and nonexcludable properties is summarized in Table 14.1. The columns of the table indicate the extent to which one person's consumption of a good fails to diminish its availability for others. Goods in the right column are nonrival and those in the left column are not. The rows of the table indicate the difficulty of excluding nonpayers from consuming the good. Goods in the top row are nonexcludable; those in the bottom row, excludable. Private goods (lower-left cell) are rival and excludable. Public goods (upper-right cell) are nonrival and nonexcludable. The two hybrid categories are commons goods (upper-left cell), which are rival but nonexcludable, and collective goods (lower-right cell), which are excludable but nonrival.

Collective goods are provided sometimes by government, sometimes by private companies. Most pure public goods are provided by government, but even private companies can sometimes find profitable ways of producing goods that are both nonrival *and* nonexcludable. An example is broadcast radio and television, which covers its costs by selling airtime to advertisers.

The mere fact that a good is a pure public good does not necessarily mean that government ought to provide it. On the contrary, the only public goods the government should even *consider* providing are those whose benefits exceed their costs. The cost of a public good is simply the sum of all explicit and implicit costs incurred to provide it. The benefit of a public good is measured by asking how much people would be willing to pay for it. Although that sounds similar to the way we measure the benefit of a private good, an important distinction exists. The benefit of an additional unit of a private good such as a cheeseburger is the highest sum

pure public good a good or service that, to a high degree, is both nonrival and nonexcludable

collective good a good or service that, to at least some degree, is nonrival but excludable

pure private good one for which nonpayers can easily be excluded and for which each unit consumed by one person means one less unit available for others

pure commons good one for which nonpayers cannot easily be excluded and for which each unit consumed by one person means one less unit available for others

Cost-Benefit

TABLE 14.1
Private, Public, and Hybrid Goods

		Nonrival	
		Low	High
Nonexcludable	High	Commons good (fish in the ocean)	Public good (national defense)
	Low	Private good (wheat)	Collective good (video streaming services)

that any individual buyer would be willing to pay for it. In contrast, the benefit of an additional unit of a public good such as an additional broadcast episode of *The Late Show with Stephen Colbert* is the sum of the reservation prices of all people who will watch that episode.

Even if the amount that all beneficiaries of a public good would be willing to pay exceeds its cost, government provision of that good makes sense only if there is no other less costly way of providing it. For example, whereas city governments often pay for fireworks displays, they almost invariably hire private companies to put on these events. Finally, if the benefit of a public good does not exceed its cost, we are better off without it.

PAYING FOR PUBLIC GOODS

Not everyone benefits equally from the provision of a given public good. For example, some people find fireworks displays highly entertaining, but others simply don't care about them, and still others actively dislike them. Ideally, it might seem that the most equitable method of financing a given public good would be to tax people in proportion to their willingness to pay for the good. To illustrate this approach, suppose Jones values a public good at $100, Smith values the same good at $200, and the cost of the good is $240. Jones would then be taxed $80 and Smith would be taxed $160. The good would be provided, and each taxpayer in this example would reap a surplus equal to 25 percent of his tax payment: $20 for Jones, $40 for Smith.

In practice, however, government officials usually lack the information they would need to tax people in proportion to their willingness to pay for specific public goods. (Think about it: If an IRS agent asked you how much you would be willing to pay to have a new freeway and you knew you would be taxed in proportion to the amount you responded, what would you say?) The following three examples illustrate some of the problems that arise in financing public goods and suggest possible solutions to these problems.

EXAMPLE 14.1	**Joint Purchase**

Will Prentice and Wilson buy a water filter?

Prentice and Wilson own adjacent summer cottages along an isolated stretch of shoreline on Cayuga Lake. Because of a recent invasion of zebra mussels, each must add chlorine to his water intake valve each week to prevent it from becoming clogged by the tiny mollusks. A manufacturer has introduced a new filtration device that eliminates the nuisance of weekly chlorination. The cost of the device, which has the capacity to serve both houses, is $1,000. Both owners feel equally strongly about having the filter. But because Wilson earns twice as much as Prentice, Wilson is willing to pay up to $800 to have the filter, whereas its value to Prentice, a retired schoolteacher, is only $400. Would either person be willing to purchase the device individually? Is it efficient for them to share its purchase?

Neither will purchase the filter individually because each has a reservation price that is below its selling price. But because the two together value the filter at $1,200, sharing its use would be socially efficient. If they were to do so, total economic surplus would be $200 higher than if they did not buy the filter.

Since sharing the filter is the efficient outcome, we might expect that Prentice and Wilson would quickly reach agreement to purchase it. Unfortunately, however, the joint purchase and sharing of facilities is often easier proposed than accomplished. One hurdle is that people must incur costs merely to get together to discuss joint purchases. With only two people involved, those costs might not be significant. But if hundreds or thousands of people were involved, communication costs could be prohibitive.

With large numbers of people, the free-rider problem also emerges (see Chapter 12, *The Economics of Information*). After all, everyone knows that the project will either succeed or fail independently of any one person's contribution to it. Everyone thus has an incentive to withhold contributions—or get a free ride—in the hope that others will give.

Finally, even when only a few people are involved, reaching agreement on a fair sharing of the total expense may be difficult. For example, Prentice and Wilson might be reluctant to disclose their true reservation prices to one another for the same reason that you might be reluctant to disclose your reservation price for a public good to an IRS agent.

These practical concerns may lead us to empower government to buy public goods on our behalf. But as the next example makes clear, this approach does not eliminate the need to reach political agreement on how public purchases are to be financed.

EXAMPLE 14.2   Head Taxes

Will government buy the water filter if there is an "equal tax" rule?

Suppose Prentice and Wilson could ask the government to help broker the water filter purchase. And suppose that the government's tax policy must follow a "nondiscrimination" rule that prohibits charging any citizen more for a public good than it charges his or her neighbor. Another rule is that public goods can be provided only if a majority of citizens approve of them. Will a government bound by these rules provide the filter that Prentice and Wilson want?

A tax that collects the same amount from every citizen is called a **head tax**. If the government must rely on a head tax, it must raise $500 from Prentice and $500 from Wilson. But because the device is worth only $400 to Prentice, he will vote against the project, thus denying it a majority. So a democratic government cannot provide the water filter if it must rely on a head tax.

> **head tax** a tax that collects the same amount from every taxpayer

A head tax is a **regressive tax**, one for which the proportion of a taxpayer's income that is paid in taxes declines as the taxpayer's income rises.

The point illustrated by this example is not confined to the specific public good considered. It applies whenever taxpayers place significantly different valuations on public goods, as will almost always happen whenever people earn significantly different incomes. An equal-tax rule under these circumstances will almost invariably rule out the provision of many worthwhile public goods.

As our third example suggests, one solution to this problem is to allow taxes to vary by income.

> **regressive tax** a tax under which the proportion of income paid in taxes declines as income rises

EXAMPLE 14.3   Proportional Income Tax

Will the government buy the filter if there is a proportional tax on income?

Suppose that Prentice proposes that the government raise revenue by imposing a proportional tax on income to finance the provision of the water filter. Will Wilson, who earns twice as much as Prentice, support this proposal?

A **proportional income tax** is one under which all taxpayers pay the same proportion of their incomes in taxes. Under such a tax, Wilson would support Prentice's proposal because if he didn't, each would fail to enjoy a public good whose benefit exceeds his share of its cost. Under the proportional tax on income, Prentice would contribute $333 toward the $1,000 purchase price of the filter and Wilson would contribute $667. The government would buy the filter, resulting in additional surpluses of $67 for Prentice and $133 for Wilson.

> **proportional income tax** one under which all taxpayers pay the same proportion of their incomes in taxes

The Economic Naturalist 14.1 example makes the point that just as equal contributions are often a poor way to pay for public goods, they are also often a poor way to share expenses within the household.

The Economic Naturalist 14.1

Why don't most married couples contribute equally to joint purchases?

Why do married couples usually pool their incomes?

Suppose Hillary earns $2,000,000 per year while her husband Bill earns only $20,000. Given her income, Hillary as an individual would want to spend much more than Bill would on housing, travel, entertainment, education for their children, and the many other items they consume jointly. What will happen if the couple adopts a rule that each must contribute an equal amount toward the purchase of such items?

This rule would constrain the couple to live in a small house, take only inexpensive vacations, and skimp on entertainment, dining out, and their children's education. It is therefore easy to see why Hillary might find it attractive to pay considerably more than 50 percent for jointly consumed goods because doing so would enable *both* of them to consume in the manner their combined income permits.

Public goods and jointly consumed private goods are different from individually consumed private goods in the following important way: *Different individuals are free to consume whatever quantity and quality of most private goods they choose to buy, but jointly consumed goods must be provided in the same quantity and quality for all persons.*

As in the case of private goods, people's willingness to pay for public goods is generally an increasing function of income. Wealthy individuals tend to assign greater value to public goods than low-income people do, not because the wealthy have different tastes but because they have more money. A head tax would result in high-income persons getting smaller amounts of public goods than they want. By increasing the total economic surplus available for all to share, a tax system that assigns a larger share of the tax burden to people with higher incomes makes possible a better outcome for both rich and poor alike. Indeed, virtually all industrialized nations have tax systems that are at least mildly **progressive**, which means that the proportion of income paid in taxes actually rises with a family's income.

Progressive taxation and even proportional taxation often have been criticized as being unfair to the wealthy, who are forced to pay more than others for public goods that all consume in common. The irony in this charge, however, is that exclusive reliance on head taxes, or even proportional taxes, would curtail the provision of public goods and services that are of greatest value to high-income families. Studies have shown, for instance, that the income elasticity of demand for public goods such as parks and recreation facilities, clean air and water, public safety, uncongested roads, and aesthetically pleasing public spaces is substantially greater than 1. Failure to rely on progressive taxation would result in gross underprovision of such public goods and services.

progressive tax
one in which the proportion of income paid in taxes rises as income rises

---

RECAP ↑

PUBLIC GOODS

A public good is both nonrival and nonexcludable. Private firms typically cannot recover the costs of producing such goods because they cannot exclude nonpayers from consuming them. Nor would charging for a public good promote efficiency, since one person's consumption of the good does not diminish its availability for others.

Both obstacles can be overcome by creating a government with the power to levy taxes. Even high-income citizens often favor progressive taxes because proportional or regressive taxes may generate insufficient revenue to pay for the public goods those taxpayers favor.

THE OPTIMAL QUANTITY OF A PUBLIC GOOD ⎯

In the examples considered thus far, the question was whether to provide a particular public good and, if so, how to pay for it. In practice, we often confront additional questions about what level and quality of a public good to provide.

Standard cost-benefit logic also applies to these questions. For example, New York City should add another rocket to a fireworks display if and only if the amount that citizens would collectively be willing to pay to see the rocket is at least as great as its cost.

Cost-Benefit

THE DEMAND CURVE FOR A PUBLIC GOOD

To calculate the socially optimal quantity of a public good, we must first construct the demand curve for that public good. The process for doing so differs in an important way from the one we use to generate the market demand curve for a private good.

For a private good, all buyers face the same price and each chooses the quantity he or she wishes to purchase at that price. Recall from Chapter 5, *Demand,* that to construct the demand curve for a private good from the demand curves for individual consumers, we place the individual demand curves side by side and add them horizontally. That is, for each of a series of fixed prices, we add the resulting quantities demanded on the individual demand curves. In Figure 14.1, for example, we add the individual demand curves for a private good, D_1 and D_2 [Figure 14.1(a) and (b)] horizontally to obtain the market demand curve for the good D [Figure 14.1(c)].

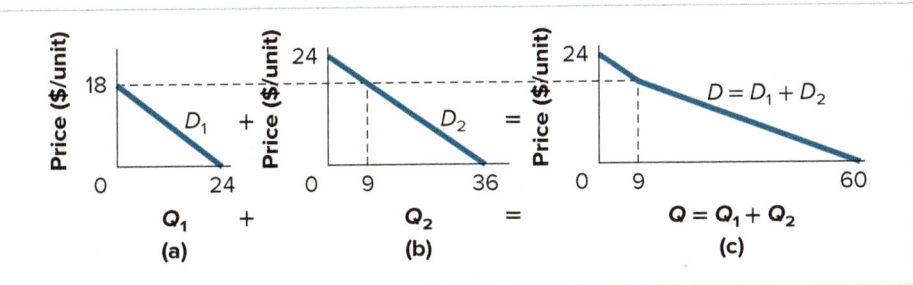

FIGURE 14.1

Generating the Market Demand Curve for a Private Good.
To construct the market demand curve for a private good (c), we add the individual demand curves (a) and (b) horizontally.

For a public good, all buyers necessarily consume the same quantity, although each may differ in terms of willingness to pay for additional units of the good. Constructing the demand curve for a public good thus entails not horizontal summation of the individual demand curves but vertical summation. That is, for each of a series of quantity values, we must add the prices that individuals are willing to pay for an additional unit of the good. The curves D_1 and D_2 in Figure 14.2(b) and (c) show individual demand curves for a public good by two different people. At each quantity, these curves tell how much the individual would be willing to pay for an additional unit of the public good. If we add D_1 and D_2 vertically, we obtain the total demand curve D for the public good [Figure 14.2(a)].

FIGURE 14.2

Generating the Demand Curve for a Public Good.
To construct the demand curve for a public good (a), we add the individual demand curves (b) and (c) vertically.

 SELF-TEST 14.2

Bill and Tom are the only demanders of a public good. If Bill's demand curve is $P_B = 6 - 0.5Q$ and Tom's is $P_T = 12 - Q$, construct the demand curve for this public good.

In the following example, we see how the demand curve for a public good might be used in conjunction with information about costs to determine the optimal level of parkland in a city.

EXAMPLE 14.4   **Using the Demand Curve to Determine Optimal Levels**

What is the optimal quantity of urban parkland?

The city government of a new planned community must decide how much parkland to provide. The marginal cost curve and the public demand curve for urban parkland are as shown in Figure 14.3. Why is the marginal cost curve upward-sloping and the demand curve downward-sloping? Given these curves, what is the optimal quantity of parkland?

Increasing
Opportunity Cost

Equilibrium

The marginal cost schedule for urban parkland is upward-sloping because of the Low-Hanging-Fruit Principle: The city acquires the cheapest parcels of land first and only then turns to more expensive parcels. Likewise, the marginal willingness-to-pay curve is downward-sloping because of the law of diminishing marginal utility. Just as people are generally willing to pay less for their fifth hot dog than for their first, they are also willing to pay less for the 101st acre of parkland than for the 100th acre. Given these curves, A^* is the optimal quantity of parkland. For any quantity less than A^*, the benefit of additional parkland exceeds its cost, which means that total economic surplus can be made larger by expanding the amount of parkland. For example, at A_0, the community would be willing to pay $200,000 for an additional acre of urban parkland, but its cost is only $80,000. Similarly, for any quantity of parkland in excess of A^*, the community would gain more than it would lose by selling off some parkland.

FIGURE 14.3

The Optimal Quantity of Parkland.

The optimal number of acres of urban parkland is A^*, the quantity at which the public's willingness to pay for additional parkland is equal to the marginal cost of parkland.

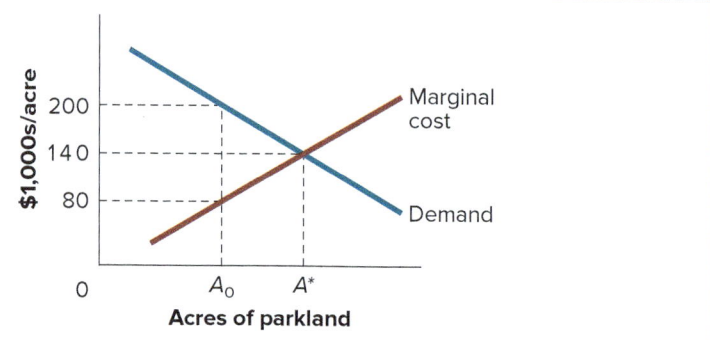

PRIVATE PROVISION OF PUBLIC GOODS

One advantage of using the government to provide public goods is that once a tax collection agency has been established to finance a single public good, it can be expanded at relatively low cost to generate revenue for additional public goods. Another advantage is that because government has the power to tax, it can summarily assign responsibility for the cost of a public good without endless haggling over who bears what share of the burden. And in the case of goods for which nonpayers cannot be excluded, the government may be the only feasible provider.

But exclusive reliance on government also entails disadvantages. Most fundamentally, the government's one-size-fits-all approach invariably requires many people to pay for public goods they don't want, while others end up having to do without public goods they want desperately. For example, many people vehemently oppose the provision of *any* sex education in the public schools, while others fervently believe that far more such instruction should be provided than is currently offered in most current public school curriculums. Mandatory taxation strikes many people as coercive, even if they approve of the particular public goods being provided.

It is no surprise, then, that governments are not the exclusive providers of public goods in any society. Indeed, many public goods are routinely provided through private channels. The challenge, in each case, is to devise a scheme for raising the required revenues. Here are some methods that seem to work.

Funding by Donation

In 2018, Americans gave more than $427 billion to private charities, many of which provide public goods to their communities. People also volunteer their time on behalf of organizations that provide public goods. When you paint your house, mow your lawn, or plant a flower garden, you are enhancing the quality of life in your neighborhood, and in that sense you are voluntarily providing a public good to your neighbors.

Development of New Means to Exclude Nonpayers

New electronic technology makes it possible to exclude nonpayers from many goods that in the past could not be thus restricted. For instance, broadcast television stations now have the ability to scramble their signals, making them available only to those consumers who purchase descrambling devices.

Private Contracting

More than 11 million Americans now live in gated private communities—private homeowners' associations that wall off contiguous properties and provide various services to residents. Many of these associations provide security services, schools, and fire protection and in other ways function much like ordinary local governments. Recognizing that individual incentives may not be strong enough to ensure socially optimal levels of maintenance and landscaping, these associations often bill homeowners for those services directly. Many of the rules imposed by these associations are even more restrictive than those imposed by local governments, a distinction that is defended on the grounds that people are always free to choose some other neighborhood if they don't like the rules of any particular homeowners' association. Many people would be reluctant to tolerate a municipal ordinance that prevents people from painting their houses purple, yet such restrictions are common in the bylaws of homeowners' associations.

Sale of By-Products

Many public goods are financed by the sale of rights or services that are generated as by-products of the public goods. For instance, as noted earlier, radio and television programming is a public good that is paid for in many cases by the sale of advertising messages. Internet services are also underwritten in part by commercial messages that pop up or appear in the headers or margins of web pages.

Given the quintessentially voluntary nature of privately provided public goods, it might seem that reliance on private provision might be preferred whenever it proved feasible. But as The Economic Naturalist 14.2 example makes clear, private provision often entails problems of its own.

The Economic Naturalist 14.2

Why do television networks favor *NFL Sunday Night Football* over *Masterpiece*?

In a given time slot, a television network faces the alternative of broadcasting either *NFL Sunday Night Football* or *Masterpiece* (formerly *Masterpiece Theatre*). If it chooses *NFL Sunday Night Football,* it will win 20 percent of the viewing audience, but only 18 percent if it chooses *Masterpiece.* Suppose those who would choose *NFL Sunday Night Football* would collectively be willing to pay $10 million for the right to see that program, while those who choose *Masterpiece* would be willing to pay $30 million. And suppose, finally, that the time slot is to be financed by a detergent company. Which program will the network choose? Which program would be socially optimal?

A detergent maker cares primarily about the number of people who will see its advertisements and will thus choose the program that will attract the largest audience—here, *NFL Sunday Night Football*. The fact that those who prefer *Masterpiece* would be willing to pay a lot more to see it is of little concern to the sponsor. But to identify the optimal result from society's point of view, we must take this difference into account. Because the people who prefer *Masterpiece* could pay *NFL Sunday Night Football* viewers more than enough to compensate them for relinquishing the time slot, *Masterpiece* is the efficient outcome. But unless its supporters happen to buy more soap in total than *NFL Sunday Night Football* viewers, the latter will prevail. In short, reliance on advertising and other indirect mechanisms for financing public goods provides no assurance that the goods chosen will maximize economic surplus.

Why do detergent companies care more about audience size than about how much people would be willing to pay to see the programs they sponsor?

Of course, the fact that the programs that best suit advertisers' needs may not be socially optimal does not mean that government decisions would necessarily be better. One can imagine, for example, a cultural affairs ministry that would choose television programming that would be "good for us" but that few of us would want to watch.

One way to avoid the inefficiency that arises when advertisers choose programming is to rely on subscription video streaming services to provide television programming. These methods allow viewers to register not just which programs they prefer but also the strength of their preferences, as measured by how much they are willing to pay.

But although a video streaming service is more likely to select the programs the public most values, it is also less efficient than broadcast TV in one important respect. As noted earlier, charging each household a fee for a subscription discourages some households from tuning in. And since the marginal social cost of serving an additional household is essentially zero, limiting the audience in this way is inefficient. Which of the two inefficiencies is more important—broadcast TV's inefficiency in choosing among programs or a video streaming service's inefficiency in excluding potential beneficiaries—is an empirical question.

In any event, the mix between private and public provision of public goods and services differs substantially from society to society and from arena to arena within any given society. These differences depend on the nature of available technologies for delivering and paying for public goods, and also on people's preferences.

EXAMPLE 14.5

The Impact of Subscription Video Streaming Services on Economic Surplus

By how much is total economic surplus reduced by Netflix's monthly fee for subscribers?

Suppose the demand curve for a month's access to the library of videos offered by Netflix is given in Figure 14.4. If the monthly subscription fee is $12, then by how much would economic surplus rise if the same library of videos were offered to consumers free of charge?

According to Figure 14.4, at a monthly fee of $12, 60 million consumers will subscribe to Netflix each month. But if the same library of videos were offered free of charge, 100 million consumers would want access. The additional economic surplus reaped by the extra 40 million consumers each month is the area of the blue triangle, which is $240 million. Since the marginal cost of giving these additional consumers access to Netflix is essentially zero, the total increase in surplus each month also would be $240 million.

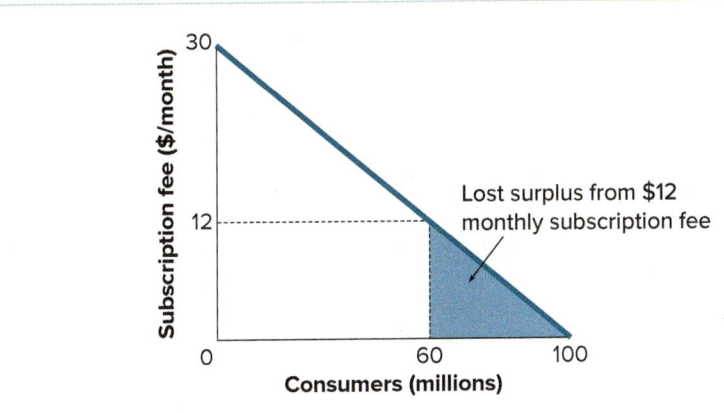

FIGURE 14.4

The Loss in Surplus from a Monthly Subscription Fee.
An additional 40 million consumers would want access to the library of videos offered by Netflix if the price were zero instead of $12 per month. The additional economic surplus is the area of the blue triangle, or $240 million per month.

In general, charging a positive price for a good whose marginal cost is zero will result in a loss in surplus. The size of the loss that results when price is set above marginal cost depends on the price elasticity of demand. When demand is more elastic, the loss in surplus is greater. Self-Test 14.3 provides an opportunity to see that principle at work.

 SELF-TEST 14.3

How would your answer to Example 14.5 have been different if the demand curve had instead been as shown below?

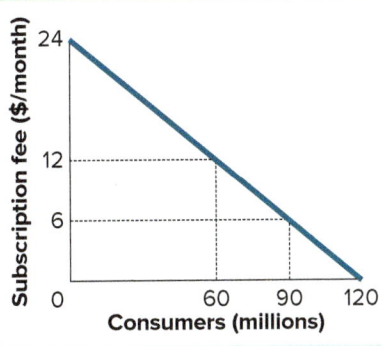

RECAP ↑

THE OPTIMAL QUANTITY OF A PUBLIC GOOD

Because the quantity of a public good must be the same for every consumer, the total demand curve for a public good is constructed by adding individual demand curves vertically. Optimal production of a public good occurs at the quantity for which the demand curve intersects the marginal cost curve for the public good.

Government need not always be the best way to provide public goods. Such goods can be provided by private organizations that rely on charitable contributions or the sale of by-products. Private for-profit companies also can become providers when new technologies such as subscription video streaming services convert public goods into collective goods.

LAWS, REGULATIONS, AND THE QUESTION OF CENTRALIZATION

The provision of public goods is not the only rationale for the existence of government. Government also creates and enforces the rules without which the efficient production of private goods would not be possible.

EXTERNALITIES AND PROPERTY RIGHTS

As we saw in Chapter 11, *Externalities, Property Rights, and the Environment,* externalities often stand in the way of socially optimal resource allocation in private activities. We saw, too, that optimal allocations are unlikely to result whenever property rights are poorly defined (for example, the tragedy of the commons). These observations suggest the existence of two additional important roles for government: the regulation of activities that generate externalities and the definition and enforcement of property rights.

These rationales for government action explain why most governments regulate activities that generate pollution, subsidize education (on the grounds that an educated public creates positive externalities), control access to fishing waters and public timberland, and enforce zoning laws. Most laws, in fact, represent attempts to define property rights or to control externalities. The law requiring motorists to drive on the right, for example, is an attempt to prevent the activities of one motorist from causing harm to others.

Proponents of minimalist government often object that the government unjustly curtails our freedom when it uses zoning laws to limit the size of the houses we build or imposes fines on motorists who violate highway speed limits. Yet the justification for such regulations is precisely the same as for the laws that prohibit your fist from occupying the same physical space as your neighbor's nose. You are free to swing your fists as you please, provided you cause no harm to others. But if your fist strikes your neighbor's nose, you become a violator of the law and subject to punishment. If the proponents of minimalist government approve of restricting behavior in this way, why do they disapprove of other attempts to discourage behaviors that cause harm to others?

Perhaps their fear is that, because externalities are so pervasive, governments that were empowered to regulate them might quickly get out of control. This is by no means an idle fear, and we emphasize that the mere fact that an externality exists does not necessarily mean that the best outcome is for the government to regulate it. As we will see in the next section, regulation entails costs of its own. The ultimate question is therefore a practical one: Will government regulation of the externality in question do more good than harm? Slogans about being free to live without government interference provide little help in answering such questions.

LOCAL, STATE, OR FEDERAL?

Framers of the U.S. Constitution were deeply skeptical of centralized government power. In drafting the Constitution, therefore, they explicitly tried to limit the powers of the federal government as much as possible, delegating most important powers to the states, which in turn delegated many of their powers to governments at the local level.

It is no surprise that the dangers of remote, centralized government ranked high among the founding fathers' concerns. After all, fresh in their memories was the autocratic treatment received by the American colonies at the hands of the monarchy in England. The founding fathers recognized that government will be more responsive the shorter the distance between officeholders and the voters who elect them.

Another obvious advantage of giving as much authority to local governments as possible is that different communities often have markedly different preferences about how much to spend on public goods, and even on what kinds of public goods to provide. When such decisions are made at the local level, people can shop for a community whose voters' preferences largely coincide with their own. Those who like high levels of public goods and services can band together and authorize high taxes to pay for them. Others who place less value on public services can choose communities in which both services and taxes are lower.

Why, given the many attractions of decisions made at the local level, did the founding fathers create federal and state governments at all? One reason is economies of scale in defense. For a country to survive politically, it must be able to deter aggression by hostile governments. A country consisting only of, say, Concord, New Hampshire, would be ill-equipped to do that. Large, well-equipped armies and navies cost a lot of money, and countries without sufficient population simply cannot afford them.

Defense, however, is not the only reason to empower governments beyond the local or state level. The problem of pollution, for example, is difficult to solve when the various sources of pollution are not subject to regulatory control by a single government. Much of the acid rain experienced in Canada, for instance, is the result of sulfur dioxide emissions from industrial sources in the upper Midwest of the United States. These emissions are beyond the reach of Canadian environmental regulations. In many instances, as with the discharge of greenhouse gases, not even a coalition of all the governments in North, Central, and South America would have power to take effective action. Carbon dioxide emitted anywhere on the planet disperses to uniform concentrations around the globe in a matter of months.

The choice between different levels of government, then, often confronts us with difficult trade-offs. Ceding the power of taxation to a federal government often entails painful compromises for voters in individual states. But the loss of political autonomy is an even less attractive option. Similarly, nations are understandably reluctant to cede any of their sovereign powers to a higher authority, but failure to take such steps may entail unacceptable environmental costs in the long run.

> **RECAP↑**
>
> **LAWS, REGULATIONS, AND THE QUESTION OF CENTRALIZATION**
>
> Government creates economic surplus not only by providing public goods but also by regulating activities that generate externalities and by defining and enforcing property rights. These rationales explain why most governments regulate pollution, subsidize education, control access to fishing waters and public timberland, and enforce zoning laws.
>
> Although the framers of the Constitution disliked centralized government power, they recognized that some government functions are not best performed at the local or even state level. Economies of scale argue for provision of defense at the national level. Externalities that transcend local boundaries provide an additional rationale for national or even international government.

CLIMATE MITIGATION: THE ULTIMATE PUBLIC GOOD?

According to a comprehensive study undertaken by McKinsey, the consulting firm, the cost of achieving the Paris Agreement's goal of net zero emissions by the year 2050 would be annual global investments of some $3.5 trillion beyond current levels.[1] But according to the U.N.'s Intergovernmental Panel on Climate Change (IPCC), meeting the net zero target won't suffice to produce climate stability. To achieve that goal, the IPCC's modeling suggests that we must also remove large quantities of CO_2 already present in the

[1]McKinsey & Co., "What Is Net Zero?" November 28, 2022, www.mckinsey.com/featured-insights/mckinsey-explainers/what-is-net-zero.

atmosphere.[2] Reforestation can help, but the 2022 IPCC report estimates that it will also be necessary to rely on direct air capture (DAC), a technology that removes existing CO_2 from the air and stores it as stable rock formations underground.

Estimates peg DAC's current cost at roughly $600 per ton of CO_2 removed, but experience with sharply declining cost trajectories for solar and wind encourages the hope that costs will fall sharply as the technology is more fully deployed. But even if its costs stabilized at $100 per ton, the cost of achieving the IPCC's removal targets between 2030 and 2070 could exceed $1.5 trillion per year. Added to the McKinsey estimate of $3.5 trillion of additional annual investment to achieve net zero emissions by 2050, the required total outlays necessary for achieving climate stability could be more than $5 trillion annually.

Since it is the wealthiest countries that are responsible for most of the greenhouse gas emissions that have contributed to the climate crisis, widely accepted norms of fairness suggest that these countries absorb a disproportionate share of the cost of mitigation. As a practical matter, because only the wealthiest countries are in a realistic position to incur the necessary expenses, it's easy to see how required annual contributions by the United States could top $1.5 trillion. Under the circumstances, it is no exaggeration to regard climate mitigation as the ultimate public good.

Some argue that climate mitigation is prohibitively costly, but that view is defensible only if we ignore the cost of failing to deal with the problem. An annual expenditure of $5 trillion is less than 5 percent of current world GDP. That's a smaller burden than missing out on just three years of economic growth—as happened in the United States in the wake of the financial crisis that began in 2008. That was hardly a welcome experience, of course, but compared to the projected damage from unchecked warming, it's essentially a rounding error.

The biggest obstacle to serious climate mitigation efforts was once widespread denial that change was even happening. But the recent frequency and intensity of floods, droughts, wildfires, and heat emergencies have persuaded most people that the climate crisis is both real and immediate.

Yet inaction persists. Psychologists say one of its causes is a perception that the battle is hopeless.[3] That perception stems in part from a belief that existing policy tools can't induce the necessary changes in behavior. But as we've attempted to explain in earlier chapters, those tools are far more powerful than is generally recognized. A much more serious obstacle to action has been a perception that because the policies required to achieve climate stability would be so costly, the world's taxpayers who live under democratic rule would be unwilling to foot the bill.

PAYING FOR CLIMATE MITIGATION

One promising development is that the private sector has already begun to undertake a significant share of the investment necessary for net-zero emissions. Because the costs of solar and wind have been falling so rapidly, electricity from new renewable sources in many areas is now cheaper than electricity generated by existing fossil-fuel facilities. For example, Texas, a state hardly known for its climate advocacy, currently produces almost twice as much near-zero emissions electricity as California. The relatively sparsely populated states of Iowa, Oklahoma, and Kansas combine to generate 1.6 times California's renewable output. Iowa, in fact, leads the nation in percentage of electricity generated from renewables (62.5 percent), and seven other states, most of them on the western plains, exceed California's 37.2 percent of power generation by renewables.[4]

---

[2]"Climate Change 2022: Mitigation of Climate Change," United Nations Intergovernmental Panel on Climate Change, 2019, www.ipcc.ch/report/sixth-assessment-report-working-group-3. The estimate can be found in Section C.3.5 (p. 25) of the *Summary for Policymakers*, www.ipcc.ch/report/ar6/wg3/downloads/report/IPCC_AR6_WGIII_SummaryForPolicymakers.pdf. The large band in the estimate reflects the uncertainty around how much the world will be exceeding its emissions "budget" at the net zero target date of 2050. Relative to existing technology, the lower bound figure of 20 gigatons is not a small number.
[3]Renee Lertzman, *Environmental Melancholia* (New York, Routledge, 2015).
[4]All figures are from U.S. Energy Information Administration, *Short-Term Energy Outlook* (STEO) reports (latest used = February 2023). "Renewables" here exclude legacy nuclear and hydroelectric power sources, which are counted separately (and would change the totals and rankings considerably) because they are changing much more slowly than the wind, solar, geothermal "nonhydro renewables" category. The latest STEO is at www.eia.gov/outlooks/steo.

In short, although extensive public investment was necessary to give solar and wind energy their initial foothold, their current low costs have now made further investment in these sources largely self-sustaining. Private incentives regarding energy sources are now much more closely aligned with society's than they were a decade ago.

But there remain clear limits on what the invisible hand can do. Cement production, for example, releases CO_2 in large quantities, but producers will take costly steps to curb those emissions only if compelled to do so, in which case society must ultimately bear the cost. The cost of removing gigatons of past emissions from the atmosphere is also one that must be borne by society. Economics offers useful advice about how we might raise the necessary revenue.

People and firms pollute not out of a desire to harm others, but because curbing pollution is costly. If clean production methods were always cheaper (as in fact they have now become for solar and wind), pollution would not have been a problem in the first place. As we saw in Chapter 11, the economist Arthur C. Pigou suggested that a good way to curb pollution was to make dirty production processes more expensive by taxing them. Such levies are commonly described as Pigouvian taxes (or as some economists call them, Pigovian taxes). Taxing pollution creates incentives to achieve any given emissions target at the lowest possible cost.

Pigouvian taxes can of course be applied to other activities that generate negative externalities. We could, and should, tax congestion, noise, vehicle weight, and a host of other consumption categories that cause injury to others. Such taxes essentially kill two birds with one stone: They raise revenue to finance climate mitigation and other valued public goods and services; and they discourage the pursuit of activities whose marginal benefits fall far short of their marginal costs.

Pigouvian taxes are in fact one of the few issues for which the traditional partisan divide in the United States and elsewhere has all but vanished among serious students of public policy. For example, N. Gregory Mankiw, a conservative Harvard economist who served as Chairman of the Council of Economic Advisers under President George W. Bush, was inspired by his enthusiasm for Pigouvian taxes to found the Pigou Club in 2006. The only requirement for membership is a willingness to attest that taxes on negative externalities are the most efficient and fair way of curbing them. The Pigou Club membership now includes a long list of economists, politicians, pundits, and others from virtually every point along the political spectrum. Liberal *New York Times* columnist Paul Krugman and anti-government crusader Grover Norquist are Pigou Club members. It would be challenging indeed to identify two people with more sharply divergent views on the membership list of any other group.

Although few taxes are viewed enthusiastically, everyone concedes, at least grudgingly, that taxes are necessary to pay for valued public services. And since we have to tax *something*, why not tax activities that cause harm to others?

Activities that emit greenhouse gases are a conspicuous example, and economists have long favored carbon taxes to curb them. Although numerous jurisdictions around the world have already enacted them, resistance to carbon taxation has remained strong in the United States. Economic analysis suggests that this resistance could be overcome by making a carbon tax revenue-neutral, which means periodically rebating the resulting revenue to taxpayers.

To see the attraction of revenue-neutrality, note first that the top 10 percent of earners worldwide account for approximately 50 percent of CO_2 emissions.[5] Energy use is less skewed in the United States than in most other countries, but here, too, top earners account for the lion's share of emissions. The most prosperous taxpayers would thus contribute most of the revenue generated by a carbon tax. It would then be a simple matter to design a rebate scheme under which 90 percent of the population received larger rebates each month than they'd paid in taxes. This would cushion the burden of the tax, and since goods with bigger carbon footprints would become more expensive, people would still face powerful incentives to choose substitutes with smaller footprints. The nonwealthy would be clear winners under this design.

---

[5]"World's Richest 10 Percent Produce Half of Carbon Emissions, While Poorest 3.5 Billion Account for Just a Tenth," Oxfam International, December 2, 2015.

Top earners would be net payers under a revenue-neutral carbon tax, but they too would come out ahead because reductions in climate-related property damage would benefit them disproportionately. Bottom line: A suitably designed revenue-neutral carbon tax would make virtually everyone better off than under current arrangements. That leaders have thus far failed to persuade voters to embrace such a tax constitutes evidence of political malpractice. Even if we were to adopt a revenue-neutral carbon tax, however, it would make no net contribution to revenues available for climate mitigation.

If countries around the globe had begun taxing carbon decades ago at rates close to the external costs of CO_2 emissions, we would not be facing a climate crisis today. But that was unfortunately never a realistic prospect. Because climatologists didn't have good estimates of emissions costs and because broad public recognition of the climate threat's severity occurred only recently, significant carbon taxes couldn't have won political support in the early going.

Even so, continuing to lobby for the adoption of carbon taxes remains a central element on climate advocates' policy agenda. But it's also one that, even if successful, would be only part of an effective mitigation program. We must also build out renewable energy grids and remove large quantities of existing CO_2 from the atmosphere, both of which will require trillions of dollars of additional investment. Taxing noise, congestion, pollutants, and other items on conventional textbook lists of negative externalities would cover only a tiny proportion of those expenses. Those who are unwilling to abandon the climate battle must therefore consider other options. We'll consider several in turn.

Some have argued that a government that issues its own currency can pay for public goods and services by simply printing money. Proponents of this approach acknowledge that it would be constrained by voters' willingness to tolerate any additional inflation that higher spending might cause. But therein lies the problem. Given the scale of the required climate mitigation measures, paying for them by printing money would provoke substantially more inflation than occurred in the wake of Russia's invasion of Ukraine. Although those increases were relatively modest by historical standards, they produced considerable political upheaval in countries around the globe.

That's why realists find it difficult to see how political support for the necessary decarbonization measures could be maintained in the face of the rapid inflation that would result if those measures were financed by printing money. Any practical path forward will therefore require reducing spending in other areas by roughly enough to offset increased spending on climate mitigation. The most practical way to accomplish that would be to impose higher taxes, which would not only generate additional revenue but also reduce taxpayers' ability to spend on emissions-producing goods and activities.

In addition to income taxes, many countries also levy taxes on the sale of goods and services. Countries in the European Union, for example, impose sales taxes (also called value-added taxes) that range from 17 to 27 percent of a good's sale price. Many object that value-added taxes are regressive, since low- and middle-income families consume significantly higher proportions of their pretax incomes than do the wealthy. EU governments have responded to this concern by using some of the revenue from value-added taxes to pay for additional social services for low- and middle-income families. Much of the revenue from the imposition of such taxes would therefore be unavailable for climate investment.

Another option for raising additional revenue is simply to make the current income tax more progressive. Critics have long objected that higher top marginal tax rates would reduce incentives to work hard and take risks. Those concerns, however, have found little support in cross-national studies, some of which use a country's number of billionaires per capita as a measure of the strength of its entrepreneurial incentives. For instance, although the top marginal tax rate in Sweden, at 52.3 percent, is more than 15 percentage points higher than in the United States, the country has almost three billionaires per million people, compared to less than two per million in the United States.[6]

---

[6]Wikipedia, https://en.wikipedia.org/wiki/List_of_countries_by_number_of_billionaires.

A more worrisome concern is that higher top marginal income tax rates could choke off savings and investment. One response to that concern would be to exempt savings from taxation, a step that has been advocated by economists from both sides of the political aisle.[7] That step would transform the current progressive income tax into a progressive consumption tax. Exempting savings would of course require significantly higher top marginal tax rates than under the current income tax.

To compute a family's taxable consumption, authorities would need only two numbers: its annual income and its annual additions to total savings. Families already document their incomes at tax time, and many also document their annual savings, as required by 401(k) accounts and similar tax-sheltered retirement savings plans. With those two numbers in hand, a family's total taxable consumption is simply its income minus its savings, less a large standard deduction—say, $10,000 per person—in recognition of the tendency of lower-income families to save at lower rates than others. Marginal tax rates on taxable consumption would start low, so that low- and middle-income families would face the same or lower tax bills as under the current income tax.

Our discussion of positional arms races in Chapter 10 suggests that a progressive consumption tax can also be interpreted as a Pigouvian tax. That's because our ability to achieve many important goals in life depends not just on how much we spend, but also on how much others spend. As the economist Richard Layard memorably wrote, "In a poor country, a man proves to his wife that he loves her by giving her a rose, but in a rich country he must give a dozen roses."[8]

If a proud family spends a little more than is customary in the hope of staging a memorable wedding reception for a beloved daughter, for example, it will raise, albeit imperceptibly, the standards that define acceptable wedding celebrations for others. The effect of any one family's extra outlays would of course be small, but their cumulative effect would be substantial. By 2018, the inflation-adjusted average expenditure on wedding receptions in the United States had passed $35,000, more than three times what it had been in 1980.

An important reason for this increase was higher spending by top earners, who benefited from the lion's share of national income growth in the decades following 1980. This group spent more on virtually everything simply because they had more money. Their more elaborate celebrations shifted expectations for others just below them, who also spent more, and so on, all the way down the income ladder.

Collectively, this extra expenditure went largely for naught, as there is no evidence that marrying couples or their guests were any happier in 2018 than their counterparts from celebrations that cost only one-third as much in 1980. One study reports that couples whose receptions cost the most were three times more likely than others to divorce in the succeeding years.[9]

One of the most robust findings from the large and contentious literature on the determinants of human well-being is that beyond a certain point—one that has long since been passed in the developed world—across-the-board increases in many forms of private consumption produce no measurable gains in health or life satisfaction.[10] A progressive consumption tax would curb the externalities associated with inequality-driven expenditure cascades in much the same way that a Pigouvian carbon tax would curb CO_2 emissions.

High-income households are of course better able than others to take advantage of tax-exempt savings opportunities, and high marginal tax rates provide a strong motive for doing so. We could expect, therefore, that although a progressive consumption tax would reduce consumption inequality over time, it would also increase wealth inequality. Because

[7]From the left: Laurence Seidman, *The USA Tax: A Progressive Consumption Tax* (Cambridge, MA: MIT Press, 2003); and from the right: Robert E. Hall and Alvin Rabushka, *The Flat Tax* (Palo Alto, CA: Hoover Institution Press, 2007).

[8]Richard Layard, "Human Satisfactions and Public Policy," *Economic Journal* 90, no. 363 (1980), p. 741.

[9]Andrew Francis-Tan and Hugo M. Mialon, "A Diamond Is Forever and Other Fairy Tales: The Relationship between Wedding Expenses and Marriage Duration," *Economic Inquiry* 53, no. 4 (October 2015), pp. 1919–1930.

[10]Carol Graham, *Happiness Around the World: The Paradox of Happy Peasants and Miserable Millionaires* (New York: Oxford University Press, 2012).

wealth inequality has already been increasing rapidly for other reasons, a progressive consumption tax would strengthen the case for maintaining a robust inheritance tax.[11]

Many prosperous voters would of course support being taxed more heavily to fund climate mitigation and other public investment. But a significant majority among the wealthy have opposed any attempt to raise their taxes. Their political campaign contributions have in fact helped elect generations of politicians who have reduced top tax rates.

That observation raises the following awkward question about the case for more progressive tax levies: If prosperous voters would be happier if the money they now spend for larger mansions, more expensive cars, and more elaborate wedding receptions were instead spent for better roads and climate mitigation, why don't they vote accordingly? The simple answer is that most believe, quite naturally, that higher taxes would make it harder to buy the luxuries they desire. But that belief is what some behavioral economists have called the mother of all cognitive illusions.

THE MOTHER OF ALL COGNITIVE ILLUSIONS

Before describing how specific mental heuristics, or rules of thumb, give rise to this illusion, it's helpful to consider the nature of cognitive illusions generally. Life is complicated. We are bombarded by terabytes of information each day, far more than we can process consciously. To cope, our nervous systems employ various heuristics. As we saw in Chapter 10, these rules of thumb often operate completely out of conscious awareness and work reasonably well much of the time. But because of important design constraints, they're imperfect.

In Figure 14.5, which square is darker, A or B? If you think A looks darker, your eyes and brain are functioning normally. But in this instance, your judgment is incorrect. In what's called the checker-shadow illusion, square A is the same shade of gray as square B. Look at the figure carefully. If your brain is functioning as nature intended, it should be telling you, "That can't be true!" And yet it is.

FIGURE 14.5

The Checker-Shadow Illusion.

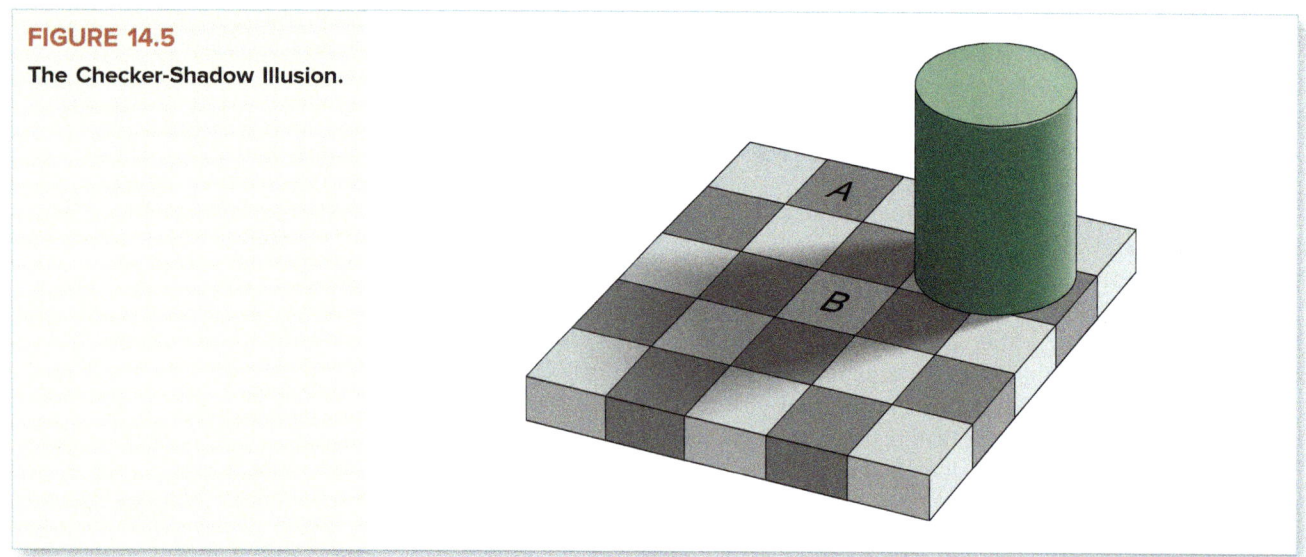

[11]Although often criticized as the "death tax," the estate tax is both an efficient and a fair way to help pay for climate mitigation and other valued public services. It functions much like a lawyer's contingency fee contract, which helps people who have been unjustly injured to obtain access to the legal system. If a lawyer believes an injury claim has merit, she may agree to represent a client on a contingency basis: If they lose in court, the client pays nothing; but if they win, the lawyer gets a share of the judgment, often roughly one-third. The estate tax is functionally equivalent to this type of contract.

The psychologist Richard Wiseman offers this explanation:

> Your eyes and brain see that the two squares are the same shade of gray, but then think, "Hold on—if a square in a shadow reflects the same amount of light as a square outside of the shadow, then in reality [square B] must be a much lighter shade of gray." As a result, your brain alters your perception of the image so that you see what it thinks is out there in the real world.[12]

That explanation, plausible though it sounds, is insufficient to convince most people. But now study the amended image in Figure 14.6 and note the complete lack of contrast between squares A and B and the added strip that joins them. Only upon seeing this second image are most people able even to consider the possibility that A and B might be the same shade of gray.

As the checker-shadow illusion dramatically illustrates, a statement that seems incontrovertibly true ("Square A is darker than square B") may in fact be false. This example should affirm at least the possibility that self-evidently true beliefs about the effect of higher taxes may be false as well.

When someone asks, "How will higher taxes affect me?" the natural first step is to try to recall how it felt the last time taxes went up. But that strategy doesn't work in the current era, since most high-income people alive today have experienced steadily declining tax rates. The top marginal tax rate in the United States was 70 percent in 1966. In 1982 it was 50 percent, and it is now just 37 percent. Apart from brief and isolated increases almost too small to notice, top marginal tax rates have fallen steadily since their 92 percent peak during World War II. Similar declines have occurred in other countries.

When Plan A fails, we go to Plan B. Because paying higher taxes means having less money to spend on other things, a plausible alternative cognitive strategy is to estimate the effect of tax hikes by recalling earlier events that resulted in lower disposable income. People might remember an occasional business reverse, for example, or a losing lawsuit, or a divorce, or a house fire, maybe even a health crisis. Rare is the life history that is completely devoid of events like these, which share a common attribute: They make people feel miserable.

More important, such events share a second feature, one that is absent from an increase in taxes: They reduce our own incomes while leaving others' incomes unaffected. Higher taxes, in contrast, reduce all incomes in tandem. This difference holds the key to understanding what behavioral economists call the mother of all cognitive illusions.

FIGURE 14.6

The Checker–Shadow Illusion Unveiled.

[12]Richard Wiseman, "Ten of the Greatest Optical Illusions," *Daily Mail*, September 25, 2010.

As most prosperous people would themselves be quick to concede, they have everything anybody might reasonably be said to need. If higher taxes pose any threat, it would be to make it more difficult for them to buy life's special extras. But "special" is an inescapably relative concept. To be special means to stand out in some way from what is expected. And almost without exception, special things are in limited supply. There are only so many penthouse apartments with sweeping views of Central Park, for instance. To get one, a wealthy New Yorker must outbid peers who also want it. The outcomes of such bidding contests depend almost exclusively on relative purchasing power. And since relative purchasing power is completely unaffected when the wealthy all pay higher taxes, the same penthouses end up in the same hands as before.

Some might object, plausibly, that higher tax rates on prosperous Americans would put them at a disadvantage relative to oligarchs from other countries in the bidding wars for trophy properties in the United States. But that disadvantage could be eliminated easily by the imposition of a purchase levy on nonresident buyers.

Again, when we try to imagine how higher taxes would affect us, our history of steadily falling tax rates prevents us thinking about how we felt when taxes rose in the past. Plan B is to recall times when our incomes fell. But most of those declines were ones in which our own incomes fell while the incomes of others stayed the same. When our relative income declines, we feel pain. But tax increases don't reduce anyone's relative income.

Emotions and memory are tightly coupled. The more closely an experience is paired with a powerful emotion, the more likely we are to remember it.[13] Strong emotions are provoked by divorces, home fires, business reverses, health crises, and other events that cause individual incomes to fall sharply. These emotions imbue the associated memories with three properties: They are vivid, painful, and easy to retrieve. Those properties greatly strengthen the illusion that tax increases will hurt.

DOES GOVERNMENT POLICY MATTER?

As noted in Chapter 1, Adam Smith's Invisible Hand Theory is widely seen as the most important single idea in economics. That he foresaw how market incentives would unleash the most spectacular and sustained rise in living standards in human history is without question an intellectual achievement of high order.

But Smith was also more circumspect about the invisible hand than his most ardent modern disciples, many of whom are disdainful of any government intervention that alters market outcomes. Some even argue that apart from the provision of national defense, it would be better to have no government at all.

Such claims are easily dismissed. If humans were more likely to flourish in societies without government, we would expect that examples of such societies would have long since emerged. And although Smith himself thought it remarkable that the pursuit of narrow self-interest *often* led to socially beneficial results, he was under no illusion that it always did so. Both in Smith's time and in ours, the only interesting question was and is how extensive the government's role should be.

As we've seen, conflicts between individual and group interests arise whenever activities entail side effects on third parties. Ronald Coase, Elinor Ostrom, and other economists have shown that it's sometimes possible to negotiate private solutions to misallocations caused by externalities. Yet for many of the biggest problems we face going forward—climate change foremost among them—private solutions fall short. We need the force of law to alter people's incentives.

Looking ahead, let's imagine a choice between two very different societies—a choice very much like the one we actually face. One society—call it A—is a continuation of long-standing trends in twenty-first-century America. In it, market forces will spur continued growth in income and wealth inequality, fueling continued increases in expenditure on cars, houses, coming-of-age celebrations, and other forms of positional consumption.

---

[13]See, for example, Elizabeth A. Phelps, "Emotion and Cognition: Insights from Studies of the Human Amygdala," *Annual Review of Psychology 57* (January 10, 2006), pp. 27–53.

Chronic budget shortfalls will produce steady pressure to reduce public spending. Investment in climate mitigation, vaccine research, hospital surge capacity, and infrastructure refurbishment will remain low. People work steadily longer hours.

The second society—call it B—adopts policies that change individual spending incentives. Those policies steer more of B's national income to green investment, infrastructure refurbishment, medical research, and hospital surge capacity. They lead people to take longer vacations and spend less on most forms of private consumption.

In short, A describes roughly the current status quo in the United States, while B describes how things might look if the country adopted policies that address some of the most important externalities that arise in market transactions.

In democratic societies, choices between alternative economic policies are made by elected officials. Some candidates favor policies that produce A while others favor ones that would produce B. Many have argued that economic analysis alone can't offer useful advice about candidate choices. On this view, people who like big cars and houses and assign little value to public services should vote for candidates who favor A, while those with different preferences should support candidates who favor B.

But there's also an opposing view. It's that votes for candidates who favor A are motivated not by well-considered preferences but rather by cognitive illusions about the effects of higher taxes and by unfamiliarity with evidence that in societies like B, most people are both happier and healthier than their counterparts in societies like A. On this view, voters who favor the status quo might want to reflect on how the policies that produce societies like A differ from those adopted by the countries listed in Table 14.2.

The countries listed in the table are the 5 happiest among the 195 countries studied in *The 2022 World Happiness Report*.[14] The rankings are based on answers to the main life evaluation question asked in the Gallup World Poll surveys from 2019 to 2021. In these and other similar surveys, higher happiness scores are closely linked to country characteristics known to promote human flourishing. Among others, these include income per capita, social support, healthy life expectancy, freedom, generosity, and absence of corruption.

The mix of policies adopted in the happiest societies closely resembles the mix described for our hypothetical society B. Compared to the United States, for instance, spending in those societies tilts more heavily toward the public sector, and top earners are taxed more heavily. Despite facing higher tax rates, the wealthy in the societies listed in Table 14.2 report significantly higher levels of life satisfaction than their American counterparts.

Are people in the happiest countries happier because the policies adopted by their countries are more conducive to human flourishing than the corresponding policies in the United States? The economic theory of how externalities shape spending decisions does not conclusively demonstrate such a causal link. But it is clearly consistent with one.

This is in any event a possibility that appears to merit further consideration.

TABLE 14.2
The World's Five Happiest Countries, 2022

1. Finland
2. Denmark
3. Iceland
4. Switzerland
5. The Netherlands

[14]*The World Happiness Report* 2022.

SUMMARY

- Our aim in this chapter was to apply principles of microeconomics to the study of the government's role in modern society. One of government's principal tasks is to provide public goods such as national defense and the criminal justice system. Such goods are, in varying degrees, nonrival and nonexcludable. The first property describes goods for which one person's consumption does not diminish the amount available for others, while the second refers to the difficulty of preventing nonpayers from consuming certain goods. *(LO1)*

- Goods that are both highly nonexcludable and nonrival are often called pure public goods. A collective good— such as a subscription video streaming service—is nonrival but excludable. Commons goods are goods that are rival but nonexcludable. *(LO1)*

- The criterion for providing the optimal quantity or quality of a public good is to keep increasing quantity or quality as long as the marginal benefit of doing so exceeds the marginal cost. One advantage of using the government to provide public goods is that once a tax collection agency has been established to finance a single public good, it can be expanded at relatively low cost to generate revenue to finance additional public goods. A second advantage is that because government has the power to tax, it can easily assign responsibility for the cost of a public good. And in the case of goods for which nonpayers simply cannot be excluded, the government may be the only feasible provider. *(LO2)*

- One disadvantage to exclusive reliance on government for public goods provision is the element of coercion inherent in the tax system, which makes some people pay for public goods they don't want, while others do without public goods they do want. Many public goods are provided through private channels, with the necessary funding provided by donations, by sale of by-products, by development of new means to exclude nonpayers, and in many cases by private contract. A loss in surplus results, however, whenever monetary charges are levied for the consumption of a nonrival good. *(LO2)*

- Because not everyone benefits equally from the provision of any given public good, charging all taxpayers equal amounts for the provision of public goods will generally not be either feasible or desirable. As in the case of private goods, people's willingness to pay for public goods generally increases with income, and most

governments therefore levy higher taxes on the rich than on the poor. Tax systems with this property have been criticized on the grounds that they are unfair to the wealthy, but this criticism ignores the fact that alternative tax schemes generally lead to worse outcomes for both rich and poor alike. *(LO2)*

- In addition to providing public goods, government serves two other important roles: the regulation of activities that generate externalities and the definition and enforcement of property rights. Despite a general view that government is more responsive the shorter the distance between citizens and their elected representatives, factors such as economies of scale in the provision of public goods and externalities with broad reach often dictate the assignment of important functions to state or national governments. *(LO3)*

- A tax on any activity not only generates revenue but also creates an incentive to reduce the activity. If the activity would have been pursued at the optimal level in the absence of a tax, taxing it will result in too little of the activity. But if an untaxed activity would have been pursued beyond its optimal level (as when it generates negative externalities), taxing it actually improves efficiency. In both cases, taxes make possible benefits from additional public goods and services. *(LO4)*

- Many wealthy voters believe that higher taxes would make it more difficult to purchase luxury goods. Behavioral economists have labeled this belief the mother of all cognitive illusions. To acquire luxury goods, which are typically in limited supply, one must outbid others who want them. And because higher taxes have no effect on relative bidding power, they do not make it harder for the wealthy to purchase luxuries. *(LO5)*

- Some critics argue that apart from providing for national defense, governments should play virtually no role in economic life. But although Adam Smith himself thought that market forces often yield socially beneficial results, he was under no illusion that they always do so. The only interesting question about government's role in the economy was for Smith, and remains, how extensive it should be. The challenge confronting market skeptics is to explain why life satisfaction levels are consistently higher in countries with higher levels of public investment. *(LO6)*

KEY TERMS

collective good	nonrival good	pure commons good
crowding out	progressive tax	pure private good
head tax	proportional income tax	pure public good
nonexcludable good	public good	regressive tax

REVIEW QUESTIONS

1. Answer the following questions related to these goods: apples, Stephen King novels, street lighting on campus, and NPR radio broadcasts. *(LO1)*
   a. Which of these goods are nonrival?
   b. Which of these goods are nonexcludable?

2. Give examples of goods that are, for the most part: *(LO1)*
   a. Rival but nonexcludable.
   b. Nonrival but excludable.
   c. Both nonrival and nonexcludable.

3. Why might even a wealthy person prefer a proportional income tax to a head tax? *(LO1)*

4. True or false: A tax on an activity that generates negative externalities will improve resource allocation in the private sector and also generate revenue that could be used to pay for useful public goods. Explain. *(LO3)*

5. Consider a good that would be provided efficiently by private market forces. Why is the direct loss in surplus that would result from a tax on this good an overstatement of the loss in surplus caused by the tax? *(LO2, LO4)*

6. Why is the effect of a carbon tax on climate stability an understatement of the tax's effect on total economic surplus? *(LO4)*

PROBLEMS

1. Two consumers, Smith and Jones, have the following demand curves for Podunk Public Radio broadcasts of recorded opera on Saturdays:

   $$\text{Smith:} \quad P_S = 12 - Q$$
   $$\text{Jones:} \quad P_J = 12 - 2Q$$

   where P_S and P_J represent marginal willingness-to-pay values for Smith and Jones, respectively, and Q represents the number of hours of opera broadcast each Saturday. *(LO2)*
   a. If Smith and Jones are the only public radio listeners in Podunk, construct the demand curve for opera broadcasts.
   b. If the marginal cost of opera broadcasts is $15 per hour, what is the socially optimal number of hours of broadcast opera?

2. Suppose the demand curves for *NFL Sunday Night Football* and *Masterpiece* are as shown in the following

diagram. A television network is considering whether to add one or both programs to its upcoming fall lineup. The only two time slots remaining are sponsored by Colgate, which is under contract to pay the network 10 cents for each viewer who watches the program, out of which the network would have to cover its production costs of $400,000 per episode. (Viewership can be estimated accurately with telephone surveys.) Any time slot the network does not fill with the *NFL Sunday Night Football* or *Masterpiece* will be filled by infomercials for a weight-loss program, for which the network incurs no production costs and for which it receives a fee of $500,000. Viewers will receive $5 million in economic surplus from watching each installment of the infomercial. *(LO2)*
   a. How will the network fill the two remaining slots in its fall lineup?
   b. Is this outcome socially efficient?
   c. By how much would total economic surplus be higher if each episode of *Masterpiece* were shown on

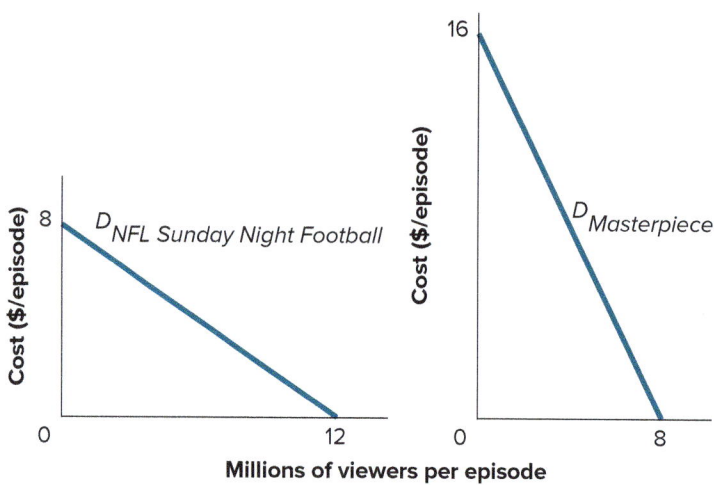

Millions of viewers per episode

PBS free of charge than if it were shown by a profit-maximizing video streaming service that charged consumers a fixed fee to watch each episode?

3. When a video streaming company chooses a subscription scheme to pay for programming, which of the following statements is true? Explain. *(LO2)*
   a. The outcome is socially efficient.
   b. The programs selected will maximize advertising revenue.
   c. The marginal cost to an additional viewer of watching the programs is lower than when advertising is used to finance programming.
   d. The outcome is always more socially efficient than when advertising is used to finance programming.
   e. The variety of programs provided is likely to rise.

4. When a group of people must decide whether to buy a shared public good or service, the free-rider problem frequently occurs because: *(LO2)*
   a. People have an incentive to understate how much the facility is really worth to them if they have to pay taxes to finance it.
   b. Each individual's needed contribution is an insignificant amount of the total required.
   c. People have an incentive to overstate how much the facility is worth to them if they don't have to pay taxes to finance it.
   d. People hope that others will value the facility enough to pay for it entirely.
   e. Only one of the above statements is not a reason for the existence of the free-rider problem.

5. The town of Smallsville is considering building a museum. The interest on the money Smallsville will have to borrow to build the museum will be $1,000 per year. Each citizen's marginal benefit from the museum is shown in the following table, and this marginal benefit schedule is public information. *(LO2, LO3)*

Citizen	Marginal benefit from museum ($/year)
Anita	340
Brandon	290
Carlena	240
Dallas	190
Eloise	140

   a. Assuming each citizen voted his or her private interests, would a referendum to build the museum and raise each citizen's annual taxes by $200 pass?
   b. A citizen proposes that the city let a private company build the museum and charge the citizens a lump-sum fee each year to view it as much as they like. Only citizens who paid the fee would be allowed to view the museum. If the private company were allowed to set a single fee, would any company offer to build the museum?
   c. A second citizen proposes allowing the private company to charge different prices to different citizens and auctioning the right to build the museum to the highest-bidding company. Again, only the citizens who pay the fee may view the museum. What is the highest bid a private company would make to supply the museum to Smallsville?

6. Jack and Jill are the only two residents in a neighborhood, and they would like to hire a security guard. The value of a security guard is $50 per month to Jack and $150 per month to Jill. Irrespective of who pays the guard, the guard will protect the entire neighborhood. *(LO2)*
   a. What is the most a guard can charge per month and still be assured of being hired by at least one of them?
   b. Suppose the competitive wage for a security guard is $120 per month. The local government proposes a plan whereby Jack and Jill each pay 50 percent of

this monthly fee and asks them to vote on this plan. Will the plan be voted in? Would economic surplus be higher if the neighborhood had a guard?

7. Refer to Problem 6. Suppose Jack earns $1,000 per month and Jill earns $11,000 per month. *(LO1, LO2)*
   a. Suggest a proportional tax on income that would be accepted by majority vote and would pay for the security guard.
   b. Suppose instead that Jack proposes a tax scheme under which Jack and Jill would each receive the same net benefit from hiring the guard. How much would Jack and Jill pay now? Would Jill agree to this scheme?
   c. What is the practical problem that prevents ideas like the one in part b from working in real-life situations?

8. The following table shows all the marginal benefits for each voter in a small town whose town council is considering a new swimming pool with capacity for at least three citizens. The cost of the pool would be $18 per week and would not depend on the number of people who actually used it. *(LO2, LO3)*

Voter	Marginal benefit ($/week)
A	12
B	5
C	2

   a. If the pool must be financed by a weekly head tax levied on all voters, will the pool be approved by majority vote? Is this outcome socially efficient? Explain.
   b. The town council instead decides to auction a franchise off to a private monopoly to build and maintain the pool. If it cannot find such a firm willing to operate the pool, then the pool project will be scrapped. If all such monopolies are constrained by law to charge a single price to users, will the franchise be sold, and if so, how much will it sell for? Is this outcome socially efficient? Explain.
   c. Suppose now that all such monopolies can perfectly price-discriminate. Will the franchise be sold, and if so, how much will it sell for? Is this outcome socially efficient? Explain.

9. Public goods are both nonexcludable and nonrival. Explain why a healthy and stable global climate is a public good (i.e., why it is nonexcludable and nonrival). *(LO4)*

10. Suppose the government would like to raise tax revenue to address the climate crisis. Why might the government decide to impose a carbon tax instead of a tax on income even if both types of taxes generate the same revenue? *(LO4)*

11. Suppose the supply curve for beef is given by $P = 1 + 0.1Q$, where P is the dollar price of a pound of beef and Q is quantity of beef in billions of pounds per year, and the demand curve for beef is given by $P = 10 - 0.2Q$. *(LO4)*
   a. What is the equilibrium price and quantity of beef bought and sold each year?
   b. Suppose that each pound of beef produced imposes a $3 cost on society due to the methane emited by cattle. Concerned about the climate crisis, the government imposes a tax of $3 on each pound of beef produced. What is the quantity of beef bought and sold each after the imposition of the tax? What impact will the tax have on the emission of methane? Does this tax make the economy more or less efficient?
   c. How much tax revenue will the tax generate? How could the government use this revenue to further address the climate crisis?

12. Suppose there are three residents in the small town of Jonesville. All three residents have nearly identical living expenses, but the first earns $100,000 per year, the second earns $50,000 per year, and the third earns no money but has a beautiful lakefront house that has been in her family for generations. Suppose the third resident decides to sell her house and leave Jonesville so she can be closer to her children. She is willing to accept the best offer she receives on the house. Both of the two remaining residents have the same preferences regarding the lake house and all other goods. *(LO5, LO6)*
   a. Assuming no one from outside Jonesville is interested in the property, which one of the two remaining residents is more likely to purchase this property? Explain.
   b. How would your answer change if both residents had to pay an income tax of 10 percent?
   c. How would your answer change if only the highest-earning resident had to pay an income tax of 20 percent?
   d. Suppose the tax revenue collected from the residents of Jonesville is used to fund improvements to the Jonesville Health Clinic. Under what conditions will the imposition of the tax make all of the residents beter off?

13. A good is positional if its value depends on how it compares with other goods in the same category. *(LO5, LO6)*
   a. Explain why public goods tend to be less positional than private goods.
   b. Explain how increasing the top marginal tax rate (the rate levied on additional income earned by top earners) could help fund public goods without compromising people's ability to purchase positional goods.

ANSWERS TO SELF-TESTS

14.1 a. The BLS website at 3 a.m. has the capacity to serve far more users than it attracts, so an additional user calling up the site does not prevent some other user from doing so. Other websites, however, do not show the nonrival property, at least during certain hours, because they attract more users than their servers can accommodate. *(LO1)*

b. The stadium at the championship game is always full, so anyone who watches the game in person prevents someone else from doing so.

c. Additional people can watch the game on television without diminishing the availability of the telecast for others.

14.2 To construct the demand curve (a), we first graph Bill's demand curve (c) and Tom's demand curve (b) and then add the two individual demand curves vertically. The equation for the demand curve is $P = 18 - 1.5\, Q$. *(LO2)*

14.3 The $12 monthly fee now excludes 60 million viewers, and the resulting loss in surplus (again the area of the blue triangle) is now $360 million. *(LO2)*

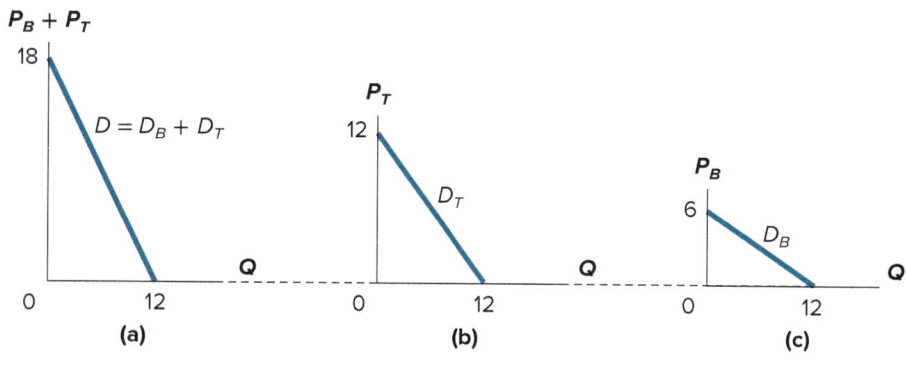

CHAPTER 15

International Trade and Trade Policy

Who gains and who loses when an economy opens up to trade?

Will Austin/Spaces Images/Blend Images

O n April 13, 1861, Southern troops fired on Fort Sumter in Charleston harbor, initiating the American Civil War. Less than a week later, on April 19, President Lincoln proclaimed a naval blockade of the South. Code-named the Anaconda Plan (after the snake that squeezes its prey to death), the blockade required the Union navy to patrol the Southern coastline, stopping and boarding ships that were attempting to land or depart. The object of the blockade was to prevent the Confederacy from shipping cotton to Europe, where it could be traded for military equipment, clothing, foodstuffs, and other supplies.

Historians are divided on the effectiveness of the Union blockade in choking off Confederate trade. In the early years of the war, the North had too few ships to cover the 3,600-mile Southern coastline, so "running" the blockade was not difficult. But in the latter part of the war the number of Union ships enforcing the blockade increased from about 90 to more than 600, and sailing ships were replaced with faster, more lethal iron-clad vessels. Still, private blockade runners attempted to elude the Union navy in small, fast ships. Because the price of raw cotton in Great Britain was between 10 and 20 times what it was in the Confederacy (a differential that indicated disruption in the normal flow of trade), blockade runners enjoyed huge profits when they were successful. But despite their efforts, by 1864 the Southern war effort was seriously hampered by a lack of military equipment and supplies, at least in part as a result of the blockade.

The use of a naval blockade as a weapon of war highlights a paradox in contemporary attitudes toward trade between nations. Presumably, an attempt by a foreign power to blockade U.S. ports would today be considered a hostile act that would elicit a strong response from the U.S. government. Yet one often hears politicians and others arguing that trade with other nations is harmful to the United States and should be restricted—in effect, that the United States should blockade its own ports! Politicians from both the Republican and Democratic Parties occasionally complain, for example, about China's exports to the United States. Some of them propose taking action against the Chinese government because, they say, it engages in unfair policies that cause Chinese products to sell in the United States for prices that are too *cheap*. Indeed, in recent years, the U.S. government enacted several policies that restrict imports of certain products from China. It also enacted other policies that restrict exports of certain products and technologies to China. So is trade a good thing or not? And if it is, why does it sometimes face determined opposition?

This chapter addresses international trade and its effects on the broader economy. We will begin by reviewing the idea of *comparative advantage,* which was introduced in Chapter 2, *Comparative Advantage.* We will show that in theory, everyone can enjoy more goods and services if nations specialize in those products in which they have a comparative advantage, and then trade freely among themselves. Furthermore, if trade is unrestricted, market forces will ensure that countries produce those goods in which they have a comparative advantage.

Having shown the potential benefits of trade, we will turn next to the reasons for opposition to trade. Although opening the economy to trade *can,* in our model, increase economic welfare overall, some groups—such as workers in industries that face competition from foreign producers—may in reality be made worse off. The fact that open trade may hurt some groups creates political pressure to enact measures restricting trade, such as taxes on imported goods (called tariffs) and limits on imports (called quotas). We will analyze the effects of these trade restrictions, along with other ways of responding to concerns about affected industries and workers through direct assistance programs.

Economists understand the frustrations with trade expressed by some groups. Indeed, economists recognize that for a displaced worker who does not expect effective direct government assistance to materialize—for example, because the worker does not expect the government to pass, implement, and sustain the relevant measures—opposing trade may appear a reasonable course of action. Economists also understand other potential concerns with trade (e.g., related to national security) that go beyond this chapter's economic analysis. However, from a purely economic point of view that takes into account both the overall size of the economic pie and how it is distributed providing direct assistance to those who are hurt by increased trade is preferable to blocking or restricting trade.

COMPARATIVE ADVANTAGE AS A BASIS FOR TRADE

Chapter 2, *Comparative Advantage,* began with the story of the Nepalese cook Birkhaman, a remarkable jack-of-all-trades who could do everything, from butchering a goat to fixing an alarm clock. Yet despite his range of skills, Birkhaman, like most Nepalese, was quite poor. The reason for Birkhaman's poverty, as we saw in Chapter 2, was precisely his versatility. Because he did so many different things, he could not hope to become as productive in each separate activity as someone who specialized entirely in that activity.

The alternative to a nation of Birkhamans is a country in which each person specializes in the activity at which he or she is relatively most efficient, or has a *comparative advantage*. This specialization, combined with trade between producers of different goods and services, allows a society to achieve a higher level of productivity and standard of living than one in which each person is essentially self-sufficient.

This insight, that specialization and trade among individuals can yield impressive gains in productivity, applies equally well to nations. Factors such as climate, natural resources, technology, workers' skills and education, and culture provide countries with comparative advantages in the production of different goods and services. For example, as we saw in Chapter 2, the large number of leading research universities in the United States gives that nation a comparative advantage in the design of technologically sophisticated computer and mobile hardware and software. Likewise, the wide international use of the English language endows the United States with a comparative advantage in producing popular films and TV shows. Similarly, France's climate and topography, together with the accumulated knowledge of generations of vintners, provides that country a comparative advantage in producing fine wines–although, as Economic Naturalist 2.3 ("How will climate change affect wine-industry specialization?") featured in Chapter 2 suggests, this comparative advantage may not last forever. Finally, Australia's huge expanses of arable land give that country a comparative advantage in producing grain.

The Principle of Comparative Advantage tells us that we can all enjoy more goods and services when each country produces according to its comparative advantage, and then trades with other countries. In the next section we explore this fundamental idea in greater detail.

Climate and long experience give France a comparative advantage in producing fine wines—for now.

PRODUCTION AND CONSUMPTION POSSIBILITIES AND THE BENEFITS OF TRADE

In this section we will consider how international trade benefits an individual country. To do so, we will contrast the production and consumption opportunities in a **closed economy**–one that does not trade with the rest of the world–with the opportunities in an **open economy**–one that does trade with other economies. Because we will make use of the production possibilities curve, which was introduced in Chapter 2, *Comparative Advantage,* we will begin by briefly reviewing that concept. We will look first at the PPC for a two-person economy and then at the PPC for a many-person economy. After reviewing the PPC, we will see how a country's production possibilities are related to its citizens' ability to consume in a closed economy versus an open economy.

closed economy an economy that does not trade with the rest of the world

open economy an economy that trades with other countries

THE TWO-WORKER PRODUCTION POSSIBILITIES CURVE

Recall that (for a two-good economy) the production possibilities curve (PPC) is a graph that shows the maximum amount of each good that can be produced, at every possible level of production of the other good.[1] To see how the PPC is constructed, let's consider a hypothetical economy, which we'll call Costa Rica, which has only two workers, Carlos and Maria. Each of these two workers can produce two goods, coffee and computers.

---

[1]For a many-good economy, the PPC shows the maximum amount of each good that can be produced at any level of production of all the other goods. Focusing on the two-good case allows us to draw the figures on the two-dimensional page. Our conclusions apply to the many-good case, however.

EXAMPLE 15.1

The PPC for a Two-Worker Economy

What is the PPC for a two-worker economy?

Two Costa Rican workers, Carlos and Maria, can each produce coffee and computers. Carlos can produce either 100 pounds of coffee or 1 computer per week. Maria can produce either 100 pounds of coffee or 2 computers per week. Both Carlos and Maria work 50 weeks per year. Find the production possibilities curve for Costa Rica.

To construct the PPC for this two-person economy, we ask first how much coffee Costa Rica could produce if both Carlos and Maria worked full-time producing coffee. Between them they can produce 200 pounds of coffee per week, so in 50 weeks they could produce 10,000 pounds of coffee. Thus if we plot coffee production on the vertical axis of the graph of Costa Rica's PPC, the vertical intercept of the PPC will be 10,000 pounds of coffee per year (point *A* in Figure 15.1). Likewise, if Carlos and Maria produced only computers, between them they could produce 3 computers per week, or 150 computers per year. So the horizontal intercept of Costa Rica's PPC is 150 computers per year (point *B* in Figure 15.1).

FIGURE 15.1

Production Possibilities Curve for a Two-Worker Economy.

In the portion of the PPC between points *A* and *C,* only Maria is producing computers, so the slope of the PPC in that range reflects Maria's opportunity cost of computers in terms of coffee production forgone. At point *C,* Maria spends all her time on computers and Carlos spends all his time on coffee. Between points *C* and *B,* any additional computers must be produced by Carlos. Thus between points *C* and *B* the slope of the PPC reflects Carlos's opportunity cost of producing computers, in terms of coffee production forgone.

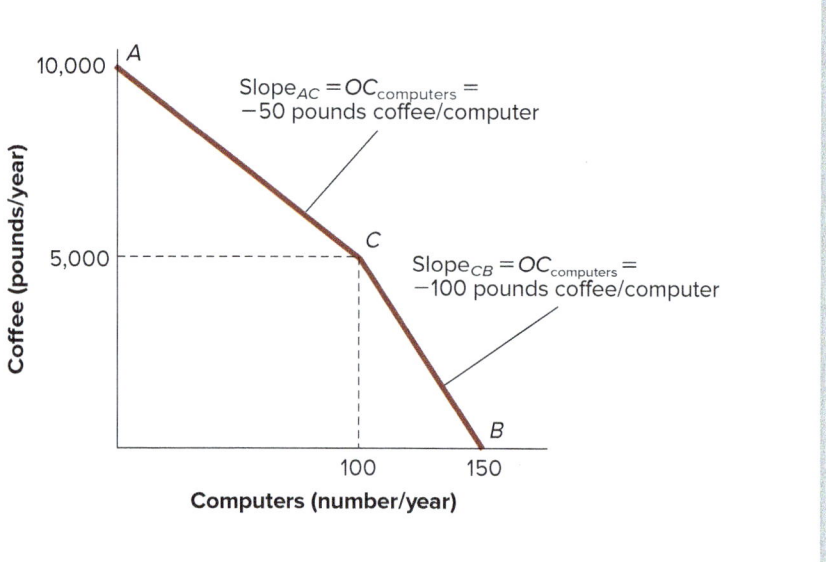

We have found where the Costa Rican PPC intersects the two axes of the graph. To find the rest of the PPC, imagine that Carlos and Maria are producing only coffee (point *A* in Figure 15.1), when they decide that they would like to have some computers as well. In this situation, which worker should switch from producing coffee to producing computers?

To answer this question, we need to find the one with a *comparative advantage* in producing computers. To do this we must calculate opportunity costs. Carlos can produce either 100 pounds of coffee or 1 computer per week. Because producing a computer leaves him one week less to devote to coffee production, which reduces his coffee output by 100 pounds, Carlos's opportunity cost of producing 1 computer is 100 pounds of coffee. Maria can produce either 100 pounds of coffee or 2 computers per week, so her opportunity cost of producing a computer is 100/2, or 50 pounds of coffee. Because Maria's opportunity cost of producing a computer is lower than Carlos's, she has a comparative advantage in producing computers. By the principle of comparative advantage, Maria should be the one to specialize in computer production. For his part, Carlos has a comparative advantage in producing coffee (see Self-Test 15.1), so he should specialize in coffee.

Starting from point A in Figure 15.1, where only coffee is produced, we can imagine that Maria begins to produce increasing numbers of computers. The slope of the line emanating from point A equals Maria's opportunity cost of producing a computer, $OC_{computers}$, where cost is measured as a negative quantity:

$$\text{Slope} = \text{Maria's } OC_{computers} = \frac{\text{loss in coffee}}{\text{gain in computers}}$$

$$= \frac{-100 \text{ pounds of coffee/week}}{2 \text{ computers/week}} = -50 \text{ pounds of coffee/computer.}$$

As Maria increases the share of her time devoted to computer production, we move down along the straight line from point A in Figure 15.1. The slope of the PPC is constant in this region at −50 pounds of coffee per computer, Maria's opportunity cost of computers.

Maria's time is limited to 50 weeks per year, however, so if she keeps increasing her computer production, she will eventually reach a point at which she produces only computers and no coffee. At that point annual production by the two workers taken together will be 100 computers (produced by Maria) and 5,000 pounds of coffee (produced by Carlos, who spends all his time producing coffee). This combination of production is shown at point C on the production possibilities curve.

Once Maria's time is fully devoted to making computers, Costa Rica can increase its computer production only if Carlos begins to build some computers, too. However, Carlos's opportunity cost, measured as pounds of coffee forgone per computer produced, is greater than Maria's. Hence at point C the slope of the PPC changes, creating a "kink" in the graph. The slope of the PPC to the right of point C is given by:

$$\text{Slope} = \text{Carlos's } OC_{computers} = \frac{\text{loss in coffee}}{\text{gain in computers}}$$

$$= \frac{-100 \text{ pounds of coffee/week}}{1 \text{ computer/week}} = -100 \text{ pounds of coffee/computer.}$$

Note that the slope of the PPC to the right of point C is more negative than the slope to the left of point C, so that the PPC declines more sharply to the right of that point. The fact that the opportunity cost of a computer increases as more computers are produced (the Principle of Increasing Opportunity Cost) implies the outwardly bowed shape that is characteristic of a production possibilities curve, as shown in Figure 15.1.

Increasing Opportunity Cost

 SELF-TEST 15.1

Example 15.1 showed that Maria has a comparative advantage in producing computers. Show by comparison of opportunity costs that Carlos has a comparative advantage in producing coffee.

THE MANY-WORKER PRODUCTION POSSIBILITIES CURVE

Although the economy considered in Example 15.1 included only two workers, the main ideas apply to economies with more workers. Suppose, for example, that we added a third Costa Rican worker, Pedro, whose opportunity cost of producing computers is higher than Maria's but lower than Carlos's. The production possibilities curve for this three-person economy would look something like Figure 15.2. Between points *A* and *C* on the PPC shown in Figure 15.2, all computers are produced by Maria, who has the greatest comparative advantage in computer production. Thus the slope of the PPC between points *A* and *C* is determined by Maria's opportunity cost, measured as the amount of coffee production forgone for each additional computer produced.

At point *C* Maria is dedicating all her time to computer production, so someone else must produce any additional computers. Pedro has the next lowest opportunity cost of producing computers, so (following the Principle of Increasing Opportunity Cost) he begins to produce computers at point *C*. The slope of the PPC between points *C* and *D* is determined by Pedro's opportunity cost, which is greater (more negative) than Maria's opportunity cost. At point *D* in Figure 15.2, Pedro is producing all the computers he can, so finally Carlos begins to produce computers as well. Thus the slope of the PPC between points *D* and *B* reflects Carlos's opportunity cost. Because opportunity cost increases as we move from left to right in the figure, the slope of the PPC becomes more and more negative, leading once again to the outwardly bowed shape.

By similar logic, we can construct a case in which there are many workers, perhaps millions. With many workers, the part of the nation's PPC that is associated with each individual worker becomes very small. As a result, the PPC for an economy with many

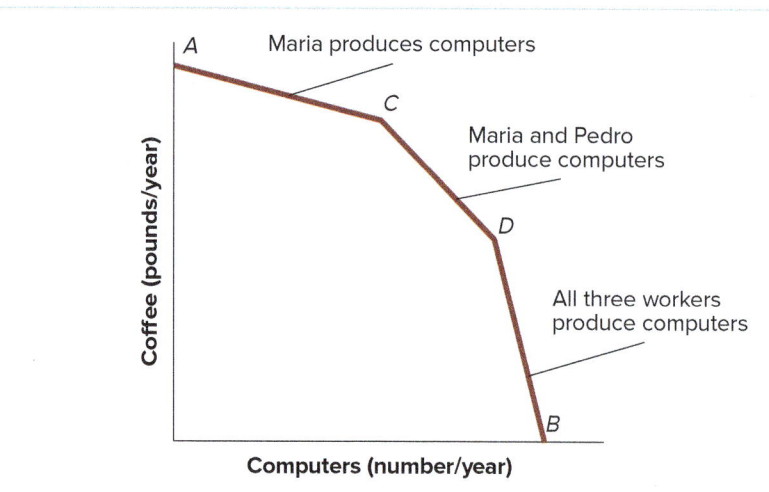

FIGURE 15.2

Production Possibilities Curve for a Three-Worker Economy.

The PPC for a three-person economy has two "kinks," at points *C* and *D*. Between points *A* and *C* only Maria produces computers, and the slope of the PPC represents her opportunity cost of producing computers. At point *C* Maria is spending all her time making computers, so any additional computers will be produced by Pedro, whose comparative advantage is the next greatest. Between points *C* and *D* the slope of the PPC is determined by Pedro's opportunity cost. At point *D* Pedro is also fully occupied producing computers, so that Carlos must begin producing them if computer production is to increase further. Between points *D* and *B* the slope of the PPC reflects Carlos's opportunity cost.

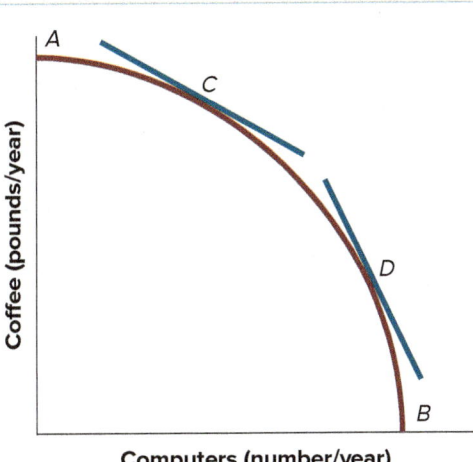

FIGURE 15.3

Production Possibilities Curve for a Many-Worker Economy.

The PPC for a many-worker economy has a smooth, outwardly bowed shape. At each point on the PPC the slope of the curve reflects the opportunity cost, in terms of coffee forgone, of producing an additional computer. For example, the opportunity cost of a computer at point *C* equals the slope of the line that just touches the PPC at that point, and the opportunity cost of a computer at point *D* equals the slope of the line that just touches the PPC there. Because the opportunity cost of producing another computer increases as more computers are produced, the slope of the PPC becomes more and more negative as we read from left to right on the graph.

workers has a smoothly bowed shape, as shown in Figure 15.3. With a smoothly curved PPC, the slope at each point still reflects the opportunity cost of producing an additional computer, as illustrated in Figure 15.3. For example, at point *C* in Figure 15.3, the opportunity cost of producing an extra computer is given by the slope of the line that just touches the PPC at that point. Because computers will be produced first by workers with the greatest comparative advantage (the lowest opportunity cost), the slope of the PPC becomes more and more sharply negative as we read from left to right in the figure.

RECAP

PRODUCTION POSSIBILITIES CURVES

- The production possibilities curve (PPC) for a two-good economy is a graph that shows the maximum amount of one good that can be produced at every possible level of production of the other good.
- The slope of a PPC at any point indicates the opportunity cost, in terms of forgone production of the good on the vertical axis, of increasing production of the good on the horizontal axis by one unit.
- The more of a good that is already being produced, the greater the opportunity cost of increasing production still further. Thus the slope of the PPC becomes more and more negative as we read from left to right, imparting the characteristic outwardly bowed shape of the curve.

CONSUMPTION POSSIBILITIES WITH AND WITHOUT INTERNATIONAL TRADE

A country's production possibilities curve shows the quantities of different goods that its economy can produce. However, economic welfare depends most directly not on what a country can *produce,* but on what its citizens can *consume.* The combinations of goods and services that a country's citizens might feasibly consume are called the country's **consumption possibilities**.

consumption possibilities
the combinations of goods and services that a country's citizens might feasibly consume

The relationship between a country's consumption possibilities and its production possibilities depends on whether the country is open to international trade. In a closed economy with no trade, people can consume only the goods and services produced within their own country. *In a closed economy, then, society's consumption possibilities are identical to its production possibilities.* A situation in which a country is economically self-sufficient, producing everything its citizens consume, is called **autarky**.

autarky a situation in which a country is economically self-sufficient

The case of an open economy, which trades with the rest of the world, is quite different. In an open economy, people are not restricted to consuming what is produced in their own country because part of what they produce can be sent abroad in exchange for other goods and services. Indeed, we will see in this section that opening an economy to trade may allow citizens to consume more of everything. Thus *in an open economy, a society's consumption possibilities are typically greater than (and will never be less than) its production possibilities.* We will illustrate this critical point with reference to the two-worker economy studied earlier in the chapter, then briefly consider the more general case of a many-worker economy.

EXAMPLE 15.2   **Costa Rica's Consumption Possibilities with Trade**

How does opening to trade affect an economy's consumption possibilities?

Two Costa Rican workers, Carlos and Maria, can produce coffee and computers as described in Example 15.1. Initially the country is closed to trade, and Maria produces only computers, while Carlos produces only coffee. Then the country opens up to trade. World prices are such that 80 pounds of coffee can be traded for 1 computer on the international market and vice versa. How does the opening of Costa Rica to trade affect Maria's and Carlos's opportunity to consume coffee and computers?

If Maria is producing only computers and Carlos is producing only coffee, then Costa Rica is at point C on the PPC shown in Figure 15.4 (which is the same as the PPC shown in Figure 15.1). At that point Maria is spending all her time producing 100 computers a year, and Carlos is spending all his time producing 5,000 pounds of coffee a year. If Costa Rica were closed to trade, Maria and Carlos could obtain more coffee only by producing fewer computers. Specifically, starting at point C on the PPC, they could obtain 50 additional pounds of coffee by giving up 1 computer—by having Maria work 1/2 week less on computers and 1/2 week more producing coffee.

If Costa Rica opens up to trade, however, then Maria and Carlos can get 80 pounds of coffee in exchange for 1 computer simply by trading computers for coffee on the international market. In other words, they can get an extra 80 pounds of coffee for each computer they give up. To illustrate the degree to which the opportunity to trade benefits Costa Rica, recall from Example 15.1 that with no trade, Maria's and Carlos's maximum coffee consumption is 10,000 pounds per year (the vertical intercept of the Costa Rican PPC). With the opportunity to trade, however, Maria can trade the 100 computers produced at point C for 8,000 pounds of coffee (80 pounds of coffee per computer × 100 computers). Together with the 5,000 pounds of coffee Carlos produces, the coffee obtained through trade raises Costa Rica's maximum annual coffee consumption from 10,000 to 13,000 pounds per year, as indicated by point F in Figure 15.4. Because trade creates the possibility for Costa Rica to consume as much as 13,000 pounds of coffee per year, point F

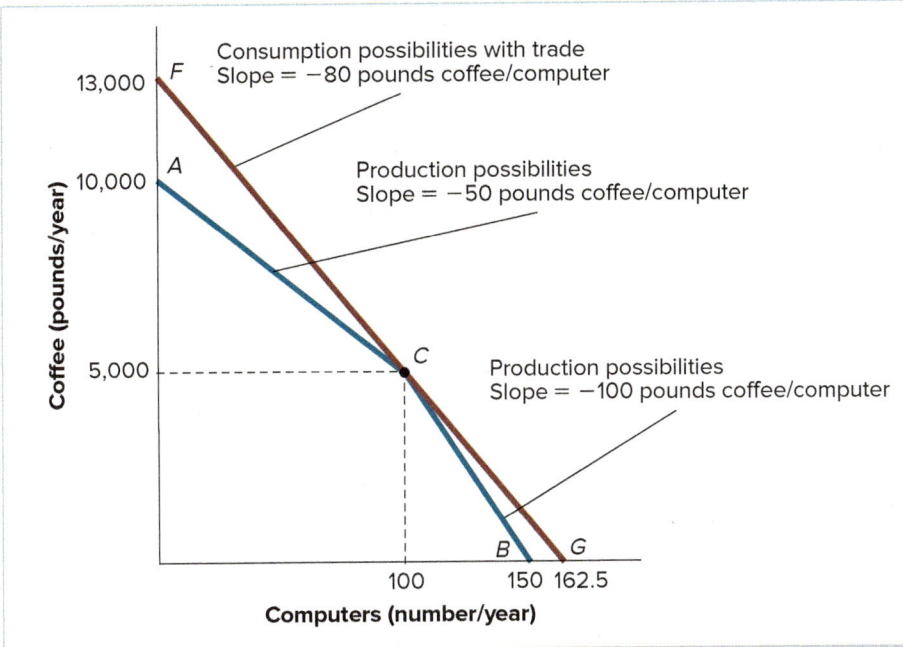

FIGURE 15.4

Costa Rica's Consumption Possibilities with Trade.

Without the opportunity to trade, Costa Rica's consumption possibilities are the same as the Costa Rican PPC, represented by line *ACB*. With the opportunity to trade, however, Costa Ricans can consume at any point along line *FG*.

is included in Costa Rica's consumption possibilities, though it would have been unattainable to the Costa Ricans before the opening up of trade.

Furthermore, with the opportunity to trade, Maria and Carlos can consume any combination of coffee and computers represented on the straight line between points *F* and *C* in Figure 15.4. This straight line has a slope of –80 pounds of coffee per 1 computer, which is the rate at which the two goods can be exchanged on the international market. So, simply by trading computers for coffee, Maria and Carlos can improve their consumption possibilities at any point except *C*, where their production and consumption possibilities are the same.

Suppose instead that, starting from point *C* on Costa Rica's PPC, Maria and Carlos decide they want to consume more computers rather than more coffee. With no ability to trade, the opportunity cost of obtaining 1 more computer at point *C* would be 100 pounds of coffee—that is, the amount of coffee that would be lost by having Carlos work 1 more week at producing an extra computer, and hence 1 week fewer at producing coffee. With trade, however, Costa Ricans can obtain an extra computer at the cost of only 80 pounds of coffee (the price of computers on the international market). In the extreme, if they wanted to consume only computers, the Costa Ricans could trade the 5,000 pounds of coffee Carlos produces at point *C* for 5,000/80 = 62.5 computers, for a total consumption (with the 100 computers Maria produces) of 162.5 computers. This maximum consumption amount is indicated by point *G* in Figure 15.4. Comparing point *G* with point *B*, we can see that the opportunity to trade increased Costa Rica's maximum consumption of computers from 150 to 162.5. (Consuming 162.5 computers a year means consuming 325 computers every two years.)

Furthermore, by trading various amounts of coffee for computers, Costa Ricans can consume any combination of computers and coffee on the straight line between points *C* and *G* in Figure 15.4. Like the segment *FC*, segment *CG* has a slope equal to –80 pounds of coffee per 1 computer, reflecting the rate at which coffee can be traded for computers on the international market. Note that since segments *FC* and *CG* have the same slopes, the line *FG* is a straight line. The line *FG* represents Costa Rica's consumption possibilities—the combinations of coffee and computers that Carlos and Maria might feasibly consume—when the Costa Rican economy is open to trade. By comparing Costa Rica's consumption possibilities without trade (line *ACB*) and with trade (line *FG*), we can see that Maria and Carlos have a wider range of consumption opportunities when their economy is open.

SELF-TEST 15.2

Prior to the opening of trade, suppose that Costa Rican residents consumed 80 computers per year. How much coffee were they able to consume each year? Suppose that the Costa Ricans open up to trade, but they choose to continue to consume 80 computers per year. Now how much coffee can they consume? In answering, use the PPC and consumption possibilities we found in Example 15.2. Does opening to trade make the Cost Ricans better off?

The same points just made in Example 15.2, which illustrates a two-worker economy, apply in the case of a many-worker economy. Figure 15.5 shows this more general case. With many workers, the PPC (curve *ACB* in the figure) is smoothly bowed. Point *A,* where the PPC intercepts the vertical axis, indicates the maximum amount of coffee the economy can produce, and point *B,* the horizontal intercept of the PPC, shows the maximum number of computers the economy can produce. The intermediate points on the PPC represent alternative combinations of coffee and computers that can be produced. As in the two-worker economy, the slope at each point on the PPC indicates the opportunity cost of producing one additional computer. The more computers that are already being produced, the greater the opportunity cost of increasing computer production still further. Hence the slope of the PPC becomes increasingly negative as we read from left to right.

Line *FG* shows the consumption possibilities for this economy if it is open to trade. This line has two key features. First, it is drawn so that it just touches the PPC at point *C* in Figure 15.5. Second, the slope of line *FG* is determined by the relative prices of coffee and computers on the world market. Specifically, as in the two-worker case (Figure 15.4), the slope of line *FG* tells us how much coffee must be exchanged on world markets to obtain an additional computer.

With access to international trade, Costa Rica can consume the greatest amount of both coffee and computers by producing at point *C* on the PPC and trading on the international market to obtain the desired combination of coffee and computers on line *FG.* (The exact combination of coffee and computers Cost Ricans will choose depends on the needs and wants of the population.)

Why should the Costa Ricans produce at point *C*? At point *C,* and only at that point, the slope of the PPC equals the slope of the consumption possibilities line, *FG.* Hence only

FIGURE 15.5

Consumption Possibilities in a Many-Worker Economy.

The PPC for a many-worker economy is the smooth, out-wardly bowed line *ACB*. If the country is open to trade, its consumption possibilities lie on the line *FG,* which just touches the PPC at point *C.* The slope of this line equals the rate at which coffee can be traded for computers at world prices. The country maximizes its consumption possibilities by producing at point *C* and then trading so as to reach its most desired point on line *FG.*

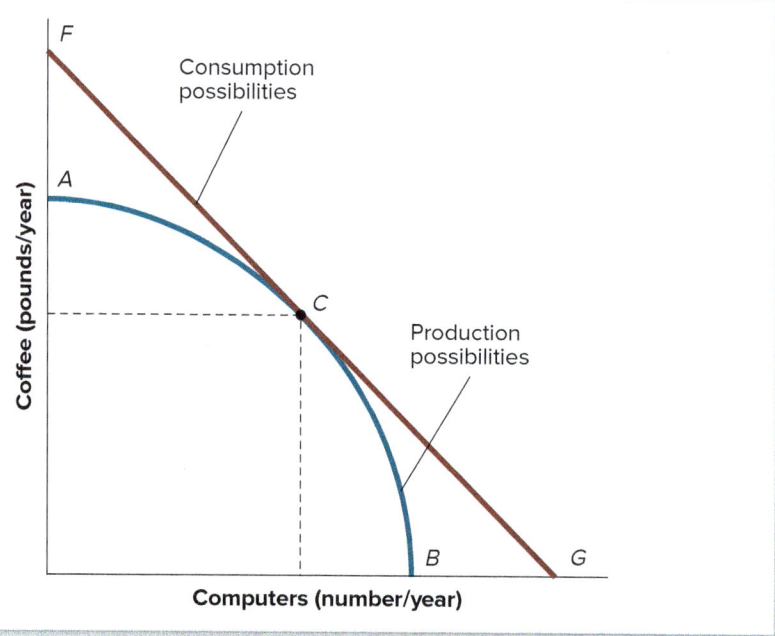

at point *C* is the opportunity cost of increasing domestic computer production equal to the opportunity cost of purchasing an extra computer on the world market. If the opportunity cost of producing a computer domestically exceeded the opportunity cost of purchasing a computer on the world market, Costa Rica would gain by reducing its computer production and importing more computers. Likewise, if the opportunity cost of producing a computer domestically were less than the opportunity cost of purchasing a computer abroad, Costa Rica would gain by increasing computer production and reducing computer imports. Costa Rica's best production combination, therefore, is at point *C,* where the domestic and international opportunity costs of acquiring an extra computer, measured in terms of coffee forgone, are equal.

We have already stated the general conclusion that can be drawn from this analysis. Once again, by opening itself up to trade, a country can consume more of *every* good than if it relied solely on its own production (a situation of *autarky*). Graphically, the consumption possibilities line in Figure 15.5 lies above the production possibilities curve, showing that through trade, Cost Rica can consume combinations of computers and coffee that would not be attainable if its economy were closed to trade.[2]

RECAP

CONSUMPTION POSSIBILITIES AND PRODUCTION POSSIBILITIES

- A country's consumption possibilities are the combinations of goods and services that its citizens might feasibly consume.
- In an economy that is closed to trade, residents can consume only what is produced domestically (a situation of autarky). Hence, in a closed economy, consumption possibilities equal production possibilities.
- The residents of an open economy can trade part of what they produce on international markets. According to the principle of comparative advantage, trade allows everyone to do better than they could otherwise. Thus, in an open economy, consumption possibilities are typically greater than, and will never be less than, production possibilities.
- Graphically, consumption possibilities in an open economy are described by a downward-sloping line that just touches the production possibilities curve (PPC). The slope of this line equals the amount of the good on the vertical axis that must be traded on the international market to obtain one unit of the good on the horizontal axis. A country maximizes its consumption possibilities by producing at the point where the consumption possibilities line just touches the PPC, and then trading so as to reach its most preferred point on the consumption possibilities line.

A SUPPLY AND DEMAND PERSPECTIVE ON TRADE

To this point we have shown that a country can improve its overall consumption possibilities by trading with other countries. In this section we will look more carefully at how international trade affects supply and demand in the markets for specific goods. We will see that when it is costly for workers and firms to change industries, opening up trade with other countries may create groups of winners and losers among producers, workers, and consumers.

Let's see how trade affects the markets for computers and coffee in Costa Rica. Figure 15.6 shows the supply and demand for computers in that country. As usual, the

[2]The single point at which consumption possibilities do *not* lie above production possibilities in Figure 15.5 is at point *C,* where production possibilities and consumption possibilities are the same. If Costa Rican residents happen to prefer the combination of computers and coffee at point *C* to any other point on *FG,* then they realize no benefit from trade.

FIGURE 15.6

The Market for Computers in Costa Rica.

If Costa Rica is closed to international trade, the equilibrium price and quantity of computers are determined by the intersection of the domestic supply and demand curves at point E. But if Costa Rica is open to trade, the domestic price of computers must equal the world price. At that price, Costa Ricans will demand q_D computers, but domestic producers will supply only q_S computers. Thus $q_D - q_S$ computers must be imported from abroad.

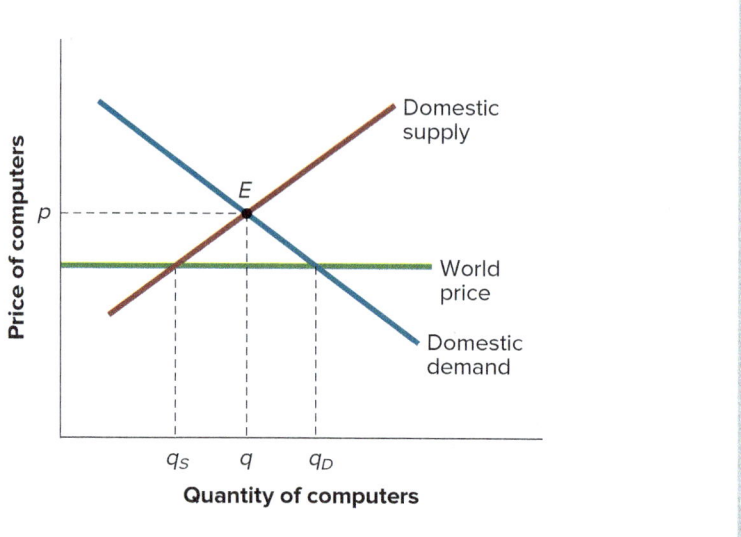

price is shown on the vertical axis and the quantity on the horizontal axis. For now, think of the price of computers as being measured in terms of coffee rather than in terms of dollars (in other words, we measure the price of computers *relative* to the price of the other good in the economy). As usual, the upward-sloping curve in Figure 15.6 is the supply curve of computers, in this case for computers produced in Costa Rica; and the downward-sloping curve is the demand curve for computers by Costa Rican residents. The supply curve for computers in Costa Rica reflects the opportunity cost of supplying computers (see Chapter 3, *Supply and Demand*). Specifically, at any level of computer production, the relative price at which Costa Rican firms are willing to supply an additional computer equals their opportunity cost of doing so. The demand curve, which tells us the number of computers Costa Ricans will purchase at each relative price, reflects the preferences and buying power of Costa Rican consumers.

If the Costa Rican economy is closed to international trade, then market equilibrium occurs where the domestic supply and demand curves intersect, at point E in Figure 15.6. The equilibrium price will be p and the equilibrium quantity, q.

If Costa Rica opens its market to trade, however, the relevant price for computers becomes the **world price** of computers, the price at which computers are traded internationally. The world price for computers is determined by the worldwide supply and demand for computers. If we assume that Costa Rica's computer market is too small to affect the world price for computers very much, the world price can be treated as fixed, and represented by a horizontal line in the figure. Figure 15.6 shows the world price for computers as being lower than Costa Rica's closed-economy price.

If Costa Ricans are free to buy and sell computers on the international market, then the price of computers in Costa Rica must be the same as the world price. (No one in Costa Rica will buy a computer at a price above the world price, and no one will sell one at a price below the world price.) Figure 15.6 shows that at the world price, Costa Rican consumers and firms demand q_D computers, but Costa Rican computer producers will supply only q_S computers. The difference between the two quantities, $q_D - q_S$, is the number of computers that Costa Rica must import from abroad. Figure 15.6 illustrates a general conclusion: *If the price of a good or service in a closed economy is greater than the world price, and that economy opens itself to trade, the economy will tend to become a net importer of that good or service.*

A different outcome occurs in Costa Rica's coffee market, shown in Figure 15.7. The price of coffee (measured relative to the price of computers) is shown on the vertical axis and the quantity of coffee on the horizontal axis. The downward-sloping demand curve in

world price the price at which a good or service is traded on international markets

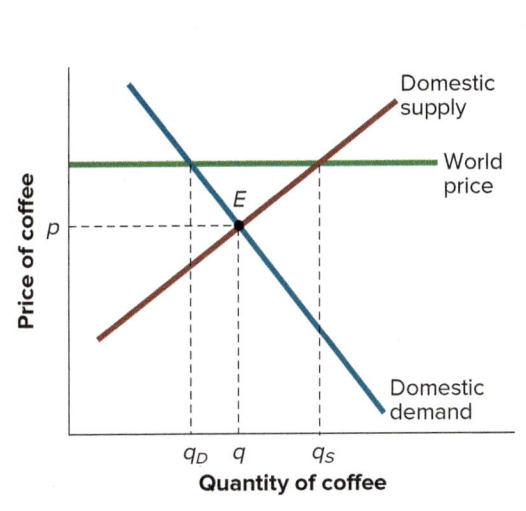

FIGURE 15.7

The Market for Coffee in Costa Rica.

With no international trade, the equilibrium price and quantity of coffee in Costa Rica are determined by the intersection of the domestic supply and demand curves (point E). But if the country opens to trade, the domestic price of coffee must equal the world price. At the higher world price, Costa Ricans will demand the quantity of coffee q_D, less than the amount supplied by Costa Rican producers, q_S. The excess coffee supplied by Costa Rican producers, $q_S - q_D$, is exported.

the figure shows how much coffee Costa Rican consumers want to buy at each relative price, and the upward-sloping supply curve how much coffee Costa Rican producers are willing to supply at each relative price. If Costa Rica's economy is closed to trade with the rest of the world, then equilibrium in the market for coffee will occur at point E, where the domestic demand and supply curves intersect. The quantity produced will be q and the price p.

Now imagine that Costa Rica opens its coffee market to international trade. As in the case of computers, if free trade in coffee is permitted, then the prevailing price for coffee in Costa Rica must be the same as the world price. Unlike the case of computers, however, the world price of coffee as shown in Figure 15.7 is *higher* than the domestic equilibrium price. How do we know that the world price of coffee will be higher than the domestic price? Recall that the price of coffee is measured relative to the price of computers, and vice versa. If the price of computers relative to the price of coffee is higher in Costa Rica than in the world market, then the price of coffee relative to the price of computers must be lower, as each price is the reciprocal of the other. More generally, as we saw in Chapter 2, *Comparative Advantage,* when two people or two countries trade with each other, neither can have a comparative advantage in *every* good and service. Thus, in an example with only two goods, if non–Costa Rican producers have a comparative advantage in computers, reflected in the lower cost of computers relative to coffee in the world market, then Costa Rican producers must have a comparative advantage in coffee. By definition, this comparative advantage implies that the opportunity cost of coffee in terms of computers must be lower in Costa Rica than in the rest of the world.

Figure 15.7 shows that at the world price for coffee, Costa Rican producers are willing to supply q_S coffee, while Costa Rican consumers want to purchase a smaller amount, q_D. The difference between domestic production and domestic consumption, $q_S - q_D$, is exported to the world market. The general conclusion of Figure 15.7 is this: *If the price of a good or service in a closed economy is lower than the world price, and that economy opens itself to trade, the economy will tend to become a net exporter of that good or service.*

These examples illustrate how the market translates comparative advantage into mutually beneficial gains from trade. If trade is unrestricted, then countries with a comparative advantage in a particular good will profit by supplying that good to the world market and using the revenue earned to import goods in which they do not have a comparative advantage. Thus the workings of the free market automatically ensure that goods will be produced where the opportunity cost is lowest, leading to the highest possible consumption possibilities for the world as a whole.

WINNERS AND LOSERS FROM TRADE

If trade is so wonderful, why do politicians so often resist free trade and "globalization"? The reason is that although free trade benefits the economy as a whole, specific groups may not benefit. Groups who are hurt by trade, and the politicians they elect, may support policies that restrict the free flow of goods and services across borders.

The supply and demand analyses shown in Figures 15.6 and 15.7 are useful in clarifying who gains and who loses when an economy opens up to trade. Look first at Figure 15.6, which shows the market for computers in Costa Rica. When Costa Rica opens its computer market to international competition, Costa Rican consumers enjoy a larger quantity of computers at a lower price. Clearly, Costa Rican computer users benefit from the free trade in computers. In general, *domestic consumers of imported goods benefit from free trade.* However, Costa Rican computer producers and their workers will not be so happy about opening their market to international competition. The fall in computer prices to the international level implies that less efficient domestic producers will go out of business, and that those who remain will earn lower profits. Unemployment in the Costa Rican computer industry will rise and may persist over time, particularly if displaced computer workers cannot easily move to a new industry. The wages paid to Costa Rican computer workers will also fall, reflecting the lower relative price of computers. We see that, in general, *domestic producers of imported goods, and workers in imported-good sectors, are hurt by free trade.*

Consumers are helped, while producers and workers are hurt, when imports increase. The opposite conclusions apply for an increase in exports (see Figure 15.7). In the example of Costa Rica, an opening of the coffee market raises the domestic price of coffee to the world price and creates the opportunity for Costa Rica to export coffee. Domestic producers of coffee benefit from the increased market (they can now sell coffee abroad as well as at home) and from the higher price of their product. Domestic workers in the coffee sector benefit too, as they are more in demand. In short, *domestic producers of exported goods, and workers in exported-good sectors, benefit from free trade.* Costa Rican coffee drinkers will be less enthusiastic, however, since they must now have to pay the higher world price of coffee and can therefore consume less. *Thus domestic consumers of exported goods are hurt by free trade.*

Free trade is *efficient* in the sense that it increases the size of the pie available to the economy. Indeed, the efficiency of free trade is an application of the Equilibrium Principle: Markets in equilibrium leave no unexploited opportunities for individuals. Despite the efficiency of free trade, however, some groups may lose from trade, which generates political pressures to block or restrict trade. In the next section we will discuss the major types of policy used to restrict trade.

The Economic Naturalist 15.1

What is the China trade shock?

The China trade shock, a term most commonly associated with economists David Autor, David Dorn, and Gordon Hanson, is used to describe the dramatic change in international trade patterns that resulted from China's rise as a major player in the global economy over the past few decades.

In a series of influential studies, these economists and their collaborators investigated the costs of the shock to U.S. workers. They found that employment has fallen in U.S. industries and regions most exposed to import competition from China—something that our theory in this chapter helps explain. However, they did not find strong evidence of simultaneous offsetting employment increases in other sectors in the same regions, suggesting that the transition of workers into sectors in which the U.S. has comparative advantage has been neither quick nor easy—something that the theory does not emphasize.

Overall, these economists conclude that workers' adjustment to trade shocks is often a slow and difficult process, and that local labor force participation rates and unemployment rates in affected regions may take a decade or more to recover. Moreover, the slow adjustment means that trade shocks could lead to prolonged economic and social problems in affected communities.

While the research underlying these conclusions is still relatively new and is still being examined, it serves as a reminder that for many workers, the short-term costs of trade may outweigh the short-term benefits. While opposition to trade among such workers is understandable, we should not conclude that the overall costs of trade outweigh the overall benefits. Rather, as these economists conclude in one of their studies:

> Better understanding when and where trade is costly, and how and why it may be beneficial, is a key item on the research agenda for trade and labor economists. Developing effective tools for managing and mitigating the costs of trade adjustment should be high on the agenda for policymakers and applied economists.[3]

RECAP

A SUPPLY AND DEMAND PERSPECTIVE ON TRADE

- For a closed economy, the domestic supply and demand for a good or service determine the equilibrium price and quantity of that good or service.
- In an open economy, the price of a good or service traded on international markets equals the world price. If the domestic quantity supplied at the world price exceeds the domestic quantity demanded, the difference will be exported to the world market. If the domestic quantity demanded at the world price exceeds the domestic quantity supplied, the difference will be imported.
- Generally, if the price of a good or service in a closed economy is lower than the world price and the economy opens to trade, the country will become a net exporter of that good or service. If the closed-economy price is higher than the world price and the economy opens to trade, the country will tend to become a net importer of the good or service.
- Consumers of imported goods, producers of exported goods, and workers in exported-good sectors benefit from trade, whereas consumers of exported goods, producers of imported goods, and workers in imported-good sectors are hurt by trade. Those groups that are hurt, and the politicians they elect, may support enacting barriers to trade.

TRADE WINNERS AND LOSERS

Winners

- Consumers of imported goods
- Producers of exported goods
- Workers in exported-good sectors

Losers

- Consumers of exported goods
- Producers of imported goods
- Workers in imported-good sectors

[3]David Autor, David Dorn, and Gordon Hanson, "The China Shock: Learning from Labor Market Adjustment to Large Changes in Trade," *Annual Review of Economics* 8 (October 2016), pp. 205–240.

PROTECTIONIST POLICIES: TARIFFS AND QUOTAS

protectionism the view that free trade is injurious and should be restricted

tariff a tax imposed on an imported good

quota a legal limit on the quantity of a good that may be imported

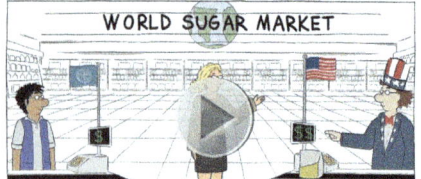

▶ Visit your instructor's Connect course and access your eBook to view this video.

Why do consumers in the United States often pay more than double the world price for sugar?

The view that free trade is injurious and should be restricted is known as **protectionism**. Supporters of this view believe the government should attempt to "protect" domestic markets by raising legal barriers to imports. (Interestingly, protectionists rarely attempt to restrict exports, even though they hurt local consumers of the exported good.) Two of the most common types of such barriers are tariffs and quotas. A **tariff** is a tax imposed on an imported good. A **quota** is a legal limit on the quantity of a good that may be imported.

TARIFFS

The effects of tariffs and quotas can be explained using supply and demand diagrams. Suppose that Costa Rican computer makers, dismayed by the penetration of "their" market by imported computers, persuade their government to impose a tariff—that is, a tax—on every computer imported into the country. Computers produced in Costa Rica will be exempt from the tax. Figure 15.8 shows the likely effects of this tariff on the domestic Costa Rican computer market. The lower of the two horizontal lines in the figure indicates the world price of computers, not including the tariff. The higher of the two lines indicates the price Costa Rican consumers will actually pay for imported computers, including the tariff. We refer to the price of computers including the tariff as p_T. The vertical distance between the two lines equals the amount of the tariff that is imposed on each imported computer.

From the point of view of domestic Costa Rican producers and consumers, the imposition of the tariff has the same effects as an equivalent increase in the world price of computers. Because the price (including the tariff) of imported computers has risen, Costa Rican computer producers will be able to raise the price they charge for their computers to the world price plus tariff, p_T. Thus the price Costa Rican consumers must pay—whether their computers are imported or not—equals p_T, represented by the upper horizontal line in Figure 15.8.

The rise in the price of computers created by the tariff affects the quantities of computers supplied and the quantities demanded by Costa Ricans. Domestic computer producers, facing a higher price for computers, increase their production from q_S to q'_S (see Figure 15.8).

FIGURE 15.8

The Market for Computers after the Imposition of an Import Tariff.

The imposition of a tariff on imported computers raises the price of computers in Costa Rica to the world price plus tariff, p_T, represented by the upper horizontal line. Domestic production of computers rises from q_S to q'_S, domestic purchases of computers fall from q_D to q'_D, and computer imports fall from $q_D - q_S$ to $q'_D - q'_S$. Costa Rican consumers are worse off and Costa Rican computer producers are better off. The Costa Rican government collects revenue from the tariff equal to the area of the pale blue rectangle.

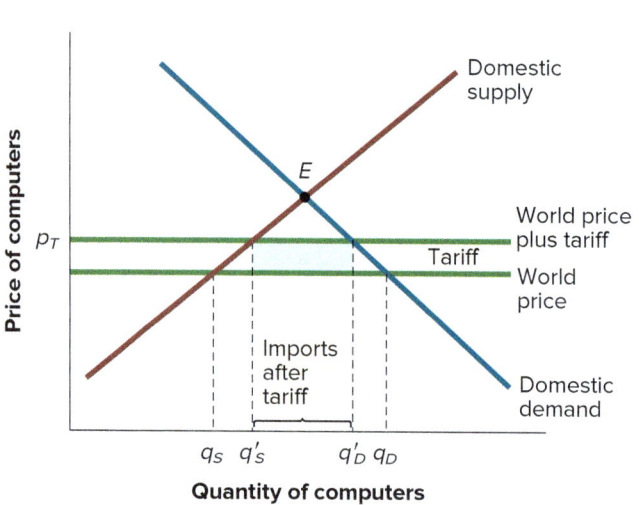

Costa Rican consumers, also reacting to the higher price, reduce their computer purchases from q_D to q'_D. As a result, the number of imported computers–the difference between domestic purchases and domestic production–falls from $q_D - q_S$ to $q'_D - q'_S$.

Who are the winners and the losers from the tariff, then? Relative to an environment with free trade and no tariff, the winners are the domestic computer producers, who sell more computers and receive a higher price for them. The clearest losers are Costa Rican consumers, who must now pay more for their computers. Another winner is the government, which collects revenue from the tariff. The blue area in Figure 15.8 shows the amount of revenue the government collects, equal to the quantity of computer imports after the imposition of the tariff, $q'_D - q'_S$, times the amount of the tariff.

EXAMPLE 15.3   A Tariff on Imported Computers

What are the effects of a tariff on trade?

Suppose that the Costa Rican market for computers is represented by Figure 15.9. Thus, if the Costa Rican economy is closed to trade, the equilibrium price for computers would be $2,000, and 2,000 computers would be bought and sold in the Costa Rican computer market every year (point E). Assuming that the world price of computers is $1,400, how would this market be affected by opening to trade, and how would it be affected by the imposition of a tariff of $400 per computer?

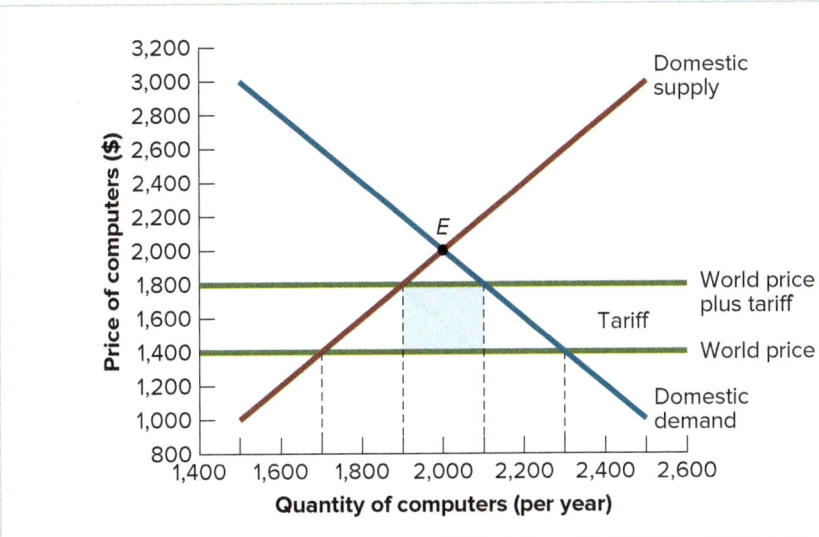

FIGURE 15.9

The Market for Computers in Costa Rica after the Imposition of an Import Tariff.

A tariff of $400 per computer raises the price of computers by $400 and reduces imports by 400 computers per year.

If the economy opens to trade, the domestic price of computers must equal the world price of $1,400. At this price, the domestic quantity demanded is 2,300 computers per year and the domestic quantity supplied is 1,700 computers per year. Imports equal the difference between the domestic quantities demanded and supplied, or 2,300 − 1,700 = 600 computers per year.

The imposition of a tariff of $400 per computer raises the price from $1,400 to $1,800. This price rise causes Costa Rican computer producers to increase their production from 1,700 to 1,900 computers per year, and it causes Costa Rican consumers to reduce their computer purchases from 2,300 to 2,100. As a result, the number of imported computers—the difference between domestic purchases and domestic production—falls from 600 to 200 (2,100 − 1,900).

Thus the tariff has raised the price of computers by $400 and reduced imports by 400 computers per year. The tariff revenue collected by the government is $400 per imported computer times 200 computers per year = $80,000 per year.

QUOTAS

An alternative to a tariff is a quota, or legal limit, on the number or value of foreign goods that can be imported. One means of enforcing a quota is to require importers to obtain a license or permit for each good they bring into the country. The government then distributes exactly the same number of permits as the number of goods that may be imported under the quota.

How does the imposition of a quota on, say, computers affect the domestic market for computers? Figure 15.10, which is similar to Figure 15.8, illustrates the effect of a quota on imported computers. As before, assume that at first there are no restrictions on trade. Consumers pay the world price for computers, and $q_D - q_S$ computers are imported. Now suppose once more that domestic computer producers complain to the government about competition from foreign computer makers, and the government agrees to act. However, this time, instead of a tariff, the government imposes a quota on the number of computers that can be imported. For comparability with the tariff analyzed in Figure 15.8, let's assume that the quota permits the same level of imports as entered the country under the tariff: specifically, $q'_D - q'_S$ computers. What effect does this ruling have on the domestic market for computers?

After the imposition of the quota, the quantity of computers supplied to the Costa Rican market is the production of domestic firms plus the $q'_D - q'_S$ imported computers allowed under the quota. Figure 15.10 shows the quantity of computers supplied inclusive of the quota. The total supply curve, labeled "Domestic supply plus quota," is the same as the domestic supply curve shifted $q'_D - q'_S$ units to the right. The domestic demand curve is the same as in Figure 15.8. Equilibrium in the domestic market for computers occurs at point F in Figure 15.10, at the intersection of the supply curve including the quota and the domestic demand curve. The figure shows that, relative to the initial situation with free trade, the quota (1) raises the domestic price of computers above the world price, to the level marked p_T in Figure 15.10; (2) reduces domestic purchases of computers

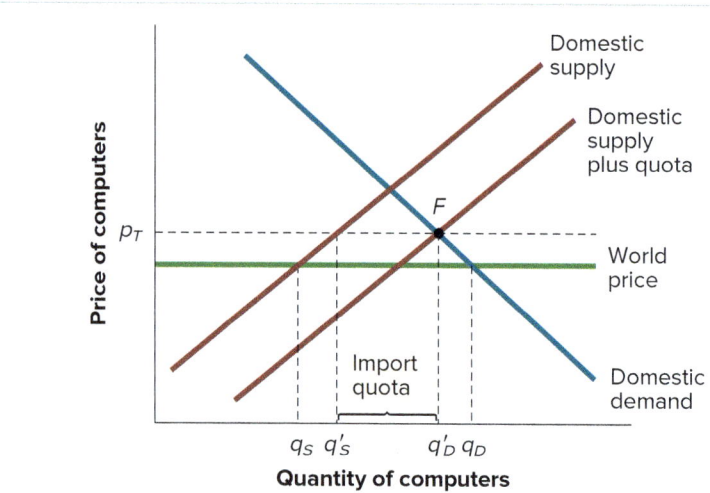

FIGURE 15.10

The Market for Computers after the Imposition of an Import Quota.

The figure shows the effects of the imposition of a quota that permits only $q'_D - q'_S$ computers to be imported. The total supply of computers to the domestic economy equals the domestic economy equals the domestic supply curve shifted to the right by $q'_D - q'_S$ units (the fixed amount of imports). Market equilibrium occurs at point F. The effects of the quota on the domestic market are identical to those of the tariff analyzed in Figure 15.8. The domestic price rises to p_T, domestic production of computers rises from q_S to q'_S, domestic purchases of computers fall from q_D to q'_D, and computer imports fall from $q_D - q_s$ to $q'_D - q'_s$. The quota differs from the tariff in that under a quota system the government collects no revenue.

from q_D to q'_D; (3) increases domestic production of computers from q_S to q'_S; and (4) reduces imports to $q'_D - q'_S$, consistent with a quota. Like a tariff, the quota helps domestic producers by increasing their sales and the price they receive for their output, while hurting domestic consumers by forcing them to pay a higher price.

Interestingly, under our assumption that the quota is set to permit the same level of imports as the tariff, the effects on the domestic market of the tariff (Figure 15.8) and the quota (Figure 15.10) are not only similar, they are *equivalent*. Comparing Figures 15.8 and 15.10, you can see that the two policies have identical effects on the domestic price, domestic purchases, domestic production, and imports.

Although the market effects of a tariff and a quota are the same, there is one important difference between the two policies, which is that a tariff generates revenue for the government, whereas a quota does not. With a quota, the revenue that would have gone to the government goes instead to those firms that hold the import licenses. A holder of an import license can purchase a computer at the world price and resell it in the domestic market at price p_T, pocketing the difference. Thus with a tariff the government collects the difference between the world price and the domestic market price of the good; with a quota, private firms or individuals collect that difference. Why then would the government ever impose a quota rather than a tariff? One possibility is that the distribution of import licenses is a means of rewarding the government's political supporters.

EXAMPLE 15.4   Effects of an Import Quota

What are the effects of an import quota on trade?

Suppose the supply of and demand for computers in Costa Rica, as well as the world price of computers, are as given in Figure 15.11. Suppose that the government imposes a quota of 200 on the number of computers that can be imported. What effect would this have on the domestic market for computers (relative to the free-trade alternative)?

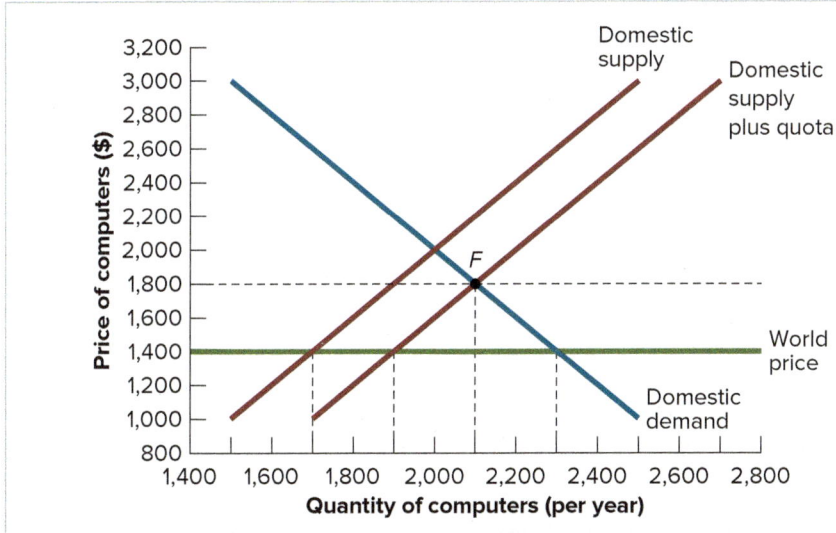

FIGURE 15.11

The Market for Computers in Costa Rica after the Imposition of an Import Quota.

A quota of 200 computers per year raises the price of computers by $400 and reduces imports by 400 computers per year.

After the quota is imposed, the equilibrium in the domestic market occurs at point *F* in the figure. As the figure shows, relative to free trade, the domestic price increases to $1,800 per computer, domestic purchases of computers decrease to 2,100, domestic production of computers increases to 1,900, and imports decrease to 200 (the difference between the 2,100 computers demanded and the 1,900 computers domestically produced).

Note that the domestic price, domestic production, and domestic demand are the same in Examples 15.3 and 15.4. Thus, under the assumptions we made, the tariff and the quota have the same effects on the domestic market for computers. The only difference between the two policies is that with a quota, the government does not get the tariff revenue it got in Example 15.3. That revenue goes instead to the holders of import licenses, who can buy computers on the world market at $1,400 and sell them in the domestic market at $1,800.

The Economic Naturalist 15.2

Why did the United States impose tariffs on imports from China?

Starting in 2018, the United States imposed several rounds of tariffs on commodities and products imported from China. The tariffs, initially ranging from 10 to 25 percent, were applied to imports worth hundreds of billions of dollars in total. In retaliation, China imposed tariffs of 5 to 25 percent on more than a hundred billion dollars' worth of goods imported from the United States.

As our analysis in this chapter predicts, studies show that the U.S. tariffs were largely reflected in higher prices for American consumers and for American producers who buy the affected goods.[4] The price of these goods increased not only when they were imported, but also, through reduced competition, when they were produced in the United States. The Chinese tariffs also hurt American producers who export to China. The overall costs of this trade war to Americans were thus substantial. Why did the United States start it?

One stated reason for imposing the tariffs was that U.S. trade negotiators were concerned that China was violating U.S. intellectual property rights, for example, by not enforcing patent laws or by requiring U.S. firms to share technology if they want to do business in China. Loss of intellectual property disadvantages U.S. producers in the long run. In this context, imposing tariffs on imports from China might be viewed as a bargaining chip in the negotiations about U.S. intellectual property rights. Concerns about worker protections, environmental protections, and regulatory differences have also historically influenced trade policy.

Another stated reason for the tariffs was national security (an issue we return to in The Economic Naturalist 15.3). Traditionally, countries have emphasized maintaining food and defense independence through local production. More recently, the COVID-19 pandemic also highlighted the vulnerability of countries that rely on trading partners for medications and medical equipment, as well as other essential supplies, while the war in Ukraine highlighted additional vulnerabilities, such as energy dependence.

While it remains to be seen how trade relations between the United States and China further develop, a range of political and economic issues between the two countries, going beyond those analyzed in this chapter, are likely to affect the negotiations.

Tariffs and quotas are not the only barriers to trade that governments erect. Importers may be subject to unnecessarily complex bureaucratic rules (so-called red tape barriers), and regulations of goods that are nominally intended to promote health and safety sometimes have the side effect, whether intentionally or unintentionally, of restricting trade. One example is European restrictions on imports of genetically modified foods. Although these

---

[4]See, for example: Mary Amiti, Stephen J. Redding, and David Weinstein, "The Impact of the 2018 Tariffs on Prices and Welfare," *Journal of Economic Perspectives* 33, no. 4 (2019), pp. 187–210; and Pablo D. Fajgelbaum, Pinelopi K. Goldberg, Patrick J. Kennedy, and Amit K. Khandelwal, "The Return to Protectionism," *Quarterly Journal of Economics* 135, no. 1 (2019), pp. 1–55.

regulations were motivated in part by concerns about the safety of such foods, they also help protect Europe's politically powerful farmers from foreign competition.

THE INEFFICIENCY OF PROTECTIONISM

Free trade is efficient because it allows countries to specialize in the production of goods and services in which they have the greatest comparative advantage. Conversely, protectionist policies that limit trade are inefficient—they reduce the total economic pie. (Recall the Efficiency Principle introduced in Chapter 3, *Supply and Demand*, that efficiency is an important social goal.) Why, then, do governments adopt such policies? The reason is similar to why some city governments impose rent controls (see Chapter 3). Although rent controls reduce economic welfare overall, some people benefit from them— namely, the tenants whose rents are held artificially below market level. Similarly, as we have seen in this section, tariffs and quotas benefit certain groups. Those who benefit from these restrictions (such as firms facing import competition, and the workers in such firms) may support politicians who promise to enact the restrictions.

Why did the U.S. impose tariffs on imports from China?

 Efficiency

The fact that free trade is efficient suggests an alternative to trade restrictions, however. Because eliminating restrictions on trade increases the overall economic pie, in general the winners from free trade will be able to compensate the losers in such a way that everyone becomes better off. Government programs that assist workers displaced by import competition are an example of such compensation. They include programs to expand job training and retraining opportunities, especially for the less-educated, who are more likely to be hurt by competition from abroad; to provide transition assistance for displaced workers, including support for internal migration within the U.S. from regions with declining industries to regions with expanding industries; to mitigate residential and educational segregation and increase the access of those left behind to employment and educational opportunities; and to promote community redevelopment in regions with declining industries.

While by no means an easy task, developing and improving such programs, and making them widely available, could do a lot to help those who lose from trade. Spreading the benefits of free trade—or at least reducing its adverse effects on certain groups— reduces the incentives of those groups to oppose free trade.

Although we have focused on the winners and losers from trade, not all opposition to free trade is motivated by economic interest. For example, many who oppose further opening to trade cite environmental concerns. Protecting the environment is an important and laudable goal, but once again the Efficiency Principle suggests that restricting trade may not be the most effective means of achieving that goal. Restricting trade lowers world income, reducing the resources available to deal with environmental problems. Furthermore, much of the income loss arising from barriers to trade is absorbed by poor nations trying to develop their economies. For this reason, leaders of developing countries are among the strongest advocates of free trade.

The Economic Naturalist 15.3

Why did the United States impose restrictions on exports to China?

In late 2022, the United States imposed bans and other controls on the export of certain products and technologies to China. The controlled list includes computer chips and items used in the development and production of semiconductors. (Both chips and semiconductors are essential components in electronic devices, from cellphones to cars.) Our analysis in this chapter predicts that such export restrictions would hurt American producers of exported goods, as well as workers in exported-good sectors. Why did the United States impose the restrictions?

As mentioned in The Economic Naturalist 15.2, the COVID-19 pandemic and Russia's war in Ukraine showed the vulnerability of global supply chains. A country may thus wish to impose *import* restrictions aimed at retaining its capacity to produce critical goods and services such as food, medicine, energy, and national defense. But could such national security concerns explain *export* restrictions?

The answer is yes. In addition to their use in consumer goods, chips and semiconductor technology are essential ingredients in other important sectors related to national security, such as artificial intelligence (AI) and advanced weapons and surveillance systems. The export restrictions imposed by the United States were part of a strategic decision by the U.S. government to cut off China's ability to access and develop such technologies motivated by a desire to maintain the United States's technological edge in key areas.

As this and the previous Economic Naturalist show, there may be reasonable exceptions to allowing unrestricted free trade. While issues such as national security are not the focus of the economic analysis of trade in this chapter, they are important considerations for policymakers. That said, from an economic point of view, restricting trade comes with a cost. Policymakers should therefore be careful when considering trade restrictions, making sure they are truly necessary, and that they are not merely being promoted by certain interest groups that stand to gain from reduced competition.

> **RECAP**
>
> **PROTECTIONIST POLICIES: TARIFFS AND QUOTAS**
> - The view that free trade is injurious and should be restricted is called protectionism.
> - The two most common types of trade barriers are tariffs, or taxes on imported goods, and quotas, legal limits on the quantity that can be imported. A tariff raises the domestic price to the world price plus the tariff. The result is increased domestic production, reduced domestic consumption, and fewer imports. A quota has effects on the domestic market that are similar to those of a tariff. The main difference is that under a quota, the government does not collect tariff revenue.
> - Trade barriers are inefficient; they reduce the overall size of the economic pie. Thus, in general, the winners from free trade should be able to compensate the losers in such a way that everyone becomes better off. Government programs to help workers displaced by import competition are an example of such compensation. They are not easy to develop and implement. Without effective compensation, however, opposition to trade by those who are hurt by it may lead to the inefficiency brought by protectionism.

SUMMARY

- According to the *Principle of Comparative Advantage,* the best economic outcomes occur when each nation specializes in the goods and services at which it is relatively most productive and then trades with other nations to obtain the goods and services its citizens desire. *(LO1)*

- The production possibilities curve (PPC) of a country is a graph that describes the maximum amount of one good that can be produced at every possible level of production of the other good. At any point the slope of a PPC indicates the opportunity cost, in terms of forgone production of the good on the vertical axis, of increasing production

of the good on the horizontal axis by one unit. The more of a good that is already being produced, the greater the opportunity cost of increasing production still further. Thus the slope of a PPC becomes more and more negative as we read from left to right. When an economy has many workers, the PPC has a smooth, outwardly bowed shape. *(LO2)*

- A country's *consumption possibilities* are the combinations of goods and services that might feasibly be consumed by its citizens. In a *closed economy*—one that does not trade with other countries—the citizens' consumption possibilities are identical to their production possibilities. But in an *open economy*—one that does trade with other countries—consumption possibilities are typically greater than, and never less than, the economy's production possibilities. Graphically, an open economy's consumption possibilities are described by a downward-sloping line that just touches the PPC, whose slope equals the amount of the good on the vertical axis that must be traded to obtain one unit of the good on the horizontal axis. A country achieves its highest consumption possibilities by producing at the point where the consumption possibilities line just touches the PPC and then trading to obtain the most preferred point on the consumption possibilities line. *(LO2)*

• In a closed economy, the relative price of a good or service is determined at the intersection of the supply curve of domestic producers and the demand curve of domestic consumers. In an open economy, the relative price of a good or service equals the *world price*—the price determined by supply and demand in the world economy. If the price of a good or service in a closed economy is greater than the world price and the country opens its market to trade, it will become a net importer of that good or service. But if the closed-economy price

is below the world price and the country opens itself to trade, it will become a net exporter of that good or service. *(LO3)*

• Although free trade is beneficial to the economy as a whole, some groups—such as domestic producers of imported goods, and workers in imported-good sectors—are hurt by free trade. Groups that are hurt by trade may support political candidates who promise to impose *protectionist* measures, such as tariffs or quotas. A *tariff* is a tax on an imported good that has the effect of raising the domestic price of the good. A higher domestic price increases domestic supply, reduces domestic demand, and reduces imports of the good. A *quota*, which is a legal limit on the amount of a good that may be imported, has the same effects as a tariff, except that the government collects no tax revenue. (The equivalent amount of revenue goes instead to those firms with the legal authority to import goods.) Because free trade is efficient, the winners from free trade should be able to compensate the losers so that everyone becomes better off. Thus policies to assist those who are harmed by trade, such as assistance and retraining for workers idled by imports, are usually preferable to trade restrictions. *(LO4)*

KEY TERMS

autarky
closed economy
consumption possibilities

open economy
protectionism
quota

tariff
world price

REVIEW QUESTIONS

1. Imagine that, all else equal, it takes U.S. workers a quarter of the time it takes Chinese workers to design a new mobile phone model. Also, imagine that it takes U.S. workers half the time it takes Chinese workers to produce a million pieces of the new model. Which of the two countries has absolute advantage, and which has comparative advantage, in designing a new model? In producing it? *(LO1)*

2. Sketch a PPC for a four-worker economy that produces two goods, hot dogs and hamburgers. Give an economic interpretation of the vertical intercept, the horizontal intercept, and the slope of the graph. *(LO2)*

3. What is meant by the "consumption possibilities" of a country? How are consumption possibilities related to production possibilities in a closed economy? In an open economy? *(LO2)*

4. A small, open economy is equally productive in producing coffee and tea. What will this economy produce if the world price of coffee is twice that of tea? Half that of tea? What will the country produce if the world price of coffee happens to equal the world price of tea? *(LO3)*

5. True or false: If a country is more productive in every sector than a neighboring country, then there is no benefit in trading with the neighboring country. Explain. *(LO3)*

6. Show graphically the effects of a tariff on imported automobiles on the domestic market for automobiles. Who is hurt by the tariff and why? Who benefits and why? *(LO4)*

7. Show graphically the effects of a quota on imported automobiles on the domestic market for automobiles. Who does the quota hurt and who benefits? Explain. *(LO4)*

PROBLEMS

McGraw Hill **connect**

1. An economy has two workers, Bella and Edward. Per day of work, Bella can pick 100 apples or 25 bananas, and Edward can pick 50 apples or 50 bananas. Bella and Edward each work 200 days per year. *(LO1, LO2)*
   a. Which worker has an absolute advantage in apples? Which has a comparative advantage? Calculate each worker's opportunity cost of picking an additional apple.
   b. Find the maximum number of each type of fruit that can be picked annually in this economy, assuming that none of the other type of fruit is picked. What is the most of each type that can be picked if each worker fully specializes according to their comparative advantage?
   c. Draw the PPC for annual production in this economy. Show numerical values for the vertical intercept, the horizontal intercept, and the slopes of each segment of the PPC.

2. A developing economy requires 1,000 hours of work to produce a television set and 10 hours of work to produce a bushel of corn. This economy has available a total of 1,000,000 hours of work per day. *(LO2)*
   a. Draw the PPC for daily output of the developing economy. Give numerical values for the PPC's vertical intercept, horizontal intercept, and slope. Relate the slope to the developing country's opportunity cost of producing each good. If this economy does not trade, what are its consumption possibilities?
   b. The developing economy is considering opening trade with a much larger, industrialized economy. The industrialized economy requires 10 hours of work to produce a television set and 1 hour of work to produce a bushel of corn. Show graphically how trading with the industrialized economy affects the developing economy's consumption possibilities. Is opening trade desirable for the developing economy? (*Hint:* When it opens to trade, the developing economy will be fully specialized in one product.)

3. Suppose that Costa Rican worker Carlos can produce either 100 pounds of coffee or 1 computer per week, and a second worker, Maria, can produce either 150 pounds of coffee or 1 computer per week. Both Carlos and Maria work 50 weeks per year. *(LO2)*
   a. Find the PPC for Costa Rica. Give numerical values for the graph's intercepts and slopes. How much of each good is produced if each worker fully specializes according to comparative advantage?
   b. World prices are such that 1 computer trades for 125 pounds of coffee on international markets. If Costa Rica is open to trade, show Costa Rica's consumption possibilities graphically. What is the most

of each good that Costa Ricans can consume when the economy is open? Compare to the situation when the economy is closed.
   c. Repeat part b under the assumption that 1 computer trades for 80 pounds of coffee on world markets.

4. Suppose that Carlos and Maria can produce coffee and computers as described in Problem 3. A third worker, Pedro, joins the Costa Rican economy. Pedro can produce either 140 pounds of coffee or 1 computer per week. Like the other two workers, Pedro works 50 weeks per year. *(LO2)*
   a. Find the PPC for Costa Rica. Give numerical values of the PPC's intercepts and slopes.
   b. Find Costa Rica's consumption possibilities if the country is open and 1 computer trades for 125 pounds of coffee on world markets. What is the most of each good that Costa Ricans can consume when the economy is open? Compare to the situation when the economy is closed.
   c. Repeat part b assuming that 1 computer trades for 200 pounds of coffee on world markets.

5. Suppose that a U.S. worker can produce 1,000 pairs of shoes or 10 industrial robots per year. For simplicity, assume there are no costs other than labor costs and firms earn zero profits. Initially, the U.S. economy is closed. The domestic price of shoes is $30 a pair, so that a U.S. worker can earn $30,000 annually by working in the shoe industry. The domestic price of a robot is $3,000, so that a U.S. worker can also earn $30,000 annually working in the robot industry.

   Now suppose that the U.S. opens trade with the rest of the world. Foreign workers can produce 500 pairs of shoes or 1 robot per year. The world price of shoes after the U.S. opens its markets is $10 a pair, and the world price of robots is $5,000. *(LO3, LO4)*
   a. What do foreign workers earn annually, in dollars?
   b. When it opens to trade, which good will the United States import and which will it export?
   c. Find the real income of U.S. workers after the opening to trade, measured in (1) the number of pairs of shoes annual worker income will buy and (2) the number of robots annual worker income will buy. Compare to the situation before the opening of trade. Does trading in goods produced by "cheap foreign labor" hurt U.S. workers?
   d. How might your conclusion in part c be modified in the short term if it is costly for workers to change industries? What policy response might help with this problem?

6. The demand and supply for automobiles in a certain country is given in the following graph. *(LO3, LO4)*
   a. Assuming that the economy is closed, find the equilibrium price and production of automobiles.

b. The economy opens to trade. The world price of automobiles is $8,000. Find the domestic quantities demanded and supplied and the quantity of imports or exports. Who will favor the opening of the automobile market to trade, and who will oppose it?

c. The government imposes a tariff of $2,000 per car. Find the effects on domestic quantities demanded and supplied.

d. As a result of the tariff, what will happen to the quantity of imports or exports, and what is the revenue raised by the tariff? Who will favor the imposition of the tariff, and who will oppose it?

7. Suppose the domestic demand and supply for automobiles is as given in Problem 6. *(LO3, LO4)*

a. The economy opens to trade. The world price of automobiles is $10,000. Find the domestic quantities demanded and supplied and the quantity of imports or exports.

b. Now assume that the government imposes a quota on automobile imports of 2,000 cars. What will happen to the quantity of imports or exports?

c. Who will favor the imposition of the quota, and who will oppose it?

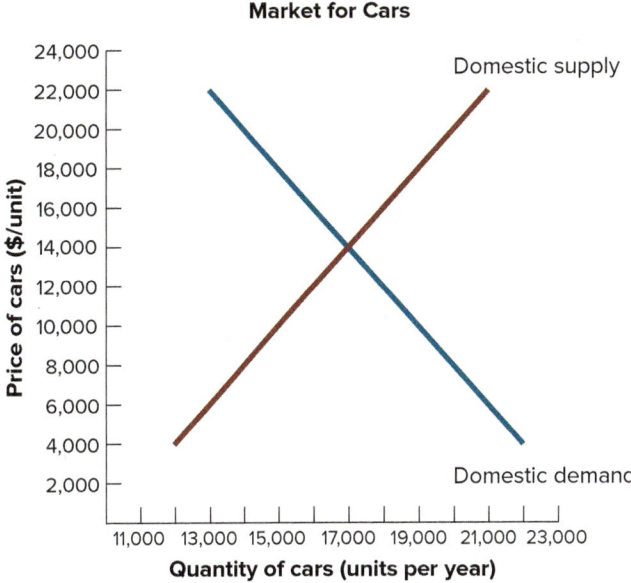

Market for Cars

ANSWERS TO SELF-TESTS

15.1 The opportunity cost of producing coffee equals the number of computers given up for each extra pound of coffee produced. Carlos can produce either 100 pounds of coffee or 1 computer per week, so his opportunity cost is given by:

$$\frac{\text{Loss in computers}}{\text{Gain in coffee}} = \frac{-1 \text{ computer/week}}{100 \text{ pounds of coffee/week}}$$
$$= -1/100 \text{ computer/pound of coffee.}$$

Maria can produce either 100 pounds of coffee or 2 computers per week, so her opportunity cost is:

$$\frac{\text{Loss in computers}}{\text{Gain in coffee}} = \frac{-2 \text{ computer/week}}{100 \text{ pounds of coffee/week}}$$
$$= -1/50 \text{ computer/pound of coffee.}$$

Since each pound of coffee Carlos produces requires the sacrifice of 1/100 of a computer, while each pound of coffee produced by Maria sacrifices 1/50 of a computer, Carlos has the smaller opportunity cost of producing coffee. Thus he has a comparative advantage in producing coffee. *(LO2)*

15.2 When the economy is closed, the Costa Ricans can obtain 80 computers by having Maria work 40 weeks making computers. If Maria works the remaining 10 weeks producing coffee and Carlos works 50 weeks producing coffee, the Costa Ricans will be able to consume $(10 + 50) \times 100 = 6,000$ pounds of coffee per year.

The world price of computers is 80 pounds of coffee, which is greater than Maria's opportunity cost of producing computers but less than Carlos's opportunity cost. Thus if the economy opens to trade, Maria will specialize in computers and Carlos will specialize in coffee. If Maria produces 100 computers, 80 of which are consumed domestically, 20 computers are available for export. Because a computer is worth 80 pounds of coffee on the world market, the 20 exported computers can be traded for 1,600 pounds of coffee. Carlos still produces 5,000 pounds of coffee. Total coffee consumption in Costa Rica is thus $1,600 + 5,000 = 6,600$ pounds. Opening to trade has allowed the Costa Ricans to consume 10 percent more coffee at no sacrifice in computers. *(LO2)*

An Algebraic Approach to Trade Analysis

Thus far, we have used a graphical approach to show how international trade and various restrictions on trade affect economic welfare. In this appendix, we illustrate how the same issues can be approached in an algebraic framework.

EXAMPLE 15A.1 A Tariff on Imported Computers

What are the effects of a tariff on trade?

Suppose the demand for computers by Costa Rican consumers is given by

$$Q^D = 3,000 - 0.5P_C$$

where Q^D is the annual quantity of computers demanded and P_C is the price per computer in dollars. The supply of computers by domestic Costa Rican producers is

$$Q^S = 1,000 + 0.5P_C$$

where Q^S is the annual quantity of computers supplied.

   a. Assuming that the Costa Rican economy is closed to trade, find the equilibrium price and quantity in the Costa Rican computer market.

   b. Assume the economy opens to trade. If the world price of computers is $1,500, find annual Costa Rican consumption, production, and imports of computers.

   c. At the request of domestic producers, the Costa Rican government imposes a tariff of $300 per imported computer. Find Costa Rican consumption, production, and imports of computers after the imposition of the tariff. How much revenue does the tariff raise for the government?

  a. To find the closed-economy price and quantity, we set supply equal to demand:

$$1,000 + 0.5P_C = 3,000 - 0.5P_C$$

Solving for P_C gives the equilibrium price, equal to $2,000 per computer. Substituting this equilibrium price into either the supply equation or the demand equation, we find the equilibrium quantity of computers in the Costa Rican market, equal to 2,000 computers per year. This equilibrium price and quantity correspond to a point like point E in Figure 15A.1.

  b. If the economy opens to trade, the domestic price of computers must equal the world price, which is $1,500. At this price, the domestic quantity demanded for computers is 3,000 − 0.5(1,500) = 2,250 computers per year; the domestic quantity supplied is 1,000 + 0.5(1,500) = 1,750 computers per year. These

FIGURE 15A.1

The Market for Computers in Costa Rica.

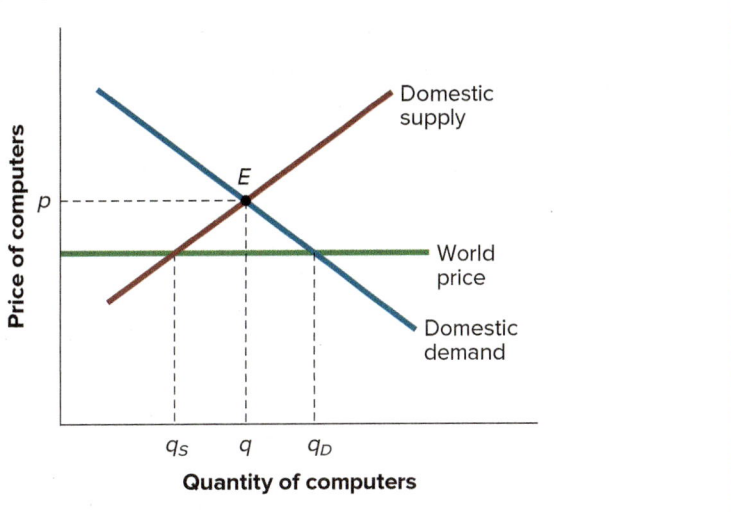

quantities correspond to q_D and q_S, respectively, in Figure 15A.1. Imports equal the difference between domestic quantities demanded and supplied, or $2{,}250 - 1{,}750 = 500$ computers per year.

c.   The imposition of a tariff of $300 per computer raises the price from $1,500 (the world price without the tariff) to $1,800. To find Costa Rican consumption and production at this price, we set the price equal to $1,800 in the demand and supply equations. Thus the domestic quantity demanded is $3{,}000 - 0.5(1{,}800) = 2{,}100$ computers per year; the domestic quantity supplied is $1{,}000 + 0.5(1{,}800) = 1{,}900$ computers per year. Imports, the difference between the quantity demanded by Costa Ricans and the quantity supplied by domestic firms, is $2{,}100 - 1{,}900 = 200$ computers per year. Thus the tariff has raised the price of computers by $300 and reduced imports by 300 computers per year. The tariff revenue collected by the government is $300/imported computer × 200 computers/year = $60,000 per year.

✅ SELF-TEST 15A.1

Repeat parts (b) and (c) of Example 15A.1 under the assumption that the world price of computers is $1,200 (the tariff is still $400). What happens if the world price is $1,800?

EXAMPLE 15A.2   Effects of an Import Quota

What are the effects of an import quota on trade?

Suppose the supply of and demand for computers in Costa Rica is as given in Example 15A.1, and the government imposes an import quota of 200 computers. Find the equilibrium price in the domestic computer market, as well as the quantities produced by domestic firms and purchased by domestic consumers.

The quantity of computers supplied by domestic Costa Rican producers was stated in Example 15A.1 to be $1{,}000 + 0.5P_C$. The quota allows 200 computers per year to be imported. Thus the total quantity of computers supplied, including both domestic production and imports, is $1{,}000 + 0.5P_C + 200$, or $1{,}200 + 0.5P_C$. Setting the quantity supplied equal to the quantity demanded, we get:

$$1{,}200 + 0.5P_C = 3{,}000 - 0.5P_C$$

Solving for P_C, we find that the price of computers in the domestic Costa Rican market is $1,800. Domestic production of computers is $1,000 + 0.5(1,800) = 1,900$ computers per year, while quantity demanded domestically is $3,000 - 0.5(1,800) = 2,100$ computers per year. The difference between domestic quantity demanded and domestic production, 200 computers per year, is made up by imports.

Note that the domestic price, domestic production, and domestic demand are the same in Examples 15A.1 and 15A.2. Thus the tariff and the quota have the same effects on the domestic market for computers. The only difference between the two policies is that with a quota, the government does not get the tariff revenue it got in Example 15A.1. That revenue goes instead to the holders of import licenses, who can buy computers on the world market at $1,500 and sell them in the domestic market at $1,800.

PROBLEMS

1. The demand for automobiles in a certain country is given by

$$D = 12,000 - 200P$$

where P is the price of a car. Supply by domestic automobile producers is

$$S = 7,000 + 50P$$

(LO2, LO3, LO4)

a. Assuming that the economy is closed, find the equilibrium price and production of automobiles.
b. The economy opens to trade. The world price of automobiles is 18. Find the domestic quantities demanded and supplied and the quantity of imports or exports. Who will favor the opening of the automobile market to trade, and who will oppose it?
c. The government imposes a tariff of 1 unit per car. Find the effects on domestic quantities demanded and supplied and on the quantity of imports or exports. Also find the revenue raised by the tariff.

Who will favor the imposition of the tariff, and who will oppose it?
d. Can the government obtain the same results as you found in part c by imposing a quota on automobile imports? Explain.

2. Suppose the domestic demand and supply for automobiles is given by Problem 1. The world price of automobiles is 16. Foreign car firms have a production cost of 15 per automobile, so they earn a profit of 1 per car. *(LO3, LO4)*
a. How many cars will be imported, assuming this country trades freely?
b. Now suppose foreign car producers are asked "voluntarily" to limit their exports to the home country to half of free trade levels. What will be the equilibrium price of cars in the domestic market if foreign producers comply? Find domestic quantities of cars supplied and demanded.
c. How will the "voluntary" export restriction affect the profits of foreign car producers?

ANSWER TO APPENDIX SELF-TEST

15A.1 If the world price of computers is $1,200, domestic demand for computers is $3,000 - 0.5(1,200) = 2,400$ computers. Domestic supply is $1,000 + 0.5(1,200) = 1,600$ computers. The difference between the quantity demanded and the quantity supplied, 800 computers, is imported. A tariff of $400 raises the domestic price of computers to $1,600. Now domestic demand is 2,200 and domestic supply is 1,800. The difference, 400 computers, equals imports. Revenue for the government is ($400/computer)(400 imported computers) = $160,000. If the world price of computers is $1,800 and there is no tariff, domestic demand is 2,100; domestic supply is 1,900; and imports are 200. A tariff of $400 raises the world price to $2,200, which is greater than the domestic price when there is no trade ($2,000). No computers are imported in this case and no tariff revenue is raised. *(LO3)*

GLOSSARY

A

absolute advantage one person has an absolute advantage over another if one takes fewer hours to perform a task than the other person

accounting profit the difference between a firm's total revenue and its explicit costs

adaptive rationality standard a variant of the rational choice model that permits additional preferences to be added if they can be shown not to handicap resource acquisition in competitive environments

adverse selection the pattern in which insurance tends to be purchased disproportionately by those who are most costly for companies to insure

allocative function of price changes in prices direct resources away from overcrowded markets and toward markets that are underserved

anchoring and adjustment an estimation technique that begins with an initial approximation (the anchor), which is then modified in accordance with additional available information (the adjustment)

asymmetric information situations in which buyers and sellers are not equally well informed about the characteristics of goods and services for sale in the marketplace

attainable point any combination of goods that can be produced using currently available resources

autarky a situation in which a country is economically self-sufficient

availability heuristic a rule of thumb that estimates the frequency of an event by the ease with which it is possible to summon examples from memory

average benefit the total benefit of undertaking n units of an activity divided by n

average cost the total cost of undertaking n units of an activity divided by n

average total cost (ATC) total cost divided by total output

average variable cost (AVC) variable cost divided by total output

B

barrier to entry any force that prevents firms from entering a new market

basic elements of a game the players, the strategies available to each player, and the payoffs each player receives for each possible combination of strategies

better-than-fair gamble a gamble whose expected value is positive

buyer's reservation price the largest dollar amount the buyer would be willing to pay for a good

buyer's surplus the difference between the buyer's reservation price and the price he or she actually pays

C

cartel a coalition of firms that agree to restrict output for the purpose of earning an economic profit

change in demand a shift of the entire demand curve

change in supply a shift of the entire supply curve

change in the quantity demanded a movement along the demand curve that occurs in response to a change in price

change in the quantity supplied a movement along the supply curve that occurs in response to a change in price

closed economy an economy that does not trade with the rest of the world

Coase theorem if, at no cost, people can negotiate the purchase and sale of the right to perform activities that cause externalities, they can always arrive at efficient solutions to the problems caused by externalities

collective good a good or service that, to at least some degree, is nonrival but excludable

commitment device a way of changing incentives so as to make otherwise empty threats or promises credible

commitment problem a situation in which people cannot achieve their goals because of an inability to make credible threats or promises

comparative advantage one person has a comparative advantage over another if his or her opportunity cost of performing a task is lower than the other person's opportunity cost

compensating wage differential a difference in the wage rate—negative or positive—that reflects the attractiveness of a job's working conditions

complements two goods are complements in consumption if an increase in the price of one causes a leftward shift in the demand curve for the other (or if a decrease causes a rightward shift)

constant (or **parameter**) a quantity that is fixed in value

constant returns to scale a production process is said to have constant returns to scale if, when all inputs are changed by a given proportion, output changes by the same proportion

consumer surplus the difference between a buyer's reservation price for a product and the price actually paid

consumption possibilities the combinations of goods and services that a country's citizens might feasibly consume

cost-plus regulation a method of regulation under which the regulated firm is permitted to charge prices that cover explicit costs of production plus a markup to cover the opportunity cost of resources provided by the firm's owners

costly-to-fake principle to communicate information credibly to a potential rival, a signal must be costly or difficult to fake

credible promise a promise to take an action that is in the promiser's interest to keep

credible threat a threat to take an action that is in the threatener's interest to carry out

cross-price elasticity of demand the percentage by which the quantity demanded of the first good changes in response to a 1 percent change in the price of the second

crowding out the tendency of increased government deficits to reduce investment spending

customer discrimination the willingness of consumers to pay more for a product produced by members of a favored group, even if the quality of the product is unaffected

D

deadweight loss the loss of consumer and producer surplus caused by disparity between price and marginal cost

decision tree (or **game tree**) a diagram that describes the possible moves in a game in sequence and lists the payoffs that correspond to each possible combination of moves

demand curve a schedule or graph showing the quantity of a good that buyers wish to buy at each price

dependent variable a variable in an equation whose value is determined by the value taken by another variable in the equation

disappearing political discourse the theory that people who support a position may remain silent because speaking out would create a risk of being misunderstood

dominant strategy one that yields a higher payoff no matter what the other players in a game choose

dominated strategy any other strategy available to a player who has a dominant strategy

E

earned-income tax credit (EITC) a policy under which low-income workers receive credits on their federal income tax

economic efficiency *See* **efficiency**

economic loss an economic profit that is less than zero

economic profit (or **excess profit**) the difference between a firm's total revenue and the sum of its explicit and implicit costs

economic rent that part of the payment for a factor of production that exceeds the owner's reservation price, the price below which the owner would not supply the factor

economic surplus the benefit of taking an action minus its cost

economics the study of how people make choices under conditions of scarcity and of the results of those choices for society

economies of scale *See* **increasing returns to scale**

efficiency (or **economic efficiency**) a condition that occurs when all goods and services are produced and consumed at their respective socially optimal levels

efficient (or **Pareto efficient**) a situation is efficient if no change is possible that will help some people without harming others

efficient point any combination of goods for which currently available resources do not allow an increase in the production of one good without a reduction in the production of the other

elastic the demand for a good is elastic with respect to price if its price elasticity of demand is greater than 1

employer discrimination an arbitrary preference by an employer for one group of workers over another

equation a mathematical expression that describes the relationship between two or more variables

equilibrium a balanced or unchanging situation in which all forces at work within a system are canceled by others

equilibrium price and equilibrium quantity the price and quantity at the intersection of the supply and demand curves for the good

excess demand (or **shortage**) the amount by which quantity demanded exceeds quantity supplied when the price of a good lies below the equilibrium price

excess profit *See* **economic profit**

excess supply (or **surplus**) the amount by which quantity supplied exceeds quantity demanded when the price of the good exceeds the equilibrium price

expected value of a gamble the sum of the possible outcomes of the gamble multiplied by their respective probabilities

explicit costs the actual payments a firm makes to its factors of production and other suppliers

external benefit (or **positive externality**) a benefit of an activity received by people other than those who pursue the activity

external cost (or **negative externality**) a cost of an activity that falls on people other than those who pursue the activity

externality an external cost or benefit of an activity

F

factor of production an input used in the production of a good or service

fair gamble a gamble whose expected value is zero

fixed cost the sum of all payments made to the firm's fixed factors of production

fixed factor of production an input whose quantity cannot be altered in the short run

free-rider problem an incentive problem in which too little of a good or service is produced because nonpayers cannot be excluded from using it

fungibility the property of an entity whose individual units are interchangeable, as money in separate accounts

G

game tree *See* **decision tree**

H

head tax a tax that collects the same amount from every taxpayer

homo economicus the narrowly self-interested, well-informed, highly disciplined, and cognitively formidable actor often assumed in traditional economic models

human capital an amalgam of factors such as education, training, experience, intelligence, energy, work habits, trustworthiness, and initiative that affects the value of a worker's marginal product

human capital theory a theory of pay determination that says a worker's wage will be proportional to their stock of human capital

hurdle method of price discrimination the practice by which a seller offers a discount to all buyers who overcome some obstacle

I

imperfectly competitive firm (or **price setter**) a firm that has at least some control over the market price of its product

implicit costs the opportunity costs of the resources supplied by the firm's owners

in-kind transfer a payment made not in the form of cash, but in the form of a good or service

income effect the change in the quantity demanded of a good that results because a change in the price of a good changes the buyer's purchasing power

income elasticity of demand the percentage by which a good's quantity demanded changes in response to a 1 percent change in income

increasing returns to scale (or **economies of scale**) a production process is said to have increasing returns to scale if, when all inputs are changed by a given proportion, output changes by more than that proportion

independent variable a variable in an equation whose value determines the value taken by another variable in the equation

inefficient point any combination of goods for which currently available resources enable an increase in the production of one good without a reduction in the production of the other

inelastic the demand for a good is inelastic with respect to price if its price elasticity of demand is less than 1

inferior good a good whose demand curve shifts leftward when the incomes of buyers increase and rightward when the incomes of buyers decrease

invisible hand theory Adam Smith's theory that the actions of independent, self-interested buyers and sellers will often result in the most efficient allocation of resources

J

judgmental and decision heuristics rules of thumb that reduce computation costs

L

labor union a group of workers who bargain collectively with employers for better wages and working conditions

law of demand people do less of what they want to do as the cost of doing it rises

law of diminishing marginal utility the tendency for the additional utility gained from consuming an additional unit of a good to diminish as consumption increases beyond some point

law of diminishing returns a property of the relationship between the amount of a good or service produced and the amount of a variable factor required to produce it; the law says that when some factors of production are fixed, increased production of the good eventually requires ever-larger increases in the variable factor

lemons model George Akerlof's explanation of how asymmetric information tends to reduce the average quality of goods offered for sale

loss aversion the tendency to experience losses as more painful than the pleasures that result from gains of the same magnitude

M

macroeconomics the study of the performance of national economies and the policies that governments use to try to improve that performance

marginal benefit the increase in total benefit that results from carrying out one additional unit of an activity

marginal cost the increase in total cost that results from carrying out one additional unit of an activity

marginal product of labor (*MPL*) the additional output a firm gets by employing one additional unit of labor

marginal revenue the change in a firm's total revenue that results from a one-unit change in output

marginal utility the additional utility gained from consuming an additional unit of a good

market the market for any good consists of all buyers or sellers of that good

market equilibrium occurs in a market when all buyers and sellers are satisfied with their respective quantities at the market price

market power a firm's ability to raise the price of a good without losing all its sales

means-tested a benefit program whose benefit level declines as the recipient earns additional income

microeconomics the study of individual choice under scarcity and its implications for the behavior of prices and quantities in individual markets

monopolistic competition an industry structure in which a large number of firms produce slightly differentiated products that are reasonably close substitutes for one another

moral hazard the tendency of people to expend less effort protecting those goods that are insured against theft or damage

N

Nash equilibrium any combination of strategy choices in which each player's choice is his or her best choice, given the other players' choices

natural monopoly a monopoly that results from economies of scale (increasing returns to scale)

negative externality *See* **external cost**

negative income tax (NIT) a system under which the government would grant every citizen a cash payment each year, financed by an additional tax on earned income

nominal price the absolute price of a good in dollar terms

nonexcludable good a good that is difficult, or costly, to exclude nonpayers from consuming

nonpositional good a good whose value does not depend heavily on how it compares with other goods in the same category

nonrival good a good whose consumption by one person does not diminish its availability for others

normal good a good whose demand curve shifts rightward when the incomes of buyers increase and leftward when the incomes of buyers decrease

normal profit the opportunity cost of the resources supplied by the firm's owners, equal to accounting profit minus economic profit

normative economic principle one that says how people should behave

O

oligopoly an industry structure in which a small number of large firms produce products that are either close or perfect substitutes

open economy an economy that trades with other countries

opportunity cost the value of what must be forgone to undertake an activity

outsourcing a term increasingly used to connote having services performed by low-wage workers overseas

P

parameter *See* **constant**

Pareto efficient *See* **efficient**

payoff matrix a table that describes the payoffs in a game for each possible combination of strategies

perfect hurdle a threshold that completely segregates buyers whose reservation prices lie above it from others whose reservation prices lie below it, imposing no cost on those who jump the hurdle

perfectly competitive market a market in which no individual supplier has significant influence on the market price of the product

perfectly discriminating monopolist a firm that charges each buyer exactly his or her reservation price

perfectly elastic demand demand is perfectly elastic with respect to price if price elasticity of demand is infinite

perfectly elastic supply supply is perfectly elastic with respect to price if elasticity of supply is infinite

perfectly inelastic demand demand is perfectly inelastic with respect to price if price elasticity of demand is zero

perfectly inelastic supply supply is perfectly inelastic with respect to price if elasticity is zero

Personal Responsibility and Work Opportunity Reconciliation Act the 1996 federal law that transferred responsibility for welfare programs from the federal level to the state level and placed a five-year lifetime limit on payment of AFDC benefits to any given recipient

positional arms control agreement an agreement in which contestants attempt to limit mutually offsetting investments in performance enhancement

positional arms race a series of mutually offsetting investments in performance enhancement that is stimulated by a positional externality

positional externality this occurs when an increase in one person's performance reduces the expected reward of another's in situations in which reward depends on relative performance

positional good a good whose value depends relatively heavily on how it compares with other goods in the same category

positive (or descriptive) economic principle one that predicts how people will behave

positive externality *See* **external benefit**

poverty threshold the level of income below which the federal government classifies a family as poor

present-aim standard of rationality a variant of the rational choice model that permits greater flexibility in assumptions about preferences

price ceiling a maximum allowable price, specified by law

price discrimination the practice of charging different buyers different prices for essentially the same good or service

price elasticity of demand the percentage change in the quantity demanded of a good or service that results from a 1 percent change in its price

price elasticity of supply the percentage change in quantity supplied that occurs in response to a 1 percent change in price

price setter *See* **imperfectly competitive firm**

price taker a firm that has no influence over the price at which it sells its product

prisoner's dilemma a game in which each player has a dominant strategy, and when each plays it, the resulting payoffs are smaller than if each had played a dominated strategy

producer surplus the amount by which price exceeds the seller's reservation price

production possibilities curve (PPC) a graph that describes the maximum amount of one good that can be produced for every possible level of production of the other good

profit the total revenue a firm receives from the sale of its product minus all costs—explicit and implicit—incurred in producing it

profit-maximizing firm a firm whose primary goal is to maximize the difference between its total revenues and total costs

profitable firm a firm whose total revenue exceeds its total cost

progressive tax one in which the proportion of income paid in taxes rises as income rises

proportional income tax one under which all taxpayers pay the same proportion of their incomes in taxes

protectionism the view that free trade is injurious and should be restricted

public good a good or service that, to at least some degree, is both nonrival and nonexcludable

pure commons good one for which nonpayers cannot easily be excluded and for which each unit consumed by one person means one less unit available for others

pure monopoly the only supplier of a unique product with no close substitutes

pure private good one for which nonpayers can easily be excluded and for which each unit consumed by one person means one less unit available for others

pure public good a good or service that, to a high degree, is both nonrival and nonexcludable

Q

quota a legal limit on the quantity of a good that may be imported

R

rational person someone with well-defined goals who tries to fulfill those goals as best he or she can

rational spending rule spending should be allocated across goods so that the marginal utility per dollar is the same for each good

rationing function of price changes in prices distribute scarce goods to those consumers who value them most highly

real price the dollar price of a good relative to the average dollar price of all other goods

regression to the mean the phenomenon that unusual events are likely to be followed by more nearly normal ones

regressive tax a tax under which the proportion of income paid in taxes declines as income rises

rent-seeking the socially unproductive efforts of people or firms to win a prize

repeated prisoner's dilemma a standard prisoner's dilemma that confronts the same players repeatedly

representativeness heuristic a rule of thumb according to which the likelihood of something belonging to a given category increases with the extent to which it shares characteristics with stereotypical members of that category

rise *See* **slope**

risk-averse person someone who would refuse any fair gamble

risk-neutral person someone who would accept any gamble that is fair or better

run *See* **slope**

S

satisficing a decision-making strategy that aims for adequate results because optimal results may necessitate excessive expenditure of resources

seller's reservation price the smallest dollar amount for which a seller would be willing to sell an additional unit, generally equal to marginal cost

seller's surplus the difference between the price received by the seller and his or her reservation price

short run a period of time sufficiently short that at least some of the firm's factors of production are fixed

shortage *See* **excess demand**

slope in a straight line, the ratio of the vertical distance the straight line travels between any two points *(rise)* to the corresponding horizontal distance *(run)*

social contagion a term used by behavioral scientists to describe how behaviors often spread from person to person in ways that resemble the spread of memes on social media

socially optimal quantity the quantity of a good that results in the maximum possible economic surplus from producing and consuming the good

statistical discrimination the practice of making judgments about the quality of people, goods, or services based on the characteristics of the groups to which they belong

status quo bias the general resistance to change, often stemming from *loss aversion*

substitutes two goods are substitutes in consumption if an increase in the price of one causes a rightward shift in the demand curve for the other (or if a decrease causes a leftward shift)

substitution effect the change in the quantity demanded of a good that results because buyers switch to or from substitutes when the price of the good changes

sunk cost a cost that is beyond recovery at the moment a decision must be made

supply curve a graph or schedule showing the quantity of a good that sellers wish to sell at each price

surplus *See* **excess supply**

T

tariff a tax imposed on an imported good

tit-for-tat a strategy for the repeated prisoner's dilemma in which players cooperate on the first move and then mimic their partner's last move on each successive move

total cost the sum of all payments made to the firm's fixed and variable factors of production

total expenditure (or **total revenue**) the dollar amount that consumers spend on a product ($P \times Q$) is equal to the dollar amount that sellers receive

total revenue *See* **total expenditure**

total surplus the difference between the buyer's reservation price and the seller's reservation price

tragedy of the commons the tendency for a resource that has no price to be used until its marginal benefit falls to zero

U

ultimatum bargaining game a game in which the first player has the power to confront the second player with a take-it-or-leave-it offer

unattainable point any combination of goods that cannot be produced using currently available resources

unit elastic the demand for a good is unit elastic with respect to price if its price elasticity of demand equals 1

V

value of the marginal product of labor (*VMPL*) the dollar value of the additional output a firm gets by employing one additional unit of labor

variable a quantity that is free to take a range of different values

variable cost the sum of all payments made to the firm's variable factors of production

variable factor of production an input whose quantity can be altered in the short run

vertical intercept in a straight line, the value taken by the dependent variable when the independent variable equals zero

W

Weber-Fechner law the relationship according to which the perceived change in any stimulus varies according to the size of the change measured as a proportion of the original stimulus

winner-take-all labor market one in which small differences in human capital translate into large differences in pay

world price the price at which a good or service is traded on international markets

INDEX

Page numbers followed by n refer notes in the text.